MASTER THE ACT ASSESSMENT® 2002

TEACHER-TESTED STRATEGIES AND TECHNIQUES FOR SCORING HIGH

ARCO™

THOMSON LEARNING

Australia • Canada • Mexico • Singapore • Spain • United Kingdom • United States

MASTER THE ACT ASSESSMENT

Get Stronger with Every Test and Watch Your Scores Rise!

YOUR PERSONAL SCORE CARD

	Self-Evaluation Test	2nd Full-Length Test	3rd Full-Length Test	4th Full-Length Test
Total English				
Usage/Mechanics				
Rhetorical Skills				
Total Math				
Pre Alg/Elem Alg				
Inter Alg/Coor Geom				
Plane Geom/Trig				
Total Reading				
Soc Studies/Science				
Lit/Humanities				
Science Reasoning				

6 THINGS YOU MUST REMEMBER THE DAY OF THE TEST TO SCORE YOUR HIGHEST!

1. **SKIP THE DIRECTIONS AND SAVE TIME.** You already know the directions from repeated practice with the exercises and sample tests in the book.

2. **SKIM THE SECTION FIRST.** Use your *MASTER THE ACT ASSESSMENT* strategies for skimming. Look for the number and types of questions. Remember your tips for answering each question type.

3. **DON'T GET LOST IN DETAILS OR BIG NUMBERS.** The unimportant is meant to distract you. Don't get sidetracked! You don't need to understand every detail to be able to answer the question.

4. **ANSWER EASY QUESTIONS FIRST.** You get the same points for easy questions as hard ones. Answer the easy ones first, read your favorite passage first, and boost your score. *But be careful:* skip to the right number on the answer sheet.

5. **WHEN IN DOUBT, GUESS.** There's no penalty for wrong answers. A blank line won't get you extra points, but guess —and you could get lucky. Eliminate answers or play hunches to improve your chances.

6. **STOP A FEW MINUTES BEFORE YOUR TIME IS UP.** When the time is almost up, look at the questions you have left. If an answer is immediately apparent, fill it in. Disqualify answers that you know are wrong and pick one of the others. If you haven't a clue, leave it blank and move on.

CHECKLIST: WHAT YOU *MUST* BRING THE DAY OF THE TEST

You *must* bring:

- ☐ **YOUR OFFICIAL ADMISSIONS TICKET**
- ☐ **PHOTO IDENTIFICATION**
- ☐ **TWO OR THREE SHARPENED #2 PENCILS WITH ERASERS**

It's a good idea to *also* bring:

- ☐ **A BATTERY-OPERATED CALCULATOR**
- ☐ **A SNACK FOR BREAK**
- ☐ **A SWEATER**

If you bring this card, too, for last-minute coaching, you'll have to leave it with other checked items outside the test room. However, **don't forget to bring this card back home with you!**

COLLEGE ADMISSIONS/FINANCIAL AID COUNTDOWN
SENIOR YEAR

SEPTEMBER
- [ ] Continue honing list of target schools, on-campus interviews and alumni interviews.
- [ ] Get financial aid information from guidance counselors and give teacher recommendations to appropriate teachers.
- [ ] Register for October ACT Assessment, October SAT I, or November SAT I.
- [ ] Begin Early Action/Early Decision steps now. Check deadlines with appropriate schools.

OCTOBER
- [ ] Register for December ACT Assessment, December SAT I, or November SAT II.
- [ ] Take October ACT Assessment, October SAT I exam.
- [ ] Draw up a master schedule of application and financial aid due dates and mark them on your calendar.
- [ ] Continue working on college essays and personal statements. Follow up on teacher recommendations.
- [ ] Submit Early Decision and Early Action applications.

NOVEMBER
- [ ] Reduce college "long list" to "short list" where applications will be sent.
- [ ] Plan Thanksgiving-break visit to college campuses.
- [ ] Get someone to proofread your applications and essays.
- [ ] Take the November SAT I or SAT II; prepare for December ACT Assessment.
- [ ] Send first-quarter grades to colleges; send test scores (include ETS numbers) for ED/EA applications and regular admissions.

DECEMBER
- [ ] Pick up any additional financial aid forms you need and attend financial aid workshops, if possible. Follow up with guidance and teachers on references letters and transcripts.
- [ ] Take ACT Assessment, SAT II subject tests this month.
- [ ] Submit all regular applications.
- [ ] If accepted on Early Decision, withdraw remaining applications. If deferred on Early Decision, send follow-up letter to college.

JANUARY
- [ ] Fill out financial aid forms. Finish and mail as soon as possible. NEVER BE LATE WITH THESE!
- [ ] Complete all applications regardless of later deadlines. Photocopy everything. If taking SAT this month, are RUSH scores required? Ask target colleges if you're not sure. Register for February ACT Assessment now.

FEBRUARY
- [ ] ACT Assessment administered this month.
- [ ] Call those colleges that didn't confirm receipt of completed applications.

MARCH
- [ ] It's not too late to apply to more schools—get any remaining applications out this month.
- [ ] Actively seek and pursue scholarship opportunities and draw up your financial aid plan to pay for next year's expenses.

APRIL
- [ ] Prepare for May AP exams.
- [ ] Plan "crunch time" visits to campuses and compare financial-aid decisions.
- [ ] Return "Wait List" cards as needed. Check admissions offices for Wait-List status.
- [ ] **Make your decision!** Send the deposit or your place won't be held; for most schools May 1st is the deadline, so do it now.
- [ ] Notify those schools you won't be attending.

MAY
- [ ] Take AP exams where appropriate.
- [ ] Check housing options: when will forms be mailed? Should you check alternative arrangements?
- [ ] Start thinking about summer employment—last chance to build up a 'nest egg' for Freshman year!

JUNE
- [ ] Write thank-you notes to anyone who helped you: guidance counselors, teachers, admissions counselors, etc.
- [ ] Make sure final high school transcripts are sent to the college you'll attend.

CONTENTS

PART 3   MASTER ACT ASSESSMENT SUBJECT REVIEWS   217

INTRODUCTION

WHY THIS IS THE ONE BOOK YOU NEED TO GET INTO YOUR FIRST-CHOICE SCHOOL

Every year, almost a million and three quarter students take a college entrance exam called the ACT Assessment, which receives its name from the initials of the company that creates and administers the test—American College Testing. This three-hour standardized test plays a crucial part in whether or not students are accepted in the college or university of their choice. Therefore, students like you actively look for ways to maximize their scores. They try to cram in the various subject areas. They receive tutoring in their weaker subjects. They enroll in test-preparation courses.

And they purchase guides to the ACT Assessment exam.

You are holding one of the best proven ways to maximize your score—ARCO's *Master the ACT Assessment*. The main idea behind this guide is simple: The best way to prepare for an exam of this type is to practice on the exam itself. You need to know the format, the kind of questions asked, the time limits, what the exam measures, and how the test-makers think.

Master the ACT Assessment brings you all this help and more.

A PERSONALIZED TIMETABLE FOR PREPARATION

This book has been written to help you succeed on the ACT Assessment no matter how long you have to prepare, how much time each day you have to devote to that preparation, or what your skill level might be. You might have bought *Master the ACT Assessment* six months before your test date or two weeks before. Your personal schedule might enable you to devote long hours to ACT Assessment preparation, or you might have only a few hours a day. You might be a math wizard, but maybe you're a bit weaker in verbal skills.

Wherever you are right now, *Master the ACT Assessment* can help *you*. You'll see how to set up a course of preparation that's tailored to your own schedule and to how much time you have before your test date. And you'll see how to focus on those areas where you need the most improvement.

PROVEN STRATEGIES TO MAXIMIZE YOUR ACT ASSESSMENT SCORE

Backed by ARCO's sixty years of test-guide experience, *Master the ACT Assessment* delivers proven strategies that can add significant points to your score. These strategies go way beyond general test-taking advice like "get a good night's sleep the night before" or "pace yourself so that you don't get delayed early on and therefore don't have time to finish." Although both tips are true, they are true of just about every test.

This guide brings you the best of these general tips, as well as proven strategies that are specific to the ACT Assessment exam, such as, "Which answer can you always skip reading in the sentence-correction part of the ACT Assessment English Test?" and "What's the best answer to try first when solving a problem in the ACT Assessment Math Test?" This is the kind of expert help that allows *you* to master the ACT Assessment.

SELF-EVALUATION TOOLS

This guide also helps you measure your readiness for taking the ACT Assessment exam. There's an initial test to give you a quick overall estimate of your test-taking skills. The estimate reveals your strengths and weaknesses. With this knowledge, you can save time and effort in preparing for the ACT Assessment while greatly increasing the effectiveness of your study.

You also see how to *continue* to measure your ACT Assessment readiness as you progress through the material in the book. When you compare the results against your initial score, you'll see which subject areas still need improvement. And when you see your scores going up over time, you have concrete proof that you're ready to take the ACT Assessment—the best confidence-booster, anxiety-reducer there is.

QUICK, THOROUGH REVIEWS OF ACT ASSESSMENT SUBJECT MATERIAL

There are four subject areas tested on the ACT Assessment exam: Standard-English skills, math skills, reading-comprehension skills, and science-reasoning skills. Within each of these subjects there's an enormous range of material; without guidance you could wander in many directions. For example, should you try to prepare for the ACT Assessment English Test by reading all of Shakespeare? By skimming a writing guide, such as the *Chicago Manual of Style*? By memorizing every grammar rule taught to you from third grade till now? Where would your preparation begin and would it ever end?

Master the ACT Assessment eliminates the guesswork of what you should study. Here is the material that actually appears on ACT Assessment exams, in the actual form in which it appears. Plus there's added help. After you work through each subject and complete the exercises, you get the opportunity to evaluate your understanding. If the self-evaluation test and the topic-area exercises show that you need still further help, don't worry. *Master the ACT Assessment* also includes a basic review of each subject covered on the exam.

FULL-LENGTH SAMPLE EXAMS

Because practice is one of the most critical components for success on a standardized examination, *Master the ACT Assessment* brings you *a full-length diagnostic exam and three additional full-length sample tests*. That's more than any other guide. This is the heart of the *Master the ACT Assessment* guide, and we'll repeat why: The best way to prepare for an exam of this type is to practice on the exam itself. Instead of the result of subject-area guesswork or teacher surveys, you get passages, problems, and questions written by experts to closely represent those used on ACT Assessment exams, followed by the answer keys and full walk-through answer explanations. Of course you expect an answer key to score your self-evaluation test, exercises, and full-length sample tests. But an answer key doesn't help you understand why your answer is wrong. That's why *Master the ACT Assessment* fully explains *why* the right answer is the right one, and what errors in thinking might have led you to choose the wrong one.

ADVICE FOR TEST REGISTRATION

If you haven't yet registered for the ACT Assessment, this guide brings you concrete help for making the registration process simpler. You see how to decide *when* it's the best time for you to take the ACT Assessment, *where* is the best site for you to take it, and *what to do* when unusual test-taking situations come up.

HELP IN INTERPRETING TEST RESULTS

ACT Assessment test results won't be expressed in that A, B, C, D, F, or 0 to 100% format you're familiar with from school. No score will be higher than 36. There will be a score for each of the four ACT Assessment sections, subscores for each area tested within a subject, a composite score, and a score range that accounts for statistical error. You'll also get a percentile score that measures you against a group of other test-takers.

What do these figures really mean? How do colleges use these figures? How should *you* use them—say, in deciding whether or not you need to retake the ACT Assessment? *Master the ACT Assessment* explains the test results clearly and helps you decide what to do next.

The guide also shows how to cancel your scores, what to do if you think your test was scored improperly, what to do when your score is delayed, even how to challenge the validity of a question.

REAL GUIDANCE FOR "AFTER THE ACT ASSESSMENT" ISSUES: COLLEGE ADMISSIONS, FINANCIAL AID, AND MORE

Sometimes the nerves and preparation leading up to the ACT Assessment make it seem as if the exam itself is the goal. But it's only one step on the path to your goal—attending the college or university of your choice. So much more is involved: choosing the college, getting teacher recommendations, and making it through the admissions procedure. And after you're accepted, there's the huge question of how to pay for tuition.

Master the ACT Assessment brings you a wealth of bonus material to help make the admissions process easier. Here are proven ways to stand out from the crowd on your application and in your admissions interview, key points to look for during a campus visit, and alternate methods of financing your education.

All in all, *Master the ACT Assessment* has all the answers you need—answers about the exam, answers to sample exams, answers to test-taking problems and situations. That's why it's the one book you need to get into your first-choice school.

HOW TO USE THIS BOOK

How can you get the most out of this book? Your first step is to read Chapter 1, which tells you all about the ACT Assessment. This chapter answers your most important questions: What's on the four ACT Assessment subject tests? What does each test look like? How are they scored? How do colleges use these scores? How do I register for the ACT Assessment? And what can I do if I have a special situation when it comes to testing?

Next, you should take the Self-Evaluation Test in Chapter 2. This is the first of the four full-length sample tests in the guide. The Self-Evaluation Test is your first real taste of the ACT Assessment—great practice in itself. It also pinpoints those areas in which you're ready for testing, as well as those areas in which you need improvement. The Self-Evaluation Test provides you with a baseline from which you'll measure all your progress. Write these scores on the Tear Card at the front of the book and watch them steadily improve as your study continues!

After you've taken the Self-Evaluation Test, read Chapter 3. This explains what each of the four subject tests measures and what you can expect from each. It then shows how to set up a personalized study plan, working with the amount of time you have right now. The chapter also explains how to handle test anxiety from now to the day of the test. Finally, to help you do the best you can the day of the test, it reveals ten proven strategies for scoring higher on the ACT Assessment.

What you do next depends on your personalized schedule. If you have the maximum time (three months or more), we suggest you work through the discussion chapters in Part 2: Strengthening Your ACT Assessment Subject Skills. There's a chapter for each subject. Here you get a more detailed explanation of what topics within the subject are covered and are walked through every type of question that will be asked. When an ACT Assessment test uses tables, charts, diagrams, or figures, you get true-to-life samples so there'll be no surprises the day of the test. Plus you get score-boosting strategies specifically designed for ACT Assessment English, Math, Reading, and Science Reasoning. At the end of each of these chapters are two exercises to see if you've understood the explanations and know how to use the strategies. A scoring guide helps you decide whether you need further review in a subject or can move on to another. Cross-referenced notes alert you to other sections in the book that might help you with a particular problem.

Summaries at the end of each chapter recap the most important points.

After finishing the subject chapter, you might decide to go to the in-depth subject review; this provides an extensive explanation of the material most likely to be tested on the ACT Assessment, as well as three exercises to give you more practice in that area. Or you might want to go directly to one of the remaining full-length sample tests. It's up to you. Whenever you *do* take one of the tests, note the results on your personal card. Your improving scores are the proof of your hard work. Scores that are slower to improve show where to focus your next efforts. Work back and forth as you need—from review and exercises, to a full-length test, back to the review. If you're doing well, toward the end you can just skim those few areas that remain a bit of a problem.

Review and practice, review and practice—this is the overall strategy for scoring higher on the ACT Assessment.

If you have a shorter timetable, remember: Chapter 3 tells you how to use the subject and review chapters to zero in at once on just those areas that give you the most trouble, so that you'll get maximum results for the most intensive study period.

Besides the subject discussions, exercises, and reviews, *Master the ACT Assessment* also brings you dozens of tips and cautions all throughout the book. These are tucked away in the margins. Read them as you come to them or save them for later. Either technique works. Margin notes also include general advice, relevant facts, and little extras to help make studying more interesting.

After you've taken the ACT Assessment, you'll have questions—from how long scores take to arrive, to how to make the best impression during a college interview, to how to finance your education when the school of your dreams finally says yes. *Master the ACT Assessment* answers those questions and dozens more, continuing even after the test to help you get into your first-choice school.

ACKNOWLEDGMENTS

We would like to thank Judith Berg, Charlotte Klaar, and Jana Gruner for their invaluable help, insight, and advice in creating this book. Their knowledge and experience provided us with critical feedback, and ultimately helped us create a comprehensive yet concise test-prep resource.

Meeting and Mastering the ACT Assessment

PREVIEW

Get to Know the ACT Assessment

To construct the best study plan—the plan that's right for *you*—you need to know what to expect from the ACT Assessment exam. This chapter takes you inside the ACT Assessment for a closer look at how the test is administered, what questions are on the test, how the test is scored, and how those scores are interpreted. You'll also learn how to register for the exam and how to make special arrangements for the exam, if necessary.

UNDERSTAND THE ACT ASSESSMENT

The ACT Assessment is a battery of multiple-choice tests used by colleges and universities to help decide which applicants to choose. Even though there are other types of standardized tests available, almost all colleges accept the ACT Assessment, and many colleges require it. The ACT Assessment is given five times each year at locations throughout the United States, Canada, and overseas, as well. This schedule enables students to apply for early admissions or to have sufficient time to re-take the test if desired or if necessary.

There are several parts to the ACT Assessment. One part is a personal interest inventory. The results of this section are useful in career planning by suggesting several occupations related to those subjects or areas that appeal to you or that are suited to your personality. It's good to know these possible career choices early because many of them have special educational requirements. Thus, the ACT Assessment not only is part of the admissions process, it can become a tool that guides your selection of courses and/or major.

In addition, the ACT Assessment includes a course and grade information questionnaire and a student profile. These help create a picture of you for the college admissions board. Each board knows from years of experience what type of student fits in well with its programs and other students. There are always exceptions, and many other elements go into the acceptance process, but the questionnaire and profile provide the board a quick "snapshot" of you.

Of course, the ACT Assessment also includes the part that concerns you most right now—the test itself. This is actually a series of tests based on a standard high school curriculum. In other words, the ACT Assessment tests what most high school students learn every day.

ROAD MAP

- *Understand the ACT Assessment*
- *Get to Know the ACT Assessment Contents and Format*
- *A Close Look at the ACT Assessment Test Components*
- *Understand How the ACT Assessment Is Scored*
- *Understand How Admissions Offices Use the Score*
- *Registering for the ACT Assessment*
- *Deciding Where to Take the ACT Assessment*
- *Know What You Need to Take on Test Day*
- *Special Registration Arrangements*

TIP

Although most colleges accept the ACT Assessment, it's always good to ensure that the colleges in which *you're* interested accept it. When you check that information, also find out what the college's deadline is for applications. This date is the cut-off for receiving all the necessary information, including ACT Assessment scores. Each college will have its own date, so check each college or university to which you're planning to apply before deciding when to schedule your ACT Assessment date.

ACT ASSESSMENT CONTENTS AND FORMAT

The ACT Assessment is a three-hour exam broken into four sections, each of which is separately timed. With breaks and with time spent listening to instructions and passing out and returning forms, the actual time spent taking the exam is four or more hours.

The four sections test Standard English skills, math skills, reading comprehension skills, and science reasoning skills. No one is expected to know every answer to every section. Because the ACT Assessment assesses the full range of students, from the less-than-average to the brilliant, there will be questions that most students will not be able to answer. That is taken into account in the scoring.

The ACT Assessment contains a total of 216 multiple-choice questions, divided among the four subject areas or sections. The following table gives you an at-a-glance look at the content breakdown.

Summary of the ACT Assessment

216 Questions – 2 hours, 55 minutes

Standard English Test – 45 minutes

40 questions on usage and mechanics

35 questions on rhetorical skills

75 QUESTIONS TOTAL

Reading Comprehension Test – 35 minutes

10 questions on prose fiction

10 questions on a humanities passage

10 questions on a social studies passage

10 questions on a natural science passage

40 QUESTIONS TOTAL

Math Test – 60 minutes

14 questions on arithmetic

10 questions on elementary algebra

9 questions on intermediate algebra

9 questions on coordinate geometry

14 questions on plane geometry

4 questions on trigonometry

60 QUESTIONS TOTAL

Science Reasoning Test – 35 minutes

15 questions on data representation

18 questions of research summaries

7 questions on conflicting opinions

40 QUESTIONS TOTAL

In the next part of this chapter, you learn what each section of the ACT Assessment contains and how it's organized.

THE ACT ASSESSMENT ENGLISH TEST

The ACT Assessment English Test lasts 45 minutes and contains 75 questions. Of those questions, 40 test your knowledge of grammar, usage, punctuation, and sentence structure. The other 35 questions address the more subtle points of writing, such as the organization of the ideas presented, the logic of the ideas, and whether the ideas are expressed in the best way possible.

The ACT Assessment English test is broken down into two areas—usage/mechanics and rhetorical skills. Usage and mechanics cover those aspects of writing where there are strict rules—grammar, usage, punctuation, sentence structure. Rhetorical skills cover writing style, how to express an idea.

USAGE AND MECHANICS

The first area might be easier for some people to grasp because "mechanically" a sentence is either right or wrong.

> *Example:* Because he needs to swap the VW Beetle for the mini-van to take the Cub Scout troop home he will go to lunch at the same time as his wife had gone.

There are two mechanical errors in the sentence. There should be a comma after "home" to separate the subordinate clause from the main clause. And there is an error in the tense of the final verb; instead of "had gone," it should be "goes." Without making these corrections, the sentence is wrong.

RHETORICAL SKILLS

Rhetorical skills involve something subtler. There might be no mechanical error, but often you can "hear" the mistake.

> *Example:* As I previously mentioned to you when explaining at last week's meeting the incredible and undisputed advantages of combining our two clubs, *The Poetry Society* and *Poets Out of the Closet*, I have written up here for your further study my thoughts on the matter, detailing the many benefits that will accrue to both organizations.

There's nothing "mechanically" wrong with this sentence. It's a complete sentence and not a fragment; the subjects and verbs within the clauses agree with each other; the punctuation is correct. However, it would be much clearer to write the following:

> At last week's meeting, I said there were benefits to combining our two clubs. Here's a note repeating why.

CAUTION

Although each ACT Assessment exam is set up roughly as described, not every ACT Assessment exam contains the same questions. The exam content can vary not only among different areas of the country, but even among students within the same test room. This might mean that the questions are in a rearranged order or that the questions themselves are different. Some exams even include "experimental" questions—questions that the test-makers are thinking of including but must first try on actual students. (Experimental questions are not included in the scoring.)

Knowing this helps you resist the temptation to look at a neighbor's sheet.

Wordiness and repetition are just two of the rhetorical errors that will appear on the test. Other areas include clarity, logic, organization, and expression. Is the passage ambiguous? Can you understand the writer's purpose? Does the writer present an argument that moves from point A, to B, to C, to D, to the conclusion? Or does the passage move from point A to B, jump to the conclusion, then double back to D, and back again to C? Is the passage well-written and original, or is it filled with cliches? Look for overall problems like these.

THE ACT ASSESSMENT MATH TEST

The ACT Assessment Math Test lasts 60 minutes and contains 60 questions. There are 14 questions on pre-algebra, which encompasses basic arithmetic and such things as linear equations and simple probability. Then there are 10 questions on elementary algebra, and then 9 questions on intermediate algebra. Coordinate geometry (9 questions) includes graphing equations, slope, distance, and midpoints. Plane geometry (14 questions) includes questions on plane figures—such as circles, squares, triangles—as well as proofs. Finally, there are 4 questions on trigonometry.

The ACT Assessment Math Test, then, is broken down into six areas: pre-algebra, elementary algebra, intermediate algebra, coordinate geometry, plane geometry, and trigonometry. These six areas are scored as three, with a subscore for pre-algebra/elementary algebra, a subscore for intermediate algebra/coordinate geometry, and a subscore for plane geometry/trigonometry. Let's look closer at the questions within this section of the ACT Assessment.

PRE-ALGEBRA/ELEMENTARY ALGEBRA

Pre-algebra covers those basic elements we tend of think of as "arithmetic"—basic whole-number operations; work with fractions, decimals, and integers; square roots, ratios, percents, and proportion. It also includes scientific notation, factors, simple linear equations, and the interpretation of data from graphs. With algebra, linear equations are replaced by quadratic equations, there are more variables, equations are solved by factoring, and problems concern properties of exponents and square roots.

INTERMEDIATE ALGEBRA/COORDINATE GEOMETRY

Intermediate algebra involves more detailed work with quadratic equations, radical expressions, absolute values, functions, complex numbers, and roots of polynomials. Coordinate Geometry takes algebraic principles and plots them out physically on a graph—a coordinate plane. Problems using graphs include plotting equalities and inequalities, and finding slopes, distances, and midpoints.

PLANE GEOMETRY/TRIGONOMETRY

Plane geometry is what we first think of when we hear the word "geometry"—plane figures such as circles, squares, triangles, trapezoids, rhombi, and others. Problems involve working with the properties of these figures—angles, arcs, parallel lines, etc.—and include the solving of geometric proofs. Trigonometry covers trigonometric functions, identities, and relations—working with sines, cosines, tangents, cotangents, secants, and cosecants.

THE ACT ASSESSMENT READING TEST

The ACT Assessment Reading Test lasts 35 minutes and contains 40 questions. The questions test your level of comprehension: do you understand a passage well enough to answer questions about it? Because reading is essential to every subject, there are 10 questions using social studies passages, 10 using natural science, 10 using prose fiction, and 10 using passages about the humanities—music, art, theater, and so on. Here's a closer look at each of these question types

Most of the questions on the ACT Assessment Reading Test have to do with comprehension: Do you understand what the author is saying?

> *Example:* After that night, Jack forbade his cousin Sarah from ever contacting him or any member of his family again, under threat of legal action.

A question of comprehension would in some way repeat the facts: Jack did not want to see his cousin Sarah ever again, he did not want his family to see Sarah ever again, and if she attempted to contact him or his family, he would see that she suffered a legal penalty.

Other questions on the test have to do with implications: What else is implied but not necessarily stated? To pick up the full implications, the sentence might need to be read within the context of the whole passage. In the previous example, possible implications are that Sarah did something "that night" which prompted Jack's reaction, that Sarah might be dangerous, or that Jack is afraid of Sarah.

Some questions have to do with style and structure, the presentation of the ideas. Does a passage present several approaches to one idea, or does it present several ideas? Does it give evidence supporting one theory or a pro-and-con debate about the theory? Does it compare and contrast two people, things, or ideas? Or does it show step-by-step how something happened?

The score breakdowns come in the subject matter of the reading material. Reading is tested in four subjects—social studies, natural sciences, prose fiction, and the humanities. These four areas are scored as two, with a subscore for social studies/natural sciences reading skills and a subscore for prose fiction/humanities reading skills.

TIP
You can use a calculator on the ACT Assessment math test, but only a simple four-function, scientific, or graphing calculator. Calculators that produce a paper tape or otherwise make noise are not allowed; neither are laptops, writing pads, or calculators with a typewriter keypad (a QWERTY keyboard). If you're not sure if your specific make and model of calculator qualifies, check the listing on the ACT Assessment Web site (www.act.org/aap/).

SOCIAL STUDIES/NATURAL SCIENCES

More scholarly material is likely to fall within these areas and includes excerpts from books, magazines, newspapers, and journals. Topics within social studies range from the history, political science, and economics you might naturally expect, to the fields of anthropology, sociology, and psychology. The natural sciences cover the physical sciences, biology, chemistry, and physics. You don't necessarily need to have taken courses in psychology or physics just to understand what a well-written passage about the topic means.

PROSE FICTION/HUMANITIES

The passages of prose fiction might be a short story in itself, or selections from short stories, novellas, and novels. The ACT Assessment does not use material from poetry or drama. The humanities questions will have passages about music, visual arts, theater, philosophy, architecture, and dance.

THE ACT ASSESSMENT SCIENCE REASONING TEST

The ACT Assessment Science Reasoning Test lasts 35 minutes and contains 40 questions. Encompassing biology, physics, chemistry, and earth science, the test measures not so much your "book knowledge" of a particular subject but your ability to interpret and analyze problems, given certain information. The test is broken into 15 questions on data representation (using graphs and tables), 18 questions on research summaries (understanding the design and results of experiments), and 7 questions on conflicting viewpoints (understanding and comparing different hypotheses).

Though it encompasses biology, physics, chemistry, and earth and space science, the Science Reasoning Test does not measure your knowledge of content in those areas. Instead, the emphasis is on the "reasoning"—if presented with adequate information, can you interpret it and draw conclusions? In other words, do you have the ability to think like a scientist?

Three areas are tested: data representation, research summaries, and conflicting hypotheses. However, in this one instance alone the ACT Assessment has no breakdown of topics for subscores. There's only one score for the Science Reasoning Test. The following sections take a closer look at the ACT Assessment Science Reasoning question types.

DATA REPRESENTATION

In this section, information is presented in the form of graphs, tables, charts, and diagrams. Questions determine not only if you can "read" the graph (that is, understand what it means), but if you can spot trends (that is, if you can make logical predictions about what will happen next).

RESEARCH SUMMARIES

These passages briefly describe experiments and their results. Questions in this area might ask about the design of the experiment or the interpretation of the results. For example, can you take the results and apply them to a new situation not described in the original passage?

CONFLICTING HYPOTHESES

Conflicting hypotheses present individual points of view about a scientific issue, the "pro" and "con" of a debate. Questions will analyze and compare the different theories for such things as logic, adequate proof, and so on. Other questions might have to do with hidden assumptions: What is the author assuming to be true about his or her position, or about the opposition's, without necessarily having the proof to back it up?

NUTS AND BOLTS: THE ACT ASSESSMENT TEST BOOKLET AND ANSWER SHEET

The format of the ACT Assessment exam should be familiar to you from standardized tests in school. All of the previously discussed questions are printed in a booklet you will receive the day of the test. Although you may mark up this booklet, for scoring purposes the answers must be put on the answer sheet, which is a separate piece of paper.

Questions for all four subject tests go on a separate answer sheet. You should be familiar with this type of answer sheet from other standardized tests—a fill-in-the-circle grid. All questions are multiple choice. The English, Reading, and Science Reasoning Tests have four choices for each answer; the Math Test has five choices for each answer.

Completely fill in the circle of your choice with your pencil. The sheets are "read" and graded by computer, so it's important that your mark is clear and complete. A check in the circle or an X through it might not be readable by the machine and possibly won't be counted even if your answer is correct. See the figure below for an example of the answer sheet and the correct way to fill in your answers (you'll see some incorrect examples there, too). Be sure to mark only one circle per question and do not to skip lines by mistake because one misplaced mark can make every answer following it wrong.

TEST 1

1 Ⓐ ● Ⓒ Ⓓ   10 Ⓕ Ⓖ ● Ⓙ   20 Ⓕ Ⓖ Ⓗ Ⓙ
2 Ⓕ Ⓖ Ⓗ ●   11 Ⓐ Ⓑ Ⓒ Ⓓ   21 Ⓐ Ⓑ Ⓒ Ⓓ
3 Ⓐ ● Ⓒ Ⓓ   12 Ⓕ Ⓖ ● Ⓙ   22 Ⓕ Ⓖ Ⓗ Ⓙ
4 ● Ⓖ Ⓗ Ⓙ   13 ● Ⓑ Ⓒ Ⓓ   23 Ⓐ Ⓑ Ⓒ Ⓓ
                14 Ⓕ Ⓖ ⊗ Ⓙ   24 Ⓕ Ⓖ Ⓗ Ⓙ

How to mark the answer sheet.

TIP
The Science Reasoning Test doesn't test your specific science knowledge, though of course it's helpful if you have it. All the information you need will be right in the passage. Very often it's not the labels that are important but rather it is the numbers and the results. So a passage might be about three different bacteria: *Clostridium botulinum, Escherichia coli, and Lactobacillus acidophilus.* It's the result, what happened to or because of the bacteria, that's important, not the names of the bacteria. You could probably substitute X, Y, and Z in this passage and in many others for the scientific terms and still understand the results and be able to answer the questions.

To help prevent test-takers from skipping answers, the ACT Assessment answer sheet is formatted a bit differently than what you might be used to seeing. Instead of each set of choices being A, B, C, and D—or A, B, C, D, and E for Math—the ACT Assessment answer sheet alternates between *sets* of answers. As you can see in the figure on the previous page, the odd-numbered questions starting with Question 1 use A, B, C, and D—or A, B, C, D, and E—then the even-numbered questions starting with Question 2 use F, G, H and J—or F, G, H, J and K for Math. This format is to help catch your attention if you miss a line and begin to fill in an answer for the wrong question.

HOW THE ACT ASSESSMENT IS SCORED

For each of the four tests, the number of correct answers is determined, giving you a raw score. The raw score for each subject is then "scaled" or calculated in such a way as to make the varying ACT Assessment exams given on that day equal to each other. So if you receive a slightly harder test than your neighbor, the increased level of difficulty will be taken into account. The scaled scores range from 1 to the highest of 36. In recent years the average score for each subject has been 21.

No single test is a completely accurate measure of a person's true ability. Everything from the weather, to the testing environment, to a person's physical and emotional well-being can affect an individual's results. To account for this, the ACT Assessment test-makers have determined that there's a 4-point "margin of error" for each subject score—that if there could be a completely accurate measure of your ability in that subject, it would fall within those four points.

In addition, within each subject you get subscores for different areas of that subject. For example, in English, you'll get a subscore for usage and mechanics and a subscore for rhetorical skills. Subscores range from 1 to the highest of 18. You'll also receive a composite score that's the average of all four subject scores.

Because everyone taking the ACT Assessment is a potential competitor for the same college seat that *you* want, the ACT Assessment results also include a percentile score. The percentile score—based on the more familiar 1–100%—measures your composite score against the composite score of other test-takers. The number indicates the percentage of students that are below you. So if you received an ACT Assessment percentile of 87%, that means you scored better than 87% of other test-takers.

HOW COLLEGE ADMISSIONS OFFICES USE THE ACT ASSESSMENT SCORE

Every college that you list on your ACT Assessment form will receive a copy of your scores, as well as your personal profile and information about your high school performance. What does a college do with the scores? Obviously, it looks for high scores, but it also takes into consideration your school record. Some people are not good test-takers: They may be better at writing reports or participating in class. Most colleges recognize these differences, although admittedly there are some that use an arbitrary ACT Assessment score to eliminate most applicants.

High ACT Assessment scores can help offset average or less-then-average high-school grades. If the ACT Assessment score is higher, colleges will look to your personal information to help explain the difference. Perhaps you received only a B in chemistry, but that was while you were also president of the debate team, sports editor for the school paper, member of the soccer team, and a representative on the student senate. Or perhaps financial need forced you to hold a part-time job throughout the school year. Or perhaps you had personal circumstances, such as a lengthy illness, that made you fall behind.

Colleges also look at the ACT Assessment scores to see if there's a balance between the different subject areas. A student's major might be Math, but he or she will also have to take classes in a variety of other subjects, depending on the particular college's requirements. So although a 36 on the ACT Assessment Math test would be wonderful (and roughly a 1 in 14,000 possibility), its being combined with a 12 on the Reading exam would make an admissions officer doubt that the applicant could pass the many courses other than Math required for a college career.

In addition, colleges use the ACT Assessment scores to measure you against this year's applicants. Admissions officers face a changing pool of applicants every year. For example, if the college received a terrific write-up in a popular national magazine or, on the other hand, a critical write-up, applications could double—or be cut in half. So what is an average score one year might be high or low another year, depending on who your actual competition is.

After a student is accepted, a college might use the ACT Assessment score together with his or her high-school performance to decide placement in freshmen classes. For example, if a particular course has three levels of study—basic, intermediate, and advanced—the ACT Assessment score might be used to place the student in the appropriate level. The score might also be used to approve a student's choice of major. For example, if a student wishes to major in physics, but his or her high-school grades and ACT Assessment Science Reasoning Test indicate a lack of ability for this difficult course of study, the college might advise the student against choosing that major and might even base acceptance on the student's willingness to change majors.

Finally, the ACT Assessment score together with high-school performance is often considered when financial aid is awarded, both as scholarships or loans.

TIP

Most colleges will officially deny using a cut-off point on ACT Assessment scores, despite whatever they do in practice. A cut-off score is a simple, time-saving way to review hundreds, even thousands of applications by eliminating those from applicants whose score is below a pre-determined minimum cut-off point. It also enables colleges to "skim" those who are generally the best students off the top of the application pile. When cut-off scores are used, just a few extra points can be crucial. That's what makes this guide so valuable, and your dedication to preparation so important.

REGISTERING FOR THE ACT ASSESSMENT

Because the ACT Assessment is a standard part of the college admissions process, most high school guidance offices have descriptive brochures on the ACT Assessment that include a registration form. The ACT Assessment is given on Saturday mornings five times during each year in February, April, June, October, and December. There are more than 5,000 testing locations throughout the United States and Canada, possibly even your own high school. It is also offered overseas. You can request which testing center you prefer.

If your guidance office does not have a brochure, you can call the ACT Assessment National Office directly (see, "How to Contact the ACT Assessment Office," later in this chapter) to request a registration form.

Online registration is also possible via the ACT, Inc. site (www.act.org/aap/). Use of a credit card is needed to pay the fee online. Whether you apply by mail or online, the fee is the same.

CALCULATING THE TESTING FEE

The basic fee is low, $21 as we go to press, except in Florida, where it's $24. The basic fee includes reporting your score to up to four colleges. However, additional fees can really boost that low basic cost. Initial registration for the ACT Assessment by telephone requires an additional $10. Late registration requires an additional $15.

Including a fifth and sixth college on your initial registration form requires an additional $6 each. If you decide to wait for your scores first, then ask that they be reported, you'll pay an additional $7 per report per test date for normal processing. Rush processing is available; the fees are determined by what level of priority is requested.

Each test date has a cut-off date for registering, so check your brochure or the Web site to make sure you apply in time without incurring the penalty. If you miss even the late cut-off, you may apply for standby testing for an additional $30. The $30 is not a guarantee that you will take the test. It only gives you the right to go to a test center and wait until all the test-takers have arrived and material has been distributed. If there is a seat left and materials left, then you may take the test.

WHEN SHOULD YOU TAKE THE ACT ASSESSMENT?

Because test results take an average of four weeks after the test date to be reported, you want to schedule the ACT Assessment accordingly, plus allow time for delays. ACT Assessment scores are always mailed and are never released by phone. That means, at the bare minimum, you should take the ACT Assessment eight weeks before the earliest college-application deadline you have.

However, you'll put yourself under considerably less pressure if you take the ACT Assessment even earlier than that. An early ACT Assessment score enables you to take the option of early admission, as well as the option of taking the test again. Even with preparation, many students take the ACT Assessment at least twice, then choose the higher of the scores. The choice of which scores to report is up to the test-taker, but scores cannot be divided. You can not, for example, take an English score from an April test date and a Math score from a June test date. Only a single date's scores will be reported.

What does all this timeline advice come down to? It means it's best to take the ACT Assessment sometime in the second semester of your junior year.

WHERE SHOULD YOU TAKE THE ACT ASSESSMENT?

It's up to you. Look at the centers listed in the brochure or on the Web site. Is your own school one of them? Would a familiar surrounding soothe you, or would nervous friends just pass their anxiety on to you? What do you know of the other test centers? Your cousin goes to one. Doesn't she always complain that her school freezes its students in the winter and roasts them in the summer? On the day of the test, when you're trying to concentrate, such things become important considerations.

If you are taking the ACT Assessment in an unfamiliar site, be sure you know how to get there and how long it takes to get there. A dry run to the site beforehand can be very helpful.

A LOOK AHEAD: WHAT YOU NEED TO DO THE DAY OF THE ACT ASSESSMENT

You must bring to the test center the following items:

- Your official admissions ticket, which you'll receive in the mail after you've registered
- Photo identification, such as your picture in the yearbook or a driver's license with picture, a physical description of you written on school letterhead by the guidance office, or a picture of you with a notarized statement stating that the picture is you
- Two or three sharpened #2 pencils with erasers

Although they're not necessary, it's also advisable to bring:

- A battery-operated four-function, scientific, or graphing calculator (all other kinds are forbidden, including calculators with paper tape, calculators with a power cord, pen input devices, laptops, electronic writing pads, and so on)
- A snack for break, such as a granola bar or a bottle of juice
- A sweater in case there's too little heat or too much air-conditioning

Of course, you will also bring a well-rested, well-fed student who is calm and confident with the knowledge that his or her ACT Assessment preparation has been the most thorough and effective possible with the help of *Master the ACT Assessment.*

SPECIAL REGISTRATION SITUATIONS

Although most of the almost one-and-three-quarter million students this year will register and take the ACT Assessment under the circumstances described above, some applicants require special consideration. In the decades that the ACT Assessment has been administered, just about every possible situation has come up and there are procedures for most.

FINANCIAL HARDSHIP

The $20 basic fee might not seem expensive to many people, but to some families it might mean the difference between buying—or not buying—a bag of much-needed groceries. After additional fees are added in for extra services, the cost can easily triple.

If you feel that the registration fee would be a financial hardship, it might be possible for you to get the fee waived. Do not contact ACT, Inc. directly; see your guidance office, which should have an ACT Assessment fee-waiver form. If you qualify for consideration, fill out the form and submit it with your registration form.

The terms for qualifying are one of the following: if the student's family receives public assistance, if the student is a ward of the state or is in a foster home, or if total family income is at or below the figure cited in the Bureau of Labor Statistics Low Standard Budget.

NON-SATURDAY TESTING

If your religious beliefs prevent you from taking the ACT Assessment on the usually scheduled Saturday dates, you can apply for a non-Saturday date. The ACT Assessment brochure has a list of non-Saturday dates and the test centers that offer them. If there is no non-Saturday test center within 50 miles of your residence, you can arrange for individualized testing from the ACT Assessment Universal Testing office (see below).

PHYSICAL ACCOMMODATIONS

Students with disabilities might need special physical accommodations to take the test, such as a different seating arrangement for a wheelchair, a large-print test booklet and answer sheet, or a sign-language interpreter to repeat the proctor's verbal instructions.

If you fall into this category, contact your guidance office. The guidance office will then give you a letter describing the accommodation needed and why it's needed, that confirms you receive a similar accommodation to take tests at school, and that verifies you do not also need extra test time. Send this letter with your registration form.

EXTENDED TEST TIME

Certain learning disabilities, physical conditions, and psychological conditions might require that a student take an untimed test in order for the results to be judged fairly. This option is available at regularly scheduled ACT Assessment test centers, but only during the October, December, and April dates. Up to five hours of total testing time is allowed.

Again, see your guidance office or contact the ACT, Inc. office. Either will provide you with a copy of a form called the *ACT Assessment Application for Extended Time National Testing.* You need to complete the form and file it with your registration.

HOMEBOUND OR CONFINED STUDENTS

Certain applicants might not be able to get to a test center at all for many reasons. They might be homebound by disability or long-term illness or might be incarcerated at the time of testing. Such students should write to the Act Universal Testing Office (see the following section, "How to Contact the ACT, Inc. Office") and describe their situation. The ACT, Inc. office will contact these students directly to arrange for individualized testing.

If you have questions about any of the above special registration situations—or any general questions—contact the ACT, Inc. office directly.

HOW TO CONTACT THE ACT, INC. OFFICE

Because of the volume of questions it handles, ACT Assessment has different phone numbers, office hours, and addresses for the various issues that come up.

- **For registration material, questions, and problems** (including lost or delayed admission tickets, test center changes, test date changes, incorrect information on an admission ticket, or cancellation of scores), call (319) 337-1270 central time from 8 a.m. to 8 p.m., Monday through Friday. Or write to ACT Assessment Registration, P.O. Box 414, Iowa City, IA 52243-0414.

- **To re-register when taking the test again,** first complete a copy of the phone worksheet in the registration booklet, make sure you have use of a touch-tone phone and a credit card, then call (800) 525-6926 twenty-four hours a day.

- **For questions about I.D. requirements** (including which forms of I.D. are acceptable and to report being denied admittance to a test center), call (319) 337-1510 central time from 8:30 a.m. to 4:30 p.m., Monday through Friday. Or write to ACT Assessment Test Administration, P.O. Box 168, Iowa City, IA 52243-0168.

- **For questions about score reports** (including additional score reports, delayed or missing score reports, and score report corrections), call (319) 337-1313 central time from 8:30 a.m. to 4:30 p.m., Monday through Friday. Or write to ACT Assessment Records, P.O. Box 451, Iowa City, IA 52243-0451.

- **For questions about special physical accommodations** for students who can take the test during regular time limits on national test dates, call (319) 337-1510 central time from 8:30 a.m. to 4:30 p.m., Monday through Friday. Or write to ACT Assessment Test Administration, P.O. Box 168, Iowa City, IA 52243-0168.

- **For questions about extended-time testing** during the regular national test dates in October, December, or April, call (319) 337-1270 central time from 8:30 a.m. to 4:30 p.m., Monday through Friday. Or write to ACT Assessment Registration, P.O. Box 414, Iowa City, IA 52243-0414.

- **For questions about extended time and alternate formats** at specially arranged times that are not during the national dates, call (319) 337-1332 central time from 8:30 a.m. to 4:30 p.m., Monday through Friday. Or write to ACT Assessment Special Testing, P.O. Box 4028, Iowa City, IA 52243-4028.

- **For questions about homebound or confined students,** call (319) 337-1332 central time from 8:30 a.m. to 4:30 p.m., Monday through Friday. Or write to ACT Assessment Universal Testing, P.O. Box 4028, Iowa City, IA 52243-4028.

- **For questions about testing outside of the United States,** call (319) 337-1448 central time from 8:30 a.m. to 4:30 p.m., Monday through Friday. Or write to ACT Assessment Universal Testing, P.O. Box 4028, Iowa City, IA 52243-4028.

- **For questions about no non-Saturday test sites within 50 miles,** call (319) 337-1332 central time from 8:30 a.m. to 4:30 p.m., Monday through Friday. Or write to ACT Assessment Universal Testing, P.O. Box 4028, Iowa City, IA 52243-4028.

- **For challenges about test questions,** request a Test Question Inquiry Form from ACT Assessment Test Administration, P.O. Box 168, Iowa City, IA 52243-0168. The form is also available online at the ACT Assessment Web site (www.act.org/aap/) so your challenge may be submitted electronically.

- **For callers using a TDD (text telephone),** call (319) 337-1524 central time from 8:30a.m. to 4:30p.m., Monday through Friday.

Summary: What You Need to Know About the ACT Assessment

- The ACT Assessment, a battery of multiple-choice tests used by colleges and universities to assess applicants, is given five times each year, across the U.S. and Canada, and overseas.

- The ACT Assessment is a three-hour exam of 216 questions, divided into four sections that test skills in Standard English, math, reading comprehension, and science reasoning. The questions are designed to cover these areas at the standard level taught in most high schools across the country.

- The ACT Assessment English test covers two broad skill sets: usage/mechanics and rhetorical skills.

- The ACT Assessment Math test covers six areas: pre-algebra, elementary algebra, intermediate algebra, coordinate geometry, plane geometry, and trigonometry.

- The ACT Assessment Reading exam tests your ability to read and interpret information from written passages drawn from four basic subject areas: social studies, natural science, prose fiction, and humanities.

- The ACT Assessment Science Reasoning test encompasses biology, physics, chemistry, and earth science. This part of the ACT Assessment tests your ability to interpret and analyze problems, based on information supplied to you in the exam.

- For each of the four ACT Assessment tests, your score is based on a "scaled score"; because the specific content of each ACT Assessment might be different, scaling is necessary to standardize your results with those of everyone else who takes the exam. Your raw score is determined by the number of correct answers on your exam; the raw score is then scaled.

- Your ACT Assessment score is only one of the factors considered by college admissions offices; they also assess your high school performance, your personal profile and circumstances, and other information you submit with your application.

- Take the ACT Assessment as early as you can, so you have time to retake it if necessary. For your scores to be available for your college applications, you should take the ACT Assessment *no less* than eight weeks before the earliest college-application deadline that you have.

If You Had to Take the Test Today: The ACT Assessment Self-Evaluation Test

How would you score if you had to take the ACT Assessment today—without any knowledge of the test contents and format, without any subject study, without any specific test-taking strategies? Doing this initial exercise will give you a general idea of what that score might be.

More importantly, this exercise gives you your first inside look at the ACT Assessment—its format, its contents, its levels of difficulty. The exercise also offers the most objective way to evaluate what your strengths and weaknesses will be under actual testing conditions. In addition, it enables you to establish a starting point for your preparation.

TAKING THE ACT ASSESSMENT SELF-EVALUATION TEST

As much as you might dread jumping into the ACT Assessment waters, the ACT Assessment diagnostic test gives you the best opportunity to evaluate where your skills are now—and where they need to be. DO NOT SKIP THIS ESSENTIAL STEP. Doing this exercise first shows your current level of readiness. Only by having this first score will you be able to measure your progress—to know which areas need to be improved and which ones need less attention, even to know that you have improved at all. Then if test nerves start to eat away at you midway through your preparation and you ask yourself "What's the use?"—you can look at your increasing scores and regain your confidence.

This self-evaluation test is the first of four full-length practice tests of the ACT Assessment included in this book. Since the results of this diagnostic test will help you form your study plan and track your progress as you prepare for the real ACT Assessment, try to simulate a genuine testing environment for yourself. Plan to do the exercise in one sitting; if you take no breaks between sections, you will need about ninety minutes. Work on a clear desk or table. Don't use notes, textbooks, or other reference material. A simple calculator may be used only where indicated. You may also use blank scrap paper to work out your answers.

Time each section, just as it would be timed under normal testing conditions. Use a stopwatch or kitchen timer, or have someone else time you. Don't try to time yourself with a clock or watch; it's too easy to lose track while you're involved in a problem. After your time is up on one section of the test, stop at once and go on to the next section. When you are done, score yourself using only those questions you answered during the time limit. Be honest. No one else will see this first score or any other score in the book. Later, for practice purposes, complete the questions you were unable to finish at the time.

Enter your answers on the answer sheet on the next page. For the sake of convenience, you may photostat the answer sheet only.

The answer key, a full explanation of every answer, and information on how to interpret your score follow the test.

THE ACT ASSESSMENT SELF-EVALUATION TEST

Answer Sheet

Section 1

1 Ⓐ Ⓑ Ⓒ Ⓓ
2 Ⓕ Ⓖ Ⓗ Ⓙ
3 Ⓐ Ⓑ Ⓒ Ⓓ
4 Ⓕ Ⓖ Ⓗ Ⓙ
5 Ⓐ Ⓑ Ⓒ Ⓓ
6 Ⓕ Ⓖ Ⓗ Ⓙ
7 Ⓐ Ⓑ Ⓒ Ⓓ
8 Ⓕ Ⓖ Ⓗ Ⓙ
9 Ⓐ Ⓑ Ⓒ Ⓓ
10 Ⓕ Ⓖ Ⓗ Ⓙ
11 Ⓐ Ⓑ Ⓒ Ⓓ
12 Ⓕ Ⓖ Ⓗ Ⓙ
13 Ⓐ Ⓑ Ⓒ Ⓓ
14 Ⓕ Ⓖ Ⓗ Ⓙ
15 Ⓐ Ⓑ Ⓒ Ⓓ
16 Ⓕ Ⓖ Ⓗ Ⓙ
17 Ⓐ Ⓑ Ⓒ Ⓓ
18 Ⓕ Ⓖ Ⓗ Ⓙ
19 Ⓐ Ⓑ Ⓒ Ⓓ

20 Ⓕ Ⓖ Ⓗ Ⓙ
21 Ⓐ Ⓑ Ⓒ Ⓓ
22 Ⓕ Ⓖ Ⓗ Ⓙ
23 Ⓐ Ⓑ Ⓒ Ⓓ
24 Ⓕ Ⓖ Ⓗ Ⓙ
25 Ⓐ Ⓑ Ⓒ Ⓓ
26 Ⓕ Ⓖ Ⓗ Ⓙ
27 Ⓐ Ⓑ Ⓒ Ⓓ
28 Ⓕ Ⓖ Ⓗ Ⓙ
29 Ⓐ Ⓑ Ⓒ Ⓓ
30 Ⓕ Ⓖ Ⓗ Ⓙ
31 Ⓐ Ⓑ Ⓒ Ⓓ
32 Ⓕ Ⓖ Ⓗ Ⓙ
33 Ⓐ Ⓑ Ⓒ Ⓓ
34 Ⓕ Ⓖ Ⓗ Ⓙ
35 Ⓐ Ⓑ Ⓒ Ⓓ
36 Ⓕ Ⓖ Ⓗ Ⓙ
37 Ⓐ Ⓑ Ⓒ Ⓓ
38 Ⓕ Ⓖ Ⓗ Ⓙ

39 Ⓐ Ⓑ Ⓒ Ⓓ
40 Ⓕ Ⓖ Ⓗ Ⓙ
41 Ⓐ Ⓑ Ⓒ Ⓓ
42 Ⓕ Ⓖ Ⓗ Ⓙ
43 Ⓐ Ⓑ Ⓒ Ⓓ
44 Ⓕ Ⓖ Ⓗ Ⓙ
45 Ⓐ Ⓑ Ⓒ Ⓓ
46 Ⓕ Ⓖ Ⓗ Ⓙ
47 Ⓐ Ⓑ Ⓒ Ⓓ
48 Ⓕ Ⓖ Ⓗ Ⓙ
49 Ⓐ Ⓑ Ⓒ Ⓓ
50 Ⓕ Ⓖ Ⓗ Ⓙ
51 Ⓐ Ⓑ Ⓒ Ⓓ
52 Ⓕ Ⓖ Ⓗ Ⓙ
53 Ⓐ Ⓑ Ⓒ Ⓓ
54 Ⓕ Ⓖ Ⓗ Ⓙ
55 Ⓐ Ⓑ Ⓒ Ⓓ
56 Ⓕ Ⓖ Ⓗ Ⓙ
57 Ⓐ Ⓑ Ⓒ Ⓓ

58 Ⓕ Ⓖ Ⓗ Ⓙ
59 Ⓐ Ⓑ Ⓒ Ⓓ
60 Ⓕ Ⓖ Ⓗ Ⓙ
61 Ⓐ Ⓑ Ⓒ Ⓓ
62 Ⓕ Ⓖ Ⓗ Ⓙ
63 Ⓐ Ⓑ Ⓒ Ⓓ
64 Ⓕ Ⓖ Ⓗ Ⓙ
65 Ⓐ Ⓑ Ⓒ Ⓓ
66 Ⓕ Ⓖ Ⓗ Ⓙ
67 Ⓐ Ⓑ Ⓒ Ⓓ
68 Ⓕ Ⓖ Ⓗ Ⓙ
69 Ⓐ Ⓑ Ⓒ Ⓓ
70 Ⓕ Ⓖ Ⓗ Ⓙ
71 Ⓐ Ⓑ Ⓒ Ⓓ
72 Ⓕ Ⓖ Ⓗ Ⓙ
73 Ⓐ Ⓑ Ⓒ Ⓓ
74 Ⓕ Ⓖ Ⓗ Ⓙ
75 Ⓐ Ⓑ Ⓒ Ⓓ

Section 2

1 Ⓐ Ⓑ Ⓒ Ⓓ Ⓔ
2 Ⓕ Ⓖ Ⓗ Ⓙ Ⓚ
3 Ⓐ Ⓑ Ⓒ Ⓓ Ⓔ
4 Ⓕ Ⓖ Ⓗ Ⓙ Ⓚ
5 Ⓐ Ⓑ Ⓒ Ⓓ Ⓔ
6 Ⓕ Ⓖ Ⓗ Ⓙ Ⓚ
7 Ⓐ Ⓑ Ⓒ Ⓓ Ⓔ
8 Ⓕ Ⓖ Ⓗ Ⓙ Ⓚ
9 Ⓐ Ⓑ Ⓒ Ⓓ Ⓔ
10 Ⓕ Ⓖ Ⓗ Ⓙ Ⓚ
11 Ⓐ Ⓑ Ⓒ Ⓓ Ⓔ
12 Ⓕ Ⓖ Ⓗ Ⓙ Ⓚ
13 Ⓐ Ⓑ Ⓒ Ⓓ Ⓔ
14 Ⓕ Ⓖ Ⓗ Ⓙ Ⓚ
15 Ⓐ Ⓑ Ⓒ Ⓓ Ⓔ

16 Ⓕ Ⓖ Ⓗ Ⓙ Ⓚ
17 Ⓐ Ⓑ Ⓒ Ⓓ Ⓔ
18 Ⓕ Ⓖ Ⓗ Ⓙ Ⓚ
19 Ⓐ Ⓑ Ⓒ Ⓓ Ⓔ
20 Ⓕ Ⓖ Ⓗ Ⓙ Ⓚ
21 Ⓐ Ⓑ Ⓒ Ⓓ Ⓔ
22 Ⓕ Ⓖ Ⓗ Ⓙ Ⓚ
23 Ⓐ Ⓑ Ⓒ Ⓓ Ⓔ
24 Ⓕ Ⓖ Ⓗ Ⓙ Ⓚ
25 Ⓐ Ⓑ Ⓒ Ⓓ Ⓔ
26 Ⓕ Ⓖ Ⓗ Ⓙ Ⓚ
27 Ⓐ Ⓑ Ⓒ Ⓓ Ⓔ
28 Ⓕ Ⓖ Ⓗ Ⓙ Ⓚ
29 Ⓐ Ⓑ Ⓒ Ⓓ Ⓔ
30 Ⓕ Ⓖ Ⓗ Ⓙ Ⓚ

31 Ⓐ Ⓑ Ⓒ Ⓓ Ⓔ
32 Ⓕ Ⓖ Ⓗ Ⓙ Ⓚ
33 Ⓐ Ⓑ Ⓒ Ⓓ Ⓔ
34 Ⓕ Ⓖ Ⓗ Ⓙ Ⓚ
35 Ⓐ Ⓑ Ⓒ Ⓓ Ⓔ
36 Ⓕ Ⓖ Ⓗ Ⓙ Ⓚ
37 Ⓐ Ⓑ Ⓒ Ⓓ Ⓔ
38 Ⓕ Ⓖ Ⓗ Ⓙ Ⓚ
39 Ⓐ Ⓑ Ⓒ Ⓓ Ⓔ
40 Ⓕ Ⓖ Ⓗ Ⓙ Ⓚ
41 Ⓐ Ⓑ Ⓒ Ⓓ Ⓔ
42 Ⓕ Ⓖ Ⓗ Ⓙ Ⓚ
43 Ⓐ Ⓑ Ⓒ Ⓓ Ⓔ
44 Ⓕ Ⓖ Ⓗ Ⓙ Ⓚ
45 Ⓐ Ⓑ Ⓒ Ⓓ Ⓔ

46 Ⓕ Ⓖ Ⓗ Ⓙ Ⓚ
47 Ⓐ Ⓑ Ⓒ Ⓓ Ⓔ
48 Ⓕ Ⓖ Ⓗ Ⓙ Ⓚ
49 Ⓐ Ⓑ Ⓒ Ⓓ Ⓔ
50 Ⓕ Ⓖ Ⓗ Ⓙ Ⓚ
51 Ⓐ Ⓑ Ⓒ Ⓓ Ⓔ
52 Ⓕ Ⓖ Ⓗ Ⓙ Ⓚ
53 Ⓐ Ⓑ Ⓒ Ⓓ Ⓔ
54 Ⓕ Ⓖ Ⓗ Ⓙ Ⓚ
55 Ⓐ Ⓑ Ⓒ Ⓓ Ⓔ
56 Ⓕ Ⓖ Ⓗ Ⓙ Ⓚ
57 Ⓐ Ⓑ Ⓒ Ⓓ Ⓔ
58 Ⓕ Ⓖ Ⓗ Ⓙ Ⓚ
59 Ⓕ Ⓖ Ⓗ Ⓙ Ⓚ
60 Ⓐ Ⓑ Ⓒ Ⓓ Ⓔ

TEAR HERE

Section 3

1	Ⓐ	Ⓑ	Ⓒ	Ⓓ	11	Ⓐ	Ⓑ	Ⓒ	Ⓓ	21	Ⓐ	Ⓑ	Ⓒ	Ⓓ	31	Ⓐ	Ⓑ	Ⓒ	Ⓓ
2	Ⓕ	Ⓖ	Ⓗ	Ⓙ	12	Ⓕ	Ⓖ	Ⓗ	Ⓙ	22	Ⓕ	Ⓖ	Ⓗ	Ⓙ	32	Ⓕ	Ⓖ	Ⓗ	Ⓙ
3	Ⓐ	Ⓑ	Ⓒ	Ⓓ	13	Ⓐ	Ⓑ	Ⓒ	Ⓓ	23	Ⓐ	Ⓑ	Ⓒ	Ⓓ	33	Ⓐ	Ⓑ	Ⓒ	Ⓓ
4	Ⓕ	Ⓖ	Ⓗ	Ⓙ	14	Ⓕ	Ⓖ	Ⓗ	Ⓙ	24	Ⓕ	Ⓖ	Ⓗ	Ⓙ	34	Ⓕ	Ⓖ	Ⓗ	Ⓙ
5	Ⓐ	Ⓑ	Ⓒ	Ⓓ	15	Ⓐ	Ⓑ	Ⓒ	Ⓓ	25	Ⓐ	Ⓑ	Ⓒ	Ⓓ	35	Ⓐ	Ⓑ	Ⓒ	Ⓓ
6	Ⓕ	Ⓖ	Ⓗ	Ⓙ	16	Ⓕ	Ⓖ	Ⓗ	Ⓙ	26	Ⓕ	Ⓖ	Ⓗ	Ⓙ	36	Ⓕ	Ⓖ	Ⓗ	Ⓙ
7	Ⓐ	Ⓑ	Ⓒ	Ⓓ	17	Ⓐ	Ⓑ	Ⓒ	Ⓓ	27	Ⓐ	Ⓑ	Ⓒ	Ⓓ	37	Ⓐ	Ⓑ	Ⓒ	Ⓓ
8	Ⓕ	Ⓖ	Ⓗ	Ⓙ	18	Ⓕ	Ⓖ	Ⓗ	Ⓙ	28	Ⓕ	Ⓖ	Ⓗ	Ⓙ	38	Ⓕ	Ⓖ	Ⓗ	Ⓙ
9	Ⓐ	Ⓑ	Ⓒ	Ⓓ	19	Ⓐ	Ⓑ	Ⓒ	Ⓓ	29	Ⓐ	Ⓑ	Ⓒ	Ⓓ	39	Ⓐ	Ⓑ	Ⓒ	Ⓓ
10	Ⓕ	Ⓖ	Ⓗ	Ⓙ	20	Ⓕ	Ⓖ	Ⓗ	Ⓙ	30	Ⓕ	Ⓖ	Ⓗ	Ⓙ	40	Ⓕ	Ⓖ	Ⓗ	Ⓙ

Section 4

1	Ⓐ	Ⓑ	Ⓒ	Ⓓ	11	Ⓐ	Ⓑ	Ⓒ	Ⓓ	21	Ⓐ	Ⓑ	Ⓒ	Ⓓ	31	Ⓐ	Ⓑ	Ⓒ	Ⓓ
2	Ⓕ	Ⓖ	Ⓗ	Ⓙ	12	Ⓕ	Ⓖ	Ⓗ	Ⓙ	22	Ⓕ	Ⓖ	Ⓗ	Ⓙ	32	Ⓕ	Ⓖ	Ⓗ	Ⓙ
3	Ⓐ	Ⓑ	Ⓒ	Ⓓ	13	Ⓐ	Ⓑ	Ⓒ	Ⓓ	23	Ⓐ	Ⓑ	Ⓒ	Ⓓ	33	Ⓐ	Ⓑ	Ⓒ	Ⓓ
4	Ⓕ	Ⓖ	Ⓗ	Ⓙ	14	Ⓕ	Ⓖ	Ⓗ	Ⓙ	24	Ⓕ	Ⓖ	Ⓗ	Ⓙ	34	Ⓕ	Ⓖ	Ⓗ	Ⓙ
5	Ⓐ	Ⓑ	Ⓒ	Ⓓ	15	Ⓐ	Ⓑ	Ⓒ	Ⓓ	25	Ⓐ	Ⓑ	Ⓒ	Ⓓ	35	Ⓐ	Ⓑ	Ⓒ	Ⓓ
6	Ⓕ	Ⓖ	Ⓗ	Ⓙ	16	Ⓕ	Ⓖ	Ⓗ	Ⓙ	26	Ⓕ	Ⓖ	Ⓗ	Ⓙ	36	Ⓕ	Ⓖ	Ⓗ	Ⓙ
7	Ⓐ	Ⓑ	Ⓒ	Ⓓ	17	Ⓐ	Ⓑ	Ⓒ	Ⓓ	27	Ⓐ	Ⓑ	Ⓒ	Ⓓ	37	Ⓐ	Ⓑ	Ⓒ	Ⓓ
8	Ⓕ	Ⓖ	Ⓗ	Ⓙ	18	Ⓕ	Ⓖ	Ⓗ	Ⓙ	28	Ⓕ	Ⓖ	Ⓗ	Ⓙ	38	Ⓕ	Ⓖ	Ⓗ	Ⓙ
9	Ⓐ	Ⓑ	Ⓒ	Ⓓ	19	Ⓐ	Ⓑ	Ⓒ	Ⓓ	29	Ⓐ	Ⓑ	Ⓒ	Ⓓ	39	Ⓐ	Ⓑ	Ⓒ	Ⓓ
10	Ⓕ	Ⓖ	Ⓗ	Ⓙ	20	Ⓕ	Ⓖ	Ⓗ	Ⓙ	30	Ⓕ	Ⓖ	Ⓗ	Ⓙ	40	Ⓕ	Ⓖ	Ⓗ	Ⓙ

TEAR HERE

The ACT Assessment Self-Evaluation Test

SECTION 1: ENGLISH

75 Questions • Time—45 Minutes

Directions: This test consists of five passages in which particular words or phrases are underlined and numbered. Alongside the passage, you will see alternative words and phrases that could be substituted for the underlined part. You must select the alternative that expresses the idea most clearly and correctly or that best fits the style and tone of the entire passage. If the original version is best, select "No Change."

The test also includes questions about entire paragraphs and the passage as a whole. These questions are identified by a number in a box.

After you select the correct answer for each question, mark the oval representing the correct answer on your answer sheet.

Passage I

An Oboist's Quest

[1]

I started playing the oboe because <u>I've heard</u> it was a
1

challenging instrument. That was <u>four years ago</u>
2

<u>and, I've</u> enjoyed learning to play the oboe as much as

I expected. However, it was not until recently that I

realized what an oboist's real challenge is: finding good

oboe reeds.

[2]

Though the reed is a small part of the instrument, <u>they</u>
3

<u>largely</u> determine the quality of the oboe's sound.

Professional oboists make their own <u>reeds, so</u> students
4

like me must buy reeds either from their teachers or

from mail-order companies.

1. A. NO CHANGE
   B. I'd have heard
   C. I've been hearing
   D. I'd heard

2. F. NO CHANGE
   G. four years ago, and I've
   H. four years ago; and I've
   J. four years ago. And, I've

3. A. NO CHANGE
   B. they determine, in large part,
   C. it largely determines
   D. it determines largely

4. F. NO CHANGE
   G. reeds. So
   H. reeds; although
   J. reeds, but

[3]

My troubles began when my teacher stopped making <u>reeds. Sending</u> all of her students on a wild goose chase

5

for the perfect reed. The problem is that there is no such thing as a perfect reed, though oboists like to daydream about it. There is also no such thing as a perfect reed supplier. Reed makers are much in demand, and the reeds are often very expensive—<u>$15 to $20 each for</u>

6

<u>something which, in my opinion, is only worth $7.</u>

[4]

Also, the reed makers tend to take their time in

sending reeds to <u>you, I usually</u> have to wait three to six

7

weeks after they've received my check in the mail. This wouldn't be a problem if I always ordered my reeds <u>in advance of the time when I need them,</u> but oboe reeds

8

are temperamental and often crack or break without warning. Thus, I need to have several back-up reeds available at all times.

[5]

I first tried buying reeds from a reed maker in Massachusetts. They were pretty good at first, but they became progressively worse <u>and lower and lower in quality</u>

9

the longer I bought them from him. It got to the point where none of the reeds he supplied worked, so I had to move on.

5. A. NO CHANGE
   B. reeds. Thus sending
   C. reeds, she sent
   D. reeds, sending

6. At this point, the writer wants to provide readers with a specific detail to substantiate her claim about the expense of oboe reeds. Which alternative does that best?

   F. NO CHANGE
   G. something that I, a student with limited funds to spend, am highly concerned about.
   H. with an additional $3 to $5 charged for shipping and handling on every order sent.
   J. although professional oboe players could probably afford to pay a relatively high price for their reeds.

7. A. NO CHANGE
   B. you, usually I
   C. you; I usually
   D. one: I usually

8. F. NO CHANGE
   G. in advance of when I need them
   H. before when they are needed
   J. ahead of time

9. A. NO CHANGE
   B. and lower in quality
   C. in quality
   D. OMIT the underlined portion.

[6]

My next source was a company in California.

However, <u>they</u> sounded like ducks quacking, so I dropped
10

them from my list.

<u>Desperate, an oboist friend of my parents was the next</u>
11

<u>person I called.</u> She helped me fix a few salvageable

reeds I owned, and soon I had several which played in

tune and had good tone. It seemed my reed troubles

were

over. <u>However, within two weeks, those</u> precious reeds
12

were all played out, and I needed more.

[7]

Recently, a friend suggested a reed maker from New

York City whose reeds, she said, were rather good. I

called him up <u>immediate,</u> and he asked me questions
13

about my playing so that he could cater to my oboe

needs. He promised to send out a supply of reeds within

a week. Imagine my disappointment when the reeds he

sent turned out to be poorly made, with unstable tones

and a thin, unpleasant sound. My search for the perfect

reed continues. It may never come to an end until I learn

to make reeds myself.

10. F. NO CHANGE
    G. their reeds
    H. the reeds of this company
    J. this company

11. A. NO CHANGE
    B. Desperate, my parents called an oboist friend of theirs.
    C. Desperate, I called an oboist friend of my parents.
    D. An oboist friend of my parents was the next person I called, desperate.

12. F. NO CHANGE
    G. However, within two weeks; those
    H. Within two weeks however; those
    J. However, within two weeks those

13. A. NO CHANGE
    B. (Place before I)
    C. (Place after I)
    D. (Leave where it is now) immediately

Items 14 and 15 pose questions about the essay as a whole.

14. The writer wishes to include the following sentence in the essay:

    Oboe reeds are made from two pieces of cane tied together with string and supported by a cylindrical piece of metal with some cork wrapped around at the base.

    That sentence will fit most smoothly and logically into Paragraph:

    F. 2, before the first sentence.
    G. 2, after the last sentence.
    H. 3, after the last sentence.
    J. 4, before the first sentence.

GO ON TO THE NEXT PAGE ➤

15. Suppose the writer were to eliminate Paragraph 4. This omission would cause the essay as a whole to lose primarily:

A. a relevant anecdote about the unreliability of many makers of oboe reeds.

B. irrelevant details about the technicalities of ordering oboe reeds through the mail.

C. relevant details about some of the difficulties oboists encounter in maintaining an adequate supply of reeds.

D. an irrelevant anecdote about the slowness of mail-order oboe reed suppliers.

Passage II

The Viking Mission—In Search of Life

[1]

A major goal of the Viking spacecraft missions of the late 1980s <u>were to determine</u> whether the soil of Mars is

16

dead, like the soil of the moon, or teeming with micro scopic life, like the soils of Earth. Soil samples brought into the Viking lander were sent to three separate biological laboratories to be tested in different ways for the presence of <u>living things indicating the existence of life.</u>

17

[2]

18 First, it was assumed that life on Mars would be

like life on <u>Earth; which is</u> based on the element carbon

19

and thrives by chemically transforming carbon compounds. Second, on Earth, where there are large

16. F. NO CHANGE
  G. was to determine
  H. were determining
  J. was the determination of

17. A. NO CHANGE
  B. beings that indicated the existence of life.
  C. creatures that contained life.
  D. life.

18. Which of the following sentences, if added here, would most clearly and accurately indicate the topic of Paragraph 2?
  F. This was a challenging scientific assignment.
  G. The tests were based on two assumptions.
  H. The Viking scientists were uncertain how to proceed.
  J. There were several main objectives being pursued in these experiments.

19. A. NO CHANGE
  B. Earth that is
  C. Earth, which is
  D. Earth—

lifeforms (like human beings and pine trees), there are also small ones (like bacteria), and the small ones are far more abundant, <u>thousands or millions of them being</u>
20
in every gram of soil. To have the best possible chance of detecting life, an instrument should look for the most abundant kind of life.

[3]

21 Specifically, the three laboratories in the lander were designed to warm and nourish any life in the Martian soil and to detect with sensitive instruments the

chemical activity <u>of the organisms.</u>
22

[4]

One characteristic of earthly plants is <u>transforming</u>
23

carbon dioxide in the air into the compounds that <u>make</u>
24
<u>them up.</u> Accordingly, one Viking experiment, called the carbon assimilation test, added radioactive carbon dioxide to the atmosphere above the soil sample.

20. F. NO CHANGE
    G. with thousands or millions of them
    H. containing thousands or millions
    J. numbering in thousands or millions

21. Which of the following sentences, if added here, would best provide a smooth transition between the previous paragraph and this one?
    A. The Viking instruments were designed, therefore, to detect carbon-based Martian microbes or similar creatures living in the soil.
    B. Thus, the Viking scientists had first to determine what kind of life they would seek before designing experiments to uncover it.
    C. The Viking mission, then, was as much a matter of biological experimentation as of interplanetary exploration.
    D. The possibility of life on other planets has fascinated humankind for as long as people have stared in wonder at the beauty and mystery of the nighttime sky.

22. F. NO CHANGE
    G. of the organism's.
    H. of the organisms'.
    J. the organisms engaged in.

23. A. NO CHANGE
    B. the transformation of
    C. to transform
    D. that they transform

24. At this point, the writer would like to provide specific details about the plant structures created out of carbon dioxide. Which alternative does that best?
    F. NO CHANGE
    G. constitute the plants' physical substance.
    H. make up their roots, branches, and leaves.
    J. make up the various parts of the plants themselves.

GO ON TO THE NEXT PAGE

The sample was then flooded with simulated Martian sunlight. 25 If any Martian life-forms converted the carbon dioxide into other compounds, the compounds could be detected by their radioactivity.

[5]

[1] Living organisms on Earth give off gases. [2] A second experiment on each lander, the gas exchange test, was designed to detect this kind of activity. [3] Plants give off oxygen, animals give off carbon dioxide,

and water is exhaled by both. [4] Nutrients and water
                              26
were added to the soil, and the chemical composition of the gas above the soil was continuously analyzed for changes that might indicate life. 27

[6]

Finally, a third experiment on each lander was
       28
based on the fact that earthly animals consume organic compounds and give off carbon dioxide. The labeled release test added a variety of radioactive nutrients to the soil and then waited to see whether any radioactive carbon dioxide would be given off.

[7]

Much to the disappointment of scientists, the Viking

25. At this point, the writer is considering the addition of the following sentence:
The Martian day is 24.6 hours long, almost the same length as the day here on Earth.
Would this be a logical and relevant addition to the essay?
A. Yes, because it provides an interesting fact about Mars, which is the planet being discussed in the essay.
B. Yes, because the length of the Martian day affects the amount of sunlight to which possible Martian life-forms are exposed.
C. No, because the length of the Martian day is basically irrelevant to the topic of the Viking experiments.
D. No, because the sunlight mentioned in the previous sentence is simulated rather than real Martian sunlight.

26. F. NO CHANGE
G. and both exhale water.
H. with both exhaling water.
J. from both water is exhaled.

27. Which of the following sequences of sentences makes this paragraph most logical?
A. NO CHANGE
B. 1, 3, 2, 4
C. 1, 4, 3, 2
D. 2, 4, 1, 3

28. F. NO CHANGE
G. (Do NOT begin new paragraph) Finally, a
H. (Do NOT begin new paragraph) A
J. (Begin new paragraph) Nevertheless, a

experiments uncovered no clear indications of Mar tian life-forms. However, the experience <u>itself</u> of
29
designing and implementing the Viking experiments was useful. It has helped scientists to clarify their understanding of terrestrial life and formulate new ideas about life beyond Earth, which may be useful as further planetary explorations are conducted in the future.

29. A. NO CHANGE
   B. (Place after implementing)
   C. (Place after was)
   D. (Place after useful)

Item 30 poses a question about the essay as a whole.

30. Suppose the writer had been assigned to write a brief essay about the results of any single scientific research project of the last twenty years. Would this essay successfully fulfill the assignment?

   F. Yes, because the essay explains that the Viking experiments failed to detect any life in the Martian soil.

   G. Yes, because the essay describes in detail the nature of the experiments conducted by the Viking researchers.

   H. No, because the Viking experiments could be considered a series of projects rather than a single project.

   J. No, because almost the entire essay is devoted to the plans for the Viking missions rather than their results.

Passage III
The Not-So-Good Old Days

[1]

Many of us look back at the turn of the century through a haze of nostalgia. Perhaps it's because <u>we've</u>
31
<u>begun</u> to feel overwhelmed by modern technology—

computers, jets, fax machines—and long for <u>an era we</u>
32
<u>like to think of as having been</u> a simpler time. Perhaps

<u>its</u> images of glowing coal stoves, the gentle aura of
33
gaslight, the sound of a horse and buggy on the pavement, the simple pleasures of the "good old summer time," that make that era seem so appealing.

31. A. NO CHANGE
   B. we began
   C. we've began
   D. we begun

32. F. NO CHANGE
   G. what we think of as
   H. a return to a period that we want to consider
   J. a part of history that we regard as being

33. A. NO CHANGE
   B. it's
   C. it may be
   D. there are

GO ON TO THE NEXT PAGE ➡

[2]

[34] Although in our imaginations we see the "Gilded Age" as a more genteel time, the reality was less pleasant. In many respects, things were really not as good as we imagine they were in "the good old days."

[3]

[1] Take, for example, those glowing coal stoves. [2] By the 1880s, those who could afford $2,000 to

$4,000—a very considerable sum for the day—might
            35
install central heating. [3] But early radiators, though cleaner than coal, filled their homes with the constant noises of "water hammer" and hissing. [4] While it
                                                          36
provided relatively little heat, coal-burning stoves were all too powerful at using up the oxygen in a room and replacing it with enough soot and dust to make a house almost uninhabitable. [37]

[4]

Then there were those horses in the street. We think nostalgically of the days before automobiles befouled

our air, but horses and buggies produced a different kind
38
of pollution. The stench was overwhelming, and there was so much manure in the streets that some observers voiced fears that America's cities would disappear like

34. Which of the alternatives best introduces the central theme of the essay and provides an appropriate transition between the first and second paragraphs?
F. Yet modern technology has been more of a boon than a bane.
G. None of us, however, have actually experienced life as it was at the turn of the century.
H. Admittedly, life in today's world has both positive and negative aspects.
J. But was that world really as idyllic as we think?

35. A. NO CHANGE
B. —a huge chunk of change for those days—
C. —which would have been a lot of money then—
D. OMIT the underlined portion.

36. F. NO CHANGE
G. Little heat though they gave,
H. Although they provided relatively little heat,
J. While relatively little heat was provided,

37. Which of the following provides the most logical ordering of the sentences in Paragraph 3?
A. NO CHANGE
B. 1, 3, 4, 2
C. 1, 4, 2, 3
D. 2, 3, 1, 4

38. F. NO CHANGE
G. one's
H. their
J. this

ancient Pompeii—but buried under something other than volcanic ash. 39

[5]

Even worse, perhaps, were those "good old summer times." There was, of course, no air conditioning, and in the cities, at least, summers were hotter than they are today, <u>because of the shorter buildings then.</u> Contempo-
40

rary clothing, too, added to the problem—<u>the garments</u>
41
<u>worn by the average person during the 1890s were</u>
<u>considerably more bulky than those worn today.</u>

[6]

Much worse could be cited—the condition of the

39. At this point, the writer is considering the addition of the following sentence:

At the turn of the century in New York City, for example, there were 150,000 horses, each of which dropped between twenty and twenty-five pounds of manure every day, which was then spread around by the buggies' wheels.

Would this be a logical and relevant addition to the essay?

A. Yes, because it provides details concerning the pollution created by horses at the turn of the century.

B. Yes, because horses remain popular as pets and companions to this day.

C. No, because it refers only to New York City, whereas the main theme of the essay is more widely applicable.

D. No, because it fails to draw a detailed comparison to the pollution created today by automobiles.

40. F. NO CHANGE

G. because lower buildings did not shield the streets from the sun as well as today's sky-scrapers.

H. since the buildings in most cities at the time weren't as tall as they are now.

J. due to the relatively low height of most buildings then.

41. Which of the alternatives most effectively supports the assertion made earlier in the sentence about the discomforts of summer clothing at the turn of the century?

A. NO CHANGE

B. most people at the time wore heavy clothes, even during the summer, despite the fact that it only made them feel hotter.

C. heavy suits, long underwear, vests for men, and voluminous dresses with multiple under-garments and girdles for women.

D. unlike today, when many people wear shorts, open-toed shoes, and thin, airy shirts or blouses on the hottest summer days.

GO ON TO THE NEXT PAGE ➤

poor, the status of women and children, <u>medical science</u>
                                              42

<u>was undeveloped;</u> the list is almost endless. <u>It's</u> prob-
                                                    43

ably true that the pace of life was slower <u>and, at least in</u>
                                                 44

<u>that respect, perhaps</u> more congenial to human sensi-

bilities a hundred years ago, the truth is that the "good

old days" really weren't so good after all.

42. F. NO CHANGE
    G. the underdevelopment of the science of medi-
       cine,
    H. the undeveloped state of medical science;
    J. the fact that medical science had not been
       developed—

43. A. NO CHANGE
    B. It may be
    C. Since it is
    D. While it's

44. F. NO CHANGE
    G. and at least, in that respect perhaps
    H. and at least in that respect, perhaps
    J. and at least—in that respect—perhaps

Item 45 poses a question about the essay as a whole.

45. The writer wishes to include the following sen-
    tence in the essay:

    The heat waves were not just unpleasant, they
    could be deadly: during the summer of 1896,
    three thousand people and two thousand horses
    died of the heat in New York City alone.

    That sentence will fit most smoothly and logi-
    cally into Paragraph:
    A. 3, after the last sentence.
    B. 5, after the first sentence.
    C. 5, after the last sentence.
    D. 6, before the first sentence.

Passage IV

Gloria Steinem, Feminist Heroine

[1]

Gloria Steinem is a political writer and activist, <u>mostly</u>
                                                       46

<u>famous</u> for her work as a leading figure in the women's

rights movement. Growing up with the lasting effects of

the Great Depression of the 1930s on her once-wealthy

family, Steinem became an independent young woman,

46. F. NO CHANGE
    G. most famous
    H. more famous
    J. famousest

working her way through elite Smith College with

minimal aid from the school or her family. While in

college, she became engaged, but her fiancé called off

the <u>wedding; because his</u> parents felt that Steinem was

       47

not wealthy enough to marry into their family. It was

one of Steinem's first encounters with the social and

economic aspects of relations between the sexes.

[2]

    After this upsetting breakup, Steinem decided to take

refuge in India, making plans to attend the universities

of Delhi and Calcutta. However, while on her way to

India, she learned that she was pregnant with her fiancé's

child. <u>This is the fiancé who had previously left her.</u>

       48

Feeling that becoming a mother was an impossible

option at that time, Steinem had an abortion in <u>England.</u>

       49

<u>Where</u> the procedure was considerably easier and safer

<u>than in</u> the United States at that time.

  50

[3]

    <u>Soon</u> Steinem was back in America, finding steady

  51

work as a writer was quite difficult, especially for a

young woman. However, she was given the opportunity

to write one of her most enduring articles while

freelancing for the now-defunct magazine *Show*. Steinem

worked undercover as a scantily-clad "bunny" hostess

47. A. NO CHANGE
    B. wedding because his
    C. wedding because, his
    D. wedding, because, his

48. F. NO CHANGE
    G. (Her fiance had already left her.)
    H. He had left Steinem, as previously mentioned.
    J. OMIT the underlined portion.

49. A. NO CHANGE
    B. England, there
    C. England. In England,
    D. England, where

50. F. NO CHANGE
    G. than
    H. as in
    J. by comparison to

51. A. NO CHANGE
    B. (Do NOT begin new paragraph) Now that
    C. (Begin new paragraph) Once
    D. (Begin new paragraph) Being that

GO ON TO THE NEXT PAGE

in a Playboy club. And wrote a ground-breaking first-
52   53
person account of the joyless lives the bunnies led.

52. F. NO CHANGE
G. club; and
H. club, and
J. club. And she

53. Which of the alternatives best emphasizes how unusual Steinem's article was?
A. NO CHANGE
B. fascinating
C. colorful
D. vivid

[4]

54 She soon enjoyed regular assignments writing for

54. Which of the following sentences provides the best transition from the previous paragraph to this one?
F. Steinem was now thirty years old.
G. This famous story helped to boost Steinem's career.
H. Undercover reporting was not Steinem's major interest, however.
J. The article has been widely reprinted and is still well-known to this day.

such magazines like *Vogue*. However, she was
55

55. A. NO CHANGE
B. magazines, that included
C. such magazines including
D. magazines like

limited to writing about "women's topics" such as
56
hairstyles and weight loss. Eventually, Steinem landed
a job with *New York* magazine, writing about politics.
She also took part in many liberal causes, and joined the
Redstockings, a feminist group.

56. F. NO CHANGE
G. hairstyles and weight loss, for example
H. including topics like hairstyles and weight loss
J. OMIT the underlined portion.

[5]

In 1963, Steinem attended a rally in support of abortion rights, and this issue; she says, helped her make the
57

57. A. NO CHANGE
B. rights, and this issue, she says, helped
C. rights; and this issue she says helped
D. rights—and this issue, she says—helped

transition to feminism. Abortion remains one of the
                                                  58
most controversial topics in American politics. Steinem
also supported causes such as the unionization of Chicano

farm workers and peace in Vietnam. Steinem soon
                                                59
stepped to the forefront of the women's rights move
ment, a tireless worker and advocate. In 1972, she co-
founded the most successful feminist publication, *Ms.*
Although the magazine was popular and influential, it
lost money due to lack of advertising, and within fifteen
years, the magazine was sold.

[6]

Steinem was now able to concentrate on her true
love—writing. She wrote many famous articles, the list
                                                    60
of which included "Marilyn," about the actress Marilyn
Monroe, and published several books, including a psychological memoir called *Revolution from Within*, a
collection of essays titled *Beyond Words*, and, most
recently, her autobiography.

58. Which of the alternatives would most effec-
    tively support the assertion made in the previous
    sentence?

    F. NO CHANGE

    G. Abortion rights was only one of the many
       causes feminists espoused during the 1960s.

    H. Many people, especially conservatives who
       oppose abortion, have been critical of her
       stand on this issue.

    J. She wanted girls in situations like the one
       she'd faced to have the option of a safe and
       legal abortion.

59. A. NO CHANGE

    B. Steinem, tirelessly working and advocating,
       soon stepped to the forefront of the women's
       rights movement.

    C. A tireless worker and advocate, Steinem
       soon stepped to the forefront of the women's
       rights movement.

    D. Soon stepping to the forefront of the women's
       rights movement, Steinem was a tireless
       worker and advocate.

60. F. NO CHANGE

    G. they included

    H. inclusive of

    J. including

Passage V

Note: The following paragraphs may or may not be arranged in the best possible order. The last
item will ask you to choose the most effective order for the paragraphs as numbered.

Movies: Economics and Artistry

[1]

The strength of the film as an art form has always
derived from cinema's role of entertaining a large and

GO ON TO THE NEXT PAGE

avid public. As early as the 1920s, during the silent movie era, a generation of filmmakers grew up whose essential vision belonged to no other <u>medium, than that</u>
61

61. A. NO CHANGE
    B. medium than that of
    C. medium, than
    D. medium; than

<u>of</u> the cinema, and <u>whose</u> public was a universal audi-
62

62. F. NO CHANGE
    G. who's
    H. for whom the
    J. which had a

ence spread across the world. <u>Their movies were watched</u>
63
<u>by people around the world.</u> Like the first dramas of

63. A. NO CHANGE
    B. People everywhere watched their movies.
    C. They made movies that people from all over the world watched.
    D. OMIT the underlined portion.

Shakespeare, their art was <u>not a product</u> of the *salon*, but
64
of the common playhouse. This is what gave such great moviemakers as Charles Chaplin, D. W. Griffith, and Sergei Eisenstein 65 their strength and freshness.

64. F. NO CHANGE
    G. a product not
    H. in no way a product
    J. not produced

[2]

However, there has always been a price to be paid for the popular appeal of movies. The salon artist has only

65. The writer is considering adding the following phrase at this point in the essay:

    (three of the movie geniuses of the 1920s, two from America, one from Europe)

    Would this phrase be a relevant and appropriate addition to the essay, and why?

    A. Yes, because it helps to clarify the role played by the three moviemakers named in the development of the art of film.
    B. Yes, because it provides interesting details about the background of the three movie makers mentioned.
    C. No, because the only information it adds, that of the moviemakers' geographic origins, is irrelevant to the theme of the essay.
    D. No, because it singles out these three moviemakers as though they were the only significant film artists of their era.

a known patron, or group of patrons, to <u>satisfy, if</u> he is
66

strong enough he can, <u>like</u> the painters of the Renais-
67

sance, mold their taste to match his own. This may also

be true of the greatest artists of the <u>movies; from</u>
68

Chaplin in the twenties to, say, Bergman or Antonioni

in the sixties. <u>Furthermore,</u> the larger <u>and more numer-</u>
69   70

<u>ous</u> the public audience and the more costly the movies

to produce, <u>equally great</u> are the pressures brought to
71

bear on the less conventional creator to make <u>your</u> work
72

conform to the pattern of the more conventional artist.
Today, the most expensive and popular movies—think
of any film by Steven Speilberg as an example—are
also the most thoroughly conventional, however skillfully crafter they may be.

[3]

66. F. NO CHANGE
    G. satisfy—if
    H. satisfy, and if
    J. satisfy. For if

67. A. NO CHANGE
    B. as
    C. similarly to
    D. as with

68. F. NO CHANGE
    G. movies. From
    H. movies. Consider
    J. movies, from

69. A. NO CHANGE
    B. But
    C. So
    D. Therefore,

70. F. NO CHANGE
    G. and greater in number
    H. in quantity
    J. OMIT the underlined portion.

71. A. NO CHANGE
    B. the greater
    C. so much greater
    D. similarly great

72. F. NO CHANGE
    G. one's
    H. his
    J. their

GO ON TO THE NEXT PAGE ➡

As the twentieth century <u>nears it's end,</u> it is clear that

73

the greatest artistic innovation of the century has been

the emergence of the movies. The worldwide popularity

of film and its power to transmit culture and values are

unprecedented in the history of art. But what makes

the movies truly unique <u>are</u> the special relationship

74

between the moviemaker and his audience.

73. A. NO CHANGE
    B. is nearing it's end
    C. draws near to its end
    D. nears its end

74. F. NO CHANGE
    G. is
    H. will be
    J. must be

Item 75 poses a question about the essay as a whole.

75. For the sake of the unity and coherence of this essay, which of the following provides the most effective ordering of the paragraphs?
    A. NO CHANGE
    B. 1, 3, 2
    C. 2, 3, 1
    D. 3, 1, 2

STOP

END OF SECTION 1. IF YOU HAVE ANY TIME LEFT, GO OVER YOUR WORK IN THIS SECTION ONLY. DO NOT WORK IN ANY OTHER SECTION OF THE TEST.

SECTION 2: MATHEMATICS

60 Questions • Time—60 Minutes

Directions: Solve each problem below and mark the oval representing the correct answer on your answer sheet.

Be careful not to spend too much time on any one question. Instead, solve as many questions as possible, and then use any remaining time to return to those questions you were unable to answer at first.

You may use a calculator on any problem in this test; however, not every problem requires the use of a calculator.

Diagrams that accompany problems may or may not be drawn to scale. Unless otherwise indicated, you may assume that all figures shown lie in a plane and that lines that appear straight are straight.

1. Of 42 horses in a stable, $\frac{1}{3}$ are black, and $\frac{1}{6}$ are white. The rest are brown. What is the number of brown horses?

   A. 7

   B. 14

   C. 21

   D. 28

   E. 35

2. A faucet is dripping at a constant rate. If at noon on Sunday 3 ounces of water have dripped from the faucet into a holding tank and if at 5 P.M. a total of 7 ounces have dripped into the tank, how many total ounces will have dripped into the tank by 2:00 A.M. on Monday?

   F. 10

   G. $\frac{51}{5}$

   H. 12

   J. $\frac{71}{5}$

   K. $\frac{81}{5}$

3. $P = (-1,2); Q = (3,5)$. What is the slope of PQ ?

   A. $\frac{3}{4}$

   B. $\frac{7}{4}$

   C. $\frac{3}{2}$

   D. $\frac{4}{3}$

   E. $\frac{7}{2}$

4. $(2,6)$ is the midpoint of the line segment connecting $(-1,3)$ to $P(x,y)$. What is the value of $2x + y$?

   F. 1

   G. 9

   H. 10

   J. 12

   K. 19

5. What is the value of $y^0 + y^{-1}$ when $y = \frac{1}{2}$?

   A. 0.5

   B. 1.50

   C. 3.00

   D. 4.00

   E. 5.00

GO ON TO THE NEXT PAGE

6. Two rectangles have the same area. One is twice as long as the other. If the longer rectangle has a length of L and a width of W, what is the perimeter of the shorter rectangle?

 F. $2L + 2W$

 G. $2L + 4W$

 H. $2L + W$

 J. $L + 4W$

 K. $4L + 2W$

7. If the average of x and y is m, and $z = 2m$, what is the average of x, y, and z?

 A. m

 B. $\dfrac{2m}{3}$

 C. $\dfrac{4m}{3}$

 D. $\dfrac{3m}{4}$

 E. $\dfrac{3}{4m}$

8. In the figure below, lines AC and AD trisect $\angle A$. What is the value of x?

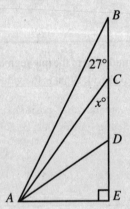

 F. 21

 G. 27

 H. 42

 J. 48

 K. 6

9. A box contains five blocks numbered 1, 2, 3, 4, and 5. John picks a block and replaces it. Lisa then picks a block. What is the probability that the sum of the numbers they picked is even?

 A. $\dfrac{9}{25}$

 B. $\dfrac{2}{5}$

 C. $\dfrac{1}{2}$

 D. $\dfrac{13}{25}$

 E. $\dfrac{3}{5}$

10. If a fleet of m buses uses g gallons of gasoline every two days, how many gallons will be needed by four buses every five days?

 F. $\dfrac{10\,g}{m}$

 G. $10gm$

 H. $\dfrac{10\,m}{g}$

 J. $\dfrac{20\,g}{m}$

 K. $\dfrac{5\,g}{4\,m}$

11. The cost of producing a certain machine is directly proportional to the number of assembly line workers required and inversely proportional to the square of the number of hours of assembly line downtime during production. If the cost was $1,500 when there were 12 workers and only two hours of downtime, how many hours of downtime was there when nine workers were producing machines at the cost of $2,000 per machine?

 A. 1

 B. 1.5

 C. 2

 D. 2.5

 E. 3

12. Which of the following is one root of the equation $x^2 - 4x + 13 = 0$?

   F. -1

   G. 5

   H. $4 + 3i$

   J. $2 - 6i$

   K. $2 + 3i$

13. In the figure below, what is the length of the perimeter of triangle OPQ?

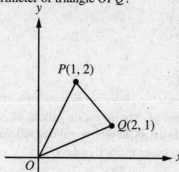

   A. $\sqrt{7}$

   B. 3

   C. $\sqrt{5} + \sqrt{2}$

   D. $\sqrt{5} + 2\sqrt{2}$

   E. $2\sqrt{5} + \sqrt{2}$

14. If $N = 3^P$ and $M = P - 1$, then, in terms of M, $\dfrac{3}{N} = ?$

   F. $\dfrac{1}{3^M}$

   G. 3^M

   H. $\dfrac{9}{3^M}$

   J. 3^{2M}

   K. 3^{1-M}

15. If A and B are positive integers, and $A^2 - B^2 = 36$, then $A = ?$

   A. 6

   B. 7

   C. 8

   D. 9

   E. 10

16. The price of a hat and scarf is $38. The hat cost $3 more than the scarf. What is the price of the scarf?

   F. $17.50

   G. $18.00

   H. $18.50

   J. $19.00

   K. $20.50

17. If $\sqrt{6}(\sqrt{3x}) = \sqrt{30}$, then $x = ?$

   A. $\dfrac{2}{5}$

   B. $\dfrac{3}{5}$

   C. $\dfrac{5}{3}$

   D. $\sqrt{3}$

   E. $\sqrt{5}$

18. If $2x - y + 4z = 7$ and $-4x + 2y - 3z = 1$, what is the value of z?

   F. -3

   G. 0

   H. 3

   J. 5

   K. It cannot be determined

19. If x and y are unequal positive integers and $xy = 36$, what is the smallest possible value of $x + y$?

   A. 12

   B. 13

   C. 15

   D. 20

   E. 37

GO ON TO THE NEXT PAGE

20. If it costs c cents per minute plus \$5 per month for long distance calls, what is the average price per minute (in cents) in a month in which n calls with an average length of 15 minutes are made?

    F. $c + \dfrac{100}{3n}$

    G. $c + 15n$

    H. $15c + \dfrac{500}{n}$

    J. $15c + \dfrac{500}{n}$

    K. $500 + \dfrac{nc}{15n}$

21. What is the area of a circle that has a diameter of π?

    A. $\dfrac{1}{4}\pi^2$

    B. $\dfrac{1}{2}\pi^2$

    C. $\dfrac{1}{4}\pi^3$

    D. $\dfrac{1}{2}\pi^3$

    E. π^3

22. A quadrilateral has angles in the ratio 1:2:3 and a fourth angle that is $31°$ larger than the smallest angle. What is the difference in degree measure between the two middle-sized angles in the quadrilateral?

    F. 16

    G. 31

    H. 47

    J. 51

    K. 63

23. A jar contains 6 numbered blocks. Four of the blocks are numbered 0 and the other two are not. If two blocks are drawn at random from the jar, what is the probability that the product of the two numbers is not zero?

    A. $\dfrac{1}{15}$

    B. $\dfrac{1}{12}$

    C. $\dfrac{2}{15}$

    D. $\dfrac{1}{6}$

    E. $\dfrac{1}{3}$

24. What is the value of $\dfrac{x^2 - 3x}{3x - 9}$ if $x = 3.03$?

    F. 1.01

    G. 1

    H. 3

    J. 101

    K. 303

25. When the tires of a taxicab are underinflated, the cab odometer will read 10% over the true mileage driven. If the odometer of a cab with underinflated tires shows m miles, what is the actual distance driven?

    A. $\dfrac{10m}{11}$

    B. $1.1m$

    C. $\dfrac{10}{11m}$

    D. $0.9m$

    E. $\dfrac{11}{10m}$

26. The ratio of Elaine's weekly salary to Carl's weekly salary was 3:2. If Elaine gets a 20% raise and Carl gets a $200 raise the ratio of their salaries will drop to 6:5. What is Elaine's salary?

    F. $200

    G. $400

    H. $480

    J. $600

    K. $720

27. P percent of $20\sqrt{3}$ is 3. $P = $?

    A. $\sqrt{3}$

    B. 3

    C. $5\sqrt{3}$

    D. $10\sqrt{3}$

    E. 20

28. In triangle ABC, the measure of $\angle B$ is 50° more than the measure of $\angle A$, and the measure of $\angle C$ is three times the measure of $\angle A$. The measure of $\angle B - \angle C$ in degrees = ?

    F. –6

    G. –4

    H. –2

    J. 0

    K. 2

29. If $2n - m = 6$, and $2n + m = 10$, $m = $?

    A. 1

    B. 2

    C. 3

    D. 4

    E. 5

30. In a group of 18 students taking Spanish or German, 12 are taking Spanish, and 4 are taking both languages. What is the number of students taking Spanish but not German?

    F. 4

    G. 6

    H. 8

    J. 10

    K. 12

31. When $x = 2$, $3x^0 + x^{-4} = $?

    A. –8

    B. 1.0625

    C. 3.0625

    D. 16

    E. 19

32. If $x = \frac{1}{2}$ and $x^2 + 2y^2 = 1$, then which of the following values is closest to the value of $|y|$?

    F. 0.1

    G. 0.2

    H. 0.4

    J. 0.5

    K. 0.6

33. If $\log_x (0.001) = 3$, then $x = $

    A. $(.001)^3$

    B. 0.01

    C. 0.1

    D. 10

    E. 1000

34. In the figure below, if $\angle ABC = 130°$, what is the area of triangle ABC?

    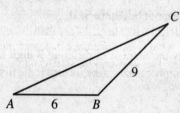

    F. $27\sin 50°$

    G. $27\cos 50°$

    H. 27

    J. $\dfrac{27}{\sin 50°}$

    K. $54\sin 50°$

GO ON TO THE NEXT PAGE

35. The cost of 4 cookies, 6 doughnuts, and 3 boxes of doughnut holes is $8.15. The cost of 2 cookies, 3 doughnuts, and 4 boxes of doughnut holes is $7.20. What is the cost of a box of doughnut holes?

    A. $.85

    B. $.95

    C. $1.05

    D. $1.15

    E. $1.25

36. Which of the following is closest to the length of the hypotenuse of a triangle with legs 3 and 5?

    F. 4

    G. 5

    H. 6

    J. 7

    K. 8

37. If $x + 2y - 3z = 5$ and $2x + 2y + 3z = 8$, then $9x + 12y = ?$

    A. 15

    B. 23

    C. 31

    D. 39

    E. It cannot be determined

38. What is the number of different 3-digit license plate numbers that can be formed if the first digit cannot be 0?

    F. 90

    G. 100

    H. 800

    J. 900

    K. 1,000

39. Three consecutive odd integers are written in increasing order. The sum of the first and second and twice the third is 46. What is the second number?

    A. 7

    B. 9

    C. 11

    D. 13

    E. 15

40. In the figure below, the area of the shaded section of the circle is 33π. What is the diameter of the circle?

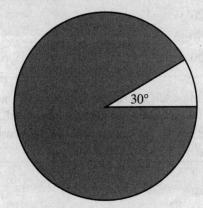

    F. 6

    G. 2π

    H. 9

    J. 12

    K. 4π

41. Jerome is 4 years older than Rodney. Two years ago, Rodney was $\frac{2}{3}$ of Jerome's age. How many years ago was Jerome twice as old as Rodney?

    A. 2

    B. 3

    C. 4

    D. 5

    E. 6

42. Point $Q(1,u)$ lies on a circle with a radius of 13 whose center is located at $(6,9)$. Which of the following is a possible value of u?

    F. -21

    G. -3

    H. 3

    J. 6

    K. 12

43. John can vacuum a hotel room in 20 minutes. Armando needs 15 minutes to do the same job. How many hours does it take them working together to vacuum 30 rooms?

    A. $\dfrac{20}{7}$

    B. 3

    C. 4

    D. $\dfrac{30}{7}$

    E. $\dfrac{50}{7}$

44. If $x = \log 2$ and $y = \log 5$, then $2y - 3x = ?$

    F. $\log \dfrac{8}{25}$

    G. $\log \dfrac{25}{8}$

    H. $\log \dfrac{25}{4}$

    J. $\log 200$

    K. $\dfrac{25}{8}$

45. A plane is flying from City A to City B at m miles per hour. Another plane flying from City B to City A travels 50 miles per hour faster than the first plane. The cities are R miles apart. If both planes depart at the same time, in terms of R and m, how far are they from City A when they pass?

    A. $\dfrac{R}{m} + 50$

    B. $\dfrac{Rm}{2m} - 50$

    C. $\dfrac{Rm}{2m + 50}$

    D. $\dfrac{R + 50}{m + 50}$

    E. $\dfrac{m + 50}{R}$

46. One x-intercept for the parabola $y = x^2 - 2x - 6$ is in which of the following intervals?

    F. $[-3,-2]$

    G. $[-2,-1]$

    H. $[-1,0]$

    J. $[0,1]$

    K. $[1,2]$

47. If $f(x) = x^2$ and $f(g(x)) = \dfrac{1}{(x^2 + 1)}$, then $g(x)$ could be which of the following?

    A. $\dfrac{1}{(x + 1)}$

    B. $\sqrt{x} + 1$

    C. $\dfrac{1}{\left(\sqrt{x^2 + 1}\right)}$

    D. $\dfrac{1}{x}$

    E. $\dfrac{1}{x^2}$

48. The numbers $-2, x, -8$ are the first three terms in a geometric progression. Which of the following could be the sum of the first six terms in the progression?

    F. -4096

    G. -2048

    H. -1024

    J. 512

    K. 1024

GO ON TO THE NEXT PAGE

49. Reduced to lowest terms, $\dfrac{4x^2 - 9}{2x^2 + x - 3} =$

    A. $\dfrac{2x+3}{x-1}$

    B. $\dfrac{2x-3}{x+1}$

    C. $\dfrac{2x+3}{x+1}$

    D. $\dfrac{2x-3}{x-1}$

    E. $\dfrac{2x^2-9}{x^2+x-3}$

50. If points P and Q have coordinates $(-1,2)$ and $(1,6)$ respectively, which of the following is the equation of a line that is a perpendicular bisector of the segment PQ?

    F. $y = -\dfrac{1}{2}x + 4$

    G. $y = \dfrac{1}{2}x + 4$

    H. $y = 2x + 4$

    J. $y = -2x + 4$

    K. $y = -2x - 4$

51. A random survey of 50 computer users was taken to determine how many used a disc drive and how many used a tape drive. The number who used both was 5 less than the number who used only a disc drive. In addition, there were 7 who used a tape drive but not a disc drive, and 2 who used neither. How many used a tape drive?

    A. 18

    B. 20

    C. 23

    D. 25

    E. 28

52. A surveyor standing at a point 50 meters from the base of a vertical cliff measures the angle of elevation to the top as 40°. She then walks another M meters directly away from the cliff until the angle of elevation to the top is 20°. M is equal to ?

    F. $50\tan 40° - 50\tan 20°$

    G. $\dfrac{50\tan 40° - 50\tan 20°}{\tan 40°}$

    H. $\dfrac{50\tan 20°}{\tan 40° - \tan 20°}$

    J. $\dfrac{50\tan 40° - 50\tan 20°}{\tan 20°}$

    K. $\dfrac{50\tan 40°}{\tan 40° - \tan 20°}$

53. $3\sqrt{2} \div 2\sqrt{8} = ?$

    A. $5\sqrt{2}$

    B. $7\sqrt{2}$

    C. $5\sqrt{8}$

    D. $5\sqrt{10}$

    E. 20

54. When Caroline travels on business, she is reimbursed $16 more per day for meals than for lodging. If she were given 50% more for lodging and $\frac{2}{3}$ as much for meals, the difference would be reversed. What is the total daily amount that Caroline is reimbursed for food and lodging?

    F. $32

    G. $48

    H. $64

    J. $72

    K. $80

55. If the numbers $-3 < M < N < 5$ are in arithmetic progression, then $M = ?$

    A. $-\dfrac{1}{3}$

    B. 0

    C. $\dfrac{1}{3}$

    D. $\dfrac{7}{3}$

    E. 3

56. Combined into a single monomial,

    $10y^2 - \dfrac{4y^4}{2y^2} =$

    F. $\dfrac{5y}{2}$

    G. $\dfrac{6}{y}$

    H. $6y^2$

    J. $8y^2$

    K. $-6y^2$

57. Given $A = \begin{bmatrix} -2 & 1 \\ 1 & 3 \end{bmatrix}$ and $B = \begin{bmatrix} x & 2 \\ 3 & y \end{bmatrix}$ and

    $2A + B = \begin{bmatrix} -5 & 4 \\ 5 & 4 \end{bmatrix}$, find xy.

    A. -2

    B. -1

    C. 0

    D. 1

    E. 2

58. If $f(x) = x + 1$, then $\dfrac{1}{f(x)} f \dfrac{1}{x} = ?$

    F. 1

    G. $\dfrac{x+1}{x}$

    H. $\dfrac{1}{x}$

    J. $\dfrac{x}{x+1}$

    K. x

59. If the slope of the line from $(-1,0)$ to $P(x,y)$ is 1 and the slope of the line from $(-4,0)$ to $P(x,y)$ is $\frac{1}{2}$, what is the value of x?

    A. -1

    B. 0

    C. 1

    D. 2

    E. 3

60. In the diagram below, O_1 and O_2 are concentric circles, and AB is tangent to O_1 at C. If the radius of O_1 is r and the radius of O_2 is twice as long, what is the area of the shaded region?

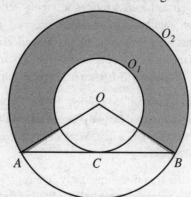

    F. $\dfrac{1}{2}\pi r^2$

    G. πr^2

    H. $1.5\pi r^2$

    J. $2\pi r^2$

    K. $3\pi r^2$

STOP

END OF SECTION 2. IF YOU HAVE ANY TIME LEFT, GO OVER YOUR WORK IN THIS SECTION ONLY. DO NOT WORK IN ANY OTHER SECTION OF THE TEST.

SECTION 3: READING

40 Questions • Time—35 Minutes

Directions: This test consists of four passages, each followed by several questions. Read each passage, select the correct answer for each question, and mark the oval representing the correct answer on your answer sheet.

Passage I—PROSE FICTION

Newland Archer was speaking with his fiance, May Welland. He had failed to stop at his club on the way up from the office where he exercised the profession of the law in the leisurely manner common to well-to-
(5) do New Yorkers of his class in the middle of the nineteenth century. He was out of spirits and slightly out of temper, and a haunting horror of doing the same thing every day at the same hour besieged his brain.

"Sameness—sameness!" he muttered, the word run-
(10) ning through his head like a persecuting tune as he saw the familiar tall-hatted figures lounging behind the plate glass; and because he usually dropped in at the club at that hour, he had passed by instead. And now he began to talk to May of their own plans, their future,
(15) and Mrs. Welland's insistence on a long engagement.

"If you call it long!" May cried. "Isabel Chivers and Reggie were engaged for two years, Grace and Thorley for nearly a year and a half. Why aren't we very well off as we are?"

(20)　　It was the traditional maidenly interrogation, and Archer felt ashamed of himself for finding it childish. No doubt she simply echoed what was said for her, but she was nearing her twenty-second birthday, and he wondered at what age "nice" women like May began
(25) to speak for themselves.

"Never, if we won't let them, I suppose," he mused, and recalled his mad outburst to his friend Jackson: "Women ought to be as free as we are—!"

It would soon be his task to take the bandage from
(30) this young woman's eyes, and bid her look forth on the world. But how many generations of women before her had descended bandaged to the family vault? He shivered a little, remembering some of the new ideas in his scientific books, and the much-cited instance of
(35) the Kentucky cave-fish, which had ceased to develop eyes because they had no use for them. What if, when he had bidden May Welland to open hers, they could only look out blankly at blankness?

"We might be much better off. We might be truly
(40) together—we might travel." Her face lit up. "That would be lovely," she admitted; she would love to travel. But her mother would not understand their wanting to do things so differently.

"As if the fact that it is different doesn't account for
(45) it!" Archer insisted.

"Newland! You're so original!" she exulted.

His heart sank. He saw that he was saying all the things that young men in the same situation were expected to say, and that she was making the answers
(50) that instinct and tradition taught her to make—even to the point of calling him original.

"Original! We're all as like each other as those dolls cut out of the same folded paper. We're like patterns stenciled on a wall. Can't you and I strike out for
(55) ourselves, May?"

He had stopped and faced her in the excitement of their discussion, and her eyes rested on him with a bright unclouded admiration.

"Goodness—shall we elope?" she laughed.

(60)　　"If you would—"

"You do love me, Newland! I'm so happy."

"But then—why not be happier?"

"We can't behave like people in novels, though, can we?"

(65)　　"Why not—why not—why not?"

She looked a little bored by his insistence. She knew very well why they couldn't, but it was troublesome to have to produce a reason. "I'm not clever enough to argue with you. But that kind of thing is rather—vulgar,
(70) isn't it?" she suggested, relieved to have hit on a word that would certainly extinguish the whole subject.

"Are you so much afraid, then, of being vulgar?"

She was evidently staggered by this. "Of course I should hate it—and so would you," she rejoined, a
(75) trifle irritably.

He stood silent, beating his walking-stick nervously against his shoe-top. Feeling that she had indeed found the right way of closing the discussion, she went on lightheartedly, "Oh, did I tell you that I showed cousin
(80) Ellen my engagement ring? She thinks it the most beautiful setting she ever saw. There's nothing like it in Paris, she said. I do love you, Newland, for being so artistic!"

1. What was Archer's reason for failing to stop at his club after leaving the office?
   A. He wanted to avoid talking with his friends there.
   B. He was afraid that his life was becoming overly routine.
   C. He disliked most of the other members of the club.
   D. He was eager to discuss the future with his fiance.

2. The reference to "the Kentucky cave-fish" (line 35) underscores Archer's concern about May Welland's:
   F. greed.
   G. timidity.
   H. immaturity.
   J. bossiness.

3. It can be inferred from the passage that Archer's engagement is expected to last:
   A. two or three months.
   B. somewhat less than a year and a half.
   C. about two years.
   D. over two years.

4. The first paragraph suggests that Archer's work as a lawyer:
   F. is not very demanding.
   G. has become tedious to him.
   H. is very lucrative.
   J. is a traditional family occupation.

5. May Welland apparently considers the idea that she and Archer might elope:
   A. frightening.
   B. romantic.
   C. fascinating.
   D. absurd.

6. The fifth paragraph (lines 26–28) suggests that Archer considers most women in the society of his time:
   F. unduly powerful.
   G. indecisive and irresponsible.
   H. unfairly dominated by men.
   J. excessively demanding.

7. Archer's reaction to being called "original" by his fiance is a feeling of:
   A. dismay.
   B. pride.
   C. bewilderment.
   D. glee.

8. Which of the following conclusions about the relationship between Archer and May Welland is best supported by the details in the passage?
   F. Archer's eagerness to accelerate their wedding is motivated by his passion for his fiance.
   G. Archer and May Welland both feel trapped in an unhappy relationship by social restrictions.
   H. Archer feels stultified by his fiance's conventionality, but feels unable to alter the situation.
   J. May Welland is eager to do whatever she can to satisfy the emotional needs of her fiance.

9. May Welland considers the discussion begun by Archer finished when she:
   A. dismisses his ideas as "vulgar."
   B. appeals to the authority of her mother.
   C. accedes to his request that their engagement be shortened.
   D. realizes that Archer truly loves her.

GO ON TO THE NEXT PAGE

10. Archer regards May Welland's attitudes as having been excessively influenced by which of the following?

    I. The traditions of her sex and class

    II. Her mother

    III. The novels she has read

    IV. Her friends Isabel and Grace

    F. I and II only

    G. II and III only

    H. I and IV only

    J. II and IV only

Passage II—SOCIAL STUDIES

From the opening days of the Civil War, one of the Union's strategies in its efforts to defeat the rebelling southern states was to blockade their ports. Compared to the Union, relatively little was manufactured in the
(5) Confederacy—either consumer goods or, more important, war materiél—and it was believed that a blockade could strangle the South into submission. But the Confederacy had 3,500 miles of coastline and, at the start of the war, the Union had only 36 ships to
(10) patrol them.

Even so, the Confederate government knew that the Union could and would construct additional warships and that in time all its ports could be sealed. To counter this, the Confederacy decided to take a radical step—
(15) to construct an ironclad vessel that would be impervious to Union gunfire. In doing so, the South was taking a gamble because, though the British and French navies had already launched experimental armor-plated warships, none had yet been tested in battle.

(20) Lacking time as well as true ship-building capabilities, rather than construct an entirely new ship, in July, 1861, the Confederacy began placing armor-plating on the hull of an abandoned U.S. Navy frigate, the steam-powered *U.S.S. Merrimack.* Rechristened the
(25) *C.S.S. Virginia,* the ship carried ten guns and an iron ram designed to stave in the wooden hulls of Union warships.

Until then, Union Secretary of the Navy Gideon Welles had considered ironclads too radical an idea, and
(30) preferred to concentrate on building standard wooden warships. But when news of the *Virginia* reached Washington, the fear it engendered forced him to rethink his decision. In October, 1861, the Union began construction of its own ironclad—the *U.S.S.*
(35) *Monitor*—which would revolutionize naval warfare.

Designed by John Ericson, a Swede who had already made substantial contributions to marine engineering, the *Monitor* looked like no other ship afloat. With a wooden hull covered with iron plating, the ship
(40) had a flat deck with perpendicular sides that went below the waterline and protected the propeller and other important machinery. Even more innovative, the ship had a round, revolving turret which carried two large guns. Begun three months after work started on
(45) the conversion of the *Virginia,* the *Monitor* was nevertheless launched in January, 1862, two weeks before the Confederacy launched its ironclad.

On March 8th, now completely fitted, the *Virginia* left the port of Norfolk, Virginia, on what was ex-
(50) pected to be a test run. However, steaming into Hampton Roads, Virginia, the Confederate ship found no fewer than five Union ships at the mouth of the James River—the *St. Lawrence, Congress, Cumberland, Minnesota,* and *Roanoke.* The first three of these were
(55) already-obsolete sailing ships, but the others were new steam frigates, the pride of the Union navy.

Attacking the *Cumberland* first, the *Virginia* sent several shells into her side before ramming her hull and sinking her. Turning next to the *Congress,* the
(60) southern ironclad sent broadsides into her until fires started by the shots reached her powder magazine and she blew up. At last, after driving the *Minnesota* aground, the *Virginia* steamed off, planning to finish off the other ships the next day. In just a few hours,
(65) she had sunk two ships, disabled a third, and killed 240 Union sailors, including the captain of the *Congress*—more naval casualties than on any other day of the war. Although she had lost two of her crew, her ram, and two of her guns, and sustained other damage, none of
(70) the nearly 100 shots that hit her had pierced her armor.

The *Monitor,* however, was already en route from the Brooklyn Navy Yard, and the next morning, March 9th, the two ironclads met each other for the first—and only—time. For nearly four hours the ships pounded
(75) at each other, but despite some damage done on both sides, neither ship could penetrate the armor-plating of its enemy. When a shot from the *Virginia* hit the *Monitor's* pilot house, wounding her captain and forcing her to withdraw temporarily, the Confederate ship
(80) steamed back to Norfolk.

Although both sides claimed victory, the battle was actually a draw. Its immediate significance was that, by forcing the withdrawal of the *Virginia*, it strengthened the Union blockade, enabling the North to con-
(85) tinue its ultimately successful stranglehold on the South. Even more important, it was a turning point in the history of naval warfare. Although neither ship ever fought again, the brief engagement of the *Monitor* and *Virginia* made every navy in the world obsolete,
(90) and, in time, spelled the end of wooden fighting ships forever.

11. According to the passage, the Confederacy wanted an ironclad vessel for all the following reasons except:

    A. an ironclad vessel might be able to withstand Union attacks.

    B. it needed open ports in order to receive supplies from overseas.

    C. the British and French navies already had ironclads.

    D. it knew that the Union would be building more warships.

12. The passage implies that the South was vulnerable to a naval blockade because of its:

    F. limited manufacturing capabilities.

    G. relatively short coastline.

    H. lack of access to natural resources.

    J. paucity of skilled naval officers.

13. According to the passage, the Confederate government chose to refit the *Merrimack* rather than build an ironclad from scratch because:

    A. it lacked sufficient funds to construct a new vessel.

    B. it had neither the time nor facilities to build a new ship.

    C. the design of the *Merrimack* was especially suitable for armor plating.

    D. it believed that converting a Union warship would damage Northern morale.

14. All of the following were unusual design features of the *Monitor* EXCEPT its:

    F. perpendicular sides.

    G. revolving gun turret.

    H. flat deck.

    J. wooden hull.

15. As it is used in line 42, the word "innovative" most nearly means:

    A. dangerous.

    B. unusual.

    C. revolutionary.

    D. clever.

16. It can be inferred from the passage that, by comparison with the design of the *Monitor*, that of the *Virginia* was more:

    F. offensively oriented.

    G. costly.

    H. versatile.

    J. traditional.

17. It can be inferred from the passage that, although construction on the *Monitor* began three months after that of the *Virginia*, the *Monitor* was completed first because:

    A. the Union had more money to spend on building its ship.

    B. the *Monitor* was less complicated to construct.

    C. the Union had greater manufacturing abilities and resources.

    D. the Confederacy did not feel compelled to hurry in completing its ship.

18. It can be inferred from the passage that the *Virginia* was able to sink or disable the *St. Lawrence, Congress,* and *Cumberland* for which of the following reasons?

    F. Its armor plating was virtually impervious to gunfire.

    G. Its steam-powered engines made it highly maneuverable.

    H. Its armor plating made it fireproof.

    J. It was capable of greater speed than the Union warships.

GO ON TO THE NEXT PAGE ▶

19. As it is used in line 69, "sustained" most nearly means:

    A. survived.

    B. inflicted.

    C. suffered.

    D. risked.

20. The author suggests that the most important long-term result of the battle between the *Virginia* and the *Monitor* was that it:

    F. enabled the Union to maintain its blockade of southern ports.

    G. demonstrated that ironclad ships represented the future of naval warfare.

    H. saved the Union navy from destruction by the *Virginia*.

    J. demonstrated the superior technological prowess of the North.

Passage III—HUMANITIES

On July 1, 1882, a brief notice appeared in the Portsmouth (England) Evening News. It read simply, "Dr. Doyle begs to notify that he has removed to 1, Bush Villas, Elm Grove, next to the Bush Hotel." So was
(5) announced the newly-formed medical practice of a 23-year-old graduate of Edinburgh University—Arthur Conan Doyle. But the town of Southsea, the Portsmouth suburb in which Doyle had opened his office, already had several well-established physicians, and
(10) while he waited for patients the young Dr. Doyle found himself with a great deal of time on his hands.

To fill it, he began writing—short stories, historical novels, whatever would keep him busy and, hopefully, bring additional funds into his sparsely-filled
(15) coffers. By the beginning of 1886, his practice had grown to the point of providing him with a respectable if not munificent income, and he had managed to have a few pieces published. Although literary success still eluded him, he had developed an idea for a new book,
(20) a detective story, and in March he began writing the tale that would give birth to one of literature's most enduring figures.

Although he was familiar with and impressed by the fictional detectives created by Edgar Allan Poe, Emile
(25) Gaboriau, and Wilkie Collins, Doyle believed he could create a different kind of detective, one for whom detection was a science rather than an art. As a

model, he used one of his medical school professors, Dr. Joseph Bell. As Bell's assistant, Doyle had seen
(30) how, by exercising his powers of observation and deduction and asking a few questions, Bell had been able not only to diagnose his patients' complaints but also to accurately determine their professions and backgrounds. A detective who applied similar intel-
(35) lectual powers to the solving of criminal mysteries could be a compelling figure, Doyle felt.

At first titled *A Tangled Skein*, the story was to be told by his detective's companion, a Dr. Ormand Sacker, and the detective himself was to be named
(40) Sherrinford Holmes. But by April, 1886, when Doyle finished the manuscript, the title had become *A Study in Scarlet*, the narrator Dr. John H. Watson, and the detective Mr. Sherlock Holmes.

A tale of revenge, in which Holmes is able to
(45) determine that two Mormons visiting England from Utah have been killed by Jefferson Hope, an American working as a London hansom cab driver, *A Study in Scarlet* was rejected by several publishers before being accepted that fall for publication by Ward, Lock
(50) & Company as part of *Beeton's Christmas Annual* in 1887. Although the author asked to be paid a royalty based on sale of the book, his publisher offered instead only a flat fee of £25 for the copyright (the equivalent of approximately $50.00 today). Doyle reluctantly
(55) accepted.

A handful of reviewers commented kindly on the story, but the reading public as a whole was unimpressed. Ward, Lock published *A Study in Scarlet* in book form the following year, while the disappointed
(60) author returned to his historical novels, with which he had finally achieved some modest success. Fictional detection, Doyle thought, was behind him. In August, 1889, however, he was approached by the editor of the American *Lippincott's Monthly Magazine*, published
(65) in Philadelphia and London, to write another Sherlock Holmes story. Although he had little interest in continuing Holmes's adventures, Doyle was still in need of money and accepted the offer.

Published in *Lippincott's* in February, 1890, and in
(70) book form later that year, *The Sign of the Four* chronicled Holmes's investigation of the murder of Bartholomew Sholto and his search for Jonathan Small and a treasure stolen by British soldiers in India. It too, however, met with little enthusiasm from the public.
(75) In the meantime, however, Doyle's other small

literary successes had enabled him to move to London, where he became a consulting physician. Fortunately, even this new London practice did not keep him very busy, leaving him time to concentrate on his writing.

(80)   In April, 1891, he submitted a short Sherlock Holmes story, "A Scandal in Bohemia," to a new magazine called *The Strand*. It was with the publication of this story, and the series of Holmes tales which followed, that the public finally took an interest in Dr. Doyle's
(85) detective, enabling him to give up his practice and turn to writing full time. Despite his own continuing lack of enthusiasm for his protagonist—he considered the Holmes stories insignificant compared to his "serious" historical novels—spurred by the public clamor for
(90) more Sherlock Holmes, Doyle eventually wrote 56 short stories and four novels in the series, and in the process created what may be the best-known character in all of English literature.

21. According to the passage, Arthur Conan Doyle began writing for all the following reasons except:

    A. his medical practice did not keep him very busy.

    B. he needed additional income.

    C. he was not interested in practicing medicine.

    D. he was fond of literary fiction.

22. As it is used in line 31, the word "deduction" most nearly means:

    F. decreasing.

    G. discounting.

    H. reducing.

    J. reasoning.

23. It can be inferred from the passage that Sherlock Holmes differed from previous fictional detectives in that:

    A. he conducted his investigations on a scientific basis.

    B. he used his own background in medicine as a source of detective methods.

    C. his cases were chronicled by a companion rather than by the detective himself.

    D. his exploits were based on the experiences of a real individual.

24. As it is used in line 36, "compelling" most nearly means:

    F. inescapable.

    G. believable.

    H. fascinating.

    J. insistent.

25. In can be inferred from the passage that the first two Sherlock Holmes tales were similar in all the following respects except:

    A. both were based on historical events.

    B. both were originally published in periodicals rather than as books.

    C. neither received a strong initial reception from the public.

    D. both were written more for financial than literary reasons.

26. The author implies that Doyle's move to London was primarily triggered by:

    F. Doyle's desire to move in literary circles.

    G. the failure of his medical practice in Southsea.

    H. an increase in Doyle's income from writing.

    J. a growing demand for Doyle's medical services.

27. The author uses the word "Fortunately" in line 77 primarily to imply that:

    A. a medical practice in London can be especially demanding.

    B. the popular demand for Doyle's writing had begun to grow at this time.

    C. Doyle's literary career was more significant than his medical practice.

    D. Doyle was strongly tempted at this time to abandon writing as a career.

GO ON TO THE NEXT PAGE

28. It can be inferred from the passage that the public finally became interested in Doyle's Sherlock Holmes stories as a result of:

    F. their continued appearance in *The Strand* magazine.

    G. the public's growing interest in detective stories.

    H. the success of Doyle's other works.

    J. the first publication of a Holmes story in the United States.

29. According to the passage, Doyle's reluctance to write further Holmes stories after 1891 was due primarily to:

    A. his belief that he was not fairly compensated for them.

    B. his lack of interest in Holmes as a character.

    C. his desire to be considered a serious author.

    D. the significant income provided by his other literary efforts.

30. Which of the following titles best summarizes the content of the passage?

    F. Arthur Conan Doyle and the Creation of the Modern Detective Story

    G. A Detective's Reluctant Chronicler: The Birth of Sherlock Holmes

    H. Physician and Author: How Arthur Conan Doyle Balanced Two Callings

    J. The Many Strands in the Character of Sherlock Holmes

Passage IV—NATURAL SCIENCE

If you've ever cupped your hand around a blinking firefly or noticed an eerie glow in the ocean at night, you are familiar with the phenomenon of bioluminescence. The ability of certain plants and animals to emit (5) light has long been a source of fascination to humans. Why do certain species of mushrooms glow? Why are midwater squids designed with ornate light-emitting organs underneath their eyes and ink glands? Why do certain particles and biological detritus floating in the (10) depths of the ocean sparkle after a physical disturbance? Are these light displays simply an example of nature in its most flamboyant mode—a case of "if

you've got it, flaunt it"—or do they serve any practical purposes?

(15) As it turns out, the manifestations of bioluminescence are as diverse as they are elegant. Yet virtually all of the known or proposed ways in which bioluminescence functions may be classed under three major rubrics: assisting predation, helping escape from preda-(20) tors, and communicating.

Many examples of the first two uses can be observed in the ocean's midwaters, a zone that extends from about 100 meters deep to a few kilometers below the surface. Almost all of the animals that inhabit the (25) murky depths where sunlight barely penetrates are capable of producing light in one way or another. Certain animals, when feeding, are attracted to a spot of light as a possible food source. Hence, other animals use their own luminescence to attract them. Just (30) in front of the angler fish's mouth is a dangling luminescent ball suspended from a structure attached to its head. What unwitting marine creatures see as food is really a bait to lure them into the angler fish's gaping maw.

(35) The uses of luminescence to elude prey are just as sophisticated and various. Some creatures take advantage of the scant sunlight in their realm by using bioluminescence as a form of camouflage. The glow generated by photophores, light producing organs, on (40) the undersides of some fishes and squids acts to hide them through a phenomenon known as countershading: the weak downward lighting created by the photophores effectively erases the animals' shadows when viewed from below against the (relatively) lighted (45) waters above.

Some marine animals use bioluminescence more actively in their own defense, turning their predators into prey. For instance, there is the so-called "burglar alarm effect," in which an animal coats an advancing (50) predator with sticky glowing tissue that makes the would-be attacker vulnerable to visually-cued hunters—like bank robbers marked by exploding dye packets hidden in stolen currency.

Bioluminescence is used not only in such interspe-(55) cific feeding frays between predators and prey, but also as an intraspecific communication facilitator. The fireflies that seem to blink on and off randomly in the summer woods are actually male and female members signaling each other during courtship. Certain fish use

(60) their luminescence as a kind of Morse code in which the female responds to the flashing of a male fish with its own flash exactly two seconds later, which the male recognizes by its timing.

(65) Bioluminescence clearly functions to help certain species ensure their survival, whether it helps them to trick predators or to mate and produce offspring. Yet, when we look at the larger evolutionary picture, bioluminescence as such is generally considered a "nonessential" characteristic. After all, closely related (70) species and even strains of the same species may have both luminous and nonluminous members, and the nonluminous ones appear just as viable and vigorous as their glowing counterparts. For instance, while many of the small marine organisms known as dino- (75) flagellates are luminous, many are not. Yet, on closer inspection, we find that the nonluminous dino- flagellates may benefit from the diversionary flashing tactics of the luminous ones. When the sea is disturbed and light flashes create phosphorescence, the species (80) which flash may provide enough light to serve the entire population. Thus, selection pressure for the development or maintenance of luminescence in additional species is not great if light generated by a part of the population serves the entire community.

(85) There are instances in which bioluminescence seems truly purposeless. What does one make of a creature, such as a newly discovered species of a tomopterid worm, that emits light for no apparent purpose? This agile swimmer with a multitude of paired legs spews (90) a bright yellow bioluminescent fluid from each of its leg pores. While other types of spewers use this strategy to create a visual distraction, this worm's display remains enigmatic, particularly since the light produced is yellow, while most midwater animals have (95) eyes that are sensitive only to blue-green. Perhaps some animal species *are* simply exploiting their capacity for flamboyance, in the same way that some humans bring a distinctively colorful flair to whatever they do.

31. The passage focuses on all of the following aspects of bioluminescence except:

   A. its role in interactions between predators and prey.

   B. its role in the evolution of various animal species.

   C. whether bioluminescence is a purely functional feature.

   D. how bioluminescent species may serve nonluminous ones.

32. From the author's description of the angler fish in lines 30–34, we can infer that this fish:

   F. is attracted to light as a possible food source.

   G. uses its light-producing organ to deter predators.

   H. dwells primarily in the ocean's midwaters.

   J. uses countershading to elude predators below.

33. The angler fish's use of bioluminescence in predation is most nearly analogous to:

   A. an exterminator's use of insecticide to poison the insects that have infested a home.

   B. a duck hunter's use of a reed-shielded blind as a hiding place from which to shoot at ducks.

   C. a trout fisherman's use of a lure designed to resemble an insect that trout love to eat.

   D. a police detective's use of a bright lamp to blind and so intimidate a suspect during questioning.

34. Each of the following statements about the use of bioluminescence in countershading is true except:

   F. The light given off by photophores underneath certain fish and squid makes the animals appear to blend in with the sunlit waters above them.

   G. Bioluminescence allows the parts of an animal normally in shadow to appear lighter.

   H. Countershading is used most effectively in regions of relatively weak sunlight.

   J. Bioluminescent animals use countershading as a way to elude predators that lurk in the sunlit waters above them.

GO ON TO THE NEXT PAGE

35. The reference to bank robbers in lines 52–54 serves mainly to:

    A. distinguish between two phenomena that appear similar but are fundamentally different.

    B. suggest a practical application for recent discoveries from natural science.

    C. point out the weaknesses in one proposed solution to a scientific conundrum.

    D. clarify a phenomenon of the animal world by comparing it to human behavior.

36. The author mentions the behavior of bioluminescent and nonluminous dionoflagellates (lines 75–78) primarily in order to illustrate:

    F. why bioluminescence is generally considered an unnecessary function in dinoflagellates.

    G. one of the functions of bioluminescence in the ocean's midwaters.

    H. why more species have not evolved with bioluminescence.

    J. how nonluminous animals may benefit from proximity to luminous ones.

37. The passage implies that, if bioluminescence were NOT a nonessential characteristic, which of the following would be true?

    A. Luminous species would be seen to thrive more successfully than closely related nonluminous ones.

    B. Nonluminous species would enjoy a reproductive advantage by comparison to luminous ones.

    C. Luminous species would gradually die out and be replaced by closely related nonluminous ones.

    D. Luminous and nonluminous species would not be observed living in close proximity to one another.

38. The phrase "selection pressure" in line 81 refers to:

    F. the potential extinction of an animal species due to the depletion of essential resources.

    G. environmental factors that favor development of a particular biological characteristic.

    H. competition among predators for a finite population of prey.

    J. selective winnowing of an animal population based on the attractiveness of specific individuals.

39. By comparison with the other species mentioned in the passage, the phenomenon of bioluminescence in the tomopterid worm discussed in lines 86–88 might best be described as:

    A. extreme.

    B. archetypal.

    C. exceptional.

    D. prototypical.

40. The author's comments about the tomopterid worm would be most seriously called into question by the discovery of which of the following?

    F. A predator of the tomopterid worm that is sensitive to yellow light

    G. Another species of tomopterid worm that produces bioluminescent blue-green fluid

    H. A prey of the tomopterid worm that does not exhibit bioluminescence

    J. Other species of midwater animals that produce bioluminescent yellow fluids

STOP

END OF SECTION 3. IF YOU HAVE ANY TIME LEFT, GO OVER YOUR WORK IN THIS SECTION ONLY. DO NOT WORK IN ANY OTHER SECTION OF THE TEST.

SECTION 4: SCIENCE REASONING

40 Questions • Time—35 Minutes

Directions: This test consists of seven passages, each followed by several questions. Read each passage, select the correct answer for each question, and mark the oval representing the correct answer on your answer sheet. You may NOT use a calculator on this test.

Passage I

Tree age is important to researchers for understanding typical life-cycles in the forest and developing sustainable forestry practices. Counting tree rings is the method that is usually used to determine the age of trees, but in tropical rain forests, such as the Amazon, tree rings may be irregular (not annual) or nonexistent.

Carbon-14 dating is another method of determining tree age. Trees take carbon dioxide, which contains some of the radioactive element carbon-14, into their tissues at a known rate. By measuring the levels of carbon-14 in a plant, scientists can determine its age. Table 2.1 lists the age and other data for trees that have emerged from the canopy in a small Amazon forest plot. The age of the trees was determined by carbon-14 dating.

Table 2.1

Tree #	Tree Species	Tree Diameter (cm)	Tree Age (Years)	Calculated Average Growth Rate (cm/yr)
1	Cariniana micrantha	140	200	0.7
2	Cariniana micrantha	100	400	0.25
3	Cariniana micrantha	140	1,400	0.1
4	Hymenolobium species	180	300	0.6
5	Hymenolobium species	90	900	0.1
6	Bagassa guianansis	120	400	0.3
7	Bagassa guianansis	150	300	0.5
8	Caryocar glabrum	130	200	0.65
9	Caryocar vilosum	120	200	0.6
10	Iryanthera grandis	160	800	0.2
11	Dipteryx odorata	120	1,200	0.1
12	Sclerolobium species	80	200	0.4

Historical patterns of forest disturbance are also important to biologists for determining the extent to which the forest is affected and the forest's pattern of recovery. The following diagram shows the catastrophic events that are known to have occurred in the area where the trees in Table 2.1 were growing.

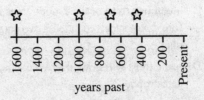

Legend: ☆ = catastrophic event

GO ON TO THE NEXT PAGE ➤

1. Looking at trees in just the *Hymenolobium* species (trees 4 and 5) in Table 2.1, researchers might conclude that:

    A. tree age is positively correlated with both tree diameter and growth rate.

    B. tree age is inversely correlated with tree diameter and positively correlated with growth rate.

    C. tree age is inversely correlated with tree diameter and growth rate.

    D. tree diameter is inversely correlated with growth rate.

2. Based on the data presented, which of the following statements is true?

    F. Trees 5 and 12 demonstrate that tree diameter is a relatively poor predictor of tree age.

    G. Trees 5 and 12 demonstrate that trees that survived a natural catastrophe will begin to grow at a faster rate because there is little competition for resources.

    H. Trees 5 and 12 demonstrate inconsistencies in the carbon-14 dating process.

    J. Trees 5 and 12 demonstrate that it is not always possible to calculate a tree's average growth rate even when the tree's diameter and age are known.

3. Looking at the catastrophe time-line and the data in Table 2.1, it is clear that:

    A. more than half of the canopy trees in the forest plot survived the most recent catastrophe.

    B. about one half of the canopy trees in the forest plot survived at least two catastrophes.

    C. about one third of the canopy trees in the forest plot survived at least two catastrophes.

    D. some trees will always survive a natural catastrophe.

4. If a tree has an age of 1,100 years and a long-term average growth rate of 0.1 cm/year, what is the diameter of the tree?

    F. 100 cm

    G. 110 cm

    H. 120 cm

    J. It cannot be determined.

5. Which of the following conclusions do the growth rates of trees 1, 2, and 3 demonstrate?

    A. Canopy trees of a single species tend to be close in age.

    B. Canopy trees of different species may have widely divergent ages.

    C. Average growth rates generally remain constant for each species.

    D. Trees of the same species may have different average growth rates at different ages.

6. Reaching the canopy, with its important resource of sunlight, is a critical goal for rain forest trees. The traditional view is that trees have a fast growth spurt to reach the canopy. The researchers in this study hypothesized that trees might reach the canopy using strategies of fast or slow growth and that both strategies might be used by trees in the same species. Which of the following findings would support their theory?

    F. It is discovered that tree 3 reached the canopy 1,200 years ago.

    G. Research on trees that have not reached the canopy show that they are all under 200 years of age.

    H. The growth rates of trees that have not reached the canopy are investigated and are found to be highly variable.

    J. The growth rates of trees that have not reached the canopy are investigated and are found to be relatively fast.

Passage II

Recently, flywheels with magnetic bearings have been designed (see figure below). These flywheels produce none of the friction associated with mechanical bearings, making them efficient energy storage devices. One application they may have is in alternative energy cars. In experimental designs, a flywheel is "spun-up" while the car is at rest with the electrical power supplied from a standard electrical outlet. After the flywheel has reached a high rate of rotation, the car can be disconnected from the socket, and the energy can be extracted from the high-speed rotating flywheel.

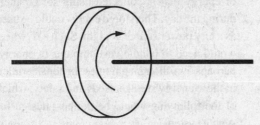

Experiment 1

Researchers looked at flywheels with different radii to gauge the effect of size on the total energy they could store. The wheels were all started at an initial frequency of 50 revolutions per second (rev/sec). All of the flywheels were *disk-type* (they had a uniform thickness along their entire radius), all were made of the same material, and all had the same thickness. After reaching the initial speed, a uniform resisting force was applied to determine how much energy it took to stop the wheel. The results of this experiment appear in Table 2.2.

Table 2.2

Radius (cm)	Energy Stored (joules)
10	100
20	1600
30	8100
40	25600

Experiment 2

Next, a disk-type flywheel with a radius of 30 cm was brought up to various initial speeds by an electric motor. The energy stored at each speed was measured. Results appear in Table 2.3.

Table 2.3

Frequency (rev/sec)	Energy Stored
40	5184
60	11664
80	20736
100	32400

Experiment 3

One of the limiting factors in the use of flywheels is the centrifugal force (the force pulling outward from the rim) that is generated as the wheel is turning. When this force becomes too great, it causes the wheel to fly apart or explode. The centrifugal force is determined by the frequency and the radius of the wheel. A doubling of the radius results in a doubling of the centrifugal force; a doubling of the frequency results in a quadrupling of the centrifugal force.

Researchers tested four wheel designs (see figure below). All of the wheels had a radius of 30 cm and the same mass; wheel thicknesses were changed to keep the mass constant. The frequency of each wheel was increased slowly until it exploded. The frequency at which this occurred as well as the energy stored in the wheel at the time was recorded. Results appear in Table 2.4.

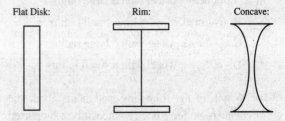
Flat Disk: Rim: Concave:

Table 2.4

Flywheel Type	Energy Stored (joules)	Strength (Maximum frequency) (rev/sec)
Flat Disk	17266	73
Rimmed	16231	42
Concave Disk	19627	72

GO ON TO THE NEXT PAGE ➤

7. The difference between Experiment 1 and Experiment 2 is:

   A. in Experiment 1, the flywheel radius is varied, while in Experiment 2, the initial speed of the flywheel is varied.

   B. in Experiment 1 the flywheel type is varied, while in Experiment 2 the initial flywheel speed is varied.

   C. in Experiment 2 the resisting force is varied, while in Experiment 1 it is uniform.

   D. in Experiment 1 the centrifugal force was varied, while in Experiment 2 it remains constant.

8. Assuming that the researchers considered energy storage and wheel strength to be of equal importance, which of the wheel designs in Experiment 3 would they conclude was optimal?

   F. Flat Disk

   G. Rimmed

   H. Concave disk

   J. The best design would depend on the wheel radius.

9. The experimental data indicate that for optimal energy storage the flywheel should be a:

   A. concave wheel with a large radius.

   B. rimmed wheel with a small radius.

   C. flat disk wheel with a large radius.

   D. concave wheel with a small radius.

10. Which of the following statements about the centrifugal force on a flywheel is best supported by the data presented?

    F. A graph of the force versus wheel radius would look similar to a graph of frequency versus energy stored.

    G. A graph of the force versus wheel radius would look similar to a graph of energy stored versus wheel strength.

    H. A graph of the force versus frequency would look similar to a graph of frequency versus energy stored.

    J. A graph of the force versus frequency would look similar to a graph of energy stored versus wheel strength.

11. A car has a disk-type flywheel with a radius of 30 cm. The disk is initially storing 120,000 joules while rotating at 64 rev/sec. When the wheel is turning at half the original speed, how much energy will remain?

    A. 10,000 joules

    B. 30,000 joules

    C. 50,000 joules

    D. 70,000 joules

12. Flywheels have been considered for the storage of energy that is collected using solar panels during the day. This stored energy could be used as a city power source at night. Such a flywheel would need to handle vast amounts of energy, perhaps 5 million megajoules. In consideration of these energy storage needs and safety, which of the following would be the best design for such a system?

    I. One very large flywheel that would turn at a relatively slow frequency

    II. Collections of small flywheels each turning at high frequencies

    III. One large flywheel that would transfer its energy to many smaller flywheels as it slowed down

    F. I only

    G. II only

    H. III only

    J. I or III only

Passage III

Lake ecosystems are highly sensitive to changes in the acid-base balance. In the last few decades there has been concern about increases in lake sulphate concentrations and pH. This has led to an environmental campaign to reduce the amount of sulphates released into the atmosphere from industrial sources.

Experiment 1

Ecologists measured the *terrestrial deposition* (land deposits) of sulphate at five alpine stations located adjacent to lakes annually between 1990 and 1998. Sulphate was measured in soil and rock samples. The averages for two-year sampling periods appear in Table 2.5.

Table 2.5

Lake	Sulphate Concentration (mg/L)			
	1990–92	1992–94	1994–96	1996–98
1	0.65	0.60	0.60	0.59
2	0.60	0.59	0.58	0.50
3	0.82	0.82	0.80	0.69
4	0.89	0.69	0.66	0.66
5	0.68	0.65	0.67	0.69

Experiment 2

In 1998, the researchers looked at the sulphate concentrations (in μequivalents/L) and pH in the lakes adjacent to the alpine stations and compared them to concentrations recorded in the same lakes in 1990. Results appear in the following figure.

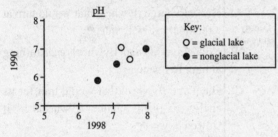

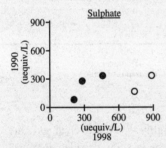

Experiment 3

In order to take into account changing climatic parameters in the study area, the researchers looked at rainfall and temperature since 1900. The results appear in the following figure.

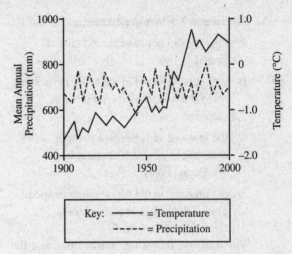

13. The researchers discovered that during the study period:

   A. the trend in sulphate lake concentration was neither up nor down, but tended to mirror terrestrial deposition trends.

   B. terrestrial deposition and lake concentrations of sulphate increased.

   C. terrestrial deposition and lake concentrations of sulphate decreased.

   D. terrestrial deposition of sulphate decreased, while lake concentrations increased.

14. One difference between Experiments 1 and 2 was:

   F. Experiment 1 was conducted over a longer period of time.

   G. Experiment 2 looked at glacial and nonglacial lakes, while Experiment 1 looked at only glacial lakes.

   H. Experiment 2 measured pH and sulphate concentrations, while Experiment 1 measured only sulphate concentrations.

   J. in Experiment 1, data was collected by analyzing rocks and soil, while in Experiment 2, air samples were taken.

GO ON TO THE NEXT PAGE

15. Experiment 2 demonstrated that:

    A. lake pH did not increase in the study period.

    B. the increase in pH in the study period was more dramatic than the increase in sulphate.

    C. the increase in sulphate was more dramatic in glacial lakes than in nonglacial lakes.

    D. the increase in pH was more dramatic in glacial lakes than in alpine lakes.

16. Which of the following statements about the sulphate concentrations measured in Experiment 1 is best supported by the data presented?

    F. Concentrations dropped in all the study areas.

    G. Concentration drops were most profound for lake 4.

    H. Concentrations dropped by about 75% for most areas.

    J. Concentrations dropped by about 50% for most areas.

17. Which of the following hypotheses might explain the findings of Experiment 2 in a way that is consistent with the findings in the other two studies?

    I. Warmer air temperatures in the lake areas may have resulted in less annual ice cover. This provided more time for the weathering, by light and wind, of sulphate-containing rocks, leading to sulphate runoff into the lakes.

    II. Drought conditions in the lake areas may have led to lower water levels, which concentrated the sulphate present.

    III. The environmental campaign failed to reduce sulphate emissions.

    A. I only

    B. III only

    C. I or II only

    D. II or III only

Passage IV

In the 1970s, a spacecraft called the Mariner 10 flew by Mercury at close range three times. These *flybys* provided clues about an intriguing planet that we know less about than any other barring Pluto. Table 2.6 shows data on Mercury, compared with the other planets in our Solar System. Some of the numbers are approximations only. A planet's *rotational period* is the time it takes to turn once on its axis, completing one planetary day. A planet's *orbital period* is the time it takes to move once around the sun, completing one planetary year.

The following figure is a plot of the density versus the radius for the terrestrial (nongaseous) planets.

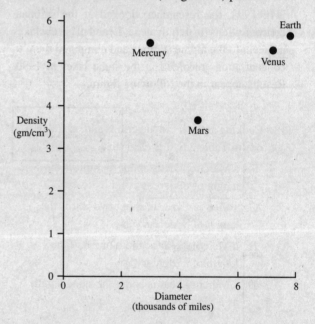

Table 2.6

Terrestrial bodies	Average density (water =1)	Average distance from sun (millions of miles)	Rotational period (earth days)	Orbital period (earth days)	Orbital eccentricity	Mean surface temp. (°C)	Description
Mercury	5.4	36	59	88	.206	179	Rocky, ferrous
Venus	5.2	67	243	225	.007	480	Rocky, ferrous
Earth	5.5	93	24 hrs	365	.017	22	Rocky, ferrous
Mars	3.9	142	25 hrs	687	.093	−23	Rocky
Jupiter	1.3	484	9 hrs	4,333	.048	−150	Gaseous
Saturn	0.7	887	10 hrs	10,760	.056	−180	Gaseous
Uranus	1.2	1,783	11 hrs	30,685	.047	−210	Icy, gaseous
Neptune	1.7	2,794	16 hrs	60,190	.009	−220	Icy, gaseous
Pluto	1	3,600	6	90,800	.25	−230	Icy, rocky, gaseous

18. Looking at the rotation periods and orbital periods in Table 2.6, it is clear that:

    F. a Mercury day is about two-thirds the length of a Mercury year.

    G. a Mercury year is about two-thirds the length of a Mercury day.

    H. a Mercury year is about one-half the length of a Mercury day.

    J. a Mercury year is about the same length as a Mercury day.

19. If the moon (a terrestrial body) has a diameter of about 4000 miles and a density of about 3.3 g/cm³, which of the following statements is most probably correct?

    A. The density versus diameter of terrestrial bodies appears to have a linear relationship.

    B. The density versus diameter of terrestrial bodies appears to have a linear relationship for Mars, Venus, and Earth only.

    C. The density versus diameter for the moon follows the linear relationship seen with the other terrestrial bodies, with the exception of Mercury.

    D. The linear relationship of density versus diameter does not appear to apply to terrestrial bodies other than the planets.

20. Which of the following is the terrestrial planet with the most eccentric orbit?

    F. Mercury

    G. Earth

    H. Jupiter

    J. Pluto

21. Which planet has a density that is most similar to that of water?

    A. Jupiter

    B. Saturn

    C. Uranus

    D. Pluto

22. Mercury has the hottest peak daytime temperature of any planet (around 973 °C). Based on this information, which of the following statements is most probably correct?

    F. Mean surface temperature is a good predictor of daytime temperature.

    G. Mercury's temperature remains stable throughout its rotational period.

    H. Temperatures plunge on Mercury at night.

    J. Nighttime temperatures are warmer on Mercury than daytime temperatures.

GO ON TO THE NEXT PAGE ▶

23. It is thought that Mercury has the largest core (dense planet center) in relation to the planet's overall size of any of the terrestrial planets. If the earth's core is approximately 3,000 miles in diameter, which of the following is a probable diameter for Mercury's core?

    A. Greater than 3,000 miles

    B. Around 2,000 miles

    C. Around 1,000 miles

    D. Around 500 miles

Passage V

Schizophrenia is a mental illness that involves the dissociation of reason and emotion, resulting in symptoms including hallucinations, hearing voices, intense withdrawal, delusions, and paranoia. The average age at which schizophrenia is diagnosed is 18 years for men and 23 years for women. It has been observed to run in families.

The cause remains a mystery, but there are several competing theories. These theories are based in part on findings from twin studies, which look at identical twins in which one or both have the disease. (Identical twins share 100% of their genetic material, while nonidentical twins share about 50%.) In 50% of the cases, when one identical twin is affected, the other will also suffer from schizophrenia. Identical twin pairs in which one individual is ill and the other is well are referred to as *discordant twins*.

Genetic Theory

One school of thought is that schizophrenia is a *genetic disorder* (one passed through the genes from parents to children). This theory gained support from the fact that schizophrenia runs in families. While it was originally believed that it was the family environment that caused this, a study has shown that children of schizophrenics adopted by families without the disease have the same risk of developing the illness as those raised by their birth parents. A final piece of evidence is the fact that the children of discordant identical twins all have the same chance of developing the illness: 17%. This indicates that even the healthy twin is somehow carrying the agent of the disease, presumably in the genes.

Infection Theory

Another school of thought is that schizophrenia arises because of a viral infection of the brain. Studies have shown that a class of viruses called "slow viruses" can linger in the brain for 20 years or longer before the infected person shows symptoms. Brain infections with viruses such as the common cold-sore virus and herpes simplex type 1 can cause symptoms that resemble schizophrenia. Schizophrenia is also more common in children born in the winter, the season when viral infections are more common. Also, one study looking at families with a history of schizophrenia showed a 70% increase in the rate of schizophrenia among children whose mothers had the flu during the second trimester of pregnancy.

24. The schizophrenia theories are similar in that:

    F. both postulate that the foundation of the illness may be laid before birth.

    G. both postulate that the family environment plays some role.

    H. both predict that the children of schizophrenics are not at greater risk than other individuals.

    J. both show that identical twins are at greater risk for schizophrenia than other individuals.

25. Which of the following findings best supports the gene theory?

    A. Parents of discordant twins report that the behavior of the twins begins to diverge at about five years of age, on average.

    B. In discordant identical twin pairs, a brain structure called the basal ganglia is activated more often in the ill twin than in the healthy twin.

    C. An identical twin of a schizophrenia sufferer is four times as likely to have the illness as a nonidentical twin of a schizophrenia sufferer.

    D. Studies have shown that viral infections sometimes infect one identical twin in the uterus and not the other.

26. The infection theory is most effective at explaining the fact that:

    I. schizophrenic patients do poorly on some memory tests.

    II. among identical twins discordant for schizophrenia, the healthy twin may have some borderline schizophrenic traits.

    III. ill twins in discordant pairs have higher rates of finger abnormalities, which can be an indication of a viral infection that occurred in the womb.

    F. I only

    G. II only

    H. III only

    J. II and III only

27. Which of the following hypotheses might supporters of both theories agree with?

    I. Individuals with schizophrenia have certain genes that predispose them to the disease, but require some kind of trigger to turn the disease on.

    II. Individuals with schizophrenia have certain genes that predispose them to viral infections of the brain.

    III. Schizophrenia is not one disease but a collection of diseases.

    A. I and II only

    B. I and III only

    C. II and III only

    D. I, II, and III

28. An identical pair of twins is found in which one was adopted at birth. Both received a diagnosis of schizophrenia as teenagers. An explanation that might be offered by supporters of the viral theory is:

    F. children are most prone to viral infections when they are school age, long after the infant in this case was adopted.

    G. the stress of being an adopted child may have triggered schizophrenia in the predisposed twin.

    H. since 50% of identical twin pairs with schizophrenia are discordant for the disease, this case does not shed light on its origin.

    J. the brains of both twins may have been infected with a slow-acting virus when they were still in the womb.

29. Which of the following studies would be logical for supporters of the genetic theory to conduct next?

    A. One that looks for finger abnormalities in the parents and grandparents of schizophrenic children

    B. One that looks for differences in the chromosomes (which hold the genes) of schizophrenic individuals and healthy individuals

    C. One that looks for scarring in the brains of schizophrenic individuals, which might be a sign of an early injury or infection

    D. One that looks at the home environments of identical twins versus nonidentical twins.

Passage VI

Researchers are experimenting with chemical sensors that could act as artificial noses. These artificial noses are capable of detecting odors indicating that meats or produce are spoiling, making them useful in the food industry. The sensors detect volatile organic compounds (VOCs), which are indicators of food quality. In an experimental system, researchers created thick films of certain *semiconductors* (materials that are neither good electrical conductors nor insulators). Each film is sensitive to a small range of VOCs. When they come into contact with these VOCs, they are *oxidized*. In this process, oxygen molecules combine with the semiconductors to form new molecules, and free electrons are released. The addition of the free electrons alters the electrical properties of the semiconductor films, and this electrical change is detected.

Experiment 1

Researchers developed artificial noses by coupling a number of different VOC detectors, similar to those described above. They then tested the ability of the

GO ON TO THE NEXT PAGE

different artificial noses to detect these VOCs. Results appear in the following figure.

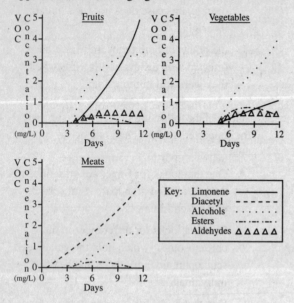

Experiment 2

The researchers sampled the air on a daily basis above a variety of stored fruits, vegetables, and meats. These air samples were injected into the column of a *chromatograph*. A chromatograph is a tool that separates mixtures into their component parts allowing researchers to identify the vapors. The results of the chromatograph experiment appear in the following figure. (Low-molecular weight alcohols, esters, and aldehydes appear grouped in the results.)

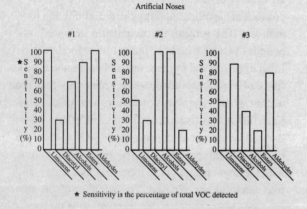

★ Sensitivity is the percentage of total VOC detected

30. Which of the following statements is best supported by the experimental data presented?

   F. Alcohols are the most important VOCs for the detection of fruit spoilage.

   G. Limonene is the most important VOC for the detection of fruit spoilage.

H. Diacetyl is the most important VOC for the detection of vegetable spoilage.

J. Esters are the most important VOCs for the detection of meat spoilage.

31. Which of the following is the most likely interpretation of the data on vegetable spoilage?

   A. Vegetables start to spoil slightly earlier than fruits.

   B. Vegetables start to spoil on about day 5, but show improvement by day 9.

   C. The concentrations of some VOCs continue to rise as vegetables decay, while others begin to wane, making them less useful as indicators.

   D. The concentrations of all VOCs begin to wane after some time, showing that they are not reliable indicators of food spoilage.

32. Which of the following statements about the artificial noses tested is best supported by the data?

   F. Nose #1 is the best indicator of meat spoilage.

   G. Nose #2 is the best indicator of vegetable spoilage.

   H. Nose #2 is the best indicator of fruit spoilage.

   J. Nose #3 is the best indicator of fruit spoilage.

33. If cost constraints limited a food processing company to one VOC detector for use in testing fruits, vegetables, and meats, which would be the best choice?

   A. A limonene detector

   B. An alcohol detector

   C. An ester detector

   D. A diacetyl detector

34. Diacetyl concentration accumulates slowly. Its first appearance signals the tenderization of the meat. If researchers were to create a patch which would appear on packaged meats indicating diacetyl presence, which of the following would be the best use of such a patch?

    F. A patch sensitive to the presence of .05 mg/L of diacetyl, alerting a grocer that the meat should be destroyed

    G. A patch indicating the presence of 2 mg/L of diacetyl, alerting a consumer that the meat should be eaten soon

    H. A patch indicating the presence of 2 mg/L of diacetyl, alerting a processing plant that the meat must be sold soon

    J. A patch indicating the appearance of 0.5 mg/L of diacetyl, alerting a consumer that the meat should be eaten soon

Passage VII

Interstellar objects (objects among the stars) in outer galaxies are often investigated using a method known as *spectroscopy*. Spectroscopy is a method of determining the atomic or molecular makeup of something by observing the object's *spectral lines*. Atoms and molecules have fixed energy levels. When an electron in an atom moves from one of its possible energy states to another, the atom releases light. This light has an energy equal to the difference in the two energy levels through which the electron moved. These energy transitions are observed as a sequence of spectral lines. Spectral lines that are close together indicate transitions in which the change in energy levels is similar.

The following figure depicts three hypothetical atoms. Energy levels are represented as horizontal segments. The distance between the segments is representative of the energy difference between the various levels. All possible transitions between energy levels are indicated by arrows.

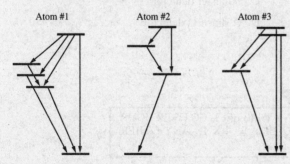

Atom #1   Atom #2   Atom #3

Scientists can observe the spectral lines of atoms that are dominant in far-away galaxies. Due to the speed at which these galaxies are traveling, these lines are shifted, but their pattern remains the same. This allows researchers to use the spectral pattern to determine which atoms they are seeing. Table 2.7 shows spectroscopic measurements made by researchers trying to determine the atomic makeup of a particular far-away galaxy. Light energy is not measured directly, but rather is determined from measuring the frequency of light, which is proportional to the energy.

Table 2.7

Frequencies measured
2096400
2092790
2021140
1940200
1946260

35. Which of the following statements is correct, based on the information in the figure?

    A. Atom #1 has five energy levels.

    B. Atom #1 has seven energy levels.

    C. Atom #3 has more energy levels than atom #2.

    D. The greatest energy transition in atom #2 is larger than the greatest transition in atom #3.

36. Which of the following statements is most likely to be incorrect, based on the information in the figure?

    F. Atom #1 would emit six spectral lines.

    G. Atom #2 would emit four spectral lines.

    H. Atom # 3 would emit five spectral lines.

    J. The number of spectral lines emitted by an atom does not necessarily match the number of energy levels.

GO ON TO THE NEXT PAGE

37. Physicists using spectroscopy to investigate the atoms depicted in the figure would observe which of the following?

   A. Atom 2 would have three spectral lines that are very close together.

   B. Atom 3 would have two spectral lines that are very close together and three more spectral lines that are relatively far from each other.

   C. Atom 3 would have three spectral lines that are very close together.

   D. Atom 1 would have three spectral lines that were close together as well as another pair of spectral lines which are very close together.

38. The researchers making the measurements for Table 2.7 might reach which of the following conclusions?

   I. The atoms appear to have five energy levels, indicating that they could be the same as atom #1.

   II. The atoms appear to be emitting two sets of two closely spaced frequencies, indicating that they could be the same as atom #3.

   III. The observed atoms do not appear to be going through any transitions in energy levels.

   F. I only

   G. II only

   H. III only

   J. II and III only

39. Atoms have "forbidden" transitions. These are transitions between energy levels that are not allowed by the laws of conservation in atomic physics. Which of the following statements concerning the atoms in the figure are true?

   A. Atom 1 has no forbidden transitions.

   B. Atom 2 has one forbidden transition.

   C. Atom 3 has no forbidden transitions.

   D. Atom 3 has more than one forbidden transition.

40. The difference in the information represented in the figure and Table 2.7 is:

   F. The figure was arrived at with spectroscopic measurements, while the information in Table 2.7 was arrived at using only a mathematical formula.

   G. The figure indicates the pattern of frequencies emitted by an atom, while Table 2.7 indicates the exact frequencies emitted by an atom.

   H. The figure indicates the number of energy levels that an atom has, while in Table 2.7 this number can be determined only by identifying the atom being observed.

   J. The figure gives an idea of the proximity of spectral lines associated with the atoms, while Table 2.7 indicates only the energy levels associated with the atoms observed.

STOP

END OF SECTION 4. IF YOU HAVE ANY TIME LEFT, GO OVER YOUR WORK IN THIS SECTION ONLY. DO NOT WORK IN ANY OTHER SECTION OF THE TEST.

SELF-EVALUATION TEST

Answer Key

Section 1: ENGLISH

1. D	16. G	31. A	46. G	61. B
2. G	17. D	32. G	47. B	62. F
3. C	18. G	33. B	48. J	63. D
4. J	19. C	34. J	49. D	64. G
5. D	20. G	35. A	50. F	65. C
6. F	21. A	36. H	51. C	66. H
7. C	22. F	37. C	52. H	67. A
8. J	23. D	38. F	53. A	68. J
9. D	24. H	39. A	54. G	69. B
10. G	25. C	40. G	55. D	70. J
11. C	26. G	41. C	56. F	71. B
12. F	27. B	42. H	57. B	72. H
13. D	28. F	43. D	58. J	73. D
14. F	29. C	44. F	59. C	74. G
15. C	30. J	45. C	60. J	75. D

Section 2: MATHEMATICS

1. C	13. E	25. A	37. D	49. D
2. J	14. F	26. J	38. J	50. F
3. A	15. E	27. C	39. C	51. D
4. K	16. F	28. H	40. J	52. J
5. C	17. C	29. B	41. E	53. B
6. J	18. H	30. H	42. G	54. K
7. C	19. B	31. C	43. D	55. A
8. J	20. F	32. K	44. G	56. J
9. D	21. C	33. C	45. C	57. E
10. F	22. F	34. F	46. G	58. H
11. B	23. A	35. E	47. C	59. D
12. K	24. F	36. H	48. G	60. G

Section 3: READING

1. B	9. A	17. C	25. A	33. C
2. H	10. F	18. F	26. H	34. J
3. B	11. C	19. C	27. C	35. D
4. F	12. F	20. G	28. F	36. J
5. D	13. B	21. C	29. C	37. A
6. H	14. J	22. J	30. G	38. G
7. A	15. C	23. A	31. B	39. C
8. H	16. J	24. H	32. H	40. F

Section 4: SCIENCE REASONING

1. C	9. A	17. A	25. C	33. B
2. F	10. H	18. F	26. H	34. J
3. C	11. B	19. C	27. D	35. A
4. G	12. F	20. F	28. J	36. F
5. D	13. D	21. D	29. B	37. D
6. H	14. H	22. H	30. G	38. G
7. A	15. C	23. B	31. C	39. B
8. H	16. G	24. F	32. G	40. F

SELF-EVALUATION TEST

Explanatory Answers

Section 1: ENGLISH

1. **D.** Since the event being described is a past event prior to another past event, the verb tense that's needed is the past perfect, not the present perfect: "I'd heard" rather than "I've heard."

2. **G.** When two independent clauses are joined by the conjunction "and," a comma is normally inserted *before* the "and" (unless the clauses are very short). It's not necessary or particularly effective to use either a semicolon (as in choice H) or a period (as in choice J) to separate these two clauses; they naturally seem to belong together.

3. **C.** Since the antecedent of the pronoun is "the reed" (singular), the pronoun should be the singular "it" rather than the plural "they."

4. **J.** The logical connector here is "but" rather than "so," since a contrast rather than a cause-and-effect relationship is being described. The semicolon in choice H is wrong; with the conjunction "although," the second clause becomes a subordinate or dependent clause, which can't stand alone as a sentence and therefore can't properly follow a semicolon.

5. **D.** In both the original wording and choice B, what follows the period is a fragment rather than a complete sentence. In choice C, the combined sentences form a run-on. Choice D avoids both errors.

6. **F.** The original phrase substantiates the writer's complaint about the high price of oboe reeds. Answers G, H, and J introduce ideas that are either completely irrelevant or slightly off the point.

7. **C.** Both the original wording and choice B create run-on sentences. The shift of pronoun to "one" in choice D sounds a little stilted, and the colon seems less appropriate than the semicolon. (Generally, the colon is best when it could be replaced with the phrase "that is," which isn't the case here.)

8. **J.** All of the answer choices are grammatically correct, but choice J is the most concise.

9. **D.** The underlined words can be omitted, because they merely repeat the idea already stated in the words "progressively worse."

10. **G.** The pronoun reference here is unclear: who or what is "they"? Choices G and H both clarify what is being referred to (the reeds, of course), but G does so more concisely.

11. **C.** The modifier "desperate" must be next to "I," since that is the person whom the modifier describes.

12. **F.** As in the original wording, the parenthetical phrase "within two weeks" should be set off from the rest of the sentence by a pair of commas.

13. **D.** The placement of the modifying word is fine, but it should be changed from an adjective to an adverb ("immediately"), since it modifies the verb "called."

14. **F.** This basic introductory information about what oboe reeds are needs to appear early in the essay.

15. **C.** The information in Paragraph 4 is relevant to the overall contents and theme of the essay, since it contributes to the explanation of why oboists have so much difficulty in getting enough good reeds for their instruments.

16. **G.** The subject of the verb is "goal," so the verb should be singular, "was" rather than "were." "To determine" is the idiomatic construction to use in this context.

17. **D.** The original wording is verbose and repetitive; so, to a lesser extent, are choices B and C. Choice D says the same thing concisely.

18. **G.** The paragraph is devoted to explaining the two underlying ideas that guided the scientists who designed the Viking experiments. Choice G sets this up accurately and clearly.

19. **C.** The semicolon in the original wording is wrong, since what follows the semicolon can't stand alone as a sentence. Changing the punctuation mark to a comma solves the problem.

20. **G.** This is the most idiomatic (normal-sounding) and clear of the alternatives. Note that choice H is definitely wrong because it's unclear who or what "contains" the thousands or millions of life-forms mentioned.

21. **A.** Having explained, in Paragraph 2, that the Viking scientists wanted to look for the most abundant forms of life, and that these were expected to take the form of soil-dwelling microbes, this sentence makes a logical transition to Paragraph 3 by beginning the explanation of how the Viking experiments were designed to search for creatures of these kinds.

22. **F.** The original wording is correct. The possessive form (using an apostrophe) isn't appropriate here, since "organisms" isn't followed by anything that is "possessed" by the organisms, nor is any such possession implied.

23. **D.** The idiomatic way to phrase this is the one in choice D: "one characteristic . . . is that they transform" etc.

24. **H.** This phrasing provides the most specific information about the plant structures that the writer is thinking about.

25. **C.** The essay is about how the Viking experiments were designed to test for life on Mars. In that context, information about how long the Martian day lasts is basically irrelevant.

26. **G.** The three clauses being strung together here should be in grammatically parallel form. Choice G carries out the parallelism.

27. **B.** Sentences 1 and 3 belong together; both describe how living organisms on Earth give off gases. Sentence 2 follows naturally after these; it connects this phenomenon to one of the Viking tests. Sentence 4 provides detail about the test, and makes a natural conclusion.

28. **F.** It makes sense to start a new paragraph here; each of the three Viking experiments gets a paragraph of its own. And since this is the last of the experiments to be described, it's appropriate to start the paragraph with the adverb "Finally."

29. **C.** This adverb sounds most natural immediately after the verb it modifies, "was."

30. **J.** Only the last paragraph of the essay deals with the *results* of the Viking mission. The rest focuses on the theoretical concepts behind the Viking experiments and the design of the experiments themselves. Thus, the essay really doesn't fulfill the assignment given.

31. **A.** The original wording is correct. The present perfect tense makes sense here, and the proper form of the verb, "begun," is used. ("Began" is the past tense and would never be used with a helping verb.)

32. **G.** All of the answer choices say more or less the same thing. Answer G does so most succinctly and clearly.

33. **B.** In this context, the contraction "its" is being used to mean "it is." Therefore, the word should contain an apostrophe: "it's."

34. **J.** The main theme of the essay is that "the good old days" weren't really very good. The rhetorical question posed in choice J introduces this theme well, and makes a good start to the second paragraph. Choice F is the best wrong answer, but it suggests that the essay will focus mainly on the advantages of modern technology, which is not true.

35. **A.** This information is relevant to the theme of the essay because it underscores the fact that the average person at the turn of the century did not have access to many advantages that would make life more pleasant in later years. The original wording is best; answers B and C are both too informal (slangy) to fit comfortably into the overall tone of the essay.

36. **H.** "It" is the wrong pronoun, of course, since what's being referred to is "coal-burning stoves," which is plural. Choice H corrects this error less awkwardly and more clearly than the alternatives.

37. **C.** The second and third sentences describe the disadvantages of central heating, which came *after* coal stoves. Therefore, they should follow the sentences about coal stoves and appear last in the paragraph.

38. **F.** The sentence begins we the first person pronoun "We," and "our" continues this construction in a logical and consistent way.

39. **A.** The proposed addition is very appropriate: it contributes in a vivid way to our understanding of the problems created by the "romantic" horse and buggy in turn-of-the-century cities.

40. **G.** The original wording is vague and fails to explain why the shorter buildings made the summers seem hotter. Choice G is the only alternative that provides the information needed to clarify the point.

41. **C.** This choice provides specific details to support the writer's point. Choices A and B merely state the idea without providing evidence to support it, and choice D digresses into a discussion of *today's* summer fashions, which is basically irrelevant.

42. **H.** This choice maintains the grammatical parallelism required to make the three items listed sound consistent.

43. **D.** The original wording creates a run-on sentence, with two independent clauses merely jammed together. Choice D fixes this by adding the appropriate subordinating conjunction "While," which clarifies the logical relationship between the two ideas and also corrects the grammatical error.

44. **F.** The phrase "at least in that respect" is a logical unit which should be kept together and set off from the rest of the sentence with a comma on either side.

45. **C.** This fact clearly belongs in Paragraph 5, where the "bad old summers" are described; and since it offers a fact that is even worse than the facts already given in that paragraph, it seems appropriate to put it at the end of the paragraph, where it can serve as the climax of that portion of the essay.

46. **G.** The correct superlative form of the adjective "famous" is "most famous"—the same kind of construction use with most adjectives that are two syllables long or longer.

47. **B.** The semicolon is wrong because what follows the punctuation mark is not an independent clause. Choices C and D are wrong because they insert an intrusive comma after the word "because," which instead should flow directly into what follows.

48. **J.** Omit this sentence, since it merely repeats information stated a few sentences earlier. It's obvious that the fiance being referred to is the same one mentioned previously.

49. **D.** The two sentences should be joined into one, since the second is a mere fragment. Choice C is grammatically correct (it fixes the fragment), but it's repetitive and awkward to mention "England" twice within three words.

50. **F.** The original wording is correct, since what's being compared is "abortion in England" with abortion "in the United States."

51. **C.** "Once" makes a better introductory word for two reasons: it clarifies the logical relationship between the two clauses, and it makes the first clause into a subordinate clause, thus avoiding the grammatical problem of a run-on sentence.

52. **H.** The best punctuation to use when two independent clauses are joined by "and" is a comma preceding the "and."

53. **A.** Since the writer wants to stress the *unusual* nature of the article, "ground-breaking" seems to be the appropriate adjective.

54. **G.** In Paragraph 3, Steinem was struggling to find work; in Paragraph 4, she is a successful writer. The sentence given in choice G explains the transition logically and gracefully.

55. **D.** This choice is the most idiomatic, graceful, and concise.

56. **F.** The details here are appropriate and help clarify the kind of writing Steinem was relegated to, so omitting them would be a poor choice. The original wording is the most graceful of the three alternatives.

57. **B.** The semicolon isn't needed here; the independent clauses are joined by "and," which calls for a comma instead. Choice B appropriately sets off the parenthetical phrase "she says" with a pair of commas.

58. **J.** This sentence is the only one that explains and demonstrates how concern over abortion rights motivated Steinem to become a committed feminist.

59. **C.** The modifying phrase "a tireless worker and advocate" must be placed next to "Steinem," since that is what the phrase modifies. Choice B and D are grammatically correct, but they sound awkward and a little unclear.

60. **J.** The simple "including" is the clearest and most concise choice for this context.

61. **B.** The comparison being drawn here calls for the phrase to be uninterrupted by commas.

62. **F.** The pronoun "whose" is perfectly correct; its antecedent is "filmmakers."

63. **D.** This sentence should be omitted; it's redundant, since it merely repeats the idea stated in the clause immediately preceding it.

64. **G.** It's better to put the word "not" after "product," to create the appropriate parallelism: "not of the salon but of the common playhouse." Now the words that follow the linked prepositions "not . . . but" are strictly parallel in form.

65. **C.** We already know, from the rest of the paragraph, that the three persons named were geniuses of the early movies. Information about where they came from seems irrelevant, since the essay doesn't discuss national differences in cinema. This phrase can be left out without losing a thing.

66. **H.** The original wording creates a run-on sentence. Choice H fixes the problem. So does choice J, but "For" doesn't connect the two ideas logically; and the dash in choice G leaves the relationship between the two ideas vague and confusing.

67. **A.** The preposition "like" is correct here, since what follows is a phrase rather than a clause.

68. **J.** Since what follows the semicolon is not an independent clause, the mark should be changed to a comma.

69. **B.** The idea in this sentence is in contrast to the idea of the previous sentence; therefore, "But" is a more logical word with which to start the sentence.

70. **J.** The underlined phrase should be omitted; it merely repeats the idea contained in the word "larger" without adding any information.

71. **B.** The idiomatic construction in English runs, "the larger . . . the greater." Once you've used the first half of a pair of phrases like these, you're committed to using the second half as well.

72. **H.** The antecedent of the pronoun is "creator," so the third-person pronoun "his" (or the less-sexist "his or her") must be used here.

73. **D.** Since this is the possessive "its" rather than the contraction meaning "it is," no apostrophe should be used.

74. **G.** The subject of the verb is "what makes the movies truly unique," which is singular in form; therefore, the singular verb "is" must be used.

75. **D.** The third paragraph should come first; it introduces the topic and places the movies in their context as the leading twentieth-century artistic innovation. The other two paragraphs, which discuss some specifics about the development of movies as an art form, follow logically after this.

Section 2: MATHEMATICS

1. **C.** $\frac{1}{3}$ of 42 is 14, and $\frac{1}{6}$ of 42 is 7. Thus, 21 horses are black or white, leaving 21 horses that are brown.

2. **J.** In 5 hours, 4 ounces $(7-3)$ of water have dripped. Therefore, the "drip rate" is $\frac{4}{5}$ of an ounce per hour. From 5:00 P.M. on Sunday until 2:00 A.M. on Monday is 9 hours, so the total that will have dripped is $7+\left(\frac{4}{5}\times 9\right)=7+\frac{36}{5}=\frac{71}{5}$ ounces.

3. **A.** $m_{PQ}=\dfrac{(5-2)}{3-(-1)}=\dfrac{3}{4}$

4. **K.** We know that the average of x and -1 must be 2. That is:

    $$2+\frac{x+(-1)}{2}$$

    Thus, $4^2=x-1$, $x=5$. Similarly, we know that the average of y and 3 must be 6. Thus: $6=\dfrac{y+3}{2}$; $12=y+3$; $y=9$. So $2x+y=19$.

    Therefore, $12=y+3$; $y=9$; $2x+y=19$.

5. **C.** Substituting $y=\frac{1}{2}$, we have $\left(\frac{1}{2}\right)^0+\left(\frac{1}{2}\right)^{-1}=1+\left(\frac{1}{2}\right)^{-1}=1+2=3$.

6. **J.** The perimeter of the longer rectangle is $2L + 2W$. The other rectangle must have a length of $\frac{1}{2}L$ and a width of $2W$, since the area is the same. Thus, the second rectangle has a perimeter of $2\left(\frac{1}{2}L\right) + 2(2W) = L + 4W$.

7. **C.** The arithmetic mean of x and y is $\frac{(x+y)}{2} = m$. This means that $x + y = 2m$, and $x + y + z = 4m$. Dividing by 3 to get the arithmetic mean of x, y and z, we have $\frac{(x+y+z)}{3} = \frac{4m}{3}$.

8. **J.** Looking first at triangle ABE, we have a right triangle with one angle of 90° and one angle of 27°. Thus, $\angle A$ must be 63°. Hence, $\angle BAC$ is one-third of that, or 21°. So, looking at triangle ABC, $\angle BCA$ must be $180° - 21° - 27° = 132°$. Since x is the supplement to that angle, $x = 48$.

9. **D.** Because each person had five choices, there are 25 possible pairs of numbers. The only way the sum could be odd is if one person picked an odd number and the other picked an even number. Suppose that John chose the odd number and Lisa the even one. John had three possible even numbers to select from, and for each of these, Lisa had two possible choices, for a total of $(3)(2) = 6$ possibilities. However, you could have had John pick an even number and Lisa pick an odd one, and there are also six ways to do that. Hence, out of 25 possibilities, 12 have an odd total and 13 have an even total. The probability is $\frac{13}{25}$.

10. **F.** Running m buses for two days is the same as running one bus for $2m$ days. If we use g gallons of gasoline, each bus uses $\frac{g}{2m}$ gallons each day. So if you multiply the number of gallons per day used by each bus by the number of buses and the number of days, you should get total usage. Thus: $\frac{g}{2m} \times 4 \times 5 = \frac{10g}{m}$.

11. **B.** Letting $C = \text{cost}$, $w = $ number of workers, and $t = $ time in hours, we have the relationship $C = k\frac{w}{t^2}$. Therefore, when $w = 12$ at $t = 2$, we have $1500 = k\frac{12}{4} = 3k$; therefore, $k = 500$. Using $k = 500$ and substituting $w = 9$ and $C = 2000$, we have:

    $$2000 = 500 \times \frac{9}{t^2} = \frac{4500}{t^2}$$

    Multiplying by t^2 and dividing by 2000, we have:

    $$t^2 = \frac{9}{4} \; ; t = \frac{3}{2} = 1.5$$

12. **K.** Using the quadratic formula with $a = 1$, $b = -4$, and $c = 13$:

    $$x = \frac{-(-4) \pm \sqrt{(-4)^2 - 4(1)(13)}}{2(1)} = \frac{4 \pm \sqrt{16 - 52}}{2} = \frac{4 \pm \sqrt{-36}}{2}$$

    $$x = \frac{4 \pm 6i}{2} = 2 \pm 3i$$

    Hence, one root is $2 + 3i$.

13. **E.** The length of OQ and OP are the same: $\sqrt{2^2 + 1^2} = \sqrt{5}$. The length of PQ is $= \sqrt{1^2 + 1^2} = \sqrt{2}$. So the perimeter is $2\sqrt{5} + \sqrt{2}$.

14. **F.** Since $P = M + 1$, $N = 3^P = 3^{M+1} = 3(3^M)$, and $\frac{1}{3^M}$.

15. **E.** Since $A^2 - B^2 = (A - B)(A + B)$, $(A - B)$ and $(A + B)$ must be factors of 36. The possibilities are as follows:

    $A - B = 1 \qquad A + B = 36$

    $A - B = 2 \qquad A + B = 18$

    $A - B = 3 \qquad A + B = 12$

    $A - B = 4 \qquad A + B = 9$

    $A - B = 6 \qquad A + B = 6$

    Only the second and fifth possibilities yield integer solutions, and in the fifth case, $A = 6$ and $B = 0$, which is not positive. The only choice that works is $A = 10$, $B = 8$, for which $A + B = 18$ and $A - B = 2$.

16. **F.** Letting h be the price of the hat and s be the price of the scarf, $h + s = 38$, and $h = s + 3$. Substituting:

    $s + s + 3 = 38$

    $2s = 35$

    $s = \$17.50$

17. **C.** Multiplying radicals gives $\sqrt{18x} = \sqrt{30}$. Hence, $18x = 30$, and $x = \frac{1}{2}$.

18. **H.** Doubling the first equation and adding it to the second gives us:

$$4x - 2y + 8z = 14$$
$$\underline{-4x + 2y - 3z = \ \ 1}$$
$$5z = 15; z = 3$$

19. **B.** The possible factors of 36 are (1,36), (2,18), (3,12), (4,9), and (6,6). The smallest possible sum is 12, but that is when x and y are equal. So we must take choice B, 13, which we get with the factors (4,9).

20. **F.** The total cost for the month is $500 + 15nc$ for $15n$ minutes of calling. Thus, the average is $\frac{500 + 15nc}{15n} = c + \frac{100}{3n}$

21. **C.** If the diameter is π, the radius is $\frac{1}{2}\pi$ and the area is $\pi r^2 = \pi\left(\frac{1}{2}\pi\right)^2 = \frac{1}{4}\pi^3$.

22. **F.** Calling the smallest angle x, the others are $2x$, $3x$, and $(x + 31)$. Because the angles in the quadrilateral must sum to 360, we get:

$$x + 2x + 3x + (x + 31) = 360$$
$$7x + 31 = 360$$
$$7x = 329; x = 47$$

That makes the degree measures of the four angles 47, 94, 141, and 78. The difference between the two in the middle is $94 - 78 = 16$.

23. **A.** Four out of 6 times, the first block drawn will be a zero. The remaining one third of the time, a non-zero number will be drawn, leaving one non-zero and four zero blocks. The chance of drawing a second non-zero block is $\frac{1}{5}$. Hence, the product will not be zero only $\frac{1}{5}$ of $\frac{1}{3} = \frac{1}{3} \times \frac{1}{5} = \frac{1}{15}$ of the time.

24. **F.** Factoring the numerator and denominator of the fraction, we see that we can divide out the common factor $(x - 3)$, thusly:

$$\frac{x^2 - 3x}{3x - 9} = \frac{x(x - 3)}{3(x - 3)} = \frac{x}{3}$$

Substituting $x = 3.03$ yields $\frac{3.03}{3} = 1.01$.

25. **A.** If the true distance is T, then the odometer will show $m = T + 0.10T = 1.1T = \left(\frac{11}{10}\right)T$. That is, $m = \frac{11}{10}T$, so $\frac{10m}{11} = T$.

26. **J.** Let Elaine's salary be $3k$, and Carl's will be $2k$. A 20% raise for Elaine will bring her salary to $(1.2)(3k) = 3.6k$, while a \$200 raise for Carl will bring his salary to $2k + 200$. Thus, $3.6k:(2k + 200) = 6:5$, or, in fractional form:

$$\frac{3.6k}{2k + 200} = \frac{6}{5}$$

Cross-multiplying: $18k = 12k + 1200$; $6k = 1200$; $k = 200$. So Elaine's salary is $3k = 600$.

27. **C.** P percent means $\frac{P}{100}$. Hence, $\frac{P}{100} \times 20\sqrt{3} = 3$ must be solved for P. Thus, $\frac{P\sqrt{3}}{5} = 3$. Multiplying by $\frac{5}{\sqrt{3}}$, and noticing that $\frac{3}{\sqrt{3}} = \sqrt{3}$ gives us $P = 5\sqrt{3}$.

28. **H.** The sum of the angles in the triangle must be 180 degrees. Letting the degree measure of $\angle A$ be x, we have $x + 50$ for B and $3x$ for C. Now:

$$x + (x + 50) + 3x = 180$$
$$5x + 50 = 180$$
$$x = 26$$

Hence, $\angle B = 76°$ and $\angle C = 78°$. Therefore, $\angle B - \angle C = -2°$

29. **B.** Adding the two equations gives us $4n = 16$, so $n = 4$. Knowing that $n = 4$, the second equation tells us that $8 + m = 10$, and $m = 2$.

30. **H.** Of the 12 students taking Spanish, 4 are taking both languages, leaving 8 taking only Spanish.

31. **C.** If $x = 2$, $x^0 = 2^0 = 1$; and $x^{-4} = 2^{-4} = \frac{1}{2^4} = \frac{1}{16} = 0.0625$. Hence, $3x^0 + x^{-4} = 3.0625$

32. **K.** If $x = \frac{1}{2}$, $x^2 + 2y^2 = \frac{1}{4} + 2y^2 = 1$ implies that $2y^2 = \frac{3}{4}$, and $y^2 = \frac{3}{8}$. Now $|y| = \sqrt{\frac{3}{8}} = \sqrt{0.375} =$ approximately 0.6.

33. **C.** The logarithmic equation is equivalent to $x^3 = 0.001$; $x^3 = \frac{1}{1000}$, for which $x = \sqrt[3]{\frac{1}{1000}}$; $x = \frac{1}{10} = 0.1$.

34. **F.** Dropping the perpendicular from C down to the extension of AB (see the diagram below), we see that $\angle CBD = 50°$ and that the altitude of the triangle, h, given by $\frac{h}{9} = \sin 50°$. Thus, $h = 9\sin 50°$, and the area of triangle ABC is thus less than $\frac{1}{2}(6)(9)\sin 50° = 27\sin 50°$.

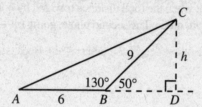

35. **E.** Using the obvious notation, we have:

    $4c + 6d + 3h = 815$

    $2c + 3d + 4h = 720$

    Multiplying the second equation by –2 and adding the equations together yields $-5h = -625$; $h = 125$.

36. **H.** By the Pythagorean Theorem, $c^2 = \sqrt{3^2 + 5^2} = \sqrt{34} =$ about 5.83, which is closest to 6.

37. **D.** Adding the two equations, we have $3x + 4y = 13$. Multiplying by 3 gives us $9x + 12y = 39$.

38. **J.** We see that we have 9 choices for the first digit, 10 choices for the second digit, and 10 choices for the third digit. Thus, the total is $9 \times 10 \times 10 = 900$.

39. **C.** Calling the smallest number x, the second is $(x + 2)$, and the third is $(x + 4)$. Therefore:

    $x + (x + 2) + 2(x + 4) = 46$

    $x + x + 2 + 2x + 8 = 46$

    $4x + 10 = 46$; $4x = 36$; $x = 9$.

    Hence, the middle number is $9 + 2 = 11$.

40. **J.** The unshaded region is a sector with a 30° angle, which is $\frac{1}{12}$ of the area of the circle. Hence, the shaded portion must be $\left(\frac{11}{12}\right)\pi r^2 = 33\pi$. Dividing by 11π and multiplying by 12, we have $r^2 = 36$. Hence, $r = 6$, and the diameter is 12.

41. **E.** Using J and R to stand for their present ages, we have:

    $J = R + 4$

    $R - 2 = \frac{2}{3}(J - 2)$

    Multiplying the second equation by 3:

    $3R - 6 = 2(J - 2)$

    Substituting from equation one:

    $3R - 6 = 2(R + 4 - 2) = 2(R + 2)$

    $3R - 6 = 2R + 4$

    $R = 10$

    Hence, Rodney is 10 and Jerome is 14. x years ago, Rodney was $10 - x$ and Jerome was $14 - x$, giving us:

    $14 - x = 2(10 - x)$

    $14 - x = 20 - 2x$

    $x = 6$

42. **G.** The equation of the circle is $(x-6)^2 + (y-9)^2 = 13^2$. Substituting $x = 1$ and $y = u$, we have:

$25 + (u-9)^2 = 169$

$(u-9)^2 = 144;\ u - 9 = \pm 12$

This gives us two possibilities: $u = -3$ or $u = 21$.

43. **D.** Since John takes 20 minutes per room, he can do 3 rooms in one hour. Armando can do 4 rooms in an hour. Thus, together they do 7 rooms in one hour. To do 30 rooms will take them $\frac{30}{7}$ hours, which is greater than 4.

44. **G.** Using the laws of logarithms, $2y - 3x = 2\log 5 - 3\log 2 = \log 5^2 - \log 2^3 = \log 25 = \log 8 = \log\left(\frac{25}{8}\right)$.

45. **C.** The planes pass at the moment when the total distance traveled by both equals R. Call this time t. The first plane, going m mph, has traveled mt miles. The second plane, going $(m+50)$ mph, has traveled $(m+50)t$. The two sum to R. Thus:

$R = mt + mt + 50t$

$R = (2m + 50)t$

Thus:

$t = \frac{R}{2m+50}$

Hence, the planes' distance from City A is m times this time:

$mt = \frac{Rm}{2m+50}$

46. **G.** Setting $y = 0$ and solving by the quadratic formula with $a = 1$, $b = -2$ and $c = -6$:

$x = \frac{-(-2)\pm\sqrt{(-2)^2-4(1)(-6)}}{2(1)} = \frac{2\pm\sqrt{28}}{2} = \frac{2\pm2\sqrt{7}}{2} = 1\pm\sqrt{7}$

Since $\sqrt{7}$ is between 2 and 3, choosing the minus sign, $1 - \sqrt{7}$ is less than -1 and greater than -2.

47. **C.** $f(g(x)) = (g(x))^2 = \frac{1}{(x^2+1)}$, and $g(x) = \pm\frac{1}{\left(\sqrt{x^2+1}\right)}$. Choose the plus sign.

48. **G.** Since the terms must have a common ratio, $\frac{-2}{x} = \frac{x}{-8}$. Cross multiplying, $x^2 = 16$, and $x = \pm 4$. For $+4$, the sixth term would be $(-2)(4)^5 = -2{,}048$, while for -4 it would be $2{,}048$.

49. **D.** Factoring numerator and denominator : $\frac{4x^2-9}{2x^2+x-3} = \frac{(2x-3)(2x+3)}{(x-1)(2x+3)}$. Dividing out the common factor $(2x + 3)$ yields $\frac{(2x-3)}{(x-1)}$.

50. **F.** The slope of PQ is $m = \frac{(6-2)}{(1-(1))} = 2$.

Hence, any line perpendicular to it has slope $-\frac{1}{2}$. Averaging the coordinates of P and Q, we see that the midpoint of PQ is $(0,4)$, which must be the y-intercept of the line we seek. Thus, $y = -\frac{1}{2}x + 4$.

51. **D.** We display the data in the Venn Diagram shown below, letting x be the number of users who have both a tape and disc drive.

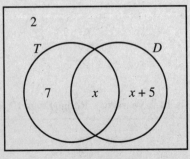

T = Tape Drive
D = Disc Drive

Totaling the numbers, we see that $2 + 7 + x + (x + 5) = 50$; $2x + 14 = 50$; $2x = 36$; $x = 18$. Knowing that $x = 18$, we can see from the diagram that the total number in T is 25.

52. **J.** Calling the height of the cliff H, and illustrating the situation with the diagram below, we see in triangle BCD that $\frac{H}{50} = \tan 40°$, that is, $H = 50\tan 40°$.

Then, in triangle ACD, we see that $\frac{H}{(50+M)} = \tan 20°$, that is, $H = 50\tan 20° + M\tan 20°$.

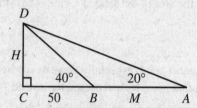

Equating the two expressions, since both are equal to H, we have:

$50\tan 40° = 50\tan 20° + M\tan 20°$

which we can solve for M by subtracting $50 \tan 20°$ from both sides and then dividing by $\tan 20°$ to give us

$M = \frac{50\tan 40° - 50\tan 20°}{\tan 20°}$

53. **B.** Since $\sqrt{8} = \sqrt{(4)(2)} = 2\sqrt{2}$, $2\sqrt{8} = 4\sqrt{2}$, and $3\sqrt{2} + 4\sqrt{2} = 7\sqrt{2}$.

54. **K.** Letting L be the amount reimbursed on lodging and M be the amount reimbursed on food, the first piece of information we have says: $M = L + 16$.

$M = L + 16$	(from first statement)
$\frac{2}{3}M = \frac{3}{2}L - 16$	(from second statement)
$-\frac{3}{2}M = -\frac{3}{2}L - 24$	(multiply first equation by $-\frac{3}{2}$)
$-\frac{5}{6}M = \qquad -40$	(add the second and third equations)
$-5M = -240$	(cross multipy)

$M = \$48 =$ cost of meals

$M \pm L + 16$, so $L = M - 16 = \$32$ for lodging. $\$48 + \$32 = \$80$

55. **A.** The numbers in an arithmetic progression have a common difference. Hence, $5 - (-3) = 3d$. That is, $8 = 3d$ and $d = \frac{8}{3}$. Thus, $M = -3 + d = -3 + \frac{8}{3} = \frac{-1}{3}$.

56. **J.** The fraction reduces to $2y^2$, and $10y^2 - 2y^2 = 8y^2$.

57. **E.** When adding the matrices, you add entries in corresponding locations. Remember to multiply each entry in A by 2 first. Thus, in the upper left-hand corner, you have $-4 + x = -5$, so $x = -1$. Similarly, in the lower right-hand corner you have

$6 + y = 4$, so $y = -2$. Hence, $xy = 2$.

58. **H.** To calculate $f\left(\frac{1}{x}\right)$, you substitute $\frac{1}{x}$ for x wherever it appears, giving $f\left(\frac{1}{x}\right) = \frac{1}{x+1}$. Combining this into a single fraction, you have $= f\left(\frac{1}{x}\right) = \frac{x+1}{1}$. Multiplying this by $\frac{1}{f(x)} = \frac{1}{(x+1)}$. The $(x + 1)$ cancels in the numerator and denominator, leaving just $\frac{1}{x}$.

59. **D.** Since the slope is the change in y divided by the change in x, the line through $(-1,0)$ having slope 1 gives us the equation:

$1 = \frac{y-0}{(x-(-1))} = \frac{y}{x+1}$

That is, $y = x + 1$.

The line through $(-4,0)$ having slope $\frac{1}{2}$ gives us the equation:

$\frac{1}{2} = \frac{y-0}{(x-(-1))} = \frac{y}{x+1}$

That is, $2y = x + 4$.

We need to know x, so substitute $x + 1$ for y in the second equation:

$2(x + 1) = x + 4$; $2x + 2 = x + 4$; $x = 2$.

60. **G.** The entire area between the two circles is the area of the larger minus the area of the smaller. Call this value A. Now, $A = \frac{1}{2}\pi(2r)^2 - \frac{1}{2}\pi r^2 = \left(\frac{3}{2}\right)\pi r^2$. Drawing the line segment from C to O forms two right triangles, each with a hypotenuse of length $2r$ and $OC = r$. Thus, angle A and angle B are each 30°, making angle $AOC = 120°$, or one third of the circle. Hence, the area of the shaded region is two-thirds of the area A and must equal πr^2.

Section 3: READING

1. **B.** The first two paragraphs make this point, especially these words from the second paragraph: "because he usually dropped in at the club at that hour, he had passed by instead."

2. **H.** Archer fears that Welland is becoming figuratively "blind," that is, unable to perceive reality because of the conventionality of her upbringing and her social surroundings. The cave-fish symbolizes his fear that Welland will never be grown-up enough to see and think for herself.

3. **B.** Paragraph 3 makes it clear that the Archer-Welland engagement will be somewhat shorter than that of Welland's friends "Grace and Thorley," which was "nearly a year and a half." However, it can't *be much* shorter than theirs; otherwise Archer would hardly be complaining about its length. Hence answer B.

4. **F.** The first paragraphs refers to the "leisurely manner" in which men of Archer's class practiced the law.

5. **D.** She laughs when she mentions the idea, and considers it "boring" to have to explain to him why it would never do. Clearly, for Welland the idea of eloping is almost too silly to discuss.

6. **H.** Archer recalls saying to his friend Jackson, "Women ought to be as free as we are—!" And earlier in the paragraph, he muses that "nice" women may begin "to speak for themselves" "Never, if we won't let them." The two statements in combination show that Archer feels that men ("we") are largely responsible for constraining women and taking away their freedom.

7. **A.** As soon as Welland says this to Archer, the author comments, "His heart sank."

8. **H.** Throughout the passage, Archer feels trapped by the "sameness" and conventionality of his relationship with Welland. Yet when she rejects his ideas about breaking out of this conventionality, he apparently is helpless to respond, and is reduced to standing silently, "beating his walking-stick nervously against his shoe-top."

9. **A.** The last three paragraphs state, twice, that Welland feels that calling the idea "vulgar" effectively dismisses the topic.

10. **F.** The third, fifth, and tenth paragraph refer to family, class, and gender traditions as the constraining forces that control Welland's attitudes. The second and eighth paragraphs refers to Welland's mother as the source of the idea that a long engagement is necessary. Welland mentions "novels" only as the kind of guide to behavior she would *never* follow, and her friends are mentioned merely for comparison's sake, not as sources of her beliefs.

11. **C.** The fact that the British and French already had (experimental) ironclads is merely mentioned in the second paragraph, not cited as a reason for the South's eagerness to build one.

12. **F.** This point is made in the second sentence of the passage.

13. **B.** See the first sentence of the third paragraph.

14. **J.** The last sentence of the third paragraph makes it obvious that wooden hulls were the rule, not the exception, among ships of the period.

15. **C.** As used in the passage, "innovative" refers to the design choices made by John Ericson, which made the *Monitor* a remarkably new type of vessel.

16. **J.** The *Virginia* was created simply by armor-plating a traditional wooden boat, whereas the *Monitor* had an entirely new design that "looked like no other ship afloat."

17. **C.** As the third paragraph suggests, the South, by comparison with the North had fewer facilities for ship-building.

18. **F.** See the last sentence of the seventh paragraph: "none of the nearly 100 shots that hit her had pierced her armor."

19. **C.** To "sustain" damage, as the word is used in this sentence, means to receive or suffer it.

20. **G.** Answer B restates the idea found in the last sentence of the passage.

21. **C.** The first two paragraphs show that Doyle pursued both writing and medicine simultaneously, apparently eager to succeed in both fields; he abandoned medicine only much later, after his writing had attained great popularity.

22. **J.** In this context, the word deduction is used to refer to the practice of drawing logical conclusions from evidence—reasoning, in other words.

23. **A.** See the first sentence of the third paragraph, which explains what made Holmes "a different kind of detective" from his fictional predecessors.

24. **H.** The word compelling is being used here to describe the effect of a character like Sherlock Holmes on readers; he compels the reader's interest because of his remarkable personal qualities.

25. **A.** Although Doyle was writing historical novels at the same time as his mystery stories, neither of the Holmes tales mentioned here is described as "based on historical events."

26. **H.** See the seventh paragraph: "Doyle's other small literary successes had enabled him to move to London."

27. **C.** If the author considers it "fortunate" that Doyle was able to concentrate on his writing rather than on practicing medicine, clearly Doyle's literary career must have been more important or worthwhile in the author's eyes than his medical work.

28. **F.** The second sentence of the last paragraph makes this point.

29. **C.** According to the last paragraph, Doyle "considered the Holmes stories insignificant compared to his 'serious' historical novels."

30. **G.** Answer H is too narrow, while answers F and J are too broad. The passage concentrates quite specifically on the origin and early history of the Holmes character, which makes answer G the best choice.

31. **B.** Each of the other answer choices is discussed in one or more paragraphs of the passage.

32. **H.** The first sentence of the third paragraph of the passage, which is where the angler fish is discussed, makes it clear that the paragraph is entirely devoted to examples of bioluminescence found in the mid-waters of the ocean.

33. **C.** Just as the angler fish uses a fake piece of food as bait to capture a hungry prey, so does the trout fisherman when he lures a trout with a tasty-looking fake insect.

34. **J.** Countershading is described in the fourth paragraph, where it is stated that this effect protects fish from predators *below* them, not above.

35. **D.** The author mentions the "exploding dye packets" that help mark a bank robber in order to clarify how some animals coat predators with glowing tissue to mark them and make them vulnerable.

36. **J.** This point is made in the first sentence of the eighth paragraph.

37. **A.** The seventh paragraph says that bioluminescence is considered nonessential because nonluminous species seem to thrive as well as luminous ones. For this, we can conclude, that, if bioluminescence were essential, the opposite would be true—luminous species would do better than nonluminous ones.

38. **G.** In the eighth paragraph, "selection pressure" is discussed specifically as an environmental force that helps promote "the development or maintenance of luminescence" among animal species. Choice G paraphrases this concept.

39. **C.** The tomopterid worm is the only example in the passage of a kind of bioluminescence that seems to have no purpose at all; thus, it is "exceptional."

40. **F.** This discovery would suggest that the tomopterid worm's bioluminescence is, in fact, useful, since it would mean that the yellow fluid it spews could help to distract dangerous predators.

Section 4: SCIENCE REASONING

1. **C.** Considering only the two trees mentioned in the question, this would be a reasonable conclusion, since the younger of the trees (tree 4) has a much larger diameter and a much faster growth rate.

2. **F.** The data in the table shows that these two trees, though they have almost the same diameter (90 cm versus 80 cm), are of vastly different ages (900 years versus 200 years). Thus, it seems clear that one cannot tell a tree's age by extrapolation from its diameter.

3. **C.** Four of the twelve trees in the table—one third of the group—are 800 years old or older, which means that they survived at least the last two catastrophes charted on the timeline.

4. **G.** This is a simple exercise in multiplication: 1,100 x 0.1 cm = 110 cm.

5. **D.** The three trees listed, all of the same species, are widely different in age and have widely varying growth rates as well. This is consistent with the conclusion stated in choice D—that trees of the same species may have different growth rates at different ages.

6. **H.** A hypothesis that trees might use more than one strategy for reaching the canopy, and that varying growth rates might consequently be found, would certainly be supported by the finding that trees growing toward the canopy do in fact exhibit widely varying growth rates.

7. **A.** The descriptions of the two experimental set-ups make it clear that the variable in Experiment 1 was the radius of the flywheel, while in Experiment 2 it was the initial speed of the flywheel.

8. **H.** The concave disk design provides the best overall results in Experiment 3. As Table 2.4 shows, that design stores considerably more energy than either of the two alternatives, while its strength is almost equal to that of the flat disk, which is the strongest. If both criteria are equally important, then the concave disk design is the best.

9. **A.** As the answer to question 8 indicates, the concave design is preferable to either the rimmed or flat disk. Experiment 1 shows that a flywheel with a larger radius is capable of storing more energy than a flywheel with a smaller radius. Thus, for optimal energy storage, a concave, large-radius wheel is best.

10. **H.** As frequency increases, centrifugal force increases even more quickly; the same relationship exists between frequency and energy stored.

11. **B.** Look at Table 2.3. By comparing the first and third lines of that table, we can see that when the speed of the flywheel is halved (from 80 to 40 revolutions per second), the amount of energy stored is quartered (from about 20,000 to about 5,000 joules). Applying this same relationship to the example in the question, we can estimate that the energy in the car flywheel will be quartered from 120,000 joules to about 30,000 joules.

12. **F.** Since safety is mentioned in the question as a primary consideration, it seems logical to choose a system that uses size rather than frequency as the primary factor for storing a large amount of energy. As Experiment 3 shows, the flywheel's frequency has a far more powerful effect on centrifugal force than does the flywheel's radius.

13. **D.** You can see in Table 2.5 that the average sulphate concentration in land deposits decreased between 1990 and 1998, while the figure shows that the amounts of sulphate in the five lakes increased during the same period. (To read the graph in the figure, compare the vertical axis—the 1990 reading—for each dot with the horizontal axis—the 1998 reading. In each case, the horizontal axis is greater.)

14. **H.** The figure includes graphs for both sulphate and pH levels, while Table 2.5 shows only sulphate readings without pH numbers.

15. **C.** You can see in the sulphate graph from the figure that the two dots furthest into the lower right-hand corner are "open" dots, representing glacial lakes. This indicates that these lakes experienced the greatest increase in sulphate levels between 1990 and 1998.

16. **G.** The concentration for lake 4 was from 0.89 milligrams per liter to 0.66, a drop of almost 26%. This is a greater decline than experienced at any of the other lakes studied.

17. **A.** The figure shows that precipitation varied within a steady range throughout the period, which isn't consistent with the idea of a serious drought, as suggested by hypothesis II. The notion that the overall level of sulphate emissions did not decrease during the period is weakened by the results of Experiment 1, which show a steady decline in terrestrial deposition of sulphates; this weakens hypothesis III. Hypothesis I, however, is not contradicted by any of the experimental findings, and in fact may help to explain why the lakes might show increased sulphates while the adjacent land areas show lower levels.

18. **F.** As you can see in the Mercury line on Table 2.6, a Mercury day is about 59 earth days, while a Mercury year is about 88 earth days. The former is about $\frac{2}{3}$ of the latter.

19. **C.** Visualize where the moon would appear on the graph shown in the figure. It would be in very much the same line as Mars, Venus, and the earth. Only Mercury seems to have a different density/diameter relationship than the other terrestrial bodies.

20. **F.** This figure can be read from Table 2.6. The only planet with a more eccentric orbit, Pluto, is not a terrestrial planet.

21. **D.** The second column of Table 2.6 provides the answer. We're told at the top of the column that the density of water has been set to equal 1. Then we see that Pluto's density happens to be exactly 1; in other words, it is virtually the same as that of water.

22. **H.** Since Mercury's mean (average) surface temperature is "only" 179°, the nighttime temperature must be very low, in order to offset and reduce the very high daytime peak.

23. **B.** If the earth's core has a diameter of about 3,000 miles, this represents about $\frac{3}{8}$ of the overall diameter of the planet. Then, if Mercury's core represents a larger fraction of the planet's overall diameter, and if Mercury's overall diameter is about 3,000 miles, then Mercury's core probably has a diameter that is around half the planet's overall diameter, or perhaps a little more. Any value in the 1,500- to 2,000-miles range would be appropriate, and only choice B fits.

24. **F.** Both the genetic theory and the infection theory attribute schizophrenia to prenatal events: in one theory, to a genetic disorder; in the other, to a prenatal infection that affects the brain of a developing infant.

25. **C.** The fact that the shared incidence of schizophrenia is four times as great between identical twins as between nonidentical twins supports the idea that shared genetic material is a major factor in the development of the disorder.

26. **H.** The phenomenon described in option III would be consistent with the idea that an infection occurred during prenatal development, thus supporting the infection theory.

27. **D.** All three hypothesis could be consistent with both theories, and, in fact, all three could help to explain how both genetic and disease factors could be involved in producing schizophrenia.

28. **J.** Those who favor the viral theory would be apt to explain the shared incidence of schizophrenia in this case as having resulted from the shared experience of a viral infection when both infants were in the womb together.

29. **B.** It would be natural from supporters of the genetic theory to want to study the genes themselves in the hope of substantiating their theory by pinpointing the actual genetic differences that cause (or help to cause) the illness.

30. **G.** As the figure shows, limonene increases steadily and dramatically as fruit ages, making this the most relevant and useful VOC for the detection of fruit spoilage.

31. **C.** You can see in the figure that the concentration of alcohols continues to rise steadily over time as vegetables decay, while some other VOCs, such as esters, rise for a time and then diminish. This state of affairs is succinctly described in choice C.

32. **G.** Since Nose #2 is highly sensitive to alcohols, which are the best indicator of vegetable spoilage, that nose would be the best choice for detecting vegetable decay.

33. **B.** An alcohol detector would be the best single choice, since that VOC is a fairly reliable indicator of spoilage for all three food groups.

34. **J.** The figure shows that a concentration level of about half a milligram of diacetyl is reached some three days after the meat is fresh. Thus, it makes sense that this would be the level at which the consumer should be alerted that the meat should soon be consumed.

35. **A.** Just count the number of horizontal lines shown in the illustration to determine the number of energy levels found in a given element. Atom #1 has five such lines; therefore, it has five energy levels.

36. **F.** As explained in the passage, the spectral lines are emitted when an atom moves from one energy level to another. Thus, the number of spectral lines observed would correspond to the number of arrows seen in the figure (since each arrow represents an energy-level transition). Understanding this lets us pick choice F as incorrect; there are seven energy transitions possible for Atom #1, so seven spectral lines would be observed, not six.

37. **D.** The passage says that the amount of space between spectral lines indicates the relative size of the change in energy levels. If two energy transitions are quite similar in size, then the spectral lines will be close; if the transitions are very different in size, the spectral lines will be far apart. Based on this, we can see that statement D is correct: the three transitions shown on the upper left-hand side of the diagram would be represented by three spectral lines that are close together, while the two transitions shown on the lower left-hand side would produce two more spectral lines that are close together.

38. **G.** In Table 2.7, the first two frequencies measured are very close; so are the last two. These would correspond to spectral lines that are close to one another, and these would reflect two pairs of similar energy transitions—the situation found in Atom #3.

39. **B.** A "forbidden" transition, as defined in the question, would be represented visually by a pair of horizontal lines that is *not* connected by an arrow. As you can see, Atoms #1 and #3 both have one or more pairs of horizontal lines that are not connected by arrows, making answers A and C wrong; Atom #3 has just one forbidden transition (between the two horizontal lines at the top), making answer D wrong. Choice B is correct because Atom #2 has one forbidden transition, between the highest and lowest energy levels, represented by the horizontal lines at the top and bottom of the diagram.

40. **F.** As the explanation for Table 2.7 says, the information in that table does not reflect direct measurement of energy but rather "the frequency of light, which is proportional to the energy." Thus, whereas the figure is generated directly by spectroscopy, the information in Table 2.7 contains information that is analogous to that derived from spectroscopy but not the same.

WHAT THIS FIRST SCORE MEANS

The results from this self-evaluation test will give you a general idea of what you might score if you had to take the ACT Assessment today. To convert the number of right answers on your self-evaluation test into an ACT Assessment scaled score, do the following:

Refer to Table 2.8 below. For each subject area, count the number of right answers and find that number in the left-hand column marked "Raw Score." Move to the right until you have the column for the appropriate subject. That is your ACT Assessment scaled score for the subject area. For example, if you had 39 right answers on your Math test, you would find the number 39 in the left-hand column, then move right to the Math column and see that you have an ACT Assessment scaled score of 23.

After you have found your scaled score for each subject, add all four scaled numbers together and divide by four. Round fractions to the nearest whole number; round $\frac{1}{2}$ upward. This number is your ACT Assessment composite score.

Table 2.8: Score Conversion Table for the Self-Evaluation Test

Raw Score	English Scaled Score	Math Scaled Score	Reading Scaled Score	Science Scaled Score
75	36			
74	35			
73	34			
72	33			
71	32			
70	31			
69	30			
68	30			
67	29			
66	29			
65	28			
64	28			
63	27			
62	27			
61	26			
60	26	36		
59	25	35		
58	25	34		
57	24	34		
56	24	33		

Raw Score	English Scaled Score	Math Scaled Score	Reading Scaled Score	Science Scaled Score
55	23	32		
54	23	31		
53	23	30		
52	22	30		
51	22	29		
50	22	29		
49	21	28		
48	21	28		
47	21	27		
46	20	27		
45	20	26		
44	20	26		
43	19	25		
42	19	25		
41	19	24		
40	18	24	36	36
39	18	23	35	34
38	18	23	33	32
37	17	23	32	30
36	17	22	31	29
35	17	22	30	28
34	16	21	29	27
33	16	21	28	27
32	15	20	27	26
31	15	20	27	25
30	14	19	26	24
29	14	19	25	24
28	14	19	25	23
27	13	18	24	23
26	13	18	23	22
25	13	18	23	22
24	12	17	22	21
23	12	17	21	21
22	12	17	20	20
21	11	16	19	20
20	11	16	18	19
19	11	16	18	19

Raw Score	English Scaled Score	Math Scaled Score	Reading Scaled Score	Science Scaled Score
18	10	15	17	18
17	10	15	16	18
16	10	15	15	17
15	9	14	15	17
14	9	14	14	16
13	9	14	14	16
12	8	13	13	15
11	8	13	13	15
10	7	13	12	14
9	7	12	11	13
8	6	12	10	12
7	6	11	8	11
6	5	11	7	10
5	4	10	6	9
4	3	8	5	8
3	2	6	4	7
2	2	5	3	5
1	1	3	2	3
0	1	1	1	1

Because each subject is divided into different topics, it's also important to know how you performed within each subject. Using the eight breakdowns listed below, circle the number if you had that answer right, then see where your subscore falls in the range of answers.

SECTION 1: ENGLISH

Usage/Mechanics: Questions 1, 2, 3, 4, 5, 7, 10, 11, 12, 13, 16, 19, 20, 22, 23, 26, 29, 31, 33, 36, 38, 42, 43, 44, 46, 47, 49, 50, 52, 55, 57, 59, 60, 61, 62, 64, 66, 67, 68, 71, 72, 73, 74

If you had 0 to 20 answers right, your subscore in this area is poor.

If you had 21 to 32 answers right, your subscore in this area is average.

If you had 33 to 43 answers right, your subscore in this area is good.

Rhetorical Skills: Questions 6, 8, 9, 14, 15, 17, 18, 21, 24, 25, 27, 28, 30, 32, 34, 35, 37, 39, 40, 41, 45, 48, 51, 53, 54, 56, 58, 63, 65, 69, 70, 75

If you had 0 to 15 answers right, your subscore in this area is poor.

If you had 16 to 23 answers right, your subscore in this area is average.

If you had 24 to 32 answers right, your subscore in this area is good.

SECTION 2: MATH

Pre-Algebra/Elementary Algebra: Questions 1, 2, 6, 7, 9, 10, 12, 16, 19, 20, 23, 25, 26, 29, 30, 35, 37, 38, 39, 41, 43, 51, 54, 55

If you had 0 to 11 answers right, your subscore in this area is poor.

If you had 12 to 17 answers right, your subscore in this area is average.

If you had 18 to 24 answers right, your subscore in this area is good.

Intermediate Algebra/Coordinate Geometry: Questions 3, 4, 5, 14, 15, 17, 18, 24, 27, 31, 32, 33, 42, 45, 48, 50, 53, 56, 59

If you had 0 to 8 answers right, your subscore in this area is poor.

If you had 9 to 13 answers right, your subscore in this area is average.

If you had 14 to 19 answers right, your subscore in this area is good.

Plane Geometry/Trigonometry: Questions 8, 11, 13, 21, 22, 28, 34, 36, 40, 44, 46, 47, 49, 52, 57, 58, 60

If you had 0 to 7 answers right, your subscore in this area is poor.

If you had 8 to 12 answers right, your subscore in this area is average.

If you had 13 to 17 answers right, your subscore in this area is good.

SECTION 3: READING

Prose Fiction: Questions 1 through 10

If you had 0 to 4 answers right, your subscore in this area is poor.

If you had 5 to 7 answers right, your subscore in this area is average.

If you had 8 to 10 answers right, your subscore in this area is good.

Social Studies: Questions 11 through 20

If you had 0 to 4 answers right, your subscore in this area is poor.

If you had 5 to 7 answers right, your subscore in this area is average.

If you had 8 to 10 answers right, your subscore in this area is good.

Humanities: Questions 21 through 30

If you had 0 to 4 answers right, your subscore in this area is poor.

If you had 5 to 7 answers right, your subscore in this area is average.

If you had 8 to 10 answers right, your subscore in this area is good.

Natural Sciences: Questions 31 through 40

If you had 0 to 4 answers right, your subscore in this area is poor.

If you had 5 to 7 answers right, your subscore in this area is average.

If you had 8 to 10 answers right, your subscore in this area is good.

SECTION 4: SCIENCE REASONING

There is no breakdown of subjects within the Science Reasoning Test.

OVERALL PERFORMANCE

Questions 1 through 40

If you had 0 to 18 answers right, your subscore in this area is poor.

If you had 19 to 29 answers right, your subscore in this area is average.

If you had 30 to 40 answers right, your subscore in this area is good.

TRACKING YOUR PROGRESS

No matter what your scores are, don't worry. *Master the ACT Assessment* will help you improve that score, whatever it is.

The following pages look at the separate subject tests of the ACT Assessment exam. There are exercises for each, as well as test-taking strategies specific to that subject. After you've worked through the subject-area discussions, you'll find a series of in-depth subject reviews. The above diagnostic has given you some ideas about which of these reviews are most important to you right now. As you complete the excercises in the subject-discussion chapters, you'll form a more complete idea of where you need to focus your pre-test practice. Finally, after the last review chapter come three full-length practice ACT Assessment exams.

With each full-length exam, you have the opportunity to analyze the results of your score, just as you did now with the self-evaluation test. The score of your next full-length exam will show the results of your diligent working through of the exercises and review. And the results of the other two exams will help you track your progress—and your growing mastery of the ACT Assessment.

Mastering the ACT Assessment: Your Plan for Success

It's time to create an ACT Assessment study plan that fits both your level of readiness for each subject area of the test, each topic within the subject area, and your own schedule. You've already begun to draw a "map" of this plan. You've pinpointed where you are now through the Self-Evaluation Test, and you know your destination: as high a score as possible on the ACT Assessment. Now you'll chart the exact route to get to your destination.

CREATING YOUR ACT ASSESSMENT STUDY PLAN

Perhaps you've already registered for the ACT Assessment and have only two weeks left before the test date; perhaps you haven't yet registered. Whichever is true, you can work out a timetable of preparation that can help boost your score.

Following are three different schedules of preparation you can either use as is or adapt. These range from having three or more months to prepare, to having just two weeks to prepare. A "middle point" of four to six weeks of preparation time is also given.

One of the most important steps for creating a study plan is not concerned with the contents of this book, and that is the issue of time. Only you can adjust your personal schedule to create the time you need to prepare. Because the results of the ACT Assessment play such a crucial role in the college or university you'll eventually attend, it's worth the sacrifice. Remember, the schedule changes are only temporary. Of course, the closer you are to your test date right now, the more adjustment is necessary.

For example, the test-taker with three or more months might have to give up a few hours of watching television or socializing with friends each week to make the time to prepare. A test-taker with only two weeks needs to find every available minute. That means a bare-bones life of school, homework, meals, showers, sleep—and ACT Assessment preparation. No phones, no friends, no television, no music; and most likely, no clubs, no sports, no part-time job. It's tough, but it's possible—and it's just for two weeks.

For every timetable, begin with the following three steps:

- **Take the Self-Evaluation Test.** If you haven't already taken the Self-Evaluation Test, do that as your first step. Arrange as-close-to-normal testing conditions as possible (a quiet place, no interruptions, use of a timer). Grade your test and find your subject scores and subscores.

- **Identify weaknesses.** Identify in each subject the type of questions on which you need the most improvement. If you ever grow short of time, you'll know this is where to concentrate your efforts.

- **Familiarize yourself with the test contents and format.** If you know what the material looks like, how the test will be presented, and how you will be asked to respond, you won't need to "reinvent the wheel" the day of the test. Besides being more comfortable with it, you'll save valuable time.

What will be the specific details of *your* ACT Assessment study plan? Out of the next three sections ("If You Have Three Months or More to Prepare," "If You Have Four to Six Weeks to Prepare," or "If You Have Two Weeks to Prepare"), turn to the one that applies to you.

IF YOU HAVE THREE MONTHS OR MORE TO PREPARE

If you have three months or more to prepare, set aside a regular time to begin your ACT Assessment preparation. Basically, you'll be reading and working through this entire book. It's long but you've given yourself plenty of time in which to do it. Spend at least three or four hours each week on preparation and accustom yourself to working for extended periods of times, as you'll be doing during the test.

After you've completed the preliminary steps listed in the preceding section, here's how the rest of *your* plan breaks down:

1. Assuming you've finished Chapters 1 and 2, finish reading this chapter. Then move on to Part 2. Read the initial sections of each subject, which tell you "What to Expect" and "Do's and Don'ts" for success.

2. Work through the two sets of practice exercises for each subject. Score yourself. If you score above-average or excellent, you can move on to the next subject.

3. If your remaining scores on the exercises still show areas of weakness, work through the entire subject review in Part 3. Pay special attention to those areas where your subscores were lowest. Work through the exercises that follow the subject review—if there's time, do all three sets of the exercises.

4. One month before the ACT Assessment, if there is any review chapter you have not yet read because your scores in that subject were above average, look over the material now. Put a check mark by those individual topics that seem unfamiliar, difficult, or confusing. If you're not sure, look at your initial subscores to pinpoint the weakest areas in your strongest subjects. Between now and the test date, review those areas.

5. Two weeks before the ACT Assessment, take at least one more full-length sample test, arranging normal test conditions for yourself. Score your test. Compare this score with the Self-Evaluation Test. Look for those areas where you might still need help. Study those parts of the review chapters.

6. The week before the ACT Assessment, finish taking the full-length sample tests. There are three altogether. You should see better overall scores. With each test you'll become more comfortable with the real ACT Assessment.

7. Two days before the ACT Assessment, re-read the last two sections of this chapter—"Minimizing Test Anxiety" and "10 Strategies for Scoring Higher on the ACT Assessment." Also re-read the "Do's and Don'ts" and "What You Need to Know" sections of the four subject chapters.

8. After taking the ACT Assessment, read Part 4, which talks about your scores, college admission, and financing your education.

IF YOU HAVE FOUR TO SIX WEEKS TO PREPARE

If you have four to six weeks to prepare, you will spend your time concentrating on your specific weaknesses. Try to schedule three long blocks of time per week to prepare.

When you've completed the preliminary steps, here's how the remainder of *your* plan breaks down:

1. Finish reading this chapter. Then move to Part 2. Out of all your subscores, rank the types of questions by priority, from the one in which you need the most improvement to the one in which you need the least improvement. Pick no more than three subjects containing these low subscores. In other words, if your four lowest subscores each occurred within a different subject, pick only the lowest three. These three subjects are where you'll spend the most time.

2. Read the initial sections of each subject, which tell you "What to Expect" and "Do's and Don'ts" for success.

3. For each of your focus subjects, work through the two sets of practice exercises. Score yourself. If you score above-average or excellent, you can move on to the next subject. If you score average or below, work through the appropriate subject review (or reviews) in Part 3. Try to work through at least one set of the exercises following the review.

4. If you have time, look over any review chapter you have not yet read. Put a check mark by those individual topics that seem unfamiliar, difficult, or confusing. Between now and the test date, review those topics.

5. The week before the ACT Assessment, take at least one more full-length sample test, arranging normal test conditions for yourself. Score your test. Compare this score with the Self-Evaluation Test. Look for the two areas where you still need the most improvement. If you have time, study those parts of the review chapters.

6. If you have time, take another full-length sample test (in addition to the diagnostic exam, there are three practice exams). With each test you'll become more comfortable with the real ACT Assessment.

7. Two days before the ACT Assessment, re-read the last sections of this chapter—"Minimizing Test Anxiety" and "10 Strategies for Scoring Higher on the ACT Assessment." Also re-read the "Do's and Don'ts" and "What You Need to Know" sections of the four subject chapters.

8. After taking the ACT Assessment, read Part 4, which talks about your scores, college admission, and financing your education.

IF YOU HAVE TWO WEEKS TO PREPARE

If you have two weeks to prepare, consider yourself to be working under "battle conditions." Eliminate every single distraction and time-consuming activity that can be suspended for two weeks. You will concentrate your time on the two lowest subscores from your Self-Evaluation Test and on short-term test-taking strategies.

After you've completed the preliminary steps recommended earlier in this chapter, here's how the rest of *your* plan breaks down:

1. Finish reading this chapter. Then move to Part 2. Out of all your subscores, rank the types of questions in priority, from the one in which you need the most improvement to the one in which you need the least improvement. Pick no more than two subjects containing these low subscores. In other words, if your four lowest subscores each occurred within a different subject, pick only the lowest two. These two subjects are where you'll spend the most time.

2. Read the initial sections of all four subjects, which tell you "What to Expect" and "Do's and Don'ts" for success.

3. For each of your focus subjects, work through the two sets of practice exercises. Score yourself. If you score above-average or excellent, you can move on to the next subject. If you score average or below, work through the subject review in Part 3. If you have time, work through one set of the exercises following the review.

4. If you have time, skim any review chapter you have not yet read. Put a check mark by those individual topics that seem unfamiliar, difficult, or confusing. Between now and the test date, review those topics.

5. Three days before the ACT Assessment, take one more full-length sample test (the diagnostic test was your first), arranging normal test conditions for yourself. Score your test. Compare this score with the Self-Evaluation Test. Look for the *one* area in which you need the most improvement. If you have time, study that part of the review chapters.

6. Two days before the ACT Assessment, take another full-length sample test, under timed conditions. This additional test will give you important practice in your test-taking skills and can help relieve your anxiety on test day.

7. The day before the ACT Assessment, re-read the last two sections of this chapter—"Minimizing Test Anxiety" and "10 Strategies for Scoring Higher on the ACT Assessment." Also re-read the "Do's and Don'ts" and "What You Need to Know" sections of the four subject chapters.

8. After taking the ACT Assessment, read Part 4, which talks about your scores, college admission, and financing your education.

MINIMIZING TEST ANXIETY

After looking over your course of action, your immediate reaction might be, "I can't do it!" And you might feel that way whether you have two weeks to prepare or three months.

You *can* do it! The only way you can't is if you convince yourself that you can't, so if you're going to spend time talking yourself into something, talk yourself into success. Mental pep talks might sound foolish, but they work. All the great athletes use them, as well as dancers, musicians, actors— anyone who needs to "perform on demand."

How do you give yourself a mental pep talk? Do it through visualization: Mentally rehearse how well the test will go.

A VISUALIZATION EXERCISE

Close your eyes and visualize yourself sitting at the test. You're calm, you're confident, and you're prepared. Breathe deeply right now and let yourself feel the calm. You're actually looking forward to the work. The test is handed out. See yourself opening it and recognizing how familiar it looks. Think, "I know this! I can do this! Sure!" See yourself calmly and confidently marking your answers.

Also visualize yourself weeks later opening the ACT Assessment envelope and reading your score. Pick a number you'd be thrilled to see and visualize it on a piece of paper right below your name. Breathe deeply right now and feel how satisfied you are with your test performance.

Try this visualization exercise often, at least once a day. It takes only minutes and can be done while you're showering, riding (not driving) to school, or going to sleep. Like most things, visualization becomes better with practice. Athletes visualize playing the "perfect game." You'll visualize taking the "perfect test."

A RELAXATION EXERCISE

It might be hard to visualize being calm and confident when your body feels like one raw nerve. A deliberate relaxation exercise can help eliminate that raw-nerve feeling.

Sit or lie quietly with closed eyes. After a few minutes begin to flex each group of muscles, hold the position for about ten seconds, then relax. Begin with your toes, squeezing them down as if you're trying to pick up a marble with each bare foot, then relax. Progress up your body, squeezing then relaxing the muscles in your ankles, calves, thighs, and so on. If you're not sure how to contract your muscles in a particular part of your body, push downward against the chair, bed, or floor with that part. Slowly tense and relax each group, working your way up to your hands, arms, shoulders, and neck. When you get to your face, do each part of your face separately. Never mind the "faces" you're making. Open your mouth wide then pucker it up to tense the muscles, wrinkle your nose, frown fiercely—then relax after each movement. After you're finished with your whole body, remain in this state of relaxation for several minutes.

AN EXERCISE IN SILLINESS

Sometimes you might not have the time or the place to do the previous exercise. Some people have found relaxing a method that might seem to be the opposite of the previous relaxation exercise. But this is another instance of "Try it, it works!"

Find a private place (an empty rest room is good if you're "in public") and engage in some very physical, very ridiculous activity. Make faces at yourself in the mirror. Practice a few operatic arias, even if—or perhaps especially if—you can't sing. Hop around and wiggle parts of your body while chanting "Shake out the willies and shake in the sillies."

Sound stupid? It sure does, but it works. In fact, the internationally famous Dale Carnegie School helps students in its public speaking courses the same way. Even as you read this, the company president of a billion-dollar corporation could be in a bathroom preparing for a major speech to stockholders by doing a Dale Carnegie exercise: shouting out the nursery rhyme, "There was a Duke of York./ He had ten thousand men./ He marched them up the hill/ and marched them down again./ And when you're up, you're up,/ and when you're down, you're down./ And when you're only halfway up,/ you're neither up nor down." And all this to the accompaniment of hand-clapping, foot-stomping, and smacking the body.

Effective as these exercises are, they're just a supplement to the more important academic preparation. But not every bit of academic preparation involves studying harder and longer. There are tips and tricks even to the ACT Assessment exam.

TEN STRATEGIES FOR SCORING HIGHER ON THE ACT ASSESSMENT

In the following chapters you'll get strategies that are specific for each subject. Here now are 10 strategies that help you score higher on the ACT Assessment no matter the subject area on which you're working.

1. **Skip the directions.** Reading the directions takes valuable time. The directions for each type of question are the same as the directions in this book. Read the directions for each type of question in the Self-Evaluation Test, the practice exercises, and the four full-length sample tests. The day of the test, just make sure the section has the same type of questions—then get to work.

2. **Skim the whole section.** Because you've just deliberately saved time by skipping the directions, you might feel a sense of urgency tugging at you to begin. Take a minute to look at the section first. Find out the kinds of questions that are being asked, how many sections there are, and how many questions.

3. **Pace yourself.** Use the knowledge you picked up from skimming to pace your work. For example, the ACT Assessment Reading Test allows you 35 minutes. In that time you have to read and answer 40 questions about four passages. This breaks down to about eight minutes to read each passage and to answer its ten questions before you need to move on to the next. Put your watch on the desk and glance at it from time to time to keep yourself on track.

4. **Answer the easy questions first.** Each section contains a mixed level of difficulty but every answer is "weighted" the same—that is, you don't get more points for answering a more difficult question. So skip the hard questions and come back to them later. Answer the easy questions first. This will give you confidence and allow more time for working on the remainders.

5. **When in doubt, guess.** In some tests you're penalized for having the wrong answer. Not in the ACT Assessment. *Only correct answers are counted.* So even if you don't have the vaguest idea of what the answer should be, you have a 1 in 4 chance (1 in 5 in Math) of being right simply by picking a random answer. If you have a hunch about one or two of the answers, or can eliminate one or two, your chances of being right are greatly improved.

6. **Don't let tough questions make your confidence slip.** Remember that almost no one gets everything right. The ACT Assessment is intended to measure the widest possible range of ability, including the six-year-old genius in senior physics who could be teaching the class. If you missed forty percent of the questions on a high school test, you'd fail. If you missed forty percent of the questions on an ACT Assessment Science Reasoning Test, you'd have an average score of 21.

7. **Frequently check your place on the answer sheet.** Yes, the use of F, G, H, J, and K for even-numbered answers helps prevent this, but losing your place can still happen, especially if you're skipping questions. Every five answers or so, double-check that the number of the question corresponds with the number of the answer. When you do skip harder questions, don't just leave them blank. Lightly circle their number on both the test booklet and on the answer sheet, so you can return to each one more quickly and to make sure you leave that line blank on the answer sheet.

   Don't panic even if you lose your place, and don't start wildly erasing. Mark where the wrong answers begin and where you noticed the error and answer correctly from that point on. If you have time, go back and correct the section you marked. If you run out of time, raise your hand. Explain to the proctor what happened and ask that you be allowed five minutes after the test with just the answer sheet to move those answers up or down a line each to the correct space. The proctor will probably say yes.

8. **Don't get sidetracked by the unimportant.** Often a question will contain an enormous amount of useless details for the sole purpose of distracting you. This is like the riddle, *"As I was going to St. Ives, I met a man with seven wives."* You don't need to understand every detail to be able to answer the question.

9. **Understand what you're being asked.** Some of the choices might be "correct"—but *not* for the question that's really being asked. Be sure you understand the question before attempting to find the answer.

10. **Stop a minute or two before your time is up.** When the time is almost up, finish the question on which you're working, then look at the questions you

have left. If an answer is immediately apparent, fill it in. If certain answers can be immediately disqualified, pick one of the others. For all the rest, just fill in the circles. A blank circle gets you nothing; guess and you could get lucky.

Bonus strategy: There's one more essential strategy for scoring higher on the ACT Assessment and you don't have to wait until the test date to use it.

That's making a study plan and following it.

Summary: What You Need to Know About Making Your Study Plan

- Whether you have only a few weeks or three months to prepare for the ACT Assessment, you can construct a workable study plan.

- When your time is limited, focus on the areas where you need the most improvement. The results of the self-evaluation test help you identify those areas.

- Anxiety won't help you prepare for or take the ACT Assessment—in fact, it can really harm your performance. Use visualization and relaxation techniques to help overcome test anxiety. You should consider visualization and relaxation exercises to be part of your total ACT Assessment study plan.

- Read, re-read, and remember the 10 strategies for higher ACT Assessment scores. These strategies can boost your confidence and your scores.

Strengthening Your ACT Assessment Subject Skills

PART 2

The ACT Assessment English Test

The ACT Assessment English Test determines how well you understand and can use "standard written English." What exactly *is* "standard written English"? That's the style of writing used in this book. It's the style of writing used for television news reports. It's the style of writing your teacher wants to see in English class. Standard written English does not allow the use of slang, colloquial or informal expressions, technical jargon, geographic or ethnic dialects, archaic language (which means language that is no longer in use, such as Shakespearean English), and creative or experimental language (which means invented words or invented uses for words, such as in James Joyce's *Ulysses*). In this chapter, you learn the types of questions you can expect on the ACT Assessment English sections, and you get an opportunity to practice your skills in answering those questions. You also learn some valuable tips that will help you succeed on ACT Assessment English questions—and you learn how to avoid some common pitfalls of the test.

WHAT TO EXPECT ON THE ACT ASSESSMENT ENGLISH TEST

The ACT Assessment tests your understanding and use of Standard English by providing passages of writing then drawing your attention to particular sentences that might or might not have mistakes in them. These might be mistakes in grammar, weaknesses in style, errors in punctuation, lapses in logic, and other writing flaws. The test questions ask you to identify the mistake, then to correct it by choosing an alternative that doesn't introduce a new mistake.

The English Test items fall into two broad categories: Usage/Mechanics and Rhetorical Skills. Usage/Mechanics refers to whether the sentence is technically correct. Check that it obeys the rules of English grammar and usage, including subject-verb agreement, correct verb tenses, parallel sentence structure, and proper use of punctuation. Rhetorical Skills refers to the overall organization of the passage, including the order of topics, clear transitions from topic to topic, clarity of expression, and the avoidance of stylistic problems like wordiness, redundancy, and vagueness.

ROAD MAP

- *Learn What to Expect on the ACT Assessment English Test*
- *Learn Strategies for Success in ACT Assessment English*
- *Practice Your Skills with ACT Assessment English Exercises*
- *Evaluate Your Understanding of ACT Assessment English*

The questions are based on five passages of 300 to 400 words each. The passages will be from nonfiction prose such as you read in magazines, books, journals, even student essays. For each passage there will be fifteen questions testing your understanding of how the passage was written—for a total of 75 questions.

QUESTIONS ON USAGE AND MECHANICS

These questions will underline part or all of a sentence and put the corresponding question number beneath the underlined portion. You will then be presented with four choices. The first choice repeats the underlined portion with no change, and three choices rephrase or eliminate the underlined portion. You must decide which of the four alternatives is best. Look for grammatical correctness, proper usage, and clarity.

Example:

1. On the day of the test, his over-protective mother packed him an ACT Assessment survival <u>kit. Ten</u> sharpened pencils, a pencil sharpener, a calculator, a pack of batteries, three different-weight sweaters, four pieces of fruit, a liter of spring water, and a box of tissues.

   A. NO CHANGE

   B. kit, ten

   C. kit; ten

   D. kit: ten

(Answer: D)

QUESTIONS ON RHETORICAL SKILLS

Questions on rhetorical skills will either underline the portion as above or have a boxed number before, after, or in the middle of a passage, which will refer to a corresponding question number. If the question is about a section of the paragraph, the boxed number will be placed at the appropriate point. If the question refers to the paragraph or passage as a whole, the boxed number will be at the end of the paragraph or passage. Questions with boxed numbers are about the passage's overall organization and will suggest changes, additions, or deletions to the passage. For these items, you must decide which alternative adds to the overall effectiveness of the passage as a piece of writing.

Example:

School Paper Editorial

The first reason why the Denville school district should not be combined with the Jackson school district is <u>the fact that</u> the schools have been sports rivals
1
for too long. Trying to unite the schools after so many years of competition would inevitably lead to friction. [2]

1. A.   NO CHANGE

   B.   because of the fact that

   C.   about

   D.   that

2. Is the author's introductory sentence effective?

   A. Yes, because it gets immediately to the problem.

   B. No, because an introduction should outline the whole subject.

   C. No, because it doesn't say how many other reasons there will be.

   D. Yes, because sports is the number one interest of most students.

(Answers: 1. D. ; 2. B.)

TIP
Reread these directions several times until you're totally familiar with them. Then the day of the test, save time by *not* reading them. This is one of your overall strategies for scoring higher on the ACT Assessment.

THE DIRECTIONS

The directions for the ACT Assessment English Test are similar to the following:

Directions: This test consists of five passages in which particular words or phrases are underlined and numbered. Alongside the passage, you will see alternative words and phrases that could be substituted for the underlined part. You must select the alternative that expresses the idea most clearly and correctly or that best fits the style and tone of the entire passage. If the original version is best, select "No Change."

The test also includes questions about entire paragraphs and the passage as a whole. These questions are identified by a number in a box.

After you select the correct answer for each question, mark the oval representing the correct answer on your answer sheet.

STRATEGIES FOR SUCCESS ON THE ACT ASSESSMENT ENGLISH TEST

Yes, you'll try to get a good night's sleep before the test, you'll try to eat a healthy breakfast, and you'll try to stay calm and focused. Although these are good pieces of advice, these tips will also help your younger sister on next week's French quiz. Here are some success strategies specifically designed to help you score higher on the ACT Assessment English Test.

Some students never learn how to skim and end up reading everything straight through, even when reviewing already-read material. But you don't need to be one of those students. Skimming is just a habit of the eye. Here are two simple ways to help acquire the habit:

1. Put your index finger at the top of the passage and let it sweep back and forth down the page more quickly than you'd normally read. Fix your gaze on the tip of your finger and follow its path. Your eyes will pick up the words around the finger.

2. Quickly read the first and last sentence of every paragraph. In most well-organized pieces of writing, you'll be able to get the major points and direction of the piece from these beginnings and endings.

SKIM THE PASSAGE BEFORE READING

Skimming a passage before reading is like checking a strange body of water before you dive in. What's the water temperature? Is the water deep enough? Are there rocks just below the surface? Checking first for general conditions alerts you to both possible dangers or a carefree experience.

Skimming alerts you to the "general conditions" of a strange passage. What's the overall structure of the piece? What's its theme or purpose? Is the style quick and breezy or slow and scholarly? Just a few seconds of skimming will help you better focus your reading.

READ THE WHOLE SENTENCE

You've skimmed then read the entire passage. You next turn your attention to the first question, which refers you to an underlined section (granted, not every question in the English section uses underlined phrases, but you learn strategies for the other English question types later in this chapter). Be sure to read the whole sentence for that question, not just the few words that are underlined, before you attempt to answer. While the mistake itself (if there is one) will be in the underlined section, the reason *why* it's a mistake often lies elsewhere in the sentence. If a pronoun is wrong, you need to know the word to which it refers. If a verb's number is wrong, you need to know the number of the subject. If a verb's tense is wrong, you need to know the tense of the rest of the sentence. Read the whole sentence first.

LISTEN FOR THE MISTAKE

Most of us make fewer grammar mistakes when we speak Standard English than when we stop and make conscious decisions about each word to use. Why? We talk before we write—speech is our primary form of communication. Throughout the day—in class, on radio, and on TV—we hear Standard English. In a way, we know most of the rules of grammar even if we cannot explain them.

On the ACT Assessment English Test, you don't have to explain a mistake. You merely have to "hear" when a mistake is being made, which in itself is relatively easy because it will be in the underlined part. Then, from the available choices, you have to "hear" the best alternative. That's another reason why reading the whole sentence is important. You need to be able to put the mistake within the context of the entire sentence in order both to hear if the underlined section sounds "funny" or "weird" and to find the right replacement.

Listening can reveal a wide range of problems, from subject-verb agreement to incorrect usage of idioms—expressions that are always said a certain way "just because" they are.

CORRECT THE MISTAKE ON YOUR OWN FIRST

After you've identified the mistake, even if you can't explain what it is, try to correct it before looking at the choices. When you have "your" correction in mind, look over the answers.

Why correct the mistake first when the correction is there to be found? For two reasons: If your exact correction is among the choices, your answer is probably right; on the other hand, if two of the remaining choices are very close to the wording of your correction, you can at least eliminate those choices that did not correct the mistake. So either way you save time.

LOOK FOR COMMON MISTAKES

Although there are many possible grammatical mistakes, the ones most commonly made fall into just a few categories. So if you can't "hear" the mistake in the underlined section, look instead to see if it contains one of these common types of errors: sentence fragments, mistakes in subject-verb agreement, problems with verb tense or verb form, incorrect referents, dangling and misplaced modifiers, parallel construction, and incorrect usage of idioms. (If you are not sure of the rules for any of these, look up the subject in the English Review in Part 3.)

Even better than having just a few mistakes to check, some of these errors frequently show up the same way on the ACT Assessment test. Here are some tips on "when to look for what."

- *Sentence fragments* are often present when an underlined section includes a period.

   Example: In the park Saturday, I threw a Frisbee to the dog in the red <u>collar. Because</u> I wanted to meet its owner.

   (Correct: collar, because.)

- *Mistakes in subject-verb agreement* are often present when an underlined verb is not relatively close to the subject.

   Example: The woman, persuaded by dozens of encouraging phone calls from her children, grandchildren, and great-grandchildren and even by multiple letters from strangers who had seen the newspaper articles, <u>are traveling</u> round the world.

   (Correct: is traveling. The subject of this sentence—the woman—is singular and therefore requires a singular verb.)

- *Incorrect idiom usage* is often present when the underlined portion and all the choices are prepositions.

   Example: It's not surprising that caffeine and coffee are viewed <u>like</u> being synonymous.

   A. NO CHANGE
   B. as like
   C. for
   D. as

   (Answer: D)

TIP
Do you need help "listening" for mistakes and corrections? Pick someone whose grammar is nearly flawless and whose voice is so distinctive you can readily hear it in your mind: a parent, a teacher, a friend, a newscaster. Then, when you're trying to hear a mistake, imagine this person saying the sentence. Try to imagine what the person would naturally say instead. If you don't have a clue, check the answer choices and decide which one of those would sound most natural—the sentence as it is, or the sentence with one of the test choices? Chances are good the sentence that sounds most natural coming from your authority is the right choice.

If you need to brush up on your English grammar and usage rules, you'll find a complete review in Chapter 8, "English Review: Grammar."

REMEMBER THAT SHORTER IS USUALLY BETTER

Occasionally, you'll find that eliminating all the answers that contain errors does not narrow your options to a single choice. You might find that two (or rarely three) answer choices all appear completely correct and equally clear, graceful, and unambiguous.

When this happens, choose whichever answer is shortest. Generally speaking, a concise, tightly worded sentence is more stylistically effective than a wordy, loosely structured one. Therefore, when all other factors appear equal, the shortest sentence is the one that the test-makers are most likely to consider correct.

DON'T ADD A NEW MISTAKE

When there are two closely worded choices or two possible ways to correct the error, be careful. Often one of the choices creates a new error. Read each choice as part of the whole sentence and "listen" for any new mistakes.

Example:

> 5. Although my brother was a talented painter, he gave up his dream of a life as an <u>artist. Making instead</u> a living as an electrical engineer and painting on weekends.
>
>   A. NO CHANGE
>   B. artist, instead making
>   C. artist. Instead he makes
>   D. artist. Rather, making
>
> (Answer: B)

Choice C corrects the error of a sentence fragment (your tip-off: The underlined portion includes a period). However, if you now read the new version of the sentence using "Instead he makes" as its opening words, you see that a new problem crops up. The phrase at the end, "and painting on weekends," doesn't grammatically match "he makes." (If it read "and paints on weekends," it would be all right.) B solves the problem without creating a new one.

FIND THE RIGHT SEQUENCE BY FINDING THE FIRST ITEM

Questions on mechanics and usage test grammar and punctuation. Questions on rhetorical skills deal with larger issues of organization, choice of contents, and style.

TIP
When you read the answer choices, you can save time by always skipping choice A. A will always repeat the underlined section the way it is in the passage. So if you think that the underlined section is correct, as it is about 25% of the time, you would choose A to indicate NO CHANGE.

CAUTION
Don't expect to find errors in vocabulary, spelling, capitalization, and hyphenation on the ACT Assessment English Test. The ACT Assessment doesn't test for these errors, so don't waste time trying to spot them.

One such item you'll certainly encounter is an overall structure question, which is often a question about the sequence of ideas. You might be asked to select the best sequence of sentences within a paragraph or the best sequence of paragraphs for the passage as a whole. Following is an example:

NOTE
Notice the bracketed numbers preceding each sentence. When you see bracketed numbers or numbers in parentheses, you can tell that the test-makers will be asking you a question about the sequence of sentences.

> [1] The immigration laws led, ultimately, to a quota system based on the number of individuals of each national origin reported in the 1890 census. [2] The United States, which was founded mainly by people who had emigrated from northern Europe, had an essentially open-door immigration policy for the first 100 years of its existence. [3] But starting in the 1880s and continuing through the 1920s, Congress passed a series of restrictive immigration laws. [4] The door to freedom hadn't been slammed shut, exactly, but it was now open only to the "right" sort of people.
>
> **Q** Which of the following sequences of sentences will make this paragraph most logical?
>
>   A. 4, 3, 1, 2
>
>   B. 2, 3, 1, 4
>
>   C. 1, 3, 2, 4
>
>   D. 2, 3, 4, 1
>
> (Answer: B)

The easiest way to find the right sequence is to find the first item—the first sentence or the first paragraph. The first item will often introduce the overall topic about which the rest of the material covers. After you've found the opening element, the others should quickly fall into place. You'll usually note some clear time sequence or progression of action that will make the correct order apparent.

EXPECT A SINGLE IDEA PER PARAGRAPH

Another type of rhetorical skills question focuses on the clear and logical development of the ideas in the passage. You may be asked to choose a sentence that would make a logical addition to the passage; you may be asked whether it would be a good idea to delete a particular sentence from the passage; or you may be asked where in the passage a certain idea would fit best.

Here's a sample of what this kind of question might look like:

> Many owners of professional baseball teams are concerned about sagging attendance figures. Various gimmicks have been tried to boost attendance, from ballpark giveaways to special "nights" honoring various ethnic groups. Teams have changed the colors of their uniforms, played rock music between innings, and set off fireworks after the game.

continues

6. The writer wishes to add another relevant example to this paragraph without straying from the purpose of illustrating the gimmicks used by baseball in an effort to improve attendance. Which of the following sentences does that best?

  F. It's hard to see what playing Goo Goo Dolls over the centerfield loudspeakers adds to the experience of a ballgame.

  G. For many sports fans, baseball is just too slow-paced; they prefer the quick, constant action of basketball.

  H. They've even tinkered with the rules of the game, introducing the so-called designated hitter.

  J. Some teams claim they are losing millions of dollars each year due to poor attendance.

(Answer: H)

The most important principle to apply to a question like this is that every paragraph should be unified around a single idea. No sentence should appear in a paragraph that doesn't clearly relate to that idea, either by explaining it, illustrating it, defending it, elaborating on it, or otherwise supporting it. In this case, only H extends the paragraph's idea.

DON'T WORRY ABOUT TINY DETAILS

There are some points of grammar that your teachers over the years might have emphasized again and again, such as "don't split infinitives; don't use dangling prepositions," and so on. Because English is a living language, its rules change over time. Although in some instances a dangling preposition is incorrect, common usage dictates that some sentences can end in a preposition. The same is true for the use of split infinitives. Because such small details of proper usage are subject to change, they don't appear on the ACT Assessment. If you find yourself considering the small details of a sentence's structure, you're unlikely to spot the more obvious mistake the sentence might contain. Don't invest time—or attention—to these small details while taking the ACT Assessment.

Also, because the test deals with larger issues of grammar, you won't be questioned on vocabulary, spelling, capitalization, and hyphenation. If you think you've spotted an error of this sort on the ACT Assessment, you haven't. Ignore it and keep looking.

AVOID THE REPETITION OF IDEAS

Another rhetorical skills question focuses on wordiness or verbosity. One way to test for this type of mistake is to look for redundancy—the needless repetition of ideas—within the sentence containing the underlined phrase. When the same concept is stated twice or more in a given sentence, the test makers are sending you a broad hint that this is an ineffective sentence that needs to be simplified. Here's an example:

1. <u>The remarkable growth in increased attendance currently being enjoyed</u> by such formerly moribund sports franchises as baseball's Cleveland Indians shows that building a new stadium can have a powerful effect on the popularity of a team.

   A. NO CHANGE
   B. The growth in attendance remarkably being enjoyed currently
   C. The remarkable growth in increased attendance currently enjoyed
   D. The remarkable attendance boom currently enjoyed

(Answer: D)

The original phrasing here contains not one but two examples of redundancy. The words "growth" and "increased" both convey the same idea. The word "being" tells you that this phenomenon is happening now—the same idea that the word "currently" expresses. Only D eliminates both redundancies without changing the meaning of the sentence (as answer B does by changing "remarkable" to "remarkably").

SUCCESS STRATEGY ROUNDUP: A LIST OF DO'S AND DON'TS

Here's the "short version" of the above advice, along with a few other miscellaneous tips, arranged in a handy list of Do's and Don'ts. After you understand each point and the reasoning behind it, you need only know the boldface sentence to jog your memory—whether you're working on the exercises at the end of this chapter, your full-length sample tests, or the ACT Assessment itself.

A list of Do's:

☑ **Skim the passage before reading it.** This will give you an idea of the overall structure, meaning, and purpose of the passage, which is especially important for questions dealing with rhetorical skills. Look for the general theme, style, and tone, and the basic sequence of ideas.

☑ **Find the grammatical error before looking at the choices.** Re-read any sentence that contains an underlined segment. Try to find the error before considering the choices. Mentally correct the error then look for the answer that matches yours. If you aren't able to correct the error, scan only that part of the choice in which the original error appeared. Then eliminate any answer that does not correct the error. You can quickly eliminate one or two choices this way.

☑ **Skip reading Answer A.** Answer A is always the same: NO CHANGE, meaning the underlined part of the sentence should remain as it is. Because A is always what you've just read in the passage itself, save time by skipping it.

☑ **Check the underlined part for the most common types of errors.** If the error isn't apparent, ask yourself these questions: Is the sentence a complete sentence? Do the subject and the verb agree? Is the tense right? Is the verb form right? Does the pronoun refer to the correct word and agree with it in person and number? Are similar ideas expressed in parallel construction? Are modifiers attached to what they're meant to modify?

☑ **Trust your ear.** If you can't identify the error, silently listen for what "sounds wrong." Even when you can't identify an error by its grammatical name, you can often hear when something sounds wrong—and also when it sounds right. Remember that, silently listen, and increase the odds of your guessing the correct answer.

☑ **When adding a sentence, stay with the central idea.** If you're asked to choose the next sentence in the paragraph, choose one that in some way further explains the main idea. Don't bring in unrelated topics.

☑ **For a sequence question, begin by finding the first sentence or the first paragraph.** Look for the sentence or the paragraph that introduces the overall topic. After you have it, the order of the other sentences or other paragraphs will be more apparent.

☑ **For style, choose the shortest.** When all the choices on a rhetorical-skills question say the same thing and all are grammatically correct, choose the shortest one. It's usually the best, most concise expression of the idea.

A list of Don'ts:

☒ **Don't try to "correct" every sentence.** NO CHANGE is the correct answer to about 25% of the questions.

☒ **Don't be distracted by wordiness.** The structural complexity of a sentence might have nothing to do with the question. Ignore anything that is not related to the question and focus only on what's being asked.

☒ **Don't choose an answer that contains a new error.** Some choices correct the original error but add a different one. Be careful when new words are added to the underlined part.

☒ **Don't worry about what's not there.** Don't look for mistakes in spelling, capitalization, and hyphenation. They're not on the test. Also, don't look for mistakes such as split infinitives and dangling prepositions. As these forms are increasingly used in daily language, the rules "against" them are weakening.

☒ **Don't try to change what isn't underlined.** If a choice includes any part of the passage that isn't underlined, eliminate it. That's not what's being questioned.

☒ **Don't separate basic sentence parts.** Subjects and verbs, verbs and objects, verbs and complements—in natural speech and in clear writing, these elements occur close to each other. So if a sentence separates, for example, the subject from the verb with a long complicated clause, look for a choice that positions subject and verb more closely together.

⊠ **Don't be fooled by fragment length.** A sentence must have a subject and a verb in the main clause to be complete. No matter how long a fragment is, if there's no subject and verb, it's not a sentence.

⊠ **Don't confuse it's with its.** This is a very common mistake. *Its* is the possessive of *it*. Because nouns form their possessive with an apostrophe, the contraction it's (the shortening of *it is*) is often mistakenly used in place of its. Reminder: its is a possessive pronoun. No possessive pronoun uses an apostrophe: *his, hers, yours, theirs, mine, ours,* and *its*.

PRACTICE EXERCISES

You've just learned some new skills for taking the ACT Assessment English Test. The following exercises will help you to practice these new skills as well as to continue to familiarize yourself with the contents and format of the ACT Assessment.

There are two English Test exercises in this chapter. Each exercise contains 30 questions and should be answered in 18 minutes. Do each exercise in one sitting in a quiet place, with no notes or reference material. Use a stopwatch or kitchen timer or have someone else watch the clock. When time is up, stop at once.

Score yourself only on those items you finished. When you're done, work through the rest of the exercise.

EXERCISES: THE ACT ASSESSMENT ENGLISH TEST

Exercise 1

30 Questions • Time—18 Minutes

Directions: This test consists of two passages in which particular words or phrases are underlined and numbered. Alongside the passage, you will see alternative words and phrases that could be substituted for the underlined part. You must select the alternative that expresses the idea most clearly and correctly or that best fits the style and tone of the entire passage. If the original version is best, select "No Change."

The test also includes questions about entire paragraphs and the passage as a whole. These questions are identified by a number in a box.

After you select the correct answer for each question, mark the oval representing the correct answer on your answer sheet.

Passage I

The Magic of Special Effects

The movies are one place where magic can come true. You can see sights you might never <u>under any</u> ₁ <u>circumstances</u> hope to see in real life—ocean liners sinking, earthquakes swallowing cities, planets exploding. You can also see sights that might never exist at <u>all;</u> ₂ <u>such as</u> rampaging monsters, battles in outer space, sky-high cities of the future.

All these are examples of the movie magic known as special effects. <u>Its the work of</u> amazingly clever ₃ and skilled effects artists.

<u>And</u> the real magic lies in how they're able to make ₄ a man in a gorilla suit into King Kong . . . tiny plastic models into huge space ships . . . and

1. A. NO CHANGE
   B. normally
   C. in daily life
   D. OMIT the underlined portion

2. F. NO CHANGE
   G. all, such as
   H. all. Such as
   J. all—such as

3. A. NO CHANGE
   B. It's the work of
   C. They're by
   D. They are the work of

4. F. NO CHANGE
   G. Nonetheless,
   H. Although
   J. Because

instructions in a computer into images of a world that no one have ever imagined before.

5

Effects artists have developed many tricks and techniques over the years. Working closely with movie directors, producers, and actors, a growing role in

6

movie making today is played by them.

[1] They can be used to save money, some movie

7

scenes would be impossibly costly to produce using ordinary methods. [2] Special effects techniques are useful to movie makers in several ways. [3] Clever use of special effects can cut those costs dramatically. [4] For example, to show an imaginary city, it would cost millions of dollars to build real buildings, roads, and so on. 8

9 Battle or disaster scenes involving explosions, floods, or avalanches can be very dangerous

5. A. NO CHANGE
   B. could ever imagine
   C. has ever imagined
   D. ever had been imagining

6. F. NO CHANGE
   G. movie making today requires them to play a growing role.
   H. they play a growing role in movie making today.
   J. their role in movie making today is a growing one.

7. A. NO CHANGE
   B. to save money. Some movie scenes
   C. for saving money, some movie scenes
   D. to save money; since some movie scenes

8. Which of the following sequences of sentences will make the paragraph most logical?
   F. 2, 1, 4, 3
   G. 3, 1, 4, 2
   H. 2, 4, 3, 1
   J. 1, 4, 3, 2

9. Which of the following sentences would provide the best transition here from the topic of the previous paragraph to the new topic of this paragraph?
   A. Today's movie makers are highly budget conscious.
   B. Some of the most exciting special effects involve computer-simulated imagery.
   C. There is a long history to the use of special effects in movies.
   D. Special effects can also make movie making safer.

GO ON TO THE NEXT PAGE

to film. Effects artists can simulate <u>such</u> in ways that

                        10

give audiences the thrill of witnessing a dangerous

event without <u>the exposing of actors</u> to real hazards.

           11

<u>Most important,</u> special effects allow movie

       12

makers to film scenes that would otherwise be

impossible. They let movies show non-existent, even

impossible worlds. [13] Special effects are a <u>movie</u>

                         14

<u>makers</u> tool for communicating a unique imaginative

experience. <u>And after all—that's</u> one of the reasons

             15

we all go to the movies.

10. F. NO CHANGE
    G. these events
    H. those
    J. it

11. A. NO CHANGE
    B. exposing actors
    C. actors being exposed
    D. actors having to be exposed

12. F. NO CHANGE
    G. To summarize,
    H. On the other hand,
    J. Nevertheless,

13. At this point, the writer is considering the addition of the following sentence:

Visions of unknown, unseen worlds have long stimulated the imaginations of human beings the world over.

Would this be a logical and relevant addition to the essay?
    A. Yes, because it emphasizes the important role that special effects play in the movies.
    B. No, because it does not directly relate to the topic of movie special effects.
    C. Yes, because it underscores the universal appeal of works of the imagination.
    D. No, because most of the world's most popular movies are produced in the United States, not "the world over."

14. F. NO CHANGE
    G. movie maker's
    H. movie makers'
    J. OMIT the underlined portion

15. A. NO CHANGE
    B. And—after all, that's
    C. And, after all, that's
    D. And that after all, is

Passage II

Cities on the Sea

[1]

Hunger has long plagued millions of the world's people, especially in the vast cities of the underdeveloped nations of Africa, Asia, and India. The food to feed the world's growing population may come largely from ocean resources. [16]

16. Which of the following sentences, if added here, would most effectively support the assertion made in the previous sentence?
    F. Fish, sea-grown plants, and even food-stuffs synthesized from algae are all examples.
    G. If population growth can be brought under control, the problem of hunger may well be alleviated.
    H. Pollution of the seas has not yet reached a level where it endangers the use of salt-water fish by humans.
    J. For thousands of years, humans have drawn nourishment from the seas around us.

[2]

Three quarter's of the earth's surface is covered
                                            17
with water. Many scientists are now looking at these vast watery regions for solutions to some pressing human dilemmas.

17. A. NO CHANGE
    B. Three quarters
    C. Three fourth's
    D. Three-quarter's

[3]

Minerals such as iron, nickel, copper, aluminum, and tin are in limited supply on the earth. Undersea mines are expected to yield fresh supplies of many of these resources. Oil and gas deposits, have been
                                            18

18. F. NO CHANGE
    G. deposits has
    H. deposits have
    J. deposits, has

discovered under the ocean floor. [19]

[4]

To take advantage of these ocean-based resources, some scientists foresee entire cities on the ocean. At first, <u>it will be built</u> close to the shore. Later,

20

floating cities might be located hundreds of miles at sea. These cities could serve many functions, <u>playing a</u>

21

<u>variety of roles</u>. Some of the people living there could harvest fish and sea plants, like farmers of the ocean. Others could operate oil and gas wells or work in undersea enclosures mining the ocean floors. <u>Also</u> the

22

floating cities could serve as terminals or stations for international travel, where ships could stop for refueling or repairs.

[5]

Much of the technology needed to build such cities <u>have already been developed</u>. Oil drilling on a large

23

scale is already conducted at sea. Rigs as large as small towns built on floating platforms or on platforms anchored into the seabed <u>serving as homes</u> to scores of

24

workers for months at a time. The same principles, on a larger scale, could be used to create ocean-going cities.

19. The writer wishes to add another relevant example to Paragraph 3. Which of the following sentences does that best?
   A. Exploration of the deepest reaches of the ocean floors has only recently begun.
   B. And the tides and thermal currents—water movements caused by temperature variations—may be future energy sources.
   C. Solar energy, too, is expected to become a major supplier of the world's future energy needs.
   D. The sea, after all, is the ultimate source of all life on Earth.

20. F. NO CHANGE
    G. they will be built
    H. they will build them
    J. it will be

21. A. NO CHANGE
    B. and play many roles.
    C. with a variety of roles to play.
    D. OMIT the underlined portion.

22. F. NO CHANGE
    G. (Place after could)
    H. (Place after serve)
    J. (Place after travel)

23. A. NO CHANGE
    B. has already been developed.
    C. have been developed already.
    D. is already developed.

24. F. NO CHANGE
    G. serving for homes
    H. have served like homes
    J. serve as homes

[6]

The cities would have to be virtually self-sufficient,
25

although shipping supplies from the mainland would be
26

costly. Each city would be a multi-story structure with
room for many kinds of facilities needed by the inhab-
27
itants. The ocean itself could provide much of the

needed food and other raw materials; while solar panels
28

and generators running on water power could provide
energy.

[7]

Many thousands of men, women, and children might
inhabit such a city. They would probably visit the
mainland from time to time, but otherwise would spend
their lives at sea as ocean-dwelling pioneers.

25. A. NO CHANGE
     B. (Begin new paragraph) The cities,
         however,
     C. (Do NOT begin new paragraph) Further-
         more, the cities
     D. (Do NOT begin new paragraph) And
         these cities

26. F. NO CHANGE
     G. since
     H. when
     J. whereas

27. A. NO CHANGE
     B. apartments, small factories, offices,
         schools, and stores.
     C. various living and other quarters to be
         used by the town's citizens.
     D. people to live and engage in other
         activities as in a land-based city.

28. F. NO CHANGE
     G. materials. While
     H. materials, while
     J. materials,

Items 29 and 30 pose questions about the essay as a whole.

29. The writer wishes to include the following sen-
     tence in the essay:

     Tourists might find the floating cities attractive
     vacation spots for boating, swimming, and
     fishing.

     That sentence will fit most smoothly and logi-
     cally into Paragraph:
     A. 3, after the last sentence.
     B. 4, before the first sentence.
     C. 4, after the last sentence.
     D. 6, after the last sentence.

GO ON TO THE NEXT PAGE

30. For the sake of the unity and coherence of this essay, Paragraph 1 should be placed:

    F. where it is now.

    G. after Paragraph 2.

    H. after Paragraph 3.

    J. after Paragraph 4.

Exercise 2

30 Questions • Time—18 Minutes

Directions: This test consists of two passages in which particular words or phrases are underlined and numbered. Alongside the passage, you will see alternative words and phrases that could be substituted for the underlined part. You must select the alternative that expresses the idea most clearly and correctly or that best fits the style and tone of the entire passage. If the original version is best, select "No Change."

The test also includes questions about entire paragraphs and the passage as a whole. These questions are identified by a number in a box.

After you select the correct answer for each question, mark the oval representing the correct answer on your answer sheet.

Passage I

The Devastation of El Niño

[1]

Throughout 1998, it seemed, whenever anything went wrong, someone could be heard exclaiming, "Blame it on El Niño!" This unusually powerful weather system received so much attention in the news media around the world that El Niño came to seem <u>like a good</u>

    1

1. A. NO CHANGE

   B. as a good

   C. as if it was a good

   D. as a

scapegoat for almost any mishap. [2]

[2]

Every year, in late December—around Christmas time—oceanic winds from the West tend to shift, causing warm water from the western Pacific to move towards South America, heating the waters along its

coast. These hot currents and the weather disturbances they cause has been dubbed El Niño—
                    3
Spanish for "the child"—because of their annual association with the Christmas holiday.

[3]

Usually, the temperature of the water increases for six months, then returns to normal. In 1998 however,
                                      4
the wind shifts occurred around April and didn't peak until January, lasting substantially longer than usual. The resulting storms and other climatic changes produced widespread flooding and erosion. And,
                                  5
among other problems, devastated Peru's population of seals and birds.

[4]

When El Niño hit, vast schools of small fish, such as anchovies and sardines, sought cooler temperatures furthest down in the depths of the Pacific
      6
than the levels where they are usually found. While this protected the fish from the unseasonable weather

2. Which of the choices best introduces a central theme of the essay and provides the most appropriate transition between the first and second paragraphs?
   F. Yet the underlying meteorological causes of El Niño remain obscure.
   G. Unfortunately, the problems it really caused for creatures living on the Pacific coast of Peru were all too real.
   H. All over the United States, people found their lives disrupted by the violent effects of El Niño.
   J. But the real effects of El Niño proved to be surprisingly mild.

3. A. NO CHANGE
   B. have been dubbed
   C. was dubbed
   D. is known as

4. F. NO CHANGE
   G. However in 1998,
   H. In 1998, however,
   J. In 1998—however,

5. A. NO CHANGE
   B. erosion; and,
   C. erosion, and,
   D. erosion and

6. F. NO CHANGE
   G. more far
   H. farther
   J. farthest

GO ON TO THE NEXT PAGE

<![CDATA[

]]>

conditions, their predators were unable to reach them at these new, greater <u>depths, thus</u> the predators had

7

no food readily available.

[5]

Aquatic mammals were hit <u>especially hardly</u>. Along

8

one Peruvian beach, the Punta San Juan, a whole season's pup production of fur seals and sea lions died, <u>as well as</u> thousands of juveniles and

9

and breeding adults. By May 13, 1998, only 15 fur seals were counted, when there are usually hundreds.

<u>On the other hand,</u> only 1,500 sea lions were

10

found in an area that usually houses 8,000.

[6]

The Humboldt penguins also faced population losses due to El Niño. These penguins normally breed twice a <u>year; but</u> in 1998, their second breeding ground was

11

flooded by 52 consecutive hours of rain. Only 50 of the 3,500 to 5,000 penguins that usually lay eggs were <u>able to do so.</u>

12

[7]

Because Peru is <u>so close in distance</u> to the Pacific

13

regions where the wind shifts and water warming of El Niño originate, it experiences the harshest effects of this unpredictable weather phenomenon. Two or three more such years may spell an end to many species of wildlife that once thrived on Peruvian shores.

7. A. NO CHANGE
   B. depths: thus
   C. depths—thus
   D. depths. Thus,

8. F. NO CHANGE
   G. hard, especially.
   H. especially hard.
   J. specially hardly.

9. A. NO CHANGE
   B. as also
   C. at the same time as
   D. so did

10. F. NO CHANGE
    G. Yet
    H. Similarly,
    J. Likewise,

11. A. NO CHANGE
    B. year, but
    C. year. And
    D. year, however

12. F. NO CHANGE
    G. capable of this.
    H. able to lay them.
    J. possible.

13. A. NO CHANGE
    B. very close in distance
    C. not distant
    D. so close

Items 14 and 15 pose questions about the passage as a whole.

14. Which of the following sentences, if added here, would best conclude the passage and effectively summarize its main idea?

    F. Two or three more such years may spell an end to many species of wildlife that once thrived on Peruvian shores.

    G. Fortunately, other countries in South America do not suffer the ill effects of El Niño to the same extent as does Peru.

    H. Government officials in Peru are currently at work to develop plans for dealing with the problems caused by El Niño the next time it strikes.

    J. However, aid from foreign countries has helped Peru to save certain of the endangered species whom El Niño has decimated.

15. Suppose the writer were to eliminate Paragraph 4. This omission would cause the essay as a whole to lose primarily:

    A. relevant details about how Pacific fish are destroyed by the effects of El Niño.

    B. irrelevant facts about feeding patterns among creatures in the southern Pacific ocean.

    C. relevant information about how El Niño affects aquatic animals on the shores of Peru.

    D. irrelevant details about the kinds of fish that live off the shores of Peru.

GO ON TO THE NEXT PAGE

Passage II

The First Thanksgiving: Turkey Day
and a Whole Lot More

Every autumn, when Thanksgiving rolls around, anxiety and stress levels in millions of American families rise. Hosting friends and relatives from all over the country and then <u>to prepare</u> one of the

16

largest meals of the year is not an easy job. But when the typical Thanksgiving dinner of today <u>is compared with</u> the celebration of the first

17

Thanksgiving, it doesn't seem like <u>quite a feat.</u>

18

<u>First, consider the menu.</u> At a typical modern-day

19

Thanksgiving, there is a roast turkey, baked yams, stuffing, cranberry sauce, gravy, and some sort of dessert—maybe ice cream and some pie or cake. Of course, you can fix everything yourself, from scratch, if you like; but if you prefer, all of the food can be purchased at a local <u>supermarket: just one trip,</u> and

20

you have all you need for your dinner.

Today's menu seems stingy by comparison to <u>the</u> <u>Pilgrims meal</u> enjoyed on the first Thanksgiving

21

in 1621. According to contemporary records, the list of foods included five deer; wild turkeys, geese, and duck; eels, lobsters, clams, and mussels fished from the ocean; pumpkin; an assortment of biscuits; hoe

16. F. NO CHANGE
   G. preparing
   H. working on preparation of
   J. doing preparation for

17. A. NO CHANGE
   B. is compared against
   C. is viewed in reference to
   D. compares with

18. F. NO CHANGE
   G. as great a feat.
   H. all that much of a feat.
   J. such a feat.

19. A. NO CHANGE
   B. Start by thinking about the food that was served.
   C. The menu is the first thing we shall discuss.
   D. The food at the first Thanksgiving was incredible.

20. F. NO CHANGE
   G. supermarket, just one trip
   H. supermarket. One trip;
   J. supermarket; one trip is all,

21. A. NO CHANGE
   B. what the Pilgrims'
   C. the meal that the Pilgrim's
   D. the dinner the Pilgrims

and ash cakes (whatever those were); popcorn balls,

22

made with corn and maple syrup; pudding; berries
of several kinds—gooseberries, cranberries, straw-
berries—plums, cherries, and bogbeans; beer made
from barley; and wine spiked with brandy. Just in case
this wasn't enough, you could fill in the

23

corners with "flint corn," a rock-hard corn ground

into a mush. ☐24 And once the dinner was served, the

22. F. NO CHANGE
    G. (what they are is unknown to me)
    H. (unheard-of today)
    J. OMIT the underlined portion.

23. A. NO CHANGE
    B. this weren't
    C. all of the above weren't
    D. one didn't find this

24. At this point, the writer is considering the addition of the following sentence:

Everything, of course, was prepared by hand;
there were no food processors, microwave ov-
ens, or other appliances to help.

Would this be a logical and relevant addition to
the essay?

    F. Yes, because it emphasizes how difficult
it was to prepare the first Thanksgiving
dinner.
    G. Yes, because many readers may not be
aware that the Pilgrims lived in a time
when technology was relatively primitive.
    H. No, because the rest of the passage does
not focus on technological differences
between 1621 and today.
    J. No, because it is unconnected to the list
of foodstuffs that occupies most of the
rest of the paragraph.

meal didn't last a few hours, but a few days—and

25

with no football on TV to distract the Pilgrims and

their friends from the serious business of eating.

    The other major difference was the guest list.

Nowadays, in many households, the whole family

comes for Thanksgiving, this provokes many groans

26

from besieged hosts. Statistics show that the average

Thanksgiving dinner boasts 23 total guests—no tiny

25. A. NO CHANGE
    B. rather a few days—
    C. but instead a few days:
    D. a few days, rather;

26. F. NO CHANGE
    G. so as to provoke
    H. the provocation of
    J. provoking

GO ON TO THE NEXT PAGE ➡

gathering, at that. [27] At the first Thanksgiving, when
Squanto, the Indian-in-residence, decided to invite

Massasoit, <u>the leader of the Wampanoags,</u>
                          28

for a little pot-luck supper, the Pilgrims weren't
expecting him to bring along the other 90
person guest list. I guess <u>they weren't overdoing it,</u>
                                                  29

afterall.

So, when the next Thanksgiving rolls around, and
<u>your tempted</u> to complain about "all this cooking—all
      30

this food—all these people!"—just be thankful it isn't
1621 and you aren't hosting the first Thanksgiving!

27. Which of the following sentences, if inserted
    here, would provide the best transition between
    the first half and the second half of the para-
    graph?
    A. We rarely have that many guests in my
       house.
    B. It could be a lot worse, however.
    C. Both family and friends are included in
       this number.
    D. And all of them show up hungry.

28. F. NO CHANGE
    G. the Wampanoag's leader,
    H. who was leading the Wampanoag's
    J. Wampanoag leader,

29. A. NO CHANGE
    B. the repast served was not, in fact,
       excessive,
    C. that dinner menu wasn't overdoing it,
    D. it wasn't too much,

30. F. NO CHANGE
    G. your feeling a temptation
    H. you're tempted
    J. there's a temptation

EXERCISE 1

1. D	7. B	13. B	19. B	25. A
2. G	8. F	14. G	20. G	26. G
3. B	9. D	15. C	21. D	27. B
4. F	10. G	16. F	22. G	28. H
5. C	11. B	17. B	23. B	29. C
6. H	12. F	18. H	24. J	30. G

1. **D.** The underlined phrase is redundant, since the words "under no circumstances" add nothing to the meaning conveyed by the word "never." It can be omitted with no loss of meaning, making the sentence more concise.

2. **G.** The semicolon in the underlined portion is wrong, since what follows it cannot stand alone as a sentence. Instead, a comma should be used.

3. **B.** When the word "its" is used in place of the words "it is," it should be spelled "it's"; the apostrophe stands for the omitted letter "i" in the contraction.

4. **F.** "And" is the most logical conjunction among the answer choices for connecting this sentence with the previous one. The other answer choices all imply a contraction or some other shift in meaning, which in fact doesn't exist.

5. **C.** The subject of the verb "have . . . imagined" is the pronoun "no one," which is singular. Therefore, the singular verb "has . . . imagined" is necessary to make the subject and verb agree in number.

6. **H.** The modifying phrase with which the sentence begins, "Working closely" etc., describes effects artists. In order to keep the modifier from "dangling," what follows the phrase should be a word naming the people being described. Thus, it's correct for the word "they" (meaning, of course, the effects artists) to immediately follow the comma. Answer H is also more concise and graceful than the other answer choices.

7. **B.** As originally written, the sentence is a run-on—two complete sentences jammed together with a comma between them. Choice B corrects the error by breaking the two sentences apart at the logical place.

8. **F.** It makes sense to start with sentence 2, which makes the general point (about the usefulness of special effects) that the rest of the paragraph then explains in more detail. And it makes sense for sentence 3 to follow sentence 4, since it refers to "those costs" described in that sentence.

9. **D.** This sentence introduces the topic around which the other sentences in the paragraph are organized.

10. **G.** The pronoun "such" is vague, leaving the reader slightly uncertain what is being referred to. (It also is awkward and non-idiomatic; i.e., "weird sounding.") "These events" refers back to the previous sentence clearly and understandably.

11. **B.** This wording is the simplest and most concise of the answer choices.

12. **F.** The words "Most important" introduce the point made in the final paragraph in a logical fashion: the idea that special effects free movie makers to depict impossible words is, arguably, the "most important" or at least most remarkable idea in the passage. The other alternative connecting words or phrases don't make as much sense in the context.

13. **B.** Since this sentence adds nothing to our understanding of movie special effects or how they are used, it can be omitted without losing anything.

14. **G.** The word "maker's" is a possessive; the sentence refers to something (the "tool" of special effects) that belongs to the movie makers. Therefore, it should be spelled with an apostrophe s, as possessives generally are.

15. **C.** The parenthetical phrase "after all" should be surrounded by commas to set it off from the rest of the sentence.

16. **F.** We're looking for a sentence that will support the idea that the hungry people of the world may be fed from resources in the sea. The sentence in answer F does this by giving several concrete examples of foods derived from the oceans.

17. **B.** The phrase "three quarters" is neither a possessive nor a contraction; it's a simple plural, and therefore should be spelled without an apostrophe.

18. **H.** There's no reason to separate the subject ("deposits") from the verb ("have been discovered") with a comma.

19. **B.** Only the sentence given in answer B offers an additional example of important resources that may be provided by the oceans.

20. **G.** Since the sentence is talking about the "cities on the ocean" mentioned in the previous sentence, the logical pronoun to use is "they" (a plural pronoun to match the plural antecedent). Choice H is wrong because it seems to refer to a "they" we can't identify—some unnamed group of people who will build the futuristic cities on the sea.

21. **D.** The words "playing a variety of roles" mean exactly the same as the words "could serve many functions" which precede them. Since the underlined phrase adds no new information to the sentence, it can and should be eliminated.

22. **G.** It's generally best for the adverb to be as close as possible to the word it modifies—in this case, the verb "could serve." It should be graceful and natural to insert it in the middle of the verb phrase: "could also serve."

23. **B.** The subject of the verb "have . . . been developed" is the singular pronoun "much." Therefore, the verb should also be singular: "has been developed."

24. **J.** As originally written, the sentence is a fragment; it has no independent verb. Answer J fixes the problem by turning the gerund "serving" into the verb "serve," whose subject is the word "rigs" way back at the start of the sentence.

25. **A.** It makes sense to start a new paragraph here. The previous paragraph talks about the existing oil-rig technology that could be used to build cities on the sea; this paragraph talks about what these new cities would be like. The ideas are distinct and deserve separate paragraphs.

26. **G.** The logical relationship between the two clauses in this sense is best expressed by the word "since"; the fact that shipping supplies from the mainland would be costly is the reason why the cities would have to be self-sufficient. "Since" states this relationship.

27. **B.** The original phrase is vague, as are choices C and D. Answer B names the kinds of facilities to be included in the new cities rather than merely alluding to them.

28. **H.** Since what follows the semicolon can't stand alone as a sentence, that punctuation mark is incorrect. It must be changed to a comma.

29. **C.** Paragraph 4 is devoted to describing the various purposes that cities on the sea might serve. The new sentence, which adds an extra example of these purposes, would make sense at the end of that paragraph.

30. **G.** Paragraph 1 describes an example of the "human dilemmas" introduced in paragraph 2. Therefore, it makes sense to have paragraph 1 follow paragraph 2.

Exercise 2

1. A	7. D	13. D	19. A	25. A
2. G	8. H	14. F	20. F	26. J
3. B	9. A	15. C	21. D	27. B
4. H	10. H	16. G	22. F	28. F
5. C	11. B	17. A	23. A	29. C
6. H	12. F	18. J	24. F	30. H

1. **A.** The conjunction "like" is correct: it's idiomatic to say that something "seems like" something else, rather than "seems as" something else.

2. **G.** Since the first paragraph talks in a somewhat light-hearted way about how people blamed all kinds of problems on El Niño, while the rest of the passage describes the very serious problems El Niño really caused, a transitional sentence is needed that says to the reader, "All kidding aside—El Niño produced some real headaches." The sentence in answer G does that.

3. **B.** The subject of the verb "has been dubbed" is plural—it's the two things "hot currents" and "weather disturbances" (a compound subject). Therefore, the plural verb "have been dubbed" is needed.

4. **H.** The parenthetical word "however" needs to be set off from the rest of the sentence by a pair of commas, one before it and one after it.

5. **C.** The last sentence of the paragraph, as originally written, is a fragment, lacking any real subject. By changing the period before it into a comma, the sentence is merged with the previous one, and "storms and . . . climatic changes" becomes the subject of the verb "devastated."

6. **H.** Two things are being compared: the greater depths the fish sought during El Niño and the lesser depths at which they normally swim. Since only two things are being compared, the comparative adjective "farther" is wanted rather than the superlative "farthest."

7. **D.** Break this sentence into two, since it's a run-on as it stands.

8. **H.** The adverb form of the adjective "hard" looks the same as the adjective: "hard." The -ly suffix isn't used in this case.

9. **A.** The conjunction "as well as" is the most graceful and idiomatic of the answer choices. Note that answer D would turn the sentence into a run-on: "So did thousands of juveniles and breeding adults" could and should stand on its own as a complete sentence.

10. **H.** Logically, the word "similarly" makes the most sense here, since what's being described in the sentence is a phenomenon that resembles the one described in the previous sentence. "Likewise" sounds awkward in this context.

11. **B.** When two potentially complete sentences are linked in one with a coordinating conjunction (in this case, "but"), it's normally correct to use a comma before the conjunction rather than some other punctuation mark.

12. **F.** The original wording is the clearest and most concise choice. Answers G and J are vague and confusing, and answer H sounds clumsy.

13. **D.** The words "in distance" are redundant, since "close" obviously refers to distance; they should be eliminated.

14. **F.** This sentence neatly ties together the various destructive effects of El Niño on wildlife living on the shores of Peru.

15. **C.** Paragraph 4 explains the indirect way El Niño affects the Peruvian mammals (by reducing the availability of their food, the schools of anchovies and sardines). It's necessary if we are to understand how El Niño affected the seals and sea lions in Peru.

16. **G.** Because it is grammatically parallel with "hosting," the present participle "preparing" is better than the infinitive "to prepare."

17. **A.** The idiomatic phrase is "compared with," not "compared against" or any of the other answer choices.

18. **J.** In this rather casual, mildly humorous essay, the phrase "such a feat" sounds both idiomatic and appropriate. The other answer choices either sound a bit awkward or are verbose by comparison.

19. **A.** The original sentence is clear and concise. The alternatives add words without adding anything to the meaning or tone of the essay.

20. **F.** Note that what follows the colon restates or summarizes what precedes it. This is a good example of the proper use of a colon.

21. **D.** Choice D states the idea most clearly of all the answer choices. The original wording is wrong, among other reasons, because the phrase "Pilgrims meal" would have to be written as the possessive "Pilgrims' meal."

22. **F.** The parenthetical phrase is appropriate in this light-hearted look back at a long-ago, slightly amazing, and mysterious holiday celebration. Answers G and H say almost the same thing, but less gracefully and idiomatically.

23. **A.** The original wording is more concise and clear than the alternatives.

24. **F.** The proposed addition fits logically into the overall theme of the essay. Note, too, that it picks up on the idea that the original Thanksgiving dinner was much harder to prepare than today's Thanksgiving dinners, which can be purchased ready-made at the supermarket (as mentioned in the second paragraph).

25. **A.** The original wording is correctly parallel to the phrase it's paired with: not "a few hours, but a few days."

26. **J.** As written, the sentence is a run-on. By changing the subject-verb pair "this provokes" into the present participate "provoking," the second half of the sentence is tightly and correctly linked with the first half, and the run-on problem is eliminated.

27. **B.** The first half of the paragraph talks about the many guests who show up at today's Thanksgiving dinners, while the second half talks about how many more guests there were at the first Thanksgiving. The sentence in choice B deftly links the two ideas.

28. **F.** The original word is both perfectly correct and idiomatic.

29. **C.** As originally worded, the underlined phrase is pretty vague; it's hard to tell what the writer is getting at. Choice C clarifies the point: the huge menu described in the previous paragraph makes sense when you consider how many people attended the dinner.

30. **H.** The contraction "you're" is necessary in this sentence, since what's intended is the same meaning as the two words "you are."

ARE YOU READY TO MOVE ON?

How well do you understand the contents and format of the ACT Assessment English Test? How well have you incorporated your new skills into your test-taking behavior?

After you've corrected each exercise, find the number below. This will give you an idea of whether you need to go to the English Review in Part 3, or whether you can move on to another subject area.

Score Key for Each Practice Exercise

Number Correct	Score	Suggested Action
0–7	Poor	Study the review chapter and complete the exercises there Study this chapter again.
8–13	Below average	Study problem areas in the review chapter; do at least one exercise there. Study this chapter again.
14–18	Average	Study this chapter again if you wish to and have time. Skim problem areas in the review chapter if you have time.
19–24	Above average	You may move on to a new subject.
25–30	Excellent	You're ready for the ACT Assessment English Test.

Summary: What You Need to Know About the ACT Assessment English Test

- The ACT Assessment English Test will include 40 questions on usage and mechanics and 35 questions on rhetorical skills. The 75 different questions will refer to five passages. You'll complete the test in one sitting that is 45 minutes long.

- Skim each passage first for overall theme, style, and organization.

- Underlined sections may be questions on either usage and mechanics or rhetorical skills. Boxed numbers always refer to questions of rhetorical skills.

- Approach each usage/mechanics item by reading the entire sentence in which the item appears and trying to identity the error *before* you look at the test choices.

- Approach each rhetorical-skills item by focusing on the central idea of the passage. Eliminate the unrelated answers.

- The easiest way to arrange a sequence is to begin by finding the first sentence or paragraph.

- The best way to say something is usually the shortest way.

The ACT Assessment Math Test

The ACT Assessment Mathematics Test determines how well you understand the basic facts and skills taught in most high school math programs. It tests your ability to take knowledge of specific math facts, formulas, techniques, and methods and to apply this knowledge by solving problems. For you to succeed on the Math sections of the ACT Assessment, you need to remember some basic information about the rules and procedures of math, and you need to be able to apply those rules to non-routine or real-world situations. In this chapter, you learn about the types of questions included on the ACT Assessment Math Tests, and you see some examples of those questions. After you've worked through the exercises at the end of this chapter, score the results and evaluate your understanding of the Math portions of the ACT Assessment.

WHAT TO EXPECT ON THE ACT ASSESSMENT MATH TEST

The ACT Assessment Math sections test your knowledge of a range of mathematical subjects. Specific topics covered include pre-algebra, elementary algebra, intermediate algebra, coordinate geometry, plane geometry, and trigonometry. Within these topics, you will need to understand the basic arithmetic operations of addition, subtraction, multiplication, and division, as well as such procedures as working with fractions and decimals, figuring out averages, and so on. You'll also need to be skilled at basic algebraic operations, including solving equations, using negative numbers and square roots, and factoring. You will need to understand the principles of geometry: concepts such as the properties of triangles, circles, and quadrilaterals, and procedures such as determining the areas and volumes of simple figures. Finally, you will be tested on basic principles of trigonometry, including solving trigonometric equations, graphing functions, and understanding the values and properties of functions.

The ACT Assessment Math Test contains 60 multiple-choice questions. The different problem types encompass straight arithmetic problems, word problems, problems in reading and interpreting graphs and charts, algebra problems, geometry problems with and without diagrams, and a few trigonometry problems. Each of the 60 questions will have 5 possible answers from which to choose.

ROAD MAP

- *Learn What to Expect on the ACT Assessment Math Test*
- *Learn Proven Strategies for Success on ACT Assessment Math*
- *Practice Your Skills with ACT Assessment Math Exercises*
- *Score Your Results and Evaluate Your Performance*
- *Review a Summary of ACT Assessment Math Facts and Tips*

Because you have 60 minutes to solve 60 problems, pace yourself. The problems will grow increasingly difficult, so don't spend too much time on any one problem, especially the beginning ones. You may use the test booklet itself as scratch paper on which to work out your calculations.

There will be a variety of problem types on the test, including the following:

Straightforward calculations:

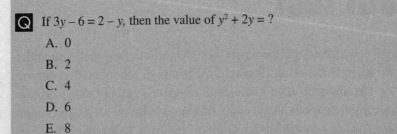

Q If $3y - 6 = 2 - y$, then the value of $y^2 + 2y = $?

   A. 0

   B. 2

   C. 4

   D. 6

   E. 8

(Answer: E)

Word problems:

Q In a group of 20 singers and 40 dancers, 20% of the singers are under 25 years old and 40% of the entire group are under 25 years old. What percent of the dancers are under 25 years old?

   A. 20%

   B. 30%

   C. 40%

   D. 50%

   E. 60%

(Answer: D)

Problems with charts, diagrams, and figures:

 Given that l_1 is parallel to l_2 in the figure below, then the value of $x + y = ?$

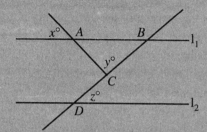

A. $90 + x$

B. $120 - y$

C. $180 - z$

D. 210

E. 270

(Answer: C)

THE DIRECTIONS

The directions for the ACT Assessment Math Test are similar to the following:

Directions: Solve each problem below and mark the oval representing the correct answer on your answer sheet.

Be careful not to spend too much time on any one question. Instead, solve as many questions as possible, and then use any remaining time to return to those questions you were unable to answer at first.

You may use a calculator on any problem in this test; however, not every problem requires the use of a calculator.

Diagrams that accompany problems may or may not be drawn to scale. Unless otherwise indicated, you may assume that all figures shown lie in a plane and that lines that appear straight are straight.

TIP

Reread these directions several times until you're totally familiar with them. Then the day of the test, save time by *not* reading them. This is one of your overall strategies for scoring higher on the ACT Assessment.

STRATEGIES FOR SUCCESS ON THE ACT ASSESSMENT MATH TEST

The ACT Assessment Math sections test your knowledge of basic math principles and procedures that you've studied in high school—you don't have to be a math wizard to succeed on this portion of the test. Timing is critical—you have 60 minutes to answer approximately 60 questions. Timing doesn't need to be a problem, though; you should be able to answer many questions in just 15 or 30 seconds. That will leave time for the more involved questions, on which you might spend two or three minutes. In other words, much of preparing for the Math sections of the ACT Assessment involves learning some good strategies and practices in advance. And yes, you'll try to get a good night's sleep before the test, you'll try to eat a healthy breakfast, and you'll try to stay calm and focused. These tips are great advice for preparing for any test. But the following sections contain some strategies that are designed—and proven—to help you score higher on ACT Assessment Math.

KNOW WHAT'S REALLY BEING ASKED

Read the question carefully. Make sure you know what's really being asked.

Most problems include a series of interrelated facts. The kinds of facts will vary depending on the kind of question.

Example:

Q Arlene has a block of wood in the form of a rectangular solid 14 inches long with a square base, which is 6 inches on a side. A right circular cylinder is drilled out of the block, as shown below. What is the volume of the wood remaining, to the nearest cubic inch?

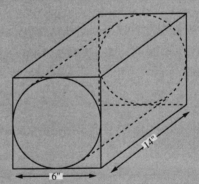

A. 54

B. 108

C. 396

D. 485

E. 495

(Answer: B)

The key to solving a problem like this is to make sure you know which fact is being asked about and what form the answer should take. If you read hastily, you might assume a particular question when, in fact, the test-makers want to focus on a different one. For example, rather than asking about when a train will arrive at City A, they might ask when the train will reach the one-third point of the trip. Rather than asking about the amount of rainfall in any particular month, as shown on a graph, they might ask about the difference between two of the months—a number that does not appear directly on the graph. And in the previous problem, rather than asking about the volume of either the cylinder or the rectangular block, for which you have figures, they have asked about the volume of the odd-shaped region that is the difference between the cylinder and the block.

KEEP MOVING WITHIN THE PROBLEM

Sitting and staring seldom leads to a solution. *Do* something, try something. Does the type of problem sound the least bit familiar? Does it at least bring to mind a procedure? Try it. The procedure might prove to be a starting point.

For example, if a problem involves fractions, try reducing them to the lowest terms or finding the lowest common denominator or translating the fractions into decimals. If a geometry diagram appears, work from the given, such as the degree measures of certain angles, to fill in other information you don't know: the complementary angle alongside the angle that's marked, for example, or the angle on the other side of the transversal which must be equal to the angle you know. If you're given a problem involving probability or permutations (varying combinations of things), just start listing all the possibilities.

Quite often, seemingly random experimentation will lead you toward the right answer. That's because the questions are written so that the numbers themselves are generally "obvious." After you see the underlying connection among the numbers, the math is usually simple.

If you need to brush up on your math skills and understanding, you have a great opportunity to do so in Chapter 9, "Math Review: From Arithmetic Through Geometry."

CAUTION
The little words in a question can make a huge difference in what's being asked: "Which of the following *may be* true?" "Which of the following *must be* true?" "Which of the following *may not be* true?" You could be asked any one of these, so pay attention and read carefully.

TIP

Rounding numbers to the nearest whole can sometimes save you valuable time on ACT Assessment Math questions—and it's a practice that goes hand-in-hand with estimating. Again, if the answer choices are close together and precise to the hundredth of a unit, rounding isn't a good technique. But in other situations, rounding will help you find the answer quickly—so you can move on.

ESTIMATE

Because the exact numbers are given for you in the answers, you can often speed through the calculations by estimating. Here's an example:

> **Q** The original price of a computer was $1,200. What was the price of the computer after two 10% markdowns?
>
> A. $960
>
> B. $972
>
> C. $980
>
> D. $1,000
>
> E. $1,072
>
> (Answer: B)

If you understand the logic behind this question, the calculations aren't difficult. You need to figure out the answer in two steps: first, subtract ten percent from the original cost of $1,200. This gives you $1,200 – $120 = $1,080. Then subtract ten percent of this new price of $1,080. This gives you $1,080 – $108 = $972. Using either your calculator or pencil and paper, the math isn't hard.

However, if you had only minutes left in which to do five more math problems, estimating would be a more useful strategy. Instead of subtracting ten percent twice in steps, you could simply subtract twenty percent at once in your head, which gives $960. Since you know the answer must be higher than that, you can quickly eliminate answer A. Then do the first step: Mentally subtract ten percent from the original cost, giving you $1080. You can eliminate answer E, as $1072 is too close to $1080 because the second ten percent hasn't been subtracted. Ten percent of $1080 is $108, close enough to a hundred that you could subtract a hundred from $1080 for an estimate of $980. Because the actual answer will be lower, and you've already eliminated $960 as too low, the answer must be $972.

Estimating isn't necessary on most ACT Assessment items; in some cases, the numbers used are so few and so simple that you might as well work with them directly. And, don't estimate when the choices are very close together. For example, if your five choices are 270, 272, 275, 278, and 282, you're going to need a precise answer that only full calculation can give. On the other hand, if your five choices are 110, 292, 348, 512, and 721, estimate. You have enough leeway for the "error" that's built into estimating. Though it's not always the best route to a solution, estimating is a handy method to use when time is short.

TRY ONE OF THE CHOICES

If you have no ideas, try one of the choices and work backward. If it doesn't lead you to the answer, it can often at least alert you to one or two that can be eliminated. Here's a very simple example:

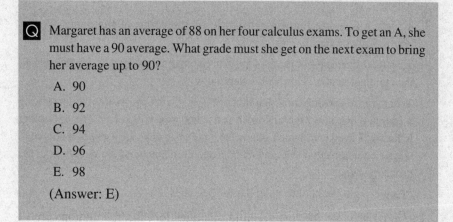

Q Margaret has an average of 88 on her four calculus exams. To get an A, she must have a 90 average. What grade must she get on the next exam to bring her average up to 90?

A. 90

B. 92

C. 94

D. 96

E. 98

(Answer: E)

Because answers are put in numerical order, choice C is always the middle answer and the most logical one to use if you're trying out possibilities. For an average of 88 on four exams, Margaret must have a total of $4 \times 88 = 352$. Adding 94 to 352 gives 446, and dividing that by 5 gives 89.2, which means it isn't high enough. By trying one number, you've just eliminated choices A, B, and C. You can now try D or E if you have time; if you have no time, pick one—as you have a 50 percent chance of being right—and move on to the next question.

TURN WORD PROBLEMS INTO EQUATIONS

If word problems are your downfall—if your eyes start to glaze at the mention of planes heading east, gallons of paint being used up, or workers working together at two different speeds—translate the unfamiliar into the familiar. Turn the words into numbers and build an equation for the answer you want.

Surprisingly, the math in most word problems is not difficult. You might have a couple of fractions to multiply or divide or a simple equation to solve, but the computations will be easy. Turning the words into numbers is usually the most difficult part. Here's how to do it:

1. **What you don't know is x.** If the question asks "What fraction of the entire job will be completed after three hours?" begin writing your equation with $x =$, where x represents that fraction of the job. Conversely, if the question asks, "How many hours will it take to do $\frac{3}{7}$ of the entire job?" then x will equal the hours of work needed. This way, after you've solved the equation, you automatically have your answer, with no further conversions needed.

Even better, instead of *x*, use *J* for the job and *H* for the time. These hints are easier to remember and help you focus on what you're really looking for.

2. **Break each phrase into a numerical expression.** Divide the problem into its smallest parts. If the part has a known number (such as "3 gallons of paint"), use the number 3. If the part doesn't have a known number, ("how many gallons," give it a letter G.

3. **Create a formula that describes the relationships of the parts.** Finally, you're back on familiar territory!

Example: Paul is eight years older than Sarah. Four years ago, Sarah was half the age Paul is now. How old is Sarah now?

What you're looking for is Sarah's age *now*. So set up your equation making *S* (Sarah's age now) the unknown for which you will solve. The only other letter we'll need is *P*, which stands for Paul's age now. Now create a couple of simple equations that state in symbols and numbers what the sentences in the problem say.

"Paul is eight years older than Sarah" becomes: $P - 8 = S$.

"Four years ago, Sarah was half the age Paul is now" becomes $S - 4 = \frac{P}{2}$. To get rid of the fraction (usually a good idea), multiply this equation through by 2: $2S - 8 = P$.

Now you can solve for *S* by substituting the expression $2S - 8$ for *P* in the first equation:

$$(2S - 8) - 8 = S$$
$$2S - 16 = S$$
$$-16 = -S$$
$$S = 16$$

So Sarah's age today is 16 (Paul is 24).

Still not sure? Do word problems still make you feel like a visitor to a strange land where you don't speak the language? Then you'll want to take along a handy "English-to-Math Dictionary" that will translate key phrases for you.

Translation Guide to Word Problems

The most difficult element of a word problem is trying to translate the relationships into mathematical procedures. A problem says *a + b = x; solve for b* and you immediately understand how *a, b,* and *x* are related and what you have to do. A word problem introduces trains and ticket sales, gallons and miles, pumpkin pies and the ages of three brothers. *How are all these people and things related?* you want to know. *What am I supposed to do?*

Following is a mini "Dictionary of Translation" that reveals what commonly used words and expressions in word problems mean in mathematical operations:

Word-Problem Word or Phrase	Mathematical Operation
added to	addition
along with	addition
amounts to	equals
and	addition
by	multiplication
decreased by	subtraction
difference	subtraction
divided by	division
each	multiplication
fewer than	subtraction
fraction	division
greater than	addition
in addition to	addition
increased by	addition
is	equals
is the same as	equals
larger than	addition
less than	subtraction
more than	addition
of	multiplication
part of	division
per	multiplication
piece	division
portion	division
product	multiplication
reduced by	subtraction
smaller than	subtraction
take away	subtraction
times	multiplication
with	addition
without	subtraction

If word problems are *your* problem, try to learn as much of the list as possible. Many of the terms—"take away," for example—are already associated with subtraction, so there actually won't be too many "foreign words" you need to translate.

CHANGE QUANTITIES INTO THE UNIT OF THE ANSWER

One common error is to give the answer in terms of the wrong unit. For example, the answer you calculate is 2 quarts; however, because the question asked for how many gallons, the correct answer is really $\frac{1}{2}$ (4 quarts = 1 gallon).

One way to avoid the error is to begin the problem by converting the units into the units demanded by the answer. So, for example, if you see that the answers are all stated in terms of square feet, while the numbers in the problem are in square yards, change them to square feet before beginning your work. (One square yard equals nine square feet.)

CONSIDER DIAGRAMS "TREASURE MAPS" TO THE SOLUTION

Diagrams, especially for geometry problems, are there for a reason. They are filled with clues to the solution. You can usually leap from what you know—the facts you are given—to what you need to know simply by using the parts of the diagram as "stepping stones." Here's an example:

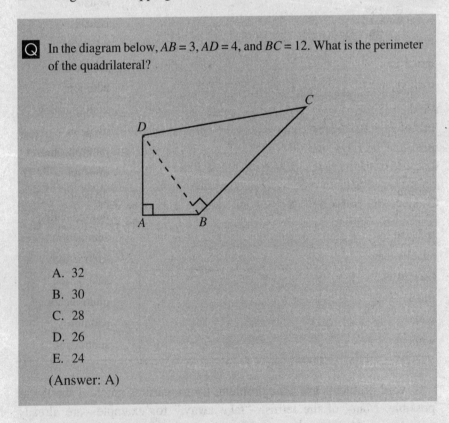

Q In the diagram below, $AB = 3$, $AD = 4$, and $BC = 12$. What is the perimeter of the quadrilateral?

A. 32

B. 30

C. 28

D. 26

E. 24

(Answer: A)

Solving a geometry problem like this one is a matter of working methodically. Just fill in the blank parts of the diagram using what you can deduce from the information you're given. (Use your pencil to mark the new facts right in the question booklet.) You'll eventually work your way to the fact about which you're being asked.

Here's how you'd apply the method to this item. This problem uses two well-known right triangles. We see that, in triangle *ABD*, one leg is 3 and one is 4, which makes $BD = 5$ (the famous "Pythagorean triple," 3-4-5). This tells us that triangle *BDC* is 5-12-13 (another famous Pythagorean triangle). Thus, *CD* is 13, and the entire perimeter is $3 + 4 + 12 + 13 = 32$.

IF THERE'S NO DIAGRAM, DRAW ONE

You don't need an art degree to sketch a diagram that will be so clear you'll see the answer at once. Here's an example:

Q One side of a rectangle with an area of 18 square inches is the diameter of a circle. The opposite side is tangent to the circle. What is the length of the circumference of the circle?

    A. 2π

    B. 6π

    C. 9π

    D. 12π

    E. 18π

    Ⓐ ● Ⓒ Ⓓ Ⓔ

Without a diagram, this is a difficult problem; with one, it's very easy. Just use the margin of your test booklet to quickly sketch a circle. Put a straight line through the center for the diameter. The diameter is also one side of the rectangle. The opposite side of the rectangle is tangent to the circle, so draw that side of the rectangle parallel to the diameter and equal to its length (by definition of being a rectangle) and passing through a point on the circle. Connect the "missing sides" of the rectangle at right angles (again, by definition). Calling the radius of the circle *r*, we see in the picture below that the rectangle has a width of *r* and a length of 2*r*.

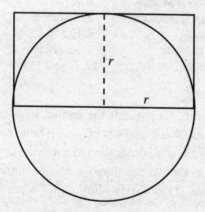

Hence, the area of the rectangle is $2r^2 = 18$, which is confirmed by the problem. Thus $r^2 = 9$, and $r = 3$. The circumference of the circle is $2\pi r = 6\pi$.

READ THE GRAPH BEFORE YOU READ THE QUESTIONS

On graph problems, spend 30 seconds analyzing the graph(s) before even looking at the questions. Look at the structural features, labels, and basic contents. This helps you find the relevant information and separate it from the mass of other information in which it is embedded. You can always return to the graph later for the details.

There are many different types of graphs. Three kinds commonly appear on the ACT Assessment: bar graphs, line graphs, and circle graphs.

A Quick Look at Bar Graphs

Bar graphs are good for making simple comparisons, such as comparing a single set of statistics (birth rates, for example) for different countries or different years. Following is an example.

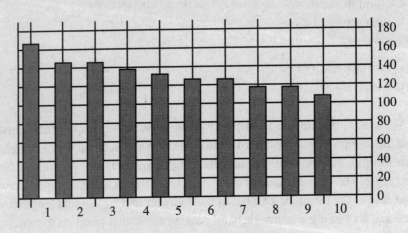

Sales of the Top Ten Industrial Corporations
in the Fortune 500, 1996 (Billions of Dollars)

1. General Motors
2. Ford Motor Company
3. Mitsui
4. Mitsubishi
5. Itochu
6. Royal Dutch/Shell
7. Marubeni
8. Exxon
9. Sumitomo
10. Toyota Motor

In this graph, each bar represents the annual sales of a different major industrial corporation. A bar graph works well here, because it makes the differences in size from one corporation to another very clear. However, if the data were more complex, this graph would be more difficult to look at and understand. A bar graph also has limitations when it comes to spotting trends.

A Quick Look at Line Graphs

Line graphs, by contrast, can be both precise and intricate. Large numbers of data points can be shown in one or more lines on a graph, and trends of increase or decrease can be easily and quickly "read" on a line graph. For these reason, line graphs are the kind of graph most often used by scientists and statisticians.

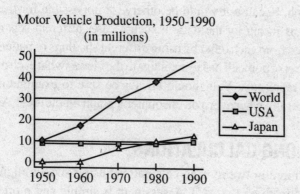

Motor Vehicle Production, 1950-1990
(in millions)

Both bar and line graphs have certain features in common:

All bar and line graphs have two axes, the horizontal (or x) axis and the vertical (or y) axis. By convention, the independent variable in an experiment or a statistical study is usually placed on the horizontal axis, and the dependent variable on the vertical axis. For example, if a chemist were studying the effect of temperature on the solubility of a substance, the independent variable would be temperature, and the dependent variable would be solubility. When the experiment was documented later, a graph of the data would have temperature along the horizontal axis and solubility on the vertical axis.

Circle Graphs

Circle graphs are used to show the breakdown of some large quantity into smaller quantities. The larger the relative size of a particular "slice of the pie," the larger the fraction of the overall quantity represented by that sector of the circle. Typical uses of a circle graph would include the division of the budget of a nation, business, or family into portions representing either different sources of income or different types of spending, and the division of a general population into particular categories (by age, religion, or occupation, for example).

Enlisted Personnel, US Armed Forces,
by Race, 1996 (Total = 419,397)

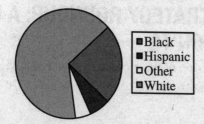

NOTE
The structural features of the graph—the labels on the axes, the units of measurement, and any information in the key—are more important than the actual data presented. If you understand the structure of the graph, you'll understand the kind of information it presents and the nature of the questions that the graph is designed to answer. After you know these things, the specific details provided by the data—the answers to the questions, in effect—are easy to look up when you need them.

All properly designed graphs are clearly labeled with the names of the variables being studied and the units of measurement (degrees, centimeters, percent, and so on). The divisions along the axes should be clearly numbered. All graphs should also have a title. Many graphs have a key providing additional information about the graph or the data. The key is usually found in one corner of the graph, or outside the limits of the graph altogether. A key is most often used when more than one line (or bar, or set of points) is plotted on one graph. Because it would be otherwise impossible for the viewer to know what is meant by the data in such a case, different sets of data are distinguished from each other by using different shadings or patterns for each line, bar, or set of points. The key explains to the viewer what each of the colors or patterns represents. You should always be sure to examine all of these features carefully whenever you encounter a graph on the ACT Assessment.

AVOID LONG CALCULATIONS

Don't get mired in twenty-step calculations using sixteen-digit numbers. Most of the math on the ACT Assessment is simple and more "method" oriented; that is, if you can discover the method, the math is usually easy. If you find yourself getting involved in long, complicated, or tricky calculations—especially ones using big numbers—stop and begin again with a clear mind. You're probably overlooking the simple shortcut that would make the calculations unnecessary. If you've already spent too much time on the question, mark it for later attention and move on. If time allows, you can return to the question later, when the answer might come to you more readily.

DON'T OVER-RELY ON YOUR CALCULATOR

The math on the ACT Assessment is specifically designed not to require the use of a calculator. It relies on reasoning and on knowing the correct procedures. If you rely too heavily on calculation, you're apt to miss the bigger picture behind the question.

You're also susceptible to certain errors with a calculator, such as hitting the wrong key, hitting the right key twice, and jamming keys. You also don't leave a visible paper trail to retrace your steps in case of a mistake.

Use a calculator if you must, but don't depend on it. Calculators work best for arithmetic calculations, square roots, and percentages; if you need to use the calculator, use it for those types of functions. And if you must use one, use one that you're familiar with, and make sure it has fresh batteries on test day.

SUCCESS STRATEGY ROUNDUP: A LIST OF DO'S AND DON'TS

Here's the short version of the previously covered advice, along with a few other miscellaneous tips, arranged in a handy list of Do's and Don'ts. After you understand each point and the reasoning behind it, you need only know the boldface sentence to jog your memory—whether you're working on the exercises at the end of this chapter, your full-length sample tests, or the ACT Assessment itself.

A list of Do's:

☑ **Keep moving within the problem.** Sitting and staring seldom leads to a solution. *Do* something. Try a procedure that seems familiar from class and appropriate to the particular problem. Even if the procedure doesn't immediately work, it might suggest something else that will.

☑ **Keep moving within the test.** Have you been working on one problem forever? There are dozens more waiting. Keep moving at a regular pace. If you're not working productively on a problem within twenty seconds, move on.

☑ **Know what's being asked.** Read carefully and make sure you know what's being asked. Also make sure you know what particular form the answer should take. For example, is the answer supposed to be a number, or coordinates for a point on a graph? Is the answer supposed to be a choice that may be true, must be true, or may not be true? *Know what's being asked.*

☑ **Round off and guess.** It's not always necessary to work with exact numbers to solve ACT Assessment math problems. Round off and save time. *When should you round off?* When the five choices are sufficiently far apart. Answers that are close together require more precise calculation.

☑ **Try one of the choices.** If you're not sure what to do, choose an answer and plug it into the question. This will often lead you to the right answer more quickly. *Which answer should you choose?* Start with C. Answers are in size order, so C will always be the middle value. If C doesn't work, you might sometimes also be able to eliminate the two larger or two smaller answers, given the information in the problem.

☑ **Turn word problems into equations.** Reduce word problems into more easily understood equations. Let *x* be that for which you want to solve (time to complete a job, distance traveled, etc.). Then turn every element of the problem into a numerical expression. After you have all the numbers and symbols, it's usually easier to see how you should build the equation that will solve the problem.

☑ **Change all units to the units of the answer.** If, for example, a problem gives you information in terms of square feet but asks for an answer in terms of square yards, it will be easier to solve the problem if you first change all the units into yards, and then begin working.

☑ **Consider diagrams "treasure maps" to the solution.** Diagrams, especially for geometry problems, are filled with clues to the solution. Examine every diagram carefully. It's there for a reason. If there's no diagram, draw one of your own. It can make the solution immediately apparent.

CAUTION
You can use a calculator on the ACT Assessment mathematics test, but not on the Science Reasoning Test. Further, you can't use a calculator that includes or is part of a pocket organizer, pen-input device, electronic writing pad, or a keyboard pad. If your calculator needs a power cord, has a paper tape, or emits beeps or other noises during operation, you won't be allowed to use it during the ACT Assessment (the ACT Assessment regulations governing the use of calculators are published in the official ACT Assessment bulletin and on the ACT Assessment Web site). A scientific calculator (that meets all of the ACT Assessment restrictions) is probably your best bet.

☑ **"Read" a graph before looking at the questions.** Think of this as skimming a reading passage before beginning to work. Look at the structure of the graph (the labels on the axes, the units of measurement, and any information in the key). This is often more important than the data itself. Refer back to the graph as often as necessary.

A list of Don'ts:

☒ **Don't get paralyzed by lengthy calculations.** Most ACT Assessment math questions do not require complicated calculations. If you understand the structure of the problem, the solution is usually evident. So if you're overwhelmed with figuring, stop and move onto the next question.

☒ **Don't get involved with large numbers.** They're difficult to work with and time-consuming. When very large numbers are given in a problem, don't assume they're part of the needed calculation. Because no problem requires a calculator, if you're calculating large numbers, you're probably overlooking the simple principle that will solve the problem.

☒ **Don't over-rely on your calculator.** No ACT Assessment Math problem requires a calculator. Using a calculator opens you to the risk of mistakes. And if you make a mistake, there's no paper trail to follow to see where the mistake occurred. Limit calculator use to basic arithmetic, percentages, and square roots. And speaking of calculators . . .

☒ **Don't bring a new calculator to the test.** Every calculator operates just a bit differently with different keys for different functions. You don't have time during the test to learn how a new calculator works. If you must use a calculator, bring one you're familiar working with—and make sure it has fresh batteries.

☒ **Don't get fooled by trick questions.** Often a question is like a riddle; it prompts an obvious answer, but the obvious answer is wrong. Other times, the answer apparently is impossible to solve, such as the area of an irregular shape. What are you overlooking? In other words, certain questions ask you to "think outside the box." However . . .

☒ **Don't expect trick questions early in the test.** Because problems are ordered in complexity from the easy to the difficult, the first third of the test will have simple questions, with correspondingly simple answers. Even the middle third will be straightforward, although harder in difficulty. Don't over-complicate things by looking for trick questions on every line.

☒ **Don't assume a guess is right just because it's one of the answers.** Although rounding off and estimating are useful, outright guessing cannot replace calculation. Often the test choices include the most common student errors, so just because "your" answer is listed doesn't mean it's right. Work it out. Don't guess answers until you're running out of time.

PRACTICE EXERCISES

You've just learned some new skills for taking the ACT Assessment Math Test. The following exercises will help you to practice these new skills as well as to continue to familiarize yourself with the contents and format of the ACT Assessment.

There are two Math Test exercises in this chapter. Each exercise contains 12 problems and should be answered in 12 minutes. Do each exercise in one sitting in a quiet place, with no notes or reference material. You may use a calculator. Use a stopwatch or kitchen timer or have someone else watch the clock. When time is up, stop at once.

Score yourself only on those items you finished. When you're done, work through the rest of the exercise.

EXERCISES: THE ACT ASSESSMENT MATH TEST

Exercise 1

12 Questions • Time—12 Minutes

Directions: Solve each problem below and mark the oval representing the correct answer on your answer sheet.

Be careful not to spend too much time on any one question. Instead, solve as many questions as possible, and then use any remaining time to return to those questions you were unable to answer at first.

You may use a calculator on any problem in this test; however, not every problem requires the use of a calculator.

Diagrams that accompany problems may or may not be drawn to scale. Unless otherwise indicated, you may assume that all figures shown lie in a plane and that lines that appear straight are straight.

1. The advertised price of potatoes is 35¢ per pound. If a bag labeled "3 pounds" actually weighs $3\frac{1}{4}$ pounds, what is the closest approximation in cents to the actual price per pound for that bag?

   A. 32
   B. 33
   C. 34
   D. 35
   E. 36

2. $P=(-1,2)$; $Q=(3,5)$. What is the slope of PQ?

   F. $\frac{3}{4}$

   G. $\frac{7}{4}$

   H. $\frac{3}{2}$

   I. $\frac{4}{3}$

   J. $\frac{7}{2}$

3. If the larger circle shown below has an area of 36π, what is the circumference of the smaller circle?

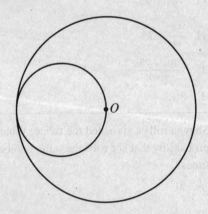

   A. 2π
   B. 4π
   C. 6π
   D. 8π
   E. 12π

4. If $r = -2$, then $r^4 + 2r^3 + 3r^2 + r = ?$
   F. −8
   G. −4
   H. 0
   I. 6
   J. 10

5. How many liters of 50% antifreeze must be mixed with 80 liters of 20% antifreeze to get a mixture that is 40% antifreeze?
   A. 80
   B. 100
   C. 120
   D. 140
   E. 160

6. Horace averaged 70 on his first m exams. After taking n more exams, he had an overall average of 75 for the year. In terms of n and m, what was Horace's average for his last n exams?
   F. $\dfrac{5m + 75}{n}$
   G. $\dfrac{5m}{n} + 75$
   H. $\dfrac{5n}{m} + 75$
   I. $\dfrac{70m + 75n}{m + n}$
   J. 80

7. Shayna rolls a six-sided die twice. What is the probability that she rolls the same number both times?
   A. 0
   B. $\dfrac{1}{36}$
   C. $\dfrac{2}{36}$
   D. $\dfrac{1}{12}$
   E. $\dfrac{7}{2}$

8. Which of the following is a common factor of both $x^2 - 4x - 5$ and $x^2 - 6x - 7$?
   F. $x - 5$
   G. $x - 7$
   H. $x - 1$
   I. $x + 5$
   J. $x + 1$

9. The diagram below shows a cube 3 units on a side with a 1×1 square hole cut through it. How many square units is the total surface area of the cube?

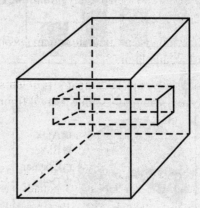

   A. 52
   B. 54
   C. 60
   D. 64
   E. 66

GO ON TO THE NEXT PAGE

Use the following information to answer questions 10–11.

The bar graph below shows the payments made by XYZ Corporation on contracts to four different suppliers last month. The same information is displayed in the pie chart.

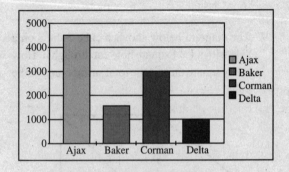

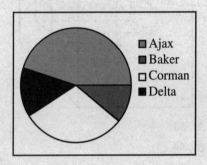

10. How many degrees are there in the angle of the sector of the pie chart representing Corman?

    F. 36

    G. 60

    H. 100

    I. 108

    J. 120

11. If Corman goes out of business and XYZ divides up its payments among the three suppliers Ajax, Baker, and Delta in the ratio of 3:2:1, how many degrees in the new pie chart will be in the sector representing Baker?

    A. 25

    B. 45

    C. 60

    D. 75

    E. 90

12. Which of the following is a correct factorization of $3x^2y^3 - 6xy^2$?

    F. $3xy^2(x - 2y)$

    G. $3xy^2(xy + 2)$

    H. $3xy^2(xy - 2)$

    I. $3x^2y(x - 2y)$

    J. $3x^2y^2(x - 2)$

Exercise 2

12 Questions • Time—12 Minutes

Directions: Solve each problem below and mark the oval representing the correct answer on your answer sheet.

Be careful not to spend too much time on any one question. Instead, solve as many questions as possible, and then use any remaining time to return to those questions you were unable to answer at first.

You may use a calculator on any problem in this test; however, not every problem requires the use of a calculator.

Diagrams that accompany problems may or may not be drawn to scale. Unless otherwise indicated, you may assume that all figures shown lie in a plane and that lines that appear straight are straight.

1. For which n is the remainder largest when 817,380 is divided by n?

   A. 4

   B. 5

   C. 6

   D. 8

   E. 9

2. Two rectangles have the same area. One is twice as long as the other. If the longer rectangle has a length of L and a width of W, what is the perimeter of the shorter rectangle?

   F. $2L + 2W$

   G. $2L + 4W$

   H. $L + 4W$

   I. $2L + W$

   J. $4L + 2W$

3. If $4x + 2y = 13$ and $4y - x = 8$, what is the value of $x + 2y$?

   A. –7

   B. –3

   C. 0

   D. 5

   E. 7

4. If the area of the rectangle in the figure below is equal to the area of the triangle, what is the perimeter of the triangle?

   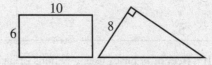

   F. 17

   G. $8 + \sqrt{15}$

   H. $8\sqrt{12}$

   I. 40

   J. 42

5. If $2^3 = \sqrt{N}$, what is N?

   A. 8

   B. 16

   C. 32

   D. 64

   E. 128

6. Four boys own a total of 150 baseball cards. If the first boy owns 28% of the cards, the second owns 24% of the cards, and the third owns three times as many cards as the fourth, what is the greatest number of cards owned by any one boy?

   F. 28

   G. 36

   H. 42

   I. 54

   J. 64

GO ON TO THE NEXT PAGE

7. If $(x - 2)(x + k) = x^2 + mx - 10$, then $mk = ?$
   A. −20
   B. −15
   C. 12
   D. 15
   E. 20

8. A box contains five blocks numbered 1, 2, 3, 4, and 5. John picks a block and replaces it. Lisa then picks a block. What is the probability that the sum of the numbers they picked is even?

   F. $\frac{9}{25}$

   G. $\frac{2}{5}$

   H. $\frac{1}{2}$

   I. $\frac{13}{25}$

   J. $\frac{3}{5}$

9. If a fleet of m buses uses g gallons of gasoline every two days, how many gallons will be needed by four buses every five days?

   A. $\frac{10g}{m}$

   B. $10gm$

   C. $\frac{10m}{g}$

   D. $\frac{20g}{m}$

   E. $\frac{5g}{4m}$

10. The ratio of the arithmetic mean of two numbers to one of the numbers is 3:5. What is the ratio of the smaller number to the larger?
    F. 1:5
    G. 1:4
    H. 1:3
    I. 2:5
    J. 1:2

11. The cost of producing a certain machine is directly proportional to the number of assembly line workers required and inversely proportional to the square of the number of hours of assembly line downtime during production. If the cost was $1,500 when there were 12 workers and only two hours of downtime, how many hours of downtime was there when nine workers were producing machines at the cost of $2,000 per machine?
    A. 1
    B. 1.5
    C. 2
    D. 2.5
    E. 3

12. Which of the following is one root of the equation $x^2 - 4x + 13 = 0$?
    F. −1
    G. 5
    H. $4 + 3i$
    I. $2 - 6i$
    J. $2 + 3i$

ANSWER KEYS AND EXPLANATIONS

Exercise 1

1. A	4. J	7. E	10. I
2. F	5. E	8. J	11. E
3. C	6. G	9. D	12. H

1. **A.** At 35¢ per pound, the 3-pound bag will be marked $1.05 or 105¢. Dividing this by the weight of the bag, we have $105 \div 3.25 \approx 32.3$. Hence, 32 is the closest answer.

2. **F.** $m_{PQ} = \dfrac{5 - 2}{3 - (-1)} = \dfrac{3}{4}$

3. **C.** The larger circle has an area of $A_L = \pi(r)^2 = 36\pi$. This means that $r^2 = 36$, and $r = 6$. The diameter of the smaller circle equals the radius of the larger one, so its radius is $\frac{1}{2}(6) = 3$. Therefore, its circumference must be $C_S = 2\pi(3) = 6\pi$.

4. **J.** Substituting: $(-2)^4 + 2(-2)^3 + 3(-2)^2 + (-2) = 16 - 16 + 12 - 2 = 10$.

5. **E.** Let x be the unknown number of liters of 50% antifreeze. The final mixture will have $(x + 80)$ liters, and the amount of antifreeze will be:

    $0.50x + 0.20(80) = 0.40(x + 80)$

    $\qquad 0.5x + 16 = 0.4x + 32$

    $\qquad 0.1x = 16; \; x = 160$

6. **G.** Because his average overall was 75, he had a total overall score of $75(m + n) = 75m + 75n$ on $n + m$ exams. Since he averaged 70 on m exams, he had a total of $70m$ on the first m. That means that his total on the last n exams was $75m + 75n - 70m = 5m + 75n$, and his average was $(5m + 75n) \div n = \frac{5m}{n} + 75$.

7. **E.** It really does not matter what number you roll on the first roll; in any case, the chance of matching it the next time you roll is $\frac{1}{6}$.

8. **J.** $x^2 - 4x - 5 = (x - 5)(x + 1)$, and $x^2 - 6x - 7 = (x - 7)(x + 1)$. The common factor is $x + 1$.

9. **D.** Each side of the square has an area of $3 \times 3 = 9$. Because there are six sides, the original cube had a surface area of 54 square units. Two 1×1 squares are now missing, making the outside area 52. The "hole" has four 3×1 rectangular sides with a total area of 12, giving a grand surface area total of 64.

10. **I.** Totaling the payments made to all four suppliers, you have $4,500 + $1,500 + $3,000 + $1,000 = $10,000. Of this total, $3,000 was paid to Corman (that is, 30% of the total). Hence, the sector representing Corman must be 30% of $360° = 108°$.

11. **E.** 25% of $10,000 is $2,500. Carmen did a total of $3,000 business. When they divided the total into the ratio 3:2:1, which is a total of 6 parts, each part is equal to $500. Baker's business increased b $1,000. $1,000 + $1,500 = $2,500, which is a quarter of the $10,000 total business represented on the chart. One-fourth of $360°$ is $90°$.

12. **H.** The first term could be thought of as $3xy^2(xy)$, and the second as $3xy^2(-2)$. Hence, we can take out the common factor $3xy^2$, leaving as the other factor $(xy - 2)$.

Exercise 2

1. D	4. I	7. D	10. F
2. H	5. D	8. I	11. B
3. E	6. I	9. A	12. J

1. **D.** 817,380 is divisible by all the numbers in the list except 8. Hence, 8 must give the largest remainder, because it is the only remainder that is not zero. To confirm, start with 5; 7,380 is divisible by 5, because it ends in 0. It is divisible by 2 because it is even, and by 4 because 80 is divisible by 4. However, it is not divisible by 8, because 380 isn't. In addition, the sum of its digits is 27, which is divisible by 3 and by 9. Because it is divisible by both 2 and 3, it is also divisible by 6.

2. **H.** The perimeter of the longer rectangle is $2L + 2W$. The other rectangle must have a length of $\frac{1}{2}L$ and a width of $2W$, since the area is the same. Thus, the second rectangle has a perimeter of $2(\frac{1}{2}L) + 2(2W) = L + 4W$.

3. **E.** We could solve the two equations simultaneously to find x and y. However, it is easier to proceed as follows: Reorder the terms in the second equation so as to start with the x term. Thus:

   $-x + 4y = 8$

   Add to this the second equation:

   $-x + 4y = 8$

   $\underline{4x + 2y = 13}$

   $3x + 6y = 21$

   Divide by 3:

   $x + 2y = 7$

4. **I.** The area of the rectangle is $6(10) = 60$. Using the legs of the right triangle as base and height (with the unknown leg called h), we have $(8)h = 60$; that is, $4h = 60$, and $h = 15$. Hence, the triangle is an 8–15–17 right triangle (one of the famous "Pythagorean triples") with a perimeter of 40.

5. **D.** $2^3 = 8$, and 8 is the square root of 64.

6. **I.** 28% of $150 = 0.28(150) = 42$. 24% of $150 = 0.24(150) = 36$. Thus, $150 - 42 - 36 = 72$ cards, which are divided between the other two boys in the ratio of 3:1. That is, one boy owns $\frac{1}{4}$ of the 72 cards (18), and other owns $\frac{3}{4}$ of them (54).

7. **D.** Using the FOIL Method: $(x - 2)(x + k) = x^2 + (k - 2)x - 2k$. Because $-2k = -10$, $k = 5$; and since $(k - 2) = m$, $m = 3$. Hence, $km = 15$.

8. **I.** Because each person had five choices, there are 25 possible pairs of numbers. The only way the sum could be odd is if one person picked an odd number and the other picked an even number. Suppose that John chose the odd number and Lisa the even one. John had three possible even numbers to select from, and for each of these, Lisa had two possible choices, for a total of $(3)(2) = 6$ possibilities. However, you could have had John pick an even number and Lisa pick an odd one, and there are also six ways to do that. Hence, out of 25 possibilities, 12 have an odd total and 13 have an even total. The probability is $\frac{13}{25}$.

9. **A.** Running m buses for two days is the same as running one bus for $2m$ days. If we use g gallons of gasoline, each bus uses $\frac{g}{2m}$ gallons each day. So if you multiply the number of gallons per day used by each bus by the number of buses and the number of days, you should get total usage. Thus: $\frac{g}{2m} \times 4 \times 5 = \frac{10g}{m}$.

10. **F.** Calling the numbers x and y, $\frac{x+y}{2:x} = \frac{3}{5}$. That is, $\frac{x+y}{2x} = \frac{3}{5}$. Cross-multiplying: $5x + 5y = 6x$; $5y = x$.

    Hence, one number is five times as large as the other, so their ratio is 1:5.

11. **B.** Letting $C = $ cost, $w = $ number of workers, and $t = $ time in hours, we have the relationship $C = k\frac{w}{t^2}$. Therefore, when $w = 12$ and $t = 2$, we have $1500 = k = 3k$; therefore, $k = 500$. Using $k = 500$ and substituting

    $w = 9$ and $C = 2000$, we have:

    $2000 = \frac{500 \times 9}{t^2} = \frac{4500}{t^2}$

    Multiplying by t^2 and dividing by 2000, we have:

    $t^2 = \frac{9}{4}$; $t = \frac{3}{2} = 1.5$.

12. **J.** Using the quadratic formula with $a = 1$, $b = -4$, and $c = 13$:

    $x = \frac{-(-4)\pm\sqrt{-4^2-4(1)(13)}}{2(1)} = \frac{4\pm\sqrt{16-52}}{2} = \frac{4\pm\sqrt{-36}}{2}$

    $x = \frac{4\pm6i}{2} = 2 \pm 3i$

    Hence, one root is $2 + 3i$.

ARE YOU READY TO MOVE ON?

How well do you understand the contents and format of the ACT Assessment Math Test? How well have you incorporated your new skills into your test-taking behavior?

After you've corrected each exercise, find the number of correct answers below. This will give you an idea of whether you need to go to the Math Review immediately following this chapter, or whether you can move on to another subject area.

Score Key for Each Practice Exercise

Number Correct	Score	Suggested Action
0–3	Poor	Study the review chapter and complete the exercises there. Study this chapter again.
4–6	Below average	Study problem areas in the review chapter; do at least one exercise. Study this chapter again.
7–8	Average	Study this chapter again if you wish to and have time. Skim problem areas in the review chapter if you have time.
9–10	Above average	You may move on to a new subject.
11–12	Excellent	You're ready for the ACT Assessment Math Test.

Summary: What You Need to Know About the ACT Assessment Math Test

- The ACT Assessment Math Test will include 14 questions on pre-algebra, 10 questions on elementary algebra, 9 questions on intermediate algebra, 9 questions on coordinate geometry, 14 questions on plane geometry, and 4 questions on trigonometry. The 60 different questions must be completed in one sitting that is 60 minutes long.

- Read diagrams and graphs before the appropriate question, looking for structural information and analyzing the data given.

- Don't get paralyzed by lengthy calculations or large numbers. The test is designed to be taken without a calculator. If you're overwhelmed by calculations and number size, you're missing the usually simple principle that will solve the problem.

- Translate word problems into equations; give numbers and symbols to every element in the word problem.

- Keep moving, both within a problem and within the test. If you're at a loss, plug the middle answer C into the equation and work backwards.

- Round off large numbers and estimate for faster, easier figuring.

- Questions are arranged from the easiest to the hardest, so don't waste time looking for trick questions early on.

- Substitute numbers for symbols to make calculations easier.

- You may use a calculator, but don't over-rely on it. The answer usually lies in concepts and shortcuts, not calculations.

The ACT Assessment Reading Test

The ACT Assessment Reading Test determines how well you understand a wide variety of written material. It tests not only what you have already learned, but it also measures your readiness to take on college-level reading. Your reading level is critical to college success, no matter what your major. In this chapter, you learn about the format and content of ACT Assessment Reading questions and the best strategies for tackling that portion of the test. You also get a chance to practice the skills and strategies you've learned on a series of timed, practice exercises that simulate the questions you will encounter on the Reading portion of the ACT Assessment.

WHAT TO EXPECT ON THE ACT ASSESSMENT READING TEST

The selections on the ACT Assessment Reading Test include the type of sophisticated, complex, and subtle reading that college students are called upon to do. In these selections, you need to do more than just understand the broad facts presented in the passage and identify the main idea. You also need to understand the relationships between the facts, to find the important details, and to see the implications, or the ideas that are suggested rather than directly stated in a piece. You will answer questions that have to do with the writer's role, such as whether an author's logic is sound or flawed and if his or her presentation is factual or opinionated. Finally, you also are asked to answer questions about the passage itself—its form, structure, and style.

A CLOSER LOOK AT ACT ASSESSMENT READING QUESTIONS AND THEIR FORMAT

The ACT Assessment Reading Test consists of four passages, from 700 to 900 words each, followed by a group of 10 questions. Both the reading and the answering of all 40 questions must be done in one 35-minute sitting. So plan on spending eight to nine minutes on each section, about half of that time on reading, the other half on answering the questions.

ROAD MAP

- *Learn What to Expect on the ACT Assessment Reading Test*
- *Understand the Format and Content of ACT Assessment Reading Questions*
- *Learn ACT Assessment Reading Strategies for Success*
- *Practice Your ACT Assessment Reading Skills*
- *Evaluate Your Progress*

The four ACT Assessment reading passages include one fiction narrative and three non-fiction selections in the areas of the natural sciences, social studies, and humanities. The fiction passage might be a short story, entire in itself, or a selection from a short story, novella, or novel. The ACT Assessment does not use material from poetry or drama. The nonfiction passages include excerpts from books, magazines, and journals and embrace a wide variety of topics. The area of social studies includes history, political science, economics, anthropology, psychology and sociology. The natural sciences include the physical sciences, biology, chemistry, and physics. Selections about the humanities might discuss music, the visual arts, theater, dance, architecture, or philosophy. There is only one passage in each main area, and any of these topics may be on a given test. You don't need to have taken a course in the subject to do well on the exam. The passage contains all of the information you need to answer the questions.

A strong vocabulary will give you a distinct edge when you tackle ACT Assessment Reading questions. For a review of important ACT Assessment vocabulary, see Chapter 10, "Reading Review: Vocabulary," later in this book.

The following example is a paragraph from a larger passage taken from the natural sciences, and the corresponding question.

 Just shaking a can of mixed nuts can show you how problematic granular material can be. The nuts don't "mix"; they "unmix" and sort themselves out, with the larger Brazil nuts on top and the smaller peanuts on the bottom. In this activity and others, granular matter's behavior apparently goes counter to the second law of thermodynamics, which states that entropy, or disorder, tends to increase in any natural system.

The passage suggests that a can of mixed nuts seems to disobey the second law of thermodynamics because it:

A. fails to mix when shaken.

B. becomes increasingly disordered over time.

C. sorts smaller nuts to the bottom rather than the top of the can.

D. does not readily separate into different kinds of nuts.

(Answer: A)

As you can see, the passage discusses the properties of granular material and includes references to such scientific principles as the laws of thermodynamics, yet no prior knowledge of the properties of granular material or the laws of thermodynamics are needed to answer the question. In this example, the last sentence of the paragraph describes the second law of thermodynamics, and it tells you that the behavior of the nuts (sorting themselves out when shaken) goes counter to that law.

LEARN THE DIRECTIONS

The directions for the ACT Assessment Reading Test are similar to the following:

> **Directions:** This test consists of four passages, each followed by several questions. Read each passage, select the correct answer for each question, and mark the oval representing the correct answer on your answer sheet.

TIP
Reread these directions several times until you're totally familiar with them. Then the day of the test, save time by *not* reading them. This is one of your overall strategies for scoring higher on the ACT Assessment.

STRATEGIES FOR SUCCESS ON THE ACT ASSESSMENT READING TEST

In other chapters of this book, you've learned general strategies and techniques that will help you prepare for success on the ACT Assessment. Getting a good night's sleep, eating a healthy breakfast, and staying calm and focused are all important to doing well on the exam. Here are some success strategies specifically designed to help you score higher on ACT Assessment Reading. As with other areas of the ACT Assessment, the Reading Test offers its own challenges. With the preparation you receive here, you can tackle the ACT Assessment Reading Test with confidence and get high scores on this critical portion of the exam.

THE THREE-STEP METHOD: PREVIEW, READ, REVIEW

The reading part of the ACT Assessment Reading Test is so time-consuming that it's tempting to jump in quickly and rush through it. However, you'll get much higher scores and remain much calmer if you use two powerful tools—patience and preparation. Do these three steps before answering any of the ACT Assessment Reading questions:

1. Preview
2. Read
3. Review

This three-stage reading method has been proven as the best way of getting the most possible information out of anything in writing. The method seems to take longer than just attacking the page but with practice you will actually be able to read more quickly—while at the same time increasing your comprehension.

This three-step method is so important, that it's worth talking a bit more about what is involved in each step.

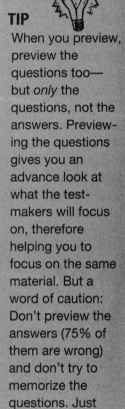

1. Preview

Preview is just another word for skim. There are two effective ways of skimming. You can either let your eyes quickly scan the page, picking up as much information as you can. Or you can actually read selected sentences from the passage: specifically, the first sentence of each paragraph in the passage, and the last sentence of the entire passage. Some people read the first and last sentence of each paragraph. Find the method that works for you.

If you're not used to skimming, use your finger as a guide for your eyes. Sweep your index finger back and forth down the page, with your gaze fixed on your fingertip. Your eyes will follow your finger, moving more quickly than you're used to, yet you will still pick up information about the passage.

What sort of information are you looking for? Look for the general content, the organization, the style. In just a few seconds you'll be able to tell, for example, whether an article is about nuclear physics or deep-sea diving, whether it's organized around an experiment or around a day in the life of a diving instructor, and whether its tone is scholarly or talky and familiar.

Knowing the content, organization, and style—and whatever else you can pick up in those few seconds—prepares you by actually making you more receptive when you read. There are no "surprises" to which to adjust. When you return to the beginning to read, you're all set for nuclear physics, or whatever.

This first step needn't take more than 30 seconds for the average ACT Assessment reading passage. Practice with a watch until you get a feel for it.

2. Read

Having previewed the passage, read it. Because the passage will be about 750 words long and the average high school student reads 250 words a minute, it should only take about three minutes.

How should you read? With a pencil in hand. Identify key points and logical connections as you find them. Underline them, circle them, or make stars at that point in the margin. The physical act of marking the text strengthens your memory of these ideas. In addition, the marks themselves make it easier to find key parts of the passage if you need to locate them later to answer a question.

Specifically, here's what to underline: the theme of the passage, the main idea of each paragraph, and the connections between the ideas. The theme of the passage is a sentence that summarizes the content. Though it's usually at the beginning of a passage, sometimes the theme is more concisely stated in the conclusion. Choose whichever you think is better. Next, each paragraph should somehow develop a point of the theme; when you find the sentence that summarizes that point (often called the topic sentence in writing class), underline it. Finally, look for the way the ideas are connected. Is this a pro-con debate? Mark one paragraph "pro" and the other "con." Is this a description of a sequence of events? Mark the paragraphs 1, 2, 3, etc; circle dates if a historical event is described.

3. Review

You skimmed the passage beforehand to prepare yourself. Now skim it again *after* reading. This helps remind you of the opening, of the main ideas you discovered through reading, and of one or two of the most important details (or at least where the details are located in the passage). Also, if the passage was particularly difficult, going back to the beginning sheds light on earlier paragraphs that you might not have fully understood at the time. Finally, because you have now previewed, then read the material, reviewing helps you better understand the overall organization you might have only glimpsed before. Basically, reviewing is a way of summing up the pieces and making them all come together in your mind.

If you marked the passage properly (which you can easily start to do with a minimum of practice), these notes form the guidelines for your review.

Because reviewing is skimming, it should take approximately the same time as skimming—about 30 seconds. In total you've spent about four minutes on the reading process, which still leaves you four minutes to answer the questions—usually more than enough time.

CONCENTRATE ON MAIN IDEAS

You've probably heard the expression "couldn't see the forest for the trees." That means being so preoccupied with individual details (the trees) that you lose sight of the overall picture (the forest). The same preoccupation often happens with reading. Certain types of passages contain innumerable details that are not essential to understanding the theme. Although the details support the theory, if you had to edit them, you would probably still have a coherent well-written passage.

It's important that you be able to distinguish between main ideas and details. The main ideas are worth focusing on; the supporting details are usually not. You can—and should—return to the passage later if a question asks for a specific detail, but the details don't need your attention up front. How can you tell one from the other? Look for these contrasts:

- **General vs. Specific.** This is the difference between saying "colors" and saying "red, green, ocher, and fuchsia." Main ideas—whether the main idea of the passage or paragraph—are broad and encompass whole categories; details explore the individual items within each category.

- **First or Last vs. Middle.** Main ideas tend to appear at the very beginning of a paragraph or passage as introduction, or at the end as conclusion. Details, on the other hand, tend to appear in the middle: in the middle of paragraphs, in the middle of the passage.

NOTE
Remember, you should plan on spending about 8 minutes on each ACT Assessment Reading passage. Using the three-step method, you will spend about half of that time reading the passage.

Step 1: 30 seconds
Step 2: 3 minutes
Step 3: 30 seconds

Total time: 4 minutes. That leaves you 4 minutes to read and answer the questions that accompany the passage. Use the exercises and practice exams in this book to work toward this timing.

- **Necessary vs. Needless.** The main idea is needed to make sense of what you're reading. Details, although they support the idea and flesh it out, are not needed for a basic understanding.

Details can be skimmed; main ideas must have your full attention.

Example: Married to Nicholas since 1804, the former Princess Alix of Hesse-Darmstadt and one of Queen Victoria's numerous grandchildren, the Tsarina (called Alexandra after her marriage), had given birth to four daughters—Olga, Tatiana, Marie, and Anastasia—between 1897 and 1901. But the laws of succession decreed that only a male could succeed the Tsar, so the birth of Alexis, which assured the continuation of the three-hundred-year-old Romanov dynasty, was a cause of great rejoicing for his parents as well throughout the vast empire.

All the details (which in this case happen to begin the paragraph and extend through the middle) are not needed for basic understanding. You don't need to remember Princess Alix's lineage, the change in her name, or the names of her daughters. The main idea is at the end: at last a son was born and the dynasty would live on.

Here is another example, this one from a typical social studies reading passage:

Do women tend to devalue the worth of their work? Do they apply different standards to rewarding their own work than they do to rewarding the work of others? These were the questions asked by Michigan State University psychologists Lawrence Messe and Charlene Callahan-Levy. Past experiments had shown that when women were asked to decide how much to pay themselves and other people for the same job, they paid themselves less. Following up on this finding, Messe and Callahan-Levy designed experiments to test several popular explanations of why women tend to shortchange themselves in pay situations.

The first two sentences in this paragraph state broad questions about women and their attitudes toward work. The sentences that follow delve into the details about the work of two psychologists who tried to explore these questions experimentally. (Subsequent paragraphs of the passage describe the experiments in even more detail.)

Thus, the first two sentences of this paragraph state the main idea—the topic around which the entire paragraph revolves. The remaining sentences give details: the names of the psychologists, the fact that they were doing follow-up work in the wake of previous experiments dealing with the same subject, and so on. The most important point for you to gather from this paragraph is the fact that the psychologists were interested in exploring women's attitudes toward work and themselves. If you understand this, you can track down specific details as needed to answer the questions.

Here's another example, this one from a natural sciences passage:

Urodeles, a class of vertebrates that includes newts and salamanders, have the enviable ability to regenerate arms, legs, tails, heart muscle, jaws, spinal cords, and other organs when these are damaged or lost. Similarly, planaria, a form of simple worm, can be sliced and diced in hundreds of pieces, with each piece giving rise to a completely new animal. However, while both urodeles and planaria have the capacity to regenerate, they use entirely different means of accomplishing this feat.

The last sentence states the main idea of this paragraph, tying together the details previously stated: both types of animals being discussed (urodeles and planaria) can regenerate organs, though they do so very differently. (Presumably, the later paragraphs of this passage will explain how.)

In this paragraph, the first sentence, dealing with urodeles, gives many specific facts that you don't need to master, including a list of some of the organs the urodele can regenerate (arms, legs, tails, and so on). The second sentence gives similar specific facts about planaria. The main idea which gives them their broader significance is the concept of regeneration—the unusual ability that unites urodeles and planaria and on which the passage as a whole focuses.

You can always return to the passage to look up a specific detail on the slim chance it will appear on a question. Don't try to understand or memorize the details if they're complicated. In a certain way, the details are a distraction. Only the main idea is fundamental to your basic understanding.

SEE HOW THE IDEAS ARE CONNECTED

Another important step in the reading process is to look for how the ideas are connected. A well-written passage does not present random ideas, but rather ideas that are logically connected to the main idea or that somehow proceed from each other. If you understand these ideas and the connections among them, you truly understand the passage as a whole.

Quite often, the structure of ideas will be made very explicit, even obvious. Consider, for example, a reading passage containing five paragraphs. Here are the opening sentences of each paragraph:

(1) Historians have long debated the reasons for the defeat of the Confederacy in the American Civil War.

(2) For decades, the dominant theory held that the North's victory was due primarily to the superior economic resources available to the Union armies.

(3) A second school of historians pointed instead to the geographic advantages enjoyed by the Northern generals.

(4) In recent years, however, more and more historians have begun to claim that, contrary to traditional Southern belief, the Northern generalship was consistently superior.

(5) In the end, perhaps the most likely explanation of the Northern victory is that it was caused by a combination of several factors.

Simply by reading these five sentences you get a very good idea of the content and structure of the whole passage. The passage deals with the issue of why the North won the Civil War. Its structure is clear-cut. Paragraph (1) sets forth the question to be discussed. Paragraphs (2), (3), and (4) each suggest a different answer to the question. And paragraph (5) concludes the passage by suggesting a possible resolution of the disagreement.

Why is it helpful to recognize the logical structure of a reading passage? It helps you in several ways:

- **The structure points out the main ideas.** Recognizing the structure makes it easy to see the main ideas of the passage. In the preceding example, the main ideas are the three separate theories being presented and discussed.

- **The structure tells the purpose of the details.** The structure tells you the purpose of the details, even when you don't know what they are. In this passage, for example, we see only the first sentence of the second paragraph, yet we can still imagine that the details will probably be specific examples of the superior resources enjoyed by the North (coal mines, factories, railroad lines, and so on).

- **The structure organizes the information.** The logical structure organizes the information in the passage, making it easy to locate any detail about which you might be asked. In this passage, if a question focuses on a detail related to the theory of Northern generalship, you'll be able to find the relevant paragraph quickly.

- **The structure explains the relationship between the ideas.** The structure explains how the main ideas are related to one another. In this case, the main ideas are three different, conflicting explanations of the same historical event.

A passage's structure is not always this clear-cut and logical, but a structure of some kind is usually present. With practice, you can learn to recognize it.

Common Types of Logical Structure

The most common ways of organizing nonfiction prose—especially the nonfiction seen on the ACT Assessment—include the following:

1. **Several theories about one idea.**

   Example: The extinction of the dinosaurs (one idea) might have been caused by an inductee food supply, an ice age, or a catastrophic event, such as a meteor strike or global flood (several theories).

   Often one theory will appear in each paragraph.

2. **One idea with several examples.**

   Example: Evidence of a global flood exterminating the dinosaurs (one idea) can be seen in fossilized remains, in abrupt changes in the earth's structure, and in the universality of the flood myth (several examples).

Again, this is often structured with one example per paragraph.

3. **Pros and cons of one idea.**

Example: Does the dinosaur record support evolution? Yes, it does (with reasons why), followed by No, it doesn't (with reasons why).

The ideas supporting the pro side might be gathered into one paragraph or might be developed into a paragraph each, depending on the length and depth of the piece. The con side would be constructed in the same way as the pro side.

4. **Compare or contrast.**

Example: A comparison between the extinction of the dinosaur and the extinction of the dodo.

Each idea would have to be viewed from both sides: natural extinction vs. manmade extinction, extinction of a whole class vs. extinction of a single species, and so on.

5. **Cause and effect.**

Example: A meteor strike caused the extinction of the dinosaurs in the following way.

The most straightforward use of cause and effect is to present reasons in chronological order: first, the meteor hit, causing massive local destruction; second, it sent up a huge cloud of dust, obscuring the sun; third, the darkened sky led to a decrease in plant life and lowered temperatures—and so on. Other methods include starting with a later event, because, for example, it's more dramatic (the final moments of the last dinosaur on earth). This is a "flashback"; afterwards the passage returns to the chronological order.

BEGIN WITH THE TYPE OF PASSAGE YOU LIKE BEST

On the day of the test, open the booklet to the Reading Test and scan the beginning of each of the four sections. You might get such diverse openings as:

1. The periodic table is a listing of each element along with its *atomic number* (the number of protons in the *nucleus* or center of the atom) and its *atomic mass* (the combined weight of protons and neutrons in the nucleus).

2. In the summer of 1904, the great Russian empire was, unlike most of the countries of Europe by that time, still under the control of one man, the 36-year-old Tsar Nicholas II, who had ruled since the death of his father, Alexander III, ten years before.

3. "Give it back," he said hotly, with one hand wiping the tears from his eyes and with the other reaching for the stuffed bear his sister now held just a few taunting inches from his fingertips.

4. The structure of a building designed by Frank Lloyd Wright—no, even just our first glimpse of it—makes our own homes and offices seem so unnatural as to be accidental; and we wonder how we could have settled for so much less for so long.

Chemistry, history, a story, and architecture: natural science, social science, fiction, and the humanities. Hopefully at least one of these categories prompted enthusiasm when you saw it. That's the first passage you should read, even if it comes later in the test section. Begin there, being careful to skip to the appropriate number on the answer sheet.

Why begin with "dessert"? You'll probably read your favorite type of passage more quickly, saving you time later. You'll also remember and understand more of it, thus answering more questions correctly. Starting with your favorite actually helps you increase your score.

DON'T PICK THE FIRST ANSWER THAT SOUNDS EITHER GOOD OR FAMILIAR

On non-math questions, answers might have degrees of "rightness and wrongness." Answer A might be plausible, but if you keep reading, you'll see that answer B sounds even better, and answer C best of all. Read every choice.

Also, don't pick an answer just because it sounds familiar. The right answer is obviously drawn from the passage; however, the wrong answer might be drawn from the passage, too. The answer sounds familiar because you've just read it, but familiarity alone doesn't guarantee accuracy. Refer back to the passage.

DON'T PICK AN ANSWER JUST BECAUSE IT'S TRUE

Most of the ACT Assessment passages will be about unfamiliar topics. Occasionally, however, you might encounter a passage on a topic you recognize or even know quite well. This can be helpful as you'll probably find the passage easy to understand.

But this can also be dangerous. You cannot bring your own knowledge or opinions to the questions and answers. You might be tempted to pick an answer choice because you happen to know it's true, or because you personally agree with it. Don't do it. The answer that is correct is the one that is based specifically on the information in the passage—even if you happen to disagree.

Example:

> **Q** The passage suggests that the murder of Rasputin was motivated primarily by:
>
> A. the growing demand among the Russian populace for true democracy.
>
> B. hostility in the popular press against both Rasputin and the imperial couple
>
> C. intrigues and jealousies among the Tsar's retinue.
>
> D. increasing disaffection with the war among many Russians.
>
> (Answer: C)

Perhaps Russian history is your favorite subject, or Rasputin your favorite historical character. You've read numerous theories explaining his murder and might even have your own theory, which might or might not be reflected in the answers. *It does not matter.* You can only choose the answer given in the passage. In this case, the correct answer is C, because that answer was supported by the information in the passage.

DEFINE WORDS BY THEIR CONTEXT

Certain questions will ask what a word means in the context of the passage. The answers might include synonyms for the definition which, under other circumstances, could be true, but for the correct ACT Assessment answer you must look for the meaning that best fits the context of the passage. Refer back to the passage to be sure.

Example:

 As used in line 12, the word "impress" most nearly means:

A. attract the favorable notice of

B. coerce

C. stamp

D. replace

After eliminating answer D, you're confused, because "impress" could mean A, B, *or* C. (Or worse, you simply pick A as the first good answer and read no further.) You must return to the passage to get the context. Conceivably, it could be any of these sentences:

Tony was eager to impress the college admissions officer with his intelligence and charm.

During the early 1800s, officers of the British Navy would sometimes impress American citizens into serving as sailors on British ships.

The king's scribe used a metal seal to impress the hot wax with the royal coat-of-arms.

Only one answer will be right, and to discover that, you must always refer back to the word's context in the passage.

SUCCESS STRATEGY ROUNDUP: A LIST OF DO'S AND DON'TS

Here's the short version of the above advice, along with a few other miscellaneous tips, arranged in a handy list of dos and don'ts. After you understand each point and the reasoning behind it, you need only know the boldface sentence to jog your memory—whether you're working on the exercises at the end of this chapter, your full-length sample tests, or the ACT Assessment itself.

A list of Do's:

☑ **Preview, read, review.** Begin each of the passages by skimming both the passage and the questions (skip the answer choices at this point). Then read the passage, keeping the questions in mind so you'll know for what to look. Afterwards, quickly review what you've just read. When answering questions, return to the passage whenever you need to.

☑ **Focus on the big ideas.** Look for the overall theme of the passage, as well as the main idea of each paragraph. The overall theme should be in the first paragraph of the passage; main ideas of each paragraph should be early in the paragraph as introduction or at the end of the paragraph as summary.

☑ **Recognize the major ways of structural organization.** Most passages will be organized in one of the following ways: several theories about one idea, one idea with several examples, pro-and-con arguments on one idea, a cause-and-effect sequence, or a comparison or contrast between two events, ideas, or people.

☑ **Read with your pencil in hand.** Underline the main idea of the passage and the main points of each paragraph. This will help you remember as well as be an easy way to return to the idea when you're answering questions. Also note important sequences, historical dates, anything you think will be important.

☑ **Start with your favorite type of reading.** By starting with your favorite type of reading, you'll read and answer questions more quickly, probably answer more questions correctly, and boost your confidence.

☑ **Read every choice before selecting your answer.** Don't stop with the first one that "sounds good" or familiar. There are degrees of rightness. Read each choice.

☑ **Define words by their context.** Some vocabulary questions will want the meaning of a word. Choose the meaning that's closest to the meaning of the word in the context of the passage.

☑ **Answer every question before going to the next passage.** Don't plan on returning to difficult questions at the end. The question will still be difficult and the passage will be fainter in your memory, requiring that you spend time reading it over again. Answer every question that you can while you're there, make reasonable guesses about the others, then move on.

A list of Don'ts:

☒ **Don't get stopped by details.** Paragraphs might be packed with details that have little to do with what you'll be asked. Skim the details. If a question does ask about them, you can return to them later.

☒ **Don't preview the answer choices.** When skimming over the passage and questions, don't look at the answers. It's time-consuming—plus 75 percent of the answers are wrong. You don't want to be looking for the wrong information when you begin the actual reading.

☒ **Don't try to answer every question from memory.** You've read the passage quickly and only once. That's usually not enough to distinguish between subtle differences in the choices. Go back to the passage and check.

☒ **Don't pick an answer simply because it's true.** One of the choices might be a statement you know to be true. Being factual does not necessarily make it the answer to the question. Understand what is being asked.

☒ **Don't be worried by the subject.** Never had an economics course? Never studied philosophy? Don't worry. You don't need prior knowledge of any subject to do well on the ACT Assessment Reading Test. All the information you need to answer the questions will be contained in the passage.

PRACTICE EXERCISES

You've just learned some new skills for taking the ACT Assessment Reading Test. The following exercises will help you to practice these new skills as well as to continue to familiarize yourself with the contents and format of the ACT Assessment.

There are two Reading Test exercises in this chapter. Each exercise contains 2 passages followed by 10 questions each and should be answered in 18 minutes. Do each exercise in one sitting in a quiet place, with no notes or reference material. Use a stopwatch or kitchen timer or have someone else watch the clock. When time is up, stop at once.

Score yourself only on those items you finished. When you're done, work through the rest of the exercise.

EXERCISES: THE ACT ASSESSMENT READING TEST

Exercise 1

20 Questions • Time—18 Minutes

Directions: This exercise consists of two passages, each followed by several questions. Read each passage, select the correct answer for each question, and mark the oval representing the correct answer on your answer sheet.

Passage I—PROSE FICTION

Shipwrecks are *a propos* of nothing. If men could only train for them and have them occur when they had reached pink condition, there would be less drowning at sea.

(5) Of the four in the dinghy, none had slept any time worth mentioning for two days and two nights previous to embarking in the dinghy, and in the excitement of clambering about the deck of a foundering ship they had also forgotten to eat heartily.

(10) For these reasons, and for others, neither the oiler nor the correspondent was fond of rowing at this time. The correspondent wondered how in the name of all that was sane there could be people who thought it amusing to row a boat. It was not an amusement; it was a diabolical

(15) punishment, and even a genius of mental aberrations could never conclude that it was anything but a horror to the muscles and a crime against the back. He mentioned to the boat in general how the amusement of rowing struck him, and the weary-faced oiler smiled in

(20) full sympathy. Previously to the foundering, by the way, the oiler had worked double-watch in the engine room of the ship.

"Take her easy, now, boys," said the captain. "Don't spend yourselves. If we have to run a surf you'll need all

(25) your strength, because we'll sure have to swim for it. Take your time."

Slowly the land arose from the sea. From a black line it became a line of black and a line of white, trees and sand. Finally, the captain said that he could make

(30) out a house on the shore.

"That's the house of refuge, sure," said the cook. "They'll see us before long, and come out after us." The distant lighthouse reared high. "The keeper ought to be able to make us out now, if he's looking through

(35) a spyglass," said the captain. "He'll notify the life-saving people."

"None of those other boats could have got ashore to give word of the wreck," said the oiler, in a low voice. "Else the life-boat would be out hunting us."

(40) Slowly and beautifully the land loomed out of the sea. The wind came again. It had veered from the northeast to the southeast.

Finally, a new sound struck the ears of the men in the boat. It was the low thunder of the surf on the

(45) shore. All but the oarsman watched the shore grow. Under the influence of this expansion, doubt and direful apprehension was leaving the minds of the men. The management of the boat was still most absorbing, but it could not prevent a quiet cheerful-

(50) ness. In an hour, perhaps, they would be ashore.

Their backbones had become thoroughly used to balancing in the boat, and they now rode this wild colt of a dinghy like circus men. The correspondent thought that he had been drenched to the skin, but happening to

(55) feel in the top pocket of his coat, he found therein eight cigars. Four of them were soaked with sea-water; four were perfectly dry. After a search, somebody produced three dry matches, and thereupon the four waifs rode impudently in their little boat, and with an assurance of

(60) an impending rescue shining in their eyes, puffed at the

big cigars and judged well and ill of all men. Everybody took a drink of water.

But then: "Cook," remarked the captain, "there don't seem to be any signs of life about your house of refuge."

(65)   "No," replied the cook. "Funny they don't see us!"

The surf's roar was dulled, but its tone was, nevertheless, thunderous and mighty. As the boat swam over the great rollers, the men sat listening to this roar. "We'll swamp sure," said everybody.

(70)   It is fair to say here that there was not a life-saving station within twenty miles in either direction, but the men did not know this fact, and in consequence they made dark and opprobrious remarks concerning the eyesight of the nation's life-savers. Four scowling men (75) sat in the dinghy and surpassed records in the invention of epithets.

"Funny they don't see us."

The lightheartedness of a former time had completely faded. To their sharpened minds it was easy to conjure (80) pictures of all kinds of incompetency and blindness and, indeed, cowardice. There was the shore of the populous land, and it was bitter and bitter to them that from it came no sign.

"Well," said the captain, ultimately. "I suppose we'll (85) have to make a try for ourselves. If we stay out here too long, we'll none of us have strength left to swim after the boat swamps."

And so the oiler, who was at the oars, turned the boat straight for the shore. There was a sudden tightening of (90) muscle. There was some thinking.

"If we don't all get ashore—" said the captain. "If we don't all get ashore, I suppose you fellows know where to send news of my finish?" They briefly exchanged some addresses and admonitions. The shore was still (95) afar.

1. In the first sentence, the narrator wishes to suggest that shipwrecks:
   A. occur all too frequently.
   B. strike at random.
   C. reflect the malign nature of the sea.
   D. usually take place at the worst of times.

2. It can be inferred from the passage that the men in the dinghy are tired because they:
   F. have been rowing the dinghy for the past two days.
   G. are unaccustomed to physical labor.
   H. have spent the previous two days on a sinking ship.
   J. had to swim a long distance to reach the dinghy.

3. In comparing the dinghy to a "wild colt" (line 52), the narrator suggests that it is:
   A. bounding roughly on the waves.
   B. too small for its four passengers.
   C. under no human control.
   D. rapidly filling with water.

4. The men in the dinghy experience a sense of "quiet cheerfulness" (line 49) because they:
   F. know that the storm that sank their ship is past.
   G. see the shore getting closer and closer.
   H. believe that the life-boat is out searching for them.
   J. think their dinghy will be able to land safely on shore.

5. When the narrator says "the four waifs rode impudently in their little boat" (lines 58–59), he is suggesting that the men:
   A. are enjoying what they know might be their last cigar.
   B. are rejoicing over their good fortune at having survived the shipwreck.
   C. believe that their skill at seamanship will save them from disaster.
   D. feel certain they will soon be rescued.

GO ON TO THE NEXT PAGE

6. It can be inferred from the passage that the other people who had been aboard the same ship as the four men in the dinghy:

   F. have already perished.

   G. are now safely on shore.

   H. are themselves afloat in other dinghies.

   J. are clinging to the wreckage of the ship.

7. The passage implies that the greatest danger to the men in the dinghy arises from the fact that:

   A. their boat is too small to safely navigate the great waves breaking on the shore.

   B. their supply of food and drinking water is rapidly being depleted.

   C. they are unable to steer their boat in the direction of the shore.

   D. they are too exhausted to row their boat toward the land.

8. As it is used in the passage, the word *dark* (line 73) means most nearly:

   F. obscure.

   G. harsh.

   H. muttered.

   J. unintelligible.

9. The passage implies that the "thinking" being done by the men in the dinghy (line 90) primarily concerns:

   A. what they must do to reach the shore safely.

   B. how they might signal their plight to those on shore.

   C. the possibility that they may drown.

   D. their bitterness over the failure of the life-savers to rescue them.

10. The passage suggests that the anger felt by the men in the dinghy toward the life-savers is:

   F. justified.

   G. excessive.

   H. ironic.

   J. misguided.

Passage II—NATURAL SCIENCE

In the early years of the twentieth century, astrophysicists turned their attention to a special category of stars, known as cepheid variables. A variable star is one whose apparent brightness changes from time to time.
(05) Among some variables, the change in brightness occurs so slowly as to be almost imperceptible; among others, it occurs in sudden, brief, violent bursts of energy.

The most impressive form of variable star is the nova, characterized by short-lived, extremely forceful explo-
(10) sions of energy. At its height, a nova may emit as much energy as 200,000 suns, and novas, especially those that are relatively close to our planet, are among the most brilliant objects in the night sky. One or two are noted in our own Milky Way galaxy each year. A nova
(15) typically goes through a number of cycles of extreme brightness followed by quiescence, repeatedly giving off huge amounts of energy and mass, until finally its mass is too small to continue the process.

The supernova, an even more spectacular object, is
(20) not a variable star but rather an exploding star, which may briefly attain a brightness equivalent to 10 billion suns before fading away forever. The single powerful burst of a supernova may leave behind a bright gaseous cloud of matter known as a nebula; the Crab nebula,
(25) first observed as a supernova in A.D. 1054, is a familiar example.

Among the true variable stars, the cepheid variables (which take their name from the constellation Cepheus, where the first such star was discovered) have special
(30) characteristics that make them an especially useful astronomical tool.

It was Henrietta Leavitt, an astronomer at the Harvard Observatory, who first examined the cepheid variables in detail. She found that these stars vary regularly in
(35) apparent brightness over a relatively short period of

time—from one to three days to a month or more. This variation in brightness could be recorded and precisely measured with the help of the camera, then still a new tool in astronomy.

(40) Leavitt also noticed that the periodicity of each cepheid variable—that is, the period of time it took for the star to vary from its brightest point to its dimmest, and back to its brightest again—corresponded to the intrinsic or absolute brightness of the star. That is, the (45) greater the star's absolute brightness, the slower its cycle of variation.

Why is this so? The variation in brightness is caused by the interaction between the star's gravity and the outward pressure exerted by the flow of light energy (50) from the star. Gravity pulls the outer portions of the star inward, while light pressure pushes them outward. The result is a pulsating, in-and-out movement that produces increasing and decreasing brightness. The stronger the light pressure, the slower this pulsation. (55) Therefore, the periodicity of the cepheid variable is a good indication of its absolute brightness.

Furthermore, it is obvious that the apparent brightness of any source of light decreases the further we are from the light. Physicists had long known that this (60) relationship could be described by a simple mathematical formula, known as the inverse square law. If we know the absolute brightness of any object—say, a star—as well as our distance from that object, it is possible to use the inverse square law to determine (65) exactly how bright that object will appear to be.

This laid the background for Leavitt's most crucial insight. As she had discovered, the absolute brightness of a cepheid variable could be determined by measuring its periodicity. And, of course, the apparent brightness (70) of the star when observed from the earth could be determined by simple measurement. Leavitt saw that with these two facts and the help of inverse square law, it would be possible to determine the distance from earth of any cepheid variable. If we know the absolute (75) brightness of the star and how bright it appears from the earth, we can tell how far it must be.

Thus, if a cepheid variable can be found in any galaxy, it is possible to measure the distance of that galaxy from earth. Thanks to Leavitt's discovery, (80) astronomical distances that could not previously be measured became measurable for the first time.

11. The primary purpose of the passage is to explain:

  A. the background and career of the astronomer Henrietta Leavitt.

  B. the development of the inverse square law for determining an object's brightness.

  C. important uses of the camera as an astronomical tool.

  D. how a particular method of measuring astronomical distances was created.

12. According to the passage, a nova differs from a supernova in all of the following ways EXCEPT that a supernova:

  F. emits its energy in a single powerful burst.

  G. may leave behind the gaseous cloud of a nebula.

  H. passes through several cycles of extreme brightness.

  J. is not a true variable star.

13. According to the passage, the cepheid variables are especially useful to astronomers because of the:

  A. regularity with which they vary in brightness.

  B. unusually great apparent brightness they exhibit.

  C. slowness of their average cycle of variation.

  D. ease with which their absolute brightness may be observed.

14. The passage states that Leavitt's work enabled astronomers to measure the distance from earth of any galaxy containing a:

  F. nebula.

  G. variable star.

  H. nova or supernova.

  J. cepheid variable.

15. According to the passage, the absolute brightness of a cepheid variable:

    A. depends upon its measurable distance from an observer on earth.

    B. may be determined from the length of its cycle of variation.

    C. changes from time to time according to a regular and predictable pattern.

    D. indicates the strength of the gravitation force exerted by the star.

16. The passage states that cepheid variables are so named after:

    F. a variable star first observed by Leavitt.

    G. the first star whose periodicity was studied by Leavitt.

    H. the constellation containing the first cepheid variable known.

    J. the first galaxy whose distance from earth was measured by Leavitt's method.

17. According to the passage, Leavitt's work provided astronomers with the means of determining which of the following?

    I. The absolute brightness of any observable cepheid variable.

    II. The apparent brightness of any object a given distance from an observer.

    III. The distance from earth of any galaxy containing an observable cepheid variable.

    A. III only

    B. I and II only

    C. I and III only

    D. I, II, and III

18. It can be inferred from the passage that a cepheid variable of great absolute brightness would exhibit:

    F. a relatively rapid variation in brightness.

    G. a correspondingly weak gravitational force.

    H. slow and almost imperceptible changes in brightness.

    J. a strong outward flow of light pressure.

19. It can be inferred from the passage that it is possible to observe each of the following with the naked eye EXCEPT the:

    A. explosion of a supernova.

    B. precise brightness of a variable star.

    C. period of greatest brightness of a nova.

    D. existence of a nebula.

20. The passage implies that Leavitt's work on cepheid variables would not have been possible without the availability of:

    F. the camera as a scientific tool.

    G. techniques for determining the distances between stars.

    H. an understanding of the chemical properties of stars.

    J. a single star whose distance from earth was already known.

Exercise 2

20 Questions • Time—18 Minutes

Directions: This exercise consists of two passages, each followed by several questions. Read each passage, select the correct answer for each question, and mark the oval representing the correct answer on your answer sheet.

Passage I—SOCIAL STUDIES

When the framers of the Constitution set to work devising the structure of the United States government, it was natural for them to consider the forms already existing in the several states. The three most basic
(5) patterns may be referred to as the Virginia, Pennsylvania, and Massachusetts models.

The Virginia model borrowed its central principal, legislative supremacy, from the thinking of the English philosopher John Locke. Locke had favored making the
(10) legislature the dominant focus of government power, and he stressed the importance of preventing a monarch, governor, or other executive from usurping that power. In line with Locke's doctrine, Virginia's constitution provided that the governor be chosen by the assembly
(15) rather than by the people directly, as were the members of a special governor's council. The approval of this council was necessary for any action by the governor.

Also derived from Locke was Virginia's bicameral legislature, in which both chambers must concur to pass
(20) a bill. Thus dividing the legislative power was supposed to prove its domination by any single faction—the so-called "division of powers" which later became an important feature of the national constitution.

Pennsylvania's constitution was probably the most
(25) democratic of any in the former colonies. Pennsylvania extended the right to vote to most adult males. (With the exception of Vermont, the other states allowed only property owners to vote; New Jersey alone extended the privilege to women.)

(30) Pennsylvanians elected the members of a single-house legislature, as well as an executive council. These bodies jointly selected the council president, who served as the state's chief executive officer; there was no governor. Neither legislators nor council members could
(35) remain in office more than four years out of seven.

The most conservative of the models was found in Massachusetts. The legislature here included two chambers. In the house of representatives, the number of legislators for a given district was based on population;
(40) in the "aristocratic" senate, representation was based on taxable wealth. The governor could veto legislature, he appointed most state officials, and he was elected independently of the legislature.

As the delegates to the Constitutional Convention
(45) began to debate the merits of these varying models, several fault lines began to appear along which the representatives of the former colonies were divided. One such line was geographic. The economic and social differences between the northern and southern states,
(50) which would lead, three generations later, to the cataclysm of the Civil War, were already making themselves felt. Dependent chiefly on the exporting of such raw materials as cotton, tobacco, and rice, the southern states strongly opposed giving Congress the power to
(55) regulate international trade, fearing the imposition of onerous taxes or tariffs. Too, the white slaveholders of the south feared federal restrictions on the practice of slavery, which was already a point of controversy between sections of the new nation.

(60) Another dividing line among the states was based on population. The less populous states opposed the notion of allocating political power based on population; they feared having the larger states, especially Virginia, New York, Massachusetts, and Pennsylvania,
(65) ride roughshod over their interests. This division to some extent echoed the north-south split, since most of the more populous states were in the north.

The debates over governmental structure quickly focused on the makeup of the legislative branch. The
(70) most populous states favored making representation in Congress proportional to population, while the

GO ON TO THE NEXT PAGE

smaller states fought for equality of representation. For a time, it appeared as though the convention might break up over this issue.

(75)   The successful resolution was a compromise originally proposed by the delegation from Connecticut, and therefore often referred to as the Connecticut Compromise, or the Great Compromise. According to this plan, which remains in effect to this day, the Congress is a (80) bicameral legislature like those in Virginia and Massachusetts. In the Senate, each state has two representatives, no matter what its size, while seats in the House of Representatives are apportioned by population. Both houses must concur in the passage of legislature, and (85) bills proposing the expenditure of government funds must originate in the House—a precaution demanded by the larger states to protect their financial interests.

The southern states won a series of specific concessions. Although the convention refused to include slaves (90) on an equal basis in the population count for Congressional representation—after all, the slaves were neither citizens nor taxpayers nor voters—it was agreed to count of the slave population, a notorious compromise long regarded as a racist blot on the constitution. The (95) north also accepted constitutional clauses forbidding export taxes and preventing Congress from interfering with the slave trade until at least 1808—over twenty years in the future. The sectional differences between north and south, and the simmering issue of slavery, (100) were thus postponed for future generations to face.

1. The author's primary purpose in writing the passage is to explain:

   A. how various models of state government influenced the debate over the U.S. Constitution.

   B. the differing roles of the legislature in each of the original American states.

   C. the contrasting forms of government found in the various original American states.

   D. the influence of John Locke's philosophy on the framers of the U.S. Constitution.

2. The state governments described in the passage varied in all of the following respects EXCEPT:

   F. the existence of the office of governor.

   G. restrictions on tenure in state offices.

   H. whether the members of the legislature were chosen directly by the people.

   J. restrictions on the eligibility of citizens to vote.

3. According to the passage, the principle purpose of the "division of powers" in the Virginia model was to:

   A. allow citizens of every social class to participate fully in government.

   B. prevent any one group from controlling the legislative power.

   C. ensure the independence of the executive from legislative manipulation.

   D. discourage the concentration of power in the hands of the governor.

4. It can be inferred from the passage that those who favored a democratic system of government would most strongly support:

   F. apportioning seats in the legislature on the basis of taxable wealth.

   G. limitation on the number of terms in office served by legislators.

   H. establishment of a bicameral legislature.

   J. granting the power to veto legislation to a popularly-elected executive.

5. According to the passage, the philosophy of John Locke most strongly influenced the governmental system of:

   A. Massachusetts.

   B. New Jersey.

   C. Pennsylvania.

   D. Virginia.

6. According to the passage, the right to vote was limited to property owners in all of the states EXCEPT:

   I. New Jersey.

   II. Pennsylvania.

   III. Vermont.

   F. II only

   G. I and II only

   H. II and III only

   J. I, II, and III

7. In can be inferred from the passage that the southern states most favored which of the following features of the new constitution?

   A. The apportionment of seats in the Senate.

   B. The apportionment of seats in the House of Representatives.

   C. The requirement that funding bills originate in the House of Representatives.

   D. The restriction of voting privileges to white male citizens.

8. As it is used in line 93, the word *notorious* most nearly means:

   F. remarkable.

   G. infamous.

   H. ingenious.

   J. celebrated.

9. According to the passage, the leaders of the southern states were concerned with defending the interests of which of the following?

   I. Slaveholders.

   II. Exporters of raw materials.

   III. The less-populous states.

   A. I only

   B. I and II only

   C. II and III only

   D. I, II, and III

10. One of the main ideas of the passage is that:

   F. resentment by the south of its treatment during the Constitutional Convention was an underlying cause of the Civil War.

   G. most white Americans at the time of the Constitutional Conventional rejected the new constitution's implicit racism.

   H. the framers of the constitution devised only temporary solutions for the rift between the northern and southern states.

   J. the issue of slavery nearly caused the failure of the Constitutional Convention.

Passage II—NATURAL SCIENCE

Today, the theory of "continental drift," which supposes that the earth's great land masses have moved over time, is a basic premise accepted by most geologists. However, this was not always so. In fact, it was not (5) until the mid-twentieth century that this concept won widespread acceptance among scientists.

Although Alfred Wegener was not the first to propose the idea that the continents have moved, his 1912 outline of the hypothesis was the first detailed descrip- (10) tion of the concept and the first to offer a respectable mass of supporting evidence for it. It is appropriate,

then, that the theory of continental drift was most widely known as "Wegener's hypothesis" during the more than fifty years of debate that preceded its ultimate acceptance (15) by most earth scientists.

In brief, Wegener's hypothesis stated that, in the late Paleozoic era, all of the present-day continents were part of a single giant land mass, Pangaea, that occupied almost half of the earth's surface. About 40 million (20) years ago, Pangaea began to break into fragments that slowly moved apart, ultimately forming the various continents we know today.

GO ON TO THE NEXT PAGE

Wegener supported his argument with data drawn from geology, paleontology, zoology, climatology, and (25) other fields. He pointed, for example, to the fact that continental margins in several regions of the globe appear to closely match one another, as though they had once been united. The fit between the land masses on either side of the Atlantic Ocean—Europe and Africa (30) on the east and North and South America on the west— is especially close. Furthermore, Wegener also showed that rock formations in Brazil and West Africa, on opposite sides of the Atlantic, are remarkably similar in age, type, and structure. This, too, was consistent with (35) the notion that the continents had once been joined.

So impressive was Wegener's array of evidence that his hypothesis could not be ignored. However, until the 1960s, most scientists were reluctant to accept Wegener's ideas. There are several reasons why this was so.

(40) First, although Wegener showed that continental movement was consistent with much of the geological and other evidence—for example, the apparent family relationships among forms of plants and animals now separated by vast expanses of ocean, once geographi- (45) cally united on the hypothetical Pangaea—he failed to suggest any causal mechanism for continental drift sufficiently powerful and plausible to be convincing.

Second, while the period during which Wegener's theory was propounded and debated saw rapid develop- (50) ments in many branches of geology and an explosion of new knowledge about the nature of the earth and the forces at work in its formation, little of this evidence seemed to support Wegener. For example, data drawn from the new science of seismology, including experi- (55) mental studies of the behavior of rocks under high pressure, suggested that the earth has far too much internal strength and rigidity to allow continents to "drift" across its surface. Measurements of the earth's gravitational field made by some of the early scientific (60) satellites offered further evidence in support of this view as late as the early 1960s.

In fact, this data pointed to a genuine flaw in Wegener's theory. He had assumed that the continental plates floated atop the ocean crust, which was relatively (65) plastic and so would permit the continents to move across its surface. This was false. The true explanation for continental movement was not uncovered until the discovery, through seismic studies, of the existence of asthenosphere, a layer of plastic, slowly-moving mate- (70) rial that lies under both the continental plates and the ocean crust at depths of 50 to 150 kilometers (30 to 80 miles). The malleability of the athenosphere permits movement of the layers above it.

Third, and perhaps most significant, Wegener's theory (75) seemed to challenge one of the most deeply-held philo- sophical bases of geology—the doctrine of uniformi- tarianism, which states that earth history must always be explained by the operation of essentially unchang- ing, continuous forces. Belief in the intervention of (80) unexplained, sporadic, and massive shaping events— known as catastrophism—was considered beyond the pale by mainstream geologists.

Wegener was not, strictly speaking, a catastrophist— he did not suggest that some massive cataclysm had (85) triggered the breakup of Pangaea—but his theory did imply a dramatic change in the face of the earth occurring relatively late in geologic history. Such a belief, viewed as tainted with catastrophism, was abhorrent to most geologists throughout the first half of this century.

11. It can be inferred from the passage that the majority of geologists today:

A. reject the theory of continental drift.

B. have softened in their opposition to catastrophism.

C. question the relevance of most of Wegener's geological evidence.

D. disagree with Wegener's idea that the continents were once united.

12. According to the passage, Wegener believed that Pangaea:

F. was destroyed in a massive cataclysm occurring about 40 million years ago.

G. consisted of several large land areas separated by vast expanses of ocean.

H. was ultimately submerged by rising oceans at the end of the Paleozoic era.

J. contained in a single land mass the basic material of all the continents that exist today.

13. It can be inferred from the passage that, by the end of the Paleozoic era:

    A. many forms of plant and animal life existed on earth.

    B. the land mass of Pangaea no longer existed.

    C. a series of unexplained catastrophes had changed the face of the earth.

    D. most of today's land forms had taken their current shape.

14. According to the passage, Wegener supported his hypothesis by pointing to the geological similarities between rock formations in West Africa and:

    F. Brazil.

    G. North America.

    H. Europe.

    J. the floor of the Atlantic Ocean.

15. The passage provides information to answer which of the following questions?

    I. What geological forces caused the breakup of Pangaea?

    II. What evidence discovered in the 1960s lent support to Wegener's hypothesis?

    III. When did Wegener's hypothesis win acceptance by most earth scientists?

    A. I only

    B. III only

    C. I and III only

    D. II and III only

16. The phrase "tainted with catastrophism" (line 88) implies that most geologists in the early twentieth century considered catastrophism:

    F. fascinating but unproven.

    G. somewhat questionable.

    H. completely incredible.

    J. demonstrably true.

17. The passage implies that the most significant reason for the opposition to Wegener's hypothesis on the part of many scientists was its:

    A. indirect challenge to a fundamental premise of geology.

    B. impossibility of being tested by experimental means.

    C. conflict with data drawn from the fossil record.

    D. failure to provide a comprehensive framework for earth history.

18. According to the passage, Wegener was mistaken in his beliefs concerning the:

    F. movements of the asthenosphere.

    G. former existence of Pangaea.

    H. plausibility of movement by the continental plates.

    J. malleability of the ocean crust.

19. As used in line 86, the word *dramatic* most nearly means:

    A. exciting.

    B. violent.

    C. large-scale.

    D. rapid.

20. The author refers to the scientific information gathered by satellites in order to suggest the:

    F. philosophical changes that ultimately led to the acceptance of Wegener's hypothesis.

    G. dramatic advances in earth science during the 1960s.

    H. differing directions taken by various earth scientists in the decades following Wegener.

    J. nature of the some of the evidence that appeared to refute Wegener.

GO ON TO THE NEXT PAGE

ANSWER KEYS AND EXPLANATIONS

Exercise 1

1. B	5. D	9. C	13. A	17. C
2. H	6. F	10. J	14. J	18. J
3. A	7. A	11. D	15. B	19. B
4. G	8. G	12. H	16. H	20. A

1. **B.** You need to read the entire paragraph to fully understand the first sentence. The point is that shipwrecks don't usually take place at convenient times; those on board ship can't prepare and train for them. Instead, they occur at random times—"*a propos* of nothing," as the first sentence says.

2. **H.** The second paragraph and the last sentence of the third paragraph combine to answer this question. They make it clear that the weariness of the men in the dinghy is a result of the fact that they have spent the last two days "clambering about the deck of a foundering [that is, sinking] ship."

3. **A.** Look at the rest of the sentence containing this phrase. It says that the men had become "used to balancing in the boat," and it compares them to "circus men." The idea is that the boat is bucking and bouncing on the waves like a bronco in a circus.

4. **G.** The (temporary) good mood of the men is attributed, in the same paragraph, to "the influence of this expansion"—namely, the growing visibility of the shore as their little boat gets closer and closer to it.

5. **D.** The description of the men smoking their cigars includes the explanatory phrase, "with an assurance of an impending rescue shining in their eyes."

6. **F.** See the eighth paragraph, where the oiler says, "None of those other boats could have got ashore to give word of the wreck." It appears from this sentence that several boats were lowered from the sinking ship, of which the dinghy is one, and that none of the others reached safety.

7. **A.** The growing fear of the men is attributed to their belief that "We'll swamp sure" in the mighty surf whose noise they hear. In other words, the waves breaking on the shore are so large and powerful that it will be impossible for them to land their boat safely. The men *are* exhausted, as choice D asserts, but the problem is not that they cannot row toward shore—they can; the problem is that they can't land safely once they get there.

8. **G.** The word "dark" is used in the phrase "dark and opprobrious remarks," describing the angry comments made by the men in the dinghy toward the life-savers, who they think are ignoring them. The context makes it clear that the remarks are harshly negative ones—"dark" in that sense only.

9. **C.** Immediately after the sentence, "There was some thinking," the men in the dinghy exchange addresses so that they can notify one another's next of kin in the event that some of them drown. Obviously, the "thinking" they are doing is about the possibility that they may not survive.

10. **J.** The fourteenth paragraph states "that there was not a life-saving station within twenty miles in either direction." Thus, it would have been impossible for any life-savers to see and rescue the shipwreck victims, and the life-savers are not to blame for the men's plight.

11. **D.** The last paragraph of the passage neatly summarizes the significance of Leavitt's work with cepheid variables.

12. **H.** It is the nova, not the supernova, that "passes through several cycles of extreme brightness." As the third paragraph makes clear, all of the other answer choices accurately describe the supernova.

13. **A.** Because the cepheid variables change in brightness according to a regular pattern, it is possible to determine their absolute brightness—and, from this, their distance. Thus, it is the regularity of their variation that makes them useful to astronomers.

14. **J.** See the first sentence of the last paragraph.

15. **B.** The sixth paragraph describes the important relationship Leavitt discovered: that the cepheid variable's periodicity (its cycle of variation) and its absolute brightness vary together. Thus, each one can be determined from the other.

16. **H.** The fourth paragraph explains that the cepheid variables are named after the constellation Cepheus, where the first cepheid variable was found.

17. **C.** As the last sentence of paragraph 6 makes clear, statement I is true; from its periodicity (which is easily observable), we can determine the absolute brightness of a cepheid variable. Statement III is supported by the last paragraph of the passage. Statement II is false because the passage doesn't suggest that Leavitt developed the method by which astronomers measured stars' apparent brightness; in fact, in paragraphs 5 and 9, Leavitt appears to take this method for granted and build upon it.

18. **J.** Paragraph 6 explains that a star with a great absolute brightness is also a star with relatively stronger light pressure; hence, the slower in-and-out pulsation and the longer periodicity that Leavitt observed.

19. **B.** We're told in the passage about how brilliant and noticeable both novas and supernovas are; and the existence of the Crab nebula since shortly after 1054 A.D. makes it obvious that it, too, must have been visible without the aid of a telescope. However, the "precise brightness of a variable star" could only be measured with the help of the camera, according to paragraph five.

20. **A.** See the last sentence of the fifth paragraph. It seems clear that the camera was a necessary tool for Leavitt's work to be possible.

Exercise 2

1. A	5. D	9. D	13. A	17. A
2. H	6. H	10. H	14. F	18. J
3. B	7. A	11. B	15. B	19. C
4. G	8. G	12. J	16. H	20. J

1. **A.** The first six paragraphs describe the various models of state government available to the framers of the constitution; the last five paragraphs discuss the debates among the framers over how to adapt these models to the needs of the new nation.

2. **H.** All of the variations mentioned in the other answer choices are noted somewhere in the passage; however, none of the state governments discussed is said to involve a legislature that is not popularly elected.

3. **B.** The second sentence of the third paragraph makes this point.

4. **G.** The fourth and fifth paragraphs describe the government of Pennsylvania, which is said to be the "most democratic" among the former colonies. Of the answer choices, only G describes a feature of this state's government.

5. **D.** See the first sentence of the second paragraph.

6. **H.** The fourth paragraph explains that only Pennsylvania and Vermont did not restrict voting to property owners.

7. **A.** Among other demands, the southern states, which were mostly small, wanted to protect their interests by having equal representation for states of all sizes rather than making representation proportional to population. Thus, the equal numbers of legislators in the Senate would have appealed to the southerners at the convention. The passage does not suggest that *any* of the states favored extension of voting privileges to non-white males, so answer D is wrong.

8. **G.** *Notorious* and *infamous* are near-synonyms; both mean "well-known and much-hated or widely despised."

9. **D.** The seventh paragraph states that the white leaders of the southern states wanted to protect their interests as exporters and as slaveholders; the last sentence of the eighth paragraph makes the point that the southern states were, for the most part, less populous than the northern states.

10. **H.** The last half of the passage develops this theme, especially in the seventh and eleventh paragraphs. It's clear that the compromises related to slavery were only temporary "band-aids" rather than permanent solutions to the problem.

11. **B.** Since most geologists today accept Wegener's hypothesis—despite its flirtation with catastrophism—it's clear that the abhorrence of catastrophism must have diminished in recent decades.

12. **J.** See the first sentence of the third paragraph, which summarizes this point neatly.

13. **A.** In the sixth paragraph, the passage explains that Wegener used the existence of similar plants and animals on widely separated continents as evidence that all the Earth's land masses were formerly connected, in the supercontinent of Pangaea. For this evidence to be valid, it would have to mean that many plants and animals existed prior to the breakup of Pangaea, which paragraph three tells us began late in the Paleozoic era.

14. **F.** The next-to-last sentence of the sixth paragraph states that rock formations in Brazil are quite similar to those in West Africa.

15. **B.** The first paragraph tells us that Wegener's hypothesis was accepted some fifty years after it was first proposed in 1912; thus, in the early 1960s. This answers question III. Question I is not answered; the passage only says (end of paragraph 6) that Wegener himself had no answer for this question. Question II is not answered; in fact, paragraph 7 refers to evidence from the 1960s that seemed to undermine, rather than support, Wegener's hypothesis.

16. **H.** The word "taint" implies that most scientists were so opposed to catastrophism that any theory with even a passing resemblance to catastrophism was considered unacceptable.

17. **A.** See the first sentence of the ninth paragraph. The "perhaps most significant" reason for many scientists' discomfort with Wegener's hypothesis was that it seemed to challenge their deep-seated belief in uniformitarianism.

18. **J.** The eighth paragraph explains Wegener's error. He believed that the ocean crust was "relatively plastic" (that is, flexible or malleable), and that this explained how the continents could drift on its surface. In fact, the ocean crust is quite rigid, as the satellite studies mentioned in paragraph seven found. The existence of the asthenosphere, which Wegener did not know about, was the correct alternative explanation.

19. **C.** As used in this passage, the word dramatic refers to changes on a vast scale—changes in the very shape and appearance of the earth's continents, in fact.

20. **J.** You'll find this stated in the last sentence of the seventh paragraph.

ARE YOU READY TO MOVE ON?

How well do you understand the contents and format of the ACT Assessment Reading Test? How well have you incorporated your new skills into your test-taking behavior?

After you've corrected each exercise, find the number below. This will give you an idea of whether you need to go to the Reading Review, or whether you can move on to another subject area.

Score Key for Each Practice Exercise

Number Correct	Score	Suggested Action
0–5	Poor	Study the review chapter and do the exercises there; then, study this chapter again.
6–8	Below average	Study problem areas in the review chapter and do at least one exercise. Study this chapter again.
9–12	Average	Study this chapter again if you wish to and have time. Skim problem areas in the review chapter if you have time.
13–15	Above average	You may move on to a new subject.
16–20	Excellent	You're ready for the ACT Assessment Reading Test.

Summary: What You Need to Know About the ACT Assessment Reading Test

- The ACT Assessment Reading Test will have four passages of 700 to 900 words, each followed by 10 questions. You'll have 35 minutes to read the four passages and to answer the forty questions.

- Preview, read, and review to get the most out of every passage on the ACT Assessment.

- Look for the main ideas; don't get caught up in the details.

- Read with pencil in hand and mark up key ideas as you find them.

- Begin with the type of reading you like best.
- Don't choose an answer merely because it seems familiar.
- Don't try to answer from memory; return to the passage to be sure you're answering correctly.
- Answer all the questions for each passage before moving on; don't plan on returning to a passage.

The ACT Assessment Science Reasoning Test

The ACT Assessment Science Reasoning Test is designed to measure your ability to understand, analyze, dissect, interpret, compare, and evaluate various kinds of scientific information. In other words, it tests your ability to think like a scientist. "Thinking like a scientist" usually proceeds along the following course: developing a theory, designing an experiment, organizing the results, and drawing conclusions. Though you won't earn a science degree in this chapter, you will learn how to succeed on the Science Reasoning portion of the ACT Assessment. You learn what the Science Reasoning questions look like, how long you can spend on each question, and the best strategies for finding the right answers within that time. You also have an opportunity to practice your skills on some questions just like those you will encounter on the real ACT Assessment.

WHAT TO EXPECT ON THE ACT ASSESSMENT SCIENCE REASONING TEST

The specific skills tested on the Science Reasoning portion of the ACT Assessment range from your ability to understand tables, graphs, figures, and diagrams, to your ability to recognize hidden assumptions underlying a theory, or to determine whether a particular piece of information strengthens or weakens an unproven hypothesis. You'll also be asked to make predictions on what might happen next in an experiment given the results so far.

The Science Reasoning Test contains seven passages of about 100 to 300 words on biology, chemistry, physics, and earth science. Each passage is followed by questions; the Science Reasoning portion of the ACT Assessment contains a total of 40 questions. You must read all the passages and answer the total of 40 questions in one 35-minute sitting. Pace yourself, as you have only five minutes to spend on each passage together with its questions. Plan to spend about two and a half minutes reading each passage and two and a half minutes answering its questions.

The biology passages may include cell biology, botany, zoology, microbiology, ecology, genetics, and evolution. Chemistry passages may include organic chemistry, inorganic chemistry, electrochemistry, biochemistry, atomic theory and properties and states of matter. Physics passages may

ROAD MAP

- *Learn about the Science Reasoning Portion of the ACT Assessment*
- *Understand the Science Reasoning Questions and Their Format*
- *Learn the Best Strategies for Success on Science Reasoning Questions*
- *Practice Your Skills and Strategies on Science Reasoning Exercises*
- *Evaluate your Science Reasoning Skills*

include mechanics, energy, thermodynamics, electromagnetism, fluids, solids, and light waves. And earth science passages may include geology, meteorology, oceanography, astronomy, and environmental sciences.

You don't need to have taken courses in any of these topics or to have prior knowledge of the field to do well on the questions. All the information you need will be given directly on the test.

Still feeling a bit uncertain about your overall knowledge of science? If so, you might benefit from a crash-course in some of the basics. You can review some of the basic principles of science in Chapter 11, "Science Reasoning Review: Understanding Data," later in this book.

THE SCIENCE REASONING QUESTIONS AND THEIR FORMAT

No matter what the field, there will be three types of Science Reasoning passages: Data Representation, Research Summaries, and Conflicting Viewpoints. The following sections introduce you to these three question types and show you examples of each.

Data Representation

A Data Representation passage will usually have one or two short paragraphs followed by one to five graphs, charts, tables, diagrams, or pictures.

Example:

The periodic table is a listing of each element along with its atomic number (the number of protons in the nucleus or center of the atom) and its atomic mass (the combined weight of protons and neutrons in the nucleus). The atomic mass is approximately equal to the number of protons and neutrons that an element has. The table is arranged into periods vertically and groups (indicated with roman numerals) horizontally. Similar chemical properties are exhibited by elements that are in the same group. Moving across a period from group I to group VII, chemical similarities decrease. Part of the table is reproduced in the following figure.

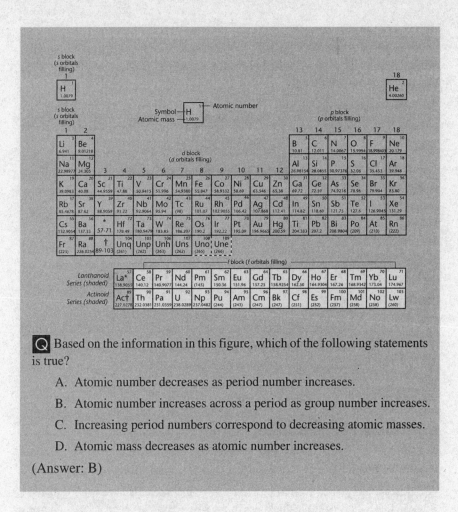

Q Based on the information in this figure, which of the following statements is true?

    A. Atomic number decreases as period number increases.

    B. Atomic number increases across a period as group number increases.

    C. Increasing period numbers correspond to decreasing atomic masses.

    D. Atomic mass decreases as atomic number increases.

(Answer: B)

Research Summaries

A Research Summaries passage has one or two short paragraphs followed by two or three descriptions of particular scientific research projects; these are usually headed *Experiment or Study 1*, *Experiment or Study 2*, and so on, and might include a summary graph.

Example:

Researchers are interested in optimizing methods for cooling electronic components such as semiconductors (a type of computer chip). Semiconductors generate heat as they operate, but excess levels of heat cause such components to malfunction or might shorten their lifespan. However, cold objects cannot be applied directly to these components, because they are too sensitive.

One cooling method that has been used is the placement of foam material between the semiconductors and a cooling plate. Foam acts as a heat conductor. Heat from the computer chip flows through the foam, towards the cooling plate. As heat is conducted through the foam in this manner, the semiconductor is cooled, and the temperature difference between the cooling plate and the

continues

semiconductor becomes smaller. Various experiments were performed to determine more about the heat conduction properties of foam.

Experiment 1

Foam pads that all had a surface area of 1 inch^2 but were of various thicknesses were inserted between a semiconductor and a cooling plate. The temperature of the cooling plate was kept constant. The semiconductor was generating 1 Watt of heat. The researchers measured the difference in temperature between the semiconductor and the cooling plate. Results appear in the following table.

Trial #	Thickness of foam (mm)	Measure temperture difference between computer chip and plate (°C)
1	1	2.2
2	2	3.9
3	4	7.2
4	6	11.0
5	8	14.2
6	10	16.3

Experiment 2

Researchers placed a foam pad between a semiconductor and a cooling plate, but in this experiment the thickness of the pad was 6 mm in all cases, and the surface area of the pad varied. The heat generated by the semiconductor remained at 1 watt. Results appear in the following table.

Trial #	Foam surface area (inches^2)	Measured temperature difference between computer chip and plate
1	0.2	17.4
2	0.4	13.3
3	0.6	11.0
4	0.8	8.3
5	1.0	7.1
6	1.5	5.3

Q Which of the following statements is supported by the data from Experiments 1 and 2?

A. Thicker foam pads are better heat conductors.

B. Heat conduction is favored by a thin foam pad with a surface area.

C. Heat dissipation was greatest when the surface area of the foam was 0.2 inches^2.

D. Using a piece of foam with a surface area of 0.8 inch^2 and a thickness of 0.6 mm appears to be equivalent to using a piece with a surface area of 1 inch^2 and a thickness of 4 mm.

(Answer: B)

Conflicting Viewpoints

A Conflicting Viewpoints passage will have one or two paragraphs followed by two or three descriptions of differing theories or ideas about a scientific question; these are usually headed *The [X] Hypothesis* or *The [Y] Theory* and, again, might include a graph.

Example:

Biologists have discovered certain genes (the basic unit of genetic material found on the chromosomes) that behave very differently depending on whether they are passed down to offspring from the father or the mother. These genes, called imprinted genes, are chemically altered in cells that give rise to eggs and sperm. These alterations result in dramatically different properties. In the imprinted genes that have been most fully studied, the female alters the gene so that certain proteins are not produced. The protein continues to be produced in the father's genes. Researchers have posed numerous theories to explain the evolution of imprinted genes. Two of the theories are presented below.

Anti-Cancer Theory

This theory holds that imprinted genes evolved to prevent cancer. The genes have been found in the placenta (an organ that develops to nourish a growing fetus). Placental tissue grows and burrows into the uterus, where the fetus develops. The ability to grow and invade tissues is also seen in aggressive cancers. Imprinted genes might have developed to ensure that the potentially dangerous placenta will not develop if there is no fetus to nourish. The female might inactivate certain growth genes in her eggs, while the sperm kept them turned on. If no fertilization took place, the growth would not occur. If a sperm did join the egg, the male's gene would ensure that the protein developed.

Protein Control Theory

A second group of biologists holds that imprinted genes developed to ensure the precise regulation of certain proteins. Genes do their work by initiating the production of different proteins. Some proteins involved in the growth of embryos might need to be regulated with great precision to ensure the healthy development of the offspring. Proponents of the protein control theory suggest that this careful regulation might be easier if only one parent is involved. Thus, one parent might turn off such genes, leaving the regulation to the other.

continues

TIP

Reminder: A *Data Representation* passage will have little text and one to five visual elements: graphs, charts, tables, diagrams, or pictures. A *Research Summaries* passage will include two or three descriptions of research projects, usually headed Experiment 1, Experiment 2, and so on, or Study 1, Study 2, and so on. Graphs summarizing the results may also appear. And a *Conflicting Viewpoints* passage will include two or three differing theories or ideas about a scientific question. They'll be given headings like The [X] Hypothesis or The [Y] Theory. Again, a graph or two might appear.

Q Supporters of the protein control theory believe that:

A. imprinted genes are used to regulate crucial proteins.

B. imprinted genes are active only in females.

C. imprinted genes should not be found in monogamous species (ones that mate for life).

D. only the male passes down imprinted genes to the offspring.

(Answer: A)

THE DIRECTIONS

The directions for the ACT Assessment Science Reasoning Test are similar to the following:

Directions: This test consists of seven passages, each followed by several questions. Read each passage, select the correct answer for each question, and mark the oval representing the correct answer on your answer sheet. You may NOT use a calculator on this test.

STRATEGIES FOR SUCCESS ON THE ACT ASSESSMENT SCIENCE REASONING TEST

Much like the Reading portion of the ACT Assessment, the Science Reasoning questions test your ability to comprehend written information. Your success on this portion of the ACT Assessment does not depend upon your scientific knowledge; instead, it depends upon your ability to read and reason. Though the scientific jargon, charts, diagrams, and figures might seem overwhelming at first, you can use some very simple techniques to work through this portion of the ACT Assessment quickly—and accurately. Here are some success strategies specifically designed to help you score higher on ACT Assessment Science Reasoning.

THE THREE-STEP METHOD: PREVIEW, READ, REVIEW

If you've already worked through the English Test chapter, you'll recognize *Preview, Read, Review* as the three-step reading method suggested there. Think of the Science Reasoning Test as a special form of reading comprehension. Some of the language might be more technical, and the information is presented not only in words but in graphs, tables, and diagrams. Nonetheless, the basic challenge is the same: to read and digest a mass of information (the "passage") and answer questions about it.

Therefore, the three-step reading method taught in Chapter 4 is an important foundation for the Science Reasoning Test. (If you haven't read Chapter 4, read just the section on "Preview, Read, Review" right now.) Here's how to apply the *Preview, Read, Review* technique to Science Reasoning.

1. *Preview the passage.* Spend about thirty seconds glancing through all of the information provided in a passage. Just skim the page, letting your eye move down the columns of type and data, absorbing as much as you can. In particular, try to determine the format of the passage: is the format Data Representation, Research Summaries, or Conflicting Viewpoints? The different formats are easy to recognize.

   Because previewing is a brief process, don't try to absorb a lot of information. You're about to read the passage in more detail, which will draw you much deeper into its contents.

2. *Read the passage.* Each one is short, a maximum of about 300 words and should take no more than a minute or two. For the visual data—tables, charts, graphs, and diagrams—read the labels on the axes or columns, the legends or keys, and explanatory sidebars. Identify the units of measurement (grams, degrees, light-years, and so on). Notice any obvious trends, patterns, or groupings in the data. Then move on. You can always refer back to the passage for the details, and in fact you should.

   During this step of the reading process, mark up the passage with your pencil. Underline main ideas, star important facts or experimental results, etc. Your sidebars will help you return more quickly to key information in the passage.

3. *Review the passage.* Spend a final thirty seconds scanning the entire passage one more time. Use this review to solidify in your mind your understanding of how the pieces of the passage fit together: the objective of the experiments, for example, or the idea behind differing theories.

   Reviewing will also help you recall where within the passage various details can be found, in the event they're asked about in the questions.

LOOK FOR THE MAIN IDEA

Every reading passage is made up of two kinds of elements: main ideas and details. The main ideas are "big" concepts—broad, general ideas which are the most important points being made by the author of the passage. If you were the author, the main ideas would be the handful of concepts you'd want people to remember after reading the passage.

The details, by contrast, are "small" concepts—narrow, specific facts that help to explain, illustrate, or support the main ideas. They're not as important to understand or remember as the main ideas.

Most Science Reasoning passages include dozens of details: the individual data points on each graph; the specific numbers that fill the grid of a table or chart; the readings or values obtained in each experiment described. There's no way you can master or memorize all of them—and there's no need to. If a question does ask about a detail, you can always return to the passage for the answer. And in fact you should, to make sure you're answering accurately.

The three different passage formats will express their main ideas in three different ways.

TIP

You should spend a total of two to three minutes on the entire three-step method for Science Reasoning questions. When you first practice answering the Science Reasoning questions, either the exercises at the end of this chapter or those in Chapter 11, make sure you work with a clock or timer. Practice the three-step method until you can consistently complete it in no more than the allotted time. This will help you get the most out of your time on this portion of the real ACT Assessment.

How to Find the Main Ideas in Data Representation Passages

In Data Representation passages, focus on what is being measured, relationships among the variables, and trends or patterns in the data. As you remember, a Data Representation passage presents a collection of scientific facts in the form of one or more graphs, tables, charts, or diagrams. To understand the information in this, you need to know what their numbers measure, how different factors affect the numbers, and what trends the numbers reveal.

Example:

The optimum population density for the survival and growth of a particular species of animal is often an intermediate one. Excessive crowding produces competition for scarce resources, such as water, food, space, and light, and encourages the spread of infectious diseases. On the other hand, a low population density has its own disadvantages, including diminished protection against attacks by predators, inability to modify the environment in a helpful fashion, and greater vulnerability to changes in temperature.

The following figure, depicting the effect of initial population density upon the rate of population growth in the flour beetle, illustrates this principle.

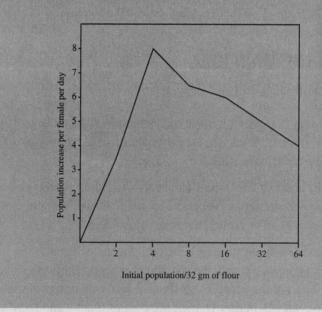

To begin, look for *what is being measured*. Reread the first sentence of the passage. It refers to "the optimum population density for the survival and growth of a particular species of animal." What is being measured is how the rate of growth in the numbers of a species is affected by the population density.

Because the passage focuses on how population density affects or influences the rate of population growth, population density is the independent variable, and rate of growth is the dependent variable. (If these scientific terms aren't familiar to you, look up the term in the glossary at the end of the Science Review chapter in Part 3.)

Next, look for *the relationships among the variables*. Here is where the graph is essential. As with virtually all line graphs, this one depicts the independent variable (population density) on the horizontal axis, and the dependent variable (rate of growth) on the vertical axis. As the dependent variable increases and decreases, the line on the graph rises and falls. While you're looking at the axes, check the scales. The horizontal scale shows initial numbers of beetles per 32 grams of flour (population density). The further to the right on this scale, the more beetles there were to start with. The vertical scale shows how fast the beetle population grew, measured in baby beetles born per female per day. The higher on this scale, the faster the population growth.

Finally, look for *the trends or patterns* in the data. In this example the trend is clearly seen in the shape of the line on the graph. Basically, the shape rises then falls; its high point is in the middle, where the horizontal scale indicates an initial population density of around 5 bugs. That's the basic trend to recognize: population growth is greatest not when the initial population density is very low or very high, but in the middle range.

These are the main ideas, and you now probably have all the information you need to answer the questions. If a specific detail is asked about (for example, "What is the rate of population increase when the initial beetle population is 32 beetles/32 grams of flour?"), you can simply look back at the graph to find the answer (4 per female per day).

How to Find the Main Idea in Research Summary Passages

In Research Summary passages, focus on the question asked, the variables being tested, and similarities and differences in the experimental results. As you remember, a Research Summary passage will pose a scientific question then describe two or three experiments or studies that attempt to answer that question. The results of the experiments are described or presented in the form of graphs or tables. The questions that follow require you to compare the experiments, recognize why they were designed as they were, and draw some basic conclusions as to what the experiments prove or don't prove.

TIP
The last sentence of the introductory material is usually important, no matter what the format. In a Data Representation passage, this sentence usually describes the relationship between the variables. In a Research Summary passage, this sentence usually describes the purpose of the experiments. In a Conflicting Viewpoints passage, this sentence usually explains the question under consideration.

Example:

It has long been known that different species of flowering plants flower at various times of the year in response to some environmental stimulus. Botanists have found that the duration and timing of light and dark conditions to which a plant is exposed, known as its photoperiod, is the crucial factor in flowering. Botanists generally classify flowering plants in three groups: long-day plants, which flower when the day length exceeds some critical value, usually in summer; short-day plants, which flower when the day length is below some critical value; and day-neutral plants, which can bloom during either long or short days.

In an effort to define more precisely the critical element in the photoperiod, scientists conducted the following experiments.

Experiment 1

A greenhouse in which conditions of light and darkness were carefully controlled was stocked with several long-day and short-day plants. These were maintained with a light regime of 14 hours of daylight alternating with 10 hours of darkness. Under these conditions, the long-day plants flowered, and the short-day plants did not.

Experiment 2

A similar greenhouse was stocked with several long-day and short-day plants. These were maintained with a light regime of 12 hours of daylight and 12 hours of darkness. The short-day plants flowered, and the long-day plants did not.

Experiment 3

In a similar greenhouse with the same assortment of plants, 12 hours of daylight and 12 hours of darkness were maintained. However, halfway through the dark period, all the plants were illuminated by a momentary flash of white light. Under these conditions, the long-day plants flowered, while the short-day plants did not.

These results are summarized in the following figure.

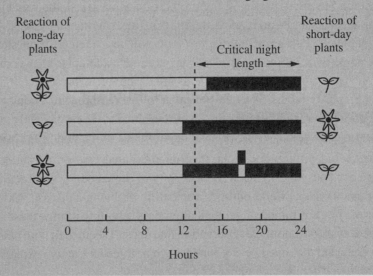

To begin, look for the question being asked. The sentence immediately preceding the experimental results tells us that purpose of the experiments was "to define more precisely the critical element in the photoperiod"; in other words, to figure out exactly to what the plants are responding when they either flower or fail to flower.

Next, look for the variables being tested. The experimenters are usually trying to determine how differing variables produce differing results or outcomes. To test this, they'll keep certain conditions in their experiments unchanged, while varying the others (hence the name "variables"). You can recognize the variables being tested by noting what is different from one experiment to the next. Some experiments might vary one condition; others will vary many conditions.

In the sample passage, the number of hours of daylight seems to be the variable tested. Then Experiment 3 introduces something new: the same number of hours of daylight and darkness, but the darkness is interrupted by a flash of light—with significantly different results. Thus, a careful description of the variable is not "hours of daylight" but rather "hours of uninterrupted darkness."

Finally, look for similarities and differences in the experimental results. Here, the results of Experiments 1 and 2 are predictable: the long-day plants flower when daylight is long and darkness is short, and the short-day plants flower when daylight is short and darkness is long. Opposite conditions produce opposite results, as you might expect. However, Experiment 3 introduces a new variable. The hours of darkness and light correspond to "short-day" conditions: twelve hours of each. But the flash of light that interrupts the "nighttime" period apparently has the effect of reversing the expected results: long-day plants flower in Experiment 3, and short-day plants don't. This suggests that the length of daylight hours isn't as crucial as the length of uninterrupted darkness.

The main ideas in a Research Summary passage, then, can be found by comparing the experiments. The ways in which they resemble one another—and, more importantly, the ways in which they differ—reveal what the scientists are interested in studying and the conclusions their work suggests.

TIP
Look carefully at the experiments, their data, and their set-ups, and use that information to determine the key variables being examined. Sometimes passages contain terminology that can be misleading, but the data never lies!

How to Find the Main Idea in Conflicting Viewpoints Passages

In Conflicting Viewpoints passages, focus on the idea to be explained, on the similarities and differences in the theories presented, and on the hidden assumptions that underlie each theory. As you remember, a Conflicting Viewpoints passage briefly outlines a scientific problem: a disease whose cause must be determined, a geological process whose workings must be described, or an astronomical observation that doesn't seem to fit with other known facts and that must be explained. Two or three alternative explanations are then offered, each under its own heading.

Example:

The salmonids are a family of fishes that includes salmon, trout, and char. Many species of salmonids are capable of navigating great distances, and they use this ability in long-range migrations, often involving thousands of miles of both ocean and fresh-water swimming. Salmon, in particular, are known for their homing behavior, in which maturing adults return to their parents' spawning (egg-laying) sites with 84 to 98 percent accuracy. Two main theories have been proposed to explain how salmon are able to navigate such great distances so successfully.

Chemoreception Theory

Salmon are one of many species of fish that are sensitive to the presence of particular chemicals in their environment, and they use stimuli provided by these chemicals and detected by the sense of smell as navigational clues. These stimuli are sometimes present over large areas of water. For example, it has been demonstrated that sockeye salmon spawned in the Fraser River in Canada can recognize water from that river in the open sea as much as 300 kilometers from its mouth.

To test the hypothesis that smell is the crucial sense for salmon navigation, scientists blocked the nasal cavities of some migrating coho salmon with absorbent cotton and marked the fish to facilitate tracing. Another group of coho salmon was differently marked and not treated in any other way. When the travels of both groups of salmon were studied, it was found that the untreated group returned accurately to their rivers of origin, and the salmon that were unable to smell selected rivers at random.

Magnetic Direction-Finding Theory

Various species of animals navigate using clues provided by the earth's magnetic field. This field, which generates magnetic lines of force running in a north-south direction, can be used in direction-finding by many birds and, some scientists believe, by some fish, including salmon.

One species of Pacific salmon, the chum, was tested for its sensitivity to magnetism in the following way. An experimental apparatus consisting of two electrical coils was built around a tank housing the salmon. When a current was run through the coils, a magnetic field was generated, capable of intensifying, weakening, or altering the earth's magnetic field, depending on the positioning of the coils. When this field was rotated 90° from the normal north-south orientation, the chum's own orientation also rotated, indicating the fish's ability to directly detect the earth's magnetic field and its responsiveness to that stimulus.

Unlike in some birds, however, whose skulls have been shown to contain particles of magnetite, a metal sensitive to magnetism, no mechanism for detecting magnetism has yet been discovered in salmon.

In a Conflicting Viewpoints passage, sometimes the theories might flatly contradict one another; other times they might be completely independent of one another or even complementary. In reality, either theory, neither, or both could be true.

To begin, look for the question to be explained. In the sample passage, the key sentence is "Two main theories have been proposed to explain how salmon are able to navigate such great distances so successfully." This makes it clear that what must be explained is the mechanism whereby salmon can find their way accurately over such long distances.

Next, look for the similarities and differences in the theories presented. For example, in the sample passage, both theories suggest that the salmon respond to environmental stimuli, as opposed, for example, to some purely internal or instinctive mechanism. On the other hand, the theories differ in the nature of the stimulus on which the salmon supposedly rely. One theory considers the sense of smell to be crucial, the other focuses on magnetism. One more difference lies in how the supposed navigational mechanism might be affected by changes in the environment.

Finally, look for the hidden assumptions that underlie each theory. Hidden assumptions are facts or ideas, not stated in the passage, that must be true if a theory is to be considered valid. Assumptions are the secret flaw in many theories. If the assumption is true, the theory might be sound, valid, and convincing. If it is false, the theory is likely to break down completely. And because the assumption is unstated—"hidden"—it is easy to overlook.

For example, in the "smell" hypothesis, one assumption is that whatever chemical gives the water in the spawning ground its distinctive "smell" must persist over time, or else the salmon couldn't recognize it when they try to return to their "home" river. In the "magnetism" hypothesis, one assumption is that if there's no magnetite in the salmon, then it must have some other substance or organ that's sensitive to magnetic fields. If any of these assumptions could be proven to be false, then the theory associated with it would crumble. Because ACT Assessment questions often ask about hidden assumptions, practice looking for them when you read a Conflicting Viewpoints passage.

KNOW THE FOUR MOST COMMON QUESTION TYPES

Most of the questions on the ACT Assessment Science Reasoning Test will fall into one of these four categories:

1. main idea
2. detail
3. inference
4. application

Main idea questions ask about one of the main ideas on which you focused in reading the passage. Earlier sections of this chapter discussed how to find the main idea in each of the Science Reasoning subject areas. These questions should be easy to answer if you've read the passage as suggested above, focusing on those elements that are most important to each type of passage.

A *detail* question focuses on one specific piece of information drawn from the passage. To answer correctly, read the question carefully, return to the passage, and find the answer. Don't try to answer from memory.

Here's a sample detail question based on a passage you read earlier in this chapter (beetles-in-the-flour):

> **Q** According to the figure, if the initial population density is 16 beetles per 32 grams of flour, what will be the rate of population increase per female per day?
>
>   A. 3
>
>   B. 5
>
>   C. 6
>
>   D. 8
>
> (Answer: C)

The answer, choice C, can be read directly from the graph that accompanies the passage.

An *inference* question requires that you make connections between two or more details that are not explicitly stated in the passage.

Using the flowering-plants passage you read earlier in the chapter, here's an example:

> **Q** On the basis of the information in the figure, the long-day plants used in the study can be expected to flower when they are housed in conditions that include:
>
>   A. a period of daylight at least twelve hours long.
>
>   B. no period of uninterrupted darkness longer than eleven hours.
>
>   C. no period of daylight shorter than twelve hours.
>
>   D. no period of uninterrupted darkness shorter than ten hours.
>
> (Answer: B)

The correct answer is choice B. To answer this item correctly, you must not only understand the overall experimental setup and the special features of Experiment 3 in the earlier passage, but also note in the figure that accompanies that passage the dotted vertical line marking what's called "critical night length." You can infer that this represents the number of hours of darkness that separate long-day from short-day plants. The line is drawn so as to mark off eleven hours of darkness (or thirteen hours of daylight), which we see must be the maximum amount of uninterrupted darkness in which a long-day plant can flower.

An *application* question requires you to apply the information in the passage to a context beyond the passage. For instance, you might be asked to evaluate a new piece of evidence that could either strengthen or weaken one of the theories presented; you could be called upon to extrapolate from the information provided to a new situation that's not included in the existing graph or table; or you might be asked how the ideas in the passage might affect some real-world problem.

Here's an example using the salmon-navigation passage you read earlier in the chapter:

> **Q** The Magnetic Direction-Finding Theory would be most greatly strengthened by the discovery that:
>
> A. chemical-sensitive organs exist in the nasal cavities of coho salmon.
>
> B. the earth's magnetic field is too weak to be detected by most species of salmon.
>
> C. particles of magnetite exist in the skulls of Pacific salmon.
>
> D. coho salmon are the only species of salmon with a highly sensitive sense of smell.
>
> (Answer: C)

The passage suggests that one weakness of the magnetic theory is the absence of any obvious mechanism by which the magnetic sensing could work. Answer C would strengthen the theory by supplying this absence. Answer B would weaken the theory rather than strengthening it, and answers A and D relate only to the Chemoreception Theory rather than the magnetic theory.

DON'T GET LOST IN NUMBERS, JARGON, OR DETAILS

Most Science Reasoning passages will include information that is not necessary to answer the question. This might be numbers in the text or on the graphs or tables, scientific terminology, or dozens of details. For example, one ACT Assessment Science Reasoning passage dealt with bacterial reproduction and listed twelve different types of bacteria using their Latin names: *Clostridium botulinum, Escherichia coli, Lactobacillus acidophilus,* and so on. Although those names were repeated on the chart, they could just as well have been labeled bacterium #1 through #12. The Latin names didn't matter.

So don't allow yourself to be distracted. Focus on the main ideas of the passage, skim the details, then answer the questions.

TIP
Though some ACT Assessment Science Reasoning questions ask about specific details, *the majority of the questions don't.* Don't spend your time trying to memorize details; when you encounter a detail question, you can return to the passage, graph, or chart to find its answer.

TIP
Even though you can't use a calculator on the Science Reasoning portion of the ACT Assessment, you won't have much trouble with the math—it's usually fairly easy in this section. And, feel free to round off numbers and estimate, especially when answer choices have broad differences.

SUCCESS STRATEGY ROUNDUP: A LIST OF DO'S AND DON'TS

Here's the "short version" of the above advice, along with a few other miscellaneous sidebars, arranged in a handy list of do's and don'ts. After you understand each point and the reasoning behind it, you need only know the boldface sentence to jog your memory—whether you're working on the exercises at the end of this chapter, your full-length sample tests, or the ACT Assessment itself.

A list of Do's:

☑ **Preview, read, review.** Think of the Science Reasoning Test as just a specialized version of the regular ACT Assessment Reading Test. Use the same skills and strategies detailed in that section, mark up the test booklet to underline main ideas, and remember that all the information you need to answer the question is right there.

☑ **Read just the labels, legends, and explanatory sidebars.** On all forms of data representation, read the labels on the axes, rows, and columns, as well as the legends and Sidebars. You don't have to read the actual point-by-point information. Notice trends, groupings, processes, and sequences, and then move on.

☑ **Find the main ideas as you read.** In Data Representation passages, focus on what is being measured, on relationships among the variables, and on trends in the data. In Research Summary passages, focus on the question of the hypothesis, on the variables being tested, and on differences in the experimental results. In Conflicting Viewpoints passages, focus on what must be explained, on similarities and differences in the theories presented, and on hidden assumptions that underlie each theory.

☑ **Know what's being asked.** Is it Experiment 3 the question asks about or Experiment 4? Table 1 or Table 2? Read carefully. Just a few words can mean the difference between the correct answer and an incorrect one.

☑ **Pay close attention to the last sentence of the introductory material.** In a Data Representation passage, the last sentence of the introductory material is where the relationship between the variables can usually be found. In a Research Summary passage, it's where the purpose of the experiments can usually be found. In a Conflicting Viewpoints passage, it's where the question under consideration can usually be found.

☑ **Look for differences in the data.** Remember that differences are more important than similarities. When comparing charts, tables, experimental design, experimental results, and so on, look for the differences. Questions are more likely to deal with differences than similarities.

☑ **Know the four type of questions.** Decide whether a question is about the main idea, details, an inference, or an application. Your approach to each will be slightly different.

☑ **Look for the change.** In any experiment, look for the variable that changes, then look to see how a change in the variable results in changes in other elements of the experiment.

A list of Don'ts:

☒ **Don't get lost in numbers, scientific jargon, and irrelevant details.** Don't try to memorize the details as you read. Just look for the main ideas. You can then refer back to passage to find the few details needed to answer questions.

☒ **Don't be thrown by math on the Science Reasoning Test.** Math on the Science Reasoning Test is very basic, and you won't be allowed to use a calculator. If you think a particular item calls for extensive calculations, you are probably misreading the question.

☒ **Don't confuse units of measurement.** Although math is secondary, it does have its role. You might be asked, for example, to take a relationship expressed in liters and apply it to a quantity of milliliters; remember to change the unit of measurement.

☒ **Don't take sides in Conflicting Viewpoints passages.** Deciding which side is right or which side you agree with is irrelevant. Trying to figure that out only wastes time and has nothing to do with the questions being asked. Focus on the information presented and the assumptions supporting each theory.

☒ **Don't accept every assumption as true.** Certain experiments will be based on faulty assumptions. If the assumption is faulty, the experimental design is faulty, and the results do not prove what the conclusion claims to prove.

PRACTICE EXERCISES

You've just learned some new skills for taking the ACT Assessment Science Reasoning Test. The following exercises will help you to practice these new skills as well as to continue to familiarize yourself with the contents and format of the ACT Assessment.

There are two Science Reasoning Test exercises in this chapter. Each exercise contains two passages and a total of 12 questions and should be answered in 10 minutes. Do each exercise in one sitting in a quiet place, with no Sidebars or reference material. Use a stopwatch or kitchen timer or have someone else watch the clock. When time is up, stop at once.

Score yourself only on those items you finished. When you're done, work through the rest of the exercise.

EXERCISES: THE ACT ASSESSMENT SCIENCE TEST

Exercise 1

12 Questions • Time—10 Minutes

Directions: This test consists of two passages, each followed by several questions. Read each passage, select the correct answer for each question, and mark the oval representing the correct answer on your answer sheet. You may NOT use a calculator on this test.

Passage I

Phytoplankton are tiny aquatic plants that are an important food source for larger animals and may be an important source of carbon (the element that is a building block of all living organisms). Phytoplankton abundance is dependent on the presence of warm surface waters. Consequently, changes in phytoplankton abundance can be used as an indicator of changes in surface water temperature.

A system for documenting phytoplankton abundance has been developed using filtering silk towed by merchant ships. The organisms color the silk green, and the intensity of the color is correlated with their abundance. The first figure shows data on the average monthly phytoplankton abundance for four decades, as determined by the color index system. Data is given for two ocean areas in the Northern Atlantic just below the arctic circle. The boundaries of these areas are depicted in the second figure.

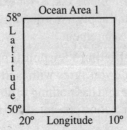

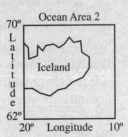

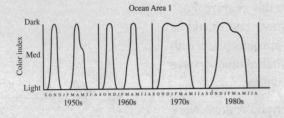

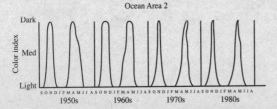

1. Based on the information in the first figure, which of the following statements concerning phytoplankton abundance in the four decades of the study is correct?

   A. There was no discernible change in patterns of phytoplankton abundance in ocean area 1.

   B. Annual phytoplankton abundance increased in ocean area 2.

   C. Annual phytoplankton abundance increased in ocean area 1 and decreased in ocean area 2.

   D. The season of high phytoplankton abundance increased in length in both ocean areas.

2. Assuming that the changes in phytoplankton abundance seen in the study occurred solely because of surface water temperature variations, the information in the figures indicates that which of the following statements is true?

   F. Surface ocean waters above latitude 62° North in the map areas cooled during the study.

   G. Surface ocean waters above latitude 50° North in the map areas cooled during the study.

   H. Surface ocean waters east of longitude 10° in the map areas warmed during the study.

   J. Surface ocean waters west of longitude 10° in the map areas cooled during the study.

3. Which of the following statements best describes typical phytoplankton abundance in ocean areas 1 and 2 in the 1950s?

   A. Abundance increased in October and remained at high levels until about June.

   B. Abundance increased slowly and fell off rapidly in two distinct periods.

   C. Abundance increased rapidly in two distinct periods and remained at peak levels for approximately three months during each of these periods.

   D. Abundance increased and fell off rapidly in two distinct periods.

4. The first figure indicates what about the changes in phytoplankton abundance?

   F. Changes occurred evenly over the course of the four decades.

   G. Changes occurred over the course of about a decade.

   H. Changes occurred over the course of about a year.

   J. Changes in area 1 were apparent earlier than changes in area 2.

5. Some researchers hypothesize that the changes in phytoplankton abundance reflect an increase in global temperature over the last century (global warming). Which of the following findings would support this hypothesis and fit the data seen in the first figure?

   A. A greater abundance of fresh water from melted ice and permafrost has begun flowing south to north from the Antarctic during the last century.

   B. A greater abundance of fresh water from melted ice and permafrost has begun flowing north to south from the Arctic during the last century.

   C. Warmer temperatures have been recorded in and around Iceland during the last century.

   D. Barring a few exceptions, phytoplankton numbers have begun to decrease dramatically in ocean areas around the globe during the last century.

6. Certain species of whales migrate annually in order to take advantage of abundant blooms of phytoplankton, one of their principal food sources. During which of the following months would a whale-watching tour in Ocean Area 1 be LEAST likely to encounter phytoplankton-eating whales?

   F. January

   G. April

   H. May

   J. August

GO ON TO THE NEXT PAGE

Passage II

Airplane wings must be designed *aerodynamically* (with consideration to the airflow over the body of the plane) to ensure efficient flight. Aerodynamic design considers *lift* and *drag*.

Lift is the force acting upwards on the plane. It is generated because the top of a wing is curved, while the bottom is flat. The air moving over the top of the wings must move faster than the air moving over the bottom. This results in a lower pressure area above the wing.

Drag is the air resistance generated by the plane. This is a force acting in opposition to the planes forward movement. The most efficient planes are those with the highest lift to drag ratio.

Researchers testing new wing designs conducted a series of experiments to measure their efficiency.

Experiment 1

Researchers tested aircraft with four wing designs (see the following figure) in a *wind tunnel* (a tunnel in which air is blown over a craft to simulate flight conditions). This test simulated flight at 400 mph. The lift and drag measured for each wing shape are recorded in Table 7.1.

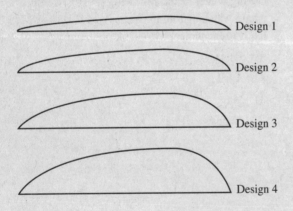

Table 7.1

Wing Design	Lift (neutrons)	Drag (neutrons)	Efficiency
1	3	.15	20:1
2	8	.2	40:1
3	10	1	10:1
4	18	2	9:1

Experiment 2

Aircraft with the four wing types depicted in the figure were tested under similar flight conditions to gauge fuel consumption. After reaching cruising altitude, the planes maintained a speed of 400 mph. The results appear in Table 7.2.

Table 7.2

Wing Design	Fuel consumption (gal/hr)
1	40
2	20
3	80
4	88

Experiment 3

Lift, drag and efficiency are dependent on airspeed. The researchers tested wing designs 1 and 2 at different speeds. Efficiency (lift to drag ratio) was recorded (Table 7.3).

Table 7.3

Airspeed (mph)	Design 1 (Efficiency)	Design 2 (Efficiency)
200	22:1	43:1
300	21:1	42:1
400	20:1	40:1
500	18:1	12:1
600	10:1	8:1

7. The most efficient wing tested in experiment 1 was:

   A. Design 1

   B. Design 2

   C. Design 3

   D. Design 4

8. A passenger plane is able to carry a fixed weight, including passengers and fuel. Which wing design would be best for such a plane?

   F. Design 1

   G. Design 2

   H. Design 3

   J. Design 4

9. In cold, damp weather, the buildup of ice on airplane wings can pose significant aerodynamic problems. Which of the following effects would you expect?

   A. As ice builds up on the top of the wing, drag increases.

   B. As ice builds up on the top of the wing, lift increases.

   C. As ice builds up on bottom of the wing, lift decreases.

   D. All of the above.

10. Which of the following test pairs reflects consistent experimental data?

    F. Experiment 1, wing design 2; Experiment 2, airspeed 200

    G. Experiment 1, wing design 1; Experiment 2, wing design 2

    H. Experiment 1, wing design 3; Experiment 3, airspeed 400

    J. Experiment 1, wing design 1; Experiment 3, airspeed 400

11. Which of the following statements about airspeed is supported by the data in Experiment 3?

    A. As airspeed increases, the lift to drag ratio increases.

    B. As airspeed increases, lift and drag increase at about the same rate.

    C. As airspeed increases, drag increases faster than lift.

    D. As airspeed increases, lift increases faster than drag.

12. New fighter jets are being designed so that the wing is modifiable, depending on the speed at which the plane is going. Which of the following would be a logical adjustment of the wing for such jets?

    F. At speeds above 500 mph, the top of the wing would become flatter.

    G. At speeds above 500 mph, the top of the wing would become more curved.

    H. At speeds above 500 mph, the bottom of the wing would become curved.

    J. None of the above.

GO ON TO THE NEXT PAGE

Exercise 2

12 Questions • Time—10 minutes

Directions: This test consists of two passages, each followed by several questions. Read each passage, select the correct answer for each question, and mark the oval representing the correct answer on your answer sheet. You may NOT use a calculator on this test.

Passage I

A greenish, potato-sized meteorite discovered in Antarctica is believed to have originated on Mars. Investigations of the meteorite have revealed a number of unusual features. Some scientists believe that these features are evidence of primitive life on Mars, while other scientists believe that they are more probably the result of nonbiological (nonliving) processes, such as hydrothermal synthesis.

Hydrothermal Synthesis Hypothesis

The meteorite crystallized slowly from *magma* (molten rock) on Mars 4.5 million years ago. About half a million years later, the rock became fractured. This was a time when Mars was much warmer and had abundant water. Deep inside the planet, in a process called *hydrothermal synthesis*, hot water and carbon seeped into the fractured rock and formed new complex *organic* compounds called polycyclic aromatic hydrocarbons (PAHs). (Organic compounds, or those that contain carbon, are formed from life processes, such as bacterial decay, as well as processes that are not associated with life, including hydrothermal synthesis and star formation.)

As the chemical environment of the planet changed over time, crystals of magnetite, iron sulfides, and carbonate formed in the rock. The crystallization of the carbonate resulted in the formation of unusual elongated and egg-shaped structures within the crystals.

Primitive Life Hypothesis

The meteorite crystallized slowly from *magma* (molten rock) on Mars 4.5 million years ago. About half a million years later, the rock became fractured. This was a time when Mars was much warmer and had abundant water. The rock was immersed in water rich in carbon dioxide, which allowed carbon to collect inside the fractured rock, along with primitive bacteria.

The bacteria began to manufacture magnetite and iron sulfide crystals, just as bacteria on earth do. As generations of bacteria died and began to decay, they created PAHs inside of the meteorite's carbon molecules. Finally, some of bacteria themselves were preserved as elongated egg-shaped fossils inside of the rock.

1. About which of the following points do the two hypotheses differ?
   A. The meteorite's age
   B. The origin of the meteorite's organic molecules
   C. The conditions on Mars when the meteorite formed
   D. The origin of the fractures in the meteorite

2. Proponents of both theories would agree that which of the following statements is true?
   F. The meteorite contains some type of fossil.
   G. Water was important for the original entry of carbon into the meteorite.
   H. The organic compounds seen in the rock were the result of decay.
   J. Magnetite crystals from Antarctica seeped into the meteorite.

3. Which of the following represents a difference in opinion between proponents of the two theories?

   A. Proponents of the Primitive Life Hypothesis maintain that Mars has changed substantially since the meteorite was formed.

   B. Proponents of the Primitive Life Hypothesis dispute the notion that PAHs can occur from processes other than bacterial decay.

   C. Proponents of the Hydrothermal Synthesis Hypothesis believe that hot water and carbon formed organic compounds in the rock.

   D. Proponents of the Hydrothermal Synthesis Hypothesis believe that the fossils found inside the meteorite were probably the remains of an organism other than a bacteria.

4. Which of the following findings would help to bolster the case of proponents of the Hydrothermal Synthesis Hypothesis?

   F. The magnetite found in the meteorite sometimes occurred in chains, similar to those produced by bacteria on earth.

   G. Glass within the meteorite hints that it was probably fractured and launched towards earth when a meteoroid or comet hit Mars.

   H. Recent studies indicate that liquid water, one of life's most fundamental necessities, does not exist on Mars.

   J. Minerals can grow into shapes that are similar to the elongated egg-shaped structures seen in the meteorite.

5. Researchers analyzing glacial ice found very low concentrations of PAHs. Which of the following additional findings would help the case of proponents of the Primitive Life Hypothesis?

   A. The meteorite contained only a small number of the thousands of PAHs, and all of the ones found are known to be associated with bacterial decay.

   B. Organic molecules were also discovered in meteorites known to have originated in the *asteroid belt* (an area orbiting the sun which is rich in asteroids).

   C. Some of the carbonates in which the PAHs were found had element ratios that are similar to those found on earth.

   D. Experiments with the weathering of rocks have shown that under certain conditions, molecules in the environment can make their way deep within a rock.

6. Which of the following experiments might help to resolve the question of whether the PAHs in the meteorite actually originated on Mars?

   F. Examine the ratios of the PAHs found in glacial ice and see if these are similar to those seen in the meteorite.

   G. Test meteorites known to have come from the moon for PAHs.

   H. Test for PAHs in meteorites known to have formed on Mars after its era of abundant water ended.

   J. All of the above.

GO ON TO THE NEXT PAGE

Passage II

Electrical circuits that allow electrical signals with some *frequencies* (number of waves per second) to pass while suppressing others are called *filters*. They are used in nearly every electronic device, from computers to VCRs. They may contain *resistors*, which resist the flow of current through a wire, *inductors*, which resist change in the current, and capacitors, which store electric charge. The following figure shows the design of three types of filters.

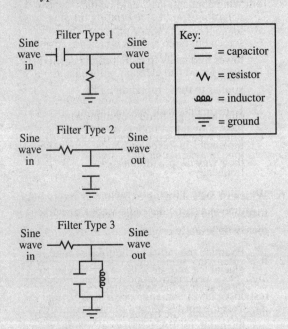

The effects of a filter can be demonstrated with a *frequency response curve*. Such a curve depicts the *amplitude* (wave height) of the output (vertical axis) as one varies the input frequency (horizontal axis), while keeping the input amplitude constant. Several experiments were conducted to test the effects of some filters.

Experiment 1

Researchers fed *sine waves* (oscillating voltage) into an electrical circuit containing the three filters depicted in the figure. The input amplitude was fixed at 2.0 volts. The amplitude of the resulting waves were measured, and the frequency response curves in the following figure were obtained.

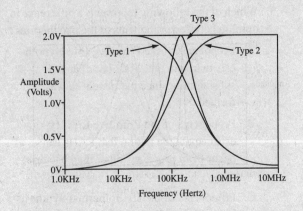

K=1000

M=1 Million

Experiment 2

A sine wave with an amplitude fixed at 2.0 volts was fed into a circuit with a type 3 filter, but in this experiment the researchers used four different values for the inductance (L). The resulting frequency response curves are shown in the following figure.

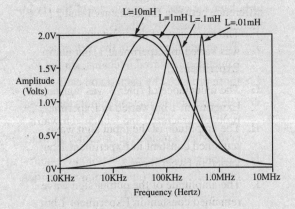

Experiment 3

Again, the researchers fed a sine wave with an amplitude fixed at 2.0 volts into a circuit with a type 3 filter. The inductance was held at .1 mH, while four different values of capacitance C were used. The resulting frequency response curves are shown in the following figure.

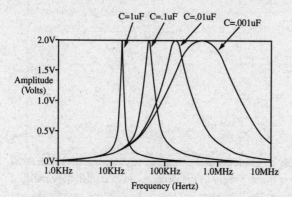

Frequency (Hertz)

7. Which of the following statements about the three filters is supported by Experiment 1?

   A. Type 1 filters out high frequencies.

   B. Type 1 filters out low frequencies.

   C. Type 2 filters out high frequencies.

   D. Type 3 filters out mid-range frequencies.

8. Which of the following accurately described the difference between Experiments 1 and 2?

   F. The frequency of the input sign wave was varied in Experiment 1, but not in Experiment 2.

   G. The inductance of filter 3 was constant in Experiment 1 but varied in Experiment 2.

   H. The amplitude of the input sign wave remained constant in Experiment 1 but varied in Experiment 2.

   J. The amplitude of the output sign wave remained constant in Experiment 1 but varied in Experiment 2.

9. When capacitance is increased for filter 3, which of the following effects occur?

   A. The output amplitude is increased.

   B. The range of frequencies that the filter does not suppress increases.

   C. A smaller range of frequencies are accepted.

   D. The accepted frequencies are in a higher range.

10. In Experiment 2, the capacitance was most likely set at:

    F. $1\mu F$

    G. $.1\mu F$

    H. $.01\mu F$

    J. $.001\mu F$

11. The frequency response curves suggest possible applications for the three filters. Which of the following applications would be most logical?

    A. Filter type 1 used by a radio receiver to screen out radio signals which are at a lower frequency than that of the desired station.

    B. Filter type 2 used in an audio circuit to eliminate high-frequency audio hum.

    C. Filter type 2 used in a radio receiver to tune in a particular radio station at a fixed frequency.

    D. Filter type 3 used in a radio receiver to tune in a particular radio station at a fixed frequency.

12. It is often very important to design filters with *high Q* (a very narrow peak in the frequency response curve). An engineer discovers that the *tuned frequency* (the frequency at which the frequency response curve peaks) of a circuit with a type 3 filter is too low. Which of the following should he do in order to raise the tuned frequency and keep a high Q filter circuit?

    F. Lower the capacitance

    G. Lower the inductance

    H. Raise the capacitance and the inductance

    J. Raise the resistance

ANSWER KEYS AND EXPLANATIONS

Exercise 1

1. C	4. G	7. B	10. J
2. F	5. B	8. G	11. C
3. D	6. J	9. D	12. F

1. **C.** You can literally "see" the answer to this question merely by glancing at the graphs in the figure. In Ocean Area 1, the two annual periods of phytoplankton abundance grew much longer as the decades passed until they merged into a single long period of abundance lasting half the year. By contrast, in Ocean Area 2, the two peaks got "thinner" as time passed, indicating a steady decrease in the phytoplankton population.

2. **F.** Only answer F gives information consistent with the data in the graphs. Ocean Area 2 is north of latitude 62°; if the waters there got cooler, it would make sense that phytoplankton abundance would decrease (see the second sentence of the passage).

3. **D.** Look at the shapes of the two peak periods in the graphs for the 1950s (roughly similar in both ocean areas). Both feature steep increases with equally steep declines, as described in answer D.

4. **G.** In both ocean areas, the most dramatic change by far appears between the 1960s and the 1970s.

5. **B.** This answer would fit both the global warming hypothesis and the data shown in the graphs in several ways. First, the graphs for Ocean Area 1, showing an increase in phytoplankton, certainly fit the notion of global warming. Second, the idea that Arctic ice is melting would fit that idea as well. Finally, the abundance of fresh water newly-melted from ice appearing in the northern reaches of the Atlantic could help to explain why phytoplankton has actually declined around Iceland: the water temperature there has gone down slightly as a result of the melting ice.

6. **J.** Of the months named, only August is a month with virtually no measurable phytoplankton in any of the four graphs for Ocean Area 1. Therefore, this is the least promising month for observing phytoplankton-eating whales.

7. **B.** The answer can easily be found in the fourth column of Table 7.1: the efficiency of design 2 (in terms of lift to drag ratio) was 40:1, a higher ratio than any of the other wings.

8. **G.** Since design 2 is most efficient according to all three experiments, it is the most desirable design.

9. **D.** Ice building up on top of the wing would increase lift, since the higher the curved upper surface of the wing, the greater the difference between the speed of air moving under the wing and above it. It would also increase drag, as suggested by the third column of Table 7.1: notice how the wings with the higher upper surface also have greater drag. Finally, ice building up under the wing would decrease the speed of air moving under the wing and so reduce lift. Thus, all three effects would occur.

10. **J.** In both experiments named here, conditions are the same: the same wing design is used, and the airspeed of 400 mph is the same. (Logically enough, the efficiency result is also the same: 40:1.)

11. **C.** Remember that "efficiency" is the same as the lift to drag ratio. Since we note in Table 7.3 that efficiency decreases as speed increases, we can tell that drag must be increasing faster than lift.

12. **F.** Consider again the results of Experiment 3 (Table 7.3). Wing design 2 is more efficient than design 1 at all of the lower speeds, but once a speed of 500 mph is reached, design 1 outperforms design 2. Thus, it appears that at high speeds a "flatter" wing design is more beneficial.

Exercise 2

1. B	4. J	7. A	10. H
2. G	5. A	8. G	11. D
3. C	6. F	9. C	12. G

1. **B.** The Hydrothermal Synthesis Hypothesis states that the PAHs (the organic molecules in the meteorite) were formed by hydrothermal synthesis, while the Primitive Life Hypothesis says that they were formed by the decay of bacteria.

2. **G.** See the fourth sentence of each of the sections describing the two hypothesis. In both cases, seeping water is described as the mechanism that allowed carbon to enter the rock.

3. **C.** This is the only true statement that also names a difference between the proponents of the two theories. Answer A describes a belief that is actually shared by proponents of both theories, while answers B and D both make false statements about what the proponents of the theories state.

4. **J.** If it's true that minerals can form "egg-shaped structures" like those found in the meteorite, this would strengthen the Hydrothermal Synthesis Hypothesis by providing an alternative explanation for these forms, which the Primitive Life proponents consider evidence of life on Mars.

5. **A.** The fact that low concentrations of PAHs were found in glacial ice (mildly) strengthens the Primitive Life Hypothesis by tending to disprove the notion that the PAHs in the meteorite seeped in after the rock landed in Antarctica. The statement in answer A would further strengthen that hypothesis by suggesting that the PAHs in the meteorite were more probably produced by bacterial decay than by non-living processes.

6. **F.** This test would at least help to eliminate—or confirm—the possibility that the PAHs found in the meteorite actually appeared there as a result of contamination from glacial ice.

7. **A.** Look at the line in the figure depicting the frequency response curve for filter type 1. It falls off dramatically in the middle of the graph, indicating that low frequencies (the left side of the graph) get through, while high frequencies (the right side of the graph) are suppressed.

8. **G.** In both experiments, the input amplitude was fixed at 2.0 volts, and the frequency was varied (along the horizontal scale of each graph). However, the inductance was varied in Experiment 2 only.

9. **C.** Look at the figure. As you go from right to left in the graph, the capacitance figures increase. And as you do so, the graphed lines form "steeper," "sharper," more "pointy" curves. This indicates that a narrower range of frequencies is being permitted through by the filter.

10. **H.** To answer this question, you need to compare Experiments 2 and 3, along with the graphs showing the results. We're told that the inductance in Experiment 3 was held at .1 mH. This corresponds with the third line from the left in the figure. Since that line most closely resembles the third line from the left in the figure—and since we're told that, for that line, the capacitance was set at .01μF—it makes sense to assume that the same capacitance must have been used to produce the matching line in Experiment 2.

11. **D.** Look at the figure. Since filter type 3 "zeroes in" on waves of a very specific frequency, allowing only those waves to pass through, it makes sense that one might use this type of filter to tune in the fixed frequency of a particular radio station (while eliminating all other competing signals).

12. **G.** As you can see from the figure, the lower the inductance, the higher the frequency at which the response curve attains its peak.

ARE YOU READY TO MOVE ON?

How well do you understand the contents and format of the ACT Assessment Science Reasoning Test? How well have you incorporated your new skills into your test-taking behavior?

After you've corrected each exercise, find the number below. This will give you an idea of whether you need to go to the Science Reasoning Review, or whether you can move on to another subject area.

Score Key for Each Practice Exercise

Number Correct	Score	Suggested Action
0–3	Poor	Study the review chapter and do the exercises there. Study this chapter again.
4–6	Below average	Study problem areas in the review chapter and do at least one exercise. Study this chapter again.
7–10	Average	Study this chapter again if you have time. Skim problem areas in the review chapter if you have time.
11–15	Above average	You may move on to a new subject.
16–20	Excellent	You're ready for the ACT Assessment Science Reasoning Test.

Summary: What You Need to Know About the ACT Assessment Science Reasoning Test

- The ACT Assessment Science Reasoning Test will contain seven passages of about 100 to 300 words long, on biology, chemistry, physics, and earth science, followed by a total of 40 questions. You will have 35 minutes to complete the test.

- Use the "Preview, Read, Review" method to tackle each passage before trying to answer the questions.

- Pay close attention to the last sentence of the introductory material in each passage.

- In Data Representation passages, look for trends (patterns) in the data. In Research Summary passages, look for differences among the experiments described. And in Conflicting Viewpoints passages, look for hidden assumptions underlying each of the theories presented.

- Identify whether questions are main idea, detail, inference, or application questions.

- Read just the labels, the axes, rows, and columns, not every bit of information in a chart. Notice trends, groupings, processes, and sequences, and then move on.

- Don't get lost in numbers, scientific jargon, and details. Only a handful of details will be asked about in the questions. Lengthy math calculations will not be necessary.

Master ACT Assessment Subject Reviews

English Review: Grammar

Reviewing twelve years of grade-, middle-, and high-school grammar in a single chapter of this book would be an exhaustive task—and exhaustive for you to study in such a concentrated time. What this chapter does, then, is focus on the rules of grammar most likely to be tested on the ACT Assessment. If you can master the rules in this chapter, you can master ACT Assessment English.

This review covers nine areas. It begins with the rules for verbs, modifying phrases, adjectives and adverbs, pronouns, connecting clauses, and punctuation. The review then covers points of grammar and logic, the use of idioms, the use of commonly confused words, and the avoidance of wordiness. A final section brings you additional resources for review in case you need extra help.

MASTERING VERBS

A *verb* is a word that shows action or a state of being. It tells what someone or something is or does. Every sentence has at least one verb; grammatically, there is no sentence if a group of words has no verb in the main clause. The "doer" of the action—the "someone or something" that "does or is" the verb—is called the *subject* of the verb.

> *Example:* An assassin killed President Lincoln.

In this sentence, *killed* is the verb, the word that shows action, and *assassin* is the subject, the doer of the action.

> *Example:* Howard is a landscape architect.

In this sentence, *is* is the verb, the word that shows a state of being, and *Howard* is the subject, the doer of the verb.

In the following sections, you learn the key rules regarding verbs covered in the ACT Assessment English Test.

A VERB MUST AGREE WITH ITS SUBJECT IN NUMBER

In a correct sentence, the verb and subject must agree in number; here, *number* refers to whether the verb and its subject are singular or plural. A singular subject and verb refer to one person or thing; a plural subject and verb refer to more than one. The number of the subject must match the

CAUTION

Subject-verb agreement can be tricky when the subject follows the verb rather than precedes it ("There were fourteen cartons left on the shelf"), when a nearby phrase refers to a group ("Among those who played a crucial role . . . was Joshua Chamberlain"), and/or when a lengthy phrase or clause separates the subject from the verb ("The purpose of such post-war international organizations as NATO, the World Bank, and the Organization of American States has been . . .").

When in doubt, find the verb in the main clause first.

number of the verb: If the subject is singular, the verb must be singular; if the subject is plural, the verb must be plural.

You can often "hear" an error in number, as in "Howard are a landscape architect" (this sentence combines a singular subject with a plural verb). It would also be wrong to write, "People was very upset by Diana's death" (a plural subject with a singular verb). In these two examples, the error in subject-verb agreement is easy to spot.

In some sentences, however, it's not as easy.

Example: Among those who played a crucial role in the Northern victory at Gettysburg were Joshua Chamberlain, a Union colonel from Maine who later enjoyed a distinguished career as an educator and politician.

The verb in the main clause of the sentence (in this example, the clause that appears first) is *were*. The simplest way to find the subject is to ask, "Who or what were?" The answer is *Joshua Chamberlain*. Now ask if the subject is singular or plural. The subject here is singular, since Joshua Chamberlain was one person. Therefore, a singular verb is needed: *were* should be changed to *was*.

The following list reviews some special situations in subject-verb agreement:

- **Collective nouns take a singular verb.** A collective noun is a noun that names a group of people or things, words like *team, group, club, class, family, collection, bunch, platoon*, and *organization*. Even names of institutions like *Harvard University*, *IBM*, and the *US Senate* may be considered collective nouns, because each refers to a large number of individuals.

- **Pronouns ending in -one, -body, and -thing take a singular verb.** These are called indefinite pronouns. There are twelve of them: someone, anyone, no one, everyone, somebody, anybody, nobody, everybody, something, nothing, anything, and everything. Although everybody and everyone refer to all people within a group, the words refer to each person of the group individually.

- **The SANAM pronouns—some, any, none, all, and most—may be either singular or plural, depending on the sentence.** In determining agreement, you usually ignore prepositional phrases that appear between the subject and the verb. A group of pronouns known by their initials (SANAM) is the exception. These pronouns may be either singular or plural, depending on how they are used in the sentence. Often the way to determine their use is to see if a prepositional phrase follows the pronoun.

Example: If most of the reporters are here, we'll begin the press conference.

In this sentence, the SANAM pronoun *most* is followed by the prepositional phrase *of the reporters*. To decide whether *most* is singular or plural, you have to look at the object of the preposition *of*. Because that object is the plural noun *reporters*, the pronoun *most* is plural and the plural verb *are* is used.

By contrast: If most of the cake is gone, I'll throw it out.

In this case, the object of the preposition *of* is the singular word *cake*. Therefore, the pronoun *most* is singular, and the singular verb *is* is used.

THE TENSE OF THE VERB MUST ACCURATELY SHOW THE SEQUENCE OF EVENTS

The tense of the verb shows the time of one event or the sequence of several events. There are six main tenses in English. *Past, present,* and *future* tenses (studied, study, will study) are the simplest to understand and usually refer to the time of one event. *Past perfect, present perfect,* and *future perfect* tenses (had studied, have studied, will have studied) show sequence. Most ACT Assessment English questions on tenses involve sequence: what is the order in which things happened?

The perfect tenses describe events occurring *before* other events. For example, an event described in the past perfect tense is one that happened *before* an event in the past tense happened:

Before she took the ACT Assessment English Test, she *had studied* for six weeks.

An event described in the present perfect tense is one that both happened *before* in the past and *continues* to happen up to the present:

He *has studied* ACT Assessment Math problems every day for an hour.

Though rarely used, there is also the future perfect tense. An event in the future perfect is one that will happen *before* another future event:

I will take the ACT Assessment next weekend; by then *I will have studied* a total of forty-seven hours.

On ACT Assessment questions about tense, a sentence or paragraph will describe two or more events occurring in a particular, unmistakable order.

Example: Lincoln announced his controversial Emancipation Proclamation, which declared all slaves held in rebel territory free, only after the North had won a significant military victory.

There are two events in this sentence: Lincoln's announcement of the Emancipation Proclamation, and the North's winning a significant military victory. What is the time sequence of these two events? The sentence makes it obvious: Lincoln announced the Proclamation in the past, and the North's victory occurred *before* that. Therefore, the announcement is in the past tense (Lincoln *announced*) and the victory is correctly in the past perfect tense (only after the North *had won*).

TIP
A handy way of remembering the number of an indefinite pronoun is to break it into two words—some *one*, every *body*, any *thing*. In a sense, each is just a singular noun with an adjective attached.

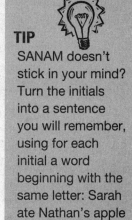

TIP
SANAM doesn't stick in your mind? Turn the initials into a sentence you will remember, using for each initial a word beginning with the same letter: Sarah ate Nathan's apple Monday.

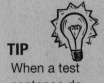

TIP

When a test sentence describes two or more events, pay attention. This could well be a sequence question. Make sure that the tenses are used clearly and that they correctly match the proper sequence of events. If not, one of them needs to be corrected.

ALWAYS USE THE PAST PARTICIPLE OF A VERB WITH THE HELPING VERB *TO HAVE*

In the preceding examples, you might have noticed that the past perfect, present perfect, and future perfect tenses all contain forms of the verb *to have*. When used to create tenses of other verbs, the verb *to have* is called an *auxiliary verb*, or, more casually, a *helping verb*.

The rule to remember is that, when you are using *to have* as an auxiliary, you must be careful to use the proper form of the basic verb. The proper form is called the *past participle*. This is one of the three principal parts of any verb. The other two parts are the *infinitive* and the *past*. The infinitive is the "to" form of the verb—*to laugh, to type, to work*. The past is the same as the simple past tense. The past participle is the part of the verb used with a form of *to have* to create the perfect tenses.

How is that part created? This is where complications—and ACT Assessment English questions—come in.

Most English verbs form both the past and the past participle the same way: by adding *-d* or *-ed* to the infinitive. Because there is no change between the past and the past participle, these verbs are called *regular* verbs. As an example, the following table gives the parts of three regular verbs.

Examples of Regular Verbs

Part	Example	Example	Example
Infinitive	to laugh	to squeeze	to consider
Past	laughed	squeezed	considered
Past Participle	laughed	squeezed	considered

However, many verbs form their past differently from adding *-d* or *-ed* to the infinitive. What's more, many of these verbs change again for the past participle. Because there is such irregularity between the three parts, these verbs are called *irregular* verbs. The following table gives examples of the parts of three irregular verbs.

Examples of Irregular Verbs

Part	Example	Example	Example
Infinitive	to fly	to go	to eat
Past	flew	went	ate
Past Participle	flown	gone	eaten

A common error with irregular verbs is to confuse the past and past participle forms, thus using the past tense where the past participle is needed.

Example: By the time Lindbergh's little plane landed on an airfield outside Paris, the exhausted pilot had flew single-handedly for over thirty hours without a break.

Because the past perfect tense is being used here, the past participle should be used; the verb should be *had flown* rather than *had flew*.

MASTERING MODIFYING PHRASES

A *modifying phrase* is a group of words that works as a unit to modify—describe or give more information about—something else in the sentence. Both adjectives and adverbs are considered modifiers; both modify—describe or give more information about—other words in the sentence. Thus, modifying phrases are groups of words that act as adjectives or adverbs. Some modifying phrases work as adjectives and modify nouns or pronouns. Others work as adverbs and modify verbs, adjectives, or adverbs.

Example: Six inches of her hair strewn on the beauty parlor's floor, Paula nervously glanced at her reflection in the mirror.

The phrase *Six inches of her hair strewn on the beauty parlor floor* works as an adjective; it modifies the noun *Paula*.

Example: After six o'clock, buses stop here once a hour.

The phrase *After six o'clock* acts as an adverb, modifying the verb *stop* by telling *when* the buses stop. Both phrases are modifying phrases.

To do your best on the ACT Assessment English Test, read through and familiarize yourself with the rules regarding modifying phrases, as discussed in the sections that follow.

A MODIFYING PHRASE MUST MODIFY A WORD OR PHRASE IN THE SAME SENTENCE

The word or phrase being modified—the person or thing being described—must be in the same sentence as the modifying phrase. If no such word or phrase appears in the same sentence, the modifying phrase is called a dangling modifier.

Example: Dismayed by the news that a top executive had suddenly accepted a job with a competitor, the price of the company's stock fell sharply the next day.

In this example, *Dismayed by the news that a top executive had suddenly accepted a job with a competitor,* is a modifying phrase, intended to describe or give more information. But information about whom or what? Who or what, exactly, was dismayed by the news? Although we understand that it

was Wall Street that was dismayed or stockholders who were dismayed, neither appears in the sentence itself. In fact, as written, the sentence states that the prices were dismayed. The modifying phrase "dangles"; there is no word or phrase to which it actually refers.

To be correct, the sentence would have to be rewritten to name the person or people who were dismayed. One possible way to rewrite would be *Dismayed by the news that a top executive had suddenly accepted a job with a competitor, stockholders sold off huge chunks of holdings and drove the stock's price down sharply.* Now the modifying phrase has a clear referent, naming the people it modifies.

A MODIFYING PHRASE MUST BE NEXT TO WHAT IT MODIFIES

A dangling modifier lacks something clear to modify. A *misplaced* modifier has something in the sentence to modify, but the two are separated in such a way that the modifier ends up describing the wrong person or thing.

> *Example:* A fabled center of monastic life during the Middle Ages, each summer thousands of visitors travel to the island of Iona near the coast of Ireland.

A fabled center of monastic life during the Middle Ages is supposed to modify the island of Iona, because that's what it describes. However, the modifying phrase is misplaced. Rather than being next to what it modifies, the modifying phrase precedes the words *each summer* and *thousands of visitors*, almost as if either of these were the fabled center. . . . One possible way to rewrite the sentence would be as follows: *A fabled center of monastic life during the Middle Ages, the island of Iona near the coast of Ireland is visited by thousands of travelers each summer.*

MASTERING ADJECTIVES AND ADVERBS

Adjectives modify (describe or give more information about) nouns or pronouns. Adjectives answer such questions as *what kind?, how many?,* or *which one?*

> *Examples:* the *blue* dress, a *moving* object, a *few* days

Adverbs modify verbs, adjectives, or other adverbs. Adverbs answer such questions as *how?, when?, where?, in what way?,* or *how often?*

> *Examples:* he ran *quickly,* she *quietly* closed the door, the phone rang *repeatedly*

The following sections discuss the basic rules for using adjectives and adverbs—information that will help you do your best on the ACT Assessment English Test.

AN ADJECTIVE CANNOT BE USED IN PLACE OF AN ADVERB

A common mistake is to use an adjective where an adverb is needed, or vice versa.

> *Example:* In the 90s, albums by Pearl Jam appeared consistent on the charts even without the exposure of music videos.

The word *consistent* is an adjective; it could be used to modify a noun (*a consistent success*) or a pronoun (*she is consistent in her habits*). However, in this sentence, an adverb is called for, because the word modified is the verb *appear*. The author wants to answer the question *how often did Pearl Jam albums appear on the charts?* To answer this question, an adverb is needed. As in many cases, the adverb here is formed by adding *-ly* to the adjective. The sentence can then easily be corrected by changing *consistent* to *consistently*.

USE A COMPARATIVE ADJECTIVE OR ADVERB TO COMPARE TWO THINGS; USE A SUPERLATIVE FOR THREE OR MORE

To compare two things, the "comparative" form of the adjective is used. The usual way to create the comparative form is to add *-er* to the adjective. To compare more than two things, the "superlative" form of the adjective is used. The usual way to create the superlative is to add *-est* to the adjective.

> *Examples:*
> (Adjective) I am tall.
> (Comparative Adjective) I am taller than my sister.
> (Superlative Adjective) But my brother David is the tallest in the family.

When an adjective has three or more syllables, adding yet another syllable makes it awkward. In this case the comparative is created by adding the separate word *more* in front of the adjective, and the superlative by adding the word *most*.

> *Example:* Keri is *beautiful*. Neve is *more beautiful*. Sarah Michelle Gellar is the *most beautiful* woman in the galaxy.

Often a writer becomes confused about whether to use the comparative or superlative form of the adjective. Just a few differences in words can change which form is called for. For example, the following two sentences say the same thing, yet each correctly uses a different form of the adjective:

TIP

The *-ly* tip-off can tell you whether a word is an adverb or an adjective. The surest way to know is to determine the word's function in the sentence: Is it modifying a noun or pronoun (making it an adjective) or is it modifying a verb, adjective, or other adverb (making it an adverb)?

To make a quick decision, look for the *-ly*. If the word ends in *-ly*, you can safely say it's an adverb. Although not every adverb ends in *-ly* (for example, **often, tomorrow, very**), words that end in *-ly* are almost always adverbs.

Of the many strange creatures that inhabit the continent of Australia, the wallaby is *more unusual* than any other.

Of the many strange creatures that inhabit the continent of Australia, the wallaby is the *most unusual*.

In the first example, the comparative form is correct because the sentence is literally comparing the wallaby to every other creature, one at a time. Thus at any one time, only two animals are being compared.

In the second example, the superlative form is correct because the wallaby is being compared to all other creatures at once.

Comparative and superlative forms of adverbs are used in much the same way. The comparative form (made with the word *more*) is used when two things are being compared; the superlative form (made with *most*) is used when three or more things are being compared.

Example: Jerry swims *quickly*. Paula swims *more quickly* than Jerry. But Karen swims *most quickly* of anyone on the swim team.

DO NOT CONFUSE THE ADJECTIVE *GOOD*, THE ADVERB *WELL*, AND THE ADJECTIVE *WELL*

This trio of words can be confusing, and because they are used quite often, it's important to get the differences straight. *Good* is an adjective with a broadly positive meaning. *Well* is the adverb form of good; it means, in effect, "in a good way." But *well* can also be an adjective meaning "healthy" or "the opposite of ill." Here is an example of each:

The singing in this high-school production sounds as *good* [adjective] as if performed by professionals.

Carrie, the understudy, sings especially *well* [adverb, that is, she sings *in a good way*].

She will have the opportunity to play the lead if Irene does not feel *well* tonight [adjective which equals *healthy*].

MASTERING PRONOUNS

A *pronoun* refers to and takes the place of a noun. Instead of saying *"Laura said that Laura was planning to go with Laura's friends to Times Square on New Year's Eve,"* you'd want to use the pronouns *she* and *her* rather than repeating the word *Laura* so often. *Laura said that she was planning to go with her friends to Times Square on New Year's Eve.* The noun that the pronoun refers to is called its *antecedent*. In this example, the noun *Laura* is the antecedent of the pronouns *she* and *her*.

The following sections outline the "rules" of pronouns and antecedents that you'll need to learn for the ACT Assessment English Test.

A PRONOUN MUST HAVE A CLEAR AND LOGICAL ANTECEDENT

A common problem is when the reader can't easily tell who or what the antecedent is supposed to be.

> *Example:* Although the hospital administrators interviewed many staff members about the repeated cases of staph infections, they had no explanation for the puzzling pattern of outbreaks.

The second half of this sentence starts with the pronoun *they*. It's impossible to tell from the context who *they* are. From a strictly grammatical point of view, the antecedent should be *staff members* as the noun closest to the pronoun; however, logically, the antecedent should be *hospital administrators*. If that was what was meant, the sentence should be rewritten. One possible revision is:

> Although they interviewed many staff members about the repeated cases of staph infections, the hospital administrators had no explanation for the puzzling pattern of outbreaks.

Now it is unmistakable who is doing what.

A PRONOUN MUST AGREE WITH ITS ANTECEDENT IN NUMBER

Just like a subject and a verb, a pronoun and its antecedent must agree in number. If the antecedent is single, the pronoun must also be single; if the antecedent is plural, the pronoun must also be plural.

This is an example of a common mistake in pronoun-antecedent agreement:

> A member of the tour group should have their tickets by the end of this week.

Who or what does the pronoun *their* refer to? That is, what is the pronoun's antecedent? *Member* is the answer, yet *member* is singular while *their* is plural. The pronoun does not agree with the noun in number and is therefore incorrect. To correct the sentence, *their* must be changed to a singular pronoun—*his* or *her*. The sentence could also be corrected by changing the noun to a plural form; for example, *Members of the tour group should have their tickets . . .*

USE SECOND- AND THIRD-PERSON PRONOUNS CONSISTENTLY

The three "persons" in grammar refer to *first person* (I, me, we, etc.), *second person* (you), and *third person* (he, she, it, they, etc.). In sentences discussing an indefinite person, English allows either second-person or

NOTE

In casual conversation people often use plural pronouns like *they, them,* and their to include both genders—while at the same time avoiding awkward constructions such as *his* or *her* or *s/he.* However, although the language is indeed changing in this regard, pairing a plural pronoun with a singular noun is still considered grammatically incorrect by most teachers, editors, and other authorities—including the ACT Assessment test-makers. On ACT Assessment English questions, check pronouns for proper agreement with their antecedents.

third-person constructions to be used. A common mistake is to mix the persons and use them inconsistently.

Example: If one lives in the northern hemisphere, on most clear winter nights you can easily see the three stars in a row that mark the belt of the hunter in the constellation Orion.

The sentence is describing how an indefinite person, meaning someone or anyone, can see Orion's belt in the winter sky. The sentence starts by using the indefinite third-person pronoun *one*. (Other such words that could have been used include the pronouns *someone* and *anyone* and expressions like *a person* or *an observer*.) However, the sentence shifts in midstream to the second person: *you* can easily see . . .

To correct the mistake, the sentence should maintain the third person throughout. Or it might use the second person, as long as that, too, is used throughout the entire sentence.

MASTERING CONNECTING CLAUSES

Clauses are groups of words that contain both a subject and a verb. A clause is called a *main* or *independent* clause if it can stand alone as a complete sentence, if it expresses a complete thought. A clause is called a *subordinate* or *dependent* clause if it cannot stand alone as a complete sentence, if it does not express a complete thought.

Conjunctions are connecting words: they connect words, phrases, or clauses. *Coordinating conjunctions* connect words, phrases, or clauses that are equal in grammatical importance. *Subordinating conjunctions* are used mainly to connect clauses. The clause introduced by a subordinating conjunction is a *dependent* clause. It is less important than a clause without such a conjunction; also its meaning is dependent on the other clause. Therefore, a dependent clause can't stand alone as a sentence.

The coordinating conjunctions are *and, or, for, nor, but,* and *yet.* Subordinating conjunctions are *because, although, after, if, when, while, since, until, before, as soon as, unless,* and *though.*

Here are a few examples of dependent clauses introduced by subordinating conjunctions:

although it had begun to rain

when the plumber arrived

because the bicycle was broken

None of the above dependent clauses is a complete thought; none can stand alone. Each needs to be connected to something else to complete the thought. Grammatically, the "something else" is an independent clause. Here are the same dependent clauses connected to an independent clause:

They stayed on the beach although it had begun to rain.

She locked the dog in the cellar when the plumber arrived.

Because the bicycle was broken, he walked to school.

The following sections discuss the connecting-clauses rules covered by the ACT Assessment English Test.

THE CONJUNCTION BETWEEN CLAUSES MUST BE LOGICAL

Each conjunction, of course, has its own meaning and cannot be used interchangeably. A test question might ask whether you recognize the proper, logical conjunction to connect two particular clauses. The answer depends on the meaning of the conjunction and whether it fits the context or not.

> *Example:* The city had fallen into ruins, and fortune-seekers from the country-side continued to pour in.

Here, two independent clauses have been joined by the coordinating conjunction *and*. Should they be? Actually the two clauses are opposed in meaning rather than complementary: *despite the fact* that the city was in ruins, fortune-seekers from the countryside continued to pour in. Given this near-contradiction, the conjunction *and* is not the best choice. Instead, *but* should be used. This more logically fits the opposition in meaning between the two clauses.

USE A SEMICOLON *(;)* TO CONNECT TWO INDEPENDENT CLAUSES

Instead of using a conjunction, independent clauses may also be connected using a semicolon *(;)*.

> *Example:* I have never needed to study more in my life; I have never been more tired.

Both clauses are independent, both express a complete thought, therefore a semicolon may be used. If the sentence instead were *I have never needed to study more in my life; because tomorrow's test affects my whole future*, the use of a semicolon would be wrong. The second part of the sentence is a dependent clause, introduced by the subordinating conjunction *because*. The semicolon should be omitted.

AVOID RUN-ON SENTENCES

A run-on sentence isn't necessarily a particularly long sentence. It might also be a sentence in which two (or more) independent clauses are incorrectly connected by being put in the same sentence without either a semicolon or a coordinating conjunction to join them properly.

Example: In addition to being a writer and lecturer, Mark Twain fancied himself an entrepreneur, he made and lost several fortunes backing various business ventures.

If this sentence were divided into two sentences after the word *entrepreneur*, either half could stand alone as a sentence. Therefore, it's a run-on sentence. Two possible corrections are to break it into two sentences or to change the comma into a semicolon.

AVOID SENTENCE FRAGMENTS

A sentence fragment is a collection of words that is punctuated as a sentence but which cannot properly stand alone as a sentence. Some sentence fragments lack either a subject or a verb. More often, the sentence fragment has both a subject and a verb, but it is a dependent rather than an independent clause. This usually happens because the clause begins either with a subordinating conjunction or with a type of pronoun called a relative pronoun, which also makes the clause dependent on another clause.

> *Example:* Carbon dating can be used in estimating the age of materials that are of organic origin only. Because the method is based on the predictable decay of carbon-based organic compounds.

The second collection of words, although punctuated as a sentence, is a fragment rather than a true sentence. It contains a subject and a verb, but it is introduced by a subordinating conjunction—the word *because*. The clause read alone is not a complete thought. To correct this particular fragment, either delete the period and unite this with the previous sentence or drop the word *because*.

MASTERING PUNCTUATION

Punctuation is the collection of marks that helps turn a string of written words into meaningful thoughts. Speech has pauses and stops, rising and falling tones of voice, and emphasis and speed to connect or separate one word from another. The written word must rely on a written system to do the same thing.

Although there are dozens of ways that punctuation can be used and misused, the ACT Assessment Test will cover the rules discussed in the following sections.

USE A COLON *(:)* TO INTRODUCE A LIST OR A RESTATEMENT

As explained in a previous section, the semicolon is used primarily to separate two independent clauses. The colon cannot be used as an alternative to the semicolon. Instead, the colon should be used to introduce a list or a restatement.

CAUTION
The length of a sentence is never an issue in its being complete. A complete sentence can be a single word. A fragment can be quite long. It all depends on whether the clauses are independent or dependent, and this in turn depends on the grammatical structure.

Example: For my term paper, I decided to write about hidden meanings in Nirvana's album *Nevermind*: references to Cobain's impending suicide, references to his wife, Courtney Love, and references to major influences in his career.

The colon is used correctly here. It alerts the reader to the fact that a list is about to be presented. However, if a list is the object of a verb or a preposition, do not use a colon before the list.

Example: For my term paper, I decided to write about hidden meanings in Nirvana's album *Nevermind,* including references to Cobain's impending suicide, references to his wife Courtney Love, and references to major influences in his career.

Here's an example of a colon used to introduce a restatement:

Barbara was named valedictorian for one reason: her exceptional academic achievement.

What follows the colon "restates" what precedes it; the words "her exceptional academic achievement" name the "one reason" mentioned before the colon.

USE COMMAS TO SEPARATE ITEMS IN A LIST OF THREE OR MORE WORDS

When three or more words, phrases, or clauses are presented in sequence, they should be separated by commas. Here are examples of each. First, look at this example of sequential words:

The Galapagos Islands boast some of the world's most unusual plants, birds, mammals, reptiles, and fish.

Here is an example of sequential phrases:

We looked for the missing gloves under the sofa, in the closet, and behind the dresser, but we never found them.

Finally, here is an example of sequential clauses:

I studied my ACT Assessment English, I studied my ACT Assessment Math, I studied my ACT Assessment Science Reasoning, and I took aspirin for my headache.

USE A PAIR OF COMMAS TO SET OFF A PARENTHETICAL PHRASE

A parenthetical phrase is an "interrupter"; it breaks into the flow of the main idea of the sentence, adding one or a few words in a convenient spot and then returning to the main idea. Although parenthetical phrases may literally be set off by parentheses (as this one is), they may also be set off from the rest

NOTE
You might have noticed in other pieces of writing that the last comma (the comma before *and*) is not always used. Once forbidden, then later required, the last comma has become optional and will not be tested on an ACT Assessment English question. The other commas, however, are not optional; they must be used.

of the sentence by a pair of commas. If the parenthetical phrase appears at the beginning or end of the sentence, only one comma is needed.

Some parenthetical phrases are frequently used: *for example, as you can see, that is, as I said before,* and so on. Whenever a phrase like this is used, it should be separated from the rest of the sentence by commas.

> *Example:* Not all men like cars; my uncle, for example, never learned to drive and can't tell a Porsche from a Volkswagen.

Another type of parenthetical phrase is an appositive, which names or describes a noun.

> *Example:* Sandy Koufax, the great left-handed Dodger pitcher, was Jack's idol during his teenage years.

DON'T USE COMMAS TO SEPARATE SENTENCE ELEMENTS THAT NATURALLY BELONG TOGETHER

Commas should not separate parts of the sentence that are naturally joined, like subject and verb, verb and object, verb and complement, and preposition and object.

> *Example:* The nineteenth-century explorers Lewis and Clark may be, two of America's most-admired historical figures.

Another common mistake of this kind is the use of a comma to set off the beginning of a parenthetical phrase but the omission of the second comma to "close off" the phrase.

> *Example:* I was surprised to find out that Christine, my girlfriend from freshman year had moved back to town.

Thus the use of only one comma ends up separating the subject *Christine* from the verb *had moved.*

USE THE APOSTROPHE *(')* CORRECTLY WHEN FORMING A POSSESSIVE OR A CONTRACTION

The apostrophe is used for two purposes in English, both of which are frequently tested on the ACT Assessment. The first use is to show possession, ownership, or some other close connection between a noun or pronoun and what follows it ("Susan's car," "the company's employees"). Form the possessive as follows:

- for a singular noun, add *'s* (the *dog's* collar)
- for a plural noun that ends in *s*, add an apostrophe (the *Jones'* apartment)
- for a plural noun that does not end in *s*, add *'s* (the *children's* teacher)
- for possessive pronouns, add nothing (*his, hers, ours,* etc.)

The apostrophe is also used in a contraction, two or more words from which letters have been removed, shortening the words into one. The apostrophe is usually inserted in place of the letters omitted. If in doubt, mentally "expand" the contraction to determine which letters have been left out; this is often a useful guide to where the apostrophe belongs.

Examples:

we've got to go = we have got to go

I'd rather not = I would rather not

she won't mind = she will not mind

it's your turn = it is your turn

you're welcome = you are welcome

TIP
Proper use of the apostrophe in a contraction is basically a matter of correct spelling. If you've had problems with this, get into the habit of noticing how contractions are spelled in good writing. It will greatly help your own writing, and it will definitely help you on the ACT Assessment.

MASTERING GRAMMAR AND LOGIC

Although the rules of grammar might sometimes seem arbitrary, they actually follow strict patterns of logic. It's like trying to compare apples and oranges. It really can't be done. One function of grammar is to establish rules so that oranges are compared to oranges and apples are compared to apples. This is logical, consistent thinking.

The following sections discuss the rules regarding grammar and logic that are covered on the ACT Assessment English Test.

ITEMS IN A LIST MUST BE GRAMMATICALLY PARALLEL

In geometry, parallel lines run in the same direction. In grammar, the rule of parallelism requires that every word, phrase, or clause in a list be constructed in the same way.

Example: Representatives to the student senate were asked to pursue often contradictory goals: boosting student acceptance of more homework, developing explanations for adding two hours to the length of each school day, and the reduction of rampant poor morale.

The sentence lists three goals of the student senate representatives. The first two are written in parallel form—that is, in phrases that begin with *gerunds* (*-ing* verbs). However, the third goal is written in a different grammatical form. Instead of a beginning with a gerund, the phrase begins with a noun. To correct the sentence, the third item should be revised to match the other two by starting with a gerund: ". . . and reducing the rampant poor morale."

TWO THINGS BEING COMPARED MUST BE GRAMMATICALLY PARALLEL

Like items in a list, items that are being compared to one another in a sentence also need to be grammatically parallel.

> *Example:* Because of advertising costs, to run for Congress today costs more than running for governor twenty years ago.

The costs of two kinds of political campaigns are being compared: a race for Congress today and a race for governor twenty years ago. As written, the sentence uses two different grammatical constructions to describe the races:

> *to run* for Congress today (infinitive)
>
> *running* for governor twenty years ago (gerund)

Either choice is correct, but using both in the same sentence is inconsistent. Correct the problem by using an infinitive in both phrases ("*to run* for Congress today costs more than *to run* for governor") or by using a gerund in both phrases ("*running* for Congress today costs more than *running* for governor").

MASTERING THE USE OF IDIOMS

After so much emphasis on logic and consistency, it seems totally illogical that idioms play such a large part in the proper use of English. An idiom, after all, is a phrase that's peculiar to a particular language and that often has no logic or rule behind its use. "That's just the way you say it" is what we tell non-native speakers. Yet despite this lack of logic, the improper use of an idiom is considered a grammatical mistake.

Because there may be no rule attached to the use of particular idioms, listen for the way you *expect* the idiom to be used, the way you've heard it used in countless conversations and lectures.

The following sections cover the rules governing idioms that are covered in the ACT Assessment English Test.

WHEN IDIOMATIC PAIRED PHRASES ARE USED, ALWAYS COMPLETE THE IDIOM

Certain idiomatic pairs of phrases must always be used together. When they aren't, the resulting sentence "sounds wrong," as if something is missing.

> *Example:* She claims her poor performance on the stage was caused as much by poor direction than by her own stage fright.

This sentence "sounds" incorrect because the idiom demands that the phrase *as much by X* always be followed by *as by Y*. It's incorrect to use the word *than* where the second *as* should be.

Another idiomatic pair that must always be used together is *the more X . . . the more Y*. For example:

The more things change, the more they stay the same.

More and *more* are often replaced by other comparatives:

The bigger they are, *the harder* they fall
The deeper the pocket, *the tighter* the purse strings
The stronger the brew, *the better* the coffee

USE THE RIGHT IDIOMATIC PREPOSITION

A variation on paired idiomatic phrases is paired idiomatic words; that is, one word is always followed by another. This happens most frequently— and most confusingly, it seems—with prepositions. Certain words always take a certain preposition. For example, one may look at, look in, look through, etc. However, one always disagrees *with* rather than disagrees against, or has scorn *for* rather than scorn at.

Example: The quarterback assured the waterboy that he had no intention to encroach on the latter's interest in the captain of the cheerleaders.

According to idiomatic usage, the word intention should be followed by the preposition *of,* so the preposition must be changed to the correct one. Because the preposition *of,* like all prepositions, must have an object, and the object must be a noun or pronoun, the verb *encroach* must also be changed to a noun form—the *gerund* (the *-ing* construction) *encroaching*. The fully corrected sentence then reads

The quarterback assured the waterboy that he had no intention of encroaching on the latter's interest in the captain of the cheerleaders.

Encroach *on* rather than encroach *against*—yet another idiom. The list goes on and on. Even native speakers can find these constructions difficult; non-native speakers must think that all idioms were invented at a drunken New Year's Eve party; that's how much sense they make.

The only proven advice is to "listen" carefully as you read test questions. If a preposition on the ACT Assessment sounds "funny," scan the answer choices to see whether the answers include a change in the preposition. If you spot another preposition that sounds better, choose it.

LEARN TO DISTINGUISH BETWEEN EASILY CONFUSED WORDS

In casual speech, so many people confuse two different words that the "incorrect" one can be mistaken for the grammatically correct one, even in more formal writing. Look over these examples and be sure to choose the right one on the ACT Assessment Test:

Examples of Easily Confused Words

Word	Definition or Distinguishing Function
likely	definition: probably destined to happen
liable	definition: legally responsible
like	function: a preposition that must take an object; cannot be used as a conjunction, as in the *He fixed it like he said he would*—incorrect
as	function: a subordinating conjunction, as in *He fixed it as he said he would*—correct
much	definition: a large quantity that can't be counted, as in *so much blood, so much sand, so much dissatisfaction*
many	definition: a large quantity that can be counted, as in *so many pints of blood, so many grains of sand, so many demonstrations of dissatisfaction*
less	definition: a decrease that can't be counted, as in *less busy than yesterday*
fewer	definition: a decrease that can be counted, as in *interrupted fewer times than yesterday*
affect	when used as a verb, meaning to influence or to move emotionally
affect	when used as a noun, meaning a feeling or an emotion
effect	when used as a verb, meaning to bring about
effect	when used as a noun, meaning result or consequence
if	indicates a condition or uncertainty
whether	indicates a choice
last	the final item in a series; indicates position
latest	the most recent; indicates time

MASTER THE ABILITY TO IDENTIFY WORDINESS

The best writing is usually the most concise writing. This is especially true in nonfiction when style and embellishment take second place to the clearest presentation of information. Wordiness can occur in several ways, and you'll want to be alert for each. The following sections discuss the things you'll need to know about eliminating wordiness when you take the ACT Assessment English Test.

AVOID VERBOSITY

Verbosity is the use of too many words. Their construction might be grammatically correct; there are simply too many words. Verbosity on the ACT Assessment Test will be fairly obvious, even exaggerated. An example used in an earlier chapter is worth repeating here:

As I previously mentioned to you when explaining at last week's meeting the incredible and undisputed advantages of combining our two clubs, *The Poetry Society* and *Poets Out of the Closet*, I have written up here for your further study my thoughts on the matter, detailing the many benefits that will accrue to both organizations.

There's nothing "mechanically" wrong with this sentence. It's a complete sentence and not a fragment; the subjects and verbs within the clauses agree with each other; the punctuation is correct. However, it would be much clearer to write

At last week's meeting, I said there were benefits to combining our two clubs. Here's a note repeating why.

AVOID CHANGING THE MEANING WHEN EDITING

Every long sentence is not necessarily verbose. When editing, be sure not to butcher the original style. Even more importantly, editing should not result in a shorter piece of writing that is confusing or that even changes the meaning of the original. Compare the three versions below:

Spielberg's *Amistad* is the filmmaker's second attempt to show that someone who is an unexcelled creator of funny, fast-paced action movies can also be a producer of films that try to deal in a serious fashion with weighty historical and moral themes. (42 words)

Spielberg's *Amistad* is the filmmaker's second attempt at dealing in a serious fashion with weighty historical and moral themes. (19 words)

Spielberg's *Amistad* is the filmmaker's second attempt to show that an unexcelled creator of funny, fast-paced action movies can also produce films dealing seriously with weighty historical and moral themes. (30 words)

Although the second version is less than half the length of the original, it loses the original meaning: the contrast between the two types of movies that Spielberg makes. The third version, being only 29% shorter, retains the meaning while expressing it more economically.

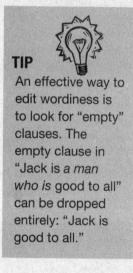

TIP
An effective way to edit wordiness is to look for "empty" clauses. The empty clause in "Jack is *a man who is* good to all" can be dropped entirely: "Jack is good to all."

AVOID REDUNDANCY

Repetition in writing sometimes serves a purpose; it might be intended style, or it might be deliberate emphasis. Needless repetition is called *redundancy*.

Example: He is taller in height than I am.

Is there a way to be taller other than height? *in height* can be deleted.

As much as 125 years ago, the science fiction writer Jules Verne wrote predictions that foretold the future existence of such modern mechanical devices as the airplane, the submarine, and even the fax machine.

We're told that Jules Verne wrote "predictions that foretold the future existence" of many things. Because *foretold* and *future existence* are contained within the meaning of *predictions*, both can be deleted.

AVOID THE PASSIVE VOICE WHEN POSSIBLE

When the subject of the verb is the doer of the action, a sentence is said to be in active voice: *Sharon built the birdhouse*. When the subject of the verb receives the action, a sentence is said to be in passive voice: *The birdhouse was built by Sharon*.

Although passive voice is sometimes appropriate, for example, when the "doer" isn't known *(Our house was vandalized while we were away)*, active voice is preferable. It is not only shorter, it is more concise and vigorous.

> *Example:* When the basic elements of the theory of natural selection were conceived by Darwin, it was unknown to him that most of the same ideas had already been developed by a rival naturalist, Charles Russel Wallace. (36 words)

Here's how the improved sentence reads when active verbs are used instead:

> When Darwin conceived the basic elements of the theory of natural selection, he didn't know that rival naturalist Charles Russel Wallace had already developed most of the same ideas. (29 words)

Unless there is a good reason to prefer the passive voice in a particular sentence, choose the active instead.

PRACTICE EXERCISES

You've just reviewed the most important points in grammar to know for success in taking the ACT Assessment English Test. The following exercises will help you to practice your new knowledge as well as to continue to familiarize yourself with the contents and format of the ACT Assessment.

There are three English Test exercises in this chapter. Each exercise contains 30 questions and should be answered in 18 minutes. Do each exercise in one sitting in a quiet place, with no notes or reference material. Use a stopwatch or kitchen timer or have someone else watch the clock. When time is up, stop at once.

Score yourself only on those items you finished. When you're done, work through the rest of the exercise.

EXERCISES: ENGLISH TEST

Exercise 1

30 Questions • Time—18 Minutes

Directions: This test consists of two passages in which particular words or phrases are underlined and numbered. Alongside the passage, you will see alternative words and phrases that could be substituted for the underlined part. You must select the alternative that expresses the idea most clearly and correctly or that best fits the style and tone of the entire passage. If the original version is best, select "No Change."

The test also includes questions about entire paragraphs and the passage as a whole. These questions are identified by a number in a box.

After you select the correct answer for each question, mark the oval representing the correct answer on your answer sheet.

Passage I

The Girls Choir of Harlem

It is rare to hear of choirs composed <u>of just girls. In</u>
                                                1
fact, for every girls' choir in the United States, there are four boys' and mixed choirs. But the Girls Choir of Harlem <u>in 1977</u> was founded, to complement the
                2
already existing and <u>justly renowned</u> Boys Choir.
                          3

<u>To this day,</u> the Boys Choir of Harlem overshadows
    4
the Girls Choir. They have been around longer <u>(1968
                                                     5
was when they were founded),</u> and have received the

1. A. NO CHANGE
   B. just of girls'.
   C. only of girls.
   D. of girls, alone.

2. F. NO CHANGE
   G. (Place after *But*)
   H. (Place after *was*)
   J. OMIT the underlined portion.

3. A. NO CHANGE
   B. famous (justly so)
   C. renowned, justly,
   D. just renowned

4. F. NO CHANGE
   G. As of today,
   H. On this day,
   J. At the moment,

5. A. NO CHANGE
   B. (having been founded in 1968)
   C. (their founding dates to 1968)
   D. (since 1968)

GO ON TO THE NEXT PAGE ➤

attention needed to gain funding and performance opportunities. The boys have appeared in some of the world's <u>most prestigious</u> musical settings. They have
6
sung a sunrise concert for the Pope on the Great Lawn

in New York's Central Park; <u>they have traveled to</u>
7
<u>Washington, D.C. and seen the Lincoln Memorial.</u>

Such glorious moments have eluded their female counterparts. During the 1980s, when funds dried up, the Girls Choir temporarily disbanded. However, in

1989, <u>the choir were</u> reassembled, and in November of
8
1997, they made their debut at Alice Tully Hall at Lincoln Center, performing music by Schumann and Pergolesi before an audience of dignitaries (including <u>the mayors wife</u>) and thousands of music lovers.
9

[1] The choir members speak confidently of some-day becoming lawyers, doctors, and politicians—jobs which once appeared out of reach to them. [2] Both the Girls Choir and the Boys Choir of Harlem act as havens for inner-city children, <u>giving</u> kids from bro-
10
ken families and poverty-stricken homes new confidence and hope for their future. [3] The boys and girls in the choirs attend the Choir Academy, a 500-student public school with a strong emphasis on singing.

6. F. NO CHANGE
   G. more prestigious
   H. very prestigious
   J. prestige-filled

7. Which of the alternative clauses would most effectively support the assertion made in the previous sentence about the musical appearances of the Boys Choir?
   A. NO CHANGE
   B. they have produced recordings enjoyed by listeners around the world.
   C. they have sung on the same bill as Luciano Pavarotti, the great Italian tenor.
   D. they sing a wide variety of music, both classical and popular.

8. F. NO CHANGE
   G. it were
   H. the choir was
   J. the girls

9. A. NO CHANGE
   B. the mayor's wife
   C. the mayors' wife
   D. a wife of the mayor

10. F. NO CHANGE
    G. they give
    H. thus giving
    J. and it gives

[4] <u>It's</u> a fine learning environment that has given the
    11

girls ambitions most of them never before considered.
12

    Now that the Girls Choir of Harlem is beginning to
receive some of the recognition that the boys have
long enjoyed, perhaps corporations and wealthy indi-

viduals will be motivated <u>for giving generously</u> to
                                    13
support the choir and ensure it will never again have to

shut down <u>for lack of money.</u>
                  14

11. A. NO CHANGE
     B. Its
     C. They offer
     D. That is

12. Which of the following sequences of sentences
     will make the paragraph most logical?
     F. 1, 4, 3, 2
     G. 2, 1, 4, 3
     H. 2, 3, 4, 1
     J. 3, 4, 1, 2

13. A. NO CHANGE
     B. generously for giving
     C. to give generously
     D. for generosity in giving

14. F. NO CHANGE
     G. because they are lacking money.
     H. as a result of money being lacking.
     J. without money.

Item 15 poses a question about the essay as a whole.

15. Suppose the writer had been assigned to write an
     essay describing the musical achievements of
     the Girls Choir of Harlem. Would this essay
     successfully fulfill the assignment?

     A. Yes, because the concert at Alice Tully Hall
        is explained in some detail.

     B. Yes, because the essay makes it clear that the
        girls in the choir are talented performers.

     C. No, because the essay discusses the Boys
        Choir as extensively as it discusses the Girls
        Choir.

     D. No, because the music performed by the
        choir is scarcely discussed in the essay.

GO ON TO THE NEXT PAGE ➤

Passage II

The Poetry of Economics

"The poetry of economics?" a reader might ask. "How can 'the dismal science' be associated with the subtlety and creativity of poetry?" <u>You're</u> skepticism

is understandable, <u>and</u> perhaps a story from an

economist's life can sketch the poetry of economics at work.

   Shortly after the Second World War, the agricultural economist Theodore Schultz, later to win a Nobel prize, spent a term based at Auburn University in <u>Alabama, he interviewed</u> farmers in the neighborhood. One day he interviewed an old and poor farm

<u>couple. And was struck</u> by how contented they seemed.

Why are you so contented, he asked, though very poor? They answered: You're wrong, Professor. We're not poor. We've used up our farm to educate four children through college, <u>remaking</u> fertile land and

well-stocked pens into knowledge of law and Latin. We are rich.

   The parents had told Schultz that the *physical* capital, <u>which economists think they understand,</u> is in

some sense just like the human capital of education. The children now owned it, and so the parents did, too.

16. F. NO CHANGE
    G. Your
    H. One's
    J. A reader's

17. A. NO CHANGE
    B. but
    C. therefore
    D. so

18. F. NO CHANGE
    G. Alabama. Where he interviewed
    H. Alabama, interviewing
    J. Alabama so as to interview

19. A. NO CHANGE
    B. couple, and was struck
    C. couple; struck
    D. couple. Struck

20. F. NO CHANGE
    G. so remaking
    H. this remade
    J. and to remake

21. A. NO CHANGE
    B. understood by economists (or so they think),
    C. that is thought by economists to be understood,
    D. OMIT the underlined portion.

Once it had been rail fences and hog pens and <u>it was</u>
                                                    22
<u>also their</u> mules. Now it was in the children's brains,

this human capital. The farm couple was rich. <u>The</u>
                                                    23
average economist was willing to accept the discovery

of human capital as soon as he understood it, which is

in fact how many scientific and scholarly discoveries

<u>get received.</u> It was an argument in a metaphor (or, if
    24
you like, an analogy, a simile, a model). A hog pen,

Schultz would say to another economist, is "just like"

Latin 101.

    The other economist would have to admit that there

was something to it. <u>Both the hog pen, and the Latin</u>
                                                    25
<u>instruction,</u> are paid for by saving. Both are valuable

assets <u>for the earning of income,</u> understanding "in-
                            26
come" to mean, as economists put it, "a stream of

satisfaction." Year after year, the hog pen and the

Latin <u>cause</u> satisfaction to stream out <u>as</u> water from a
        27   28
dam. Both last a long time, but finally wear out—when

the pen falls down and the Latin-learned brain dies.

    And the one piece of "capital" can be made into the

22. F. NO CHANGE
    G. also
    H. as well
    J. OMIT the underlined portion.

23. A. NO CHANGE
    B. (Begin new paragraph) The
    C. (Begin new paragraph) So the
    D. (Do NOT begin new paragraph) Yet the

24. F. NO CHANGE
    G. are received.
    H. become received.
    J. have their reception.

25. A. NO CHANGE
    B. Both the hog pen and the Latin instruction
    C. The hog pen, and the Latin instruction as well,
    D. Both the hog pen, and also the Latin instruction,

26. F. NO CHANGE
    G. for income's earning,
    H. for earning income,
    J. with which income may be earned,

27. A. NO CHANGE
    B. causes
    C. produce
    D. makes

28. F. NO CHANGE
    G. similarly to
    H. as with
    J. like

GO ON TO THE NEXT PAGE ▶

other. An educated farmer, <u>because of his degree in</u>

29

<u>agriculture from Auburn,</u> can get a bank loan to build

a hog pen; and when his children grow up he can sell

off the part of the farm with the hog pen to pay for

another term for Junior and Sis up at Auburn, too. 30

29. A. NO CHANGE

    B. due to having a degree from Auburn in agriculture,

    C. as a result of a degree in agriculture from Auburn

    D. OMIT the underlined portion

30. The writer wants to link the essay's opening and conclusion. If inserted at the end of the essay, which of the following sentences best achieves this effect?

    F. The wisdom of the farmer is greater, in the end, than the wisdom of the economics professor.

    G. Human capital is a concept based on a metaphor—and metaphor is the essential tool of poetry.

    H. Thus, education is the most valuable form of human capital, even for the farmer.

    J. Physical capital and human capital are ultimately not so different after all.

Exercise 2

30 Questions • Time—18 Minutes

Directions: This test consists of two passages in which particular words or phrases are underlined and numbered. Alongside the passage, you will see alternative words and phrases that could be substituted for the underlined part. You must select the alternative that expresses the idea most clearly and correctly or that best fits the style and tone of the entire passage. If the original version is best, select "No Change."

The test also includes questions about entire paragraphs and the passage as a whole. These questions are identified by a number in a box.

After you select the correct answer for each question, mark the oval representing the correct answer on your answer sheet.

Passage I

Note: The paragraphs that follow may or may not be in the most appropriate order. Item 15 will ask you to choose the most logical sequence for the paragraphs.

A People's Art, for Good and Ill

[1]

During the early years of movies—say, from 1910
                                                1
to 1940—the greatness of film as an art form lay in its
own ingenuity and invention. And this in every instance originated in cinema's role <u>as entertaining</u> a
                                                    2
large and avid public. Between 1920 and 1930, a
generation of filmmakers grew up who were not failed
novelists or <u>playwrights who'd had no success</u> but
                                                3
moviemakers, through and through. Their essential

vision belonged to no other medium <u>with the excep-</u>
                                                        4
<u>tion of</u> the cinema, and this made it vital and exciting.

[2]

Furthermore, their public was a universal audience
of ordinary people, spread across the world.
<u>Comparable to</u> the first dramas of <u>Shakespeare,</u> their
        5   6
art was not a product of the palace, the mansion, or

1. A. NO CHANGE
   B. —say from 1910, to 1940—
   C. —from 1910, say to 1940—
   D. —from 1910 to 1940, say;

2. F. NO CHANGE
   G. of entertaining
   H. to entertain
   J. as entertainers on behalf of

3. A. NO CHANGE
   B. playwrights lacking success
   C. playwrights without any successes
   D. unsuccessful playwrights

4. F. NO CHANGE
   G. than
   H. aside from
   J. from

5. A. NO CHANGE
   B. As were
   C. Not dissimilarly to
   D. Like

6. F. NO CHANGE
   G. Shakespeare, some of whose plays have been made into outstanding motion pictures,
   H. Shakespeare, who also wrote a number of highly-acclaimed narrative and lyric poems,
   J. Shakespeare, although he lived nearly three centuries before the invention of the movies,

GO ON TO THE NEXT PAGE ➤

the village square, but rather of the common play-
                                    7
house where working people sat shoulder to shoulder
with the middle class and the well-to-do. This is what
gave the early movie makers the strength and freshness we still perceive in their art.

                    [3]

Thus, today, with movies more popular than ever,
and with box-office receipts for the great international
                                    8
hit films running into hundreds of millions of dollars,

movies are becoming more and more conventional,
                                    9
unimaginative, and stale. The freshness of the early

movie makers has been lost.
                    10

                    [4]

However, there is a price to be paid for this demo-
                11
cratic appeal to the common person. The artist who

serves an elite audience has a known patron only, or
                                            12
group of patrons, to satisfy. If he is strong enough, he
can, like the painters of the Renaissance, mold their

7. Which of the choices is most consistent with the writer's point concerning the style of the early moviemakers?
   A. NO CHANGE
   B. the private club,
   C. the tenements of the poor,
   D. the athletic arena,

8. Which of the alternative clauses most effectively supports the writer's point concerning the current situation of moviemakers?
   F. NO CHANGE
   G. and with movie stars like Harrison Ford known and admired by millions of people around the world,
   H. and with thriving motion picture industries not only in Hollywood but in many other countries,
   J. and with more opportunities for talented young filmmakers than ever before,

9. A. NO CHANGE
   B. conventional—unimaginative—
   C. conventionally unimaginative,
   D. conventional; unimaginative;

10. F. NO CHANGE
    G. have been
    H. are being
    J. will be

11. A. NO CHANGE
    B. Fortunately,
    C. Surprisingly,
    D. Therefore,

12. F. NO CHANGE
    G. (Move after *has*)
    H. (Move after *satisfy*)
    J. OMIT the underlined portion.

taste in the <u>image of his own</u>. This can also be true of

13

the greater and more resolute artists of the cinema, from Chaplin in the nineteen twenties to, say, Bergman or Antonioni in the sixties. But the larger the audience and the more costly the movies to produce, <u>great</u>

14

<u>become</u> the pressures brought to bear on the less conventional creator to make his work conform to the pattern of the more conventional creator.

13. A. NO CHANGE
    B. of his taste.
    C. like his own.
    D. of his own personal taste.

14. F. NO CHANGE
    G. so much greater become
    H. greater are
    J. the greater

Item 15 poses a question about the essay as a whole.

15. For the sake of the unity and coherence of this essay, Paragraph 3 should be placed:
    A. where it is now.
    B. before Paragraph 1.
    C. before Paragraph 2.
    D. after Paragraph 4.

Passage II

Regeneration, A Natural Miracle

Urodeles, a kind of vertebrate that <u>include</u> such

16

small, lizard-like creatures as newts and salamanders,

have an enviable ability <u>few</u> other animals enjoy. They

17

can regenerate arms, legs, tails, heart muscle, jaws, spinal cords, and other organs that are injured or destroyed by accidents or <u>those who prey on them.</u>

18

16. F. NO CHANGE
    G. includes
    H. comprise
    J. numbers

17. A. NO CHANGE
    B. only few
    C. nearly no
    D. scarcely no

18. F. NO CHANGE
    G. animals who eat them
    H. predatory animals
    J. predators

GO ON TO THE NEXT PAGE ➤

[19] Planaria, a kind of simple worm, have their

20

own form of regenerative power. A single worm can

19. Which of the following sentences, if added here, would provide the best transition between the first paragraph and the second?
    A. Urodeles are not the only creatures with this amazing ability.
    B. Scientists have long marveled at the regenerative power of urodeles.
    C. Regeneration affords to those creatures that possess it a kind of immortality.
    D. There are dozens of different species of urodeles living in North America.

20. F. NO CHANGE
    G. Planaria—a kind of simple worm,
    H. A simple kind of worm, known as planaria,
    J. Planaria, simply a kind of worm,

be sliced and diced into hundreds of pieces, and each

21

piece giving rise to a completely new animal.

21. A. NO CHANGE
    B. each piece gives rise
    C. with each piece giving rise
    D. each one rising

However, while both urodeles and planaria have the

22

capacity to regenerate, they use different means to

accomplish this amazing feat.

22. F. NO CHANGE
    G. Furthermore,
    H. And
    J. Meanwhile,

In effect, urodeles turn back the clock. When injured, the animal first heals the wound at the site of the

23

missing limb. Then various specialized cells at the

23. A. NO CHANGE
    B. (Place after *When*)
    C. (Place after *wound*)
    D. (Place after *limb*)

site, such like bone, skin, and blood cells, seem to lose

24

their identity.

24. F. NO CHANGE
    G. such as
    H. namely
    J. as

They revert into unspecialized cells, like those in

25

25. A. NO CHANGE
    B. to the form of
    C. to being
    D. toward being

the embryo before birth. <u>Ultimate,</u> as the new limb
                            26

takes shape, the cells take on the specialized roles they

had previously cast off.

   <u>By contrast,</u> planaria regenerate using special cells
          27

called neoblasts. Scattered within the body, these

neoblasts remain in an unspecialized state, <u>this</u>
                                              28

<u>enables</u> them to turn into any cell type <u>that may be</u>
                                            29

<u>needed.</u> Whenever planaria are cut, the neoblasts

migrate to the site and begin to grow and develop.

Soon, an entirely new animal is formed from the

broken fragments <u>from an old one.</u>
                    30

26. F. NO CHANGE
    G. So,
    H. Thus,
    J. Ultimately,

27. A. NO CHANGE
    B. Nonetheless,
    C. In fact,
    D. Otherwise,

28. F. NO CHANGE
    G. thus able
    H. enabling
    J. enabled in this way

29. A. NO CHANGE
    B. which are necessary.
    C. for which there is a requirement.
    D. one may want.

30. F. NO CHANGE
    G. that are part of the old.
    H. of the old.
    J. out of the old one.

Exercise 3

30 Questions • Time—18 Minutes

Directions: This test consists of two passages in which particular words or phrases are underlined and numbered. Alongside the passage, you will see alternative words and phrases that could be substituted for the underlined part. You must select the alternative that expresses the idea most clearly and correctly or that best fits the style and tone of the entire passage. If the original version is best, select "No Change."

   The test also includes questions about entire paragraphs and the passage as a whole. These questions are identified by a number in a box.

   After you select the correct answer for each question, mark the oval representing the correct answer on your answer sheet.

Passage I

Tunnel Vision: The Bane of Business

<u>Businesses don't</u> always get into trouble because
1

they are badly run or inefficient. Sometimes, well-

managed companies fail <u>because their leaders don't</u>
2

<u>understand, simply,</u> how the world is changing around

them. What happened to Wang, the office automation

company, is a classic example.

In the early 1980s, Wang represented the preemi-

nent office automation capability in the world—

<u>so much so that in many offices the name "Wang" had</u>
3

<u>become a synonym for "office automation."</u> With a

reputation for quality and with proprietary hardware

and software that guaranteed the uniqueness of its

product, Wang had built a market position <u>seeming</u>
4

<u>unassailable.</u>

<u>Yet</u> in less than a decade, Wang faded to near
5

<u>obscurity. Shrinking</u> dramatically and surviving only
6

by transforming itself to use its software and engineer-

ing strengths in completely different ways. In place of

Wang's specialized computer systems, versatile

1. A. NO CHANGE
    B. A business doesn't
    C. No business
    D. Businesses may not

2. F. NO CHANGE
    G. because, simply, their leaders don't under-
       stand
    H. because their leaders fail simply at under-
       standing
    J. because their leaders simply don't under-
       stand

3. The writer intends to emphasize the degree to
    which Wang dominated its marketplace in the
    early 1980s. If all of these statements are true,
    which best accomplishes the writer's goal?
    A. NO CHANGE
    B. only IBM had a better reputation among
       corporate leaders around the world.
    C. the company's founder was generally re-
       garded as one of the world's most successful
       businesspeople.
    D. with many thousands of employees in scores
       of offices around the globe.

4. F. NO CHANGE
    G. seemingly unassailable.
    H. that seemed unassailable.
    J. that was unassailable, or so it seemed.

5. A. NO CHANGE
    B. Although
    C. And
    D. For

6. F. NO CHANGE
    G. obscurity, shrinking
    H. obscurity. It shrank
    J. obscurity; shrinking

personal computers <u>linked together in networks</u> had
7

become the dominant office tools. The new personal

computers first transformed the market for office

automation networks <u>then wiping out</u> the old market.
8

Wang <u>had saw itself</u> as a specialized kind of com-
9

puter company using large machines to serve entire

companies. <u>It's</u> excellence and leadership in innova-
10

tion <u>was highly respected,</u> and it was important to
11

Wang *not to lose* that position. That view led Wang to

stick to its familiar business until it was too late. It

failed to see the opportunity presented by the personal

computer. Eventually, Wang did attempt to move into

personal computers, but by this time the company's

opportunity to move forward was gone. <u>Wang had</u>
12

<u>been badly outmaneuvered and was left with no</u>

<u>market.</u>

Sometimes a business leader stumbles into this kind

of trap by waiting to see what develops, trading time

7. A. NO CHANGE
   B. linked, network-style, together
   C. that were linked together forming networks
   D. linked to form networks together

8. F. NO CHANGE
   G. and then wiping out
   H. wiping out subsequently
   J. and then wiped out

9. A. NO CHANGE
   B. had seen itself
   C. itself had been seen
   D. having seen itself

10. F. NO CHANGE
    G. Its
    H. Their
    J. Wangs'

11. A. NO CHANGE
    B. was respected highly
    C. were highly respected
    D. had won high respect

12. Which of the following sentences, if added here, would best summarize the point of the paragraph and provide a clear transition to the next paragraph?
    F. NO CHANGE
    G. Today, Wang is developing new business niches that it hopes will bring it renewed success in the future.
    H. Wang's reputation for excellence remained untarnished.
    J. The market for personal computers continues to grow.

GO ON TO THE NEXT PAGE ➤

for the prospect of more information <u>and a decrease in</u>

                                    13

<u>uncertainty.</u> Sometimes the leader is simply so afraid

to lose that he or she <u>is incapable of</u> the bold action

                                14

required for success. <u>Regardlessly,</u> the leader is oper-

                          15

ating with limited vision, and the company suffers as

a result.

13. A. NO CHANGE
    B. and less uncertainty.
    C. or certainty.
    D. but a smaller degree of uncertainty.

14. F. NO CHANGE
    G. is unable for taking
    H. finds it impossible to perform
    J. can not do

15. A. NO CHANGE
    B. In either case,
    C. Anyway,
    D. Because

Passage II

The Unblinking Eye

Photography <u>is of course a</u> visual art like many

                        16

others, including painting, drawing, and the various

forms of printmaking. But photography is unique

<u>as one of these</u> arts in one respect: the person, place,

    17

event, or other subject <u>that have been</u> photographed is

                                18

always real, captured by a photographer who is an on-

the-spot eyewitness to its reality. A painting may

depict a scene that is <u>partly or in whole</u> imaginary—a

                        19

knight battling a dragon, a city beneath the sea, or the

features of a woman who never existed. But a photo-

graph is a document <u>reflecting</u> with more or less

                      20

completeness and accuracy something that was actu-

ally happening as the shutter clicked.

16. F. NO CHANGE
    G. is, of course, a
    H. is of course, a
    J. is—of course, a

17. A. NO CHANGE
    B. as a member of these
    C. compared to other
    D. among these

18. F. NO CHANGE
    G. that has been
    H. having been
    J. OMIT the underlined portion.

19. A. NO CHANGE
    B. in part or entirely
    C. partly or wholly
    D. partly, or in its entirety,

20. F. NO CHANGE
    G. to reflect
    H. that reflect
    J. for reflecting

Viewers <u>have an awareness concerning</u> this feature
                                    21
of photography, of course, which explains why photos
(and, today, film and television footage) of world
events can have <u>such a powerful</u> emotional and intel-
                              22
lectual impact. The photographed image of a starving

child in Africa or India 23 conveys the reality of a
tragedy halfway around the world with an immediacy

and force <u>shared by no purely verbal report.</u>
                          24

25 Photos can indeed mislead when the photographer, either deliberately or inadvertently, exaggerates or omits crucial details of the real-life scene, or

21. A. NO CHANGE
    B. are wary concerning
    C. have awareness of
    D. are aware of

22. F. NO CHANGE
    G. so much powerful
    H. so powerful
    J. the power of

23. The writer is considering adding the following
    phrase at this point in the essay:
    —its belly distended, eyes sunken, ribs
    protruding—
    Would this phrase be a relevant and appropriate
    addition to the essay, and why?
    A. No, because the kind of image it conveys is
       excessively familiar from newspapers and
       television.
    B. Yes, because it suggests vividly the power of
       a photographic image to move the viewer
       emotionally.
    C. No, because it distracts the reader's attention
       from the writer's point about the nature of
       photography.
    D. Yes, because it encourages the reader to take
       action on behalf of children starving in dis-
       tant lands.

24. F. NO CHANGE
    G. not shared by any report that is purely verbal.
    H. more than can be had by any purely verbal
       report.
    J. beyond that of a report which is verbal,
       purely.

25. Which of the following sentences, if added here,
    would most effectively provide a transition to
    the new paragraph?
    A. Words, of course, can be used to deceive.
    B. Not all photographers are interested in de-
       picting social or political problems.
    C. This is not to say that the camera never lies.
    D. It takes true artistry to produce compelling
       photographs.

GO ON TO THE NEXT PAGE ➤

freezing on film a momentary image that distorts or
26

falsifies the flow of reality. When photography is

enrolled in the service of political, social, or commer-
27

cial causes, such deceptions are all too common. [28]

Nonetheless, no conscientious photographer will be

guilty of them. At its best, photography is unequalled
29

as a purveyor of truth, and this is the goal of every self-
30

respecting camera artist.

26. F. NO CHANGE
    G. freezes
    H. by freezing
    J. to freeze

27. A. NO CHANGE
    B. for the purpose of serving
    C. so as to promote
    D. in helping to create interesting in

28. The writer is considering adding the following sentence at this point in the essay:

    Computer-generated imagery is even more prone to distortion and fabrication than photography.

    Would this sentence be a relevant and appropriate addition to the essay, and why?

    F. No, because the topic of computer-generated imagery is unrelated to the main theme of the essay.
    G. Yes, because computer-generated imagery is now widely used in advertisements and other commercial presentations.
    H. No, because most people are well aware that computer-generated images are often distorted.
    J. Yes, because, like photography, computer-generated imagery is a form of visual art.

29. A. NO CHANGE
    B. involved with such.
    C. a party to these things.
    D. among those who take part in them.

30. F. NO CHANGE
    G. for
    H. yet
    J. so

ANSWER KEYS AND EXPLANATIONS

Exercise 1

1. C	7. C	13. C	19. B	25. B
2. G	8. H	14. F	20. F	26. H
3. A	9. B	15. D	21. A	27. A
4. F	10. F	16. G	22. J	28. J
5. D	11. A	17. B	23. B	29. A
6. F	12. H	18. H	24. G	30. G

1. **C.** It's more graceful, idiomatic, and clear to leave the prepositional phrase "of girls" intact, putting the modifying adverb "only" in front of the phrase rather than in the middle of it.

2. **G.** In most sentences, a modifying phrase like "In 1977," telling when the event described in the sentence takes place, fits best at the beginning. In this case, it would slip in nicely after the introductory conjunction "But."

3. **A.** The idiomatic phrase "justly renowned" is perfectly clear and correct as used in the original sentence.

4. **F.** The other answer choices change the meaning of the phrase in a way that isn't logical, given the context. The sentence is explaining how and why the Boys Choir overshadows the Girls Choir, given the history of the two organizations. Thus, it makes sense to introduce the sentence with the phrase "To this day," which says that the Boys Choir still overshadows the younger Girls Choir, even 20 years after the Girls Choir was founded.

5. **D.** All the answer choices say the same thing; choice D does it most concisely.

6. **F.** Since all of the world's musical settings are being compared (at least implicitly), the superlative adjective "most prestigious" is needed, rather than the comparative "more prestigious" or some other form.

7. **C.** The writer is trying to suggest that the Boys Choir has performed on many "prestigious" occasions. The concert for the Pope is an example; so is performing on the same bill as Pavarotti. The other statements, while interesting, don't describe prestigious occasions for musical performances.

8. **H.** The collective noun "choir" is normally treated, for grammatical purposes, as a singular word; therefore, it should be paired with the singular verb "was reassembled" rather than the plural "were."

9. **B.** The correct form of the possessive here would be "the mayor's wife."

10. **F.** The original wording is grammatically correct and clear. Choice G would turn the sentence into a run-on; choice H needlessly adds the word "thus"; and choice J uses the pronoun "it," whose antecedent and meaning aren't clear in the context.

11. **A.** The original "It's" is perfectly correct. In this context, "it's" means "it is," so the form of the word including an apostrophe is right.

12. **H.** Sentence 1 draws a conclusion based on the rest of the paragraph, so it logically belongs last. Sentence 2 introduces the paragraph's overall topic, so it makes sense to put that one first. And sentences 3 and 4 clearly belong together, in that order.

13. **C.** The idiomatic expression is, "motivated to do something" rather than "motivated for doing something."

14. **F.** The phrase "for lack of money" is an idiomatic and familiar one. Choices G and H are verbose and awkward by comparison; choice J is vague and hard to understand.

15. **D.** Read the explanation of the assignment carefully: the writer has been asked to "describe the musical achievements" of the choir. The essay we've read explains a bit about the choir's history and its importance in the lives of its inner-city members, but it really doesn't describe their musical achievements.

16. **G.** In this context, what's needed is the possessive "your" rather than the contraction "you're" (= you are).

17. **B.** The logical conjunction here is "but," since there is a contrast in meaning between the skepticism referred to in the first half of the sentence and the explanation offered in the second half, which is intended to disarm that skepticism.

18. **H.** As written, the sentence is a run-on; the second half of the sentence, beginning "he interviewed," could stand alone as a sentence. Choice H fixes this by making the last five words into a modifying phrase that explains what Schultz did in Alabama, tacked neatly on to the rest of the sentence.

19. **B.** It's incorrect to handle this as two sentences, since what follows the period is lacking a subject for the verb "was struck." As shown in choice B, the two should be unified, so that "he" becomes the subject for both verbs: "interviewed" and "was struck."

20. **F.** The original word is grammatically correct and logical in meaning.

21. **A.** The original wording is more clear and idiomatic than either of the two alternatives (choices B and C). It would be wrong to delete the phrase altogether (choice D), since it ties into one of the main ideas of the essay: how Schultz used a poetic metaphor to explain a new economic idea through analogy with an old, familiar idea.

22. **J.** For the sake of parallelism, eliminate these words. The list should simply read, "rail fences and hog pens and mules."

23. **B.** It makes sense to begin a new paragraph here, since the main idea has changed. The previous paragraph summarizes the old farm couple's concept of "human capital"; the new paragraph, which begins at this point, discusses how metaphors can help to explain new theoretical concepts.

24. **G.** The phrase "get received" is very slangy, too much so for the context of this fairly serious, formal essay on economics. "Are received," which means much the same thing, is more appropriate.

25. **B.** The commas in the original are needless; among other flaws, they separate the subject of the sentence (it's the compound subject "hog pen" and "Latin instruction") from its verb ("are paid for"). The subject and the verb shouldn't be separated by commas unless it's unavoidable.

26. **H.** This wording is the most concise and graceful of the four alternatives.

27. **A.** The plural verb "cause" is necessary, since the compound subject "hog pen" and "Latin" is plural.

28. **J.** What follows the underlined word is the noun phrase "water from a dam." Therefore, the preposition "like" is correct. (The conjunction "as" would be correct only if what followed was a clause, such as "water pours from a dam.")

29. **A.** All three alternatives mean much the same thing, but the original wording is clearest and most graceful. To omit the underlined words would obscure the point of the sentence, which is that the educated farmer can use his knowledge to produce concrete wealth (a hog pen).

30. **G.** This sentence serves the stated purpose best because it summarizes the main point of the essay by linking its opening and closing paragraphs, using the concept of "the poetry of economics" as the connecting theme.

Exercise 2

1. A	7. B	13. A	19. A	25. C
2. G	8. F	14. J	20. F	26. J
3. D	9. A	15. D	21. C	27. A
4. G	10. F	16. G	22. F	28. H
5. D	11. A	17. A	23. A	29. A
6. F	12. G	18. J	24. G	30. H

1. **A.** The punctuation in the original is correct. It sets off the entire parenthetical phrase with a pair of dashes (one correct way to do it), and separates the additional interjection, "say," from the rest of the phrase with a comma of its own.

2. **G.** It's idiomatic to speak of one's "role of doing something," rather than, for example, a "role as doing something" or the other choices.

3. **D.** The underlined phrase should be grammatically parallel to "failed novelists." "Unsuccessful playwrights" fits.

4. **G.** The normal idiom is, "no other X than Y."

5. **D.** The simple preposition "Like" is the clearest and most concise way of expressing the desired meaning.

6. **F.** Answers G, H, and J all offer parenthetical clauses that could be inserted after the word "Shakespeare" in the essay. However, in each case, the additional information provided is only marginally relevant to the topic of the essay. The original version, with none of these clauses, is the best.

7. **B.** The writer is contrasting the humble audiences for the first movies with the elite audience for other forms of art. To fit this notion, "the private club" makes more logical sense than any of the other answer choices.

8. **F.** The point of the paragraph—and the major point of the essay—is that the large amounts of money involved in modern movie making have taken away some of the freshness and creativity of movies as an art form. To support this point, the original clause is the best.

9. **A.** The original punctuation is correct. The three adjectives, "conventional, unimaginative, and stale," are being listed in a series, and it's proper to separate the items in the list by commas.

10. **F.** "Has been" is correct; it's a singular verb, to match the singular subject "freshness."

11. **A.** The conjunction "However" logically introduces this paragraph, which shifts the topic of the essay from the freshness of the early movies to the conventionality produced by the money pressures felt by today's movie makers. "However" suggests the change in theme.

12. **G.** The adverb "only" sounds most natural, and its meaning is clearest, when it follows "has": The sequence makes it clear that the writer is implying, "only a *known* patron, not a vast collection of *unknown* patrons like those in the movie audience."

13. **A.** The original wording is understandable, grammatical, and idiomatically correct.

14. **J.** The proper idiomatic pairing is, "the more costly . . . the greater."

15. **D.** Since paragraph 3 offers a conclusion based on the existence of financial pressures in today's movie industry, it's logical to put that paragraph after the paragraph in which those pressures are described—paragraph 4.

16. **G.** The subject of the verb "include" is the pronoun "that," which can be either singular or plural. To tell which it is, refer back to its antecedent, which is "kind." Since "kind" is singular, so is "that"; so the singular verb "includes" is needed.

17. **A.** The original wording is best. Each of the other answer choices is non-idiomatic and awkward-sounding.

18. **J.** All four answer choices say much the same thing. Therefore, the concise single-word alternative "predators" is better than the other, more wordy versions.

19. **A.** This sentence makes for the best transition, since it leads the reader from the topic of urodeles toward the second type of animal being discussed, planaria, which are also capable of regeneration.

20. **F.** The apposite phrase "a kind of simple worm," which briefly describes "planaria," is appropriately set off from the rest of the sentence by being enclosed within a pair of commas.

21. **C.** It's incorrect to use the conjunction "and" at the start of this phrase. Instead, the preposition "with" links the phrase to the rest of the sentence in a way that makes it meaning and its relation to the other parts of the sentence clear.

22. **F.** Up to this point, the essay has described a similarity between urodeles and planaria: both can regenerate. Now, a difference will be discussed: their varying means of accomplishing this. Thus, the connecting word "However," which suggests a change in theme, makes sense.

23. **A.** This sentence is telling what the animal first does when injured. (Later, we'll learn what the animal does second.) Thus, the adverb "first" most directly modifies the verb "heals," which means it should be placed as close as possible to that verb. The original location, therefore, is the best one.

24. **G.** "Such like" is not idiomatic; "such as" is.

25. **C.** The idiomatic expression to use with the verb "revert" is "to being."

26. **J.** What's needed in this context is the adverb "ultimately" rather than the adjective "ultimate." It modifies the entire sentence by telling *when* the event described takes place: at the end of the entire regeneration process.

27. **A.** "By contrast" sets up an appropriate transition from the previous paragraph, which discussed how urodeles regenerate, to this one, which shifts to the topic of how planaria regenerate.

28. **H.** The sentence as originally worded is a run-on; the second half of the sentence, beginning with "this enables," could stand alone as a sentence. Choice H fixes the problem by turning the second half of the sentence into a modifying phrase clearly attached to the first half of the sentence.

29. **A.** The original wording is the clearest way of stating the idea. Choice B is wrong because of the plural verb "are" (it should be singular, to match its subject, "which," referring back to "cell type"); choice D is wrong because of the weird use of the pronoun "one." (Whom could it possibly refer to?)

30. **H.** The idiomatic phrasing "of the old" implies "of the old [animal]," grammatically parallel to the phrase "an entirely new animal" earlier in the sentence.

Exercise 3

1. A	7. A	13. B	19. C	25. C
2. J	8. J	14. F	20. F	26. G
3. A	9. B	15. B	21. D	27. A
4. H	10. G	16. G	22. F	28. F
5. A	11. C	17. D	23. B	29. A
6. G	12. F	18. G	24. F	30. F

1. **A.** The original wording is the best choice. Note that answers B and C are wrong because they shift to a singular construction ("business" rather than "businesses,"), which doesn't fit with the pronoun "they" later in the sentence.

2. **J.** Choice J is the most concise and graceful alternative. One clue: Note that both the original wording and choice G include commas around the adverb "simply," which is often a telltale sign of unnecessary awkwardness.

3. **A.** The clause in the original sentence does the best job of underscoring Wang's preeminent position in the office automation marketplace. The other statements suggest vaguely related ideas, but none clearly states that Wang was number one in its field, as the original clause does.

4. **H.** Choices F and G are unclear in their reference; choice J is wordy and awkward. Choice H makes the point clearly and concisely.

5. **A.** The dramatic shift in tone between the first paragraph (describing Wang's former greatness) and the second paragraph (describing its later collapse) is appropriately signaled by the "Yet."

6.　**G.** The sentence in the original essay beginning with the word "shrinking" is actually a fragment. Choice G fixes this by attacking it to the previous sentence, where it becomes a long phrase modifying "Wang."

7.　**A.** All four answer choices say much the same thing; choice A does it most concisely and gracefully.

8.　**J.** The subject of the sentence is "computer"; the writer's intention is to have a compound verb, "transformed" and "wiped out." Choice J sets up this structure and makes the relationship between the various parts of the sentence quite clear.

9.　**B.** The correct past participle of the verb "to see" is "seen"; whenever an auxiliary (helping) verb is used, "seen" should be used, not "saw."

10.　**G.** In this sentence, "its" is being used as the possessive form of the pronoun "it." Therefore, no apostrophe should be used. (In this way, of course, "its" and other possessive pronouns, such as "yours" and "hers," differ from other possessives.)

11.　**C.** The plural verb "were" must be used, since the subject is also plural: the compound "excellence and leadership."

12.　**F.** This paragraph describes the missteps that led Wang to ignore the personal computer market until it was too late, severely damaging Wang's business prospects. Only the sentence in choice F summarizes this information accurately.

13.　**B.** The hypothetical business leader discussed in this sentence is trading time for two other things: "more information" and "a decrease in uncertainty." Since two similar things are being listed, it would be desirable for them to be described in grammatically parallel terms: "more information and less uncertainty."

14.　**F.** It's perfectly idiomatic to speak of someone being "incapable of [bold] action." Thus, the original wording is correct.

15.　**B.** There's no such word as "regardlessly." The answer choice which best fits the context is B; the phrase "in either case" refers back to the two causes of business leaders' hesitation to act described in the previous two sentences.

16.　**G.** The parenthetical phrase "of course" should be set off from the rest of the sentence by a pair of matching bookends: two commas, one before the phrase and one after.

17.　**D.** The most concise and graceful wording is choice D.

18.　**G.** The singular verb "has been" is needed; its subject, "that," is singular, since it refers back to the singular antecedent "subject." Answer J is wrong because the sentence becomes a bit confusing when the underlined words are eliminated altogether.

19.　**C.** The two adverbs should be grammatically parallel to one another, as they are in choice C.

20.　**F.** The alternatives versions are all less idiomatic and "normal-sounding" than the original.

21.　**D.** This version makes the point in fewer, clearer words than either version A or C. Note that answer B distorts the meaning of the sentence: "wariness" and "awareness" are two very different things.

22.　**F.** The original version is grammatically correct and idiomatic.

23.　**B.** The point of the paragraph is the emotional impact that a vivid photograph can have. The interjected phrase strengthens this point by calling to mind an image that clearly illustrates this impact.

24.　**F.** This version is the shortest and most concise way of saying what all four answer choices say.

25.　**C.** The topic of the new paragraph is the fact that photos—despite their inherent realism—can be used to mislead. Choice C establishes a clear transition to this topic by making it clear that the writer does not want to exaggerate the claims for the realism of photography stated previously in the essay.

26.　**G.** The verb "freezes" should be used in order to maintain grammatical parallelism with the verbs "exaggerates" and "omits" earlier in the sentence.

27.　**A.** The other answer choices are awkward and less idiomatic than this version.

28. **F.** If this were a more general essay on the topic of truth and falsehood in art, then a digression on the new computer-generated imagery and its capacity for deception might be relevant and interesting. However, this essay deals solely with photography; in this context, a sentence on computer images seems out of place.

29. **A.** By comparison to this phrasing, the others sound awkward and a little vague.

30. **F.** The logical connection between the two halves of the sentence is best conveyed by "and." There is no sharp contrast between the two, so "yet" is wrong, nor is there a cause-and-effect relationship, which eliminates "for" and "so."

ARE YOU READY TO MOVE ON?

How well do you understand the contents and format of the ACT Assessment English Test? How well have you incorporated your review knowledge into your test-taking behavior?

After you've corrected each exercise, find the number in the table below. This will give you an idea of whether you still need improvement.

Score Key for Each Practice Exercise

Number Correct	Score	Suggested Action
0–7	Poor	Study Chapters 4 and 8 again. See "Additional Resources for Review," below.
8–13	Below average	Study problem areas in Chapters 4 and 8. See "Additional Resources for Review," below if you have time.
14–18	Average	Skim problem areas in Chapters 4 and 8 if you wish to and have time.
19–24	Above average	You may move on to a new subject.
25–30	Excellent	You're ready for the ACT Assessment English Test.

ADDITIONAL RESOURCES FOR REVIEW

After reviewing this chapter and trying to apply your knowledge on additional practice exercises and sample tests, you might still want help in English grammar, usage, or rhetoric. You might be looking further than the ACT Assessment's reach. However, get as much help as you think you need.

Here are some suggested titles for English review:

The Elements of Style, Third Edition. William Strunk, Jr., and E.B. White. Allyn & Bacon, 1979.

Essential English Composition for College-Bound Students, Third Edition. Leo Lieberman and Jeffrey Spielberger. ARCO. 1993.

Grammar for Grownups. Val Drummond. Harper Perennial, 1993.

Painless Grammar. Rebecca Elliott. Barron's Educational Series, 1997.

Math Review: From Arithmetic Through Geometry

Instead of reviewing every principle of every possible Math topic, this ACT Assessment Review concentrates on the topics that appear most frequently on the test. What test-takers will be happy to know is that most of these topics are part of the regular curriculum taught to virtually every high school ninth- and tenth-grade student. That means the ACT Assessment Math Test has no hidden surprises, which should be an enormous boost to your confidence level.

The Review includes the basic facts, formulas, and concepts you need to refresh yourself, as well as examples of how these concepts might be turned into actual ACT Assessment test questions. The Review here—and the ACT Assessment Math Test itself—begins at the lowest level of difficulty with basic arithmetic operations and pre-algebra, then goes on to cover elementary and intermediate algebra, and coordinate and plane geometry. At the end there is a brief survey of certain principles in trigonometry; though on the test itself, these problems make up less than 10% of the exam. There is no calculus in this Review and none on the test. Immediately after the review are three more practice exercises. A final section brings you additional resources for review in case you need extra help.

ARITHMETIC

NUMBERS AND THE NUMBER LINE

We can think of the real numbers as points on a line. To represent this, we usually draw a horizontal line, with one point on the line chosen to represent zero. All the positive numbers are to the right of zero, and all the negative numbers are to the left of zero. Therefore, the numbers get larger as you go from left to right.

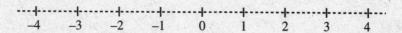

The *absolute value* of any number N is symbolized by $|N|$ and is simply the number without its sign. Thus, $|8| = 8$, $|-7| = 7$, and $|0| = 0$.

ROAD MAP

- *Review the Basics of ACT Assessment Arithmetic*
- *Review the Basics of ACT Assessment Algebra*
- *Review the Basics of ACT Assessment Geometry*
- *Review the Basics of ACT Assessment Coordinate Geometry*
- *Practice Your Skills on ACT Assessment Exercises*

The absolute value can be thought of as the distance of the number from zero. The further you get from zero, the larger the absolute value. So numbers far to the left are negative numbers with large absolute values.

When a number line is shown on the ACT Assessment, you can safely assume that the line is drawn to scale and that any numbers that fall between the markings are at appropriate locations. Thus, 2.5 is halfway between 2 and 3, and –0.4 is four-tenths of the way from 0 to –1. However, always check the scale, because the "tick marks" do not have to be at unit intervals!

Example 1: On the number line shown below, where is the number which is less than D and half as far from D as D is from G?

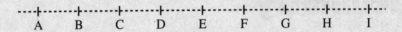

Solution: First, any number less than D must lie to the left of D. (Get it? Left = less!) The distance from D to G is 3 units. Thus, the point we want must be $1\frac{1}{2}$ units to the left of D—that is, halfway between B and C.

Example 2: On the number line shown below, which point corresponds to the number 2.27?

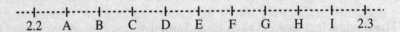

Solution: Since the labeled end points are 2.2 and 2.3, the ten intervals between must each be one-tenth of the difference. Hence the tick marks must represent hundredths. That is, A = 2.21, B = 2.22, and so on. Thus, we know that G = 2.27.

LAWS OF ARITHMETIC AND ORDER OF OPERATIONS

In carrying out arithmetic or algebraic operations, you should use the famous mnemonic (memory) device Please My Dear Aunt Sally to recall the correct order of operations. The operations of Powers, Multiplication, Division, Addition, and Subtraction should be carried out in that order reading from left to right.

If we want to indicate a change in order, we place the operation in parentheses, creating one number. Always calculate the number in parentheses first. Thus, $16 - 3 \times 4 = 16 - 12 = 4$, because we multiply before adding. However, if we want the number $16 - 3$ to be multiplied by 4, we must write it this way: $(16 - 3) \times 4 = 13 \times 4 = 52$.

The basic laws of arithmetic were originally defined for whole numbers, but they carry over to all numbers. You should know all of them from past experience. They are:

- *The commutative law.* It doesn't matter in which order you add or multiply two numbers. That is:

  $a + b = b + a$

  $ab = ba$

- *The associative law*, also called the *regrouping law*. It doesn't matter how you group the numbers when you add or multiply more than two numbers. That is:

  $a + (b + c) = (a + b) + c$

  $a(bc) = (ab)c$

- *The distributive law* for multiplication over addition. This law can be represented as follows:

  $a(b + c) = ab + ac$

  It means you can add first and then multiply, or multiply each term in the sum by the same amount and then add the two products. Either way the result is the same.

- *The properties of zero and one.* Zero times any number is zero. Zero added to any number leaves the number unchanged. One times any number leaves the number unchanged.

- *The additive opposite.* For every number n, there is a number $-n$ such that $n + (-n) = 0$. This number is the additive opposite.

- *The multiplicative inverse.* For every number n except 0, there is a number $\frac{1}{n}$ such that $(\frac{1}{n})(n) = 1$. Division by n is the same as multiplication by $\frac{1}{n}$, and division by zero is never allowed.

Example: (a) What is the value of $\frac{3+B}{4\times 3-3B}$ if $B = 3$? (b) What value is impossible for B?

Solution: (a) The fraction bar in a fraction acts as a "grouping symbol," like parentheses, meaning we should calculate the numerator and denominator separately. That is, we should read this fraction as $(3 + B) \div (4 \times 3 - 3 \times B)$. When $B = 3$, the numerator is $3 + 3 = 6$, and the denominator is $12 - 3 \times 3 = 12 - 9 = 3$. Therefore, the fraction is $\frac{6}{3} = 2$.

(b) Since we cannot divide by zero, we cannot let $4 \times 3 - 3 \times B = 0$. But in order for this expression to equal zero, $4 \times 3 = 3 \times B$. By the commutative law, $B = 4$. Thus, the only value that B cannot have is 4.

DIVISIBILITY RULES

A *factor* or *divisor* of a whole number is a number that divides evenly into the given number, leaving no remainder. For example, the divisors of 24 are 1, 2, 3, 4, 6, 8, 12, and 24 itself.

A *proper divisor* is any divisor except the number itself. Thus, the proper divisors of 24 are 1, 2, 3, 4, 6, 8, and 12. If you want to know whether k is a divisor of n, try to divide k into n and see whether there is any remainder. If the remainder is zero, then n is divisible by k.

There are several useful rules for testing for divisibility by certain small numbers. These are summarized in the table below.

Table 9.1: Rules for Testing Divisibility

Number	Divides into a Number N if . . .
2	N is even; that is, it ends in 2, 4, 6, 8, or 0.
3	The sum of the digits of N is divisible by 3.
4	The last two digits form a number divisible by 4.
5	The number ends in 5 or 0.
6	The number is divisible by 2 and 3.
8	The last three digits form a number divisible by 8.
9	The sum of the digits of N is divisible by 9.
0	The number ends in 0.

Example 1: Consider the number 7,380. How many numbers in the table above do not divide evenly into 7,380?

Solution: 7,380 is divisible by all the numbers in the table except 8. Do you see why? To start with, 7,380 is divisible by 10 and 5 because it ends in 0. It is divisible by 2 because it is even, and by 4 because 80 is divisible by 4. However, it is not divisible by 8 because 380 isn't. In addition, the sum of its digits is 18, which is divisible both by 3 and by 9. Since it is divisible by both 2 and 3, it is also divisible by 6.

Example 2: Which numbers in the following list are divisible by 3, 4, and 5, but not by 9?

15,840

20,085

23,096

53,700

79,130

Solution: The easiest thing to look for is divisibility by 5. Just ask, does the number end in 5 or 0? By inspection, we can eliminate 23,096, which ends in 6. We want the number to be divisible by 4, which means it must be even and its last two digits must form a number divisible by 4. That knocks out the number ending in 5 (which is odd), as well as 79,130, because 30 is not divisible by 4.

This leaves 15,840 and 53,700. The digits of 15,840 add up to 18, while those of 53,700 total 15. Both are divisible by 3, but 15,840 is also divisible by 9. Therefore, only 53,700 meets all the conditions.

DIVISIBILITY IN ADDITION, SUBTRACTION, AND MULTIPLICATION

If you add or subtract two numbers that are both divisible by some number k, then the new number formed will also be divisible by k. Thus, 28 and 16 are both divisible by 4. If you take their sum, 44, or their difference, 12, they too are divisible by 4.

If you multiply two numbers together, any number that divides either one also divides the product. Thus, if j divides M and k divides N, then jk divides MN.

If two numbers being multiplied have a common divisor, then the product is divisible by the square of that number. Thus, $21 \times 15 = 315$ is divisible by 7, because 7 divides 21, and by 5, because 5 divides 15. It is also divisible by $35 = 5 \times 7$, and by 9, because $9 = 3^2$ and 3 divides both 21 and 15.

Example 1:

 If a and b are whole numbers and $3a = 2b$, which of the following must be true?

A. a is divisible by 2, and b is divisible by 3.

B. a and b are both divisible by 2.

C. a and b are both divisible by 3.

D. a is divisible by 3, and b is divisible by 2.

E. None of the above

Solution: The correct answer is A. If $3a$ equals $2b$, then $3a$ must be divisible by 2, which means a must be divisible by 2, since 3 is not. Similarly, $2b$ must be divisible by 3, which means b must be divisible by 3, since 2 is not.

You should be especially aware of the divisibility properties of even and odd numbers.

- *Even numbers* are those that are divisible by 2: 0, 2, 4, 6, . . .
- *Odd numbers* are not divisible by 2: 1, 3, 5, 7, . . .

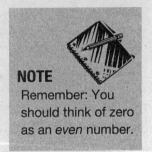

NOTE

Remember: You should think of zero as an *even* number.

Certain simple but very useful results follow from these definitions:

- If you add or subtract two even numbers, the result is even.
- If you add or subtract two odd numbers, the result is even.
- Only when you add or subtract an odd and an even number is the result odd. Thus, 4 + 6 is even, as is 7 − 3. But 4 + 3 is odd.
- When you multiply any whole number by an even number, the result is even.
- Only when you multiply two odd numbers will the result be odd. Thus, (4)(6) and (4)(7) are both even, but (3)(7) is odd.

Example 2: If $3x + 4y$ is an odd number, is x odd or even, or is it impossible to tell?

Solution: $4y$ must be even, so for the sum of $3x$ and $4y$ to be odd, $3x$ must be odd. Since 3 is odd, $3x$ will be odd only if x is odd. Hence, x is odd.

Example 3: If $121 − 5k$ is divisible by 3, may k be odd?

Solution: The fact that a number is divisible by 3 does not make it odd. (Think of 6 or 12.) Therefore, $121 − 5k$ could be odd or even. It will be odd when k is even and even when k is odd. (Do you see why?) Thus, k could be odd or even. For example, if $k = 2$, $121 − 5k = 111$, which is divisible by 3; and if $k = 5$, $121 − 5k = 96$, which is divisible by 3.

COMPARING FRACTIONS

Two fractions $\frac{a}{b}$ and $\frac{c}{d}$ are defined to be equal if $ad = bc$. For example, $\frac{3}{4} = \frac{9}{12}$ because $(3)(12) = (4)(9)$. This definition, using the process known as *cross-multiplication*, is very useful in solving algebraic equations involving fractions. However, for working with numbers, the most important thing to remember is that multiplying the numerator and denominator of a fraction by the same number (other than zero) results in a fraction equal in value to the original fraction. Thus, by multiplying the top and the bottom of $\frac{3}{4}$ by 3, we have $\frac{3}{4} = \frac{(3)(3)}{(3)(4)} = \frac{9}{12}$.

Similarly, dividing the numerator and denominator of a fraction by the same number (other than zero) results in a fraction equal in value to the original fraction. It is usual to divide through the top and the bottom of the fraction by the greatest common factor of both numerator and denominator to reduce the fraction to lowest terms. Thus, by dividing the top and the bottom of $\frac{15}{25}$ by 5, we have $\frac{15}{25} = \frac{15 \div 5}{25 \div 5} = \frac{3}{5}$.

For all positive numbers, if two fractions have the same denominator, the one with the larger numerator is larger. If two fractions have the same numerator, the one with the smaller denominator is larger. For example, $\frac{5}{19}$ is smaller than $\frac{8}{19}$, but $\frac{8}{17}$ is larger than $\frac{8}{19}$.

Example 1: If b and c are both positive whole numbers greater than 1, and $\frac{5}{c} = \frac{b}{3}$, what are the values of b and c?

Solution: Using cross-multiplication, $bc = 15$. The only ways 15 can be the product of two positive integers is as $(1)(15)$ or $(3)(5)$. Since both b and c must be greater than 1, one must be 3 and the other 5. Trying both cases, it is easy to see that the only possibility is that $b = 3$ and $c = 5$, making both fractions equal to 1.

Example 2: Which is larger, $\frac{4}{7}$ or $\frac{3}{5}$?

Solution: The first fraction named has a larger numerator, but it also has a larger denominator. To compare the two fractions, rewrite both with the common denominator 35 by multiplying the top and bottom of $\frac{4}{7}$ by 5 and the top and bottom of $\frac{3}{5}$ by 7 to yield $\frac{20}{35}$ and $\frac{21}{35}$ respectively. Now, it is easy to see that $\frac{3}{5}$ is the larger.

Example 3: Which is larger, $\frac{-6}{11}$ or $\frac{13}{-22}$?

Solution: First of all, it does not matter where you put the minus sign—top, bottom, or opposite the fraction bar; if there is one minus sign anywhere in a fraction, the fraction is negative.

Next, remember: In comparing negative numbers, the one with the larger absolute value is the smaller number. So start by ignoring the signs, and compare the absolute values of the fractions. If the two fractions had a common denominator or numerator, it would be easy. So, multiply the top and bottom of $\frac{6}{11}$ by 2 to yield $\frac{12}{22}$, and it is easy to see that $\frac{13}{22}$ is the larger. Hence, $\frac{13}{-22}$ has the greater absolute value, meaning that $\frac{-6}{11}$ is the larger number.

Of course, you could have solved either of these last two examples on a calculator. Dividing the numerator by the denominator will yield a decimal. Thus, in Example 2, as a decimal $\frac{4}{7} = 0.571 \ldots$ and $\frac{3}{5} = 0.6$. Try Example 3 this way for yourself.

ARITHMETIC WITH FRACTIONS

Multiplication and Division

When multiplying two fractions, the result is the product of the numerators divided by the product of the denominators. In symbols, $\frac{a}{b} \times \frac{c}{d} = \frac{ac}{bd}$. Thus, $\frac{3}{5} \times \frac{10}{9} = \frac{2}{3}$.

Don't forget that the resulting fraction can be reduced to lowest terms by canceling out like factors in numerator and denominator. Thus, $\frac{3}{5} \times \frac{10}{9} = \frac{2}{3}$.

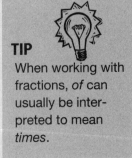

TIP
When working with fractions, *of* can usually be interpreted to mean *times*.

Example 1: Jasmine earns $\frac{3}{4}$ of what Sidney earns, and Sidney earns $\frac{2}{3}$ of what Paul earns. What fraction of Paul's salary does Jasmine earn?

Using J, S, and P to stand for the people's earnings respectively, we have:

$$5 = \frac{2}{3}P; \, J = \frac{3}{4}S$$

Thus:

$$J = \frac{3}{4} \times \frac{2}{3}P = \frac{1}{2}P$$

Example 2: Pedro has half as many CDs as Andrea has, and Marcia has $\frac{3}{5}$ as many CDs as Andrea. What fraction of Marcia's number of CDs does Pedro have?

Solution: Using P, A, and M to stand for the number of CDs each owns respectively, we have:

$$P = \frac{1}{2}A; \, M = \frac{3}{5}A$$

Thus:

$$\frac{P}{M} = \frac{\frac{1}{2}A}{\frac{3}{5}A} = \frac{1}{2} \times \frac{5}{3} = \frac{5}{6}$$

So Pedro has $\frac{5}{6}$ as many CDs as Marcia.

Addition and Subtraction

To add or subtract fractions with the same denominator, simply add or subtract the numerators. For example, $\frac{5}{17} + \frac{3}{17} = \frac{8}{17}$, and $\frac{5}{17} - \frac{3}{17} = \frac{2}{17}$.

However, if the denominators are different, you must first rewrite the fractions so they will have the same denominator. That is, you must find *a common denominator*. Most books and teachers stress that you should use the *least common denominator (LCD),* which is the least common multiple (LCM) of the original denominators. This will keep the numbers smaller. However, any common denominator will do!

If you are rushed, you can always find a common denominator by just taking the product of the two denominators. For example, to add $\frac{5}{12} + \frac{3}{8}$, you can multiply the denominators 12 and 8 to find the common denominator 96. Thus:

$$\frac{5}{12} + \frac{3}{8} = \frac{5 \times 8}{12 \times 8} + \frac{3 \times 12}{8 \times 12} = \frac{40}{96} + \frac{36}{96} = \frac{76}{96}$$

Now you can divide both the numerator and the denominator by 4 to reduce the fraction to its lowest terms; that is: $\frac{76}{96} = \frac{19}{24}$.

To find the least common denominator, you must first understand what a least common multiple is. Given two numbers M and N, any number that is divisible by both is called a *common multiple* of M and N. The *least common multiple (LCM)* of the two numbers is the smallest number that is divisible by both. For example, 9 and 12 both divide into 108, so 108 is a common multiple; but the LCM is 36.

For small numbers, the easiest way to find the LCM is simply to list the multiples of each number (in writing or in your head) until you find the first common multiple. For example, for 9 and 12 we have the following multiples:

$$9 \quad 18 \quad 27 \quad \underline{36} \quad 45 \ldots$$

$$12 \quad 24 \quad \underline{36} \quad 48 \quad 60 \ldots$$

The first number that appears in both lists is 36.

The traditional method for finding the LCM, which is the method that translates most readily into algebra, requires that you find the *prime factorization* of the numbers.

Every whole number is either prime or composite. A *prime* is a whole number greater than 1 for which the only factors (divisors) are 1 and the number itself. Any whole number that is not prime is *composite*.

All composite numbers can be factored into primes in an essentially unique way. To find an LCM, you must find the smallest number that contains all the factors of both numbers. Thus, 9 factors as (3)(3), and 12 factors as (2)(2)(3). The LCM is the smallest number that has all the same factors: that is, two 3s and two 2s. Since (3)(3)(2)(2) = 36, the LCM is 36.

This definition also extends to sets of more than two numbers. Thus, the LCM of 12, 15, and 20 must contain all the prime factors of all three numbers: (2)(2)(3); (3)(5); (2)(2)(5). So the LCM is (2)(2)(3)(5) = 60. Now to add $\frac{5}{12} + \frac{3}{8}$ using the smallest possible numbers, we find the LCM of 12 and 8, which is 24. Then, we write $\frac{5}{12} = \frac{10}{24}$ and $\frac{3}{8} = \frac{9}{24}$. Thus:

$$\frac{5}{12} + \frac{3}{8} = \frac{10}{24} + \frac{9}{24} = \frac{19}{24}$$

Example 3: Find the LCM for 18 and 30.

Solution: Using prime factorization, 18 = (2)(3)(3), and 30 = (2)(3)(5). Since the factors 2 and 3 are common to both numbers, we need only multiply in one extra 3 to get the factors of 18 and a 5 to get the factors of 30. Thus, the LCM = (2)(3)(3)(5) = 90.

Example 4: Mario figures that he can finish a certain task in 20 days. Angelo figures that he can finish the same task in 25 days. What fraction of the task can they get done working together for seven days?

Solution: In seven days, Mario would do $\frac{7}{20}$ of the entire task. In the same week, Angelo would do $\frac{7}{25}$ of the entire task. Therefore, together they do $\frac{7}{20} + \frac{7}{25}$ of the whole job.

Now we have to add two fractions that have the same numerator. Can we add them directly by just summing the denominators? No! To add directly, it is the bottoms that must be the same! Instead, we must find a common denominator. The LCD is 100. Thus:

$$\frac{7}{25} + \frac{7}{20} = \frac{28}{100} + \frac{35}{100} = \frac{63}{100}$$

$\frac{63}{100}$ may also be expressed as 0.63 or 63%. Do you know why? If not, read the next section carefully.

FRACTIONS, DECIMALS, AND PERCENTS

Every fraction can be expressed as a *decimal*, which can be found by division. Those fractions for which the prime factorization of the denominator involves only 2's and 5's will have terminating decimal expansions. All others will have repeating decimal expansions. For example, $\frac{3}{20} = 0.15$, while $\frac{3}{11} = 0.272727\ldots$

To convert a number given as a decimal into a fraction, you must know what the decimal means. In general, a decimal represents a fraction with a denominator of 10, or 100, or 1,000, ..., where the number of zeros is equal to the number of digits to the right of the decimal point. Thus, for example, 0.4 means $\frac{4}{10}$; 0.52 means $\frac{52}{100}$; and $0.103 = \frac{103}{1000}$.

Decimals of the form 3.25 are equivalent to *mixed numbers*; thus, $3.25 = 3 + \frac{25}{100}$. For purposes of addition and subtraction, mixed numbers can be useful, but for purposes of multiplication or division, it is usually better to convert a mixed number into an *improper fraction*. Thus:

$$3\frac{1}{4} = \frac{13}{4}$$

How did we do that? Formally, we realize that $3 = \frac{3}{1}$, and we add the two fractions $\frac{3}{1}$ and $\frac{1}{4}$, using the common denominator 4. In informal terms, we multiply the whole number part (3) by the common denominator (4), and add the numerator of the fraction (1) to get the numerator of the resulting improper fraction. That is, $(3)(4) + 1 = 13$.

Example 1: If $\frac{0.56}{1.26}$ reduced to lowest terms is $\frac{a}{b}$, and a and b are positive whole numbers, what is b?

Solution: Rewriting both numerator and denominator as their fractional equivalents, $0.56 = \frac{56}{100} = \frac{14}{25}$, and $1.26 = 1 + \frac{26}{100} = 1 + \frac{13}{50} = \frac{63}{50}$.

We now accomplish the division by inverting the denominator of the fraction and multiplying. Thus:

$$\left(\frac{14}{25}\right)\left(\frac{50}{63}\right) = \frac{4}{9}$$

As you can see, $b = 9$.

Of course, you could also solve this example by changing the numerator and denominator of the original fraction to whole numbers. You would multiply both the top and the bottom by 100 to move both decimal points two places to the right; thus, $\frac{0.56}{1.26} = \frac{56}{126}$. Now you can divide out the common factor of 14 in the numerator and the denominator to reduce the fraction to $\frac{4}{9}$.

Per<u>cent</u> means per <u>hundred</u> (from the Latin word *centum* meaning "hundred"). So that, for example, 30% means 30 per hundred, or as a fraction $\frac{30}{100}$, or as a decimal 0.30.

To convert a number given as a percent to decimal form, simply move the decimal point two places to the left. To convert a decimal to a percent, reverse the process—move the decimal point two places to the right.

To avoid confusion, keep in mind the fact that, when written as a percent, the number should look bigger. Thus, the "large" number 45% = 0.45, and the "small" number 0.73 = 73%.

Example 2: In a group of 20 English majors and 30 history majors, 50% of the English majors and 20% of the history majors have not taken a college math course. What percent of the entire group have taken a college math course?

Solution: Start with the English majors. Since 50% = 0.50, 50% of 20 = (0.50)(20) = 10. For the history majors, 20% = 0.20; 20% of 30 = (0.20)(30) = 6. Hence, a total of 16 out of 50 people in the group have not taken math, which means that 34 have. As a fraction, 34 out of 50 is $\frac{34}{50}$ = 0.68 = 68%.

> **TIP**
> If you divide on a calculator, you will find that 0.56 ÷ 1.26 = 0.4444444..., which you might recognize as $\frac{4}{9}$. Here is a good trick to remember: Any repeating decimal can be written as the repeating portion divided by an equal number of 9s. Thus, 0.333... = $\frac{3}{9}$ = $\frac{1}{3}$; 0.279279279... = $\frac{279}{999}$ = $\frac{31}{111}$.

AVERAGES

There are three common measurements used to define the typical value of a collection of numbers. However, when you see the word *average* with no other explanation, it is assumed that what is meant is the *arithmetic mean*. The average in this sense is the sum of the numbers divided by the number of numbers in the collection. In symbols, $A = \frac{T}{n}$.

So, for example, if on four math exams you scored 82, 76, 87, and 89, your average at this point is (82 + 76 + 87 + 89) ÷ 4 = 334 ÷ 4 = 83.5.

Example 1: At an art show, Eleanor sold six of her paintings at an average price of $70. At the next show, she sold four paintings at an average price of $100. What was the overall average price of the 10 paintings?

Solution: You can't just say the answer is 85, the average of 70 and 100, because we do not have the same number of paintings in each group. We need to know the overall total. Since the first six average $70, the total received for the six was $420. Do you see why? (70 = $\frac{T}{6}$; therefore, T = (6)(70) = 420). In the same way, the next four paintings must have brought in $400 in order to average $100 apiece. Therefore, we have a total of 10 paintings selling for $420 + $400 = $820, and the average is $\frac{\$820}{10}$ = $82.

Example 2: Erica averaged 76 on her first four French exams. To get a B in the course, she must have an 80 average on her exams. What grade must she get on the next exam to bring her average to 80?

Solution: If her average is 76 on four exams, she must have a total of $(4)(76) = 304$. In order to average 80 on five exams, her total must be $(5)(80) = 400$. Therefore, she must score $400 - 304 = 96$ on her last exam. Study hard, Erica!

The other measurements used to define the typical value of a set of numbers are the *median*, which is the middle number when the numbers are arranged in increasing order, and the *mode*, which is the most common number.

Example 3: Which is greater for the set of nine integers {1, 2, 2, 2, 3, 5, 6, 7, 8}, the mean minus the median or the median minus the mode?

Solution: The median (middle number) is 3, the mode is 2 and the mean is $(1 + 2 + 2 + 2 + 3 + 5 + 6 + 7 + 8) \div 9 = 4$. Thus, the mean minus the median is $4 - 3 = 1$, and the median minus the mode is $3 - 2 = 1$. The two quantities are equal.

ALGEBRA

SIGNED NUMBERS

Addition and Subtraction

To add two numbers of the same sign, just add them and attach their common sign. So $7 + 9 = 16$, and $(-7) + (-9) = -16$. You could drop the parentheses and instead of $(-7) + (-9)$ write $-7 - 9$, which means the same thing. In other words, adding a negative number is the same thing as subtracting a positive number.

When adding numbers of opposite signs, temporarily ignore the signs, subtract the smaller from the larger, and attach to the result the sign of the number with the larger absolute value. Thus, $9 + (-3) = 6$, but $(-9) + 3 = -6$. Again, we could have written $9 + (-3) = 9 - 3 = 6$ and $(-9) + 3 = -9 + 3 = -6$.

When subtracting, change the sign of the second number (the *subtrahend*) and then use the rules for addition. Thus, $7 - (-3) = 7 + 3 = 10$ and $-7 - 3 = -7 + (-3) = -10$.

Example 1: Evaluate $-A - (-B)$ when $A = -5$ and $B = -6$.

Solution: All the minus signs can be confusing. However, if you remember that "minus a minus is a plus," you can do this in two ways. The first is to realize that if $B = -6$, then $-B = +6$, and if $A = -5$, then $-A = 5$ Thus, $-A - (-B) = 5 - 6 = -1$.

Alternatively, you can work with the letters first: $-A - (-B) = -A + B = -(-5) + (-6) = 5 - 6 = -1$.

Multiplication and Division

If you multiply two numbers with the same sign, the result is positive. If you multiply two numbers with opposite signs, the result is negative. The exact same rule holds for division. Thus $(-4)(-3) = +12$, and $(-4)(3) = -12$. For division, it doesn't matter which is negative and which positive; thus $(-6) \div (2) = -3$, and $(6) \div (-2) = -3$, but

$$(-6) \div (-2) = +3.$$

If you have a string of multiplications and divisions to do, if the number of negative factors is even, the result will be positive; if the number of negative factors is odd, the result will be negative. Of course, if even one factor is zero, the result is zero, and if even one factor in the denominator (divisor) is zero, the result is undefined.

Example 2: If $A = (234,906 - 457,219)(35)(-618)$ and $B = (-2,356)(-89,021)(-3,125)$, which is larger, A or B?

Solution: Don't actually do the arithmetic! 457,219 is greater than 234,906, so the difference is a negative number. Now, A is the product of two negative numbers and a positive number, which makes the result positive. B is the product of three negative numbers and must be negative. Every positive number is greater than any negative number, so A is greater than B.

Example 3:

 If $\frac{AB}{MN}$ is a positive number, and N is negative, which of the following are NOT possible?

   F. A is positive, and B and M are negative.

   G. A, B, and M are negative.

   H. A, B, and M are positive.

   J. B is positive, and A and M are negative.

   K. M is positive, and A and B are negative.

Solution: The correct answer is G. To determine the sign of the fraction, we can just think of A, B, M, and N as four factors. Knowing that N is negative, the product of the other three must also be negative in order that the result be positive. The only possibilities are that all are negative, or one is negative and the other two are positive. This works only for case G.

LAWS OF EXPONENTS

In an expression of the form b^n, b is called the base and n is called the *exponent* or *power*. We say, "b is raised to the power n." (Notice: $b^1 = b$; hence, the power 1 is usually omitted.) If n is any positive integer, then b^n is the product of n b's. For example, 4^3 is the product of three 4's, that is, $4^3 = 4 \times 4 \times 4 = 64$.

Certain rules for operations with exponents are forced upon us by this definition.

- $b^m \times b^n = b^{m+n}$. That is, when multiplying powers of the same base, keep the base and add the exponents. Thus, $3^2 \times 3^3 = 3^{2+3} = 3^5 = 243$.

- $(ab)^n = a^n b^n$ and $\left(\frac{a}{b}\right)^n = \frac{a^n}{b^n}$

  That is, to raise a product or quotient to a power, raise each factor to that power, whether that factor is in the top or bottom. Thus, $(2x)^3 = 2^3 x^3 = 8x^3$, and $\left(\frac{2}{x}\right)^3 = \frac{2^3}{x^3} = \frac{8}{x^3}$.

- $(b^m)^n = b^{nm}$. That is, to raise to a power to a power, retain the base and multiply exponents. Thus, $(2^3)^2 = 2^6 = 64$.

- $\frac{b^n}{b^m} = b^{n-m}$ if $n > m$, and $\frac{b^n}{b^m} = \frac{1}{b^{m-n}}$ if $n < m$. That is, to divide powers of the same base, subtract exponents. For example, $\frac{4^5}{4^2} = 4^3 = 64$, and $\frac{4^2}{4^5} = \frac{1}{4^3} = \frac{1}{64}$.

For various technical reasons, $x^0 = 1$ for all x except $x = 0$, in which case it is undefined. With this definition, one can define b^{-n} in such a way that all the laws of exponents given above still work even for negative powers! This definition is $b^{-n} = \frac{1}{b^n}$

Now you have the choice of writing $\frac{x^3}{x^5}$ as $\frac{1}{x^2}$ or as x^{-2}

Example 1: If $x = 2$, which is larger, 1.10 or $x^0 + x^{-4}$?

Solution: If $x = 2$, $x^0 = 2^0 = 1$, and $x^{-4} = 2^{-4} = = 0.0625$. Hence, $x^0 + x^{-4} = 1.0625$, which is less than 1.10.

Example 2:

Q Which of the following expressions is equivalent to $\frac{(2x)^3}{x^7}$?

A. $\frac{1}{8x^4}$

B. $\frac{8}{x^{-4}}$

C. $(8x)^{-4}$

D. $8x^{-4}$

E. $\frac{x^4}{8}$

Solution: The correct answer is D. Cubing the numerator, we cube each factor. Since $2^3 = 8$, we have $\frac{(2x)^3}{x^7} = \frac{8x^3}{x^7}$.

We now divide x^3 by x^7 by subtracting the exponents: $3 - 7 = -4$. Notice that we could have written $8x^{-4}$ as $\frac{8}{x^4}$.

Be alert to the properties of even and odd powers. Even powers of real numbers cannot be negative. This rule applies to both positive and negative integer powers. Thus, x^2 is positive, as is x^{-2} except for $x = 0$, when x^2 is zero and x^{-2} is undefined (because you cannot divide by zero).

Odd powers are positive or negative depending upon whether the base is positive or negative. Thus, $2^3 = 8$, but $(-2)^3 = -8$. Zero to any power is zero, except zero to the zero, which is undefined.

Example 3: If $x < 0$ and $y > 0$, what is the sign of $-4x^4y^3$?

Solution: x^4 is positive, because it has an even power. y^3 is positive because y is, and -4 is obviously negative. The product of two positives and a negative is negative. Thus,

$-4x^4y^3$ is negative.

Example 4: If $x^4 + 3y^2 = 0$, what is the sign of $2x - 6y + 1$?

Solution: Since neither x^4 nor $3y^2$ can be negative, the only way their sum can be zero is if both x and y are zero. Therefore, $2x - 6y + 1 = +1$, which is positive.

RATIO, PROPORTION, AND VARIATION

A fractional relationship between two quantities is frequently expressed as a *ratio*. A ratio can be written as a fraction, $\frac{b}{a}$, or in the form $b:a$ (read "b is to a"). A *proportion* is a statement that two ratios are equal. To say, for example, that the ratio of passing to failing students in a class is 5:2 means that if we set up the fraction $\frac{P}{F}$ representing the relationship between the number of passing and failing students, it should reduce to $\frac{5}{2}$. If we write this statement as $P:F :: 5:2$, we read it "P is to F as 5 is to 2," and it means $\frac{P}{F} = \frac{5}{2}$.

Often, a good way to work with information given in ratio form is to represent the numbers as multiples of the same number.

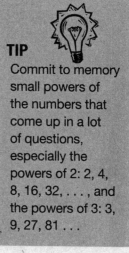

TIP
Commit to memory small powers of the numbers that come up in a lot of questions, especially the powers of 2: 2, 4, 8, 16, 32, . . . , and the powers of 3: 3, 9, 27, 81 . . .

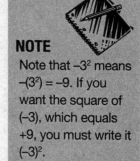

NOTE
Note that -3^2 means $-(3^2) = -9$. If you want the square of (-3), which equals $+9$, you must write it $(-3)^2$.

Example 1:

 The ratio of Democrats to Republicans in a certain state legislature is 5:7. If the legislature has 156 members, all of whom are either Democrats or Republicans (but not both), what is the difference between the number of Republicans and the number of Democrats?

    A. 14

    B. 26

    C. 35

    D. 37

    E. 49

Solution: The correct answer is B. Let the number of Democrats be $5m$ and the number of Republicans be $7m$, so that $D:R :: 5m:7m = 5:7$. The total number of legislators is $5m + 7m = 12m$, which must be 156. Therefore, $12m = 156$, and $m = 13$. Thus, the difference is $7m - 5m = 2m = 2(13) = 26$.

When you are told that one quantity, say y, *varies directly* with (or as) x, that means simply that $y = kx$, where k is some constant.

To say that y varies directly with x^2 or x^3 or any given power means that $y = kx^2$ or kx^3. If you are told that y varies inversely with x, it means that $y = \frac{k}{x}$. Similarly, if y varies inversely with x^n, it means that $y = \frac{k}{x^n} = kx^{-n}$.

Usually, the problem is to first determine k (the *constant of proportionality*) and then solve further.

Example 2: The time it takes to run a computer sorting program varies directly with the square of the number of items to be sorted. If it takes 7 microseconds to sort a list of 12 items, how long will it take to sort 40 items?

Solution: Letting t = time in microseconds and x = the number of items to be sorted, the relationship must be $t = kx^2$. When $x = 12$, $k = 7$. Therefore, $7 = k(12)^2 = 144k$. Hence, $k = \frac{7}{144}$. Thus, $y = \frac{7}{144}x^2$. When $x = 40$, $y = \frac{7}{144}(40)^2 = \frac{7(1600)}{144}$ = about 77.8.

Example 3: The time it takes to paint a wall is directly proportional to the area of the wall and inversely proportional to the number of painters. If 3 painters can paint 1000 square feet of wall in 6 hours, how many square feet can 8 painters paint in 15 hours?

Solution: The relationship must be $t = k\left(\frac{A}{p}\right)$, where t = time, A = area, and p = number of painters. Hence, when $A = 1000$ and $p = 3$, $6 = k\left(\frac{1000}{8}\right)$. That is, $6 = 125k$ and $k = \frac{6}{125}$. Now we substitute $p = 8$ and $t = 15$ into $t = \left(\frac{6}{125}\right)\left(\frac{A}{p}\right)$, yielding $15 = \left(\frac{6}{125}\right)\left(\frac{A}{8}\right) = \frac{3A}{500}$. Multiplying by 500 and dividing by 3, we have $A = 1500$.

SOLVING LINEAR EQUATIONS

To solve a linear equation, remember these rules:

- If you add or subtract the same quantity from both sides of an equation, the equation will still be true and will still have the same roots (solutions).

- If you multiply or divide both sides of an equation by any number except zero, the equation will still be true and will still have the same roots.

Use these two properties to isolate the unknown quantity on one side of the equation, leaving only known quantities on the other side. This is known as *solving for the unknown*.

Example 1: If $14 = 3x - 1$ and $B = 6x + 4$, what is the value of B?

Solution: From the first equation, $3x - 1 = 14$. Add 1 to both sides:

$$3x - 1 = 14$$
$$\underline{1 = 1}$$
$$3x = 15$$

Divide both sides by 3:

$$\frac{3x}{3} = \frac{15}{3}; x = 5$$

Of course, the question asked for B, not x. So we substitute $x = 5$ into $B = 6x + 4$ and get $B = 6(5) + 4 = 34$.

Example 2: If $\frac{2x}{3} + 2 = a$ and $y = 2x + 6$, what is the value of y in terms of a?

Solution: How do we do this? We realize that if we knew what x was in terms of a, then we could substitute that expression for x into $y = 2x + 6$ and have y in terms of a. In other words, we want to solve $\frac{2x}{3} + 2 = a$ for x.

Multiply through by 3 to clear the fractions. Be careful: use the distributive law and multiply every term on both sides by 3. You should now have:

$$2x + 6 = 3a$$

Now add −6 to both sides of the equation:

$$2x + 6 = 3a$$
$$\underline{-6 = -6}$$
$$2x = 3a - 6$$

Now divide by 2:

$$\frac{2x}{2} = \frac{3a - 6}{2}; x = \frac{3a - 6}{2}$$

Substituting:

$$y = 2\left(\frac{3a - 6}{2}\right) + 6$$
$$y = 3a - 6 + 6$$
$$= 3a$$

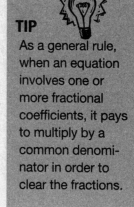

TIP
As a general rule, when an equation involves one or more fractional coefficients, it pays to multiply by a common denominator in order to clear the fractions.

SOLVING LINEAR INEQUALITIES

The statement that a number M is less than another number N means that $N - M$ is positive. In other words, when you subtract a smaller number from a larger number, the result is positive. In symbols, this can be expressed: $M < N$ or $N > M$.

On the number line, if $M < N$, we can infer that M lies to the left of N. This means, in particular, that any negative number is less than any positive number. It also implies that, for negative numbers, the one with the larger absolute value is the smaller number.

Inequalities (also called *inequations*) can be solved in the same way as equations are. When working with inequalities, remember these rules:

- If you add or subtract the same quantity from both sides of an inequation, it will still be true in the same sense. Thus, $14 > 7$ and $14 - 5 > 7 - 5$.
- If you multiply or divide both sides of an inequation by the same positive number, the inequation will still be true in the same sense. Thus, $3 < 8$ and $(6)(3) < (6)(8)$
- If you multiply or divide both sides of an inequation by the same negative number, the inequation will still be true, but with the sense *reversed*. Thus, $4 < 9$; but if you multiply by (-2), you get $-8 > -18$. (Remember, for negative numbers, the one with the larger absolute value is the smaller number.)

Notice that theses rules hold whether you are working with $<$ (is less than) and $>$ (is greater than) or $\leq$ (is less than or equal to) and $\geq$ (is greater than or equal to). Use them to isolate the unknown quantity on one side of the inequality, leaving only known quantities on the other side. This is known as *solving for the unknown*. Solutions to inequalities can be given in algebraic form or displayed on the number line.

Example 1: For what values of x is $12 - x \geq 3x + 8$?

Solution: We solve this just like an equation. Start by adding the like quantity $(x - 8)$ to both sides in order to group the x terms on one side and the constants on the other; thus:

$$12 - x \geq 3x + 8$$
$$\underline{x - 8 = x - 8}$$
$$4 \geq 4x$$

Now divide both sides by 4, which does not change the sense of the inequality, yielding:

$$1 \geq x$$

Hence, the inequality will be true for any number less than or equal to 1 and false for any number greater than 1. For example, if $x = 3$, $12 - x = 9$ and $3x + 8 = 17$, and the inequality is not satisfied. Graphically, this can be shown as in the figure below.

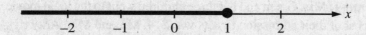

Notice that the darkened section is the set of solution values, and the solid dot at $x = 1$ indicates that the value 1 is included in the solution set. By contrast, see the figure below. It shows the solution set for $x < 2$, where the open circle shows that $x = 2$ is not included.

Example 2: If $A < 2 - 4B$, can you tell how large B is in terms of A? Can you tell how small B is?

Solution: We are really being asked to solve the inequality for B. To start, we add -2 to both sides, thus:

$$A < 2 - 4B$$
$$\underline{-2 = -2}$$
$$A - 2 < -4B$$

Next divide by -4, remembering to reverse the inequality, thus:

$$\frac{A - 2}{-4} > B; \quad \frac{2 - A}{4} > B$$

Notice two things here. When we changed the denominator on the left-hand side from -4 to $+4$, we also changed the sign of the numerator, by changing $(A - 2)$ to $(2 - A)$. Of course, this is the equivalent of multiplying the numerator and the denominator by -1.

Also, this tells us what B is less than, nothing about what B is greater than. For example, if A were 6, then $B < -1$, but B could be -100 or -1000 or anything else "more negative" than -1.

SOLVING TWO LINEAR EQUATIONS WITH TWO UNKNOWNS

Many word problems lead to equations in two unknowns. Usually, one needs as many equations as there are unknowns to solve for all or some of the unknowns: in other words, to solve for two unknowns, two independent equations are needed; to solve for three unknowns, three equations are needed, and so on. However, there are exceptions.

You should know two methods for solving two equations with two unknowns. They are the *method of substitution* and the *method of elimination by addition and subtraction.* We shall illustrate both methods by example. The first example uses the method of substitution.

Example 1: Mrs. Green and her three children went to the local movie. The total cost of their admission tickets was $14. Mr. and Mrs. Arkwright and their five children went to the same movie, and they had to pay $25. What was the cost of an adult ticket and what was the cost of a child's ticket?

Solution: Expressing all amounts in dollars, let x = cost of an adult ticket, and let y = cost of a child's ticket.

For the Greens:

$$x + 3y = 14$$

For the Arkwrights:

$$2x + 5y = 25$$

The idea of the method of substitution is to solve one equation for one variable in terms of the other and then substitute that solution into the second equation. Here, we solve the first equation for x, because that is the simplest one to isolate:

$$x = 14 - 3y$$

Substitute this value into the second equation:

$$2(14 - 3y) + 5y = 25$$

This gives us one equation with one unknown that we can solve:

$$28 - 6y + 5y = 25$$

$$-y = -3; y = 3$$

Now that we know $y = 3$, we put this into $x = 14 - 3y$ to get:

$$x = 14 - 3(3) = 5$$

Thus, the adult tickets were $5.00 each and the children's tickets were $3.00 each.

Here is an example using the method of elimination.

Example 2: Paula and Dennis both went to the bakery. Paula bought 3 rolls and 5 muffins for a total cost of $3.55. Dennis bought 6 rolls and 2 muffins for a total cost of $3.10. What was the price of one roll?

Solution: Let us express all amounts in cents. Let r = the cost of a roll; let m = the cost of a muffin. Paula paid:

$$3r + 5m = 355$$

Dennis paid:

$$6r + 2m = 310$$

The idea of the method of elimination is that adding equal quantities to equal quantities gives a true result. So we want to add some multiple of one equation to the other equation such that when the two equations are added together, one variable will be eliminated.

In this case, it is not hard to see that if we multiply the first equation by -2, the coefficient of r will become -6. Then, if we add the two equations, r will drop out. Here's how it works:

-2 times the first equation is: $-6r - 10m = -710$

The second equation is: $6r + 2m = 310$

Adding: $-8m = -400$

Dividing by -8, $m = 50$. We now substitute this into either of the two equations. Let's use the second:

$6r + (2)(50) = 310$

$6r = 210; r = 35$

Thus, muffins are 50¢ each and rolls are 35¢.

WORD PROBLEMS WITH ONE OR TWO UNKNOWNS

There are word problems of many different types. Many, like age or coin problems, involve only common sense. For others, there are specific formulas or pieces of factual knowledge that can be helpful.

For example, for *consecutive integer problems*, you need to know that consecutive integers differ by 1; therefore, a string of such numbers can be represented by $n, n + 1, n + 2, \ldots$

Consecutive even or odd integers differ by 2, so a string of such numbers can be represented as $n, n + 2, n + 4, \ldots$

Travel problems usually require you to use the formula $d = rt$; that is, Distance equals Rate times Time.

Example 1: Sally is 6 years older than Manuel; three years ago, Sally was twice as old as Manuel. How old is Sally today?

Solution: If you have trouble setting up the equations, try plugging in possible numbers. Suppose that Sally is 20 today. If Sally is 6 years older than Manuel, how old is Manuel? He is 14. You get from 14 to 20 by *adding* 6. So if S is Sally's age and M is Manuel's, $S = M + 6$.

Three years ago, Sally was $S - 3$, and Manuel was $M - 3$. So, from the second sentence, we know that $S - 3 = 2(M - 3)$ or $S - 3 = 2M - 6$. Thus, $S = 2M - 3$.

Now, substituting $S = M + 6$, into the second equation:

$M + 6 = 2M - 3$

$M = 9$

Which means that Sally is $9 + 6 = 15$.

Example 2: Three consecutive odd integers are written in increasing order. If the sum of the first and second and twice the third is 46, what is the second number?

Solution: Calling the smallest number x, the second is $x + 2$, and the third is $x + 4$. Therefore:

$$x + (x + 2) + 2(x + 4) = 46$$

$$x + x + 2 + 2x + 8 = 46$$

$$4x + 10 = 46$$

$$4x = 36; x = 9$$

Hence, the second number is $9 + 2 = 11$.

Example 3: It took Andrew $1\frac{1}{2}$ hours to drive from Aurora to Zalesville at an average speed of 50 miles per hour. How fast did he have to drive back in order to reach Aurora in 80 minutes?

Solution: The distance from Aurora to Zalesville must be given by $d = rt = (50)(1.5) = 75$ miles. Since 80 minutes is 1 hour and 20 minutes, or $1\frac{1}{3} = \frac{4}{3}$ hours, we must solve the equation $75 = \frac{4}{3} r$. Multiplying by 3, we have $225 = 4r$; then, dividing by 4, $r = 56.25$ mph.

MONOMIALS AND POLYNOMIALS

In any group of algebraic and arithmetic expressions, each expression is called a *term. Monomial* describes a single term; for example, we might say that $2x + 3y^2 + 7$ is the sum of three terms or three monomials.

Technically, if we enclose an algebraic expression in parentheses, it becomes one term, so that we could say that $(x + 2y) + (3x - 5y^2)$ is the sum of two monomials. But usually, when we talk about a monomial, we mean a term that is a single product of certain given constants and variables, possibly raised to various powers. Examples might be $7, 2x, -3y^2, 4x^2z^5$. Each of these is a monomial.

In a monomial, the constant factor is called the *coefficient of the variable factor*. Thus, in $-3y^2$, -3 is the coefficient of y^2. If we restrict our attention to monomials of the form Ax^n, the sums of such terms are called *polynomials*. Polynomials with two terms are called *binomials*, and those with three terms are called *trinomials*. Expressions like $3x + 5$, $2x^2 - 5x + 8$, and $x^4 - 7x^5 - 11$ are all examples of polynomials.

In a polynomial, the highest power of the variable that appears is called the *degree of the polynomial*. The three examples just given are of degree 1, 2, and 5, respectively.

Example 1: Find the value of $3x - x^3 - x^2$ when $x = -2$.

Solution: Substitute -2 every place you see an x, thus:

$$3(-2) - (-2)^3 - (-2)^2 = -6 - (-8) - (+4) = -6 + 8 - 4 = -2$$

Monomials with identical variable factors can be added or subtracted by adding or subtracting their coefficients. Thus: $3x^2 + 4x^2 = 7x^2$, and $3x^4 - 9x^4 = -6x^4$.

To multiply monomials, take the product of their coefficients and take the product of the variable parts by adding exponents of factors with like bases. Thus:

$$(-4xy^2)(3x^2y^3) = -12x^3y^5$$

Monomial fractions can be reduced to lowest terms by dividing out any common factors of the coefficients and then using the usual rules for subtraction of exponents in division. For example:

$$\frac{6x^3y^5}{2x^4y^3} = \frac{3y^2}{x}$$

Example 2: Combine into a single monomial $9y - \dfrac{6y^3}{2y^2}$.

Solution: The fraction reduces to $3y$, and $9y - 3y = 6y$.

COMBINING POLYNOMIALS AND MONOMIALS

Polynomials are added or subtracted simply by combining like monomial terms in the appropriate manner. Thus, $(2x^2 + 5x - 3) + (3x^2 + 5x - 12)$ is summed by removing the parentheses and combining like terms, to yield $5x^2 + 10x - 15$.

Example 1: What is the sum of $(3a^2b^3 - 6ab^2 + 2a^3b^2)$ and $(5a^2b^3 - 2a^3b^2)$?

Solution: Removing the parentheses, we combine the terms with identical literal parts by adding their coefficients:

$$(3a^2b^3 - 6ab^2 + 2a^3b^2) + (5a^2b^3 - 2a^3b^2)$$

$$= 3a^2b^3 - 6ab^2 + 2a^3b^2 + 5a^2b^3 - 2a^3b^2$$

$$= 8a^2b^3 - 6ab^2$$

Notice that the $2a^3b^2$ and $-2a^3b^2$ terms exactly cancelled out.

To multiply a polynomial by a monomial, use the distributive law to multiply each term in the polynomial by the monomial factor. For example, $2x(2x^2 + 5x - 11) = 4x^3 + 10x^2 - 22x$.

When multiplying a polynomial by a polynomial, repeatedly apply the distributive law to form all possible products of the terms in the first polynomial with the terms in the second.

The most common use of this is in multiplying two binomials, such as $(x + 3)(x - 5)$. In this case, there are four terms in the result: $x \times x = x^2$; $x(-5) = -5x$; $3 \times x = 3x$; and $3(-5) = -15$; but the two middle terms are added together to give $-2x$. Thus, the product is $x^2 - 2x - 15$.

$$(x + 3)(x - 5) = x^2 + (-5x + 3x) - 15$$

$$= x^2 - 2x - 15$$

Be sure to remember these special cases:

- $(x + a)^2 = (x + a)(x + a) = x^2 + 2ax + a^2$
- $(x - a)^2 = (x - a)(x - a) = x^2 - 2ax + a^2$

Example 2: If m is an integer, and $(x - 6)(x - m) = x^2 + rx + 18$, what is the value of $m + r$?

Solution: The product of the last terms, $6m$, must be 18. Therefore, $m = 3$. If $m = 3$, then the sum of the outer and inner products becomes $-6x - 3x = -9x$, which equals rx. Hence, $r = -9$, and $m + r = 3 + (-9) = -6$.

FACTORING MONOMIALS AND THE DIFFERENCE OF SQUARES

Factoring a monomial from a polynomial simply involves reversing the distributive law. For example, if you are looking at $3x^2 - 6xy$, you should see that $3x$ is a factor of both terms. Hence, you could just as well write this expression as $3x(x - 2y)$. Multiplication using the distributive law will restore the original formulation.

Example 1: If $x - 5y = 12$, which is greater, $15y - 3x$ or -35?

Solution: We can see that $15y - 3x = -3(x - 5y)$. Hence, it must equal $-3(12) = -36$, which is less than -35.

When you multiply $(a - b)$ by $(a + b)$ using the FOIL method, the middle terms exactly cancel out, leaving just $a^2 - b^2$. Thus, the difference of two squares, $a^2 - b^2 = (a - b)(a + b)$.

For example, $x^2 - 16$ can be thought of as $x^2 - 4^2 = (x - 4)(x + 4)$.

However, the sum of two squares—$b^2 + 16$, for example—cannot be factored.

TIP

This fact about the differences of two squares can be handy. For example, you can find $101^2 - 99^2$ as $(101 - 99)(101 + 99) = 2(200) = 400$.

Example 2:

 If x and y are positive integers, and $x - 2y = 5$, which of the following is the value of $x^2 - 4y^2$?

   A. 0

   B. 16

   C. 45

Solution: Since $x^2 - 4y^2 = (x - 2y)(x + 2y) = 5(x + 2y)$, $x^2 - 4y^2$ must be divisible by 5. Therefore, 16 is not possible. If the result is to be zero, $x + 2y = 0$, which means that $y = -2x$, so that both numbers cannot be positive. Hence, the expression must equal 45, which you get if $x = 7$ and $y = 1$. So the answer is C.

Example 3: If x and y are positive integers, and $y^2 = x^2 + 7$, what is the value of y?

Solution: If we rewrite the equation as $y^2 - x^2 = 7$ and factor, we have $(y - x)(y + x) = 7$. Thus, 7 must be the product of the two whole numbers $(y - x)$ and $(y + x)$. But 7 is a prime number which can only be factored as 7 times 1. Of course, $(y + x)$ must be the larger of the two; hence, $y + x = 7$, and $y - x = 1$.

Adding the two equations gives us $2y = 8$; $y = 4$. (Of course, $x = 3$, but we weren't asked that.)

OPERATIONS WITH SQUARE ROOTS

The square root of a number N, written $\sqrt{N}$, is a number that when squared produces N. Thus, $\sqrt{4} = 2$, $\sqrt{9} = 3$, $\sqrt{16} = 4$, and so on.

The symbol $\sqrt{}$ is called the *radical* sign, and many people refer to $\sqrt{N}$ as *radical N*. When we write $\sqrt{N}$, it is understood to be a positive number. So when you are faced with an algebraic equation like $x^2 = 4$, where you must allow for both positive and negative solutions, you must write $x = \pm \sqrt{4} = \pm 2$ (where $\pm$ is read as *plus or minus*).

You should be aware that $\sqrt{0} = 0$ and $\sqrt{1} = 1$. Square roots of negative numbers are not real numbers. All positive numbers have square roots, but most are irrational numbers. Only perfect squares like 4, 9, 16, 25, 36, . . . have integer square roots.

If you assume that you are working with non-negative numbers, you can use certain properties of the square root to simplify radical expressions. The most important of these rules is: $\sqrt{AB} = \sqrt{A} \times \sqrt{B}$.

This can be used to advantage in either direction. Reading it from right to left, we may write $\sqrt{3} \times \sqrt{12} = \sqrt{36} = 6$. But you should also know how to use this rule to simplify radicals by extracting perfect squares from "under" the radical. Thus, $\sqrt{18} = \sqrt{9} \times 2 = 3\sqrt{2}$.

The key to using this technique is to recognize the perfect squares in order to factor in a sensible manner. Thus, it would do you little good to factor 18 as 3×6 in the preceding example, since neither 3 nor 6 is a perfect square.

Example: If $\sqrt{5} \times \sqrt{x} = 10$, which is larger, $\sqrt{x}$ or $2\sqrt{5}$?

Solution: Since $10 = \sqrt{100}$ and $\sqrt{5} \times \sqrt{x} = \sqrt{5x}$, we know that $5x = 100$ and $x = 20$. But $20 = 4 \times 5$, so $\sqrt{20} = 2\sqrt{5}$. Hence, the two quantities are equal.

TRINOMIAL FACTORING AND QUADRATIC EQUATIONS

When you multiply two binomials $(x + r)(x + s)$ using the FOIL method, the result is a trinomial of the form $x^2 + bx + c$, where b, the coefficient of x, is the sum of the constants r and s, and the constant term c is their product.

Trinomial factoring is the process of reversing this multiplication. For example, to find the binomial factors of $x^2 - 2x - 8$, we need to find two numbers whose product is -8 and whose sum is -2. Since the product is negative, one of the numbers must be negative and the other positive. The possible factors of 8 are 1 and 8 and 2 and 4. In order for the sum to be -2, we must choose -4 and $+2$. Thus, $x^2 - 2x - 8 = (x - 4)(x + 2)$.

This technique can sometimes be used to solve quadratic equations. If you have an equation like $x^2 - 7x + 6 = 0$, you can factor the trinomial. To do this, you need two numbers whose product is $+6$ and whose sum is -7. Since the product is positive, both must be of the same sign, and since the sum is negative they must both be negative. It is not hard to see that -6 and -1 are the only correct options.

Once the trinomial is factored, the equation becomes $(x - 1)(x - 6) = 0$. Of course, the only way a product of two or more numbers can be zero is if one of the numbers is zero. Thus, either:

$$x - 1 = 0 \text{ or } x - 6 = 0$$

$$x = 1 \text{ or } x = 6$$

Example: The area of a rectangle is 60 and its perimeter is 32. What are its dimensions?

Solution: The area of a rectangle is determined by the formula $A = LW$, its perimeter by the formula $P = 2L + 2W$. In this case, we have $LW = 60$ and $2L + 2W = 32$. Dividing by 2, $L + W = 16$. Therefore, $L = 16 - W$, which we substitute in $LW = 60$, giving:

$$(16 - W)W = 60$$

$$16W - W^2 = 60$$

Grouping everything on the right-hand side, we have

$$0 = W^2 - 16W + 60$$

Now, factoring:

$$0 = (W - 10)(W - 6)$$

This yields $W = 10$ or $W = 6$.

Of course, if $W = 6$, $L = 10$, and if $W = 10$, $L = 6$. Either way, the dimensions are 6×10.

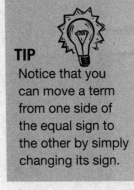

TIP
Notice that you can move a term from one side of the equal sign to the other by simply changing its sign.

THE QUADRATIC FORMULA

Some quadratic equations are not solvable by factoring using rational numbers. For example, because $x^2 + x + 1$ has no factors using whole numbers, $x^2 + x + 1 = 0$ has no rational roots (solutions).

In other cases, rational roots exist, but they are difficult to find. For example, $12x^2 + x - 6 = 0$ can be solved by factoring, but the solution is not easy to see:

$$12^2 + x - 6 = (3x - 2)(4x + 3)$$

Setting each factor equal to zero:

$$3x - 2 = 0 \text{ or } 4x + 3 = 0$$

yields $x = \dfrac{2}{3}$ or $x = \dfrac{3}{4}$.

What can you do when faced with such a situation? You use the *quadratic formula*, which states that, for any equation of the form $ax^2 + bx + c = 0$, the roots are:

$$x = \frac{-b \pm \sqrt{b^2 - 4ac}}{2a}$$

Example 1: If $6x^2 - x - 12 = 0$, what is the smallest integer greater than x?

Solution: Use the quadratic formula to solve for x. We identify a, b, and c as $a = 6$, $b = -1$, and $c = -12$. We substitute into the formula, yielding:

$$x = \frac{-(-1) \pm \sqrt{-1^2 - 4(6)(-12)}}{2(6)} = \frac{1 \pm \sqrt{1 + 288}}{12} = \frac{1 \pm \sqrt{289}}{12} = \frac{1 \pm 17}{12}$$

Using the plus sign:

$$x = \frac{1 + 17}{12} = \frac{18}{12} = \frac{3}{2}$$

Using the minus sign:

$$x = \frac{1 - 17}{12} = \frac{-16}{12} = -\frac{4}{3}$$

Both possible values of x are less than 2.

COMPLEX NUMBERS

Sometimes, when applying the quadratic formula, the *discriminant*, $d = b^2 - 4ac$, will be a negative number. In such a case, you have to deal with the square root of a negative number. Such a number is called *imaginary*. In general, if N is any positive number, then $\sqrt{-N}$ is written as $i\sqrt{N}$, where i is the square root of -1.

Numbers of the form bi, where b is a real number, are called *pure imaginary numbers*. For example, $\sqrt{-4} = i\sqrt{4} = 2i$ and $\sqrt{-3} = i\sqrt{3}$ are both pure imaginary numbers.

Numbers of the form $a + bi$, where a and b are both real numbers are called *complex numbers*. Thus, complex numbers have both a real and an imaginary part.

When doing arithmetic with complex numbers, just think of i as an unknown, like x, except whenever you get an i^2 in a computation, replace it with -1.

Example 1:

Q If $z = 4 + 3i$ and $w = 3 - 4i$, $zw - \dfrac{z}{w} = ?$

A. $14 - i$

B. $7 - 25i$

C. $24 - 6i$

D. $24 - 8i$

E. $7 - i$

Solution: The correct answer is D. Multiplying $(4 + 3i)(3 - 4i)$ by the FOIL method yields $12 - 7i - 12i^2$. Replacing i^2 by -1, we have $12 - 7i - 12(-1)$ $= 12 - 7i + 12 = 24 - 7i$.

To find $\frac{z}{w}$ in the form $a + bi$ so that we can subtract it from zw, we need to rationalize the denominator of the fraction by multiplying the numerator and denominator of the fraction by the *complex conjugate* of w. (The complex conjugate of $a + bi = a - bi$.) When you multiply these two, the term involving i drops out, and you end up with just $a^2 + b^2$. Thus:

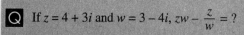

$$\frac{z}{w} = \left(\frac{4 + 3i}{3 - 4i}\right) \times \frac{3 + 4i}{3 + 4i} = \frac{12 + 25i + 12i^2}{3^2 + 4^2} = \frac{25i}{25} = i$$

Hence, $zw = \frac{z}{w} = (24 - 7i) - i = 24 - 8i$.

Example 2:

 Which of the following is one root of $x^2 - 4x + 5 = 0$?

F. $4 - i$

G. $2 - i$

H. $2 + 2i$

J. $3i$

K. $2 - 2i$

Solution: The correct answer is G. Using the quadratic formula with $a = 1$, $b = -4$, and $c = 5$, we have:

$$x = \frac{-(-4) \pm \sqrt{4^2 - 4(1)(5)}}{2(1)} = \frac{4 \pm \sqrt{16 - 20}}{2} = \frac{4 \pm \sqrt{-4}}{2} = \frac{4 \pm 2i}{2}$$

Dividing each term in the numerator by the denominator 2 gives us $x = 2 \pm i$. Since we can choose either + or –, we see that $2 - i$ is one root.

HIGHER ROOTS AND FRACTIONAL EXPONENTS

The symbol $\sqrt[n]{x}$ is used to represent the nth root of the number x. The nth root of x is that number which, when raised to the nth power, gives x as a result. For example, $\sqrt[3]{8} = 2$ because $2^3 = 8$.

Roots can also be represented by using fractional exponents. To be precise, we define $x^{\frac{1}{n}} = \sqrt[n]{x}$. In particular, the $\frac{1}{2}$ power of a number is its square root. So, for example:

$$16^{\frac{1}{2}} = \sqrt[2]{16} = \sqrt{16} = 4$$

and

$$125^{\frac{1}{3}} = \sqrt[3]{125} = 5$$

In addition, other fractional powers can be defined by using the laws of

exponents. That is, one can interpret an expression like $x^{\frac{3}{5}}$ to mean $\left(x^{\frac{1}{5}} \right)^3$

because $\frac{3}{5} = \left(\frac{1}{5} \right)(3)$. Thus:

$$32^{\frac{3}{5}} = \left(\sqrt[5]{32} \right)^3 = 2^3 = 8$$

Negative fractional powers can be similarly calculated by remembering that $x^{-n} = \frac{1}{x^n}$.

For example, to calculate $8-$, we first find $8^{\frac{2}{3}} = \left(\sqrt[3]{8} \right)^2 = 2^2 = 4$.

Now, $8-$ is the reciprocal of 8; that is, $\frac{1}{4}$.

Example 1: Find the value of $\dfrac{3x^0 + x^{\frac{1}{2}}}{2 + x^{-\frac{3}{4}}}$ if $x = 16$.

Solution: Let's calculate the numerator and denominator separately. In the numerator, $x^0 = 1$ for any x and, $x^{\frac{1}{2}} = \sqrt{x}$. Hence, $3(16^0) + 16^{\frac{1}{2}} = 3(1) + \sqrt{16} = 3 + 4 = 7$.

In the denominator, $16^{-\frac{3}{4}} = \frac{1}{8}$, which means that the denominator is $\frac{16}{8} + \frac{1}{8} = \frac{17}{8}$. So the original expression is equal to

$$\frac{7}{\frac{17}{8}} = 7\left(\frac{8}{17}\right) = \frac{56}{17}$$

FUNCTIONS

Two variables, say x and y, may be related in a number of ways. In a *function* or *functional relationship*, one variable, usually x, is called the *independent variable*. The other, usually y, is the *dependent variable*. For every choice of x, precisely one y is defined. As x varies, y varies in an exactly predictable fashion.

In this situation, we say that "y is a function of x," meaning that the value of y is determined by the value of x. The function itself is denoted by f (or g, or h, . . .). The collection of possible values of the independent variable is called the *domain* of f. The y-value associated with a given x-value is denoted by $f(x)$ (read f of x). The collection of possible values of the dependent variable is called the range of f.

If an expression $f(x)$ defines a function, then the y corresponding to any specific x can be found by simply substituting that value for x in the expression $y = f(x)$.

Example 1: Suppose that the relation between x and y is given by $y = f(x)$, where $f(x) = x^2 + 3x - 4$. Find $f(1)$ and $f(2 + a)$.

Solution: To find the value of the function for any number, we substitute that number for x in the expression for $f(x)$. In essence, we think of this function as $f(\ ) = (\ )^2 + 3(\ ) - 4$, and then we fill in the blanks. So to find $f(1)$, we substitute 1 for x wherever it appears, thus:

$$f(1) = (1)^2 + 3(1) - 4 = 1 + 3 - 4 = 0$$

So $f(1) = 0$. In the same manner:

$$f(2 + a) = (2 + a)^2 + 3(2 + a) - 4$$

$$= 4 + 4a + a^2 + 6 + 3a - 4$$

$$= a^2 + 7a + 6$$

Example 2:

 Letting $f(x) = x^2$ and $g(x) = x + 3$, find each of the following:

A. $g(2)f(5)$

B. $f(g(1))$

C. $g(f(x))$

Solutions:

A. $g(2) = 2 + 3 = 5$; $f(5) = 5^2 = 25$; $g(2)f(5) = 5(25) = 125$.

B. To find $f(g(1))$, first find $g(1) = 1 + 3 = 4$. Now $f(g(1)) = f(4) = 4^2 = 16$.

C. To find $g(f(x))$, substitute $f(x)$ every place you see an x in $g(x) = x + 3$. In other words, $g(f(x)) = f(x) + 3$. But, since $f(x) = x^2$, $g(f(x)) = x^2 + 3$.

Two functions f and g for which $f(g(x)) = g(f(x)) = x$ are called inverse functions. When this occurs, $g(x)$ is called f-inverse and denoted $f(-1(x))$. The functions are called inverses because they "undo" one another. That is, for any value x, calculating $f(x)$ and substituting the result into $f(-1)$ brings you right back to the value x, where you started.

Example 3:

 Which of the following functions is $f^{-1}(x)$ for $f(x) = 3x + 2$?

A. $-3x + 2$

B. $\dfrac{x - 2}{3}$

C. $\dfrac{1}{3x + 2}$

D. $\dfrac{1}{3x} + 2$

E. $\dfrac{1}{3}x + \dfrac{1}{2}$

Solution: The correct answer is B. If you try calling each of these expressions in turn $g(x)$ and calculate $f(g(x)) = 3[g(x)] + 2$, you will see that only for B will the result be $f(g(x)) = x$. Thus, $f(g(x)) = x \left(\frac{x-2}{3}\right) + 2 = x - 2 + 2 = x$.

You may want to check for yourself that $g(f(x)) = x$.

EXPONENTIALS AND LOGARITHMS

Among the most important examples of inverse functions are the *exponential and logarithmic functions*. For any constant $b > 0$ and 1, the exponential functions $f(x) = b^x$ and $g(x) = \log_b x$ are inverse functions. That is, $\log_b b^x = x$ and $b^{\log_b x} = x$. That is, the logarithm is the exponent. b is called the base of the logarithm.

The two most frequently encountered bases are 10, the base for *common logarithms*, and e, the base for *natural logarithms*. You should know that the symbol $\log x$ with no base shown is assumed to be the logarithm to the base 10. The symbol $\ln x$ is used as shorthand for the natural logarithm. That is, $\ln x = \log_e x$. Thus, $\log 10^x = x$; $10^{\log x} = x$; $\ln e^x = x$; and $e^{\ln x} = x$.

The main properties of the exponential functional are determined by the laws of exponents. It is important to recognize that the relationships $b^k = N$ and $\log_b N = K$ are equivalent. That is, any relationship between the variables written in logarithmic form may be rewritten in exponential form, and vice versa.

Example 1: If $\log_x 125 = 3$, what is x?

Solution: This statement is equivalent to $x^3 = 125$, for which we can see by inspection that $x = 5$.

There are certain properties of the logarithm that you should know that also follow from the laws of exponents.

- $\log_b M + \log_b N = \log_b MN$

- $\log_b M - \log_b N = \log_b \dfrac{M}{N}$

- $\log_b \dfrac{1}{M} = -\log_b M$

- $k\log_b M = \log_b M^k$

You should also know that $\log_b 1 = 0$, and that the $\log_b M$ is only defined for positive values of M; that is, the log is undefined for zero or negative values.

Example 2:

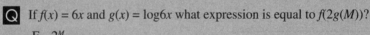

Ⓠ If $f(x) = 6x$ and $g(x) = \log 6x$ what expression is equal to $f(2g(M))$?

    F. 2^M

    G. 6^M

    H. M^6

    J. M^2

    K. 6^{2M}

Solution: The correct answer is J. $2g(M) = 2\log_6 M + \log_6 M^2$. Hence, $f(2g(x)) = M^2$

GEOMETRY

ANGLES, COMPLEMENTS, AND SUPPLEMENTS

An *angle* is formed when two *rays* originate from the same point. Angles are usually measured in *degrees* or *radians*. As on the ACT Assessment exam, we shall use only degree measure.

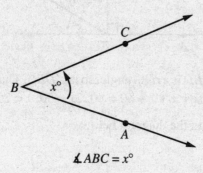

$\angle ABC = x°$

A *straight angle* has a measure of 180°. Any two angles that sum to a straight angle are called *supplementary*. Thus, two angles that measure 80° and 100° are supplementary.

Two equal supplementary angles are 90° each, and a 90° angle is called a *right angle*. Two angles that sum to a right angle are called *complementary*. Thus, 25° is the complement of 65°.

Angles less than 90° are called *acute*, and angles between 90° and 180° are called *obtuse*. The sum of all the angles around a given point must total to 360°.

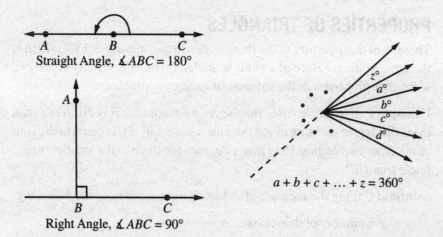

Straight Angle, $\angle ABC = 180°$

Right Angle, $\angle ABC = 90°$

$a + b + c + \ldots + z = 360°$

Example 1: Find x in the diagram below.

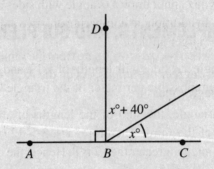

Solution: Since $\angle ABD$ is a right angle, so is $\angle DBC$. Thus, $x + (x + 40) = 90$. Removing parentheses: $x + x + 40 = 90$; $2x = 50$; $x = 25$.

Example 2: Find x in the diagram below.

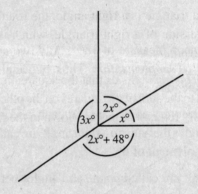

Solution: $8x + 48 = 360$; $8x = 312$; $x = 39$.

PROPERTIES OF TRIANGLES

The sum of the measures of the three angles in any triangle is $180°$, which is the same as the measure of a straight angle. This fact is usually combined with other properties in the solution of geometric problems.

Example 1: In triangle ABC, the degree measure of $\angle B$ is $30°$ more than twice the degree measure of $\angle A$, and the measure of $\angle C$ is equal to the sum of the other two angles. How many degrees are there in the smallest angle of the triangle?

Solution: Calling the measure of $\angle A$ in degrees x, we have the following:

$x = $ number of degrees in $\angle A$

$2x + 30 = $ number of degrees in $\angle B$

$x + (2x + 30) = 3x + 30 = $ number of degrees in $\angle C$

Summing, we have $x + 2x + 30 + 3x + 30 = 180$. Combining like terms: $6x + 60 = 180$; $6x = 120$; $x = 20$.

Clearly, $2x + 30$ and $3x + 30$ are larger than x, so the smallest angle is $20°$.

In a triangle, the sum of the lengths of any two sides must exceed the length of the third. Thus, you cannot draw a triangle with sides of lengths 3, 6, 10, because $3 + 6 < 10$. In addition, in comparing any two sides, the longer side will be opposite the larger angle.

Example 2: A triangle has sides with lengths of 5, 12, and x. If x is an integer, what is the minimum possible perimeter of the triangle?

Solution: In any triangle, the sum of the lengths of any two sides must exceed the length of the third. Therefore, $x + 5 > 12$, which means that $x > 7$. The smallest integer greater than 7 is 8. Hence, the minimum possible perimeter is $5 + 12 + 8 = 25$.

Can you see why the maximum perimeter of this triangle is 33?

THE PYTHAGOREAN THEOREM

When one angle in a triangle is a right angle, the triangle is called a *right triangle*. The longest side of a right triangle, which is opposite the right angle, is called the *hypotenuse*.

The *Pythagorean Theorem* tells us that the square on the hypotenuse of a right triangle is equal to the sum of the squares on the other two sides (or *legs*). In symbols, we usually remember this as shown in the figure below.

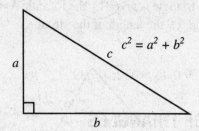

In practice, you should remember some well-known *Pythagorean triples*, that is, sets of whole numbers such as 3-4-5 for which $a^2 + b^2 = c^2$. Right triangles whose sides correspond to the numbers that make up a Pythagorean triple appear commonly on the ACT Assessment. Other less easily recognized Pythagorean triples are 5-12-13, 8-15-17, and 7-24-25. In addition, look for multiples of the triples, such as 6-8-10 or 15-20-25.

There are other important cases that yield non-integer solutions for the lengths of the sides of a right triangle. For example, the hypotenuse of a triangle with one leg of length 1 and the other of length 2 can be found by writing $c^2 = 1^2 + 2^2$. Thus, $c^2 = 5$ and $c = \sqrt{5}$.

Example 1: Find x in the diagram below.

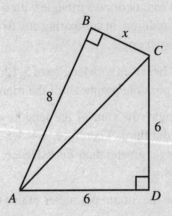

Solution: Using the Pythagorean Theorem in triangle ACD, the theorem tells us that $6^2 + 6^2 = c^2$. Hence, $c^2 = 72$. In triangle ABC, letting x represent the length of BC, $72 = c^2 = x^2 + 8^2$. That is, $x^2 = 72 - 64 = 8$. Thus, $x = \sqrt{8} = 2\sqrt{2}$.

THE AREA OF A TRIANGLE

In any triangle, you can construct a line from one *vertex* (point) perpendicular to the opposite side. (Sometimes that side may have to be extended outside the triangle, as shown in the second case below.) This line is called the *altitude* or *height*. The area of a triangle is given by the formula $A = \frac{1}{2}bh$, where $b =$ the length of the base and $h =$ the length of the altitude.

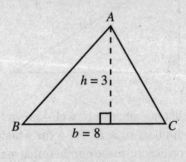

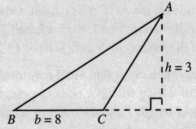

Both triangles shown in the diagram above have the same area: $A = \frac{1}{2}(8)(3) = 12$.

Example 1: In triangle ABC, $AB = 6$, $BC = 8$, and $AB = 10$. Find the altitude from vertex B to side AC.

Solution: Since the sides are 6-8-10, the triangle is a disguised 3-4-5 right triangle with AC being the hypotenuse. Drawing the triangle as described produces the diagram below.

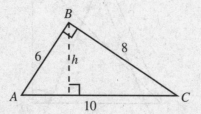

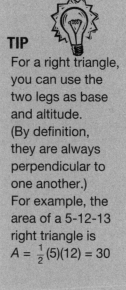

TIP

For a right triangle, you can use the two legs as base and altitude. (By definition, they are always perpendicular to one another.) For example, the area of a 5-12-13 right triangle is $A = \frac{1}{2}(5)(12) = 30$

By using the two legs as base and height, the area of the triangle must be $A = \frac{1}{2}(6)(8) = 24$. By using the hypotenuse and the unknown altitude, the area must be $A = \frac{1}{2}(10)(h) = 5h$. Therefore, $5h = 24$, and $h = 4.8$.

ISOSCELES AND EQUILATERAL TRIANGLES

A triangle with two sides of equal length is called an *isosceles triangle*. If all three sides are equal, it is called an *equilateral triangle*. The angles opposite the equal sides in an isosceles triangle (as shown in the diagram below) are equal in measure; thus, if two angles in a triangle are equal, the triangle is isosceles. If all three angles are equal, the triangle is equilateral. In particular, this tells us that for an equilateral triangle each angle has a degree measure of 60°.

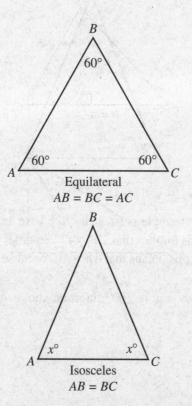

Equilateral
$AB = BC = AC$

Isosceles
$AB = BC$

Here is a good example of how this fact can be used in a problem.

Example 1: If in triangle ABC, as shown in the figure below, $AC = BC$ and $x \leq 50$, what is the smallest possible value of y?

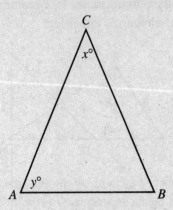

Solution: Since sides AC and BC are of equal length, the two base angles, $\angle A$ and $\angle B$, must be equal. As always, the three angles must total $180°$. Hence, $x + 2y = 180$, which means that $y = \frac{180-x}{2} = 90 - \frac{1}{2}x$.

Now, the smallest possible value for y is achieved when x is as large as possible; that is, when $x = 50$, for which $y = 65$.

Example 2: In the triangle shown below, $AB = BC$. Which is longer, AC or AB?

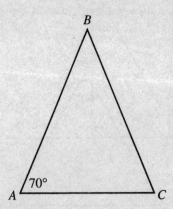

Note: Diagram not drawn to scale

Solution: Since the triangle is isosceles, the base angles are equal. Thus, $\angle A = \angle C = 70°$. This implies that $\angle B = 40°$ (in order to reach the full $180°$ in the triangle). But that means that $AB > AC$, because it is the side opposite the larger angle.

SPECIAL RIGHT TRIANGLES

These are two special right triangles whose properties you should be familiar with. The first is the *isosceles right triangle*, also referred to as the *45°-45°-90° triangle*. By definition, its legs are of equal length, and its hypotenuse is $\sqrt{2}$ times as long as either leg.

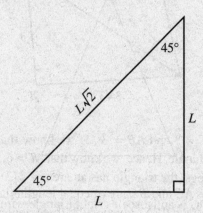

The other important right triangle is the *30°-60°-90° triangle*. You can see by dropping an altitude that this is half of an equilateral triangle. Hence, the shorter leg is half the hypotenuse, and the longer leg (the one opposite the 60° angle) is $\sqrt{3}$ times the shorter leg.

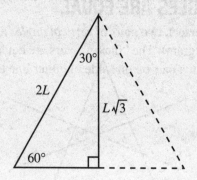

Example 1: Find the area of the region shown in the diagram below.

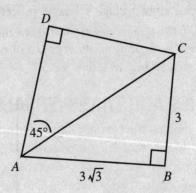

Solution: Since $BC = 3$ and $AB = 3\sqrt{3}$, we know that triangle ABC is a $30°$-$60°$-$90°$ right triangle. Hence, we know that $AC = 6$, and taking one-half the product of the legs, the triangle has an area of $\frac{1}{2}(3)(3\sqrt{3}) = \frac{9}{2}\sqrt{3}$.

Since triangle ADC is an isosceles right triangle with a hypotenuse of 6, each leg must be $\frac{6}{\sqrt{2}}$. Again, taking one-half the product of the legs, the triangle has an area of $\frac{1}{2}(\frac{6}{\sqrt{2}}) = \frac{18}{2} = 9$.

Adding the two areas, we have $9 + \frac{9}{2}\sqrt{3}$.

VERTICAL ANGLES ARE EQUAL

When two lines intersect, two pairs of *vertical angles* are formed (as shown in the following diagram). The "facing" pairs are equal and, of course, the two angles that form a pair on one side of either line add up to $180°$.

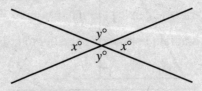

Example 1: In the diagram below, which is larger, $x + y$ or $w + z$?

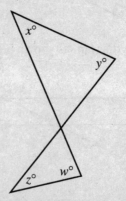

Solution: We know that the sum of the angles in any triangle is 180°. Letting the measure of $\angle ABC$ be m, we have, in the upper triangle, $x + y = 180 - m$.

Similarly looking at the larger triangle, we know that $w + z = 180 - n$.

Therefore, $x + y = w + z$. The quantities named are equal.

PARALLEL LINES AND TRANSVERSALS

If you start with two lines parallel to one another and draw a line that crosses them, the crossing line is called a *transversal*. The intersection of the transversal with the parallel lines creates several sets of related angles. In particular, the *corresponding angles* (labeled C in the diagram below) and the *alternate interior angles* (labeled A in the diagram below) are always equal.

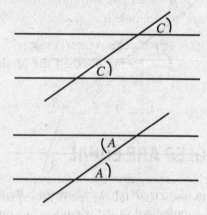

Combining these properties with your knowledge about vertical angles and the angles in a triangle can lead to interesting examples.

Example 1: In the diagram below, l_1 is parallel to l_2. Find x.

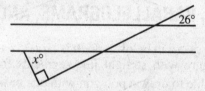

Solution: We'll label the diagram as shown below.

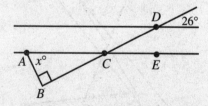

We see that $\angle DCE = 26°$, which makes $\angle ACB = 26°$. Since triangle ABC is a right triangle, x is the complement of 26°, or 64°.

Example 2: In the diagram below, l_1 is parallel to l_2. Find x.

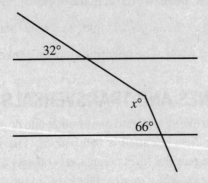

Solution: Extend the line AB as shown in the diagram below.

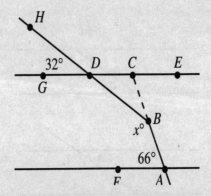

Look at the angles in triangle BCD. As alternate interior angles, $\angle BCE = \angle BAF = 66°$, so its supplement in the triangle, $\angle C$, must equal 114°. As vertical angles, $\angle CDB = \angle HDG = 32°$. Therefore, in the triangle, $\angle D = 32°$. Since the three angles in the triangle must sum to 180°, $\angle B = 34°$. x is the supplement to 34°—that is, 140°.

RECTANGLES, PARALLELOGRAMS, AND OTHER POLYGONS

Any geometric figure with straight line segments for sides is called a *polygon*. It is possible to draw a polygon with one or more interior angles greater than 180°, as illustrated in the figure below.

However, if all the interior angles in the polygon are less than 180°, we have a *convex polygon*. The sum of the angle measurements in any convex polygon is $180(n-2)$, where n is the number of vertices. Thus, for a triangle, $n=3$, and the sum is 180. For a *quadrilateral* (a four-sided figure), $n=4$, and the sum is 360. For a *pentagon* (a five-sided figure), $n=5$, and the angle sum is 540, and so on.

To find the *perimeter* of a polygon (the distance around the figure), simply add together the lengths of all the sides. Of course, it may require some thinking to determine each length.

To find its area, connect the vertices by line segments to divide the polygon into triangles; then sum the areas of these triangles.

Example 1: Find the area of figure *ABCDE* shown below.

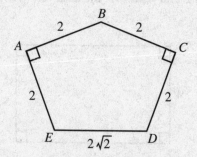

Solution: Drawing the line segments *BE* and *BD* divides the region into three triangles as shown. Triangles *ABE* and *BCD* are both 45°-45°-90° right triangles, making $BE = BD = 2\sqrt{2}$.

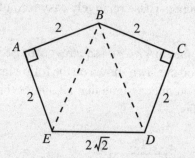

This makes the central triangle an equilateral triangle. The area of each of the two outer triangles is $\frac{1}{2}(2)(2) = 2$, so the two together have an area of 4. The center triangle has a base whose length is $2\sqrt{2}$. If you draw the altitude, you get a 30°-60°-90° right triangle with a shorter leg whose length is $\sqrt{2}$. This makes the height $\sqrt{3}$ times that, or $\sqrt{6}$. This gives an area of $\frac{1}{2}(2\sqrt{2})(\sqrt{6}) = \sqrt{12} = 2\sqrt{3}$. Hence, the total area of the polygon is $4 + 2\sqrt{3}$.

A *parallelogram* is a quadrilateral in which the pairs of opposite sides are parallel. The opposite angles in a parallelogram are equal, and the opposite sides are of equal length (see the figure below).

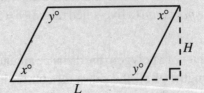

The area of a parallelogram is determined by its length times its height; that is, $A = LH$, as labeled in the diagram.

If the angles in the parallelogram are right angles, we have a *rectangle*. For a rectangle of length L and width W, the area is $A = LW$, and the perimeter is $P = 2L + 2W$.

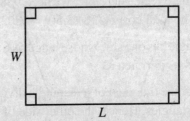

For example, the area of a rectangular garden that is 20 yards long and 10 yards deep is $(20)(10) = 200$ square yards. However, to put a fence around the same garden (that is, around its perimeter) requires $2(20) + 2(10) = 60$ running yards of fencing. These relatively easy formulas can lead to some tricky questions.

Example 2: If sod comes in 4×4 foot squares costing $3.50 per square, how much will it cost to sod the lawn shown on the following page (all distances indicated in feet)? You may assume that all angles that appear to be right angles are right angles.

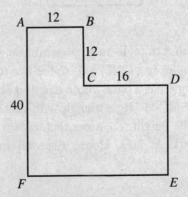

Solution: Completing the rectangle as shown in the figure below, we see that the large rectangle *AGEF* is $40 \times 28 = 1{,}120$ square feet.

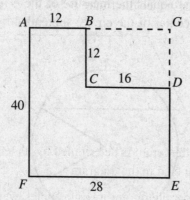

The smaller rectangle *BGDC* is $12 \times 16 = 192$ square feet. Hence, the area that must be sodded is $1{,}120 - 192 = 928$ square feet. Now, each 4×4 foot piece of sod is 16 square feet. Therefore, we need $928 \div 16 = 58$ squares of sod at \$3.50 each. The total cost is $(58)(3.50) = \$203$.

Example 3: A rectangle has one side whose length is 6 and a diagonal whose length is 10. What is its perimeter?

Solution: Notice that the diagonal of a rectangle divides the rectangle into two identical right triangles. Hence, the other side of this rectangle can be found by the Pythagorean Theorem. We recognize that side 6 and diagonal 10 implies that we have a 6-8-10 right triangle, so the unknown side is 8. The perimeter is, therefore, $2(6) + 2(8) = 28$.

BASIC PROPERTIES OF CIRCLES

A line segment from the center of a circle to any point on the circle is called a *radius* (plural *radii*). All radii of the same circle are equal in length. A line segment that passes through the center of the circle and cuts completely across the circle is called a *diameter*. A diameter is, of course, twice as long as any radius. Thus, $d = 2r$.

Any line cutting across a circle is called a *chord*, and no chord can be longer than the diameter. A portion of a circle is called an *arc*. Any arc has a degree measure that equals the measure of the *central angle* (an angle whose vertex is the center of the circle) subtended by it, as shown in the figure below.

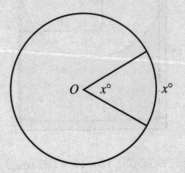

Example 1: If the arc *PS* in the diagram below has a degree measure of 62°, is the chord *PS* longer or shorter than the radius of the circle?

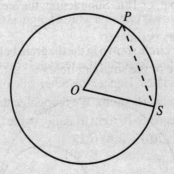

Solution: Since all radii are equal, triangle *OPS* is isosceles, and the angles at *P* and *S* must be equal. Suppose each is *x*. Now, $2x + 62 = 180$. Hence, $x = 59$. Therefore, *PS* is opposite the largest angle in the triangle and must be the longest side. That is, *PS* is longer than a radius.

THE AREA AND CIRCUMFERENCE OF A CIRCLE

The distance around a circle (analogous to the perimeter of a polygon) is its *circumference*. For any circle of radius *r*, the circumference is given by the formula $C = 2\pi r$; that is, the circumference equals twice the radius times π (a constant, designated by the Greek letter pi, whose value is approximately 3.1415 or $\frac{22}{7}$).

The area of the same circle is given by the formula $A = \pi r^2$; that is, the area equals pi times the radius squared.

Example 1: Find the area of the shaded region shown in the diagram below. (The curved side is a *semicircle*; that is, an arc equal to half a complete circle.)

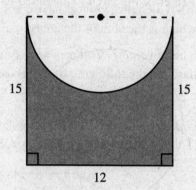

Solution: The dotted line completes the rectangle, whose area is $12 \times 15 = 180$ square units. The radius of the arc must be 6, since its diameter is 12. The area of the whole circle would be $\pi r^2 = \pi(6^2) = 36\pi$. Hence, the area of the semi-circle is half of that, or 18π. Subtracting, the area of the shaded region is $180 - 18\pi$.

Example 2: The larger circle shown in the diagram below has an area of 36π. Find the circumference of the smaller circle.

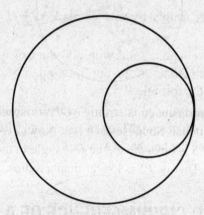

Solution: The larger circle has an area of $AL = \pi(r)^2 = 36\pi$. This means that $r^2 = 36$, and $r = 6$. The diameter of the smaller circle equals the radius of the larger one, so its radius is $\frac{1}{2}(6) = 3$. Therefore, its circumference must be $2\pi(3) = 6\pi$.

VOLUMES

A solid (three-dimensional) figure with straight line edges and flat surfaces is called a *polyhedron*. The surfaces bounding the solid are called *faces*. The edges of a polyhedron have lengths; its faces have areas; and the entire figure has a *surface area*, which is the sum of the areas of all its faces.

A solid figure also has a *volume*. Volumes are expressed in cubic units. You should be familiar with the following formulas for volumes of regular polyhedrons:

- A *rectangular solid* is a polyhedron with rectangular faces at right angles to one another. (Think of a typical cardboard box, like a shoebox.)

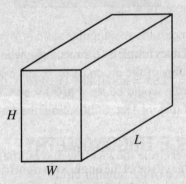

Its volume is determined by the formula $V = LWH = \text{Length} \times \text{Width} \times \text{Height}$

- A *cube* is a rectangular solid with all edges of equal length; that is $L = W = H = s$. (Think of one die from a pair of dice.) Its volume is determined by the formula $V = s^3$.
- A right circular cylinder is a solid with a circular base and a side perpendicular to the base. (Think of a soda can.) Its volume is the area of the base times the height, or $V = \pi r^2 h$.

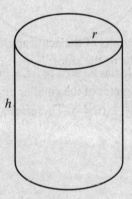

Example 1: Find the length of a rectangular solid with a height of 6 that is twice as long as it is wide, if its volume is the same as that of a cube with a total surface area of 864 square inches.

Solution: Let x = the width of the rectangular solid. Now, $2x$ = length. The volume of the rectangular solid is $V = 6(x)(2x) = 12x^2$.

Since the cube has six square faces, its total surface area is 6 times the area of one face. In symbols, $6s^2 = 864$. Dividing by 6, $s^2 = 144$, and $s = 12$. Hence, the volume of the cube is $123 = 1,728$. Since the two solids have the same volume:

$$12x^2 = 1728; x^2 = 144; x = 12$$

The length of the rectangular solid, which is twice the width, is thus 24.

Example 2: Which has the greater volume, a rectangular solid that is 6 feet long and has a square base with sides 4 feet long, or a cylinder with a length of 7 feet and a diameter of 4 feet?

Solution: The volume of the rectangular solid is $V = (4)(4)(6) = 96$ square feet. The radius of the cylinder is 2, so its volume is: $V_C = \pi(2)^2(7) = 28\pi$.

Since π = about $\frac{22}{7}$, 28π = about 88. Therefore, the rectangular solid is larger.

RIGHT TRIANGLE TRIGONOMETRY

The usual convention is to label the angles of a right triangle A, B, and C, with C the right angle. We then label the sides opposite the respective angles as a, b, and c, as shown in the figure below.

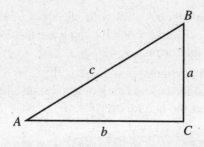

The *trigonometric functions* of the acute angles are then defined in terms of the ratios of the lengths of the sides. For angle A, we have:

$$\sin A = \frac{a}{c}$$

$$\cos A = \frac{b}{c}$$

$$\tan A = \frac{a}{b}$$

$$\cot A = \frac{b}{a}$$

$$\sec A = \frac{c}{b}$$

$$\csc A = \frac{c}{a}$$

The trigonometric functions for angle B are defined similarly. The important things to remember are:

$$\text{sine} = \frac{\text{opposite}}{\text{hypotenuse}}$$

$$\text{cosine} = \frac{\text{adjacent}}{\text{hypotenuse}}$$

$$\text{tangent} = \frac{\text{opposite}}{\text{adjacent}}$$

It is convenient to also know that for any angle x, $\tan x = \frac{\sin x}{\cos x}$.

The other trigonometric functions can be found by using the following simple identities:

$$\cot x = \frac{1}{\tan x} \qquad\qquad \csc x = \frac{1}{\sin x}$$

$$\sec x = \frac{1}{\cos x}$$

These relationships between sides and angles make possible the solution of many interesting problems.

Example 1:

Q A 60-foot-long guy wire is attached to the top of a 45-foot pole, as shown in the figure below. Using the table of values given below, which of the following is closest to the angle the wire makes with the ground?

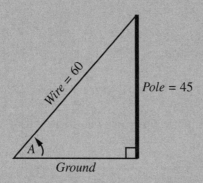

Angle	Sin	Cos	Tan
41	0.6561	0.7547	0.8693
42	0.6691	0.7431	0.9004
43	0.682	0.7314	0.9325
44	0.6947	0.7193	0.9657
45	0.7071	0.7071	1
46	0.7193	0.6947	1.0355
47	0.7314	0.682	1.0723
48	0.7431	0.6691	1.1106
49	0.7547	0.6561	1.1504
50	0.766	0.6428	1.1918

A. 49°

B. 47°

C. 45°

D. 43°

E. 41°

Solution: The correct answer is A. Using the relationship $\sin A = \frac{a}{c}$ with $a = 45$ and $c = 60$, we have $\sin A = \frac{45}{60} = \frac{3}{4} = 0.75$. Referring to the table, we see that $\sin 49° = .7547$, which is the closest among the four choices. Hence, choice A is correct.

Example 2:

 A vertical pole casts a shadow 50 feet long when the sun is at an angle of elevation of 42°, as shown in the figure below. Using the table on the preceding page, what is the height of the pole to the nearest foot?

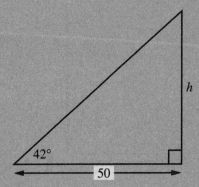

F. 55

G. 50

H. 45

J. 40

K. 35

Solution: The correct answer is H. Calling the unknown height h, we have $\tan A = \frac{h}{50}$. From the table, we see that $\tan 42° = 0.9004$; multiplying by 50, we have $h = 50(0.9004) = 45.02$, or 45 feet to the nearest foot.

COORDINATE GEOMETRY

THE MIDPOINT FORMULA

Given two points $P(x_1, y_1)$ and $Q(x_2, y_2)$, the midpoint M of the line segment PQ has the following coordinates:

$$x_M = \frac{x_1 + x_2}{2}, y_M = \frac{y_1 + y_2}{2}$$

In words: To find the coordinates of the midpoint of a line segment, simply average the coordinates of the end points. For example, the midpoint between (3,4) and (2,–2) is

$$x_M = \frac{3+2}{2} = \frac{5}{2}, y_M = \frac{4+(-2)}{2} = \frac{2}{2} = 1$$

Hence, the midpoint is $\left(\frac{5}{2}, 1\right) = (2.5, 1)$.

Example 1: If (2,6) is the midpoint of the line segment connecting (–1,3) to $P(x,y)$, which is larger, $2x$ or y?

Solution: We know that the average of x and –1 must be 2. That is, $2 = \frac{x+(-1)}{2}$, or $4 = x - 1$; $x = 5$.

Similarly, we know that the average of y and 3 must be 6. Thus, $6 = \frac{y+3}{2}$, or $12 = y + 3$; $y = 9$.

Since $2x = 10$, $2x > y$.

Example 2: If $b < 6$, is (3,b) closer to $P(0,2)$ or $Q(6,10)$?

Solution: We see that (3,6) is the midpoint of PQ. Therefore, in the x-direction, (3,b) will be equidistant from both P and Q. However, if $b < 6$, then b must be closer to 2 than to 10. Therefore, (3,b) is closer to (0,2) than to (6,10).

THE DISTANCE FORMULA AND EQUATIONS FOR CIRCLES

Given two points $P(x_1,y_1)$ and $Q(x_2,y_2)$, the distance from P to Q is given by the formula:

$$d = \sqrt{(x_1 - x_2)^2 + (y_1 - y_2)^2}$$

In words, the distance is the square root of the sum of the change in x squared plus the change in y squared. This can be symbolized as follows:

$$d = \sqrt{(\Delta x)^2 + (\Delta y)^2}$$

For example, the distance from (6,2) to (3,–1) is $d = \sqrt{(6-3)^2 + (3-(-1))^2}$

Thus:

$$d = \sqrt{3^2 + 4^2} = \sqrt{9 + 16} = \sqrt{25} = 5$$

Example 1: The point (4,t) is equidistant from points (1,1) and (5,3). What is the value of t?

Solution: Since the distances from the two given points are the same, we use the distance formula twice and equate the results, thus:

$$\sqrt{(4-1)^2 + (t-1)^2} = \sqrt{(5-4)^2 + (3-t)^2}$$

$$\sqrt{9 + (t^2 - 2t + 1)} = \sqrt{1 + (9 - 6t + t^2)}$$

$$\sqrt{10 - 2t + t^2} = \sqrt{10 - 6t + t^2}$$

Squaring both sides:

$$10 - 2t + t^2 = 10 - 6t + t^2$$

Subtracting $t^2 + 10$ from both sides leaves:

$$-2t = -6t$$

$$4t = 0; t = 0$$

Since all points on a circle are equidistant from its center, you can use the distance formula to prove that the equation for a circle whose radius is r and whose center is at the origin is $x^2 + y^2 = r^2$.

Similarly, the equation for a circle whose radius is r and whose center is at (h,k) is $(x - h)^2 + (y - k)^2 = r^2$.

Example 2: The point $(t,-1)$ lies on a circle whose radius is 5 and whose center is at $(4,2)$. What are the possible values of t?

Solution: Since every point on the circle must be 5 units from the center, we know that $(t,-1)$ must be 5 units from $(4,2)$. Using the equation for the circle with $h = 4$ and $k = 2$, and $r = 5$, we have:

$$(x - 4)^2 + (y - 2)^2 = 25$$

Letting $x = t$ and $y = -1$:

$$(t - 4)^2 + (-1 - 2)^2 = 25$$

Expanding, we have:

$$t^2 - 8t + 16 + 9 = 25$$

We subtract 25 from both sides to yield:

$$t^2 - 8t = 0$$

This factors as $t(t - 8) = 0$, with two possible solutions, $t = 0$ or $t = 8$.

SLOPE OF A LINE

Given two points $P(x_1, y_1)$ and $Q(x_2, y_2)$, the slope of the line passing through P and Q is given by the formula:

$$M = \frac{y_1 - y_2}{x_1 - x_2}$$

In words, this says that the slope is the change in y divided by the change in x, or $M = \frac{\Delta y}{\Delta x}$.

For example, the slope of the line passing through $(6,4)$ to $(3,-1)$ is $\frac{4-(-1)}{6-3} = \frac{5}{3}$.

(Notice that it doesn't matter which point you consider the first point and which the second, as long as you are consistent in the top and bottom of the fraction. Try it!)

Example 1: The points $(-1,-1)$, $(3,11)$, and $(1,t)$ lie on the same line. What is the value of t?

Solution: Since the slope of a line is the same for any two points on the line, and since $M = \frac{y_1 - y_2}{x_1 - x_2}$ using $(-1,-1)$ and $(3,11)$, we must have:

$$M = \frac{11 - (-1)}{3 - (-1)} = \frac{12}{4} = 3.$$

Now, using the pair $(-1,-1)$ and $(1,t)$, $3 = \frac{t-(-1)}{1-(-1)} = \frac{t+1}{2}$.

Multiplying by 2, $6 = t + 1$; $t = 5$.

EQUATIONS OF LINES

The equation that defines a straight line is usually remembered as $y = mx + b$, where m is the slope and b is the y-intercept. When $m = 0$, we have the equation $y = b$, which has as its graph a horizontal straight line crossing the y-axis at $(0,b)$. The exceptional case is the vertical line, which is defined by the equation $x = a$, where a is the common x-value of all the points on the line. (Of course, $x = 0$ is the y-axis, and, naturally, $y = 0$ is the x-axis.)

Parallel lines have the same slope, and perpendicular lines (other than the vertical and horizontal case) have slopes that are negative reciprocals.

Example 1: Find the equation of a straight line parallel to the line with equation $y = 2x - 5$ that passes through the point $(-1,4)$.

Solution: By inspection, the given line has slope 2. Any line parallel to it must also have slope 2, and, therefore, must have equation $y = 2x + b$. To determine b, we use the fact that any point that lies on the line must satisfy the equation. Therefore, substituting the coordinates of the point $(-1,4)$ into the equation must yield a correct equation. Thus:

$$4 = 2(-1) + b;\ 4 = -2 + b;\ b = 6$$

The equation is $y = 2x + 6$.

Example 2: Find the equation of a straight line perpendicular to the line with equation $y = \frac{2}{3}x - 4$ that has y-intercept 9.

Solution: The given line has slope $\frac{2}{3}$. Any line perpendicular to it must have as its slope the negative reciprocal of $\frac{2}{3}$, that is, $-\frac{3}{2}$. Since the line we want has y-intercept 9, its equation must be $y = -\frac{3}{2}x + 9$. It is possible to multiply this equation by 2 to get $2y = -3x + 18$, which could also be written $3x + 2y = 18$.

Example 3: Find the equation of the line that is the perpendicular bisector of the line segment connecting points $P(-1,1)$ and $Q(3,5)$.

Solution: PQ has a slope of $M = \frac{5-(-1)}{3-(-1)} = \frac{4}{4} = 1$.

Hence, the perpendicular bisector must have as its slope the negative reciprocal of 1, which is -1. Thus, its equation must be $y = -x + b$. Since the line bisects the segment, it must pass through the midpoint of PQ, which we find by averaging the coordinates of the endpoints to get $(1,2)$. Substituting: $2 = -1 + b$; $b = 3$, and the equation is $y = -x + 3$.

SYSTEMS OF EQUATIONS WITH NON-UNIQUE SOLUTIONS

As we mentioned above, any equation of the form $Ax + By = C$ is the equation of a straight line because (unless $B = 0$), it can be rewritten in the form $y = mx + b$ by using a little algebra. Hence, when you try to solve two linear equations with two unknowns simultaneously, you could think of the process as trying to find the coordinates of the point of intersection of two lines.

Of course, a problem arises if the two lines have the same slope. In such a situation, there are two possibilities. The first is that the lines are parallel and have no point of intersection. In that case, the equations are called *inconsistent* (or *incompatible*) and there is *no* solution.

The other possibility is that the two equations are really two different forms of the same equation. In that case, you have only one line and there is an infinite number of solutions; any point (x,y) that lies on the line is at the "intersection" of the two (identical) lines.

Example 1: A certain store sells blouses and skirts at a fixed price regardless of style or size. Marla bought 4 blouses and 6 skirts and was charged $380 before taxes. Arlene went to the same store; she bought 2 blouses and 3 skirts and was charged $195 before taxes. What was the price of a blouse?

Solution: Letting b = the price of a blouse and s = the price of a skirt, we have for Marla $4b + 6s = 380$, and for Arlene $2b + 3s = 195$.

If we multiply the second equation by –2 and add it to the first, we have:

$$4b + 6s = 380$$
$$\underline{-4b - 6s = -390}$$
$$0 = -10$$

But this is impossible! This means that the two equations represent parallel lines, and there is no solution. Someone must have made a mistake in calculating either Marla's or Arlene's bill, so there is no correct way to answer the question as posed.

Example 2: Juan has a package containing some 2¢ stamps and some 5¢ stamps with a total value of 62¢. If Juan had 3 more than twice as many 2¢ stamps as he now has, and twice as many 5¢ stamps, the assortment would be worth $1.30. What is the greatest number of 5¢ stamps Juan may have?

Solution: Let x be the number of 2's and y be the number of 5's. Expressing the given information in cents, we have $2x + 5y = 62$ and $2(2x + 3) + 5(2y) = 130$.

Expanding the second equation:

$$4x + 6 + 10y = 130$$

$$4x + 10y = 124$$

If we attempt to solve by elimination, we can multiply the first equation by -2 and add it to the second equation:

$$-4x - 10y = -124$$

$$\underline{4x + 10y = 124}$$

$$0 = 0$$

It is certainly true that $0 = 0$, but it is not much help! Actually, we see that the second equation is simply double the first. So really we have two equations—two definitions of the same line—yielding an infinite number of solutions.

However, the question posed can be answered. Since the nature of the given information implies that both x and y must be positive integers (there is no way to have a *negative* number of stamps), the greatest possible value of y is when $x = 1$, for which $y = 12$.

PARABOLAS AND QUADRATIC EQUATIONS

The graph of the quadratic function $y = ax^2 + bx + c$ is a *parabola*. Visually, the graph of a parabola will "open up" if $a > 0$, and will "open down" if $a < 0$. In either case, the vertex or turning point of the parabola will be found at $x = \frac{-b}{2a}$, and the curve will be symmetrical with respect to the line $x = \frac{0b}{2a}$.

Naturally, there is a strong relationship between the graph and the solution to the equation $ax^2 + bx + c = 0$, which must be solved to find the x-intercepts of the graph.

If the equation has two real distinct roots, then the curve crosses the x-axis at two points. If there are two identical roots, then that value will be the x-coordinate of the vertex, and the curve will be tangent to the axis at that point. If the roots are both complex, then the curve will never cross the x-axis.

Example 1: Find the coordinates of the vertex of the parabola $y = x^2 - 4x + 3$.

Solution: The x-coordinate of the vertex is $x = -\frac{b}{2a} = -\frac{-4}{2(1)} = 2$.

Substituting, the y-coordinate is $y = (2)^2 - 4(2) + 3 = -1$. Hence, the vertex is $(2, -1)$.

Just for the sake of completeness, you should see that the curve opens up (because $a = 1$) and that it has y-intercept $(0,3)$ and x-intercepts $(1,0)$ and $(3,0)$. The graph is shown below.

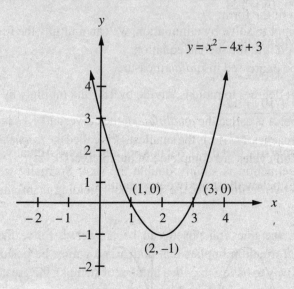

Example 2: Find the x-intercepts and coordinates of the vertex for the parabola $y = -2x^2 - 4x + 6$.

Solution: Finding the x-intercepts means finding the values of x for which $y = 0$; that is, the roots of the equation $-2x^2 - 4x + 6 = 0$.

Dividing by -2, we have $x^2 + 2x - 3 = 0$, which factors as $(x - 1)(x + 3) = 0$. Therefore, $x = 1$ and $x = -3$. The x-intercepts are $(0,1)$ and $(0,-3)$. The x-coordinate of the vertex is $x = -\frac{b}{2a} = -\frac{-4}{2(-2)} = -1$.

By substitution, the y-value is 8. Hence, the coordinates are $(-1,8)$. It is not an accident that the x-coordinate of the vertex falls halfway between the roots. That is a result of the symmetry of the curve. Again, for the sake of completeness, the graph is shown below. Notice that it opens down because $a = -2$.

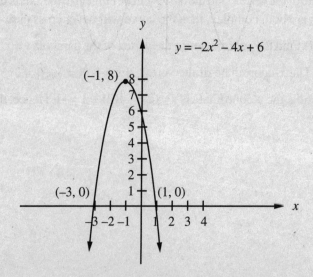

TRIGONOMETRIC GRAPHS

The trigonometric functions all have graphs. In particular, you should be comfortable with the sine and cosine curves. Remember that when you look at a function of the form:

$$y = A\sin kx \text{ or } y = A\cos kx$$

x should be expressed in *radian* measure.

To convert degrees to radians, divide by 180 and multiply by π.

The number A is called the *amplitude* of the curve, and $|A|$ is maximum value that y reaches. ($-|A|$ is the smallest.) k is called the *frequency* and tells how many full cycles are completed in the interval $[0, 2\pi]$.

The graphs below illustrate two possibilities.

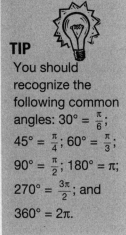

TIP
You should recognize the following common angles: $30° = \frac{\pi}{6}$; $45° = \frac{\pi}{4}$; $60° = \frac{\pi}{3}$; $90° = \frac{\pi}{2}$; $180° = \pi$; $270° = \frac{3\pi}{2}$; and $360° = 2\pi$.

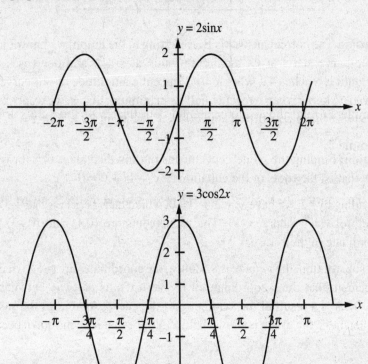

Example 1:

 What is the smallest possible positive value of x for which $4\cos 2x = 2$?

   A. $\dfrac{\pi}{12}$

   B. $\dfrac{\pi}{6}$

   C. $\dfrac{\pi}{4}$

   D. $\dfrac{\pi}{3}$

   E. $\dfrac{\pi}{2}$

Solution: The correct answer is B. Referring to the graph, we know that the cosine curve starts at its maximum value at $x = 0$ and decreases there after until it reaches -1, when $x = \pi$. Since the amplitude of our curve is 4, we want to know when it reaches half its maximum; that is, we want to solve $\cos 2x = \frac{1}{2}$. Since $\cos 60° = \frac{1}{2}$ and $60° = \frac{\pi}{3}$, we want $2x = \frac{\pi}{3}$ or $x = \frac{\pi}{6}$.

Example 2:

 For which value of b will the graph of $y = \sin 4x$ complete 3 full cycles in the interval $[0,b]$?

   F. $\dfrac{\pi}{4}$

   G. $\dfrac{\pi}{2}$

   H. $\dfrac{3\pi}{4}$

   J. π

   K. $\dfrac{3\pi}{2}$

Solution: The correct answer is K. The function has a frequency of 4. Therefore, it will complete four full cycles in the interval $[0, 2\pi]$. Hence, it will complete three full cycles in $\frac{3}{4}$ of that time, and $\frac{3}{4}(2\pi) = \frac{3\pi}{2}$.

OTHER ACT ASSESSMENT MATH TOPICS

THE ADDITION PRINCIPLE FOR COUNTING

If a set A has m elements, and a set B has n elements, and the two sets have no elements in common, then the total number of elements in the two sets combined is $m + n$. But if there are k elements common to the two sets, then the total in the combined set is $m + n - k$. In other words, when summing the two sets, you must take into account the double counting of elements common to both groups.

This kind of situation is usually handled most easily by displaying the given information in a Venn Diagram, as shown in the examples that follow.

Example 1: Helena applied to 12 colleges for admission. Sergei applied to 10. Between them they applied to 16 different colleges. How many colleges received applications from both students?

Solution: Let H be the set of colleges to which Helena applied, and let S be those to which Sergei applied. Letting x be the number that are common to both sets, the diagram shown below displays the data.

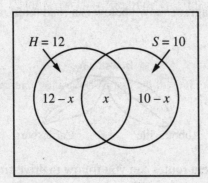

The central region is that common to both sets, and we can see that the total is $(12 - x) + x + (10 - x) = 16$. Removing parentheses and combining like terms, we have $22 - x = 16$; $x = 6$.

Example 2: A survey of voters shows that 43% listen to radio news reports, 45% listen to TV news reports, and 36% read a daily newspaper. What is the maximum possible percent that do all three?

Solution: If the three sets were totally disjointed, that is, had no overlap, the sum of the percentages would be 100%. The extent of various kinds of overlap will show up as an excess over 100%. Everyone in two of the three categories will be counted twice, and everyone in all three categories will be counted three times.

If we total 43 + 45 + 36, we find that we have accounted for 124% of the voters, a 24% overcount. Therefore, the number common to all three cannot be greater than one-third of that, or 8%. This maximum of 8% is reached only if no one falls into two out of three categories, so that the entire overcount is the result of people in all three categories.

THE MULTIPLICATION PRINCIPLE FOR COUNTING

Suppose a process can be broken down into two steps. If the first step can be performed in m ways, and if, for each of those ways, the second step can be performed in n ways, then the total number of ways of performing the operation is $T = mn$. This is known as the *multiplication principle for counting*.

For example, suppose that a jar contains five blocks of different colors. We pick a block, record the color, and then pick a second block without replacing the first. The number of possible color combinations is $(5)(4) = 20$, since there are five possible colors to be drawn from in the first step and four possible colors in the second step. This process extends to more than two steps in the natural way.

Example 1: The diagram shown below is a road map from Abbottsville to Cartersburg.

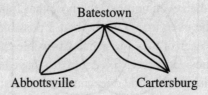

How many different routes can you follow to drive from Abbottsville to Cartersburg if you go through Batestown only once?

Solution: You have 3 choices for a road from Abbottsville to Batestown and 4 roads from Batestown to Cartersburg. Hence, by the multiplication principle, the total number of routes is $3 \times 4 = 12$.

Example 2: How many different 3-digit license plate numbers can you form if the first digit cannot be 0?

Solution: By the natural extension of the multiplication principle to a three-step process, we see that you have 9 choices for the first digit (1,2,3 . . . 9), 10 choices for the second digit (0,1,2 . . . 9), and the same 10 choices for the third digit. Thus, the total is $9 \times 10 \times 10 = 900$.

As a natural extension of the multiplication principle, it is not hard to show that the number of distinct arrangements of n distinguishable objects in a row is n *factorial* calculated as follows:

$$n! = n(n-1)(n-2) \ldots (2)(1)$$

For example, there are $4! = 4 \times 3 \times 2 \times 1 = 24$ ways of arranging the four symbols ♣, ♦, ♥, and ♠ in a straight line.

Example 1: If the five starting members of a basketball team are lined up randomly for a photograph, what is the chance that they will be in order of height from shortest to tallest, left to right?

Solution: There are 5 distinguishable people, who can be arranged in $5! = 5 \times 4 \times 3 \times 2 \times 1 = 120$ ways. In only one of these ways will they be in the correct order. Therefore, the chance is $\frac{1}{120}$.

PROBABILITY

To find the probability of an event, divide the number of outcomes favorable to the event by the total number of possible outcomes. For example, if a bag contains 12 blue marbles and 9 red marbles, the probability that a marble selected at random is blue is the number of blue marbles divided by the total number of marbles, which is $\frac{12}{21} = \frac{4}{7}$.

Example: A box contains five blocks numbered 1, 2, 3, 4, and 5. Johnnie picks a block and replaces it. Lisa then picks a block. What is the probability that the sum of the numbers they picked is even?

Solution: Since each had 5 choices, there are 25 possible pairs of numbers. The only way the sum could be odd is if one person picked an odd number and the other picked an even number. Suppose that Johnnie chose the odd number and Lisa the even one. Johnnie had 3 possible even numbers to select from, and for each of these, Lisa had 2 possible choices, for a total of $(3)(2) = 6$ possibilities. However, you could also have had Johnnie pick an even number and Lisa pick an odd one, and there are also 6 ways to do that. Hence, out of 25 possibilities, 12 have an odd total and 13 have an even total. The probability of an even total, then, is $\frac{13}{25}$.

ARITHMETIC AND GEOMETRIC PROGRESSIONS

A sequence of numbers $a_1, a_2, a_3, \ldots, a_n$ is said to form an arithmetic progression if there is a constant (unchanging) difference between successive terms. That is, calling this difference d, we have $a_{k+1} = a_k + d$ for $k = 1, 2, 3, \ldots$ This means that we can write $a_k = a_1 + (k-1)d$. Usually, for simplicity, we write simply a for a_1 and write:

$$a_k = a + (k-1)d$$

The last (nth) term of the sequence is frequently abbreviated L, and we have:

$$L = a + (k-1)d$$

The sum of the terms in the progression is then the average of the first and last terms times the number of terms. As a formula:

$$S = n\left(\frac{a+L}{2}\right)$$

or:

$$S = n\left(\frac{2a+(n-1)d}{2}\right)$$

Example 1:

Q What is the sum of the first ten terms of the sequence $-5, -2, 1, 4, \ldots$?

A. 17.5

B. 22

C. 40.5

D. 85

E. 135

Solution: The correct answer is D. The first term is -5. The common difference, $d = 3$. Hence, the tenth (last) term is $-5 + 9(3) = 17$, and the first and last terms average 8.5. Therefore, the sum is $10(8.5) = 85$.

A sequence of numbers $a_1, a_2, a_3, \ldots, a_n$ is said to form a geometric progression if each term is a constant multiple of the preceding one. That is, the ratio of successive terms is a constant. Calling the common ratio r, we have $a_{k+1} = a_k r$ for $k = 1, 2, 3, \ldots$ which means that we can write $a_k = a_1 r^{k-1}$. Usually, for simplicity, we use a for a_1 and write:

$$a^k = ar^{k-1} \text{ for } k = 1, 2, 3, \ldots, n$$

The last (nth) term is an $= ar^{n-1}$. The sum of the terms in the progression is given by the formula:

$$S = a\left(\frac{1-r^n}{1-r}\right)$$

Example 2:

 If the fourth term of a geometric progression is 5 and the seventh term is –40, what is the sum of the first five terms?

F. $\dfrac{-55}{8}$

G. $\dfrac{19}{8}$

H. 3

J. $\dfrac{33}{8}$

K. $\dfrac{55}{8}$

Solution: The correct answer is F. If the fourth term is 5 and the seventh term is –40, we have two equations: $ar^3 = 5$ and $ar^6 = -40$.

Dividing the second by the first, we have:

$$\frac{ar^6}{ar^3} = \frac{-4}{5};\ r^3 = -8$$

This yields $r = -2$. Since $ar^3 = 5$ and $r^3 = -8$, $a = \frac{-5}{8}$. The sum of the first five terms, then, is:

$$S = -\frac{5}{8}\left(\frac{1-(-2)^5}{1-(-2)}\right) = -\frac{5}{8}\left(\frac{33}{3}\right) = -\frac{55}{8}$$

MATRICES

A *matrix* (plural *matrices*) is a rectangular array of numbers. The rows of the matrix are numbered from top to bottom, and the columns are numbered from left to right. Matrices with the same "shape," that is, having the same numbers of rows and columns, can be added and subtracted by adding or subtracting like entries in their positions.

Example 1: Find the sum of these two matrices:

$$A = \begin{pmatrix} 2 & 6 \\ 3 & -1 \end{pmatrix} \qquad B = \begin{pmatrix} 4 & 0 \\ 2 & 1 \end{pmatrix}$$

Solution: The two matrices are both the same shape (2 × 2), and we can simply add the entries to get:

$$A + B = \begin{pmatrix} 6 & 6 \\ 5 & 0 \end{pmatrix}$$

To multiply a matrix A by a *scalar* (number) k, multiply every entry in A by k. For example:

$$3\begin{pmatrix} 2 & 6 \\ 3 & -1 \end{pmatrix} = \begin{pmatrix} 6 & 18 \\ 9 & -3 \end{pmatrix}$$

To form the product of a row matrix and a column matrix. The product, RC, of a row matrix R with a column matrix C can be defined only if the number of entries in each is the same. When this occurs, the product is a number which is the sum of the products of the respective entries.

For example, if $R = (1\ 2\ 3)$ and $C = \begin{pmatrix} 4 \\ 5 \\ 6 \end{pmatrix}$,

then

$$RC = (1\ 2\ 3)\begin{pmatrix} 4 \\ 5 \\ 6 \end{pmatrix} - (1)(4) + (2)(5) + (3)(6) = 32$$

Given two matrices A, which is $m \times n$, and B, which is $n \times p$, their product, AB, can be formed because the number of columns in the first matrix is equal to the number of rows in the second. The resulting matrix will be $m \times p$, and the entry in row number i, column number j is the product of row i of A and column j of B.

Example 2:

Q If $A = \begin{pmatrix} 2 & 6 \\ 3 & -1 \end{pmatrix}$ and $B = \begin{pmatrix} 4 & 3 & -2 \\ 2 & 1 & 5 \end{pmatrix}$ then the entry in

the second row, third column of AB will be

F. -11

G. -1

H. 1

J. 11

K. 20

Solution: The correct answer is F. We need to find the product of the second row of A and the third column of B, that is:

$$(3\ -2)\begin{pmatrix} -2 \\ 5 \end{pmatrix} = (3)(-2) + (-1)(5) = -11$$

PRACTICE EXERCISES

You've just reviewed the most important points in arithmetic, algebra, geometry, and trigonometry for success in taking the ACT Assessment Math Test. The following exercises will help you to practice your new knowledge as well as to continue to familiarize yourself with the contents and format of the ACT Assessment.

There are three Math Test exercises in this chapter. Each exercise contains 12 problems and should be answered in 12 minutes. Do each exercise in one sitting in a quiet place, with no notes or reference material. You may use a calculator. Use a stopwatch or kitchen timer or have someone else watch the clock. When time is up, stop at once.

Score yourself only on those items you finished. When you're done, work through the rest of the exercise.

EXERCISES: ACT ASSESSMENT MATH

Exercise 1

12 Questions • Time—12 Minutes

Directions: Solve each problem below and mark the oval representing the correct answer on your answer sheet.

Be careful not to spend too much time on any one question. Instead, solve as many questions as possible, and then use any remaining time to return to those questions you were unable to answer at first.

You may use a calculator on any problem in this test; however, not every problem requires the use of a calculator.

Diagrams that accompany problems may or may not be drawn to scale. Unless otherwise indicated, you may assume that all figures shown lie in a plane and that lines that appear straight are straight.

1. If a fleet of seven taxicabs uses 180 gallons of gasoline every two days, how many gallons will be used by four taxicabs during a seven-day week?

   A. 180
   B. 240
   C. 300
   D. 360
   E. 420

2. If $a = -1$ and $b = -2$, what is the value of $(2 - ab^2)^3$?

   F. 27
   G. 64
   H. 125
   I. 216
   J. 343

GO ON TO THE NEXT PAGE

3. If four boxes of books each weighing at least 20 pounds have an average weight of 60 pounds, and if one of the boxes weighs 80 pounds, what is the maximum possible weight of the heaviest box in pounds?

A. 90

B. 100

C. 110

D. 120

E. 140

4. A quadrilateral has angles in the ratio 1:2:3 and a fourth angle that is 31° larger than the smallest angle. What is the difference in degree measure between the two middle-sized angles in the quadrilateral?

F. 16

G. 31

H. 47

I. 51

J. 63

5. What is the area of the region shown below, if the curved side is a semicircle?

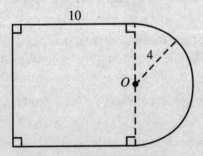

A. $20 + 4\pi$

B. $20 + 6\pi$

C. $40 + 6\pi$

D. $60 + 8\pi$

E. $80 + 8\pi$

6. How many gallons of milk that is 2% butterfat must be mixed with milk that is 3.5% butterfat to yield 10 gallons that is 3% butterfat?

F. 3

G. $\dfrac{10}{3}$

H. $\dfrac{7}{2}$

I. $\dfrac{11}{3}$

J. 4

Use the following information to answer questions 7–8.

An advertisement for a men's clothing store reads, "Men's shirts $22 each; 3 for $55. Receive a 10% discount on any sale of $100 or more."

7. What is the total cost of eight shirts?

A. $136.80

B. $138.60

C. $154.00

D. $158.40

E. $176.00

8. What is the greatest number of shirts you can buy if you have $100 to spend?

F. 4

G. 5

H. 6

I. 7

J. 8

9. What is the larger value of x if $x^2 + 6x + 8 = 0$?

A. –6

B. –4

C. –2

D. 2

E. 4

10. In the figure below, *M* is the midpoint of *RS*. What is the area of triangle *MOP*?

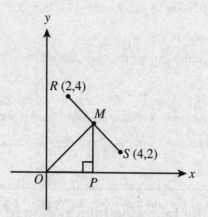

F. $\sqrt{7}$

G. 3

H. 3.5

I. 4

J. 4.5

Use the following information to answer questions 11–12.

The maximum speed of airplanes has increased from the 30 miles per hour that the Wright Brothers' first plane flew in 1903 to the much greater speeds possible today. The following graph shows increases in the air speed record from 1903 to 1967.

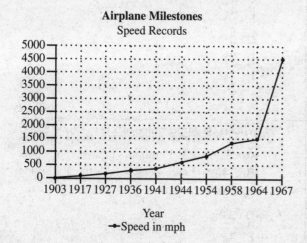

11. In approximately what year did a plane first fly over 500 miles per hour?

A. 1940

B. 1941

C. 1943

D. 1948

E. 1950

12. The air distance from New York to Los Angeles is about 3,000 miles. How much longer (in hours) would it take a plane flying at the 1944 record speed to fly that distance than a plane flying the same distances at the 1964 record speed?

F. 2

G. 2.5

H. 3

I. 4

J. 6

GO ON TO THE NEXT PAGE

Exercise 2

12 Questions • Time—12 Minutes

Directions: Solve each problem below and mark the oval representing the correct answer on your answer sheet.

Be careful not to spend too much time on any one question. Instead, solve as many questions as possible, and then use any remaining time to return to those questions you were unable to answer at first.

You may use a calculator on any problem in this test; however, not every problem requires the use of a calculator.

Diagrams that accompany problems may or may not be drawn to scale. Unless otherwise indicated, you may assume that all figures shown lie in a plane and that lines that appear straight are straight.

1. If 6 drums of oil will heat 5 identical buildings for 3 days, how many days will 10 drums of oil last when heating 2 of the same buildings?

   A. 10

   B. 12

   C. 12.5

   D. 14.5

   E. 18

2. In the figure below, the centers of all three circles lie on the same line. The medium-sized circle has a radius twice the size of the radius of the smallest circle, and the smallest circle has a radius whose length is 2. What is the area of the shaded region?

   F. 3π

   G. 4π

   H. 6π

   I. 8π

   J. 10π

3. At a certain bakery, the cost of 4 rolls, 6 muffins, and 3 loaves of bread is $9.10, and the cost of 2 rolls, 3 muffins, and a loaf of bread is $3.90. What is the cost of a loaf of bread?

   A. $1.05

   B. $1.10

   C. $1.20

   D. $1.25

   E. $1.30

4. If x and y are positive integers, and $x - 2y = 5$, which of the following could be the value of $x^2 - 4y^2$?

   F. -3

   G. 0

   H. 14

   I. 45

   J. 51

5. John can vacuum a hotel room in 20 minutes. Armando needs 15 minutes to do the same job. How many hours does it take them working together to vacuum 30 rooms?

   A. $\dfrac{20}{7}$

   B. 3

   C. 4

   D. $\dfrac{30}{7}$

   E. $\dfrac{50}{7}$

6. A plane is flying from City A to City B at m miles per hour. Another plane flying from City B to City A travels 50 miles per hour faster than the first plane. The cities are R miles apart. If both planes depart at the same time, in terms of R and m, how far are they from City A when they pass?

   F. $\dfrac{R}{m} + 50$

   G. $\dfrac{Rm}{2m} - 50$

   H. $\dfrac{Rm}{2m + 50}$

   I. $\dfrac{R + 50}{m + 50}$

   J. $\dfrac{m + 50}{R}$

7. When the units and tens digits of a certain two-digit number are reversed, the sum of the two numbers is 121 and the difference is 9. What is the tens digit of the original number?

   A. 1
   B. 3
   C. 4
   D. 6
   E. 7

8. $\sqrt{\dfrac{5}{\sqrt{25}}} = ?$

   F. $\dfrac{\sqrt{5}}{5}$

   G. 1

   H. $\sqrt{5}$

   I. $2\sqrt{5}$

   J. $m5\sqrt{5}$

9. If x and y are positive integers, and $x + y = 10$, what is the value of $|x - y|$ when $x^2 + y^2$ is as small as possible?

   A. 0
   B. 2
   C. 4
   D. 6
   E. 8

10. If $\log_x(0.001) = 3$, then $x = ?$

   F. $(.001)^3$
   G. 0.01
   H. 0.1
   I. 10
   J. 1000

11. Which of the following is the inverse function for $f(x) = \dfrac{2x}{x+4}$?

   A. $g(x) = \dfrac{4x}{x - 2}$

   B. $g(x) = \dfrac{4x}{2 - x}$

   C. $g(x) = \dfrac{x - 4}{2x}$

   D. $g(x) = \dfrac{-2x}{x + 4}$

   E. $g(x) = \dfrac{4x}{x + 2}$

12. Which of the following is an equation of the straight line that has y-intercept 2 and is perpendicular to the line $3x - 5y = 11$?

   F. $5x - 3y = 2$
   G. $5x + 3y = 2$
   H. $3x - 5y = 9$
   I. $3x - 5y = -10$
   J. $5x + 3y = 6$

GO ON TO THE NEXT PAGE

Exercise 3

12 Questions • Time—12 Minutes

Directions: Solve each problem below and mark the oval representing the correct answer on your answer sheet.

Be careful not to spend too much time on any one question. Instead, solve as many questions as possible, and then use any remaining time to return to those questions you were unable to answer at first.

You may use a calculator on any problem in this test; however, not every problem requires the use of a calculator.

Diagrams that accompany problems may or may not be drawn to scale. Unless otherwise indicated, you may assume that all figures shown lie in a plane and that lines that appear straight are straight.

1. Andover and Diggstown are 840 miles apart. On a certain map, this distance is represented by 14 inches. Lincoln and Charleston are 630 miles apart. On the same map, what is the distance between them in inches?

   A. $9\frac{1}{2}$

   B. 10

   C. $10\frac{1}{2}$

   D. 11

   E. $11\frac{1}{2}$

2. Combined into a single monomial, $10y^2 - \frac{4y^4}{2y^2} = $?

   F. $\frac{5y}{2}$

   G. $\frac{6}{y}$

   H. $6y^2$

   I. $8y^2$

   J. $-6y^2$

3. In the (x,y) coordinate plane, what is the distance from $P(-2,8)$ to $Q(3,-4)$?

   A. $\frac{12}{5}$

   B. $\sqrt{17}$

   C. $\sqrt{145}$

   D. 13

   E. 18

4. In the figure below, what is the area of the region shown?

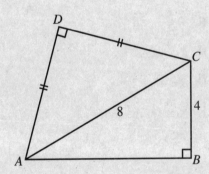

   F. $8\sqrt{3}$

   G. 16

   H. $12 + 4\sqrt{3}$

   I. $8 + 8\sqrt{3}$

   J. $16 + 8\sqrt{3}$

5. The figure below shows a square garden with a 1-yard-wide concrete path around it. If the area of the walkway is 80 square yards, what is the length of one side of the garden in yards?

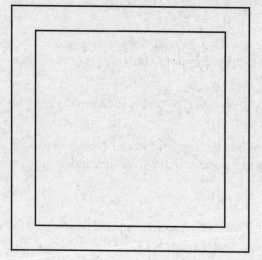

A. 36
B. 38
C. 40
D. 64
E. 80

6. If $A < 2 - 4B$, which of the following is true?

F. $\dfrac{2-A}{4} > B$

G. $\dfrac{2-A}{4} < B$

H. $B > 4A + 2$

I. $B < 4A + 2$

J. None of the above

7. If $9^{2x} = 3^{3x-4}$, then $x = ?$

A. -4

B. $-\dfrac{4}{3}$

C. 1

D. $\dfrac{4}{3}$

E. 4

8. If $x = 4.04$, what is the value of $\dfrac{(x^2-16)}{(4x+16)}$?

F. 0.01

G. 0.04

H. 1.01

I. 1.04

J. 4.01

9. If $x < y < -1$, which of the following expressions is greatest?

A. $\dfrac{x}{y}$

B. $\dfrac{y}{x}$

C. $\left(\dfrac{y}{x}\right)^2$

D. 0

E. $\left(\dfrac{x}{y}\right)^2$

10. The length of a walk-in closet is 4 feet greater than its width. Its area is 60 square feet. How many feet wide is the closet?

F. 4

G. 6

H. 8

I. 10

J. 12

GO ON TO THE NEXT PAGE

11. If $\frac{1}{x} - \frac{4}{3} = \frac{2}{x}$, what is the value of x?

   A. -3

   B. $-\frac{4}{3}$

   C. $-\frac{3}{4}$

   D. $\frac{3}{4}$

   E. $\frac{4}{3}$

12. Reduced to lowest terms, $\frac{4x^2-9}{2x^2+x-3} = ?$

   F. $\frac{2x+3}{x-1}$

   G. $\frac{2x-3}{x+1}$

   H. $\frac{2x+3}{x+1}$

   I. $\frac{2x-3}{x-1}$

   J. $\frac{2x^2-9}{x^2+x-3}$

ANSWER KEYS AND EXPLANATIONS

Exercise 1

1. D	4. F	7. B	10. J
2. I	5. E	8. H	11. C
3. D	6. G	9. C	12. I

1. **D.** Running 7 cabs for 2 days is the same as running one cab for 14 days, while running 4 cabs for 7 days is the same as running one cab for 28 days. Thus, you simply need twice as much gasoline! Here's another way to look at this: The fact that we use 180 gallons of gasoline by running 7 cabs for 2 days means that we use 180 gallons running one cab for 14 days. In other words, each cab uses $\frac{180}{14}$ gallons each day. So if you multiply the number of gallons per day used by each cab by the number of cabs and the number of days, you should get total usage. That is: $\frac{180}{14} \times 4 \times 7 = 360$.

2. **I.** Substituting, $[2 - (-1)(-2)^2]^3 = [2 - (-4)]^3 = 6^3 = 216$.

3. **D.** If the boxes have an average weight of 60 pounds, then the four must total 240 pounds. Because one weighs 80, the other three total 160. The largest box could weigh 120, with the other two each weighing 20.

4. **F.** Calling the smallest angle x, the others are $2x$, $3x$, and $(x + 31)$. Because the angles in the quadrilateral must sum to 360, we get:

$$x + 2x + 3x + (x + 31) = 360$$

$$7x + 31 = 360$$

$$7x = 329; x = 47$$

That makes the degree measures of the four angles 47, 94, 141, and 78. The difference between the two in the middle is $94 - 78 = 16$.

5. **E.** The dotted line divides the region into a rectangle and a semi-circle. Because the radius of the circular arc is 4, the diameter of the circle is 8, and that is the width of the rectangle. The length is 10. Hence, its area is 80. The area of the whole circle would be $\pi r^2 = \pi(4^2) = 16\pi$. Hence, the area of the semi-circle is half of that, or 8π. Therefore, the total area is $80 + 8\pi$.

6. **G.** Let g be the number of gallons that is 2% butterfat. Then $10 - g$ will be the amount that is 3.5% butterfat. The total amount of butterfat is:

$$0.02g + 0.035(10 - g) = 0.03(10)$$

$$0.02g + 0.35 - 0.035g = 0.3$$

Now, multiply by 1000 to clear out the decimals:

$$20g + 350 - 35g = 300$$

$$-15g = -50; g = \frac{10}{3}$$

7. **B.** Eight shirts are two sets of three, plus two singles, which will cost $110 plus $44, or $154. Then you get a $15.40 discount (10%), bringing the final cost to $138.60.

8. **H.** If you buy five shirts, you get three for $55 plus two more for $22 each, for a total of $99. But if you buy six shirts (two sets of three), you pay $110 less a 10% discount of $11, bringing your cost down to $99. The extra shirt is free!

9. **C.** Factoring: $x^2 + 6x + 8 = (x + 2)(x + 4) = 0$. Therefore:

$$x + 2 = 0 \text{ or } x + 4 = 0$$

$$x = -2 \text{ or } x = -4$$

The larger root is -2.

10. **J.** The midpoint has coordinates that are the average of the end points; that is, (3,3). Hence, the triangle is an isosceles right triangle with legs 3 units long and an area equal to $\frac{1}{2}bh = (\frac{1}{2})(3)(3) = 4.5$.

11. **C.** In 1941, the record was under 500 miles per hour, and in 1944, it was over 500 mph. The line graph seems to cross the 500 grid line at about 1943.

12. **I.** The 1964 record was 1,500 mph. To fly 3,000 miles at this speed would take 2 hours. In 1944, the speed record was 500 mph. To fly 3,000 miles at that speed would take 6 hours, or 4 hours longer.

Exercise 2

1. C   4. I   7. D   10. H

2. I   5. D   8. G   11. A

3. E   6. H   9. A   12. J

1. **C.** Letting x be the unknown number of days, we know that the ratio of "number of drums" to "number of building-days" must be constant; that is, $6:15 = 10:2x$. Written as a fractional equation: $\frac{6}{15} = \frac{10}{2x}$. Thus, $\frac{2}{5} = \frac{5}{x}$. Cross-multiplying: $2x = 25$; $x = 12.5$.

2. **I.** The smallest circle has a radius of 2, the medium circle has a radius of 4, and the diameter of the large circle must be 12, which makes its radius 6. The area of a semi-circle is half that of the entire circle; that is, $\frac{1}{2}r^2$. The area of the shaded region is the area of the largest semi-circle minus the areas of the two smaller ones; that is, $\frac{1}{2}\pi(36) - \frac{1}{2}\pi(16) - \frac{1}{2}\pi(4) = 8\pi$.

3. **E.** Letting r, m, and b be the prices in cents of rolls, muffins, and bread respectively yields two equations:

    $4r + 6m + 3b = 910$

    $2r + 3m + b = 390$

    If we multiply the second equation by –2 and add the two together, we have:

    The first equation: $4r + 6m + 3b = 910$

    –2 times the second equation: $\underline{-4r - 6m - 2b = -780}$

                                      $b = 130$

    Hence, the price of a loaf of bread is $1.30.

4. **I.** Because $x^2 - 4y^2 = (x - 2y)(x + 2y) = 5(x + 2y)$, $x^2 - 4y^2$ must be divisible by 5. Therefore, –3, 14, and 51 are not possible answers (none is divisible by 5). If the result is to be zero, $x + 2y = 0$, which means that $y = -2x$; so both numbers cannot be positive. Hence, the expression must equal 45, which you get if $x = 7$ and $y = 1$.

5. **D.** Since John takes 20 minutes per room, he can do 3 rooms in one hour. Armando can do 4 rooms in an hour. Thus, together they do 7 rooms in one hour. To do 30 rooms will take them $\frac{30}{7}$ hours, which is greater than 4.

6. **H.** The planes pass at the moment when the total distance traveled by both equals R. Call this time t. The first plane, going m mph, has traveled mt miles. The second plane, going $(m + 50)$ mph, has traveled $(m + 50)t$. The two sum to R. Thus:

    $R = mt + mt + 50t$

    $R = (2m + 50)t$

Thus:

$$t = \frac{R}{2m+50}$$

Hence, the planes' distance from City A is m times this time:

$$mt = \frac{Rm}{2m+50}$$

7. **D.** Calling the number $10t + u$, when we reverse the digits, we get $10u + t$. The sum is then $(10t + u) + (10u + t) = 11t + 11u = 121$. Dividing by 11, we have $t + u = 11$. Taking the difference: $(10t + u) - (10u + t) = 9t - 9u = 9$, and dividing by 9: $t - u = 1$. Finally, adding:

$$t + u = 11$$
$$\underline{t - u = 1}$$
$$2t = 12;\ t = 6$$

8. **G.** Because $\sqrt{25} = 5$, $\frac{\sqrt{25}}{5} = 1$, and $\sqrt{1} = 1$.

9. **A.** If $x = 5$ and $y = 5$, $x^2 + y^2 = 50$. For any other choice—say, 6 and 4—the sum is larger. Hence, the value of $x^2 + y^2$ is least when $x = y$ and $|x - y| = 0$.

10. **H.** The logarithmic equation is equivalent to $x^3 = 0.001$; $x^3 = \frac{1}{1000}$, for which $x = \sqrt[3]{\frac{1}{1000}}$; $x = \frac{1}{10} = 0.1$.

11. **A.** To find the inverse function, write y for $f(x)$, and then interchange x and y in the original equation and solve for y in terms of x. Thus, $y = \frac{2x}{x-4} \rightarrow x = \frac{2t}{y-4}$. Multiplying by $(y-4)$, we have $xy - 4x = 2y$. Bringing $2y$ to the left side and $4x$ to the right gives us: $xy - 2y = 4x$; $y(x-2) = 4x$, and dividing by $(x-2)$, $y = \frac{4x}{x-2}$.

12. **J.** Solving $3x - 5y = 11$ for y, we have $5y = 3x - 11$; $y = \frac{3}{5}x - \frac{11}{5}$. Hence, the slope is $m = \frac{3}{5}$. The slope of the perpendicular line must be $m = -\frac{5}{3}$; combined with the y-intercept $b = 2$, we have the equation $y = -\frac{5}{3}x + 2$. Multiply by 3: $3y = -5x + 6$; add $5x$ to both sides: $5x + 3y = 6$.

Exercise 3

1. C	4. J	7. A	10. G
2. I	5. B	8. F	11. C
3. D	6. F	9. E	12. I

1. **C.** The actual distance and the distance on the map must be in the same proportion. That is: $630:840 = x:14$, where x is the unknown distance. In fractions: $\frac{630}{840} = \frac{x}{14}$; $\frac{3}{4} = \frac{x}{14}$. Cross-multiplying: $4x = 42$; $x = 10.5$.

2. **I.** The fraction reduces to $2y^2$, and $10y^2 - 2y^2 = 8y^2$.

3. **D.** By the distance formula, $d = \sqrt{(3-[-2])^2 + (-4-8)^2} = \sqrt{25 + 144} = \sqrt{169} = 13$.

4. **J.** Because $BC = 4$ and $AC = 8$, we know that triangle ABC is a 30°-60°-90° right triangle. Hence, we know that $AB = 4\sqrt{3}$. Taking one-half the product of the legs, the triangle has an area of $\frac{1}{2} \times 4 \times (4\sqrt{3}) = 8\sqrt{3}$. Because triangle ADC is an isosceles right triangle with a hypotenuse of 8, each leg must be $\frac{8}{\sqrt{2}}$. Again, taking one-half the product of the legs, the triangle has an area of $\frac{1}{2} \times \frac{8}{\sqrt{2}} \times \frac{8}{\sqrt{2}} = \frac{64}{4} = 16$. Adding the two areas, we have $16 + 8\sqrt{3}$.

5. **B.** Calling the side x, then the entire area including the walkway is $(x + 2)^2$. The area of the garden is x^2, and the difference is the area of the walkway. Thus:

$$(x + 2)^2 - x^2 = 80$$

$$x^2 + 2x + 4 - x^2 = 80$$

$$2x + 4 = 80$$

$$2x = 76; x = 38$$

6. **F.** Add -2 to both sides, thus:

$$A < 2 - 4B$$

$$\underline{-2 = -2}$$

$$A - 2 < -4B$$

Divide by -4, remembering to reverse the inequality:

$$\frac{2 - A}{4} > B$$

7. **A.** In order to equate exponents, the bases must be the same. We can rewrite: $9^{2x} = (3^2)^{2x} = 3^{4x}$, and now we can equate $4x = 3x - 4$, yielding $x = -4$.

8. **F.** Factoring the numerator and denominator of the fraction, we see that we can divide out the common factor $(x + 4)$ thus:

$$\frac{x^2 - 16}{4x + 16} = \frac{(x - 4)(x + 4)}{4(x + 4)} = \frac{x - 4}{4}$$

Substituting $x = 4.04$ yields $\frac{0.004}{4} = 0.01$.

9. **E.** Because $x < y < -1$, the ratios $\frac{x}{y}$ and $\frac{y}{x}$ are both positive numbers, but $\frac{y}{x} < 1$, while $\frac{x}{y} > 1$. Therefore, $(\frac{x}{y})^2 > \frac{x}{y}$, and must be the greatest.

10. **G.** Calling the width w, the length is $w + 4$, and the area is $w(w + 4) = 60$. Thus, $w^2 + 4w - 60 = 0$. Factoring, $(w - 6)(w + 10) = 0$ gives us two roots: $w = 6$ and $w = -10$. Of course, we need the positive root, 6 (since there's no such thing as "negative width").

11. **C.** Clear fractions by multiplying each term in the equation by the least common denominator, $3x$, yielding $3 - 4x = 6$; $-3 = 4x$; $x = \frac{-3}{4}$.

12. **I.** Factoring numerator and denominator: $\frac{4x^2 - 9}{2x^2 + x - 3} = \frac{(2x - 3)(2x + 3)}{(x - 1)(2x + 3)}$. Dividing out the common factor $(2x + 3)$ yields $\frac{2x - 3}{x - 1}$.

ARE YOU READY TO MOVE ON?

How well do you understand the contents and format of the ACT Assessment Math Test? How well have you incorporated your review knowledge into your test-taking behavior?

After you've corrected each exercise, find the number of correct answers below. This will give you an idea of whether you still need improvement.

Score Key for Each Practice Exercise

Number Correct	Score	Suggested Action
0–3	Poor	Study Chapters 5 and 9 again. See Additional Resources for Review below.
4–6	Below average	Study problem areas in Chapters 5 and 9. See Additional Resources for Review below if you have time.
7–8	Average	Skim problem areas in Chapters 5 and 9 if you have time.
9–10	Above average	You may move on to a new subject.
11–12	Excellent	You're ready for the ACT Assessment Math Test.

ADDITIONAL RESOURCES FOR REVIEW

If you want to review and practice math in greater depth than the information in this book permits, browse the shelf at your local store and find a book that interests you. Scan the introductory material and directions to see if it is clearly written.

Also check the Table of Contents to see that the book covers topics specifically included on the ACT Assessment. Many books do not; other books include much more than you need. You want to be sure that you're focusing this extra study time on ACT Assessment-specific material.

Here's a selection of worthwhile math review books you may want to consider.

> *Forgotten Algebra* by Barbara Lee Bleau. Second Edition. Barron's Educational Series, 1994.
>
> *Algebra the Easy Way* by Douglas Downing. Third Edition. Barron's Educational Series, 1996.
> (This book is unique—a math review in the form of a fantasy novel. Many find this a charming and fun way to study the topic. Unfortunately, the other books

in Barron's "Easy Way" series don't use the same concept.)

Geometry the Easy Way by Lawrence S. Leff. Third Edition. Barron's Educational Series, 1997.

Math Smart by Marcia Lerner. Princeton Review, 1996. Also *Math Smart II: Algebra, Geometry, Trigonometry.*

Math the Easy Way by Anthony Prindle and Katie Prindle. Third Edition. Barron's Educational Series, 1996.

Kaplan Math Power by Robert Stanton. Simon & Schuster, 1997.

10

Reading Review: Vocabulary

For many students, vocabulary is the heart of better reading comprehension. Think of words simply as tools. The more tools you have at your disposal, the more you can do. For example, a carpenter can build a birdhouse with just a hammer, saw, and nails. But to build an entire house, he or she needs many more tools: level, plane, vise, screwdriver, screws, wrench, ruler—and those are needed just to begin. The more words you know, the more you'll comprehend when you read—no matter what the subject—and the easier you'll find the entire ACT Assessment Test.

Instead of studying any random "difficult" word you might come upon, you can focus your time and effort on the vocabulary here. This review first brings you overall strategies for building your vocabulary. Then it gives a list of the words most commonly used on the ACT Assessment, along with their definitions and sample sentences. Some of these words might appear surprisingly easy and familiar; when that's the case, the word often has different meanings and you might be tested on being able to distinguish their correct use. Immediately after this "common word list" are three more practice exercises in reading. A final section brings you additional resources for review in case you need extra help.

MASTER STRATEGIES FOR BUILDING YOUR VOCABULARY

You might not think strategies and vocabulary building can be said in the same breath. After all, for a bigger vocabulary, what more is involved than memorization? The answer is a great deal more. Memorization will only provide you with a bigger "list" of words; in some ways it's nothing more than a glorified exercise in spelling. The Master Strategies here help make these words part of your working vocabulary—and that's the key to scoring higher on the ACT Assessment.

LEARN A FEW WORDS EVERY DAY

The saying is "An apple a day keeps the doctor away"—*not* "Eat a whole bushel of apples the next time you feel sick." But that's the approach many students take with vocabulary: They try to cram years', worth of vocabulary into a few nights' study or even a single sitting.

ROAD MAP

- *Learn the Top Strategies for Building Your ACT Assessment Vocabulary*
- *Review the ACT Assessment Word List*
- *Review the Most Common Prefixes and Suffixes*
- *Practice Your ACT Assessment Vocabulary Skills*
- *Evaluate Your Skills and Options for Further Study*

This method is ineffective because vocabulary must be learned over time. Unlike, say, spelling, vocabulary takes more than just memorization and several exposures. You need time to "digest" the word and make it part of your vocabulary.

So the first and most basic strategy behind building your vocabulary is simple: *Learn just a few words at a time, and work on vocabulary every day.* Fifteen minutes a day will put hundreds of new words at your command before you take the ACT Assessment.

ACTIVELY USE WHAT YOU'VE LEARNED AND LEARN WHAT YOU USE

There's another saying: "Use a word three times and it's yours forever." Vocabulary building involves active application of what you've learned. Looking up a word's definition is a start (although most vocabulary tools already provide a definition). Then write original sentences for the word and use it daily. These are the best ways to solidify your memory of its meaning.

If you're an active "vocabulary builder," you won't limit yourself to just the ACT Assessment words below. You'll want the widest ranging vocabulary possible. To do that, besides looking at the list below, also go through the dictionary at random and pick up a few new words each day. Even better, keep a word journal of both the words below and any unfamiliar word you encounter in reading or in conversation. If you hear or read something unfamiliar, you don't have to stop right then to grab a dictionary and write a sentence. Just add it to your journal as a source of new words. The extra benefit of adding words you actually read or hear is that you're learning what you already "use." These words are part of your actual life, as opposed to opening up the dictionary and finding that your new word for the day, for example, is *hermeneutics* (the science of interpretation).

LEARN TO RECOGNIZE ROOT WORDS

If you've studied Latin or even Greek, you have a distinct advantage in learning vocabulary. Many English words have their roots, their beginnings, in Latin and Greek. Other languages share Latin and Greek as roots, so if you know Spanish or Italian, you might be coming at the same Latin root from another angle. And, because English itself has borrowed from so many different sources, any knowledge you have of any other language is also extremely helpful.

Here's an example of how root words work. Suppose you've never heard of the ACT Assessment vocabulary word, *discredit.* You don't know what this English word means. However, you *do* know just from looking at it that the Latin root word is *credere*, meaning *to believe.* If you also know that the prefix *dis-* means the negative of whatever word to which it's attached, you come up with the word dis-believe. The exact meaning is actually closer to *cause disbelief* rather than disbelieve itself, but knowing the root and the prefix would enable you to make an excellent guess on an ACT Assessment question.

Another benefit of learning root words is that once you know the root, you usually have the key to not just one but several words, all variations on the root. From *credere*, for example, comes *discredit*—and also *credential, credible, credit, credo, credulous,* and *incredible,* all of which have to do with belief or believing in some way.

HOW TO USE YOUR ACT ASSESSMENT WORD LIST

Following is a list of the words most commonly used on the ACT Assessment in passages, question stems, and answer choices. There are about 500 primary words likely to appear in one form or another, and hundreds more related words using either a variant or the same root. For each primary word there is a definition and a sample sentence. For many words, the root is also given.

Your vocabulary review should be an active process. Go down the list and check every word you don't know or about which you feel hesitant. Every day study the definition of a few of these checked words. Copy the word and its definition into your journal. Jot down its part of speech. Look at its variations. Find the root if it's not given here. Write an original sentence. Identify it in your reading material. Use it in class, on tests, and in reports.

Seeing and using the word in all these contexts will help you remember it now, then understand it better when you see it again on the ACT Assessment.

WORDS MOST LIKELY TO APPEAR ON THE ACT ASSESSMENT TEST

abbreviate (verb) to make briefer, to shorten. *Because time was running out, the speaker had to abbreviate his remarks.* abbreviation (noun).

 root: from the Latin *brevis* meaning short. The same root is also found in the word *brevity*.

abide (verb) to withstand. *It's extremely difficult to abide criticism when you feel that it is undeserved.*

abstain (verb) to refrain, to hold back. *After his heart attack, he was warned by the doctor to abstain from smoking, drinking, and over-eating.* abstinence (noun), abstemious (adjective).

abstract (adjective) intangible; apart from concrete existence. *The most difficult concepts for most students to learn are those which are most abstract.* abstraction (noun).

absurdly (adverb) in a meaningless or ridiculous manner. *Absurdly, the doctor asked the man with the broken arm if he was feeling well.* absurd (adjective).

accouterments (noun) accessories or equipment. *Other than his weapons, the equipment a soldier carries is considered accouterments.*

acrimonious (adjective) biting, harsh, caustic. *The election campaign became acrimonious, as the candidates traded insults and accusations.* acrimony (noun).

root: from the Latin *acer* meaning sharp. The same root is also found in the words *acerbity, acrid,* and *exacerbate.*

adaptable (adjective) able to be changed to be suitable for a new purpose. *Some scientists say that the mammals outlived the dinosaurs because they were more adaptable to a changing climate.* adapt (verb), adaptation (noun).

adept (adjective) highly skilled or proficient. *Although with today's electronic calculators it's not absolutely essential, most accountants are nevertheless adept at arithmetic.*

admirable (noun) deserving the highest esteem. *Honesty has always been considered a particularly admirable trait.* admirably (adverb).

adulation (noun) extreme admiration. *Few young actors have received greater adulation than did Marlon Brando after his performance in* A Streetcar Named Desire. adulate (verb), adulatory (adjective).

adversary (noun) an enemy or opponent. *When the former Soviet Union became an American ally, the United States lost its last major adversary.*

adversity (noun) misfortune. *It's easy to be patient and generous when things are going well; a person's true character is revealed under adversity.* adverse (adjective).

aeons (noun) immeasurably long periods of time. *Although it hadn't actually been that long, it seemed to the two friends that it had been aeons since they'd seen each other.*

allege (verb) to state without proof. *Some have alleged that Foster was murdered, but all the evidence points to suicide.* allegation (noun).

alleviate (verb) to make lighter or more bearable. *Although no cure for AIDS has been found, doctors are able to alleviate the sufferings of those with the disease.* alleviation (noun).

root: from the Latin *levis* meaning light. The same root is also found in the words *levitate* and *levity.*

ambiguous (adjective) having two or more possible meanings. *The phrase, "Let's table that discussion" is ambiguous; some think it means, "Let's discuss it now," while others think it means, "Let's save it for later."* ambiguity (noun).

root: from the Latin *ambo* meaning both. The same root is also found in the words *ambidextrous* and *ambivalent.*

ambivalent (adjective) having two or more contradictory feelings or attitudes; uncertain. *She was ambivalent toward her impending marriage; at times she was eager to go ahead, while at other times she wanted to call it off.* ambivalence (noun).

anachronistic (adjective) out of the proper time. *The reference, in Shakespeare's Julius Caesar, to "the clock striking twelve" is anachronistic, since there were no striking timepieces in ancient Rome.* anachronism (noun).

   root: from the Greek *chronos* meaning time. The same root is also found in the words chronic, chronicle, chronograph, chronology, and synchronize.

anomaly (noun) something different or irregular. *The tiny planet Pluto, orbiting next to the giants Jupiter, Saturn, and Neptune, has long appeared to be an anomaly.* anomalous (adjective).

anonymity (noun) the state or quality of being unidentified. *Fatigued by years in the public eye, the president had begun to long for anonymity.* anonymous (adjective).

anxiety (noun) apprehension, worry. *For many people, a visit to the dentist is a cause of anxiety.* anxious (adjective).

apprenticeship (noun) a period of time during which one learns an art or trade. *Before the advent of law schools, a young person interested in becoming an attorney generally entered into an apprenticeship with an already established lawyer.*

aptitude (noun) natural ability or talent. *It was clear, even when he was a very young child, that Picasso had an extraordinary aptitude for art.*

arable (adjective) able to be cultivated for growing crops. *Rocky New England has relatively little arable farmland.*

arbiter (noun) someone able to settle dispute; a judge or referee. *The public is the ultimate arbiter of commercial value: it decides what sells and what doesn't.*

   root: from the Latin *arbiter* meaning judge. The same root is also found in the words *arbitrage*, *arbitrary*, and *arbitrate*.

arbitrary (adjective) based on random or merely personal preference. *Both computers cost the same and had the same features, so in the end I made an arbitrary decision about which to buy.*

aristocratic (adjective) of the nobility. *Having been born a prince, and raised to succeed his father on the throne, the young man always had an aristocratic air about him.* aristocracy (noun).

artisans (noun) skilled workers or craftsmen. *During the Middle Ages, hundreds of artisans were employed to build the great cathedrals.*

assiduous (verb) working with care, attention, and diligence. *Although Karen is not a naturally gifted math student, by assiduous study she managed to earn an A in trigonometry.* assiduity (noun).

associate (verb) to join or become connected. *After many years of working on her own, the attorney decided to associate herself with a large law firm.* associate (noun).

astute (adjective) observant, intelligent, and shrewd. *Safire's years of experience in Washington and his personal acquaintance with many political insiders make him an astute commentator on politics.*

asymmetrical (adjective) not balanced. *If one of the two equal-sized windows is enlarged, the room's design will become asymmetrical.* asymmetry (noun).

audible (adjective) able to be heard. *Although she whispered, her voice was picked up by the microphone, and her words were audible throughout the theater.* audibility (noun).

   root: from the Latin *audire* meaning to hear. The same root is also found in the words audition, auditorium, and auditory.

auditory (adjective) of, relating to, or experienced through hearing. *Attending a symphony concert is primarily an auditory rather than a visual experience.*

behavioral (adjective) relating to how humans or animals act. *Psychology is considered a behavioral science because it concerns itself with human actions and reactions.* behavior (noun).

benevolent (adjective) wishing or doing good. *In old age, Carnegie used his wealth for benevolent purposes, donating large sums to found libraries and schools.* benevolence (noun).

   root: from the Latin *bene* meaning well. The same root is also found in the words *benediction, benefactor, beneficent, beneficial, benefit,* and *benign.*

blithely (adverb) in a gay or cheerful manner. *Much to everyone's surprise, the condemned man went blithely to the gallows, smiling broadly at the crowd.* blithe (adjective).

bombastic (adjective) inflated or pompous in style. *Old-fashioned bombastic political speeches don't work on television, which demands a more intimate style of communication.* bombast (noun).

buttress (noun) something that supports or strengthens. *The endorsement of the American Medical Association is a powerful buttress for the claims made about this new medicine.* buttress (verb).

candor (noun) openness, honesty, frankness. *In his memoir about the Vietnam War, former defense secretary McNamara describes his mistakes with remarkable candor.* candid (adjective).

capitulate (verb) to surrender or cease resisting. *After many proposals over a number of years, the young woman finally decided to capitulate and marry her suitor.* capitulation (noun).

carnivorous (adjective) meat-eating. *The long, dagger-like teeth of the Tyrannosaurus make it obvious that this was a carnivorous dinosaur.* carnivore (noun).

   root: from the Latin *vovare* meaning to eat. The same root is also found in the words *devour, omnivorous,* and *voracious.*

cataloguing (verb) creating a list or register. *The man was so busy cataloguing his library that he had no time to read.* catalogue (noun).

censure (noun) blame, condemnation. *The news that Senator Packwood had harassed several women brought censure from many feminists.* censure (verb).

characterize (verb) to describe the qualities of. *Although I am reluctant to characterize the man, I must say that he seems to me dishonest and untrustworthy.* characterization (noun).

chauvinism (noun) a prejudiced belief in the superiority of one's own group. *The company president's refusal to hire any women for upper management was indicative of his male chauvinism.*

circuitous (adjective) winding or indirect. *We drove to the cottage by a circuitous route so we could see as much of the surrounding countryside as possible.*

circumlocution (noun) speaking in a roundabout way; wordiness. *Legal documents often contain circumlocutions which make them difficult to understand.*

   root: from the Latin *circus* meaning a circle. The same root is also found in the words *circumference, circumnavigate, circumscribe, circumspect,* and *circumvent.*

circumscribe (verb) to define by a limit or boundary. *Originally, the role of the executive branch of government was clearly circumscribed, but that role has greatly expanded over time.* circumscription (noun).

circumvent (verb) to get around. *When Jerry was caught speeding, he tried to circumvent the law by offering the police officer a bribe.*

cogent (adjective) forceful and convincing. *The committee members were won over to the project by the cogent arguments of the chairman.* cogency (noun).

cognizant (adjective) aware, mindful. *Cognizant of the fact that it was getting late, the master of ceremonies cut short the last speech.* cognizance (noun).

   root: from the Latin *cognoscere* meaning to know. The same root is also found in the words *cognition, cognitive, incognito,* and *recognize.*

ONLINE "WORD OF THE DAY"
For more vocabulary help, try Wordsmith's Word of the Day at www.wordsmith.org/ words/today.html for an ever-changing selection.

cohesive (adjective) sticking together, unified. *An effective military unit must be a cohesive team, all its members working together for a common goal.* cohere (verb), cohesion (noun).

colloquial (adjective) informal in language; conversational. *Some expressions from Shakespeare, such as the use of thou and thee, sound formal today but were colloquial English in Shakespeare's time.*

communal (adjective) of or pertaining to a group. *Rather than have dinner separately, the members of the team chose to have a communal meal.*

conciliatory (adjective) seeking agreement, compromise, or reconciliation. *As a conciliatory gesture, the union leaders agreed to postpone a strike and to continue negotiations with management.* conciliate (verb), conciliation (noun).

concise (adjective) expressed briefly and simply; succinct. *Less than a page long, the Bill of Rights is a concise statement of the freedoms enjoyed by all Americans.* concision (noun).

root: from the Latin *caedere* meaning to cut. The same root is also found in the words *decide*, *excise*, *incision*, and *precise*.

conditioned (adjective) trained or prepared for a specific action or process. *In Pavlov's famous experiments, by ringing a bell when he was about to feed them, he conditioned his dogs to salivate at the sound of the bell.*

condolence (noun) pity for someone else's sorrow or loss; sympathy. *After the sudden death of Princess Diana, thousands of messages of condolence were sent to her family.* condole (verb).

root: from the Latin *dolere* meaning to feel pain. The same root is also found in the words *dolorous* and *indolent*.

configuration (noun) the arrangement of the parts or elements of something. *The configuration of players on a baseball field is governed both by tradition and by the rules of the game.* configure (verb).

conjure (verb) to call to mind or evoke. *The scent of magnolia always conjures up images of the Old South.*

connoisseur (noun) an expert capable of acting as a critical judge. *There was no question that the woman's discriminating palate made her a connoisseur of vintage wines.*

constructive (adjective) serving to advance a good purpose. *Although simply complaining about someone's behavior generally does no good, constructive criticism can sometimes bring about positive change.*

consummate (verb) to complete, finish, or perfect. *The deal was consummated with a handshake and the payment of the agreed-upon fee.* consummate (adjective), consummation (noun).

contaminate (verb) to make impure. *Chemicals dumped in a nearby forest had seeped into the soil and contaminated the local water supply.* contamination (noun).

contemporary (adjective) modern, current; from the same time. *I prefer old-fashioned furniture rather than contemporary styles. The composer Vivaldi was roughly contemporary with Bach.* contemporary (noun).

   root: from the Latin *tempus* meaning time. The same root is also found in the words *temporal, temporary,* and *temporize.*

contraband (noun) goods or merchandise whose exportation, importation, or possession is illegal. *Illegal drugs smuggled across the border are considered contraband by U.S. legal authorities.*

convergence (noun) the act of coming together in unity or similarity. *A remarkable example of evolutionary convergence can be seen in the shark and the dolphin, two sea creatures that developed from different origins to become very similar in form.* converge (verb).

converse (noun) something that is contrary or opposite. *While women often wear clothes similar to those of men, the converse is generally not true.*

convoluted (adjective) twisting, complicated, intricate. *Tax law has become so convoluted that it's easy for people to violate it accidentally.* convolute (verb), convolution (noun).

   root: from the Latin *volvere* meaning to roll. The same root is also found in the words *devolve, involve, revolution, revolve,* and *voluble.*

coveted (verb) desired something belonging to another. *Although the law firm associate congratulated his coworker on becoming a partner, in his heart he had coveted the position.* covetous (adjective), covetousness (noun).

credulity (noun) willingness to believe, even with little evidence. *Con artists fool people by taking advantage of their credulity.* credulous (adjective).

criterion (noun) a standard of measurement or judgment. (The plural is *criteria.) In choosing a design for the new taxicabs, reliability will be our main criterion.*

   root: from the Greek *krinein* meaning to choose. The same root is also found in the words *criticize* and *critique.*

culpable (adjective) deserving blame, guilty. *Although he committed the crime, because he was mentally ill he should not be considered culpable for his actions.* culpability (noun).

cultivate (verb) to foster the growth of. *She was so impressed on first hearing Bach's Brandenburg Concertos that she decided to return to school to cultivate her knowledge of Baroque music.*

cumulative (adjective) made up of successive additions. *Smallpox was eliminated only through the cumulative efforts of several generations of doctors and scientists.* accumulation (noun), accumulate (verb).

customary (adjective) commonly practiced or used. *It is considered customary for a groom to give his best man a gift either immediately before or after the wedding.*

daunting (adjective) intimidating. *Many recent college graduates consider the prospect of taking on a full-time job a daunting one.* daunt (verb), dauntingly (adverb).

debacle (noun) a great disaster or failure. *The French considered Napoleon's defeat at the hands of the British at Waterloo a debacle of the first magnitude.*

decorous (adjective) having good taste; proper, appropriate. *The once reserved and decorous style of the British monarchy began to change when the chic, flamboyant young Diana Spencer joined the family.* decorum (noun).

decry (verb) to criticize or condemn. *Cigarette ads aimed at youngsters have led many to decry the marketing tactics of the tobacco industry.*

delegate (verb) to give authority or responsibility. *The president delegated the vice-president to represent the administration at the peace talks.* delegate (noun).

deleterious (adjective) harmful. *About thirty years ago, scientists proved that working with asbestos could be deleterious to one's health, producing cancer and other diseases.*

　　root: from the Latin *delere* meaning to destroy. The same root is also found in the word *delete*.

delineate (verb) to outline or describe. *Naturalists had long suspected the fact of evolution, but Darwin was the first to delineate a process—natural selection—through which evolution could occur.*

demise (noun) death. *The demise of Queen Victoria, after more than sixty years on the throne, was followed almost immediately by the coronation of her son Edward as king of England.*

denigrate (verb) to criticize or belittle. *The firm's new president tried to explain his plans for improving the company without seeming to denigrate the work of his predecessor.* denigration (noun).

depicted (verb) represented in a picture, sculpture or words. *In his novel* Lincoln, *Gore Vidal depicted the president not as the icon we had always known but rather as a shrewd and wily politician.* depiction (noun).

derivative (adjective) taken from a particular source. *A person's first attempts at original poetry are apt to be derivative of whatever poetry he or she most enjoys reading.* derivation (noun), derive (verb).

desolate (adjective) empty, lifeless, and deserted; hopeless, gloomy. *Robinson Crusoe was shipwrecked and had to learn to survive alone on a desolate island. The murder of her husband left Mary Lincoln desolate.* desolation (noun).

despair (verb) to lose all hope or confidence. *Having been unable to find a job for several months, the editor began to despair of ever securing a new position.* despair (noun), desperation (noun).

detached (verb) free from involvement. *Because judges have no stake in the cases brought before them, they are able to take a detached view of the proceedings.* detachment (noun).

deter (verb) to discourage from acting. *The best way to deter crime is to insure that criminals receive swift and certain punishment.* deterrence (noun), deterrent (adjective).

determined (verb) decided conclusively. *After reviewing all the evidence, the jury determined that the defendant was not guilty of the crime.* determination (noun), determinedly (adverb).

deviate (verb) to depart from a standard or norm. *Having agreed upon a spending budget for the company, we mustn't deviate from it; if we do, we may run out of money soon.* deviation (noun).

devious (adjective) tricky, deceptive. *Milken's devious financial tactics were designed to enrich his firm while confusing or misleading government regulators.*

dictate (verb) to speak or act domineeringly. *Whether we consider it fair or not, those to whom we report at work generally have the authority to dictate our actions.* dictator (noun), dictatorial (adjective).

diffident (adjective) hesitant, reserved, shy. *Someone with a diffident personality should pursue a career that involves little public contact.* diffidence (noun).

diffuse (verb) to spread out, to scatter. *The red dye quickly became diffused through the water, turning it a very pale pink.* diffusion (noun).

digress (verb) to wander from the main path or the main topic. *My high school biology teacher loved to digress from science into personal anecdotes about his college adventures.* digression (noun), digressive (adjective).

diminish (verb) to make less or to cause to appear to be less. *By a series of foolish decisions, the committee chairman substantially diminished his authority among the other members.* diminution (noun).

diminutive (adjective) unusually small, tiny. *Children are fond of Shetland ponies because their diminutive size makes them easy to ride.* diminution (noun).

WORDS ON WORDS
"How forcible are right words." Job 6:25

discern (verb) to detect, notice, or observe. *I could discern the shape of a whale off the starboard bow, but it was too far away to determine its size or species.* discernment (noun).

discipline (noun) control gained by enforcing obedience or order. *Those who work at home sometimes find it difficult to maintain the discipline they need to be productive.* discipline (verb), disciplinary (adjective).

disclose (verb) to make known; to reveal. *Election laws require candidates to disclose the names of those who contribute money to their campaigns.* disclosure (noun).

discredit (verb) to cause disbelief in the accuracy of some statement or the reliability of a person. *Although many people still believe in UFOs, among scientists the reports of "alien encounters" have been thoroughly discredited.*

   root: from the Latin *credere* meaning to believe. The same root is also found in the words *credential, credible, credit, credo, credulous,* and *incredible.*

discreet (adjective) showing good judgment in speech and behavior. *Be discreet when discussing confidential business matters: for example, don't talk in the presence of strangers on the elevator.* discretion (noun).

discrepancy (noun) a difference or variance between two or more things. *The discrepancies between the two witnesses' stories show that one of them must be lying.* discrepant (adjective).

disingenuous (adjective) pretending to be candid, simple, and frank. *When Texas billionaire H. Ross Perot ran for president, many considered his "jest plain folks" style disingenuous.*

disparage (verb) to speak disrespectfully about, to belittle. *Many political ads today both praise their own candidate and disparage his or her opponent.* disparagement (noun), disparaging (adjective).

disparity (noun) difference in quality or kind. *There is often a disparity between the kind of high-quality television people say they want and the low-brow programs they actually watch.* disparate (adjective).

disproportionate (adjective) imbalanced in regard to size, number, or degree. *Many people spend a disproportionate amount of their income on housing.* disproportion (noun).

dissemble (verb) to pretend, to simulate. *When the police questioned her about the crime, she dissembled innocence.*

dissipate (verb) to spread out or scatter. *The windows and doors were opened, allowing the smoke that had filled the room to dissipate.* dissipation (noun).

dissonance (noun) lack of music harmony; lack of agreement between ideas. *Most modern music is characterized by dissonance, which many listeners find hard to enjoy. There is a noticeable dissonance between two common beliefs of most conservatives: their faith in unfettered free markets and their preference for traditional social values.* dissonant (adjective).

   root: from the Latin *sonare* meaning to sound. The same root is also found in the words *consonance, sonar, sonic,* and *sonorous.*

distinctive (adjective) serving to identify or distinguish. *The teams in a football game can be easily distinguished by their distinctive uniforms.* distinctively (adverb).

divulge (verb) to reveal. *The people who count the votes for the Oscar awards are under strict orders not to divulge the names of the winners.*

dogmatic (adjective) holding firmly to a particular set of beliefs, often with little or no basis. *Believers in Marxist doctrine tend to be dogmatic, ignoring evidence that contradicts their beliefs.* dogmatism (noun).

durable (adjective) long-lasting. *Denim is a popular material for work clothes because it is strong and durable.*

   root: from the Latin *durare* meaning to last. The same root is also found in the words *durance, duration,* and *endure.*

duress (noun) compulsion or restraint. *Fearing that the police might beat him, he confessed to the crime, not willingly but under duress.*

eclectic (adjective) drawn from many sources; varied, heterogeneous. *The Mellon family art collection is an eclectic one, including works ranging from ancient Greek sculptures to modern paintings.* eclecticism (noun).

ecumenical (adjective) general or worldwide in influence, extent, or application. *With hundreds of millions of adherents on every continent, the Roman Catholic Church is truly ecumenical.*

eerie (adjective) weird, strange. *The cobwebs hanging about its rooms gave the old mansion an eerie quality.*

efficacious (adjective) able to produced a desired effect. *Though thousands of people today are taking herbal supplements to treat depression, researchers have not yet proved them efficacious.* efficacy (noun).

egalitarian (adjective) asserting or promoting the belief in human equality. *Although the French Revolution was initially an egalitarian movement, during the infamous Reign of Terror human rights were widely violated.* egalitarianism (noun).

egregious (adjective) obvious, conspicuous, flagrant. *It's hard to imagine how the editor could allow such an egregious error to appear.*

   root: from the Latin *grex* meaning herd. The same root is also found in the words *aggregate, congregate,* and *gregarious.*

YOU ARE WHAT YOU SAY
Just as the correctness of your speech can make you perceived as someone who's bright or dull, the extent of your vocabulary can make you be perceived as someone who's interesting or boring. A wider vocabulary adds appeal to your words.

elevate (verb) to lift up. *When an individual successfully completes a difficult task, it generally tends to elevate his or her self-esteem.* elevation (noun).

elliptical (adjective) very terse or concise in writing or speech; difficult to understand. *Rather than speak plainly, she hinted at her meaning through a series of nods, gestures, and elliptical half-sentences.*

elongate (verb) lengthen, extend. *Because the family was having such a good time at the beach, they decided to elongate their stay for several more days.* elongation (noun).

elusive (adjective) hard to capture, grasp, or understand. *Though everyone thinks they know what "justice" is, when you try to define the concept precisely, it proves to be quite elusive.* elude (verb).

   root: from the Latin *ludere* meaning to play. The same root is also found in the words *delude, illusion, interlude,* and *ludicrous.*

embodied (verb) represented, personified. *Although his natural modesty would have led him to deny it, Mahatma Ghandi has been said to have embodied all the virtues of which man is capable.* embodiment (noun).

emend (verb) to correct. *Before the letter is mailed, please emend the two spelling errors.* emendation (noun).

eminent (adjective) noteworthy, famous. *Vaclav Havel was an eminent author before being elected president of the Czech Republic.* eminence (noun).

empathy (noun) imaginative sharing of the feelings, thoughts, or experiences of another. *It's easy for a parent to have empathy for the sorrow of another parent whose child has died.* empathetic (adjective).

empirical (adjective) based on experience or personal observation. *Although many people believe in ESP, scientists have found no empirical evidence of its existence.* empiricism (noun).

emulate (verb) to imitate or copy. *The British band Oasis admitted their desire to emulate their idols, the Beatles.* emulation (noun).

encirclement (noun) the act of surrounding or going around completely. *The greatest fear of the Soviet leadership was the encirclement of their nation by a collection of hostile countries.* encircle (verb).

enclave (noun) a distinctly bounded area enclosed within a larger unit. *Since the late nineteenth century, New York City's Greenwich Village has been famous as an enclave for artists.*

encroach (verb) to go beyond acceptable limits; to trespass. *By quietly seizing more and more authority, Robert Moses continually encroached on the powers of other government leaders.* encroachment (noun).

encumbered (verb) burdened or weighed down. *Having never worked in the field before, the young architect was not encumbered by the traditions of the profession.* encumbrance (noun).

enervate (verb) to reduce the energy or strength of someone or something. *The stress of the operation left her feeling enervated for about two weeks.*

engage (verb) to hire or employ. *When the entrepreneur recognized that he was unable to handle the day-to-day responsibilities of his business, he engaged an assistant.* engagement (noun).

engender (verb) to produce, to cause. *Disagreements over the proper use of national forests have engendered feelings of hostility between ranchers and environmentalists.*

enhance (verb) to improve in value or quality. *New kitchen appliances will enhance your house and increase the amount of money you'll make when you sell it.* enhancement (noun).

enlighten (verb) to furnish knowledge to. *Because the young woman knew her parents disliked her boyfriend, she neglected to enlighten them about her plans for marriage.* enlightenment (verb).

enmity (noun) hatred, hostility, ill will. *Longstanding enmity, like that between the Protestants and Catholics in Northern Ireland, is difficult to overcome.*

enthrall (verb) to enchant or charm. *When the Swedish singer Jenny Lind toured America in the nineteenth century, audiences were enthralled by her beauty and talent.*

entice (verb) to lure or tempt. *Hoping to entice her husband into bed, the woman put on a provocative negligee.*

enviable (adjective) extremely desirable. *After months without work, the job-seeker suddenly found himself in the enviable position of having two offers from which to choose.*

envision (verb) to picture in one's mind. *Despite her best efforts, the mother found it impossible to envision what her son would be like as an adult.*

ephemeral (adjective) quickly disappearing; transient. *Stardom in pop music is ephemeral; most of the top acts of ten years ago are forgotten today.*

epistemological (adjective) of the branch of philosophy that investigates the nature and origin of knowledge. *The question of how we come to learn things is an epistemological one.* epistemology (noun).

equanimity (noun) calmness of mind, especially under stress. *Roosevelt had the gift of facing the great crises of his presidency—the Depression, the Second World War—with equanimity and even humor.*

　　root: from the Latin *anima* meaning mind or spirit. The same root is also found in the words *animate, magnanimous, pusillanimous,* and *unanimous.*

TIP

If you don't know the root, look at the word's context; the meaning surrounds it. You might not know the word *unconscionable*. But if it appeared in the sentence, *"He was so unconscionable a killer that at the trial he laughed in the face of the victim's mother,"* you'd have a fair understanding of the word.

equilibrium (noun) a state of intellectual or emotional balance. *Due to the tragedies the man had endured, and their negative effect on his life, it took some time before he could regain his equilibrium.*

eradicate (verb) to destroy completely. *American society has failed to eradicate racism, although some of its worst effects have been reduced.*

   root: from the Latin *radix* meaning root. The same root is also found in the word *radical*.

espouse (verb) to take up as a cause; to adopt. *No politician in American today will openly espouse racism, although some behave and speak in racially prejudiced ways.*

ethic (noun) a moral principle or value. *In recent years, many people have argued that the unwillingness of young people to work hard shows that the work ethic is disappearing.* ethical (adjective).

evanescent (adjective) vanishing like a vapor; fragile and transient. *As she walked by, the evanescent fragrance of her perfume reached me for just an instant.*

evident (adjective) obvious, apparent. *Since the new assistant clearly had no idea of what her boss was talking about, it was evident that she had lied about her experience in the field.* evidence (noun).

evolving (verb) developing or achieving gradually. *Although he had been a difficult child, it was clear that the young man was evolving into a very personable and pleasant adult.* evolution (noun).

exacerbate (verb) to make worse or more severe. *The roads in our town already have too much traffic; building a new shopping mall will exacerbate the problem.*

exasperate (verb) to irritate or annoy. *Because she was trying to study, Sharon was exasperated by the yelling of her neighbors' children.*

   root: from the Latin *asper* meaning rough. The same root is also found in the word *asperity*.

exculpate (verb) to free from blame or guilt. *When someone else confessed to the crime, the previous suspect was exculpated.* exculpation (noun), exculpatory (adjective).

exert (verb) to put forth or bring to bear. *Parents often must exert their power over children, although doing so too often can hurt the child's self-esteem.* exertion (noun).

exhilaration (noun) the act of being made happy, refreshed or stimulated. *Diving into a swimming pool on a hot day generally provides people with a sense of exhilaration.* exhilarate (verb).

exonerate (verb) to free from blame. *Although Jewell was suspected at first of being involved in the bombing, later evidence exonerated him.* exoneration (noun), exonerative (adjective).

expedite (verb) to carry out promptly. *As the flood waters rose, the governor ordered state agencies to expedite their rescue efforts.*

exploitation (noun) the act of making use of a person or thing selfishly or unethically. *The practice of slavery was a cruel case of human exploitation.* exploit (verb).

expropriate (verb) to seize ownership of. *When the Communists came to power in China, they expropriated most businesses and turned them over to government-appointed managers.* expropriation (noun).

   root: from the Latin *proprius* meaning own. The same root is also found in the words *appropriate*, *property*, *proprietary*, and *proprietor*.

extant (adjective) currently in existence. *Of the seven ancient "Wonders of the World," only the pyramids of Egypt are still extant.*

extenuate (verb) to make less serious. *Karen's guilt is extenuated by the fact that she was only twelve when she committed the theft.* extenuating (adjective), extenuation (noun).

extol (verb) to greatly praise. *At the party convention, speaker after speaker rose to extol their candidate for the presidency.*

extricate (verb) to free from a difficult or complicated situation. *Much of the humor in the TV show* I Love Lucy *comes in watching Lucy try to extricate herself from the problems she creates by fibbing or trickery.* extricable (adjective).

extrinsic (adjective) not an innate part or aspect of something; external. *The high price of old baseball cards is due to extrinsic factors, such as the nostalgia felt by baseball fans for the stars of their youth, rather than the inherent beauty or value of the cards themselves.*

exuberant (adjective) wildly joyous and enthusiastic. *As the final seconds of the game ticked away, the fans of the winning team began an exuberant celebration.* exuberance (noun).

fabricate (verb) to construct or manufacture. *Because the young man didn't want his parents to know where he'd spent the evening, he had to fabricate a story about studying in the library.* fabrication (noun).

facile (adjective) easy; shallow or superficial. *The one-minute political commercial favors a candidate with facile opinions rather than serious, thoughtful solutions.* facilitate (verb), facility (noun).

   root: from the Latin *facere* meaning to do. The same root is also found in the words *facility*, *factor*, *facsimile*, and *faculty*.

fallacy (noun) an error in fact or logic. *It's a fallacy to think that "natural" means "healthful"; after all, the deadly poison arsenic is completely natural.* fallacious (adjective).

felicitous (adjective) pleasing, fortunate, apt. *The sudden blossoming of the dogwood trees on the morning of Matt's wedding seemed a felicitous sign of good luck.* felicity (noun).

fleshiness (noun) fatness or corpulence. *Although he had been thin as a young man, as he aged he developed a certain amount of fleshiness that dieting never entirely eliminated.* fleshy (adjective).

flexibility (noun) the state of being pliable or adaptable. *Because the job required someone who would be able to shift quickly from one task to another, the manager was most interested in candidates who showed flexibility.* flexible (adjective).

format (noun) the shape and size of something. *The format of a book, i.e., its height, width, and length, is an essential factor in determining how much it will cost to produce.*

formidable (adjective) awesome, impressive, or frightening. *According to his plaque in the Baseball Hall of Fame, pitcher Tom Seaver turned the New York Mets "from lovable losers into formidable foes."*

fortuitous (adjective) lucky, fortunate. *Although the mayor claimed credit for the falling crime rate, it was really caused by several fortuitous trends.*

fractious (adjective) troublesome, unruly. *Members of the British Parliament are often fractious, shouting insults and sarcastic questions during debates.*

fragment (verb) a part broken off or detached. *Even though the girl overheard only a fragment of her parents' conversation, it was sufficient for her to understand that they had decided to get a divorce.* fragmentation (noun).

fraternize (verb) to associate with on friendly terms. *Although baseball players aren't supposed to fraternize with their opponents, players from opposing teams often chat before games.* fraternization (noun).

   root: from the Latin *frater* meaning brother. The same root is also found in the words *fraternal*, *fraternity*, and *fratricide*.

frenetic (adjective) chaotic, frantic. *The floor of the stock exchange, filled with traders shouting and gesturing, is a scene of frenetic activity.*

functionally (adverb) in relation to a specific task or purpose. *Although the man knew the letters of the alphabet, since he could not read an entire sentence he was considered functionally illiterate.* function (noun).

gargantuan (adjective) huge, colossal. *The building of the Great Wall of China was one of the most gargantuan projects ever undertaken.*

genial (adjective) friendly, gracious. *A good host welcomes all visitors in a warm and genial fashion.*

genre (noun) kind or sort. *Surprisingly, romance novels constitute the literary genre that produces more book sales than any other.*

geometric (adjective) increasing or decreasing through multiplication. *When two people give birth to two children, who marry two others and give birth to four children, who in turn marry two others and give birth to eight children, the population grows at a geometric rate.* geometrically (adverb).

graft (verb) to unite or join two things. *When one uses a computer, it is possible to easily graft two existing documents together.*

grandiose (adjective) overly large, pretentious, or showy. *Among Hitler's grandiose plans for Berlin was a gigantic building with a dome several times larger than any ever built.* grandiosity (noun).

gratuitous (adjective) given freely or without cause. *Since her opinion was not requested, her harsh criticism of his singing seemed a gratuitous insult.*

gregarious (adjective) enjoying the company of others; sociable. *Marty is naturally gregarious, a popular member of several clubs and a sought-after lunch companion.*

grotesque (adjective) outlandish or bizarre. *The appearance of the aliens depicted in the film* Independence Day *is so different from that of human beings as to be grotesque.*

guileless (adjective) without cunning; innocent. *Deborah's guileless personality and complete honesty make it hard for her to survive in the harsh world of politics.*

gullible (adjective) easily fooled. *When the sweepstakes entry form arrived bearing the message, "You may be a winner!" my gullible neighbor tried to claim a prize.* gullibility (noun).

hackneyed (adjective) without originality, trite. *When someone invented the phrase, "No pain, no gain," it was clever, but now it is so commonly heard that it seems hackneyed.*

hardheadedness (noun) the quality of being stubborn or willful. *Hardheadedness is not a quality most people admire, because those who possess it can be extremely difficult to deal with.* hardheadedly (adverb).

harried (adjective) harassed. *At the height of the Saturday dinner hour, the manager of a restaurant is likely to feel harried and overwhelmed.* harry (verb).

heinous (adjective) very evil, hateful. *The massacre by Pol Pot of over a million Cambodians is one of the twentieth century's most heinous crimes.*

hierarchy (noun) a ranking of people, things, or ideas from highest to lowest. *A cabinet secretary ranks just below the president and vice president in the hierarchy of the executive branch.* hierarchical (adjective).

humanistic (adjective) concerned with human beings and their capacities, values, and achievements. *The humanistic philosophers of the Renaissance regarded humankind as the pinnacle of creation.* humanism (noun).

TIP
If a word is totally unfamiliar to you, be sure to look up its pronunciation when you're looking up its meaning. You want to be able to use it in your speech as well as in writing.

humility (noun) the quality of being humble. *The president was an extremely powerful man, but his apparent humility made him seem to be very much like everyone else.*

iconoclast (noun) someone who attacks traditional beliefs or institutions. *Comedian Dennis Miller enjoys his reputation as an iconoclast, though people in power often resent his satirical jabs.* iconoclasm (noun), iconoclastic (adjective).

idiosyncratic (adjective) peculiar to an individual; eccentric. *Cyndi Lauper sings pop music in an idiosyncratic style, mingling high-pitched whoops and squeals with throaty gurgles.* idiosyncrasy (noun).

idolatry (noun) the worship of a person, thing, or institution as a god. *In Communist China, Chairman Mao was the subject of idolatry; his picture was displayed everywhere, and millions of Chinese memorized his sayings.* idolatrous (adjective).

imminent (adjective) about to incur, impending. *In preparation for his imminent death, the man called his attorney to draw up a last will and testament.* imminence (noun).

impartial (adjective) fair, equal, unbiased. *If a judge is not impartial, then all of her rulings are questionable.* impartiality (noun).

impeccable (adjective) flawless. *The crooks printed impeccable copies of the Super Bowl tickets, impossible to distinguish from the real things.*

impetuous (adjective) acting hastily or impulsively. *Ben's resignation was an impetuous act; he did it without thinking, and he soon regretted it.* impetuosity (noun).

implicit (adjective) understood without being openly expressed; implied. *Although most clubs had no written rules excluding blacks and Jews, many had an implicit understanding that no blacks or Jews would be allowed to join.*

imposing (adjective) impressive because of bearing, size or dignity. *Because the man was well over six feet tall and weighed in excess of three hundred pounds, most people found him to be an imposing figure.*

impunity (noun) exemption from punishment or harm. *Since ambassadors are protected by their diplomatic status, they are generally able to break minor laws with impunity.*

impute (verb) to credit or give responsibility to; to attribute. *Although Sarah's comments embarrassed me, I don't impute any ill will to her; I think she didn't realize what she was saying.* imputation (noun).

inarticulate (adjective) unable to speak or express oneself clearly and understandably. *A skilled athlete might be an inarticulate public speaker, as demonstrated by many post-game interviews.*

root: from the Latin *articulus* meaning joint or division. The same root is also in the word *articulate*.

inception (noun) the beginning of something. *After her divorce, the woman realized that there had been problems from the very inception of her marriage.*

incipient (adjective) beginning to exist or appear. *The company's chief financial officer recognized the firm's incipient financial difficulties and immediately took steps to correct them.*

incisive (adjective) expressed clearly and directly. *Franklin settled the debate with a few incisive remarks that summed up the issue perfectly.*

inclination (noun) a disposition toward something. *The young woman had a strong inclination to have as many children as possible, mainly because she came from a large and happy family herself.* incline (verb).

incompatible (adjective) unable to exist together; conflicting. *Many people hold seemingly incompatible beliefs: for example, supporting the death penalty while believing in the sacredness of human life.* incompatibility (noun).

inconsequential (adjective) of little importance. *When the stereo was delivered, it was a different shade of gray than I expected, but the difference was inconsequential.*

inconsistency (noun) the quality of being irregular or unpredictable. *The inconsistency of the student's work made it extremely difficult for his teachers to accurately gauge his abilities.* inconsistent (adjective).

incorrigible (adjective) impossible to manage or reform. *Lou is an incorrigible trickster, constantly playing practical jokes no matter how much his friends complain.*

incremental (adjective) increasing gradually by small amounts. *Although the initial cost of the Medicare program was small, the incremental expenses have grown to be very large.* increment (noun).

indelible (adjective) permanent or lasting. *Meeting President Kennedy left an indelible desire in young Bill Clinton to someday live in the White House himself.*

indeterminate (adjective) not definitely known. *The college plans to enroll an indeterminate number of students; the size of the class will depend on the number of applicants and how many accept offers of admission.* determine (verb).

indicative (adjective) serving to point out or point to. *The fact that when the man got home he yelled at his children for no good reason was indicative of his bad day at the office.* indication (noun), indicate (verb).

indifferent (adjective) unconcerned, apathetic. *The mayor's small proposed budget for education suggests that he is indifferent to the needs of our schools.* indifference (noun).

indistinct (adjective) unclear, uncertain. *We could see boats on the water, but in the thick morning fog their shapes were indistinct.*

indomitable (adjective) unable to be conquered or controlled. *The world admired the indomitable spirit of Nelson Mandela; he remained courageous despite years of imprisonment.*

induce (verb) to cause. *The doctor prescribed a medicine which is supposed to induce a lowering of the blood pressure.* induction (noun).

indulgent (adjective) lenient. *Abraham Lincoln was so indulgent of his children that while he was president he let them run freely through the Oval Office without reprimanding them.* indulgence (noun), indulge (verb).

inevitable (adjective) unable to be avoided. *Once the Japanese attacked Pearl Harbor, American involvement in World War II was inevitable.* inevitability (noun).

inexhaustible (adjective) incapable of being entirely used up. *For many years we believed that the world's supply of fossil fuels was inexhaustible, but we now know that eventually it will be necessary to find other sources of energy.*

inexorable (adjective) unable to be deterred; relentless. *It's difficult to imagine how the mythic character of Oedipus could have avoided his evil destiny; his fate appears inexorable.*

influential (adjective) exerting or possessing the power to cause an effect in an indirect manner. *While the pope has direct authority only over Roman Catholics, he is also influential among members of other faiths.* influence (noun), influence (verb).

inherent (adjective) naturally part of something. *Compromise is inherent in democracy, since everyone cannot get his way.* inhere (verb), inherence (noun).

initiative (noun) the first step or opening move. *At those times when no one seems able to make a decision, someone must take the initiative to get things going.* initiation (noun), initiate (verb).

innate (adjective) inborn, native. *Not everyone who takes piano lessons becomes a fine musician, which shows that music requires innate talent as well as training.*

innocuous (adjective) harmless, inoffensive. *I was surprised that Andrea took offense at such an innocuous joke.*

innovative (adjective) characterized by introducing or beginning something new. *The innovative design of its new computer gave the company an advantage over its competitors.* innovation (noun).

insecure (adjective) not confident or sure. *The tenth-grade girl was very bright, but because she was not as attractive as some of her classmates she felt insecure about talking to boys.* insecurity (noun).

insipid (adjective) flavorless, uninteresting. *Most TV shows are so insipid that you can watch them while reading without missing a thing.* insipidity (noun).

insistence (noun) firm in stating a demand or opinion. *The man's insistence that Orson Welles—rather than Humphrey Bogart—had starred in* Casablanca *made it clear that he was quite ignorant about movies.* insistent (adjective), insist (verb).

inspiration (noun) the action or power of moving the intellect or emotions. *The individual who is able to persevere, despite adversity, often serves as an inspiration to the rest of us.* inspire (verb).

instinct (noun) a natural aptitude or ability. *The films for children produced by Walt Disney's studio were invariably successful because Disney had an instinct for what children would like to see.* instinctive (adjective).

insular (adjective) narrow or isolated in attitude or viewpoint. *New Yorkers are famous for their insular attitudes; they seem to think that nothing important has ever happened outside of their city.* insularity (noun).

integrity (noun) honesty, uprightness; soundness, completeness. *"Honest Abe" Lincoln is considered a model of political integrity. Inspectors examined the building's support beams and foundation and found no reason to doubt its structural integrity.*

intensity (noun) great concentration, force or power. *The intensity of the emotions evoked by the film* Gone With the Wind *have for more than fifty years brought viewers to tears.* intense (adjective), intensify (verb).

interaction (noun) mutual or reciprocal influence. *It is the successful interaction of all the players on a football team that enables the team to win.* interact (verb).

interminable (adjective) endless or seemingly endless. *Addressing the UN, Castro announced, "We will be brief"—then delivered an interminable four-hour speech.*

   root: from the Latin *terminare* meaning to end. The same root is also found in the words *coterminous, exterminate, terminal*, and *terminate*.

interrogation (noun) the act of formally and systematically questioning someone. *The results of the jewel thief's interrogation enabled the police to catch his accomplices before they could flee the country.* interrogate (verb).

intimidating (verb) frightening. *A boss who is particularly demanding can often be intimidating to members of his or her staff.* intimidation (noun).

intransigent (adjective) unwilling to compromise. *Despite the mediator's attempts to suggest a fair solution, the two parties were intransigent, forcing a showdown.* intransigence (noun).

intrepid (adjective) fearless and resolute. *Only an intrepid adventurer is willing to undertake the long and dangerous trip by sled to the South Pole.* intrepidity (noun).

   root: from the Latin *trepidus* meaning alarmed. The same root is also found in the word *trepidation*.

intricate (adjective) complicated. *The plans for making the model airplane were so intricate that the boy was afraid he'd never be able to complete it.* intricacy (noun).

intrusive (adjective) forcing a way in without being welcome. *The legal requirement of a search warrant is supposed to protect Americans from intrusive searches by the police.* intrude (verb), intrusion (noun).

intuitive (adjective) known directly, without apparent thought or effort. *An experienced chess player sometimes has an intuitive sense of the best move to make, even if she can't explain it.* intuit (verb), intuition (noun).

inundate (verb) to flood; to overwhelm. *As soon as playoff tickets went on sale, eager fans inundated the box office with orders.*

   root: from the Latin *unda* meaning wave. The same root is also found in the word *undulate*.

invariable (adjective) unchanging, constant. *When writing a book, it was her invariable habit to rise at 6 and work at her desk from 7 to 12.* invariability (noun).

   root: from the Latin *varius* meaning various. The same root is also found in the words *prevaricate, variable, variance, variegated,* and *vary*.

inversion (noun) a turning backwards, inside-out, or upside-down; a reversal. *Latin poetry often features inversion of word order; for example, the first line of Vergil's Aeneid: "Arms and the man I sing."* invert (verb), inverted (adjective).

   root: from the Latin *vertere* meaning to turn. The same root is also found in the words *adversary, adverse, reverse, vertical,* and *vertigo*.

inveterate (adjective) persistent, habitual. *It's very difficult for an inveterate gambler to give up the pastime.* inveteracy (noun).

invigorate (verb) to give energy to, to stimulate. *As her car climbed the mountain road, Lucinda felt invigorated by the clear air and the cool breezes.*

invincible (adjective) impossible to conquer or overcome. *For three years at the height of his career, boxer Mike Tyson seemed invincible.*

inviolable (adjective) impossible to attack or trespass upon. *In the president's remote hideaway at Camp David, guarded by the Secret Service, his privacy is, for once, inviolable.*

irresponsible (adjective) lacking a sense of being accountable for one's actions. *The teenager was supposed to stay home to take care of her younger brother, so it was irresponsible for her to go out with her friends.*

irresolute (adjective) uncertain how to act, indecisive. *When McGovern first said he supported his vice president candidate "one thousand percent," then dropped him from the ticket, it made McGovern appear irresolute.* irresolution (noun).

jeopardize (verb) to put in danger. *Terrorist attacks jeopardize the fragile peace in the Middle East.* jeopardy (noun).

jettison (verb) to discard. *In order to keep the boat from sinking, it was necessary to jettison all but the most essential gear.*

juxtapose (verb) to put side by side. *It was strange to see the old-time actor Charlton Heston and rock icon Bob Dylan juxtaposed at the awards ceremony.* juxtaposition (noun).

laboriously (adverb) in a manner marked by long, hard work. *The convicts laboriously carried the bricks from one side of the prison yard to the other.* laborious (adjective).

latent (adjective) not currently obvious or active; hidden. *Although he had committed only a single act of violence, the psychiatrist said he had probably always had a latent tendency toward violence.* latency (noun).

laudatory (adjective) giving praise. *The ads for the movie are filled with laudatory comments from critics.*

   root: from the Latin *laus* meaning praise. The same root is also found in the words *applaud, laud, laudable,* and *plaudit.*

lenient (adjective) mild, soothing, or forgiving. *The judge was known for his lenient disposition; he rarely imposed long jail sentences on criminals.* leniency (noun).

lethargic (adjective) lacking energy; sluggish. *Visitors to the zoo are surprised that the lions appear so lethargic, but in the wild lions sleep up to eighteen hours a day.* lethargy (noun).

liability (noun) an obligation or debt; a weakness or drawback. *The insurance company had a liability of millions of dollars after the town was destroyed by a tornado. Slowness afoot is a serious liability in an aspiring basketball player.* liable (adjective).

liberation (noun) the act of freeing, as from oppression. *The liberation of the inmates of the Nazi concentration camps was an event long anticipated by the Jews of the world.* liberate (verb).

lucid (adjective) clear and understandable. *Hawking's* A Short History of the Universe *is a lucid explanation of modern scientific theories about the origin of the universe.* lucidity (noun).

ludicrous (adjective) laughable because of obvious absurdity. *The man with the lampshade on his head was a ludicrous sight to the others at the party.*

luminous (adjective) emitting or reflecting light. *Because of their happiness, brides are often described as being luminous on their wedding days.*

malediction (noun) curse. *In the fairy tale "Sleeping Beauty," the princess is trapped in a death-like sleep because of the malediction uttered by an angry witch.*

　root: from the Latin *malus* meaning bad. The same root is also found in the words *malefactor, malevolence, malice,* and *malicious.*

malevolence (noun) hatred, ill will. *Critics say that Iago, the villain in Shakespeare's* Othello, *seems to exhibit malevolence with no real cause.* malevolent (noun).

malinger (verb) to pretend illness to avoid work. *During the labor dispute, hundreds of employees malingered, forcing the company to slow production and costing it millions in profits.*

malleable (adjective) able to be changed, shaped, or formed by outside pressures. *Gold is a very useful metal because it is so malleable. A child's personality is malleable and deeply influenced by the things her parents say and do.* malleability (noun).

mandate (noun) order, command. *The new policy on gays in the military went into effect as soon as the president issued his mandate about it.* mandate (verb), mandatory (adjective).

　root: from the Latin *mandare* meaning to entrust or to order. The same root is also found in the words *command, demand,* and *remand.*

masquerading (verb) disguising oneself. *In Mark Twain's classic novel* The Prince and the Pauper, *the prince was masquerading as a peasant boy while the peasant boy pretended to be the prince.*

mastery (noun) possession of consummate skill. *The brilliance of William Butler Yeats' poetry exemplifies his mastery of the English language.*

mediate (verb) to reconcile differences between two parties. *During the baseball strike, both the players and the club owners were willing to have the president mediate the dispute.* mediation (noun).

　root: from the Latin *medius* meaning middle. The same root is also found in the words *intermediate, media,* and *medium.*

mediocrity (noun) the state of being middling or poor in quality. *The New York Mets, who'd finished in ninth place in 1968, won the world's championship in 1969, going from horrible to great in a single year and skipping mediocrity.* mediocre (adjective).

meditative (adjective) characterized by reflection or contemplation. *His unusual quietness and the distant look in his eyes suggested that he was in an uncharacteristically meditative mood.* meditation (noun).

menacing (adjective) threatening or endangering. *When their father gave the children a menacing look, they immediately quieted down and finished their dinner.* menace (noun), menace (verb).

mercurial (adjective) changing quickly and unpredictably. *The mercurial personality of Robin Williams, with his many voices and styles, made him perfect for the role of the ever-changing genie in* Aladdin.

mete (verb) to deal out or dole. *As late as the 19th century, a leather whip called the "cat-o-nine-tails" was used to mete out punishment in the British navy.*

minuscule (adjective) very small, tiny. *Compared to the compensation received by the people who head large corporations in the United States, the salary of the average American worker seems minuscule.*

misconception (noun) a mistaken idea. *Columbus sailed west under the misconception that he would reach the shores of Asia that way.* misconceive (verb).

mitigate (verb) to make less severe; to relieve. *Wallace certainly committed the assault, but the verbal abuse he'd received helps to explain his behavior and somewhat mitigates his guilt.* mitigation (noun).

modesty (noun) a moderate estimation of one's own abilities. *It's unusual to find genuine modesty in politicians, as they must have healthy egos if they are to convince others of their abilities to lead.* modest (adjective).

modicum (noun) a small amount. *The plan for your new business is well designed; with a modicum of luck, you should be successful.*

  root: from the Latin *modus* meaning measure. The same root is also found in the words *immoderate, moderate, modest, modify,* and *modulate.*

mollify (verb) to soothe or calm; to appease. *Carla tried to mollify the angry customer by promising him a full refund.*

momentous (adjective) important, consequential. *Standing at the altar and saying "I do" is a momentous event in anyone's life.*

monarchical (adjective) of or relating to a ruler, such as a king. *Because he was raised with the knowledge that one day he would rule Russia, Czar Nicholas II perceived all that went on around him from a monarchical point of view.* monarch (noun).

mosaic (noun) a picture or decorative design made by combining small colored pieces, or something resembling such a design. *The diversity of America's population makes it a mosaic of races, religions, and creeds.*

mundane (adjective) everyday, ordinary, commonplace. *Moviegoers in the 1930s liked the glamorous films of Fred Astaire because they provided an escape from the mundane problems of life during the Great Depression.*

munificent (adjective) very generous; lavish. *Ted Turner's billion-dollar donation to the UN is probably the most munificent act of charity in history.* munificence (noun).

mutable (adjective) likely to change. *A politician's reputation can be highly mutable, as seen in the case of Harry Truman—mocked during his lifetime, revered afterward.*

   root: from the Latin *mutare* meaning to change. The same root is also found in the English words *immutable, mutant,* and *mutation.*

mutually (adverb) of or regarding something shared in common. *The terms of the contract were so generous to both parties that they considered the deal mutually beneficial.* mutual (adjective).

mythical (adjective) of or relating to a traditional story not based on fact. *Although in the Middle Ages people believed in the existence of unicorns, they are mythical beasts.*

nocturnal (adjective) of the night; active at night. *Travelers on the Underground Railroad escaped from slavery to the North by a series of nocturnal flights. The eyes of nocturnal animals must be sensitive in dim light.*

notorious (adjective) famous, especially for evil actions or qualities. *Warner Brothers produced a series of movies about notorious gangsters such as John Dillinger and Al Capone.* notoriety (noun).

novice (noun) beginner, tyro. *Lifting your head before you finish your swing is a typical mistake committed by the novice at golf.*

   root: from the Latin *novus* meaning new. The same root is also found in the words *innovate, novelty,* and *renovate.*

noxious (adjective) harmful or injurious to health. *Because of the noxious fumes being emitted by the factory, the government forced the owners to shut it down.*

nuance (noun) a subtle difference or quality. *At first glance, Monet's paintings of water lilies all look much alike, but the more you study them, the more you appreciate the nuances of color and shading that distinguish them.*

nurture (verb) to nourish or help to grow. *The money given by the National Endowment for the Arts helps nurture local arts organizations throughout the country.* nurture (noun).

obdurate (adjective) unwilling to change; stubborn, inflexible. *Despite the many pleas he received, the governor was obdurate in his refusal to grant clemency to the convicted murderer.* obduracy (noun).

   root: from the Latin *durus* meaning hard. The same root is also found in the words *durable* and *endure.*

objective (adjective) dealing with observable facts rather than opinions or interpretations. *When a legal case involves a shocking crime, it may be hard for a judge to remain objective in her rulings.* objectivity (noun).

oblivious (adjective) unaware, unconscious. *Karen practiced her oboe with complete concentration, oblivious to the noise and activity around her.* oblivion (noun), obliviousness (noun).

obscure (adjective) little known; hard to understand. *Mendel was an obscure monk until decades after his death, when his scientific work was finally discovered. Most people find the writings of James Joyce obscure; hence the popularity of books that explain his books.* obscure (verb), obscurity (noun).

obstinate (adjective) stubborn, unyielding. *Despite years of effort, the problem of drug abuse remains obstinate.* obstinacy (noun).

obtrusive (adjective) overly prominent. *Philip should sing more softly; his bass is so obtrusive that the other singers can barely be heard.* obtrude (verb), obtrusion (noun).

officiate (verb) to perform a function, ceremony, or duty. *Although weddings can be performed by judges, it is customary to have a clergyman officiate at such ceremonies.* official (noun).

oligarchy (noun) government by a small faction of people or families. *Saudi Arabia, which is almost entirely controlled by one large family, is a good example of an oligarchy.* oligarchic (adjective).

onerous (adjective) heavy, burdensome. *The hero Hercules was ordered to clean the Augean Stables, one of several onerous tasks known as "the labors of Hercules."* onus (noun).

opportunistic (adjective) eagerly seizing chances as they arise. *When Princess Diana died suddenly, opportunistic publishers quickly released books about her life and death.* opportunism (noun).

opulent (adjective) rich, lavish. *The mansion of newspaper tycoon Hearst is famous for its opulent decor.* opulence (noun).

ostentatious (adjective) overly showy, pretentious. *To show off his wealth, the millionaire threw an ostentatious party featuring a full orchestra, a famous singer, and tens of thousands of dollars worth of food.*

ostracize (verb) to exclude from a group. *In Biblical times, those who suffered from the disease of leprosy were ostracized and forced to live alone.* ostracism (noun).

overindulge (verb) to yield to whims or desires to an excessive degree. *When offered tables laden with food at weddings and other such gatherings, many people overindulge and afterward find that they've eaten too much.* overindulgence (noun).

palatability (noun) the state of being acceptable to the taste, the mind, or the sensibilities. *The woman had never eaten lobster before, so to test its palatability she took just a tiny bite.* palatable (adjective).

panacea (noun) a remedy for all difficulties or illnesses, a cure-all. *Because the snake oil salesman promised that his product would cure everything from lumbago to an unhappy love life, it was considered a panacea by those foolish enough to buy it.*

pariah (noun) outcast. *Accused of robbery, he became a pariah; his neighbors stopped talking to him, and people he'd considered friends no longer called.*

parochial (adjective) narrowly limited in range or scope; provincial. *Those who grow up in small towns, as opposed to large cities, tend to be less worldly, and consequently often take a more parochial view of things.* parochialism (noun).

partisan (adjective) reflecting strong allegiance to particular party or cause. *The vote on the president's budget was strictly partisan: Every member of the president's party voted yes, and all others voted no.* partisan (noun).

paternal (adjective) fatherly. *In the past, people often devoted their entire lives to working for one company, which in turn rewarded them by treating them in a paternal manner.* paternity (noun).

pathology (noun) disease or the study of disease; extreme abnormality. *Some people believe that high rates of crime are symptoms of an underlying social pathology.* pathological (adjective).

  root: from the Greek *pathos* meaning suffering. The same root is also found in the words *apathy, empathy, pathetic, pathos,* and *sympathy.*

patina (noun) the surface appearance of something grown beautiful with use or age. *The patina that had grown over the bridge made it glow in the morning sunlight.*

pellucid (adjective) very clear; transparent; easy to understand. *The water in the mountain stream was cold and pellucid. Thanks to the professor's pellucid explanation, I finally understand relativity theory.*

  root: from the Latin *lux* meaning light. The same root is also found in the words *elucidate, lucid,* and *translucent.*

penitent (adjective) feeling sorry for past crimes or sins. *Having grown penitent, he wrote a long letter of apology, asking forgiveness.*

permeate (verb) to spread through or penetrate. *Little by little, the smell of gas from the broken pipe permeated the house.*

perceptive (adjective) quick to notice, observant. *With his perceptive intelligence, Holmes was the first to notice the importance of this clue.* perceptible (adjective), perception (noun).

perfidious (adjective) disloyal, treacherous. *Although he was one of the most talented generals of the American Revolution, Benedict Arnold is remembered today as a perfidious betrayer of his country.* perfidy (noun).

  root: from the Latin *fides* meaning faith. The same root is also found in the words *confide, confidence, fidelity,* and *infidel.*

persevere (adjective) to continue despite difficulties. *Although several of her teammates dropped out of the marathon, Laura persevered.* perseverance (noun).

perspective (noun) point of view. *Those politicians who are more disposed to change than to tradition are generally thought of as having a liberal rather than a conservative perspective.*

perspicacity (noun) keenness of observation or understanding. *Journalist Murray Kempton was famous for the perspicacity of his comments on social and political issues.* perspicacious (adjective).

 root: from the Latin *specere* meaning to look. The same root is also found in the words *circumspect, conspicuous, inspect, introspective, spectacle, spectator,* and *speculate.*

peruse (verb) to examine or study. *Mary-Jo perused the contract carefully before she signed it.* perusal (noun).

pervasive (adjective) spreading throughout. *As news of the disaster reached the town, a pervasive sense of gloom could be felt everywhere.* pervade (verb).

pigmented (verb) colored. *The artist pigmented his landscape with such variety that the picture was a riot of color.* pigment (noun).

placate (verb) to soothe or appease. *The waiter tried to placate the angry customer with the offer of a free dessert.* placatory (adjective).

plastic (adjective) able to be molded or reshaped. *Because it is highly plastic, clay is an easy material for beginning sculptors to use.*

plausible (adjective) apparently believable. *The idea that a widespread conspiracy to kill President Kennedy has been kept secret for over thirty years hardly seems plausible.* plausibility (noun).

pluralist (noun) one who believes in the intrinsic value of all cultures and traditions. *Anyone who firmly believes in the advantages of multiculturalism can be said to be a pluralist.*

policing (verb) regulating, controlling, or keeping in order. *The Federal Communications Commission is responsible for policing the television industry to see that it complies with government regulations.*

portability (noun) the quality of being capable of being carried. *One of the great advantages of battery-powered radios is their portability.* portable (adjective).

pragmatism (noun) a belief in approaching problems through practical rather than theoretical means. *Roosevelt's approach toward the Great Depression was based on pragmatism: "Try something," he said; "If it doesn't work, try something else."* pragmatic (adjective).

precision (noun) exactness. *If all the parts of an engine aren't built with precision, it is unlikely that it will work properly.* precise (adjective).

WORDS ON WORDS
"Words may be deeds." Aesop, *Fables.*

predatory (adjective) living by killing and eating other animals; exploiting others for personal gain. *The tiger is the largest predatory animal native to Asia. Microsoft has been accused of predatory business practices that prevent other software companies from competing with them.* predation (noun), predator (noun).

predilection (noun) a liking or preference. *To relax from his presidential duties, Kennedy had a predilection for spy novels featuring James Bond.*

predominant (adjective) greatest in numbers or influence. *Although hundreds of religions are practiced in India, the predominant faith is Hinduism.* predominance (noun), predominate (verb).

   root: from the Latin *dominare* meaning to rule. The same root is also found in the words English *dominate, domineer, dominion,* and *indomitable.*

prepossessing (adjective) attractive. *Smart, lovely, and talented, she has all the prepossessing qualities that mark a potential movie star.*

prerequisite (noun) something that is required as a prior condition. *Generally speaking, a high school diploma is a prerequisite for matriculating at a university.*

presumptuous (adjective) going beyond the limits of courtesy or appropriateness. *The senator winced when the presumptuous young staffer addressed him as "Chuck."* presume (verb), presumption (noun).

pretentious (adjective) claiming excessive value or importance. *For an ordinary shoe salesman to call himself a "Personal Foot Apparel Consultant" seems awfully pretentious.* pretension (noun).

primarily (adverb) at first, originally. *When people have children, their priorities change: they are no longer primarily individuals but, rather, primarily parents.* primary (adjective).

proficient (adjective) skillful, adept. *A proficient artist, Louise quickly and accurately sketched the scene.* proficiency (noun).

proliferate (verb) to increase or multiply. *Over the past fifteen years, high-tech companies have proliferated in northern California, Massachusetts, and other regions.* proliferation (noun).

prolific (adjective) producing numerous offspring or abundant works. *With more than one hundred books to his credit, Isaac Asimov was one of our most prolific authors.*

promulgate (verb) to make public, to declare. *Lincoln signed the proclamation that freed the slaves in 1862, but he waited several months to promulgate it.*

propagate (verb) to cause to grow; to foster. *John Smithson's will left his fortune for the founding of an institution to propagate knowledge, without saying whether that meant a university, a library, or a museum.* propagation (noun).

propriety (noun) appropriateness. *Some people had doubts about the propriety of Clinton's discussing his underwear on MTV.*

prosaic (adjective) everyday, ordinary, dull. *"Paul's Case" tells the story of a boy who longs to escape from the prosaic life of a clerk into a world of wealth, glamour, and beauty.*

provocative (adjective) likely to stimulate emotions, ideas, or controversy. *The demonstrators began chanting obscenities, a provocative act that they hoped would cause the police to lose control.* provoke (verb), provocation (noun).

  root: from the Latin *vocare* meaning to call. The same root is also found in the words *evoke, invoke, revoke, vocal,* and *vocation.*

proximity (noun) closeness, nearness. *Neighborhood residents were angry over the proximity of the sewage plant to the local school.* proximate (adjective).

  root: from the Latin *proximus* meaning near or next. The same root is also found in the word *approximate.*

pseudonym (noun) a fictitious name. *When an author does not want a book to carry his own name, he uses a pseudonym.* pseudonymous (adjective).

pugnacious (adjective) combative, bellicose, truculent; ready to fight. *Ty Cobb, the pugnacious outfielder for the Detroit Tigers, got into more than his fair share of brawls, both on and off the field.* pugnacity (noun).

  root: from the Latin *pungere* meaning to jab or to prick. The same root is also found in the words *pugilist, punctuate, puncture,* and *pungent.*

punctilious (adjective) very concerned about proper forms of behavior and manners. *A punctilious dresser like James would rather skip the party altogether than wear the wrong color of tie.* punctilio (noun).

quell (verb) to quiet, to suppress. *It took a huge number of police to quell the rioting.*

querulous (adjective) complaining, whining. *The nursing home attendant needed a lot of patience to care for the three querulous, unpleasant residents on his floor.*

quintessential (adjective) regarding the purest essence of something. *Tom Clancy, author of* The Hunt for Red October *and other best-sellers, is the quintessential writer of techno-thrillers.* quintessence (noun).

reciprocate (verb) to make a return for something. *If you'll baby-sit for my kids tonight, I'll reciprocate by taking care of yours tomorrow.* reciprocity (noun).

reclusive (adjective) withdrawn from society. *During the last years of her life, actress Greta Garbo led a reclusive existence, rarely appearing in public.* recluse (noun).

reconcile (verb) to make consistent or harmonious. *Roosevelt's greatness as a leader can be seen in his ability to reconcile the demands and values of the varied groups that supported him.* reconciliation (noun).

reconstruct (verb) to build or create again. *Because the South was so thoroughly destroyed during the Civil War, it was necessary to start from scratch and reconstruct the entire region.* reconstruction (noun).

refinement (noun) polish, cultivation. *Although the man came from a humble background, by making an effort to educate himself he managed over the years to develop a very high level of refinement.* refine (verb).

refute (adjective) to prove false. *The company invited reporters to visit their plant in an effort to refute the charges of unsafe working conditions.* refutation (noun).

reincarnation (noun) rebirth in a new body or form of life; a fresh embodiment. *Many of those who voted for Bill Clinton for president hoped that he would be a reincarnation of John F. Kennedy.* reincarnate (verb).

rejoinder (noun) an answer or reply. *The man's rejoinder to the accusation that he had murdered his partner was that he had committed no crime.*

relevance (noun) connection to the matter at hand; pertinence. *Testimony in a criminal trial may be admitted only if it has clear relevance to the question of guilt or innocence.* relevant (adjective).

relinquish (verb) to surrender or give up something. *In order to run for Congress, the man had to relinquish his membership in the "restricted" country club.*

renovate (verb) to renew by repairing or rebuilding. *The television program* This Old House *shows how skilled craftspeople renovate houses.* renovation (noun).

renunciation (noun) the act of rejecting or refusing something. *King Edward VII's renunciation of the British throne was caused by his desire to marry an American divorcee, something he couldn't do as king.* renounce (verb).

replete (adjective) filled abundantly. *Graham's book is replete with wonderful stories about the famous people she has known.*

reprehensible (adjective) deserving criticism or censure. *Although Pete Rose's misdeeds were reprehensible, not all fans agree that he deserves to be excluded from the Baseball Hall of Fame.* reprehend (verb), reprehension (noun).

repudiate (verb) to reject, to renounce. *After it became known that Duke had been a leader of the Ku Klux Klan, most Republican leaders repudiated him.* repudiation (noun).

reputable (adjective) having a good reputation; respected. *Find a reputable auto mechanic by asking your friends for recommendations based on their own experiences.* reputation (noun), repute (noun).

   root: from the Latin *putare* meaning to reckon. The same root is also found in the words *compute, dispute, impute*, and *putative*.

resilient (adjective) able to recover from difficulty. *A pro athlete must be resilient, able to lose a game one day and come back the next with confidence and enthusiasm.* resilience (adjective).

respectively (adverb) in the order given. *On arriving home, the woman kissed her husband and son respectively.*

resurrect (verb) to bring back to life, practice, or use. *When Rob's novel became a best-seller, he decided to resurrect one he'd written years before to see if that book would sell as well.* resurrection (noun).

revitalize (verb) give new life or vigor to. *Although he had been extremely popular at one time, Frank Sinatra had fallen from favor before his role in the film* From Here to Eternity *revitalized his career.* revitalization (noun).

rework (verb) revise. *After playwrights create first drafts of their plays, they generally rework them until they feel they're strong enough to be performed.*

rigorous (adjective) characterized by strictness or severity. *In order to make sure that they are tough enough, Marine recruits are put through rigorous training before they're allowed to join the Corps.* rigor (noun).

romanticize (verb) to treat in an idealized manner. *Although World War II was one of the grimmest conflicts in history, most films about it romanticized it for propaganda reasons.* romantic (adjective).

sanctimonious (adjective) showing false or excessive piety. *The sanctimonious prayers of the TV preacher were interspersed with requests that the viewers send him money.* sanctimony (noun).

   root: from the Latin *sanctus* meaning holy. The same root is also found in the words *sanctify, sanction, sanctity*, and *sanctuary*.

scrutinize (verb) to study closely. *The lawyer scrutinized the contract, searching for any sentence that could pose a risk for her client.* scrutiny (noun).

secrete (verb) to emit; to hide. *Glands in the mouth secrete saliva, a liquid that helps in digestion. The jewel thieves secreted the necklace in a tin box buried underground.*

sedate (verb) to reduce stress or excitement by administering a drug for that purpose. *The woman was so upset by the events of the day that she had to be sedated to fall asleep.* sedative (adjective).

sedentary (adjective) requiring much sitting. *When Officer Samson was given a desk job, she had trouble getting used to sedentary work after years on the street.*

   root: from the Latin *sedere* meaning to sit. The same root is also found in the words *sedate, sedative*, and *sediment*.

sermonizing (verb) speaking in a didactic or dogmatic manner. *Because he was hardly in a position to give advice to anyone, the man's sermonizing only served to irritate his listeners.* sermon (noun).

shortcomings (noun) deficiencies or flaws. *Although the woman believed her father had many outstanding qualities, it did not keep her from recognizing his shortcomings.*

simplification (noun) the state of being less complex or intricate. *As a result of years of complaints by the public, the Internal Revenue Service has embarked on a simplification program designed to make tax forms more understandable to those responsible for filling them out.* simplify (verb).

simulated (adjective) imitating something else; artificial. *High-quality simulated gems must be examined under a magnifying glass to be distinguished from real ones.* simulate (verb), simulation (noun).

   root: from the Latin *simulare* meaning to resemble. The same root is also found in the words *similarity, simulacrum, simultaneous*, and *verisimilitude*.

solace (verb) to comfort or console. *There was little the rabbi could say to solace the husband after his wife's death.* solace (noun).

sophisticated (adjective) worldly-wise or complex. *While many people enjoy drinking domestic beers, those with more sophisticated tastes often prefer imported brews.* sophistication (noun).

spurious (adjective) false, fake. *The so-called Piltdown Man, supposed to be the fossil of a primitive human, turned out to be spurious, though who created the hoax is still uncertain.*

squabble (verb) to engage in trivial quarrels. *When he has a bad day at the office, he often goes home and squabbles with his wife.*

stabilizing (adjective) making reliable or dependable. *He was quite wild as a teenager, but since marriage his wife has had a stabilizing influence on him.* stability (noun), stabilize (verb).

stagnate (verb) to become stale through lack of movement or change. *Having had no contact with the outside world for generations, Japan's culture gradually stagnated.* stagnant (adjective), stagnation (noun).

stimulus (noun) something that excites a response or provokes an action. *The arrival of merchants and missionaries from the West provided a stimulus for change in Japanese society.* stimulate (verb).

stoic (adjective) showing little feeling, even in response to pain or sorrow. *A soldier must respond to the death of his comrades in stoic fashion, since the fighting will not stop for his grief.* stoicism (noun).

strenuous (adjective) requiring energy and strength. *Hiking in the foothills of the Rockies is fairly easy, but climbing the higher peaks can be strenuous.*

stylistically (adverb) relating to the way something is said, done, or performed. *While Jim Croce's music was stylistically close to folk, it was usually categorized as rock.*

sublimate (verb) to divert the expression of an instinctual desire or impulse into one that is socially acceptable. *He was so attracted to the woman when he first met her that he wanted to kiss her, but he knew he had to sublimate that desire if he didn't want to frighten her away.* sublimation (noun), subliminal (adjective).

subtle (adjective) not immediately obvious. *Because the aroma of her perfume was so subtle, it took several moments before he even noticed it.* subtlety (noun).

succumb (verb) to give in or give up. *Although he had serious reservations about joining the company, he knew that if they continued to pursue him he would eventually succumb to their blandishments.*

superficial (adjective) on the surface only; without depth or substance. *Her wound was superficial and required only a light bandage. His superficial attractiveness hides the fact that his personality is lifeless and his mind is dull.* superficiality (noun).

superfluous (adjective) more than is needed, excessive. *Once you've won the debate, don't keep talking; superfluous arguments will only bore and annoy the audience.* superfluity (noun).

suppress (verb) to put down or restrain. *As soon as the unrest began, thousands of helmeted police were sent into the streets to suppress the riots.* suppression (noun).

surfeit (noun) an excess. *Most American families have a surfeit of food and drink on Thanksgiving Day.* surfeit (verb).

surreptitious (adjective) done in secret. *Because Iraq has avoided weapons inspections, many believe it has a surreptitious weapons development program.*

surrogate (noun) a substitute. *When the congressman died in office, his wife was named to serve the rest of his term as a surrogate.* surrogate (adjective).

surveillance (noun) close observation of someone or something. *The detective knew that, if she kept the suspect under surveillance long enough, he would eventually do something for which he could be arrested.*

suspend (verb) to stop for a period, to interrupt. *When the young man was caught speeding for the third time, the judge suspended his license.*

symmetrical (adjective) having balanced proportions. *Although the human face appears symmetrical, its component parts are never perfectly balanced.* symmetry (noun).

synchronize (verb) to make to occur at the same time. *The generals planning the invasion wanted to synchronize the air, sea, and land attacks for maximum power.* synchronicity (noun).

tactile (adjective) relating to the sense of touch. *The thick brush strokes and gobs of color give the paintings of van Gogh a strongly tactile quality.* tactility (noun).

   root: from the Latin *tangere* meaning to touch. The same root is also found in the words *contact, contiguous, tangent,* and *tangible.*

tangential (adjective) touching lightly; only slightly connected or related. *Having enrolled in a class on African-American history, the students found the teacher's stories about his travels in South America only of tangential interest.* tangent (noun).

tedium (noun) boredom. *For most people, watching the Weather Channel for twenty-four hours would be sheer tedium.* tedious (adjective).

temerity (noun) boldness, rashness, excessive daring. *Only someone who didn't understand the danger would have the temerity to try to climb Everest without a guide.* temerarious (adjective).

temperance (noun) moderation or restraint in feelings and behavior. *Most professional athletes practice temperance in their personal habits; too much eating or drinking, they know, can harm their performance.* temperate (adjective).

temperament (noun) the manner of behaving characteristic of a specific individual. *Her temperament was such that she was argumentative and generally difficult to deal with.* temperamental (adjective).

tenacious (adjective) clinging, sticky, or persistent. *Tenacious in pursuit of her goal, she applied for the grant unsuccessfully four times before it was finally approved.* tenacity (noun).

   root: from the Latin *tenere* meaning to hold. The same root is also found in the words *retain, tenable, tenant, tenet,* and *tenure.*

tensile (adjective) capable of being extended or stretched. *While ropes are not tensile, rubber bands are made to be so.*

terrestrial (adjective) of the Earth. *The movie* Close Encounters *tells the story of the first contact between beings from outer space and terrestrial humans.*

titanic (adjective) huge, colossal. *Because of the size of the armies arrayed against each other, the battle of Gettysburg was a titanic one.*

transcendent (verb) rising above or going above the limits of. *Although she had been baptized as a child, when the young woman underwent a second baptism as an adult it was a transcendent emotional experience for her.* transcendence (noun).

transgress (verb) to go past limits; to violate. *If Iraq has developed biological weapons, then it has transgressed the UN's rules against weapons of mass destruction.* transgression (noun).

transient (adjective) passing quickly. *Long-term visitors to this hotel pay at a different rate than transient guests who stay for just a day or two.* transience (noun).

transition (noun) a passage from one state to another. *In retrospect, the young man recognized that his joining the army had served as a transition from childhood to adulthood.*

transitory (adjective) quickly passing. *Public moods tend to be transitory; people may be anxious and angry one month, relatively contented and optimistic the next.*

translucent (adjective) letting some light pass through. *Blocks of translucent glass let daylight into the room while maintaining privacy.*

transmute (verb) to change in form or substance. *In the middle ages, the alchemists tried to discover ways to transmute metals such as iron into gold.* transmutation (noun).

trite (adjective) boring because of over-familiarity; hackneyed. *Her letters were filled with trite expressions, like "All's well that ends well," and "So far so good."*

triviality (noun) the condition or quality of being of little importance of significance. *Lacking anything of interest to talk about, the man's conversation was a study in triviality.* trivial (adjective).

truism (noun) something which is obvious or self-evident. *That one must be careful when driving a car is such a truism that it seems hardly worth mentioning.*

truncate (verb) to cut off. *The manuscript of the play appeared truncated; the last page ended in the middle of a scene, halfway through the second act.*

turbulent (adjective) agitated or disturbed. *The night before the championship match, Martina was unable to sleep, her mind turbulent with fears and hopes.* turbulence (noun).

root: from the Latin *turba* meaning confusion. The same root is also found in the words English *disturb, perturb*, and *turbid*.

tyrannical (adjective) despotic or oppressive. *The American colonists felt so oppressed by King George's tyrannical rule that they believed it necessary to rebel against him.* tyrant (noun), tyrannize (verb).

> **WORDS ON WORDS**
>
> "Speech is civilization itself. The word, even the most contradictory word, preserves contact—it is silence which isolates." Thomas Mann, *The Magic Mountain*, 1924

uncouth (adjective) crude, unrefined. *The man behaved in such an ill-mannered and obnoxious way that almost everyone who met him considered him to be uncouth.*

unctuous (adjective) characterized by false or affected earnestness. *The man's manner was so unctuous that people felt that he could not be trusted.*

undomesticated (adjective) not comfortable with or accustomed to a home environment. *Unlike dogs, which have lived with people for centuries, undomesticated animals like wolves do not make good pets.*

uneasiness (noun) the state of lacking comfort or a sense of security. *The prospective bride's uneasiness about the plans for the wedding led her to double-check everything that had to be done.* uneasy (adjective).

unimagined (adjective) not even conceived of. *The author's first book was so successful that it led not to unimagined wealth and fame.*

unnerving (verb) upsetting. *Being involved in even a minor automobile accident is invariably an unnerving experience.*

unpalatable (adjective) distasteful, unpleasant. *Although I agree with the candidate on many issues, I can't vote for her, because I find her position on capital punishment unpalatable.*

unparalleled (adjective) with no equal; unique. *Tiger Woods's victory in the Masters golf tournament by a full twelve strokes was an unparalleled accomplishment.*

unstinting (adjective) giving freely and generously. *Eleanor Roosevelt was much admired for her unstinting efforts on behalf of the poor.*

untenable (adjective) impossible to defend. *The theory that this painting is a genuine van Gogh became untenable when the artist who actually painted it came forth.*

untimely (adjective) out of the natural or proper time. *The untimely death of a youthful Princess Diana seemed far more tragic than Mother Teresa's death of old age.*

unveiling (noun) an act of uncovering or making public. *The culmination of the ceremony was the unveiling of the statue which had been commissioned to honor the late president.*

unyielding (adjective) firm, resolute, obdurate. *Despite criticism, Cuomo was unyielding in his opposition to capital punishment; he vetoed several death penalty bills as governor.*

usurper (noun) someone who takes a place or possession without the right to do so. *Kennedy's most devoted followers tended to regard later presidents as usurpers, holding the office they felt he or his brothers should have held.* usurp (verb), usurpation (noun).

utilitarian (adjective) purely of practical benefit. *The design of the Model T car was simple and utilitarian, lacking the luxuries found in later models.*

utilize (verb) to make use of. *When one does research for a book it's not always possible to utilize all the information that's been gathered in the process.* utilization (noun).

utopian (adjective) impractically idealistic. *Although there have been many utopian communities founded over the centuries, due to their impractical nature none has ever survived more than a few years.* utopia (noun).

vacillation (noun) inability to take a stand. *The young man's vacillation over getting married made it impossible for him and his girlfriend to set a date for the wedding.* vacillate (verb).

validate (verb) to officially approve or confirm. *The election of the president is validated when the members of the Electoral College meet to confirm the choice of the voters.* valid (adjective), validity (noun).

vanity (noun) excessive pride in one's appearance or accomplishments. *The man's vanity was so extreme that, despite evidence to the contrary, he believed that everyone else thought as well of him as he did himself.* vain (adjective).

venerate (verb) to admire or honor. *In Communist China, Chairman Mao Zedong was venerated as an almost god-like figure.* venerable (adjective), veneration (noun).

vestige (noun) a trace or remainder. *Today's tiny Sherwood Forest is the last vestige of a woodland that once covered most of England.* vestigial (adjective).

vex (verb) to irritate, annoy, or trouble. *Unproven for generations, Fermat's last theorem was one of the most famous, and most vexing, of all mathematical puzzles.* vexation (noun).

vindicate (verb) to confirm, justify, or defend. *Lincoln's Gettysburg Address was intended to vindicate the objectives of the Union in the Civil War.* vindication (noun).

virtually (adverb) almost entirely. *As a result of chemotherapy, he was virtually free of the cancer that had threatened his life.* virtual (adjective).

virtuoso (noun) someone very skilled, especially in an art. *Vladimir Horowitz was one of the great piano virtuosos of the twentieth century.* virtuosity (noun).

    root: from the Latin *virtus* meaning strength. The same root is also found in the word *virtue*.

vivacious (adjective) lively, sprightly. *The role of Maria in* The Sound of Music *is usually played by a charming, vivacious young actress.* vivacity (noun).

    root: from the Latin *vivere* meaning to live. The same root is also found in the words *revive, vital, vivid,* and *vivisection.*

TIP
This list will give you a "feel" for the type of word that will appear on the ACT Assessment—in addition to the words that commonly *do* appear. This is useful so that you can pass over that "word for the day" random selection if it turns out to be something like chemotaxonomy (the classification of organisms by comparison of biochemical analysis). You'll know it just doesn't "feel" ACTish.

volatile (adjective) quickly changing; fleeting, transitory; prone to violence. *Public opinion is notoriously volatile; a politician who is very popular one month may be voted out of office the next.* volatility (noun).

vulnerable (adjective) open to damage or attack. *In baring her soul to her friend, the woman recognized that she was making herself extremely vulnerable.*

wield (verb) to exercise or exert (power or influence). *Because others tend to be afraid of him, when a dictator wants to wield his authority he only has to express his desires, and whatever he wants is done immediately.*

zealous (adjective) filled with eagerness, fervor, or passion. *A crowd of the candidate's most zealous supporters greeted her at the airport with banners, signs, and a marching band.* zeal (noun), zealot (noun), zealotry (noun).

PREFIX AND SUFFIX TABLES

Scattered throughout the word list in this chapter are notations about word *roots*. The root is one of the three word parts that are used to build most words. The *suffix* and *prefix* are the other two word parts that you should know in order to deconstruct and define words.

A prefix is an addition *before* a word that changes the meaning of the root, becoming a variation on the basic meaning. Prefixes shape or give a new direction to the word. Giving direction is perhaps the best way to describe it, because you'll notice that most prefixes are prepositions. The following table lists some of the more common prefixes that you will encounter in words on the ACT Assessment.

Prefixes

Prefix	Meanings
a, ab	apart, away, from, off, without
ad	at, near, to, toward
ante	before, in front
anti	against, opposite
bi	twice, two
co, com, con	jointly, together, with
de	away, down, from, off, reversal, undoing
di	apart; *also* double or two
dis	apart, away from, lack of, reversal, undoing
dys	bad, faulty
em, en	cause to be in, put into, put upon, restrict
e, ef, ex	away from, former, out of
equa, equi	equal, even

Prefix	Meanings
extra	beyond the bounds of, outside
fore	before, front, preceding
hyper	excessive, over, undue, unusual
hypo	less than, under
im, in	in, into, within; *also* not or without
inter	among, between, reciprocal
mis	mistake, reversal, wrongly
multi	many
non	not, absence of
ob, oc, of, op	against, on, over, toward
para	beside, beyond, next to
peri	about, around
poly	many
post	after, behind
pre	before, in advance of, in front
pro	before, favoring, for, forward
re	again, back, backward, undo
semi	half, somewhat
sub, sup	below, beneath, less than, under
super	above, exceeding limits, over
trans	across, beyond, through
un	not, reversal

A suffix is an addition *after* a word that changes the meaning of the root, becoming a variation on the basic meaning. Suffixes shape the word, often changing its part of speech from, say, a verb to a noun or a noun to an adjective. The following table lists some common suffixes, many of which are used in words on the ACT Assessment.

Suffixes

Suffix	Meanings
able, ible	capable of, fit for, tending to
age	act, condition, place of, result of
al	relating to
ance, ence	act, condition of, process of, relating to
ary	relating to, connected with
ate	function of, one who does or is
en	made of, to make (the root)

continues

Suffixes (cont.)

Suffix	Meanings
er, or	person or thing that does (the root)
ful	able to, full of
hood	condition of, class of persons
ion	action of, condition of
ish	belonging to, being like (the root), somewhat
ism	condition of, practice of, system of
ist	one who does, one who favors
ite	person associated with (the root)
ive	relating to, tending to
ize	to make, to subject to
less	not having, without, unable to
ly	similar in appearance or manner; *also* every
ment	act of having done, result of
ness	having the characteristics of
ory, tory	relating to, place of
ous	full of, like, possessing
tion, sion	act of doing, state of being
ty	quality, state of being

PRACTICE EXERCISES

You've just acquired some powerful new help for taking the ACT Assessment Reading Test. The following exercises will help you to practice these new skills as well as to continue to familiarize yourself with the contents and format of the ACT Assessment.

There are three Reading Test exercises in this chapter. Each exercise contains 2 passages followed by 10 questions each and should be answered in 18 minutes. Do each exercise in one sitting in a quiet place, with no notes or reference material. Use a stopwatch or kitchen timer or have someone else watch the clock. When time is up, stop at once.

Score yourself only on those items you finished. When you're done, work through the rest of the exercise.

EXERCISES: READING TEST

Exercise 1

20 Questions • Time—18 Minutes

Directions: This exercise consists of two passages, each followed by several questions. Read each passage, select the correct answer for each question, and mark the oval representing the correct answer on your answer sheet.

Passage I—HUMANITIES

Often considered the beginning of modernism in painting, the French impressionists of the late 19th Century—Manet, Degas, Pissarro, Monet, and others—had a far-reaching effect on artists around the (5) world, as much for the philosophy underlying their work as for the new painterly esthetic they pioneered. For although the impressionists expressly disavowed any interest in philosophy, their new approach to art had significant philosophical implications. The view of (10) matter that the impressionists assumed differed profoundly from the view that had previously prevailed among artists. This view helped to unify the artistic works created in the new style.

The ancient Greeks had conceived of the world in (15) concrete terms, even endowing abstract qualities with bodies. This Greek view of matter persisted, so far as painting was concerned, into the nineteenth century. The impressionists, on the other hand, viewed light, not matter, as the ultimate visual reality. The philosopher (20) Taine expressed the impressionist view of things when he said, "The chief 'person' in a picture is the light in which everything is bathed."

In impressionist painting, solid bodies became mere reflectors of light, and distinctions between one object (25) and another became arbitrary conventions; for by light all things were welded together. The treatment of both color and outline was transformed as well. Color, formerly considered a property inherent in an object, was seen to be merely the result of vibrations of light on the (30) object's colorless surface. And outline, whose function had formerly been to indicate the limits of objects, now marked instead merely the boundary between units of pattern, which often merged into one another.

The impressionist world was composed not of sepa- (35) rate objects but of many surfaces on which light struck and was reflected with varying intensity to the eye through the atmosphere, which modified it. It was this process that produced the mosaic of colors that formed an impressionist canvas. "Light becomes the sole sub- (40) ject of the picture," writes Mauclair. "The interest of the object upon which it plays is secondary. Painting this conceived becomes a purely optic art."

From this profoundly revolutionary form of art, then, all ideas—religious, moral, psychological—were ex- (45) cluded, and so were all emotions except certain aesthetic ones. The people, places, and things depicted in an impressionist picture do not tell a story or convey any special meaning; they are, instead, merely parts of a pattern of light drawn from nature and captured on (50) canvas by the artist.

Paradoxically, the impressionists' avowed lack of interest in subject matter made the subject matter of their work particularly important and influential. Prior to the impressionist revolution, particular themes and (55) subjects had been generally deemed more suitable than others for treatment in art. Momentous historic events; crucial incidents in the lives of saints, martyrs, or heroes; the deeds of the Greek and Roman gods; the images of the noble, wealthy, and powerful—these (60) dominated European painting of the eighteenth and early nineteenth centuries.

The impressionists changed all that. If moral significance is drained from art, then any subject will serve as well as any other. The impressionists painted life as they (65) found it close to hand. The bustling boulevards of modern Paris; revelers in smoky cafes, theatres, and

GO ON TO THE NEXT PAGE

nightclubs; working-class families picnicking by the Seine—these are typical of the images chosen by the impressionists. It was not only their formal innovations (70) that surprised and disturbed the academic critics of their day. The fact that they chose to depict the "low life" of contemporary Paris rather than the exalted themes preferred by their predecessors made some wonder whether what the impressionists created was art at all.

(75)   In this regard as in so many others, the impressionists were true precursors of twentieth-century painting. Taking their cue from the impressionists, modernists from the cubists to the pop artists have expanded the freedom of the creator to make art from anything and (80) everything. Picasso, Braque, and Juan Gris filled their still lifes with the machine-made detritus of a modern city, even pasting actual printed labels and torn sheets of newsprint into their pictures and so inventing what came to be called collage. Six decades later, Andy (85) Warhol carried the theme to its logical conclusion with his pictures of Campbell's soup cans, depicted in a style as grandiose and monumental as any king or prophet in a neo-classical painting. Among its other messages, Warhol's work is proclaiming, "If art is a game of (90) surfaces—an experiment in color and light—then the beauty and importance of a tin can is equal to that of Helen of Troy." In this, he was a true kin—if a distant one—to Degas, Renoir, and Pissarro.

1. The author of the passage is primarily concerned with explaining:

   A. how new scientific ideas concerning light and color have affected the visual arts.

   B. the philosophical implications of the impressionist style of painting.

   C. the artistic techniques that the impressionist painters were the first to develop.

   D. the influence of thinkers like Taine and Mauclair on impressionist painting.

2. The main point of the last paragraph is that the impressionists deeply influenced twentieth century painters in their:

   F. choice of subject matter.

   G. treatment of light.

   H. use of art to tell stories.

   J. application of collage techniques.

3. According to the passage, the impressionist painters differed from the ancient Greeks in that they:

   A. considered color to be a property inherent in objects.

   B. regarded art primarily as a medium for expressing moral and aesthetic ideas.

   C. treated the objects depicted in a painting as isolated, rather than united in a single pattern.

   D. treated light, rather than matter, as the ultimate reality.

4. According to the passage, an impressionist painting is best considered:

   F. a harmonious arrangement of solid physical masses.

   G. a pattern of lights of varying intensities.

   H. a mosaic of outlines representing the edges of objects.

   J. an analysis of the properties of differing geometric forms.

5. The passage suggests that the impressionist painters regarded the distinctions among different kinds of objects to be painted as:

   A. primarily of psychological interest.

   B. arbitrary and essentially insignificant.

   C. reflecting social and political realities.

   D. suggestive of abstract truths.

6. The passage suggests that an impressionist painter would be most likely to depict which of the following scenes?

   F. A military victory by a Roman general.

   G. A can of Campbell's soup.

   H. Coffee drinkers in a Parisian restaurant.

   J. The death of a Christian martyr.

7. It can be inferred from the passage that the impressionist approach to painting was:

    A. highly objective.

    B. politically motivated.

    C. profoundly religious.

    D. ultimately conservative.

8. It can be inferred that the "low life" mentioned by the author in line 71 refers mainly to the:

    F. activities of the criminal underworld in nineteenth century France.

    G. everyday existence of middle-class and working-class Parisians.

    H. exploits of figures from Greek and Roman mythology.

    J. hand-to-mouth poverty in which most impressionist painters were forced to live.

9. The author refers to Helen of Troy (line 92) as an example of the kind of subject matter preferred by:

    A. many pre-impressionist painters.

    B. the impressionists.

    C. Picasso, Braque, and Gris.

    D. Andy Warhol.

10. It can be inferred from the passage than an impressionist painter would be most likely to agree with which of the following statements?

    F. A picture is significant primarily as a symbol of the artist's mental state.

    G. The highest purpose of art is to teach philosophical truths.

    H. The quality of a picture has nothing to do with the nature of the objects it depicts.

    J. An artist should strive to recreate on canvas the inner nature of objects from real life.

Passage II—NATURAL SCIENCE

Community cancer clusters are localized patterns of excessive cancer occurrence. The following passage discusses the difficulties involved in identifying common causes for community cancer clusters.

(5) Community cancer clusters are viewed quite differently by citizen activists than by epidemiologists. Environmentalists and concerned local residents, for instance, might immediately suspect environmental radiation as the culprit when a high incidence of cancer (10) cases occurs near a nuclear facility. Epidemiologists, in contrast, would be more likely to say that the incidences were "inconclusive" or the result of pure chance. And when a breast cancer survivor, Lorraine Pace, mapped twenty breast cancer cases occurring in her West Islip, (15) Long Island, community, her rudimentary research efforts were guided more by hope—that a specific environmental agent could be correlated with the cancers—than by scientific method.

When epidimiologists study clusters of cancer cases (20) and other non-contagious conditions such as birth defects or miscarriage, they take several variables into account, such as background rate (the number of people affected in the general population), cluster size, and specificity (any notable characteristics of the individual (25) affected in each case). If a cluster is both large and specific, it is easier for epidemiologists to assign blame. Not only must each variable be considered on its own, but it must also be combined with others. Lung cancer is very common in the general population. Yet when a (30) huge number of cases turned up among World War II shipbuilders who had all worked with asbestos, the size of the cluster and the fact that the men had had similar occupational asbestos exposures enabled epidemiologists to assign blame to the fibrous mineral.

(35) Furthermore, even if a cluster seems too small to be analyzed conclusively, it may still yield important data if the background rate of the condition is low enough. This was the case when a certain vaginal cancer turned up almost simultaneously in a half-dozen young women. (40) While six would seem to be too small a cluster for meaningful study, the cancer had been reported only once or twice before in the entire medical literature. Researchers eventually found that the mothers of all the afflicted women had taken the drug diethylstilbestrol (45) (DES) while pregnant.

GO ON TO THE NEXT PAGE ➡

Although several known carcinogens have been discovered through these kinds of occupational or medical clusters, only one community cancer cluster has ever been traced to an environmental cause. Health officials (50) often discount a community's suspicion of a common environmental cause because citizens tend to include cases that were diagnosed before the afflicted individuals moved into the neighborhood. Add to this the problem of cancer's latency. Unlike an infectious disease (55) like cholera, which is cased by a recent exposure to food or water contaminated with the cholera bacterium, cancer may have its roots in an exposure that occurred ten to twenty years earlier. Citizens also conduct what one epidemiologist calls "epidemiologic gerrymander- (60) ing," finding cancer cases, drawing a boundary around them, and then mapping this as a cluster.

Do all these caveats mean that that the hard work of Lorraine Pace and other community activists is for naught? Not necessarily. Together with many other (65) reports of breast cancer clusters on Long Island, the West Islip situation highlighted by Pace has helped epidemiologists lay the groundwork for a well-designed scientific study.

11. The "hope" mentioned in line 16 refers specifically to Pace's desire to:
   A. help reduce the incidence of breast cancer in future generations.
   B. determine the culprit responsible for her own breast cancer case.
   C. refute the dismissive statements of epidemiologists concerning her research efforts.
   D. identify a particular cause for the breast cancer cases in West Islip.

12. The case of the World War II shipbuilders with lung cancer (lines 29–34) is an example of:
   F. an occupational cluster.
   G. a medical cluster.
   H. a radiation cluster.
   J. an environmental cluster.

13. The case of six young women with vaginal cancer (lines 38–45) is an example of a cluster that has:
   A. a high background rate and is fairly specific.
   B. a low background rate and is fairly specific.
   C. a high background rate and small size.
   D. a low background rate and is non-specific.

14. The passage suggests that the fact that "only one community cancer cluster has ever been traced to an environmental cause" (lines 48–49) is most likely due to the:
   F. methodological difficulties in analyzing community cancer clusters.
   G. reluctance of epidemiologists to investigate environmental factors in cancer.
   H. lack of credibility of citizen activists in claiming to have identified cancer agents.
   J. effectiveness of regulations restricting the use of carcinogens in residential areas.

15. As it is used in line 50, the word *discount* most nearly means:
   A. exacerbate
   B. doubt
   C. ridicule
   D. heed

16. In lines 49–53 ("Health officials . . . into the neighborhood"), the author suggests that activists may mistakenly consider a particular incidence of cancer as part of a community cluster despite the fact that:
   F. the affected individual never worked with any carcinogenic material.
   G. the cancer was actually caused by a long-ago exposure.
   H. a high background rate suggests a purely random incidence.
   J. the cancer actually arose in a different geographic location.

17. The reference to cancer's "latency" in line 54 refers to the tendency of cancer to:

    A. exist in a dormant or hidden form.

    B. spread through the body at a surprisingly rapid rate.

    C. pass through phases of apparent cure and recurrence.

    D. be masked by other, unrelated illnesses.

18. The "epidemiological gerrymandering" which the author describes in lines 59–60 is most closely analogous to:

    F. a toddler's declaring that all the toys in one area of the school playground are now his property.

    G. a school principal's redistributing students in two classrooms so that each classroom has the same number of gifted students.

    H. a politician's drawing of election district boundaries so as to give one political party control of a majority of districts.

    J. a nurse's erasing information on a patient's chart and substituting false data.

19. As it is used in line 62, the word *caveats* refers to the:

    A. incidence of "gerrymandering" by citizens concerned about cancer.

    B. potential flaws in amateur studies of cancer clusters.

    C. warnings by activists concerning environmental dangers in their communities.

    D. tendencies of activists to assume environmental causes for cancer.

20. The author suggests that the work of concerned citizens who map cancer clusters:

    F. has proven the existence of several environmental causes of cancer.

    G. frequently involves the manipulation of data in order to strengthen a case.

    H. has sometimes paved the way for further studies by trained epidemiologists.

    J. is normally of little or no value to the scientific community.

Exercise 2

20 Questions • Time—18 Minutes

Directions: This exercise consists of two passages, each followed by several questions. Read each passage, select the correct answer for each question, and mark the oval representing the correct answer on your answer sheet.

Passage I—PROSE FICTION

Although Bertha Young was thirty she still had moments like this when she wanted to run instead of walk, to take dancing steps on and off the pavement, to bowl a hoop, to throw something up in the air and catch it
(5) again, or to stand still and laugh at—nothing—at nothing, simply.

What can you do if you are thirty and, turning the corner of your own street, you are overcome, suddenly, by a feeling of bliss—absolute bliss!—as though you'd
(10) suddenly swallowed a bright piece of that late afternoon sun and it burned in your bosom, sending out a little shower of sparks into every particle, into every finger and toe . . . ?

Oh, is there no way you can express it without being
(15) "drunk and disorderly?" How idiotic civilization is! Why be given a body if you have to keep it shut up in a case like a rare, rare fiddle?

"No, that about the fiddle is not quite what I mean," she thought, running up the steps and feeling in her bag
(20) for the key—she'd forgotten it, as usual—and rattling

GO ON TO THE NEXT PAGE ➡

the letter-box. "It's not what I mean, because—Thank you, Mary"—she went into the hall. "Is nurse back?"

"Yes, M'm."

"I'll go upstairs." And she ran upstairs to the nursery.

(25)   Nurse sat at a low table giving Little B her supper after her bath. The baby had on a white flannel gown and a blue woolen jacket, and her dark, fine hair was brushed up into a funny little peak. She looked up when she saw her mother and began to jump.

(30)   "Now, my lovey, eat it up like a good girl," said Nurse, setting her lips in a way that Bertha knew, and that meant she had come into the nursery at another wrong moment.

"Has she been good, Nanny?"

(35)   "She's been a little sweet all the afternoon," whispered Nanny. "We went to the park and I sat down on a chair and took her out of the carriage and a big dog came along and put its head on my knee and she clutched its ear, tugged it. Oh, you should have seen her."

(40)   Bertha wanted to ask if it wasn't rather dangerous to let her clutch at a strange dog's ear. But she did not dare to. She stood watching them, her hands by her side, like the poor little girl in front of the rich little girl with the doll.

(45)   The baby looked up at her again, stared, and then smiled so charmingly that Bertha couldn't help crying:

"Oh, Nanny, do let me finish giving her supper while you put the bath things away."

"Well, M'm, she oughtn't to be changed hands while
(50) she's eating," said Nanny, still whispering. "It unsettles her; it's very likely to upset her."

How absurd it was. Why have a baby if it has to be kept—not in a case like a rare, rare fiddle—but in another woman's arms?

(55)   "Oh, I must!" said she.

Very offended, Nanny handed her over.

"Now, don't excite her after her supper. You know you do, M'm. And I have such a time with her after!"

Thank heaven! Nanny went out of the room with the
(60) bath towels.

"Now I've got you to myself, my little precious," said Bertha, as the baby leaned against her.

She ate delightfully, holding up her lips for the spoon and then waving her hands. Sometimes she wouldn't let
(65) the spoon go; and sometimes, just as Bertha had filled it, she waved it away to the four winds.

When the soup was finished Bertha turned round to the fire.

"You're nice—you're very nice!" said she, kissing
(70) her warm baby. "I'm fond of you. I like you."

And, indeed, she loved Little B so much—her neck as she bent forward, her exquisite toes as they shone transparent in the firelight—that all her feeling of bliss came back again, and again she didn't know how to
(75) express it—what to do with it.

"You're wanted on the telephone," said Nanny, coming back in triumph and seizing *her* Little B.

1. It can be inferred from the passage that Nanny is afraid that Bertha will make the baby:

   A. overly excited.

   B. unwilling to finish her supper.

   C. physically ill.

   D. unwilling to have a bath.

2. Bertha's feelings toward Nanny may best be described as a mixture of:

   F. resentment and despair.

   G. timidity and jealousy.

   H. contempt and hostility.

   J. exasperation and affection.

3. When the narrator compares the body to "a rare, rare fiddle" (line 17), she suggests that Bertha feels:

   A. excessively frail and vulnerable.

   B. precious yet difficult to handle.

   C. unable to express her feelings.

   D. giddy, confused, and anxious.

4. It can be inferred from the third paragraph (lines 14–17) that Bertha believes that revealing her emotions openly will:

   F. expose her to social disapproval.

   G. cause people to doubt her sanity.

   H. hurt the feelings of those she loves.

   J. make others think she is intoxicated.

5. The comparison of Bertha to "the poor little girl" (line 43) primarily suggests Bertha's:

   A. desire to spend more time with Little B.

   B. wish that her family had more money.

   C. emotional and psychological immaturity.

   D. yearning for some sign of friendship from Nanny.

6. We can infer that what the narrator considers "absurd" (line 52) is:

   F. Nanny's gingerly treatment of Little B.

   G. the class distinctions that separate Nanny and Bertha.

   H. the powerful love for Little B that Bertha is feeling.

   J. Nanny's haughty attitude toward Bertha.

7. The facial expression worn by Nanny in the eighth paragraph (lines 30–33) suggests that she:

   A. does not enjoy feeding Little B.

   B. is tired of working as a nurse for another woman's child.

   C. dislikes when Bertha visits the nursery.

   D. wishes to hide the nature of her relationship with Little B.

8. We can infer from the word "triumph" in line 77 that Nanny:

   F. is happy that Little B has finished eating her supper.

   G. feels proud of her ability to control the activities of the household.

   H. wishes she had a baby of her own.

   J. is glad to be able to take Little B out of Bertha's arms.

9. The passage suggests that the "bliss" experienced by Bertha is basically:

   A. a form of maternal love.

   B. impossible to fully explain.

   C. a desire to rebel against civilization.

   D. a sign of her immaturity.

10. Given the way she is presented in the passage, Bertha can best be described as:

    F. emotional and impulsive.

    G. rigidly self-controlled.

    H. vain and insecure.

    J. arrogant and demanding.

Passage II—SOCIAL STUDIES

As the climate in the Middle East changed beginning around 7000 B.C.E., conditions emerged that were conducive to a more complex and advanced form of civilization in both Egypt and Mesopotamia. The pro-
(05) cess began when the swampy valleys of the Nile in Egypt and of the Tigris and Euphrates rivers in Mesopotamia became drier, producing riverine lands that were both habitable and fertile, and attracting settlers armed with the newly developed techniques of
(10) agriculture. This migration was further encouraged by the gradual transformation of the once-hospitable grasslands of these regions into deserts. Human population became increasingly concentrated into pockets of settlement scattered along the banks of the great rivers.

(15) These rivers profoundly shaped the way of life along their banks. In Mesopotamia, the management of water in conditions of unpredictable drought, flood, and storm became the central economic and social challenge. Villagers began early to build simple earthworks, dikes,

GO ON TO THE NEXT PAGE

(20) canals, and ditches to control the waters and reduce the opposing dangers of drought during the dry season (usually the spring) and flooding at harvest time.

Such efforts required a degree of cooperation among large numbers of people that had not previously existed. (25) The individual village, containing only a dozen or so houses and families, was economically vulnerable; but when several villages, probably under the direction of a council of elders, learned to share their human resources in the building of a coordinated network of water- (30) control systems, the safety, stability, and prosperity of all improved. In this new cooperation, the seeds of the great Mesopotamian civilizations were being sown.

Technological and mathematical invention, too, were stimulated by life along the rivers. Such devices as the (35) noria (a primitive waterwheel) and the Archimedean screw (a device for raising water from the low riverbanks to the high ground where it was needed), two forerun- ners of many more varied and complex machines, were first developed here for use in irrigation systems. Simi- (40) larly, the earliest methods of measurement and compu- tation and the first developments in geometry were stimulated by the need to keep track of land hold- ings and boundaries in fields that were periodically inundated.

(45) The rivers served as high roads of the earliest com- merce. Traders used boats made of bundles of rushes to transport grains, fruits, nuts, fibers, and textiles from one village to another, transforming the rivers into the central spines of nascent commercial kingdoms. Mud (50) from the river banks originally served as the region's sole building material, as well as the source of clay for pottery, sculpture, and writing tablets. With the opening

of trade, other materials became available. Building stones such as basalt and sandstone were imported, as (55) was alabaster for sculpture, metals such as bronze, copper, gold, and silver, and precious and semiprecious gemstones for jewelry, art, and decoration.

Eventually, Middle Eastern trade expanded surpris- ingly widely; we have evidence suggesting that, even (60) before the establishment of the first Egyptian dynasty, goods were being exchanged between villagers in Egypt and others as far away as Iran.

By 3500 B.C.E., Mespotomanian society was flour- ishing. The major archeological source from which we (65) derive our knowledge of this period is the city of Uruk, site of the modern Al Warka. Two major structures from the time are the so-called Limestone Temple, an im- mense structure about the size of an American football field (250 × 99 feet), and the White Temple, built on a (70) high platform some 40 feet above the plain. Associated discoveries include several outstanding stone sculp- tures, beautifully decorated alabaster vases, clay tab- lets, and many cylinder seals, which were both artistic expressions and symbols of personal identification used (75) by Mesopotamian rulers. Clearly, a complex and ad- vanced civilization was in place by the time these artifacts were created.

Historians have observed that similar developments were occurring at much the same time along the great (80) river valleys in other parts of the world—for example, along the Indus in India and the Hwang Ho in China. The history of early civilization has been shaped to a remarkable degree by the relationship of humans and rivers.

11. The primary purpose of the passage is to explain:
    A. how primitive technologies were first developed in the ancient Middle East.
    B. how climatic changes led to the founding of the earliest recorded cities.
    C. the influence of river life on the growth of early Mesopotamian civilization.
    D. some of the recent findings of researchers into early human history.

12. It can be inferred from the passage that, prior to 7000 B.C.E., relatively more of the Mesopotamian population could be found in:
    F. grasslands away from the rivers.
    G. mountainous regions.
    H. villages along the riverbanks.
    J. deserts areas far from the rivers.

13. According to the passage, the unpredictability of water supplies in Mesopotamia had which of the following social effects?

   I. It led to warfare over water rights among rival villages.

   II. It encouraged cooperation in the creation of water-management systems.

   III. It drove farmers to settle in fertile grasslands far from the uncontrollable rivers.

   A. I only

   B. II only

   C. II and III only

   D. Neither I, II, nor III

14. As it is used in line 49, the word *nascent* most nearly means:

   F. powerful.

   G. emerging.

   H. crude.

   J. wealthy.

15. According to the passage, the earliest trade routes in the ancient Middle East:

   A. were those between various centrally-ruled commercial kingdoms.

   B. were those that linked villages in Egypt with others in Iran.

   C. served to link the inhabitants of small villages with the dynastic kings who ruled them.

   D. connected villages that were scattered along the banks of the same river.

16. The author states that the trade good imported into Mesopotamia included:

   I. alabaster.

   II. clay tablets.

   III. semiprecious stones.

   F. I only

   G. III only

   H. I and III only

   J. II and III only

17. It can be inferred from the passage that the emergence of complex civilizations in the Middle East was dependent upon the previous development of:

   A. basic techniques of agriculture.

   B. symbolic systems for writing and mathematical computation.

   C. a system of centralized government.

   D. a method of storing and transferring wealth.

18. The main purpose of the seventh paragraph (lines 63–77) is to describe the:

   F. recent work of archeologists in studying Mesopotamian society.

   G. political and social structures that evolved in Mesopotamia.

   H. artistic styles favored by Mesopotamian craftspeople.

   J. archeological evidence of high Mesopotamian culture.

19. The passage implies that the size of the Limestone Temple suggests which of the following characteristics of Mesopotamian society?

   A. Its access to building materials imported from distant regions.

   B. Its fascination with the use of mathematical models in architecture.

   C. Its focus on the priesthood as the source of political and economic power.

   D. Its ability to marshal significant material and human resources for a building project.

GO ON TO THE NEXT PAGE

20. The author refers to emerging civilizations in India and China primarily in order to emphasize the:

   F. importance of water transportation in the growth of early trade.

   G. relatively advanced position enjoyed by the Middle East in comparison to other regions.

   H. rapidity with which social systems developed in the Middle East spread to other places.

   J. crucial role played by rivers in the development of human cultures around the world.

Exercise 3

20 Questions •Time—18 Minutes

Directions: This exercise consists of two passages, each followed by several questions. Read each passage, select the correct answer for each question, and mark the oval representing the correct answer on your answer sheet.

Passage I—HUMANITIES

It is widely believed that every word has a correct meaning, that we learn these meanings principally from teachers and grammarians (except that most of the time we don't bother to, so that we ordinarily speak "sloppy
(5) English"), and that dictionaries and grammars are the supreme authority in matters of meaning and usage. Few people ask by what authority the writers of dictionaries and grammars say what they say.

I once got into a dispute with an Englishwoman over
(10) the pronunciation of a word and offered to look it up in the dictionary. The Englishwoman said firmly, "What for? I am English. I was born and brought up in England. The way I speak *is* English." Such self-assurance about one's own language is not uncommon among the En-
(15) glish. In the United States, however, anyone who is willing to quarrel with the dictionary is regarded as either eccentric or mad.

Let us see how dictionaries are made and how the editors arrive at definitions. What follows applies, inci-
(20) dentally, only to those dictionary offices where first-hand, original research goes on—not those in which editors simply copy existing dictionaries. The task of writing a dictionary begins with reading vast amounts of the literature of the period or subject that the dictio-
(25) nary is to cover. As the editors read, they copy on cards every interesting or rare word, every unusual or peculiar occurrence of a common word, a large number of common words in their ordinary uses, and also the sentences in which each of these words appears, thus:

(30) pail

The dairy *pails* bring home increase of milk

Keats, *Endymion*, I, 44-45

That is to say, the context of each word is collected, along with the word itself. For a really big job of
(35) dictionary writing, such as the *Oxford English Dictionary* (usually bound in about twenty-five volumes), millions of such cards are collected, and the task of editing occupies decades. As the cards are collected, they are alphabetized and sorted. When the sorting is
(40) completed, there will be for each word anywhere from two to three to several hundred illustrative quotations, each on its card.

To define a word, then, the dictionary editor places before him the stack of cards illustrating that word; each
(45) of the cards represents an actual use of the word by a writer of some literary or historical importance. He reads the cards carefully, discards some, rereads the rest, and divides up the stack according to what he thinks are the several senses of the word. Finally, he writes his
(50) definitions, following the hard-and-fast rule that each definition must be based on what the quotations in front of him reveal about the meaning of the word. The editor cannot be influenced by what *he* thinks a given word *ought* to mean. He must work according to the cards or
(55) not at all.

The writing of a dictionary, therefore, is not a task of setting up authoritative statements about the "true meanings" of words, but a task of *recording,* to the best of one's ability, what various words have meant to authors
(60) in the distant or immediate past. *The writer of a dictionary is a historian, not a lawgiver.* If, for example, we had been writing a dictionary in 1890, or even as late as 1919, we could have said that the word "broadcast" means "to scatter" (seed and so on) but we could not
(65) have decreed that from 1921 on, the commonest meaning of the word should become "to disseminate audible messages, etc., by radio transmission."

To regard the dictionary as an "authority," therefore, is to credit the dictionary writer with gifts of prophecy
(70) which neither he nor anyone else possesses. In choosing our words when we speak or write, we can be *guided* by the historical record afforded us by the dictionary, but we cannot be *bound* by it, because new situations, new experiences, new inventions, new feelings, are always
(75) compelling us to give new uses to old words. Looking under a "hood," we should ordinarily have found, five hundred years ago, a monk; today, we find a motorcar engine.

The way in which the dictionary writer arrives at his
(80) definitions merely systematizes the way in which we all learn the meanings of words, beginning at infancy, and continuing for the rest of our lives. Let us say that we have never heard the word "oboe" before, and we overhear a conversation in which the following sen-
(85) tences occur:

He used to be the best *oboe* player in town . . . Whenever they came to that *oboe* part in the third movement, he used to get very excited . . . I saw him one day at the music shop, buying a new reed for his
(90) *oboe*. . . He never liked to play the clarinet after he started playing the *oboe* . . . He said it wasn't much fun, because it was too easy.

Although the word may be unfamiliar, its meaning becomes clear to us as we listen. After hearing the first
(95) sentence, we know that an "oboe" is "played," so that it must be either a game or a musical instrument. With the second sentence the possibilities as to what an "oboe" may be are narrowed down until we get a fairly clear idea of what is meant. This is how we learn by verbal
(100) context.

1. The author describes the attitude of the English-woman (lines 9–13) primarily in order to illustrate the fact that the:

    A. English tend to view the language habits of Americans with disdain.

    B. pronunciation of words is not of great importance.

    C. dictionary is not an authority on how language should be used.

    D. English are more careful in their use of language than are Americans.

2. It can be inferred that the author regards the attitude of the typical American toward the dictionary as resulting from:

    F. a misunderstanding of the role of the dictionary writer.

    G. an unwarranted self-assurance on the part of most people who speak English.

    H. an excessive sense of respect for those in positions of authority.

    J. a mistaken belief that the meanings of words never change.

GO ON TO THE NEXT PAGE ➡

3. The author uses the word "context" in line 33 to refer to the:

   A. primary meaning of a word.

   B. sentence in which a word appears.

   C. significance of the author who uses a word.

   D. way in which the definition of a word changes through time.

4. The *Oxford English Dictionary* is mentioned in the passage as an example of a dictionary that:

   F. is largely copied from the work of previous dictionaries.

   G. attempts to describe how words should be used as well as how they have been used.

   H. reflects the language of England rather than that of the United States.

   J. is based on very extensive first-hand research.

5. As it is used in line 60, the word *immediate* most nearly means:

   A. instantaneous.

   B. recent.

   C. ancient.

   D. rapid.

6. As it is used in line 26, the word *peculiar* most nearly means:

   F. incorrect.

   G. unintelligible.

   H. specific.

   J. distinctive.

7. The author's explanation, in the sixth paragraph (lines 56–67), concerning the meaning of the word "broadcast," illustrates how language may change as a result of:

   A. the careless misuse of words.

   B. changes in technology.

   C. the appearance of a new dictionary.

   D. new interpretations of linguistic history.

8. The main idea of the seventh paragraph (lines 68–78) is that:

   F. no one can foresee how language will change in the future.

   G. the dictionary is a largely useless tool for most writers.

   H. careful writers are guided by the historical meanings of the words they choose.

   J. most dictionaries are outdated as soon as they are published.

9. The author uses the example of the word "oboe" to illustrate how word meanings are learned:

   A. in infancy.

   B. by those who edit dictionaries.

   C. from hearing them used in conversation.

   D. from dictionary definitions.

10. It can be inferred from the passage that the author would most strongly agree with which of the following statements?

    F. Every word has a correct meaning.

    G. The writer of a dictionary is basically a historian.

    H. Anyone willing to quarrel with the dictionary is eccentric or mad.

    J. Grammars are the supreme authority in matters of usage.

Passage II—NATURAL SCIENCE

(The article from which this passage is excerpted was written in 1986.)

Around the turn of the century, two major innovations in the field of forensic science were added to the repertoire of scientific crime-fighting tools. One was fingerprinting; the other was blood-typing. Only in the (5) last ten years, however, have scientists begun to believe that genetic markers in blood and other body fluids may someday prove as useful in crime detection as fingerprints.

The standard ABO blood typing originated in the (10) work of Austrian pathologist Karl Landsteiner. He found in 1901 that four basic blood types existed and that these were transmitted from generation to generation according to the recently rediscovered laws of inheritance developed by Gregor Mendel earlier in the (15) century.

The four blood types classified by Landsteiner are known as A, B, AB, and O. Their names derive from the presence or absence of two substances, designated A and B, found on the surface of some blood cells. Persons (20) with blood type A have red blood cells with substance A on their surface. Their blood also contains an antibody which reacts defensively against blood cells with substance B on their surface. Conversely, persons with blood type B have substance B on the surface of their red (25) blood cells, as well as an antibody against substance A.

When a person of either of these blood types is transfused with blood of the opposite type, the antibodies swing into action, destroying the transfused cells. (Indeed, it was the failure of many blood transfusions (30) that had first led physicians to suspect the existence of mutually incompatible blood groups.)

Blood type AB contains both substances and neither antibody; it can harmlessly receive a transfusion of any blood type. Hence its designation as the "universal (35) recipient." Blood type O contains neither substance and both antibodies; it reacts negatively to blood types A, B, and AB, and can receive only type O blood. However, type O blood may be safely transfused into any recipient, since it lacks any substance that could cause a (40) negative reaction; therefore, type O is the "universal donor."

In addition to their obvious importance in medical treatment, the four basic blood types of the ABO system have long been used by police as a form of negative (45) identification. Testing traces of blood found in or around a crime scene could help rule out suspects who were members of a different blood group. Added sophistication came with the discovery of additional subgroups of genetic markers in blood (such as Rh factor, by which (50) an individual's blood type is generally designated as either positive [+] or negative [−], depending on whether or not the factor is present) and with the discovery that genetic markers are present not only in blood but in other body fluids, such as perspiration and saliva.

(55) These discoveries were still of limited use in crime detection, however, because of the circumstances in which police and scientists must work. Rather than a plentiful sample of blood freshly drawn from a patient, the crime laboratory is likely to receive only a tiny fleck (60) of dried blood of unknown age from an unknown "donor" on a shirt or a scrap of rag that has spent hours or days exposed to air, high temperature, and other contaminants.

British scientists found a method for identifying (65) genetic markers more precisely in small samples. In this process, called electrophoresis, a sample is placed on a tray containing a gel through which an electrical current is then passed. A trained analyst reads the resulting patterns in the gel to determine the presence of various (70) chemical markers.

Electrophoresis made it possible to identify several thousand subgroups of blood types rather than the twelve known before. However, the equipment and special training required were expensive. In addition, (75) the process could lead to the destruction of evidence. For example, repeated tests of a blood-flecked shirt— one for each marker—led to increasing deterioration of the evidence and the cost of a week or more of laboratory time.

(80) It remained for another British researcher, Brian Wrexall, to demonstrate that simultaneous analyses, using inexpensive equipment, could test for ten different genetic markers within a 24-hour period. This development made the study of blood and fluid samples a (85) truly valuable tool for crime detection.

GO ON TO THE NEXT PAGE ▶

11. The author of the passage is mainly concerned with describing:

    A. how advances in crime detection methods have led to new discoveries in science.

    B. various ways in which crime detection laboratories assist the police.

    C. the development of new scientific tools for use in crime detection.

    D. areas of current research in the science of crime detection.

12. According to the passage, a person of blood type AB could safely donate blood to a person of which blood type?

    I.   Type A.

    II. Type B.

    III. Type AB.

    IV. Type O.

    F. III only

    G. I or III only

    H. II or III only

    J. III or IV only

13. According to the passage, a person of blood type B– would have blood cells containing which of the following?

    I.   Substance A.

    II. Substance B.

    III. Antibodies against substance A.

    IV. Rh factor.

    A. I only

    B. II only

    C. II and III only

    D. II and IV only

14. The passage implies that the practice of transfusing blood from one patient to another began:

    F. prior to the twentieth century.

    G. after the work of Landsteiner.

    H. when electrophoresis became widely available.

    J. around the middle of the twentieth century.

15. It can be inferred from the passage that blood typing is useful to forensic scientists only in cases where:

    A. the crime victim's blood is readily accessible.

    B. the blood type of every potential suspect is previously known.

    C. blood from the perpetrator is found at the crime scene.

    D. a fresh sample of blood from the suspect is available.

16. At the time this passage was written, blood-typing as a crime-detection tool, by comparison with fingerprinting, was:

    F. less costly.

    G. more precise.

    H. less effective.

    J. more widely used.

17. It can be inferred from the passage that electrophoresis resembles fingerprinting in that both:

    A. provide a form of negative identification in crime detection.

    B. may be used to help identify those who were present at the time of a crime.

    C. were developed by scientists at around the same time.

    D. must be employed almost immediately after a crime to be effective.

18. The passage implies that electrophoresis may help scientists determine:

    F. whether or not a sample of blood could have come from a particular person.

    G. the age and condition of a dried specimen of blood or other body fluid.

    H. the means by which the victim of a violent crime was probably attacked.

    J. the age, gender, and ethnic background of an unknown criminal suspect.

19. According to the passage, Wrexall's refinement of electrophoresis led to:

    A. more accurate test results.

    B. easier availability of fluid samples.

    C. wider applicability of the tests.

    D. more rapid testing.

20. According to the passage, all of the following may reduce the usefulness of a fluid sample for crime detection EXCEPT:

    F. the passage of time.

    G. discoloration or staining.

    H. exposure to heat.

    J. exposure to contaminants.

ANSWER KEYS AND EXPLANATIONS

Exercise 1

1. B	5. B	9. A	13. B	17. A
2. F	6. H	10. H	14. F	18. H
3. D	7. A	11. D	15. B	19. B
4. G	8. G	12. F	16. J	20. H

1. **B.** The first sentence of the passage announces this topic, and the whole passage sticks closely to it.

2. **F.** The last three paragraphs of the passage discuss the influence of the impressionists on the choices of subject matter made by later artists; and, we are told, at the start of the last paragraph, "In this regard as in so many others, the impressionists were true precursors of twentieth-century painting."

3. **D.** The second paragraph of the passage expresses this idea: see the third sentence in particular ("The Impressionists, on the other hand, viewed light, not matter, as the ultimate visual reality").

4. **G.** The third and fourth paragraphs make this point clear, especially the first sentence of the fourth paragraph, which refers to "light . . . reflected with varying intensity to the eye."

5. **B.** The first sentence of the third paragraph states this point explicitly.

6. **H.** This scene is most similar to the typical impressionist scenes listed in the seventh paragraph. Choices F and J sound like typical subjects of the pre-impressionists (see paragraph six), and the Campbell's soup can, of course, is associated with Andy Warhol, six decades after the impressionists (paragraph eight).

7. **A.** This summarizes the fifth paragraph, which explains how the impressionists excluded all ideas and most emotions from their art. If virtually all human feelings and thoughts are eliminated, the result is an extreme objectivity.

8. **G.** This answer seems to best fit the list of typical impressionist subjects given in the fourth sentence of paragraph six.

9. **A.** Helen of Troy, a heroine of Greek legend, would epitomize the kind of subject European painters in the eighteenth and early nineteenth centuries might have favored (according to paragraph six).

10. **H.** The fifth paragraph is the key. It tells us that the impressionists were not interested in the "meaning" of the things they painted—only in the pattern of light they created. Hence, the nature of the objects depicted is irrelevant.

11. **D.** Refer back to the sentence in which the word "hope" appears. It says that Pace wanted to "correlate" something in the environment with the incidence of cancer, which is the same idea paraphrased in choice D.

12. **F.** Since the workers were all exposed to asbestos on the job, it seems clear that their cancers were an example of an occupational cluster.

13. **B.** The story told in the third paragraph involves a "low background rate" because the number of people in the general population who suffer from this kind of cancer is very small; it is a "fairly specific" cluster (according to the definition given in the second paragraph) because of the notable characteristic shared by all the victims—all had taken DES while pregnant.

14. **F.** Paragraph four, from which this observation is taken, is devoted to describing the difficulties experts have in gathering and interpreting information about cancer clusters with suspected environmental causes.

15. **B.** We're told that health officials "discount" local suspicions because of the imprecision with which community members gather data. In other words, the officials are dubious about these suspicions.

16. **J.** As the sentence says, "citizens tend to include cases that were diagnosed before the afflicted individuals moved into the neighborhood."

17. **A.** Read the sentence *after* the one in which the word "latency" is used; it explains exactly what is meant by this concept.

18. **H.** The "gerrymandering" described in the passage involves community activists drawing boundaries to fit their preconceived ideas or wishes, just as a politician does when he draws an election district boundary to produce a particular electoral result.

19. **B.** The sentence in which the word "caveats" appears refers back to the previous paragraph, which describes the doubts the experts have about the work amateurs do in studying cancer clusters.

20. **H.** This restates the idea found in the very last sentence of the passage.

Exercise 2

1. A	5. A	9. B	13. B	17. A
2. G	6. F	10. F	14. G	18. J
3. C	7. C	11. C	15. D	19. D
4. F	8. J	12. F	16. H	20. J

1. **A.** The fourteenth and eighteenth paragraphs make this point: "It unsettles her; it's very likely to upset her," and "Now, don't excite her after her supper."

2. **G.** Paragraph 12 provides good evidence for both points. Bertha "does not dare to" criticize Nanny's handling of the baby, even indirectly; and we're told that she feels "like the poor little girl in front of the rich little girl with the doll" when she sees Nanny with Little B. Later, she expresses unhappiness over the fact that her baby is "in another woman's arms." Clearly, Bertha is both a little jealous of Nanny and a little intimidated by her.

3. **C.** Reread the third paragraph, which contains the metaphor being asked about. Bertha is frustrated over keeping her body "shut up in a case like a rare, rare fiddle" because she is eager to find some way of expressing the feeling of "bliss" she is experiencing.

4. **F.** The key sentence is "How idiotic civilization is!" which makes it clear that Bertha restrains her emotions out of concern about the judgment "civilization" (i.e., society) would pass upon her if she expressed them openly.

5. **A.** Bertha is clearly well-to-do (since she employs a nanny and, apparently, another servant—Mary, from paragraph four). Thus, the literal answer B cannot be correct. The rest of the scene between Bertha, Nanny, and Little B makes it clear that Bertha longs for a closer connection to her own child, and that she and Nanny are subtly competing to "own" the baby.

6. **F.** The exclamation "How absurd it was" is made in response to Nanny's expression of concern that Little B will be "unsettled" or "upset" by Bertha.

7. **C.** The sentence states that Nanny's pursed lips indicate that Bertha "had come into the nursery at another wrong moment." (Note the word "another," which suggests that she is forever "intruding" into the nursery.) Clearly Bertha is somehow unwelcome in her own child's room.

8. **J.** Nanny is "triumphant" in the final sentence because she is able to send Bertha away (to answer the telephone) and can reclaim "*her* Little B." As we've already seen, much of the passage deals with the subtle competition between these two women for the attention and love of the baby.

9. **B.** The first two paragraphs of the passage describe this emotion rather fully. Both make it clear that the "bliss" Bertha feels is caused by no specific event but rather is something that happens "suddenly," "turning the corner of your own street"—with no apparent explanation.

10. **F.** The passage describes Bertha as overwhelmed by her own feelings, struggling to control her expression of her emotions, unable to refrain from "crying" out her wishes (though somewhat afraid to do so). The words "emotional and impulsive" seem appropriate to summarize Bertha's personality—at least, on the day when this passage takes place.

11. **C.** The first sentence of the second passage neatly summarizes its main theme. Note how virtually all of the ideas and details in the passage relate to the influence of the rivers on early Mesopotamian civilization.

12. **F.** See the next-to-last sentence of the first paragraph, which says that people moved to the riverbanks as "the once-hospitable grasslands" turned into deserts.

13. **B.** The third paragraph of the passage describes how the need for water-management systems encouraged cooperation among large groups of Mesopotamian villagers. Statement I is not supported by the passage, and Statement III is contradicted by the last sentence of the first paragraph.

14. **G.** *Nascent* means "being born." It is generally used figuratively, as it is here, to mean "newly emerging" or "taking shape."

15. **D.** See the first sentence of the fifth paragraph.

16. **H.** See the fifth paragraph, which lists the items that the Mesopotamians imported. Clay tablets, we're told there, were not imported goods; rather, they were made out of "mud from the river banks," which of course was available locally.

17. **A.** In the first paragraph, we're told that the development of great civilizations in the Middle East began when the river valleys attracted "settlers armed with the newly developed techniques of agriculture."

18. **J.** This paragraph describes the archeological findings from the city of Uruk, from which "we derive our knowledge of this period" (i.e., the high point of Mesopotamian culture).

19. **D.** The last sentence of the seventh paragraph summarizes the point: "a complex and advanced civilization was in place by the time these artifacts were created." The great size of the Limestone Temple would support this idea because it suggests that the Mesopotamians were able to bring together large amounts of money, raw materials, talent, and power in order to complete so enormous a project.

20. **J.** The last paragraph, where India and China are mentioned, is used to make the point that life along river valleys has played a crucial role in the development of civilization in many parts of the world.

Exercise 3

1. C	5. B	9. C	13. C	17. B
2. F	6. J	10. G	14. F	18. F
3. B	7. B	11. C	15. C	19. D
4. J	8. F	12. F	16. H	20. B

1. **C.** The Englishwoman described in the anecdote feels that she has no need to consult the dictionary because she is as much of an authority on the proper use of language as any reference book. The author seems to agree with her. Hence, answer C.

2. **F.** The first paragraph explains the mistaken attitude that most Americans have toward the "authority" of the dictionary, and the rest of the passage is devoted to explaining why it is wrong by showing the reader what the true function of the dictionary writer is.

3. **B.** As the example (showing how the poet Keats used the word "pail" in a sentence) illustrates, the *context* collected by the dictionary editors is simply the sentence in which the word appears.

4. **J.** Notice the second sentence of the third paragraph, in which the author mentions that his purpose is to explain what first-hand dictionary research is like. He then alludes to the *Oxford English Dictionary* as an example of a project for which such research was undertaken.

5. **B.** The author draws a contrast between "the distant past" and "the immediate past." Thus, he is using the word *immediate* to mean the opposite of *distant*—that is, "recent."

6. **J.** According to the author, dictionary editors strive to collect "every unusual or peculiar occurrence of a common word." The context makes it clear that *peculiar* is being used here to mean "distinctive" or "special."

7. **B.** As you can see by rereading the last sentence of the sixth paragraph, the new meaning of "broadcast" came about as a result of the invention and popularity of radio. Therefore, the story illustrates how new technology may create the need for a new word meaning. (The example of the word "hood" in the very next paragraph illustrates the same point.)

8. **F.** As the paragraph states, "new situations, new experiences . . . are always compelling us to give new uses to old words." Therefore, a dictionary writer cannot predict how language will change, and shouldn't be expected to do so.

9. **C.** The author quotes several sentences from an imaginary overheard conversation which illustrate the meaning of the word "oboe." The anecdote shows how one might learn such a word by listening to a similar conversation. Although the author says that we learn words in this way "beginning at infancy," this particular example doesn't relate to infancy, since babies don't normally talk about oboes; thus, answer A is wrong.

10. **G.** The italicized sentence in the sixth paragraph states this very point. The other three answer choices are all stated in the first two paragraphs as elements of the mistaken attitude the author attributes to most Americans.

11. **C.** The passage deals with the development and use of blood-typing as a crime-fighting tool; other aspects of blood-typing, such as its role in medical treatment, are mentioned only as side issues.

12. **F.** A person of blood type AB has blood cells with both substance A and substance B on their surface. This, types A, B, and O would all react badly to AB blood, since they all contain some antibodies that would be triggered by it. Only type AB can safely receive an AB blood transfusion.

13. **C.** Cells of blood type B– (B negative) would contain substance B and antibodies against substance A; they would not contain Rh factor (otherwise, they would be designated B+, as stated in paragraph six).

14. **F.** The parenthetical sentence in the fourth paragraph says that Landsteiner's investigation into blood types was triggered by the "failure of many blood transfusions." If this is so, then blood transfusion must have been a well-known practice prior to 1901, when Landsteiner made his major discovery.

15. **C.** Since the object of the forensic scientist is to discover the perpetrator of a crime, blood-typing can only be useful when a sample of blood from the (presumed) criminal is found at the crime scene.

16. **H.** The last sentence of the first paragraph makes it clear that, at the time the passage was written, fingerprinting was more useful in crime detection than blood-typing.

17. **B.** Both fingerprinting and electrophoresis can be used as a means of identifying the person who produced a given sample of blood, from which their presence at a crime scene may be inferred. Choice A is wrong because only fingerprinting is referred to in the passage as a "negative" form of identification (see the sixth paragraph of the passage).

18. **F.** The ninth paragraph of the passage suggests this idea. The fact that electrophoresis can identify thousands of blood subgroups suggests that this method is capable of narrowing down the identity of a blood "donor" quite specifically.

19. **D.** The last paragraph explains that Wrexall showed how "simultaneous analyses" could produce useful results within 24 hours—in other words, "more rapid testing."

20. **B.** All of the answer choices except choice B are explicitly mentioned somewhere in the passage.

ARE YOU READY TO MOVE ON?

How well do you understand the contents and format of the ACT Assessment Reading Test? How well have you incorporated your new vocabulary into your test-taking behavior?

After you've corrected each exercise, find the number below. This will give you an idea of whether you still need improvement.

Score Key for Each Practice Exercise

Number	Correct Score	Suggested Action
0–5	Poor	Study Chapters 6 and 10 again. See "Additional Resources for Review," below.
6–8	Below average	Study problem areas in Chapters 6 and 10 again. See "Additional Resources for Review," below if you have time.
9–12	Average	Skim problem areas in Chapters 6 and 10 if you have time.
13–15	Above average	You may move on to a new subject.
16–20	Excellent	You're ready for the ACT Assessment Reading Test.

ADDITIONAL RESOURCES FOR REVIEW

After reviewing this chapter and trying to apply your knowledge on additional practice exercises and sample tests, you might still want help in Reading. "Real" reading—of newspapers, magazines, journals, and books— is always helpful. If you would like specific titles that deal with vocabulary building and reading techniques, take a look at one or more of the following:

Word Smart by Adam Robinson *et. al.* Princeton Review, 1993.

Kaplan Word Power by Meg F. Schneider. Simon & Schuster, 1997.

The two previously listed books help increase your vocabulary knowledge, with an emphasis on words often found on the ACT Assessment and other standardized tests.

Merriam Webster's Vocabulary Builder by Mary Wood Cornog. Merriam Webster, 1994.

1000 Most Important Words by Norman Schur. Ballantine, 1982.

These two books are small, "mass-market" sized paperbacks which focus on vocabulary building. Neither is specifically focused on the ACT Assessment exam; however, both are interesting and well written and include many words that are highly appropriate for ACT Assessment preparation.

Read Better, Remember More by Elizabeth Chesla. Learning Express, 1997.

Improving Reading Comprehension and Speed by Marcia J. Coman and Kathy L. Heavers. NTC, 1997.

These last two books help you improve your reading skills. Neither is focused specifically on the ACT Assessment, but the techniques they teach can easily be applied to the exam.

Science Reasoning Review: Understanding Data

The purpose of the ACT Assessment Science Reasoning Test is to "measure the interpretation, analysis, evaluation, reasoning, and problem-solving skills associated with science." What it comes down to is a test of your ability to think like a scientist; it's a test of skills rather than of facts.

This review focuses on the three scientific skills measured on the ACT Assessment Science Reasoning exam: interpreting the numbers on a graph, chart, or table; trying to figure out what the results of an experiment do and don't prove; and comparing different theories of some natural phenomenon. These three skills are tested by the three different reading passages: Data Representation, Research Summaries, and Conflicting Viewpoints. The review provides you with the key science-thinking strategies needed to do well on each. Immediately after the review are three more practice exercises. A final section brings you additional resources for review in case you need extra help.

HOW TO READ TABLES, GRAPHS, AND CHARTS

When a scientist shares data, he or she faces the challenge of how to present the information in the best way. The presentation must describe the phenomenon being observed in unambiguous, concrete terms, usually involving numbers: *How many? How large? How hot? How fast? How bright?* and so on. In a well-designed, properly performed experiment, the data cannot be disputed even when conclusions drawn from the data are. The presentation of data must also make it possible for experiments to be duplicated exactly (an important criterion for the acceptance of any new discovery or theory) and for variations or discrepancies to be quantified.

There are many ways to present data. One is to simply describe the separate points of information within a paragraph in a list-like fashion. However, a long list of numbers within a block of text is difficult to grasp; surrounded by words, the numbers lose their relationships to each other, making patterns and trends nearly impossible to observe. Also, if a specific number is sought, it cannot be easily found except through reading the entire text.

A much better way of presenting numerical data is through a pictorial representation that's largely non-verbal—the use of tables, graphs, and charts.

AN IN-DEPTH REVIEW OF TABLES

Suppose you wanted to present the mean distances of the solar system's nine planets from the sun, as the distances relate to each planet's orbital period (the time it takes for a planet to orbit the Sun) and its orbital speed. You could begin a rather lengthy paragraph saying that Mercury is 36,000,000 miles from the sun, having an orbital period of 88 days, and an orbital speed of 29.75 miles per second. Venus is next closest, being 67,000,000 miles from the sun and having an orbital period of 225 days and an orbital speed of 21.76 miles per second. Earth is the third planet from the sun, a distance away of 93,000,000 miles, with an orbital period of 1 year and an orbital speed of 18.51 miles per second. Mars is next, being 141,000,000 miles from the sun, with an orbital period of 1 year and 323 days, and an orbital speed of 14.99 miles per second . . . and so on. Even though in this instance the relationships here are fairly obvious, the information is not immediately apparent nor readily accessible.

On the other hand, you could put all of the same information into a table. A table puts forth the data in a clear, easy-to-follow fashion, as well as makes the relationships between the variables very clear. See the following table.

Mean Distance from the Sun, Orbital Period, and Orbital Speed for the Nine Planets in Earth's Solar System

Planet	Mean Distance from the Sun (miles)	Orbital Period	Orbital Speed (miles per second)
Mercury	36,000,000	88 days	29.75
Venus	67,000,000	225 days	21.76
Earth	93,000,000	1 year	18.51
Mars	141,000,000	1 yr, 323 days	14.99
Jupiter	480,000,000	12 years	8.12
Saturn	900,000,000	29.5 years	5.99
Uranus	1,800,000,000	84 years	4.23
Neptune	2,800,000,000	164 years	3.38
Pluto	3,600,000,000	247.7 years	2.95

The information as presented in the table is in a much more useful format than mere description. Rather than being forced to read through a paragraph to find one particular set of data—say, for Saturn—we can now find the values in which we are interested with a glance. We find the name Saturn in the left-most column and simply follow the row of information to find its distance from the sun (900,000,000 miles), its orbital period (29.5 years), and its orbital speed (5.99 miles per second). More importantly, information in a table reveals patterns, trends, and relationships between the different variables.

VARIABLES AND TRENDS

How do variables relate to each other? When one variable increases and the other increases, or when one variable decreases and the other decreases, we say that the relationship between the two variables is a *direct relationship*. When one variable increases and the other decreases, we say that the relationship between the two variables is an *inverse relationship*.

The table makes it fairly easy to see three relationships among the variables in the example. First, we can see that as a planet's mean distance from the Sun increases, its orbital period also *increases*. Second, we can see that as a planet's mean distance from the Sun increases, its orbital speed *decreases*. Finally, we can see that as the orbital speed decreases, the orbital period *increases*. So the table shows one direct relationship (mean distance and orbital period) and two inverse relationships (mean distance and orbital speed; as well as orbital period and orbital speed).

If the increase or decrease in one variable is proportional to the increase or decrease in another variable, the relationship is called a *proportional relationship*. This means that the ratio between two variables is constant. For example, if for every 50,000-mile increase from the sun, the orbital period increased 100 days, we could call this a proportional relationship. The ratio between the two variables is always the same.

AN IN-DEPTH REVIEW OF GRAPHS

Any series of numbers can be represented by a line. This is the basis of all graphs. When variables such as the corresponding sets of numbers from a table are plotted on a line, the trends and relationships become even more apparent than when those same numbers are in that table. See the following figure, which plots just the relationship between the distance from the sun and orbital speed.

NOTE
A variable is anything in an experiment that changes. The *independent variable* is the experimental condition that is deliberately changed or varied to test its effect on something else. In this example, the independent variable is the distance from the sun: How does distance from the sun affect orbital period and orbital speed? Orbital period and orbital speed are called the *dependent variables*; their "result" depends on the independent variable.

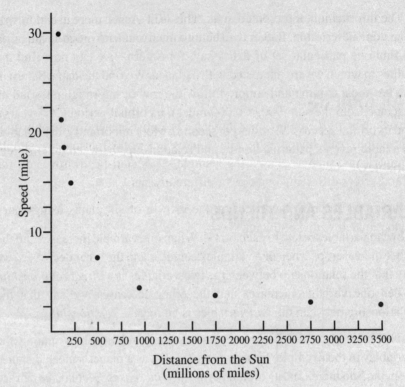

Fig. 11.1.

The relationship shown in this figure is an inverse relationship: as distance increases, speed decreases. However, it is not a *proportional relationship*. The relationship or ratio between the two variables changes. If the ratio were constant, we could connect the points on the graph and form a straight line. However, because in reality the line would be curved if we connected the points, the relationship is not proportional. The rate of decrease in orbital speed diminishes with distance from the Sun. In other words, the farther away from the Sun a planet is, the less its orbital speed is decreased from that of its neighbor nearer the Sun. Hence, the gradual "flattening out" of the curve as it moves toward the right side of the graph.

A common format of ACT Assessment questions is to give you a graph and to ask for results based on information not given on the graph. The answer can be easily calculated because, if a relationship between variables is proportional, you can extend the straight line indefinitely until the information "appears."

Practically speaking, you can physically extend the line in the test booklet only so far. Fortunately, however, there's a simple equation for calculating a straight line. This will enable you to predict what the dependent variable *(y)* will be, when the independent variable *(x)* is given. The formula is $y = mx + b$; x and y are the variables, m is the slope (the ratio or the simple linear relationship between the variables), and b is the y intercept (the value of y when the value of x is zero). The y intercept is often zero itself. (Look over the topic "Equations of Lines" in your Math Review if this is not familiar from coordinate geometry.)

Use this formula to predict results. The ACT Assessment question will give you one variable, which you put into the formula to produce the other variable.

BAR GRAPHS

There are many different types of graphs. Scientists generally use only two: bar graphs and line graphs. Bar graphs are good for making simple comparisons, such as comparing a single set of statistics (birth rates, for example) for different countries or different years.

Figure 11.2 shows the effect on the growth of six plants using water contaminated with a pollutant.

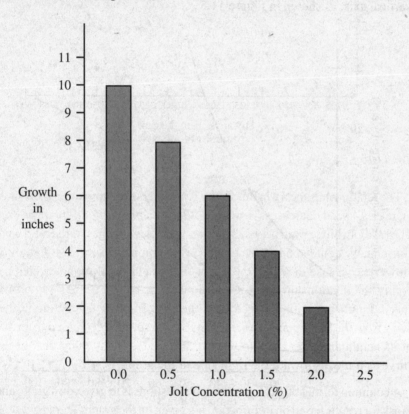

Fig. 11.2.

In Figure 11.2, each bar represents the growth of a different plant fed with a different concentration of a pollutant in water. The height of each bar represents the amount each plant grew.

This type of graph makes the differences in growth caused by varying the concentration of pollutant very clear. However, if the data were more complex, this graph would be more difficult to look at and understand. For example, if a hundred different pollutants were tested, the results would be too complex for a bar graph and still have recognizable trends.

NOTE
The formula for a straight line ($y = mx + b$) calculates y when x, the independent variable, is given. Sometimes, however, an ACT Assessment question might give you y, the dependent variable, and ask you to calculate x. *Be careful to note which variable you've been given.* If you're given y, you must rearrange the formula (beginning $x =$) for the answer to be in terms of x.

LINE GRAPHS

By contrast, line graphs can be both precise and intricate, even when multiple variables are measured. For this reason, line graphs are the kind of graph most often used by scientists.

For example, if a chemist was studying the effect of temperature on the solubility of several substances, the independent variable would be temperature, and the dependent variable would be solubility. With all other factors constant (such as the volume of the solvent, the pressure, etc.), any changes in the solubility of each substance could clearly and unambiguously be attributed to temperature. To document the experiment, a graph of the data would have temperature along the horizontal axis and the solubility on the vertical axis, as shown in Figure 11.3.

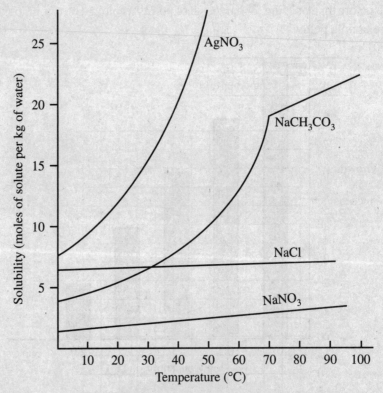

Fig. 11.3.

By noting the independent and dependent variables in this graph, we can tell that the question the graph is designed to answer is, "How does temperature affect the solubility of these four different substances?" After you know this, the specific details provided by the data—the answers to the ACT Assessment questions, in effect—are easy to look up if you need them.

Notice that the above figure has more than one line. Each line shows the solubility of a different solute, with the name of the solute next to the line. The lines could also have been drawn using different colors or using different styles (dots, dashes, solid, wavy) to make the contrast between substances clearer. In that case, the grapher could have identified each line separately in a legend or key (such is used in the next example). Because the independent and dependent variables are the same for each solute—temperature and solubility—they can be placed on the same axes. Presenting all the lines on the same graph allows comparisons between substances to be made easily.

Whether bar or line, all properly-designed graphs have axes clearly labeled with the names of the variables being studied and the units of measurement used (degrees, centimeters, percent, and so on). The divisions along the axes should be clearly numbered. All graphs should also have a title. Many graphs have a legend or key providing additional information about the graph or the data. The key is usually found in one corner of the graph or outside the limits of the graph altogether. A key is most often used when more than one line (or bar, or set of points) is plotted on one graph. See the example below.

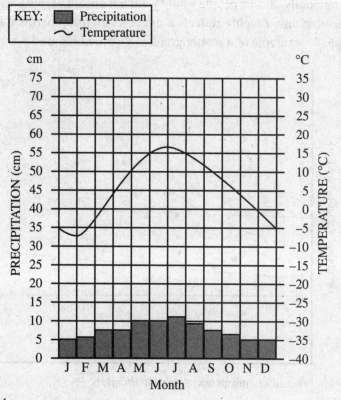

Fig. 11.4.

TIP

The structural features of a graph—the labels on the axes, the units of measurement, and any information in the key—are more important than the specific data presented. If you understand the structure of the graph, you'll understand the kind of information it presents and the nature of the questions that the graph is designed to answer.

Because it would be otherwise impossible for the viewer to know what is meant by the data in such a case, different sets of data are distinguished from each other by using different colors or patterns for each line, bar, or set of points. The key explains to the viewer what each of the colors or patterns represents. Always be sure to examine all of these features carefully whenever you encounter a graph.

NOTE

Obviously, a best-fit line will show the basic pattern or trend, but it *cannot* be used to determine any actual, specific values. Think of it as a highly simplified or rough depiction of a relationship that, in the real world, is complicated and variable.

SCATTER GRAPHS

As we've seen, a line graph is created by plotting data points on graph paper (or by entering these points into a computer which creates the graph automatically). These points are then connected to create a line. If these points are not connected, the graph is called a *scatter graph*. This style of graph is often used when the points cannot be connected into a smooth line, perhaps because the relationship between the independent and dependent variables is complex or influenced by other, secondary factors.

For example, we know that, in a general way, a person's height and weight tend to vary together: NBA basketball players, who are usually very tall, usually weigh a lot as well, while professional jockeys are usually both short and light. But other factors (like diet) play a role in determining height and weight, and there are certainly exceptions to the general relationship: there are some people who are quite tall but very thin and some people who are short and fat. Thus, a graph depicting the height and weight data sets for twenty randomly-chosen people would yield not a neat line, but a scattering of points that only roughly reflects a direct relationship between the two variables. An example of a scatter graph is shown in Figure 11.5.

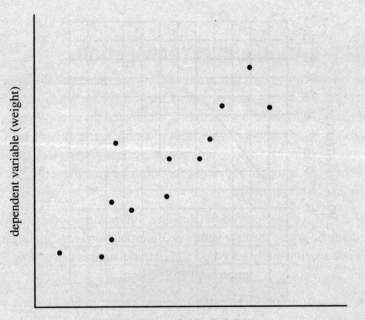

Fig. 11.5.

It is sometimes difficult to interpret trends from a scatter graph. To help, a "best-fit" line can be drawn in (see Figure 11.6). The best-fit line is designed to lie as close as possible to each of the data points. Some points might lie right on the line, others might lie on either side of it, but in general all the points should come close to it.

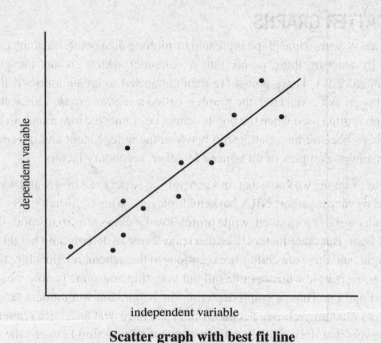

Scatter graph with best fit line

Fig. 11.6.

INTERPOLATION AND EXTRAPOLATION

We mentioned previously that certain ACT Assessment questions might ask you to predict results given one of the variables. When data form a continuous line (that is, a smooth line, either straight or curved), it can be represented by an equation. When this is the case, you can "work backward" by using the equation to determine specific values. Thus, you can use such a line (or its equation) to get values for points beyond those that have been determined experimentally.

The name for this procedure is either *interpolation* or *extrapolation*, depending on where the new values lie. Interpolation is calculating a value *between* experimentally tested points. Extrapolation is calculating a value *beyond* experimentally tested points.

For example, from the bar graph we saw earlier in Figure 11.2, we can assume that if the concentration of pollutant had been 0.25% for a seventh plant, this plant would have grown nine inches. Although this concentration wasn't tested, the graph and its equation can be used to infer this result. And because the results of this seventh plant would fall between the results of the 0.0% concentration and the 0.5% concentration actually tested, calculating for this seventh plant is interpolation.

Another example of interpolation is shown in Figure 11.7. The known data points—that is, those points determined experimentally—lie on the curved line. Interpolation, again, is calculating a result that lies between points actually tested.

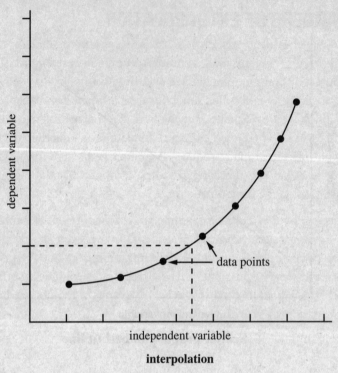

interpolation

Fig. 11.7.

Similarly, the lines on graphs can be extended *beyond* the limits of the experimentally tested values. Extending the line in this way is called extrapolation (see Figure 11.8). This is part of the power of graphs.

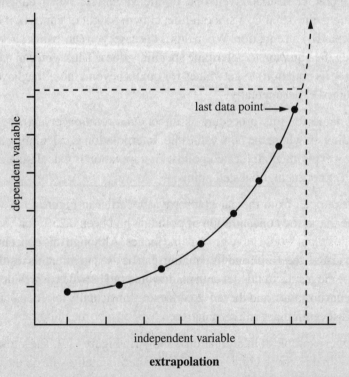

extrapolation

Fig 11.8.

THE DANGERS OF EXTRAPOLATION

It's not always valid to make predictions by simply extending a trend line into infinity. Doing this makes the sometimes faulty assumption that the relationship will continue unchanged indefinitely. If the line shows the results of a carefully controlled laboratory experiment, for example, then the assumption is safer to make. But an observation of natural phenomenon might not always be predicted as easily. Sometimes a quantitative change somewhere "off the graph" produces a qualitative change, bringing new factors to bear that can dramatically alter an observed relationship at a particular point on the trend line.

Population growth is a classic example of the limitations of extrapolation. As long as the resources of food, water, and living space are plentiful, a population (whether human, animal, or plant) might continue to grow over time in accordance with predictable ratios, based on the number of offspring generated by each individual. Figure 11.9 graphs a theoretical line for projected population growth.

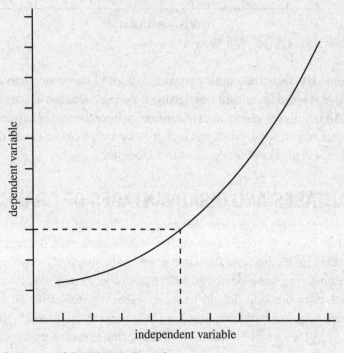

Fig. 11.9. Protected Population Growth

But because this isn't a carefully controlled lab experiment, the same line in reality can't be extended forever. At some point, resources will begin to be scarce; food, water, and even clean air might run out. Famine and disease will take their toll. Among humans, there will also be the important, though somewhat unpredictable, results of warfare and artificial contraception— birth control. In reality, the trend line could eventually take a dramatic turn, as shown in Figure 11.10 below.

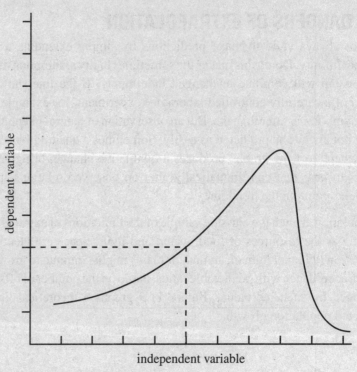

Fig. 11.10. Actual Population Growth

So scientists must be cautious when extrapolating trend lines, which means that *you* should be cautious when answering questions about extrapolation. An intelligent assessment of limiting factors that could influence the trend must be part of any analysis that goes beyond what has been directly observed in nature or demonstrated in a laboratory.

ADVANTAGES AND DISADVANTAGES OF GRAPHS

Graphs share with tables the advantage of making data points easily accessible. As we've seen, values can be found on one axis. By then tracing from the axis to the line and from this point on the line to the other axis, we can determine the corresponding value on the other axis. The superiority of the graph over the table lies in its clear visual representation of a trend, tendency, or underlying relationship. When there is no such trend or relationship, then a table of values is probably more useful and appropriate than a graph.

As an example, perhaps someone studied the relationship between height and ACT Assessment scores. Because there's no tendency for taller (or shorter) people to score higher (or lower) on the ACT Assessment, there's no true trend line here—just a bunch of random points which, when connected, produce no coherent shape. The resulting graph might look something like the one shown in Figure 11.11, with the experimental results literally "all over the map." In other words, there's no clear relationship between the independent and dependent variables. This data would perhaps be more meaningfully presented in table form.

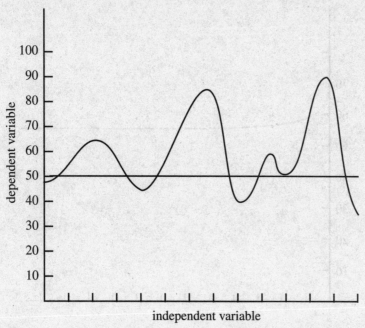

Fig. 11.11.

Although graphs and tables each have their place in the representation of data, graphs have some basic advantages. Lines and patterns are easier to remember than numbers and are capable of catching the eye and stimulating the imagination. Many people do not respond to numbers but have an immediate response to pictures.

Also, graphs can condense a large amount of information into a small space. If the experiment of the plants watered with a pollutant had been conducted using hundreds of different concentrations and the results listed in a table, the table containing all those values would have to be hundreds of lines long. But all the concentrations could be represented on a single line graph no larger than any of those we've already seen.

Now, how about the disadvantages of presenting information in graphs? A major disadvantage of graphs is that they can be less accurate than the numbers they represent. One reason is that values are sometimes rounded, either to make plotting easier or (a little less honestly) to better fit the pattern that the scientist has found—or hoped to find. The condensation of data, just described as an advantage, can also lead to imprecision. When a single graph is used to illustrate hundreds of thousands of individual pieces of data, any one case, or handful of cases, will be hard to pick out.

Graphs are also subject to subtle manipulation. One way of doing this is by adjusting the scale of values or the *baseline* of the graph. The baseline is the line from which any increase or decrease in a variable is measured. To see this manipulation in action, look at the two graphs shown in Figures 11.12 and 11.13. The baseline forms, literally, the "bottom line" of the graph and usually has a value of zero, as in the top graph in the figure. However, sometimes the baseline is set at a different value, as shown in the bottom graph.

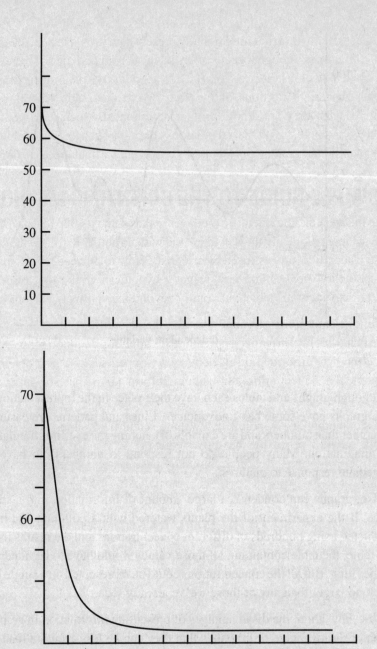

Fig.11.12 & Fig.11.13.

In the second graph, the baseline has been shifted up to emphasize the decline in the value of the dependent variable. The drop from 70 to around 52, which is noticeable but modest in the first graph, appears dramatic in the second graph. Such manipulation can be completely innocent, intending to make the data easier to read, for example, or to highlight crucial variations. However, an adjustment like this can also emphasize certain features of the data, sometimes in a misleading manner. If the variable in these graphs represented, for example, the quantity of air pollutants being produced by a certain factory, the company managing the factory would probably prefer having the second graph published in the local newspaper, because it makes the decline in emissions appear to be so much greater.

Honest scientists do not intentionally present data in a false or misleading way. Sometimes, though, because they have such a good idea of the effect they hope to demonstrate even before they examine the data, scientists will emphasize certain portions of the data or certain trends without fully realizing what they are doing. Similarly, journalists, social and political activists, and others with biased opinions also have been known to deliberately manipulate graphic presentations to force a particular conclusion.

A SIMPLE GUIDE TO THE SCIENTIFIC METHOD

Mere mention of "the scientific method" makes some people feel as if they have the most illogical minds in the world with no ability to follow the step-by-step analytical process used by scientists. How to proceed from hypothesis to theory (never mind how to get a hypothesis in the first place) is mysterious, uncomfortable, and totally beyond the "normal" person.

Well, scientists are "normal" too, and the scientific method is nothing more than a highly formalized procedure for applying common sense. At its heart, the scientific method itself is very simple: identify a problem or phenomenon, collect information about it, form a hypothesis about it, and test the hypothesis.

Understanding a few points that go into scientific thinking is necessary before moving on to the next two type of ACT Assessment Science Reasoning questions, Research Summary passages and Conflicting Viewpoints passages.

INDUCTIVE AND DEDUCTIVE REASONING

Scientists employ two types of logic to explain the natural and physical world, known as inductive and deductive reasoning.

Inductive reasoning moves from the specific to the general. Scientists do this when they use data from experiments or observations as the basis for a more general theory. Gregor Mendel (1822–84) developed his theory of genetics based on his observations on many generations of pea plants. Mendel collected extensive data regarding the characteristics of over 28,000 of these plants and the ways in which those characteristics were transmitted from one generation to the next, with particular traits emerging as dominant and others receding in importance over time.

Needing a way to explain what he saw, Mendel was able to find certain statistical relationships among the data he collected, from which he determined that independent units of heredity, now called genes, formed the basis by which traits were continually recombined from one generation to the next. Mendel's mental leap from specific observation to a general theory that explained those observations was a classic example of inductive reasoning.

Deductive reasoning, on the other hand, involves applying general laws to specific cases. Scientists do this when they use existing theories to explain experimental results or observations. Suppose a scientist observed that a particular characteristic in humans—for example, the hereditary condition known as sickle-cell anemia—was transmitted from one generation to the next following the same statistical relationships that Mendel observed in his pea plants. This scientist could use deduction to determine that Mendel's Laws of Heredity apply to the inheritance of the sickle-cell trait, and on this basis make specific predictions about who is or is not likely to develop the disease.

Induction and deduction, in combination, form the underpinnings of the scientific method. As you'll see, both processes are involved in the development of a scientific theory.

STARTING WITH A HYPOTHESIS

The scientific method, in simple terms, involves first forming a hypothesis and then testing that hypothesis through observation, experimentation, and/or prediction.

A hypothesis is a tentative explanation for some natural phenomenon, one which has not been tested or verified in any way. Think of a hypothesis as an educated guess about why something happens or about the nature of the relationship between two or more variables. Nearly all scientific research starts with a hypothesis.

On reflection, you might think it odd to start with a proposed explanation. Why not simply gather data at random first, and wait until later to develop a hypothesis? Forming a hypothesis first sets out a clear direction and goal for the subsequent observations and experiments. It also forces the scientist to think at length about what factors are likely to be influential and what scientific elements are involved.

Starting with a poor hypothesis usually leads to time-wasting, dead-end experiments. A good hypothesis must pass certain tests. Generally, it must fit into the totality of the existing scientific framework. A hypothesis that runs contrary to the current body of scientific thinking is unlikely to gain favor in the scientific community, unlikely even to be examined, debated, or tested. This is because the theorems and laws in all the branches of science are highly interdependent. If a new hypothesis is based on the assumption that some major element in the dominant world view of science is wrong, it's likely that many other elements must be assumed to be wrong as well. Most scientists would consider this both unlikely and too difficult to be worth testing.

Because much of what we believe today about the natural world has been demonstrated over time by extensive experimentation and a generally consistent body of observations, scientists are reluctant to accept a hypothesis that would require either a drastic rethinking of basic scientific principles or a wholesale junking of previously observed results. This helps to explain, for example, why few serious scientists are interested in experiments to test the existence of psychic phenomena (ESP, telekinesis, clairvoyance, and so forth). There is so much evidence, experience, and theory suggesting the physical impossibility of these phenomena that it seems to be a waste of precious limited resources to invest time and effort in studying them.

Nonetheless, it is true that hypotheses which dramatically diverge from the common body of knowledge will occasionally be proven true through experimentation or observation. Darwin's Theory of Evolution and Einstein's Theory of Relativity are two examples. Both were revolutionary in that they forced scientists to rethink certain basic assumptions they had previously taken for granted—the immutability of species in the case of Darwin, and traditional ideas about the nature of gravity, matter, and energy in the case of Einstein. Such theories are rare, but they are integral to scientific advancement.

Another requirement for a good hypothesis is that it may not disagree with any observed phenomena. Furthermore, anything that can be deduced logically from the hypothesis also may not disagree with any observable phenomena. This test can often be used to rule out an incorrect hypothesis before any experimentation is done. Galileo (1564–1642), the Italian physicist and astronomer, used this test when attempting to form a hypothesis regarding the motion of falling bodies. He had initially hypothesized that the speed of a falling body would be proportional to the distance the body traveled; in other words, the greater the height from which an object fell, the faster it would fall. However, a logical deduction from this hypothesis was that the time required for two objects to fall different distances would be the same, which is contradicted by actual observation of falling objects. Thus Galileo was able to eliminate this as a working hypothesis.

TESTING A HYPOTHESIS

After a good hypothesis has been chosen, the next step is to test the hypothesis through experiment, observation, and/or prediction. The method(s) to be used will depend on the nature of the hypothesis. Mendel was able to perform genetic experiments using pea plants because of their short life cycle, which made it possible to study many generations of plants in just a few years. Similar experiments in human genetics are impossible, because of the length of human generations and because of ethical and moral considerations.

In some fields of science, prediction is the crucial test of a hypothesis. The Copernican model of the solar system (with the Sun at its center) was largely confirmed because of its success in predicting such phenomena as eclipses. Similarly, Einstein's General Theory of Relativity was strongly supported in 1919 when, during a solar eclipse, starlight was observed to bend in the vicinity of the Sun in a manner predicted by Einstein.

NOTE

The following quote aptly sums up the principle of "simplest is best":

"*Entities are not to be multiplied without necessity*." William of Ockham (1285–1349), English philosopher.

This principle is called Ockham's Razor, or "the law of parsimony." It means that, when choosing between several possible explanations for phenomena, it is generally best to choose the simplest one. Only if the simplest explanation fails would you resort to the more complex explanation.

The Basics of Experimental Design

Modern scientific observation and experimentation are generally very rigorous, strictly ordered, and highly accurate. To achieve this it is important that experiments be well designed, carefully executed, and precisely documented. The experimental methods and techniques must be consistent and clear. An experiment's crucial goals are objectivity and reproducibility.

Objectivity refers to the need to design an experiment so as to eliminate the effects of personal bias on the part of any experimenter or of anyone who participates in analyzing the resulting data. Bias need not be conscious; in fact, the most insidious and difficult-to-eliminate forms of bias are so subtle that the experimenter is unaware they exist. For example, even if the experimenter has no "preference" for a particular outcome to an experiment, he or she might unconsciously hope merely that the experiment will yield results that are clear and "interesting." A bias as slight as this might influence how an experimenter "reads" the results, producing slight errors in the observation or recording of data that, cumulatively, might have a major impact on the accuracy of the research.

To reduce or eliminate such bias, experiments are often designed to be "blind." In a blind experiment, the experimenter is prevented from knowing which test subjects represent the variable and which represent the control. For example, suppose an experiment is being performed to test the effect of a new drug on laboratory rats. The new drug will be placed in the food of the test group, but not in the food of the control group. If this experiment were blind then the experimenter would have no knowledge about which rat is being fed the drug until after all the data has been collected. By doing this, the experimenter will have no way of knowing what results to expect from each individual rat.

Blind experiments are especially common in research involving human subjects. Such experiments are often designed to be "double blind," meaning that neither the experimenter nor the subjects know who represents the control group. If a new drug was tested on people, the test group would receive a pill containing the drug, and the control group would receive a pill containing no active ingredients (known as a placebo), but all subjects would believe that they were receiving the new drug.

Besides the experimental design, the experimental protocol, or written procedure to be followed in conducting the experiment, must be carefully planned so as to remove any opportunity for experimental bias to affect the results. For example, decisions as to the timing of steps in the experiment, the selection of subjects, and other methodologies must not be left to the discretion of the experimenter but must be deliberately predetermined. For example, if an experimenter needed seedlings from a nursery, he or she might arbitrarily choose "a representative sampling"; in truth, however, the experimenter might consciously or unconsciously choose very healthy or very sickly plants, whichever would help prove the particular hypothesis.

Experimental protocol, written beforehand, would eliminate this flaw by instituting a random selection process: every tenth seedling would be chosen for the experiment.

The second crucial goal in experimental design is *reproducibility*. Reproducibility means that an experiment must be capable of being reproduced exactly so as to test the validity of the results. One hallmark of scientific knowledge is that, within specified parameters, it is broadly and generally applicable. Subject to specified conditions such as air pressure, pure water will boil at exactly the same temperature everywhere in the world.

Several years ago some scientists claimed to have successfully produced the phenomenon known as "cold fusion." If true, this would have been an epochal scientific discovery with enormous practical implications; fusion is a powerful energy source, and cold fusion (i.e. fusion at a temperature close to normal room temperature) would have the potential of being an incredibly cheap, virtually unlimited form of energy. The excitement quickly turned to disappointment and anger when the scientists' description of their experiments proved to be too vague to be reproducible, and attempts to duplicate their work failed to yield any noteworthy amount of energy. It was understood that reproducibility was the crucial test of the significance of these remarkable claims—and they failed.

Generally speaking, the more reproducible the experiment, the more likely the results are to be accepted by the scientific community at large and, in time, integrated into the scientific canon. However, each branch of science has its own acceptable level of reproducibility. In the social and psychological sciences, "human factors" are so pervasive—indeed, they are the very subject matter of these sciences—that true reproducibility and universality of results is almost never achieved.

WHAT YOU NEED TO KNOW ABOUT VARIABLES

Nearly all experiments are designed with certain elements in common. Two of these basic elements are the independent and dependent variables.

The independent variable is so named because it is adjusted independently of other factors. Usually the independent variable is controlled by the experimenter, although there are many instances in which it is not under any control and may only be observed. A planet's distance from the sun in the first table in this chapter is an obvious example. In any case, it's desirable to have one and only one independent variable in a given experiment. Experiments with two or more independent variables are harder to reproduce. It's also difficult to draw reliable conclusions from them because it's usually impossible to determine with certainty the relative importance of each variable—or the unpredictable ways that two or more variables might affect each other. Ideally, scientists need to be able to account for all the phenomena they observe, or else they cannot say for sure why changes occur.

CAUTION

An experiment without a control group severely limits the conclusions that can be drawn from it. Thus, the health cures claimed by medical charlatans can often be discounted because no control group is tested. Many people would have recovered anyway without treatment by the charlatan. Without a matched control group for comparison's sake, any data about such medical claims are more or less meaningless.

THE ROLE OF THE CONTROL

Another element used in nearly all experiments is the control. The control is an experimental subject for which all the relevant variables, including the independent variable, are held constant. Because the independent variable is held constant, any changes observed in the control must be caused by other factors. These changes can then be accounted for throughout the rest of the experiment.

For example, in testing a new experimental therapy for AIDS, researchers might study two groups of patients: a group receiving the new treatment and a control group that is not receiving the new treatment. It would be important to match the two groups as closely as possible in every other way. The average age, the severity of AIDS symptoms, and the nature of any other health problems suffered should be as similar as possible in both groups. If this is done, and if the experimental group shows a markedly better rate of recovery than the control group, it would be reasonably good evidence that the improvement is due to the new therapy rather than any other factor.

HOW TO READ RESEARCH SUMMARIES

Having reviewed the steps of the scientific method and what goes into solid experimental design, you're now ready to look at the way Research Summaries will be presented on the ACT Assessment Test and what to look for in a passage so as to be able to answer the questions. Read the sample below:

Enzymes are special proteins which act as catalysts to speed up chemical reactions in cells. Enzymes catalyze reactions by first having their active site bind to its *substrate*, usually the molecule which is undergoing reaction. The ability of an enzyme to bind substrate is called its activity. Thus, activity is also a measure of how well an enzyme catalyzes a reaction. The active site of an enzyme is very specific for its substrate. This specificity is created by the three-dimensional shape of the enzyme. However, this three-dimensional shape is dependent upon environmental factors, such as temperature and pH, a measure of acidity.

If the shape of the enzyme is changed, the enzyme might no longer be able to bind to its substrate. In this case, the enzyme is said to be *denatured*. Extremes of either temperature or pH can cause enzymes to denature.

A scientist isolated three enzymes from a mammalian cell. These enzymes will be denoted Enzyme A, Enzyme B, and Enzyme C.

Experiment 1

A scientist placed samples of Enzyme A into twelve different tubes. Each tube contained a buffer solution at a different pH such that the first tube was at pH = 1, the second tube at pH = 2, the third tube at pH = 3, and so on up to the twelfth tube, which was at pH = 12. The scientist then added an indicator which would turn the solution yellow if bound by the enzyme. Thus, the solution would turn more yellow when more indicator was bound. The temperature for all the tubes was 25° C. This procedure was repeated for Enzyme B and Enzyme C. The scientist was then able to create the following graph:

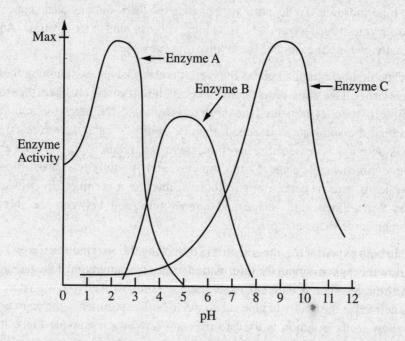

Experiment 2

A sample of Enzyme A was placed into a single tube containing a buffer solution at the pH which gave the greatest activity in Experiment 1. The tube was then brought to near freezing, and a sample was taken and tested for activity by addition of the same indicator above. The tube was then gradually warmed, with samples taken every five degrees and tested for activity. The process was repeated for Enzyme B and Enzyme C. The scientist was then able to create this graph:

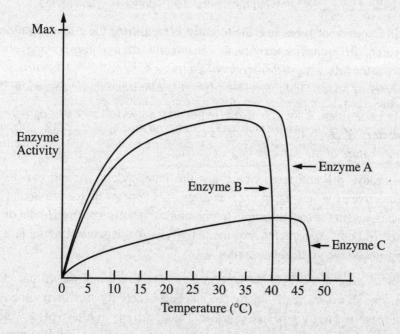

Five terms are defined within the first experiment: *enzyme, substrate, activity, denature,* and *pH*. An enzyme catalyzes reactions; that is, it speeds them up. The reactant that the enzyme catalyzes is the substrate. Activity, in the special sense in which the word is used here, is the ability of an enzyme to bind substrate. To denature is to change the three-dimensional shape of an enzyme in such a way that it is no longer able to bind to its substrate. And finally, pH is a measure of the acidity of a substance.

The first paragraph explains that certain relationships exist among these five terms. If the three-dimensional shape of the enzyme is changed, then the ability of the enzyme to bind the substrate is lessened. If the enzyme's ability to bind the substrate is lessened, then its ability to catalyze the reaction (i.e. activity) is lessened. Therefore, there is a relationship between the three-dimensional shape of the enzyme and its activity. Furthermore, we learn that, in certain circumstances, there is a relationship between the three-dimensional shape and temperature, and between the three-dimensional shape and pH.

In both experiments, the scientist is observing the enzyme's activity. We know this by combining the information in the first paragraph of the passage with the description of the two experimental protocols. Activity, we've seen, is defined as the ability to bind substrate. In both experiments, the degree of yellow in the solution is used to measure how much enzyme binds the indicator; thus, the degree of yellow indicates the enzyme's activity. The activity, then, is the dependent variable. In Experiment 1, the independent variable is pH. In Experiment 2, the independent variable is temperature.

What is the hypothesis for each experiment? You'll notice that none is given. The hypothesis is implicit in the independent and dependent variables being tested and the relationships among the various elements in the experiment. This is how the Research Summaries will be set up, so you must train yourself to look at an experiment and determine the hypothesis yourself.

In Experiment 1, because the scientist is measuring the effect of varying levels of pH on enzyme activity, we can infer that the hypothesis being tested here is the following: *The activity of Enzymes A, B, and C is dependent to a greater or lesser extent upon the pH level of the surrounding solution.*

In Experiment 2, the scientist is hypothesizing as follows: *The activity of Enzymes A, B, and C is dependent to a greater or lesser extent upon the temperature of the surrounding solution.*

Because pH and temperature are the independent variables of their respective experiments, in the first graph, pH appears on the horizontal or *x*-axis, and in the second graph, temperature appears on the horizontal or *x*-axis. In both experiments enzyme activity is the dependent variable and appears on the vertical or *y*-axis.

What are the results of the experiments? The first graph shows that each enzyme shows the tendency first to increase in activity as pH rises, then to decrease in activity as pH rises further. Thus, each enzyme has a pH at which it displays maximum activity. This differs for each enzyme. For Enzyme A, the pH at which maximum activity occurs is around 2; for Enzyme B, it is around 6; for Enzyme C, it is around 10. The second graph shows that each enzyme has the tendency to slowly increase in activity as temperature rises. This increase eventually levels out, and the enzyme activity is stable over a range of temperatures. Then it suddenly drops off, quickly falling to no activity. The temperatures at which the enzyme activity rises and suddenly falls differ from enzyme to enzyme. In addition, Enzymes A and B attain a markedly higher level of activity than Enzyme C.

How are the two graphs similar and different? Does the information in each graph support the other? The graphs are similar in that they both present data regarding the activity levels of the same three enzymes (A, B, and C). However, the independent variable is different in each. There is no direct relationship between the two graphs; each shows the effect of enzyme activity on a different key variable. Therefore, the graphs do not support or contradict each other because each shows activity as a function of a different variable.

UNDERSTANDING HOW SCIENTISTS COMPARE CONCLUSIONS

Earlier, we said that data, if compiled and recorded accurately, cannot be disputed, but the conclusions drawn from data can be. Scientists often disagree with the conclusions of their peers. The level of disagreement varies from time and time, and sometimes even between the different branches of science. This represents the third type of passage you'll see on the Science Reasoning Test. You'll be tested on your ability to understand and compare the conflicting viewpoints.

Currently, for example, the field of paleontology (the study of ancient life, as recorded in fossil remains) is one in which disagreement even about fairly fundamental matters is frequent. The origins of the human species are still hotly debated, and each new discovery seems to create a new controversy. In this case, one cause of the debate lies in the fact that the data (the fossils) can be interpreted in a variety of ways. And because of the random destruction wrought by time, and the inaccessibility of many fossils, there are also many gaps in the fossil record that can be filled at present only by speculation and educated guesses.

By contrast, there is currently relatively little debate about fundamental principles among chemists. This is because the field of chemistry as presently conceived appears to be fairly complete. Almost every new discovery can be explained in a way that agrees with the current body of knowledge. Only on the rare occasion when a new discovery seems to disagree with previous theories or ideas do chemists sometimes argue.

However, this isn't to suggest that everything that can be known about chemistry *is* known. Occasionally a particular field which appears to be a more or less settled body of knowledge is revolutionized by a new theory or a dramatic series of discoveries. For example, the field of earth science had been relatively calm for almost two centuries until the 1960s when the new theory of plate tectonics exploded onto the scene. Then earth science became a hotbed of scientific controversy. Perhaps a similar upheaval might someday shake the virtual unanimity that chemistry enjoys today.

THE SCIENTIFIC VIEW OF COMPLEX SYSTEMS

Sometimes different conclusions are possible when scientists examine a complex system in which there are several interrelated variables. Because of the complexity of living systems—referring not only to individual creatures but to the interconnected webs of life that make up an ecological system—there is often disagreement among biologists concerning cause and effect, the forces behind ecological change, and so on. Biological complexity is difficult to eliminate even under experimental conditions because eliminating variables often upsets the equilibrium of the system. As a result, ecologists often argue. The different conclusions they draw about the systems they study might all be logically correct and consistent with the data. The differences are due to the fact that different ecologists will give different weights to the same complexly interconnected variables.

HOW SCIENTISTS IDENTIFY SIGNIFICANT FACTORS

When you think like a scientist in an effort to form a conclusion about the cause of some observed phenomenon, you must first decide what factors are important in the situation under scrutiny. When there are many different factors to consider, this might be difficult. The process of isolating the most significant factors is often best managed through gradual elimination of the unimportant or irrelevant factors. Consider the following situation:

Jane was walking to school one day in November when she noticed that about two dozen small orange fish, which she had previously seen swimming in the pond next to the school, were floating on top of the water, dead. Looking more closely, Jane could find no other sign of animal life in the pond, but she did observe that there were dozens of frogs on the lawn next to the pond. (She couldn't recall noticing frogs near the pond before.)

The day was sunny and mild, but Jane knew that the previous night there had been a severe storm of rain mixed with sleet; the local temperature had plummeted below freezing for the first time that autumn. Jane also noticed that the Squmb River emptied into the pond. She knew that the Squmb River flowed past an operational nuclear power plant about two miles upstream. Jane went to school. Later that morning, when she happened to glance outside during history class, she saw the school's custodian emptying yesterday's lunch leftovers into the pond.

Here is a mystery. What caused the death of the fish in the pond? Let's consider each element in the situation, beginning by eliminating all the factors which are unlikely to be relevant. Could the frogs somehow be responsible for the death of the fish? This seems implausible. Frogs are obviously not predators of fish. And although it is possible that the frogs and the fish might compete for some resources—they might both eat some of the same insects, for example—it seems unlikely that dozens of fish would die suddenly because the frogs managed to eat up all of their food. We can probably eliminate the frogs as a relevant factor in this case.

Next, consider the role that the weather could have played. It is possible that the sudden cold killed the fish. However, two factors make this unlikely. First, we know that water usually acts as an insulator; water temperatures change much more slowly than air temperatures, which is why the pond did not freeze overnight, despite the cold weather. (Remember, Jane saw the dead fish floating on the liquid surface of the pond.) The fact that the frogs are alive also tends to weaken this hypothesis. If the cold had killed the fish, it probably would have killed the frogs, too.

That leaves us with two other pieces of evidence: the existence of the nuclear power plant upstream and the dumping of cafeteria wastes in the water. It's possible that either cause might have killed the fish, because either could have introduced some unhealthful chemicals into the pond. How could Jane determine which factor was responsible?

It would be pretty tough to set up experimental conditions, controlling for all but a single variable, in the real world, as in Jane's pond. Thus, Jane would probably need to make an educated guess about the cause of the dead fish. Additional data could certainly be gathered. Jane could ask the custodian about the nature of the refuse he had dumped into the pond. His answer, if accurate, could help clarify whether any toxic substances were involved.

Jane could also conduct some research into the activities of the nuclear power plant. How recently did it begin operating? If the plant had been on line for several years, with the fish thriving until now, it would tend to weaken the argument that the plant is the cause of the fish's demise. What pollutants, if any, are known to be emitted into the stream by the plant? Government records are likely to exist that might shed light on this question. Did any substantive change in the plant's operations occur just prior to the death of the fish? If so, it could be relevant to an explanation.

As you can see, the mystery of the fish pond is unlikely to have an easy-to-find solution. Real-life scientific issues like this one generally lead to disagreements among researchers. However, disagreement is not necessarily a bad thing. Very often, disagreement spurs on research, as scientists in the different camps search for the proof that their theory is correct.

HOW TO READ CONFLICTING VIEWPOINTS PASSAGES

The mystery of the dead fish is just a simple example of possibly conflicting conclusions that might arise given the same data. Here is an ACT Assessment Conflicting Viewpoints passage, as well as what you should look for so as to be able to answer the questions. Read the sample below:

The origin of modern humans and the evolutionary path by which our ancestors first emerged has long been the subject of heated debate. Of particular interest is exactly where and when modern humans (Homo sapiens) evolved, and the relationship between modern humans and so-called Neanderthal man (generally considered to be a primitive form of Homo sapiens). Three varying theories concerning these issues are presented below.

Theory 1

Homo erectus (a primitive ancestor of *Homo sapiens*—modern humans) evolved in Africa about 1.6 million years ago and soon after spread to all parts of the Old World. The Neanderthals and all other primitive forms of *Homo sapiens* then evolved from *Homo erectus*. In time, these primitive forms evolved into modern humans. This was the first proposed theory, based originally on fossil dating which suggested a continuous time line leading, one by one, from *Homo erectus* to the various primitive forms (including Neanderthal) and, from these, on to modern humans. Since then, new fossil discoveries have been accounted for (with varying success) by using this theory.

Theory 2

Homo erectus evolved in Africa about 1.6 million years ago and soon spread to all parts of the Old World. Neanderthals are evolutionarily descended from those *Homo erectus* individuals which migrated to the Old World. However, the Neanderthals did not evolve into modern humans. Rather they represent a now-extinct side branch on the evolutionary tree of the genus *Homo*. *Homo sapiens* evolved independently of Neanderthals in the Old World, eventually supplanted the Neanderthal population, and later evolved into modern humans. This is based on fossil evidence that suggests that the Neanderthals were too primitive (based primarily upon cranial measurements taken of fossilized skulls) to possibly have been ancestors of modern humans. However, the skulls of other early *Homo sapiens* show traits which seem to follow the evolutionary line to modern humans.

Theory 3

Homo erectus evolved in Africa about 1.6 million years ago and soon spread to all parts of the Old World. The Neanderthals are evolutionarily descended from those *Homo erectus* individuals that migrated to the Old World, as are the other primitive *Homo* forms which were determined to be direct ancestors of *Homo sapiens* according to the evidence in Theory 2. However, according to this theory, modern humans actually evolved separately in Africa, and did not spread to the rest of the world until about 90,000 years ago. This is based on evidence taken from mitochondrial DNA (DNA which resides in the mitochondria and which passes undisturbed from mother to child). Mitochondrial DNA suggests that all modern humans can trace their lineage to a single group of individuals living in southern Africa about 90,000 years ago.

As with all Conflicting Viewpoints passages, look for the assumptions beneath each theory. Theory 1 assumes that the *Homo sapiens* evolution must have been a continuous event, stemming from the first *Homo erectus* to enter the Old World. Theory 2 also assumes that *Homo sapiens* evolved from the *Homo erectus* population in the Old World. However, it assumes that the Neanderthals were too primitive to have been an ancestor of modern humans. Thus there were two branches on the evolutionary tree. Theory 3 assumes that modern humans evolved in Africa and are not related to primitive *Homo sapiens* in the Old World, including Neanderthal. This assumes that there are three or more branches on the human evolutionary tree, and that these evolutionary changes took place in drastically different places.

The three different theories rely on three different sources of evidence. Theory 1 cites the evidence of fossils with weight given to dating techniques. Theory 2 cites the evidence of fossils, but this time weight is given to features (mainly of skulls), not dating. Theory 3 cites the evidence of mitochondrial DNA.

Note the assumptions behind each theory and the evidence relied on by each theory. This will help you better understand the questions on this part of the Science Reasoning Test.

SCIENTIFIC TERMS AND CONCEPTS MOST LIKELY TO BE ON YOUR ACT ASSESSMENT

The following terms and concepts have been chosen as those most likely to appear on the ACT Assessment Science Reasoning Test. The terms are drawn from the fields of biology, chemistry, earth sciences, and physics. The test-makers know you might not have studied a specific field, for example, physics. However, in the minimum two years of high school science you've presumably taken, you have probably been exposed to most of these words. You should have the broad background of scientific knowledge necessary to give you some understanding of the term when it's put in the context of a Science Reasoning passage.

This list is a helpful way to refresh your memory of crucial science topics you've studied throughout your high school years. It'll also highlight for you the topics or areas in which your background is strongest and weakest.

HOW TO USE YOUR SCIENTIFIC TERMS LIST

Go down the list and check every word you don't know or are hesitant about. If the following definition is not sufficient to jog your memory, you might want to review the relevant topics using your favorite science textbook or study guide. Because you tend to remember information you like, the terms have been broken down into the four fields of biology, chemistry, earth sciences, and physics. This way you can quickly pinpoint areas that need attention.

Assuming you've allowed yourself three months or more, work on about ten minutes' worth of words each day. If you wish, write the definition of each unfamiliar word into a notebook to make your own Scientific Terms journal.

Putting the definition in your journal will help you remember the word better when you see it again on the ACT Assessment.

SCIENTIFIC TERMS AND CONCEPTS GLOSSARY

Chemistry

acid—a substance capable of donating hydrogen ions. This is called the Bronsted-Lowry definition. Alternately, the Lewis definition says that an acid is any species that accepts electron pairs. This definition is more general. Acids have a sharp, sour taste; vinegar is an example.

activation energy—the minimum collision energy required between two molecules for a reaction to occur.

atom—the smallest unit of an element, composed of electrons, protons, and neutrons, that still has all the properties of that element.

atomic mass—the average mass of the atoms of a given element. Atomic mass is measured in atomic mass units. One atomic mass unit has been set at one-twelfth the mass of the carbon-12 atom.

Avogadro's number—the number of atoms in 12 grams of carbon-12, equal to 6.022×10^{23}. This constant is used in various chemical and physical calculations and formulas.

base—a substance capable of accepting hydrogen ions. This is known as the Bronsted-Lowry definition. (By corollary, bases dissolved in water increase the amount of hydroxide ion [OH].) Alternately, the Lewis definition says that a base is any species that donates lone-pair electrons. This definition is more general. Bases are slippery.

boiling point—the temperature at which the liquid and gas phases of a substance are in equilibrium.

buffer—a solution that maintains a constant pH despite the addition of small amounts of acid or base. A buffer is usually made by mixing a weak acid with its conjugate weak base.

calorie—the amount of heat required to raise one gram of water one degree $C°$.

catalyst—a substance that takes part in a chemical reaction and causes it to go faster. The catalyst itself is not a reactant and undergoes no chemical change.

chromatography—a method of fractionation in which a mobile phase containing the mixture to be separated is passed over a stationary phase which displays some affinity for the materials in the mobile phase. This affinity may be based upon polarity, size, or some form of reversible binding ability (such as between an enzyme and its substrate). The stationary phase must be carefully chosen so as to maximize the differences in affinity for the various substances in the mobile phase.

compound—a substance containing two or more elements.

concentration—the ratio between solute and solvent in a solution.

conservation of mass—the law which states that in every chemical reaction there must be an equal quantity of matter before and after the reaction.

covalent bond—a bond formed between two atoms by the sharing of electrons.

crystal—a solid in which the particles are arranged in a repeating geometrical pattern.

electron—a negatively charged subatomic particle.

empirical formula—the chemical formula of a compound that shows the relative number of atoms of each element in terms of the smallest integers. Thus, the empirical formula shows the ratio of elements within a compound.

energy—a property of matter which describes the ability to do work. Energy takes many forms, including potential energy and kinetic energy (see *enthalpy*).

enthalpy—a measurement of the energy of a system due to the movement of its particles. At constant pressure, the enthalpy change of a system is equal to the heat absorbed.

entropy—a measurement of the disorder of a system. A fundamental law is that the enthalpy of the universe is constantly increasing. However, in many reactions the enthalpy is decreased (i.e. the system is more ordered after the reaction than before). (Biological systems tend to employ reactions which increase the order of the system. To do this, they must create more disorder in the surrounding environment. This is one of the reasons many reactions in biological systems require a great input of energy.)

fractional distillation—the separation of two or more components of a liquid solution on the basis of their different boiling points. This is done by repeated evaporation and recondensation of the components.

fractionation—the separation of a mixture into its parts.

free energy—the chemical potential energy of a chemical substance or system.

functional group—a group of atoms in a molecule (usually organic) that exhibit characteristic properties. Examples of functional groups commonly encountered are alcohols (–OH), aldehydes and ketones (–C=O; in ketones this group is internal), carboxylic acid (–COOH), and amines ($-NH_2$).

gas—a phase of matter having no definite shape and a volume that is defined only by the size of the container. The gaseous phase is the most energetic phase for a given substance.

heat—the means by which energy is transferred from a hot body to a colder body.

WORDS ON SCIENCE

"The great tragedy of Science [is] the slaying of a beautiful hypothesis by an ugly fact." Thomas Henry Huxley, "Biogenesis and Abiogenesis," 1870.

hydrogen bond—the strong dipole-dipole interaction that forms between a hydrogen atom bonded to a strongly electronegative atom (such as oxygen) and a lone-pair electron on a nearby electronegative atom. Hydrogen bonds are very weak. (Millions of hydrogen bonds are constantly forming and unforming in a glass of water. These bonds are responsible for the special properties of water, such as its elevated boiling point.)

inhibitor—a substance that slows the rate of a reaction. There are three main types of inhibitors: competitive, uncompetitive, and mixed inhibitors.

ion—an atom or group of atoms that has gained or lost one or more electrons. This causes the atom or group of atoms to become either negatively or positively charged.

ionic bond—a bond formed through the attraction of two ions of opposite charge.

isomers—two forms of a chemical compound that have the same chemical formula but a different spatial configuration.

liquid—a phase of matter in which a substance has no definite shape but has a definite volume. Matter in the liquid phase has a kinetic energy intermediate between that of mass in solid phase and mass in the gaseous phase.

lone-pair electrons—an unshared pair of electrons in the outermost orbital of an atom.

mass—the measure of the amount of matter.

matter—anything which exhibits the property of inertia (see listing below, under "Physics").

melting point—the temperature at which the liquid and solid phases of a substance are in equilibrium.

molality—the number of moles of solute present per kilogram of solvent. Because one kilogram of water has a volume of one liter, molality is also the number of moles of solute present per liter of water, and the molality and molarity of such solutions are equal.

molarity—The number of moles of solute present per liter of solute.

mole—The amount of a substance consisting of Avogadro's number of elementary particles (atoms or molecules). Therefore, one mole of any substance contains 6.022×10^{23} elementary particles.

molecular formula—the chemical formula of a compound that specifies the actual number of atoms of each element in a compound.

molecular mass—the mass of a molecule, found by summing the atomic masses of each of the atoms within the molecule.

neutron—a neutrally charged subatomic particle

nucleus—the small, positively charged center of an atom, composed of protons and neutrons.

orbital—one of several spaces around the nucleus of an atom, each of which can be occupied by up to two electrons. All the electrons in a given orbital must have the same energy level, energy sublevel, and spatial orientation.

oxidation—the loss of electrons.

pH—a measure of the hydronium ion concentration in a solution. $pH = -\log[H_3O^+]$.

polarity—asymmetrical charge distribution over a molecule. Such a molecule is called a dipole.

pressure—the force exerted by moving particles on a specified unit area. Thus, pressure may be expressed as pounds (the force) per square inch (the unit area).

proton—a positively charged subatomic particle.

reaction rate—the rate of formation of product in a reaction.

reduction—the gain of electrons.

salt—a compound consisting of the positive ion of a base and the negative ion of an acid.

solid—a phase of matter in which a substance has definite shape and volume. The atoms in a solid have the lowest kinetic energy of the three phases, because their molecules are relatively fixed in space.

solution—a homogeneous mixture of a solute and solvent. The solute is that which is dissolved in the solvent.

temperature—a measure of the average kinetic energy of molecules.

titration—a technique in which small amounts of an acid or base of known concentration and pH are added to a solution in order to determine the pH of the solution. By using an indicator or a pH meter, the experimenter can observe the change in pH caused by these additions, and from this data and from the known pH and volume of acid or base added, the pH of the solution can be determined.

van der Waals forces—weak forces of attraction between two molecules. These forces do not result in a bond. Rather, they represent the attraction of the electrons of one atom for the protons of another, in much the same way opposite pole of a magnet attract each other.

Biology

alternation of generations—The succession of haploid and diploid phases in a sexually reproducing organism. In most animals, only the gametes are in the haploid phase. In fungi, algae, and plants, the haploid phase may be the dominant phase, although in vascular plants the diploid is dominant.

amino acid—a compound made up of carbon, hydrogen, nitrogen, and oxygen and containing one of more than 20 different possible side groups.

The general formula for amino acids is $H_2N-CHR-COOH$, where R is the side group.

asexual reproduction—reproduction involving the cells of only one parent. As such, there is no fusion of nuclei and no transfer of genetic material. Thus the offspring is genetically identical to the parent. There are five types of asexual reproduction: binary fission, budding, sporulation, regeneration, and vegetative reproduction.

autotroph—an organism which manufactures organic food from inorganic sources. Plants are autotrophs.

carbohydrate—a compound made up of carbon, hydrogen, and oxygen with the general formula $C_n(H_2O)_m$. Carbohydrates are commonly known as sugars and are the primary sources of cellular energy. Examples of carbohydrates are starch and cellulose.

cell—the basic unit of organization in all living things. Any cell is surrounded by a plasma membrane, which separates the interior environment from the exterior and regulates the passage of materials into and out of the cell. All cells also must contain the hereditary material of the cell and some structures capable of processing energy. There are two distinct types of cells: prokaryotic cells and eukaryotic cells.

chemosynthesis—the process by which chemical energy is trapped and converted into usable forms of energy. Nitrogen-fixing bacteria do this.

chromosome—a structure composed of DNA and sometimes protein that contains some or all of the genetic material of a cell.

circulation—the process by which materials are transported throughout the body. The circulatory system in humans consists of the blood vessels (arteries, veins, and capillaries) and the heart. This system is a closed circulatory system. Some lower animals, such as the hydra, have an open circulatory system.

diffusion—the process by which molecules pass across a porous membrane. Diffusion may be passive, in which case the molecules cross from the region of highest concentration to the region of lowest concentration, or either facilitated or active, in which cases the passage is helped in some way so as to not be entirely dependent upon the concentration.

digestion—the process by which large, insoluble molecules are broken down into small, soluble molecules. Digestion may be intracellular or extracellular.

DNA—the fundamental hereditary material of all living organisms. George Watson and Francis Crick elucidated the double-stranded nature of the DNA molecule and the helix structure it assumes. DNA molecules make up the gene. DNA molecules are composed of nucleotides, which consist of a 5-carbon sugar (deoxyribose), a phosphate, and a nitrogen base. The nitrogen base determines the nucleic acid. In DNA, there are four types of nitrogen bases (adenine, thymine, guanine, and cytosine), and therefore four types of nucleic acids. These four bases also are the basis for the genetic code. Key to the continuation of life is the fact that DNA can reproduce with a high degree of accuracy.

egestion—the removal of undigested material.

enzyme—a protein which acts as a catalyst in chemical reactions. Enzymes have binding sites on their surface, which is generally where the reaction occurs.

eukaryote—an organism whose genetic material is contained within a nucleus. All life-forms other than the viruses and bacteria are eukaryotes.

evolution—the process by which organisms change from generation to generation. Evolution is a gradual change involving random genetic mutations. Charles Darwin suggested that genetic mutations resulting in physiological changes will sometimes confer an advantage to the organism over its competitors. This advantage leads to natural selection, which is the driving force behind all evolutionary change.

excretion—the removal of cellular waste products from an organism.

gene—a unit of a chromosome that contains all the genetic information to create a single polypeptide.

genetics—the study of heredity, founded by Gregor Mendel. There are three main laws in genetics which Mendel developed. The first is the Law of Dominance, which states that when organisms containing pure contrasting traits are crossed, only one of the traits will be expressed in the offspring. The trait which is expressed is the dominant trait; the trait not expressed is the recessive trait. The second law is the Law of Segregation, which states that alleles segregate during gamete formation and then recombine. The third law is the Law of Independent Assortment, which states that alleles on different genes assort independently during gamete formation.

genotype—the exact description of the genetic makeup of an organism.

heterotroph—an organism which obtains pre-made organic food from other sources. These organisms are unable to make organic food from inorganic sources. Animals are heterotrophs.

homeostasis—the maintenance of a steady state.

ingestion—the process of taking in food.

lipid—a large, oily organic molecule. Examples are fats, oils, and steroids. Lipids can be converted into twice the cellular energy of carbohydrates, and are therefore used to store energy in the body.

meiosis—The process by which specialized reproductive cells in sexually reproducing organisms are created. These reproductive cells are called gametes, and they are special in that they are haploid (having only one set of chromosomes). Because normal cells are usually diploid (having two sets of chromosomes) meiosis involves the halving of the number of chromosomes. Meiosis occurs in two phases and results in four haploid cells.

metabolism—the process by which complex, high-energy compounds are broken down by organisms into usable forms of energy.

mitosis—the process of cell division in which the chromosomes replicate so that there are two exactly similar sets of genetic material in the cell. The cell then divides into two cells, with each cell taking one set of chromosomes. The result is two cells that are genetically identical.

nucleus—The centrally located chamber in eukaryotic cells which contains the chromosomes. It is bounded by a double membrane and is the information center of the cell.

nutrition—all the activities by which an organism obtains and processes materials necessary for energy, growth, reproduction, and regulation.

osmosis—the process by which water passes across a porous membrane. In osmosis, water will flow from a region with a low concentration of dissolved molecules to a region with a high concentration of dissolved molecules.

phenotype—the description of the traits observable in an organism. These traits are the result of the genetic makeup of the organism as well as environmental factors.

photosynthesis—the process by which visible light is trapped and converted into usable forms of energy. Plants and green algae do this. Photosynthesis occurs in two reactions, the light and dark reactions. A byproduct of the light reaction is oxygen. Photosynthesis occurs in the chlorophyll of plants.

prokaryote—an organism whose genetic material is not contained within a nucleus, but rather free in the cytoplasm. This is the simplest form of cell. Bacteria and viruses are prokaryotes.

protein—a compound made up of many amino acids linked together end to end. Proteins are integral to building many structural features in the cell. Enzymes are also proteins.

regulation—the coordination and control of life activities. In all animals, regulation involves chemical control. In higher animals, regulation also involves nerve control.

reproduction—there are two types of reproduction, asexual and sexual. Asexual reproduction involves only one parent. There are three main types of asexual reproduction; fission, budding, and spore formation. Sexual reproduction involves two parent cells. If these cells are the same, then the joining of these cells is called conjugation. If these cells are different, then the joining of these cells is called fertilization.

respiration—the conversion of chemical energy in food by oxidation into forms which can be used to drive the chemical reactions essential to life. The two types of respiration are aerobic and anaerobic respiration.

RNA—the material through which the genetic information in DNA is converted into the proteins for which it codes. RNA has a different 5-carbon sugar (ribose) and instead of the nitrogen base thymine it has uracil. RNA is single stranded. There are two main types of RNA: messenger RNA (mRNA), and transfer RNA (tRNA).

sexual reproduction—reproduction in which the cells of two parents combine through the process of fertilization to produce a fertilized egg cell which develops into a new, genetically unique organism. During the process of fertilization, there is an exchange of genetic material which allows for genetic variation.

synthesis—the process by which materials necessary for energy, growth, reproduction, and regulation are made by an organism from energy sources obtained from the environment.

tissue—a group of similar cells which are organized into a single unit and which perform the same function. Tissue types in animals include epithelial (such as skin, and the linings of the lungs, digestive tract, and blood vessels), muscle, nerve, connective/supportive, blood, and reproductive tissue. Tissues in animals group together to form organs. Tissue types in plants include conducting (xylem and phloem), growing, supporting, storage, and reproductive tissue.

transport—the process by which materials are absorbed and circulated throughout an organism.

vitamin—a compound which the body cannot synthesize for itself but which is necessary in small quantities for life functions. Vitamins come in a variety of structurally unrelated forms. Many vitamins work as coenzymes (i.e. they are necessary to make certain enzymes active).

Earth/Space Sciences

asteroid—a large celestial body composed mostly of rock. Asteroids usually are under the influence of a star's gravitational field, but have larger, more eccentric orbits than planets.

atmosphere—the gaseous layer that envelopes the earth. The thickness of the earth's atmosphere is about 1,100 km. It consists of three layers: the troposphere, the stratosphere, and the mesosphere. The earth's atmosphere is important in that it shields the earth from harmful radiation and excessive heat. It also prevents the earth from cooling too rapidly at night.

biosphere—the portion of the earth which supports life, including most of the hydrosphere, the lower portions of the atmosphere, and nearly all of the earth's surface.

climate—all the characteristics of weather, including precipitation, temperature, and humidity, which a particular region experiences over a long period of time. The averages of all these factors constitute the climate for a particular place.

community—all the microorganisms, plants, and animals inhabiting a given location which interact and are ecologically integrated.

compression cementation—the process by which sediment is cemented together into sedimentary rock due to the large compression forces exerted by heavy layers of overlying material.

condensation—the changing of water from a gas to a liquid, involving the removal of heat from the water. The heat is then released into the atmosphere in the form of latent heat, so called because the temperature remains the same during this process.

conduction—the transfer of heat through solids. This occurs because, when a solid is heated, its atoms will move faster. Random collisions between these atoms and those neighboring will cause the neighboring atoms to also move faster. This process repeats until the heat has transferred across the solid.

convection—the transfer of heat through the air.

crystallization—the process by which igneous rock is formed from molten magma.

depression—an area of low atmospheric pressure around which winds travel anti-clockwise in the Northern Hemisphere and clockwise in the Southern Hemisphere. Depressions tend to occur when warm air meets cold air. Because the cold air is heavier than the warm air, the warm air rises above the cold, causing winds as well as cloud formation.

earthquake—a shifting of the rock layers of the earth's crust, most commonly caused by either the movement of tectonic plates or the eruption of volcanoes. Earthquakes emit two kinds of shock waves: P-waves and S-waves. P-waves travel through both liquids and solids, while S-waves travel only through solids.

ecosystem—all of the organisms of a particular habitat together with the environment in which they live.

electromagnetic energy—the energy exhibited by the earth due to its magnetic field.

environment—all of an organism's surroundings. This includes all of the species which influence the organism as well as temperature, humidity, light, and so on.

erosion—the physical process by which rocks are corroded and converted into other forms by the action of heat, cold, gases, water, wind, gravity, and plant life. The process of erosion is key to the formation of sedimentary rock and soil.

evaporation—the changing of water form a liquid to a gas. Heat must be added to the water in this process. (This is why your skin feels cooler when water evaporates from it.)

galaxy—a grouping of hundreds of millions of stars. All these stars interact gravitationally and orbit around a common center. The galaxy in which the earth exists is called the Milky Way galaxy.

geocentric model—the model of the solar system which sets the earth at the center of the solar system and has all of the celestial bodies rotating around the earth. This model is unnecessarily complicated and was eventually abandoned in favor of the heliocentric model.

geomagnetism—the magnetic phenomena exhibited by the earth and its atmosphere. The study of geomagnetism often centers on the study of the earth's gravitational field and the changes which occur in it.

greenhouse effect—the effect of atmospheric carbon dioxide, water, and other trace gases on the average temperature at the surface. This effect is caused by the absorption by these substances of energy radiated from the earth.

heliocentric model—the model of the solar system which has the sun at the center with the planets rotating around it. In this model, the apparent motion of the stars is explained by the rotation of the earth.

hydrological cycle (water cycle)—the cycle whose primary components are (1) the evaporation of moisture from the surface of the earth, due to the warming of the sun's rays, (2) the carrying of this moisture into higher levels of the atmosphere, (3) the condensation of water vapor into clouds, and (4) the return of water to the surface as precipitation.

hydrosphere—the layer of water on the surface of the earth. This includes all the oceans, as well as the rivers, lakes, etc. It is estimated to cover about 70.8% of the earth's surface.

igneous rock—rock formed during the cooling and crystallization of a hot, molten fluid from the earth's core called magma. Igneous rock makes up over 95% of the earth's crust.

infiltration—the process by which water passes into the earth through the soil.

lithosphere—the layer of the earth's crust composed of rock and extending for about 100 km below the surface. The lithosphere is composed of two shells, known as the crust and the upper mantle. These are in turn divided into tectonic plates. See *Tectonic Plate Theory*.

mantle and core—the heavy interior of the earth, which constitutes most of the earth's mass. The core is composed of a molten layer surrounding a solid center. It is the source of much of the earth's heat. The mantle, on the other hand, is solid and rigid.

metamorphic rock—rock formed by the process of metamorphism, which involves partial melting and recrystallization of sedimentary or igneous rock. An example is marble, which is caused by the metamorphosis of limestone.

metamorphism—a process of structural change in rocks induced by heat and pressure.

meteorology—the study of the earth's atmosphere, specifically the day-to-day variations of weather conditions.

moon—a large celestial body travelling in orbit around a planet.

orbit—the path an object takes when travelling around a large body due to its gravitational force.

permeability—a measure of the rate at which water passes through particles. Permeability is dependant upon porosity, which is a measure of the amount of space between particles. Larger particles have a greater porosity and therefore a greater permeability.

planet—a large celestial body travelling in orbit around a star. There is currently much debate as to what exactly differentiates a planet from other large bodies in space, such as asteroids.

pollutant—any substance found in the environment in levels above that normally found and which may cause harm.

population—all the members of a species inhabiting a given location.

precipitation—the moisture that falls to the earth's surface. Examples are rain, snow, sleet, and hail.

radiation—energy absorbed by the earth's atmosphere from space. Most of the radiation we are subjected to comes from the sun, called insolation (short for incoming solar radiation).

runoff—the water which is unable to infiltrate the surface of the earth, and thus runs down into streams, rivers, lakes, and so on.

satellite—any object which travels around a large body (such as a planet or a sun) due to the gravitational forces exerted by that body upon the object.

sedimentary rock—rock formed from the products of weathering on other rocks. This happens when water and carbon dioxide break up and dissolve small pieces of rock.

solar energy—the energy released by the sun, in the form of light, heat, and other types of radiation.

star—a large celestial body composed of incandescent gases, largely hydrogen and helium. A star radiates energy created by internal nuclear fusion reactions, in which two lighter atoms are fused to create a single heavier atom and a release of energy. Thus, hydrogen nuclei are fused to create helium (a process called hydrogen burning), and then helium nuclei are fused to eventually create carbon (helium burning). As a result of these reactions, the density of a star is constantly increasing as it ages, and its increasingly powerful gravitational field constantly causes it to contract.

sublimation—the change from a solid to a gas without passing through the liquid phase.

sun—a star which has planets orbiting within its gravitational field.

system—a grouping of planets, all rotating around a star (sun) due to the gravitational forces exerted by it.

Tectonic Plate Theory—the theory which states that the tectonic plates of the earth's crust and upper mantle move about, collide, and separate over time. Tectonic Plate Theory explains the relative positions of the continents and the formation of large mountain ranges such as the Himalayas, as well as natural phenomena such as earthquakes.

terrestrial radiation—the radiation of energy from the earth's surface into space. This generally occurs at night when temperatures are cooler.

transpiration—the process by which plants release moisture to the atmosphere.

weather—the state of the atmosphere at a particular time and place. Elements of weather include temperature, humidity, cloudiness, precipitation, wind, and pressure.

Physics

acceleration—the rate of velocity change over a given period of time. This is given by the equation $a = \Delta v / \Delta t$. Because velocity is a component of acceleration, acceleration is a vector quantity (see *vector*).

amplitude—the distance from the crest or the trough to the center of a wave.

angular acceleration—the change in angular velocity.

angular velocity—velocity around a circular path.

centripetal acceleration—acceleration towards a central point. When bodies move in a circular motion, their velocity at any one time is tangential to the circle. Thus, for the body to continue to move circularly, the velocity must constantly be moving towards the center. Thus, it is accelerating towards the center. This acceleration is what accounts for centripetal force.

conductor—something through which electric charges may move. Conductors, however, vary in terms of how easily they allow charge to move through. This is because of resistance.

diffraction—the bending of waves caused when a wave encounters an opening which is the same size as its wavelength.

efficiency—as applied to an engine, the ratio of the net work done by the system to the heat added to the system at the higher temperature.

electric charge—a fundamental measure based upon the idea that the electron represents a negative charge. Charge is measured in coulombs, where one coulomb equals 6.25×10^{18} electrons. Charge can either be negative or positive, depending upon whether it is likely to repel or attract electrons.

electric current—in a circuit, the amount of charge flowing past a certain point per unit of time. Current is represented by the letter I and is measured in amperes or coulombs per unit time. Thus, $I = \frac{Q}{T}$, where Q is charge.

electric field—that region in space in which a charge can experience an electric force. Electric fields can act to move charges from one point to another.

electric force—the force generated between charges as a result of the repulsive or attractive characteristics described in the Law of Electrostatics.

electromagnetic induction—the creation of a magnetic field as a result of the flow of an electric current.

force—any phenomena that pulls or pushes a mass. Force is a vector quantity, described by the formula F = ma.

frequency—the number of cycles of a wave that pass a particular point per unit time.

gravity—the force which pulls masses toward the earth. Gravity accelerates all masses at 9.8 m/s^2 and is always perpendicular to the surface of the earth.

inertia—the characteristic of mass which dictates that the motion of a mass will not change unless an outside force is applied to it.

interference—what happens when two waves come together. Interference results in a change in amplitude. If the change is additive (i.e. the amplitudes of the two waves are added) then the interference is constructive. If the opposite occurs, it is destructive interference.

kinetic energy—the energy of a body associated with its motion, defined as $k = \frac{1}{2}mv^2$.

Law of Electrostatics—states that like charges repel each other, while opposite charges attract each other.

magnetic field—the region in space in which a charge can experience a magnetic force. Magnetic fields flow out of the North Pole and into the South Pole.

magnetism—the property of a charge in motion, caused by the revolution of atoms around the nucleus of an atom. The direction of the magnetic effect is determined by the direction in which the electron spins around its axis.

momentum—the quantity of motion an object possesses, dependent upon the mass of the object and the velocity at which it travels. Thus, p (momentum) $= mv$. If two objects of unequal size are traveling at the same speed, the object with the greater mass has more momentum. Likewise, if two objects of equal size are traveling at different speeds, then the object with the greater speed has more momentum. Momentum is dependent upon velocity (a vector quantity), and is thus a vector quantity.

period—the time it takes for one complete wave to pass a certain point.

polarization—the selective passage of waves that only vibrate in a particular plane.

potential energy—energy dependent upon relative position as opposed to motion. Potential energy is caused by gravity or elasticity. Thus, an object's potential energy is dependent upon either its distance from the earth or the degree to which a coiled spring attached to the object has been stretched. Potential energy can be changed into kinetic energy either by dropping the object or releasing the spring.

reflection—the bouncing of a wave off a surface. Reflection of light is responsible for the formation of images in mirrors.

refraction—the bending of light as it passes from one medium to a second medium. Because different media will allow light to pass through at different speeds (i.e., different optical densities), there will be a change in velocity when light makes such a transition. This velocity change is responsible for refraction.

resistance—the opposition of current flow. When resistance occurs in a conductor, some of the kinetic energy from the moving particles is converted into heat.

scalar—a quantity that has magnitude but no direction. Examples of scalars are mass, length, time density, energy, and temperature.

speed—the distance traveled by a body over a given period of time. S (speed) = d/t (distance/time).

thermodynamic efficiency—the ideal efficiency an engine would have if it could be operated in a purely reversible fashion.

torque—the force which causes the rotation of a mass about a fixed point.

vector—a quantity that has both magnitude and direction. Examples of vectors are velocity, force, acceleration, momentum, electric field strength, and magnetic field strength. It is very important when describing vector quantities that both the magnitude and strength be described. The magnitude of force, for example, is important, but without knowing the direction of the force we cannot know how the force acts on the body. Because vectors have direction, we must be able to quantify the directional qualities of a vector. This is done by breaking a vector into two components. These components are given by the formula $A_x = A \cos \theta$ and $A_y = A \sin \theta$, where θ is the angle at which the vector is traveling relative to its origin or the body on which it acts.

velocity—the combination of the magnitude of speed with its direction. Thus the equation for the magnitude of velocity is the same as that for speed, d/t. However, some direction must also be specified using the components found above (see *vector*).

wave—any disturbance that propagates through a material medium (mechanical waves) or space (electromagnetic waves).

wavelength—the distance between a point on a wave to the same point on the next wave.

work—done on an object whenever a force moves the object some distance. Work is the product of the force causing the motion and the distance the object moves, or $W = F\Delta d$.

PRACTICE EXERCISES

You've just reviewed the most important points in science for success in taking the ACT Assessment Science Reasoning Test. The following exercises will help you to practice your new knowledge as well as to continue to familiarize yourself with the contents and format of the ACT Assessment.

There are three Science Reasoning Test exercises in this chapter. Each exercise contains two passages and a total of 12 questions and should be answered in 10 minutes. Do each exercise in one sitting in a quiet place, with no notes or reference material. Use a stopwatch or kitchen timer or have someone else watch the clock. When time is up, stop at once.

Score yourself only on those items you finished. When you're done, work through the rest of the exercise.

EXERCISES: SCIENCE TEST

Exercise 1

12 Questions • Time—10 minutes

Directions: This test consists of two passages, each followed by several questions. Read each passage, select the correct answer for each question, and mark the oval representing the correct answer on your answer sheet. You may NOT use a calculator on this test.

Passage I

Environmental levels of the *organic volatile chemical* benzene are of concern to public health officials because studies have shown that continual exposure to high concentrations of this compound can cause leukemia. Organic volatile chemicals are carbon containing compounds which are easily vaporized and therefore are present in the air. Experiments to test for the presence of such chemicals were devised.

Experiment 1

Researchers outfitted individuals in urban, suburban, and rural areas with monitoring instruments that they could wear throughout the day. These instruments recorded the concentrations of benzene they were exposed to as they went about their normal activities. Other monitoring devices were used to record the benzene output of various known sources in the participants' environment. The average percentage of total benzene that participants were exposed to from various sources as well as the average percentage of total output from these sources are given in Table 11.1.

Table 11.1

Sources	% of total benzene emissions	% of total benzene exposure
Automobiles	80%	20%
Industry	15%	4%
Household sources (e.g., stored paints and gasoline)	4.5%	35%
Cigarettes	0.5%	41%

Experiment 2

The researchers decided to look at whether other volatile organic compounds were found in greater concentrations indoors or outdoors. Residents from two areas wore monitoring devices that recorded the levels of a number of volatile organic compounds that they were exposed to during outdoor and indoor activities for several days. The first area was a highly industrial New Jersey city and the other was a rural township in Maine. The average exposure levels of residents in these areas are listed in Table 11.2.

GO ON TO THE NEXT PAGE

Table 11.2

Volatile chemical	NJ Industrial (μ/m^3)		Maine Rural Township (μ/m^3)	
	indoor	outdoor	indoor	outdoor
Trichloroethane	21	4	14	3
Tetrachloroethylene	9	3	8	1
Chloroform	5	0.2	2	0.1
O-oxylene	5	3	3	2
Styrene	5	0.5	1	0.2

Experiment 3

Fine particles in the air, particularly breathable particles (those that are 10 microns or smaller and are able to penetrate into the lungs), are another environmental concern. Large population studies have suggested that elevated outdoor concentrations of fine particles are associated with premature death. Most fine particles form through processes of combustion, such as cooking, burning candles, smoking, or burning firewood.

Researchers wanted to see what the total levels of such particles were indoors and outdoors and how these levels compared with an individual's exposure levels. Monitors that recorded levels of breathable particles were put inside and outside the homes of one individual from both of the communities in Experiment 2. These individuals were also asked to wear monitoring devices for one day and one night. The results from this experiment are shown in Table 11.3.

Table 11.3

	Day			Night		
	Personal Exposure μ/m^3	Indoor Levels μ/m^3	Outdoor Levels μ/m^3	Personal Exposure μ/m^3	Indoor Levels μ/m^3	Outdoor Levels μ/m^3
NJ Indust. City	152	98	100	75	65	95
Maine Rural Township	149	95	93	73	72	90

1. The results of Experiment 1 indicate that which of the following statements is true?

   A. Automobiles and industrial pollution are not significant sources of benzene emissions.

   B. The largest sources of benzene output were also the sources that caused the highest individual exposures.

   C. Cigarettes caused more benzene emissions than any other source tested.

   D. An individual's highest exposure to benzene was more likely to occur indoors than outdoors.

2. One of the differences between Experiment 1 and Experiment 2 is that:

   F. Experiment 1 did not investigate a volatile compound.

   G. Experiment 2 showed that people are exposed to higher levels of volatile organic compounds indoors, a finding that was contradicted by Experiment 1.

   H. Experiment 1 looked at compound emission levels, while Experiment 2 looked only at compound exposure levels.

   J. Experiment 2 looked at the average compound exposure levels from a pool of data, while Experiment 1 looked at individuals' compound exposure levels.

3. Which of the following hypotheses would best explain the results seen in Experiment 3?

   A. Moving about stirs up a personal cloud of breathable particles.

   B. Industrial sites tend to perform most combustion activities in the night hours, thus raising particle levels at night.

   C. Particles formed during cooking and smoking tend to remain suspended for at least 24 hours, so that daytime levels generally do not drop off at night.

   D. Exposure to breathable particles is largely attributable to automobile exhaust.

4. If the researchers conducting Experiment 3 added another study subject and found that he had a daytime indoor exposure level of 75 micrograms/meter^3, which of the following would be the most likely daytime personal exposure level for this individual?

   F. 65 micrograms/meter^3

   G. 75 micrograms/meter^3

   H. 85 micrograms/meter^3

   J. 125 micrograms/meter^3

5. Researchers hypothesized that volatile organic compounds follow the same pattern of personal exposure versus indoor exposure levels as that seen with breathable particles in Experiment 3. If this hypothesis is correct, which of the following is probably closest to the actual indoor level of trichloroethane in the rural Maine township?

   A. 1 micrograms/meter^3

   B. 6 micrograms/meter^3

   C. 15 micrograms/meter^3

   D. 19 micrograms/meter^3

6. To prove the hypothesis in Question 5, researchers would need to do which of the following?

   F. Conduct Experiment 2 again, but ask the subjects to wear monitoring devices only during the day.

   G. Conduct Experiment 3 again, this time asking all of the subjects from Experiment 2 to participate.

   H. Conduct Experiment 2 again, but this time place monitors in the indoor settings in addition to those worn by individuals.

   J. Conduct Experiment 2 again, but break down the individual exposure levels into those encountered during the day and during the night.

GO ON TO THE NEXT PAGE

Passage II

In small communities, infectious organisms such as Varicella-zoster virus, which causes chickenpox, occasionally become extinct. The threshold at which such extinctions occur is known as the critical community size. Extinctions are followed by a period in which there are no infections until the virus is reintroduced from an outside source.

Researchers collected data on these extinctions or *fadeouts* in various communities before the development of the chickenpox vaccine. Fadeouts were defined as a period of three or more weeks in which there were no new reported cases of the infection. They then attempted to develop computer models of the patterns of fadeouts seen using information about the dynamics of the infection. The first of the following figures shows the real data on chickenpox versus the data generated by two different computer models. The second of the figures demonstrates the different assumptions made by the two models concerning the duration of the *infectious period* (the period in which an individual can transmit the infection to another individual). This was the only difference between the two models.

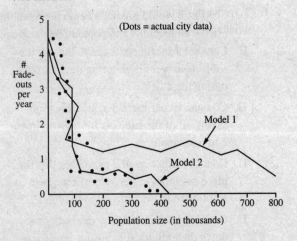

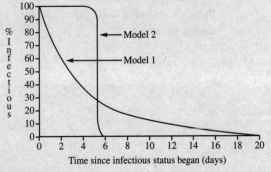

7. The critical community size for chickenpox is:
   A. Over 1 million
   B. About 700,000
   C. About 400,000
   D. Under 100,000

8. The difference between models 1 and 2 is:
   F. Model 1 predicts a more concentrated infectious period, compared with model 2.
   G. Model 1 predicts more individuals will be infectious after six days, compared with model 2.
   H. Model 2 predicts a greater number of individuals will be infectious in the early days of the infectious period, compared with model 1.
   J. All of the above.

9. Which of the following statements is best supported by the first figure?
   A. As the number of viruses climbs toward 1 million, the number of fadeouts per year declines.
   B. As a community population increases, the discrepancy between the predictive abilities of the two models increases.
   C. Model 1 is better at predicting annual fadeouts for communities under 300,000, while model 2 is better at predicting annual fadeouts for communities over 300,000.
   D. Both models overestimate the number of annual fadeouts for chickenpox.

10. In a community with a population of 300,000, the number of fadeouts per year:
    F. is below 1.
    G. is above 1.
    H. is more variable than in a population below 100,000.
    J. is lower than in a population of 500,000.

11. Which of the following statements might explain the difference in the abilities of models 1 and 2 to predict the actual number of annual fadeouts of chickenpox?

   A. Model 2 predicts that there will be more individuals spreading infection in the early infectious period, resulting in a lower number of predicted fadeouts, compared with model 1.

   B. Model 1 predicts that there will be some individuals spreading infection in the late infectious period, reducing the number of predicted fadeouts, compared with model 2.

   C. Model 2 predicts that there will be a longer infectious period in larger communities, increasing the number of predicted fadeouts, compared with model 1.

   D. Model 2 assumes a more constant rate of movement from an infectious to a non-infectious status.

12. If the researchers used another computer model for chickenpox using the assumption about the infectious period depicted below (see the following figure, model 3), what could you expect this model to predict?

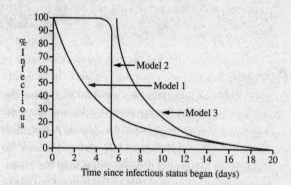

   F. Model 3 would predict more annual fadeouts than model 1.

   G. Model 3 would predict more annual fadeouts than model 2, but less than model 1.

   H. Model 3 would underestimate the number of annual fadeouts.

   J. Model 3 would predict a better correlation between fadeouts and population size than models 1 or 2.

Exercise 2

12 Questions • Time—10 minutes

Directions: This test consists of two passages, each followed by several questions. Read each passage, select the correct answer for each question, and mark the oval representing the correct answer on your answer sheet. You may NOT use a calculator on this test.

Passage I

Individuals usually have two copies of each *gene* (the basic unit of genetic material, found on the *chromosomes*), one from their mother and one from their father. Genetic or inherited diseases are those that can be passed down to the next generation through the genes. These diseases follow a number of patterns. Two of the basic ones are *dominant* and *recessive* inheritance.

In a genetic disease with a recessive inheritance pattern, an individual will not be affected by the disease unless he or she is passed two copies of the disease gene, one from each parent. An individual who is passed one copy of the disease gene is called a *healthy carrier*. He or she will not have the disease, but can still pass the gene on to an offspring. The first of the following figures shows a family with this type of genetic disease.

In a disease with a dominant inheritance pattern, any individual with a copy of the disease gene will have the disease. (Depending on the disease, individuals with two copies may have an accelerated or more severe disease course, or may be unable to survive). There is no such thing as a healthy carrier with this type of disease. The second figure shows a family with this type of genetic disease.

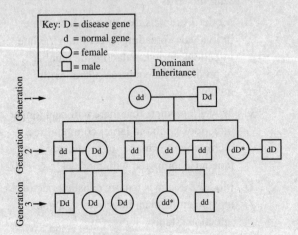

1. Which of the following is the correct number of healthy carriers in the third generation of the family depicted in the first figure?

A. None

B. 2

C. 5

D. 6

2. Which of the following is the correct number of family members with the disease in the first figure?

F. 0

G. 2

H. 10

J. 12

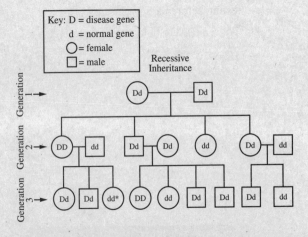

3. Which of the following statements about the first figure is true?

  A. The mother in the first generation had to have at least one parent with the disease.

  B. The father in the first generation had to have at least one parent who had one or more of the disease genes.

  C. The children of the healthy carriers in the family could end up with the disease even if the other parent is not a carrier.

  D. The daughter marked with an asterisk in the third generation could pass the disease on to her children.

4. Which of the following statements about the family in the second figure is true?

  F. Either the mother or father of the first generation father must have had the disease.

  G. Either the mother or father of the first generation mother must have been a carrier of the disease gene.

  H. There are three healthy carriers in the second generation.

  J. The couple marked with an asterisk in the second generation will be unable to have any healthy children.

5. What is the correct number of individuals with the disease in the second figure?

  A. 5

  B. 6

  C. 7

  D. There is not enough information to determine this.

6. If the generation 3 daughter marked with an asterisk in the family in the second figure was planning on having children, which of the following would be accurate advice for her regarding genetic testing?

  F. She should be tested to rule out the possibility that one or more of her children would be carriers of the disease gene, but she could be sure that none of them would develop the disease.

  G. Both she and her husband need to be tested to rule out the possibility that they are healthy carriers of the disease gene.

  H. Testing is unnecessary for the daughter; she is not carrying the disease gene.

  J. Testing one of the parents is sufficient to rule out the disease in their children.

7. The family in the following figure has a genetic disease that follows either the dominant or recessive pattern. Which of the following statements concerning this family is true?

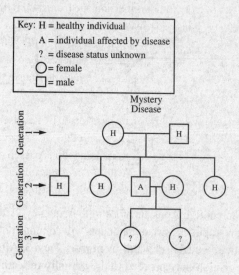

  A. Either the father or mother in the first generation is not carrying the disease gene.

  B. The family is definitely not suffering from a dominantly inherited genetic disorder.

  C. The healthy son in the second generation would have no reason to undergo genetic testing before having children.

  D. We can be sure that both of the affected son's daughters will have the disease.

GO ON TO THE NEXT PAGE

Passage II

Interferometry is a highly sensitive method of measuring distances that are close to the wavelength of light. An interferometer (depicted in the following figure) uses a *partially reflecting mirror* (one which reflects half the light and allows the other half to continue through) to split a *coherent* light source, such as a laser beam.

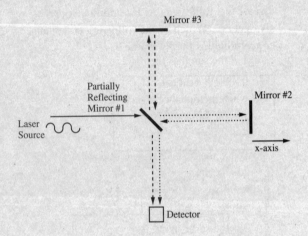

Coherent light consists of a single frequency. After the light is split, the two components will continue until they are reflected backwards by mirrors 2 and 3. After this reflection they proceed to the partially reflecting mirror again, and each path has a component (about a half) that proceeds to the light detector. The detector receives the sum of the two components of light, each with its own phase (shift of the wave with respect to a fixed spot).

Two experiments using an interometer were conducted.

Experiment 1

In Experiment 1, researchers moved mirror 2 backwards slowly, thereby lengthening the path that one component of the light travels and changing its phase. The light received by the detector was recorded at a number of positions. The following figure shows some of their findings along with the phase relationship of the waves that they deduced from these results.

Measured Light Intensity (milliwatts)	Mirror Position along x-axis (nanometers)	Phase relationship of the two different light components
1	0	
35	75	
57	150	
35	225	
1	300	

Experiment 2

In Experiment 2, researchers used various light sources with different frequencies (number of waves per second). With each source, they moved mirror 2 backwards slowly, recording the light received by the light detector at each position. The results of this experiment are shown in the following figure.

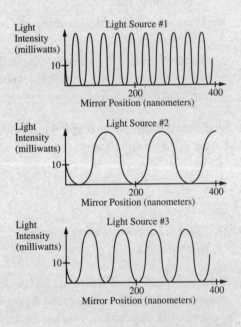

8. The factor that was varied in Experiment 1 is:

    F. the angle of the partially reflecting mirror.

    G. the wavelength (distance from one peak to the next) of one component of the light.

    H. the frequency of one component of the light.

    J. the phase of one component of the light.

9. Experiment 1 demonstrates that the lowest light intensity values occur in which situation?

   A. Only when mirror 2 is at 0 nanometers.

   B. When the two light components have different frequencies.

   C. When the light component waves are 180% out of phase (troughs occur in one component where peaks occur in the other).

   D. When the light component waves are in phase (troughs and peaks match).

10. In the figure, the asterisk on the graph 1 of light source 1 represents which of the following?

    F. A mirror position at which the two light components are in phase.

    G. A mirror position where the light intensity is the same as at 300 nm in the figure.

    H. A mirror position at which the light source is at its highest frequency.

    J. A mirror position at which the entire light source is reflected by the partially reflecting mirror.

11. Which of the following statements about the light sources in the figure is most accurate?

    A. Light source 1 is always in phase.

    B. Light source 2 has the longest wavelength.

    C. Light source 3 has a shorter wavelength than light source 1.

    D. The greatest light intensity was detected from light source 1.

12. In the figure, peak light detection should occur:

    F. when the distance from the laser to mirror 1 is the same as the distance from the laser to mirror 2.

    G. when the distance from the laser to mirror 1 is the same as the distance from the laser to the light detector.

    H. When the distance from mirror 1 to mirror 2 is the same as the distance from mirror 1 to mirror 3.

    J. When the distance from the laser to mirror 3 is the same as the distance from mirror 1 to the light detector.

Exercise 3

12 Questions • Time—10 minutes

Directions: This test consists of two passages, each followed by several questions. Read each passage, select the correct answer for each question, and mark the oval representing the correct answer on your answer sheet. You may NOT use a calculator on this test.

Passage I

Schizophrenia is a mental illness that involves the dissociation of reason and emotion, resulting in symptoms including hallucinations, hearing voices intense withdrawal, delusions, and paranoia. The average age at which schizophrenia is diagnosed is 18 years for men and 23 years for women. It has been observed to run in families.

The cause remains a mystery, but there are several competing theories. These theories are based in part on findings from twin studies, which look at identical twins in which one or both have the disease. (Identical twins share 100% of their genetic material, while nonidentical twins share about 50%.) In 50% of the cases, the other will also suffer from schizophrenia. Identical twin pairs in which one individual is ill and the other is well are referred to as *discordant twins*.

Genetic Theory

One school of thought is that schizophrenia is a *genetic disorder* (one passed through the genes from parents to children). This theory gained support from the fact that schizophrenia runs in families. While it was originally believed that it was the family environment that caused this, a study has shown that children of schizophrenics adopted by families without the disease have the same risk of developing the illness as those raised by their birth parents. A final piece of evidence is the fact that the children of discordant identical twins all have the same chance of developing the illness: 17%. This indicates that even the healthy twin is somehow carrying the agent of the disease, presumably in the genes.

Infection Theory

Another school of thought is that schizophrenia arises because of a viral infection of the brain. Studies have shown that a class of viruses called "slow viruses" can linger in the brain for 20 years or longer before the infected person shows symptoms. Brain infections with viruses such as the common cold sore virus and herpes simplex type I can cause symptoms that resemble schizophrenia. Schizophrenia is also more common in children born in the winter, the season when viral infections are more common. Also, one study looking at families with a history of schizophrenia showed a 70% increase in the rate of schizophrenia among children whose mothers had the flu during the second trimester of pregnancy.

1. The schizophrenia theories are similar in that:
   A. both postulate that the foundation of the illness may be laid before birth.
   B. both postulate that the family environment plays some role.
   C. both predict that the children of schizophrenics are not at greater risk than other individuals.
   D. both show that identical twins are at greater risk for schizophrenia than other individuals.

2. Which of the following findings best supports the gene theory?
   F. Parents of discordant twins report that the behavior of the twins begins to diverge at about five years of age, on average.
   G. In discordant identical twin pairs, a brain structure called the basal ganglia is activated more often in the ill twin than in the healthy twin.
   H. An identical twin of a schizophrenia sufferer is four times as likely to have the illness as a nonidentical twin of schizophrenia sufferer.
   J. Studies have shown that viral infections sometimes infect one identical twin in the uterus and not the other.

3. The infection theory is most effective at explaining the fact that:

I. schizophrenic patients do poorly on some memory tests.

II. among identical twins discordant for schizophrenia, the healthy twin may have some borderline schizophrenic traits.

III. ill twins in discordant pairs have higher rates of finger abnormalities, which can be an indication of a viral infection that occurred in the womb.

   A. I only

   B. II only

   C. III only

   D. II and III only

4. Which of the following hypotheses might supporters of both theories agree with?

I. Individuals with schizophrenia have certain genes that predispose them to the disease, but require some kind of trigger to turn the disease on.

II. Individuals with schizophrenia have certain genes that predispose them to viral infections of the brain.

III. Schizophrenia is not one disease but a collection of diseases.

   F. I and II only

   G. I and III only

   H. II and III only

   J. I, II, and III

5. An identical pair of twins is found in which one was adopted at birth. Both received a diagnosis of schizophrenia as teenagers. An explanation that might be offered by supporters of the viral theory is:

   A. children are most prone to viral infections when they are school age, long after the infant in this case was adopted.

   B. the stress of being an adopted child may have triggered schizophrenia in the predisposed twin.

   C. since 50% of identical twin pairs with schizophrenia are discordant for the disease, this case does not shed light on its origin.

   D. the brains of both twins may have been infected with a slow acting virus when they were still in the womb.

6. Which of the following studies would be logical for supporters of the genetic theory to conduct next?

   F. One that looks for finger abnormalities in the parents and grandparents of schizophrenic children

   G. One that looks for differences in the chromosomes (which hold the genes) of schizophrenic individuals and healthy individuals

   H. One that looks for scarring in the brains of schizophrenic individuals, which might be a sign of an early injury or infection

   J. One that looks at the home environments of identical twins versus non-identical twins

Passage II

Seychelles warblers are insect-eating birds that usually lay one egg a year. Young warblers, particularly the females, often remain with their parents for several years helping them prepare and care for the next *hatchlings* (newly hatched birds), rather than mating themselves. A *breeding pair* (mating male and female) stays in the same territory from year to year.

Two experiments regarding the breeding behavior of the Seychelles warblers were performed.

Experiment 1

Biologists rated the territories of Seychelles warblers based on the density of insects available. They followed 100 breeding pairs in high- and low-quality territories over one breeding season, recording the breeding success (determined by the survival of a hatchling to leave the nest) for pairs with various numbers of helpers (previous offspring remaining with the mating pair). The results are seen in Table 11.4.

GO ON TO THE NEXT PAGE ➡

Table 11.4

Helper #	Reproductive Success (%)
High-Quality Territory	
0	86%
1	94%
2	95%
3	79%
Low-Quality Territory	
0	75%
1	65%
2	66%
3	64%

Experiment 2

The researchers hypothesized that Seychelles warblers might be able to adjust the *sex ratio* (number of males versus number of females) of their hatchlings depending on territory quality or number of helpers present. They again looked at 100 breeding pairs with various numbers of helpers in high- and low-quality territories and recorded the sex of their offspring for one breeding season. The results appear in Table 11.5.

Table 11.5

Helper #	Male Hatchlings (%)	Female Hatchlings (%)
High-Quality Territory		
0	15%	85%
1	13%	87%
2	78%	22%
3	76%	24%
Low-Quality Territory		
0	75%	25%
1	80%	20%
2	79%	21%
3	74%	26%

7. Which of the following statements about the design of Experiments 1 and 2 is most accurate?

   A. Experiment 1 investigated breeding success, while Experiment 2 investigated sex ratios for hatchlings.

   B. Experiment 1 followed warblers for several breeding seasons, while Experiment 2 followed them for only one season.

   C. Experiment 1 looked at the effect of varying helper number, while Experiment 2 was concerned only with responses to variations in territory quality.

   D. Experiment 1 followed breeding pairs, while Experiment 2 followed the helpers of breeding pairs.

8. Which of the following graphs best depicts the relationship between helper number and male hatchlings in a high-quality territory?

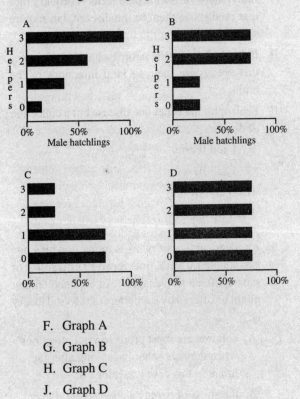

   F. Graph A

   G. Graph B

   H. Graph C

   J. Graph D

9. Based on the information in the passage, which of the following statements about reproductive success in Seychelles warblers is most accurate?

   A. Reproductive success in low-quality territories goes up with helper number.

   B. Reproductive success in high-quality territories goes down with helper number.

   C. Reproductive success is dependent on helper number but not on territory quality.

   D. Reproductive success in high-quality territories goes up if there are one or two helpers, and down if there are more than two.

10. Which of the following statements about helper number is correct?

   F. Helper number has no effect on the sex ratios of hatchlings.

   G. Helper number has no effect on the sex ratio · of hatchlings in low-quality territories.

   H. Warblers with zero or one helper have a greater proportion of female hatchlings.

   J. Warblers with zero or one helper have a greater proportion of male hatchlings.

11. Which of the following theories fits the data collected in Experiments 1 and 2?

   A. In high-quality areas, one or two helpers are useful, but more than two will put a drain on resources. Therefore breeding pairs with several helpers will adjust the sex-ratios of their hatchlings to favor males.

   B. Breeding pairs in low-quality territories need the most help in raising their hatchling and will adjust the sex-ratios of their hatchlings in an attempt to gain more males.

   C. All breeding pairs benefit from at least one helper and will adjust the sex ratios of their hatchlings to favor females if they have no helpers.

   D. Male hatchlings require more resources than female hatchlings, so only birds in high-quality territories with several helpers will adjust the sex ratios of their hatchlings to favor males.

12. Assuming that the hypothesis of the researchers conducting Experiment 2 is correct, which of the following results would you expect from experiments in which breeding pairs and their helpers were moved to different territories?

   F. Breeding pairs with several helpers moved from high-quality territories to low-quality territories switched to having more male hatchlings.

   G. Breeding pairs with one helper moved from high-quality territories to low-quality territories attempted to increase their helper number.

   H. Breeding pairs with one or two helpers moved from low-quality territories to high-quality territories switched to having mainly female hatchlings.

   J. Breeding pairs with two or more helpers moved from low-quality territories to high-quality territories did not change the sex ratios of their hatchlings.

ANSWER KEYS AND EXPLANATIONS

Exercise 1

1. D	4. J	7. C	10. F
2. H	5. B	8. J	11. A
3. A	6. H	9. B	12. H

1. **D.** Since cigarettes and household sources produce the lion's share of individuals' benzene exposure (75% of the total), it seems clear that indoor rather than outdoor sources are responsible for the highest exposure levels.

2. **H.** In Experiment 1, emission levels were compared to exposure levels; by contrast, in Experiment 2, only exposure levels were studied, while emission levels were ignored.

3. **A.** The real anomaly in Table 7.6 is the high daytime "personal exposure" levels, which far exceed all the other numbers in the chart (which are all roughly comparable to one another, whether daytime or nighttime levels are considered). Of the four answer choices, answer A does the most to explain this result: if "moving about" stirs up a cloud of particles, this would explain why people have high personal exposure levels during the day, which subside at night (when they go to bed).

4. **J.** Consider the second column of values in Table 7.6. The indoor exposure levels for the two experimental subjects shown there are quite close—98 and 95. If the third subject has an indoor exposure level of 75, that would be about 20% lower than either of the first two subjects. Now, if the personal exposure level varies by a similar amount, we'd expect the third subject to have a personal exposure level about 20% below 150—somewhere in the neighborhood of 120. Hence, answer J.

5. **B.** We see in Table 7.6 that the actual indoor levels of breathable particles are about the personal exposure levels as recorded by monitoring devices. If the same relationship holds true for trichloroethane, then the level of 14 would be reduced by the same amount, to about 9.

6. **H.** Experiment 2 measured only personal exposure levels, while Experiment 3 monitored the indoor and outdoor environments as well. To test whether the results of Experiment 3 would be duplicated with the compounds tested in Experiment 2, indoor environmental monitors would have to be added to the experiment.

7. **C.** The crucial data for answering this question are the dots in the figure, which show actual communities in which fadeouts occurred. Since all of the dots appear to the left of the 400,000 population mark, we can see that that represents the level at which fadeouts of the virus are no longer likely to occur.

8. **J.** All of the statements given in answers F, G, and H are true, as seen in the figure. The infectious period predicted in model 1 is less concentrated than in model 2 (see how long it takes for the "tail" of Model 1 to disappear at the right end of the graph). Model 1 predicts that more people will be infected after 6 days than does model 2 (there's a severe drop-off in infected individuals just prior to day 6, according to model 2). And model 2 shows a much higher infection rate in the early days than does model 1 (its curve is at the very top of the scale).

9. **B.** In the figure, notice how, at community sizes under 100,000 (the left end of the graph), the two curves of model 1 and model 2 track one another closely. (They are also both quite accurate as compared to the dots, which indicate actual experience of fadeouts.) Beyond the 100,000 population level, however, the curves gradually diverge more and more.

10. **F.** Compare the height of the dots at the 300,000 population level with the vertical scale at the left-hand side of the graph. The dots are below the one-per-year level; hence answer F.

11. **A.** To answer this question, you need to consider data from both graphs. Only statement A fits the information in both figures: Model 2 does predict a larger number of infectious people early in the cycle, and it also predicts a smaller number of fadeouts than does model 1.

12. **H.** Since the new model 3 predicts both a high number of infectious individuals in the early days (as does model 2), while also extending their recovery period over a long period of time (as does model 1), both factors would tend to reduce the number of predicted fadeouts. As a result, model 3 would probably be less accurate than model 2, erring on the side of predicting fewer fadeouts than would actually occur.

Exercise 2

1. C	4. F	7. B	10. F
2. G	5. C	8. J	11. B
3. B	6. H	9. C	12. H

1. **C.** As the key explains, the disease gene is represented by a capital D, while the normal gene is represented by a lowercase d. Thus, a healthy carrier would be a person with one disease gene and one normal gene, or a Dd combination. There are five such people depicted in the third generation of the figure.

2. **G.** Only people who have two disease genes—DD—will suffer from a disease transmitted as a recessive trait. In the figure, we see just two such people: a female (circle) in generation 2 and a female in generation 3.

3. **B.** Since the father (the square) in generation 1 has one disease gene D, he must have had a parent from whom he inherited that gene.

4. **F.** As with the father in generation 1 in the figure, we see that the disease gene D is present in the father of this family. And since this is a dominant trait, whichever parent of that individual transmitted the disease gene to him must also have suffered from the disease.

5. **C.** Anyone in the figure with even a single disease gene D will suffer from the disease. There are seven such individuals in the chart: one in generation 1, three in generation 2, and three more in generation 3.

6. **H.** Since the individual in question has genes labeled dd, she has two normal genes and does not need to worry about the possibility of transmitting a disease gene to her children.

7. **B.** The disease cannot be a dominant trait. We can tell this because the male in generation 2 who is affected by the disease (center of chart) has two healthy parents. If he had inherited a dominant disease trait from one of his parents, one or both of them would be affected by the disease as well.

8. **J.** By gradually moving mirror 2, the phase of the component of the light reflected by that mirror was gradually altered as well.

9. **C.** Look at the first and last lines in the figure. In the last column, you can see that the phase relationship is 180° out of synch on both lines. And in the first column, the light intensity is at its lowest—just one milliwatt.

10. **F.** Since, as the figure shows, light intensity is at its greatest when the two light components are in phase, then the "high points" in the figure (including the one marked with an asterisk) must represent such moments.

11. **B.** In the graphs in the figure, wavelength is represented by the horizontal distance from peak to peak or from trough to trough of the wavy lines. Since this distance is greatest in the second graph, light source 2 must have the longest wavelength.

12. **H.** As the figure suggests, maximum light intensity occurs when the two light components are perfectly in phase. The best way to ensure this happening would be for the distance traveled by the two light sources to be exactly equal, as is the case in the situation described in answer H.

Exercise 3

1. A	4. J	7. A	10. G
2. H	5. D	8. G	11. A
3. C	6. G	9. D	12. J

1. **A.** Both the genetic theory and the infection theory attribute schizophrenia to prenatal events: in one theory, to a genetic disorder; in the other, to a prenatal infection that affects the brain of a developing infant.

2. **H.** The fact that the shared incidence of schizophrenia is four times as great between identical twins as between nonidentical twins supports the idea that shared genetic material is a major factor in the development of the disorder.

3. **C.** The phenomenon described in option III would be consistent with the idea that an infection occurred during prenatal development, thus supporting the infection theory.

4. **J.** All three hypotheses could be consistent with both theories. In fact, all three could help to explain how both genetic and disease factors could be involved in producing schizophrenia.

5. **D.** Those who favor the rival theory would be apt to explain the shared incidence of schizophrenia in this case as having resulted from the shared experience of a viral infection when both infants were in the womb together.

6. **G.** It would be natural from supporters of the genetic theory to want to study the genes themselves in the hope of substantiating their theory by pinpointing the actual genetic differences that cause (or help to cause) the illness.

7. **A.** As the descriptions of the experiments make clear, Experiment 1 measured breeding success in relation to the quality of the birds' territory and the number of "helpers" the birds had, while Experiment 2 measured the ratio of male to female hatchlings against the same two variables.

8. **G.** This graph accurately reflects the data found in the upper half of Table 7.8.

9. **D.** As you can see in Table 7.7, the highest level of reproductive success in high-quality territories is found when one or two helpers are present (94% and 95% success); the rate falls off when a third helper appears (79%).

10. **G.** Look at the lower half of Table 7.8. In low-quality territories, the percentage of male hatchlings varies in a narrow, seemingly random range (between 74% and 80%) as the number of helpers varies, suggesting that the number of helpers has no real effect on the sex ratio among hatchlings there.

11. **A.** This is the only theory that even begins to explain the curious data in Table 7.8, in which all warbler pairs except low-helper pairs in high-quality territories produce more male offspring than female. If we assume that a shortage of resources favors male hatchlings (who perhaps have some different behavior from females; greater aggressiveness in pursuit of food, for example), then the pattern in Table 7.8 becomes at least understandable and consistent.

12. **J.** Since all warbler pairs with two or more helpers have high male-to-female hatchling ratios—regardless of whether they are in high-quality or low-quality territories—one would expect no change in the ratio even with a change from one territory to another.

ARE YOU READY TO MOVE ON?

How well do you understand the contents and format of the ACT Assessment Science Reasoning Test? How well have you incorporated your review knowledge into your test-taking behavior?

After you've corrected each exercise, find the number below. This will give you an idea of whether you need further help, or whether you can move on to another subject area.

Score Key for Each Practice Exercise

Number Correct	Score	Suggested Action
0–3	Poor	Study Chapters 7 and 11 again. See "Additional Sources for Review," below.
4–6	Below average	Study problem areas in Chapters 7 and 11. See "Additional Sources for Review," below if you time.
7–10	Average	Skim problem areas in Chapters 7 and 11 if you have time.
11–15	Above average	You may move on to a new subject.
16–20	Excellent	You're ready for the ACT Assessment Science Reasoning Test.

ADDITIONAL RESOURCES FOR REVIEW

If you want to review a specific science field—biology, chemistry, physics, or earth science—to feel more comfortable with the science passages on the ACT Assessment, refer to your high school textbook or favorite review book on the subject.

The three books listed below are more general guides, written to be interesting and user-friendly, that can help sharpen your understanding of "how science works." The last two, in particular, are fun to read and contain drawings and cartoons that illuminate as they entertain.

Thinking Physics: Practical Lessons in Critical Thinking. Lewis Carroll Epstein. Insight Press, 1997.

Science Matters: Achieving Scientific Literacy. Robert M. Hazen and James Trefil. Anchor Books, 1991.

The Five Biggest Ideas in Science. Charles M. Wynn and Arthur W. Wiggins. Wiley, 1997.

Three Full-Length Practice ACT Assessment Exams

PREVIEW

PRACTICE EXAMINATION 1

Answer Sheet

1. English Test

1 (A) (B) (C) (D)	20 (F) (G) (H) (J)	39 (A) (B) (C) (D)	58 (F) (G) (H) (J)
2 (F) (G) (H) (J)	21 (A) (B) (C) (D)	40 (F) (G) (H) (J)	59 (A) (B) (C) (D)
3 (A) (B) (C) (D)	22 (F) (G) (H) (J)	41 (A) (B) (C) (D)	60 (F) (G) (H) (J)
4 (F) (G) (H) (J)	23 (A) (B) (C) (D)	42 (F) (G) (H) (J)	61 (A) (B) (C) (D)
5 (A) (B) (C) (D)	24 (F) (G) (H) (J)	43 (A) (B) (C) (D)	62 (F) (G) (H) (J)
6 (F) (G) (H) (J)	25 (A) (B) (C) (D)	44 (F) (G) (H) (J)	63 (A) (B) (C) (D)
7 (A) (B) (C) (D)	26 (F) (G) (H) (J)	45 (A) (B) (C) (D)	64 (F) (G) (H) (J)
8 (F) (G) (H) (J)	27 (A) (B) (C) (D)	46 (F) (G) (H) (J)	65 (A) (B) (C) (D)
9 (A) (B) (C) (D)	28 (F) (G) (H) (J)	47 (A) (B) (C) (D)	66 (F) (G) (H) (J)
10 (F) (G) (H) (J)	29 (A) (B) (C) (D)	48 (F) (G) (H) (J)	67 (A) (B) (C) (D)
11 (A) (B) (C) (D)	30 (F) (G) (H) (J)	49 (A) (B) (C) (D)	68 (F) (G) (H) (J)
12 (F) (G) (H) (J)	31 (A) (B) (C) (D)	50 (F) (G) (H) (J)	69 (A) (B) (C) (D)
13 (A) (B) (C) (D)	32 (F) (G) (H) (J)	51 (A) (B) (C) (D)	70 (F) (G) (H) (J)
14 (F) (G) (H) (J)	33 (A) (B) (C) (D)	52 (F) (G) (H) (J)	71 (A) (B) (C) (D)
15 (A) (B) (C) (D)	34 (F) (G) (H) (J)	53 (A) (B) (C) (D)	72 (F) (G) (H) (J)
16 (F) (G) (H) (J)	35 (A) (B) (C) (D)	54 (F) (G) (H) (J)	73 (A) (B) (C) (D)
17 (A) (B) (C) (D)	36 (F) (G) (H) (J)	55 (A) (B) (C) (D)	74 (F) (G) (H) (J)
18 (F) (G) (H) (J)	37 (A) (B) (C) (D)	56 (F) (G) (H) (J)	75 (A) (B) (C) (D)
19 (A) (B) (C) (D)	38 (F) (G) (H) (J)	57 (A) (B) (C) (D)	

2. Math Test

1 (A) (B) (C) (D) (E)	16 (F) (G) (H) (J) (K)	31 (A) (B) (C) (D) (E)	46 (F) (G) (H) (J) (K)
2 (F) (G) (H) (J) (K)	17 (A) (B) (C) (D) (E)	32 (F) (G) (H) (J) (K)	47 (A) (B) (C) (D) (E)
3 (A) (B) (C) (D) (E)	18 (F) (G) (H) (J) (K)	33 (A) (B) (C) (D) (E)	48 (F) (G) (H) (J) (K)
4 (F) (G) (H) (J) (K)	19 (A) (B) (C) (D) (E)	34 (F) (G) (H) (J) (K)	49 (A) (B) (C) (D) (E)
5 (A) (B) (C) (D) (E)	20 (F) (G) (H) (J) (K)	35 (A) (B) (C) (D) (E)	50 (F) (G) (H) (J) (K)
6 (F) (G) (H) (J) (K)	21 (A) (B) (C) (D) (E)	36 (F) (G) (H) (J) (K)	51 (A) (B) (C) (D) (E)
7 (A) (B) (C) (D) (E)	22 (F) (G) (H) (J) (K)	37 (A) (B) (C) (D) (E)	52 (F) (G) (H) (J) (K)
8 (F) (G) (H) (J) (K)	23 (A) (B) (C) (D) (E)	38 (F) (G) (H) (J) (K)	53 (A) (B) (C) (D) (E)
9 (A) (B) (C) (D) (E)	24 (F) (G) (H) (J) (K)	39 (A) (B) (C) (D) (E)	54 (F) (G) (H) (J) (K)
10 (F) (G) (H) (J) (K)	25 (A) (B) (C) (D) (E)	40 (F) (G) (H) (J) (K)	55 (A) (B) (C) (D) (E)
11 (A) (B) (C) (D) (E)	26 (F) (G) (H) (J) (K)	41 (A) (B) (C) (D) (E)	56 (F) (G) (H) (J) (K)
12 (F) (G) (H) (J) (K)	27 (A) (B) (C) (D) (E)	42 (F) (G) (H) (J) (K)	57 (A) (B) (C) (D) (E)
13 (A) (B) (C) (D) (E)	28 (F) (G) (H) (J) (K)	43 (A) (B) (C) (D) (E)	58 (F) (G) (H) (J) (K)
14 (F) (G) (H) (J) (K)	29 (A) (B) (C) (D) (E)	44 (F) (G) (H) (J) (K)	59 (F) (G) (H) (J) (K)
15 (A) (B) (C) (D) (E)	30 (F) (G) (H) (J) (K)	45 (A) (B) (C) (D) (E)	60 (A) (B) (C) (D) (E)

3. Reading Test

1 Ⓐ Ⓑ Ⓒ Ⓓ	11 Ⓐ Ⓑ Ⓒ Ⓓ	21 Ⓐ Ⓑ Ⓒ Ⓓ	31 Ⓐ Ⓑ Ⓒ Ⓓ
2 Ⓕ Ⓖ Ⓗ Ⓙ	12 Ⓕ Ⓖ Ⓗ Ⓙ	22 Ⓕ Ⓖ Ⓗ Ⓙ	32 Ⓕ Ⓖ Ⓗ Ⓙ
3 Ⓐ Ⓑ Ⓒ Ⓓ	13 Ⓐ Ⓑ Ⓒ Ⓓ	23 Ⓐ Ⓑ Ⓒ Ⓓ	33 Ⓐ Ⓑ Ⓒ Ⓓ
4 Ⓕ Ⓖ Ⓗ Ⓙ	14 Ⓕ Ⓖ Ⓗ Ⓙ	24 Ⓕ Ⓖ Ⓗ Ⓙ	34 Ⓕ Ⓖ Ⓗ Ⓙ
5 Ⓐ Ⓑ Ⓒ Ⓓ	15 Ⓐ Ⓑ Ⓒ Ⓓ	25 Ⓐ Ⓑ Ⓒ Ⓓ	35 Ⓐ Ⓑ Ⓒ Ⓓ
6 Ⓕ Ⓖ Ⓗ Ⓙ	16 Ⓕ Ⓖ Ⓗ Ⓙ	26 Ⓕ Ⓖ Ⓗ Ⓙ	36 Ⓕ Ⓖ Ⓗ Ⓙ
7 Ⓐ Ⓑ Ⓒ Ⓓ	17 Ⓐ Ⓑ Ⓒ Ⓓ	27 Ⓐ Ⓑ Ⓒ Ⓓ	37 Ⓐ Ⓑ Ⓒ Ⓓ
8 Ⓕ Ⓖ Ⓗ Ⓙ	18 Ⓕ Ⓖ Ⓗ Ⓙ	28 Ⓕ Ⓖ Ⓗ Ⓙ	38 Ⓕ Ⓖ Ⓗ Ⓙ
9 Ⓐ Ⓑ Ⓒ Ⓓ	19 Ⓐ Ⓑ Ⓒ Ⓓ	29 Ⓐ Ⓑ Ⓒ Ⓓ	39 Ⓐ Ⓑ Ⓒ Ⓓ
10 Ⓕ Ⓖ Ⓗ Ⓙ	20 Ⓕ Ⓖ Ⓗ Ⓙ	30 Ⓕ Ⓖ Ⓗ Ⓙ	40 Ⓕ Ⓖ Ⓗ Ⓙ

4. Science ReasoningTest

1 Ⓐ Ⓑ Ⓒ Ⓓ	11 Ⓐ Ⓑ Ⓒ Ⓓ	21 Ⓐ Ⓑ Ⓒ Ⓓ	31 Ⓐ Ⓑ Ⓒ Ⓓ
2 Ⓕ Ⓖ Ⓗ Ⓙ	12 Ⓕ Ⓖ Ⓗ Ⓙ	22 Ⓕ Ⓖ Ⓗ Ⓙ	32 Ⓕ Ⓖ Ⓗ Ⓙ
3 Ⓐ Ⓑ Ⓒ Ⓓ	13 Ⓐ Ⓑ Ⓒ Ⓓ	23 Ⓐ Ⓑ Ⓒ Ⓓ	33 Ⓐ Ⓑ Ⓒ Ⓓ
4 Ⓕ Ⓖ Ⓗ Ⓙ	14 Ⓕ Ⓖ Ⓗ Ⓙ	24 Ⓕ Ⓖ Ⓗ Ⓙ	34 Ⓕ Ⓖ Ⓗ Ⓙ
5 Ⓐ Ⓑ Ⓒ Ⓓ	15 Ⓐ Ⓑ Ⓒ Ⓓ	25 Ⓐ Ⓑ Ⓒ Ⓓ	35 Ⓐ Ⓑ Ⓒ Ⓓ
6 Ⓕ Ⓖ Ⓗ Ⓙ	16 Ⓕ Ⓖ Ⓗ Ⓙ	26 Ⓕ Ⓖ Ⓗ Ⓙ	36 Ⓕ Ⓖ Ⓗ Ⓙ
7 Ⓐ Ⓑ Ⓒ Ⓓ	17 Ⓐ Ⓑ Ⓒ Ⓓ	27 Ⓐ Ⓑ Ⓒ Ⓓ	37 Ⓐ Ⓑ Ⓒ Ⓓ
8 Ⓕ Ⓖ Ⓗ Ⓙ	18 Ⓕ Ⓖ Ⓗ Ⓙ	28 Ⓕ Ⓖ Ⓗ Ⓙ	38 Ⓕ Ⓖ Ⓗ Ⓙ
9 Ⓐ Ⓑ Ⓒ Ⓓ	19 Ⓐ Ⓑ Ⓒ Ⓓ	29 Ⓐ Ⓑ Ⓒ Ⓓ	39 Ⓐ Ⓑ Ⓒ Ⓓ
10 Ⓕ Ⓖ Ⓗ Ⓙ	20 Ⓕ Ⓖ Ⓗ Ⓙ	30 Ⓕ Ⓖ Ⓗ Ⓙ	40 Ⓕ Ⓖ Ⓗ Ⓙ

TEAR HERE

Practice Examination 1

1. ENGLISH TEST

75 Questions • Time—45 Minutes

Directions: This test consists of five passages in which particular words or phrases are underlined and numbered. Alongside the passage, you will see alternative words and phrases that could be substituted for the underlined part. You must select the alternative that expresses the idea most clearly and correctly or that best fits the style and tone of the entire passage. If the original version is best, select "No Change."

The test also includes questions about entire paragraphs and the passage as a whole. These questions are identified by a number in a box.

After you select the correct answer for each question, mark the oval representing the correct answer on your answer sheet.

Passage I

On Coping in Another Culture

Language schools are booming, partially <u>though</u> in
1
an era of global trade, businessmen realize that foreign languages can be a valuable asset. But a little learning is a dangerous <u>thing unless</u> you can really handle a
2
language, it is best to limit yourself to a few gracious phrases. Much more important is an awareness of non-verbal behavior and the cultural nuances of the country you <u>were visiting</u>.
3

The first thing you need to <u>know, however</u>, is
4
whether you are dealing with a "low-context" or a "high-context" culture. Low-context cultures, such as those of the United States, England and Germany, spell things out verbally and rely on a more literal

1. A. NO CHANGE
    B. because
    C. since
    D. OMIT the underlined portion.

2. F. thing, and
    G. thing, unless
    H. thing. Unless
    J. thing; however

3. A. NO CHANGE
    B. have visited
    C. will have visited
    D. are visiting

4. F. NO CHANGE
    G. know, indeed
    H. know
    J. believe, therefore

GO ON TO THE NEXT PAGE ➡

interpretation of the spoken word. <u>There</u> tends to be no

5

gap between what is said and what is meant.

On the other hand, high-context <u>cultures, which</u>

6

<u>reside in Spain, France, Mexico, Japan, communicate</u>

more by nuance and implication, <u>for that reason</u> rely-

7

ing less on actual words than on gestures and situa-

tions. What remains <u>unsaid is</u> often what is most

8

important.

[9] The Japanese will listen and nod their heads and encourage you to go on, no matter what they think. This is a show of respect. The closest anyone will come to saying no is, "It is very difficult," or, "We will

5. A. NO CHANGE
   B. their
   C. they're
   D. it

6. F. NO CHANGE
   G. cultures, such as reside in Spain, France, Mexico and Japan, communicate
   H. cultures: Spain, France, Mexico, Japan, communicate
   J. cultures—Spain, France, Mexico, Japan— communicate

7. A. NO CHANGE
   B. and for that reason
   C. which is why they
   D. OMIT the underlined portion.

8. F. NO CHANGE
   G. unsaid that is
   H. unsaid, which is
   J. unsaid is not

9. Which of the following sentences best continues to develop and support the theme of the essay while providing a smooth transition between the preceding paragraph and this one?
   A. In Japan, for example, people will never say no or openly disagree with you.
   B. One of the best examples of this would be the culture of Japan.
   C. Mexicans and Japanese are famous for being gracious hosts.
   D. High-context cultures often prize politeness and expressive mannerisms.

give this positive study." [10] If someone is truly

interested in what you are proposing, <u>you will engage</u>
                              11
<u>in a dialogue on the subject</u> rather than simply
encouraging you to speak.

   Gestures too are potential sources of miscommuni-

cation. <u>Even</u> handshakes differ in subtle ways from
              12
country to country. The British handshake is firm and
used infrequently. In Italy and France, a gentler grip
will make a better impression. The Germans and
Danes nod their heads when they shake hands as a
gesture of respect, but someone <u>not knowing this</u>
                                    13
might misinterpret their attitude as being aggressive.
Likewise, looking directly into someone's eyes, which
is a staple of Anglo-American trust-building, is

10. Given that all are true, which of the following
    sentences, if added here, would best enhance the
    illustration of that aspect of Japanese culture
    being discussed while at the same time main-
    taining the flow of the paragraph?

    F. The Japanese have developed a complex
       set of rules aimed at saving face.

    G. What this really means is "Let's forget the
       whole business."

    H. It is, therefore, best not to state your own
       disagreement too boldly.

    J. It is crucial for the Japanese to take into
       account the ranking order within any
       group.

11. A. NO CHANGE

    B. they could engage you in a dialogue on the
       subject

    C. you will be engaged in a dialogue on the
       subject

    D. he or she will engage you in a dialogue on
       the subject

12. F. NO CHANGE

    G. Because

    H. And particularly

    J. While even

13. A. NO CHANGE

    B. who does not know this

    C. wary of this

    D. whom is unaware of this

GO ON TO THE NEXT PAGE

considered too aggressive in most countries of the Orient. [14] 15

14. Which of the following sentences, if added here, would best conclude the paragraph and tie it back to the main idea of the essay?

F. Even a classic American O.K. sign is considered vulgar in countries such as Brazil and Greece.

G. Thus it is imperative to take care in making gestures while abroad and to follow the lead of your hosts.

H. If, however, you find you are unsure how to read the codes of another culture, you can at least pay attention and strive to be polite on your own.

J. Because of the variety of meanings that can be ascribed to a single gesture, it is important to study cultural habits before arriving in a foreign country.

Item 15 poses a question about the essay as a whole.

15. Suppose the writer had been assigned to write an essay exploring the distinction between low-context and high-context cultures. Would this essay successfully fulfill that assignment?

A. Yes, because the essay focuses on patterns of difference between high-context and low-context cultures.

B. Yes, because the essay describes in detail the contrast between Japanese and German customs.

C. No, because the essay only makes the distinction within a more general treatment of cultural differences.

D. No, because the essay fails to define the terms "low-context" and "high-context" and give clear examples.

Passage II
The Decline of Leisure

<1>

When I think of the decline of leisure, I picture a scene witnessed not too long ago by me on a river in

16. F. NO CHANGE

G. which was witnessed not to long ago

H. that I witnessed not too long ago

J. I was witness to, not too long ago

16

Idaho. I went there to <u>fly-fish on</u> a warm September
17

day. Beside the lazy rush of the current, there was a

much more frenetic rush of canoes and rafts and

rowboats full of <u>fishermen, rowing furiously, staking</u>
18

<u>out beachheads and casting</u> with the intensity of a

competition.

<2>

In high season, fishing on the West's great rivers is

like entering gold rush days. [19] The grand landscape

is crowded with anglers who <u>managed</u> to carve time
20

from their hectic schedules, and most are practicing a

capital-intensive form of leisure.

<3>

Today's fishermen don't feel they are for real unless

they're sporting <u>every one of</u> the right clothes and
21

equipment, the gear they've seen in magazines and

catalogues. Fashionable rods and reels, polarized

glasses, the right hat, rain jacket, boots, waders, and

17. A. NO CHANGE
B. fly-fish, on
C. fly-fish, but on
D. fly-fish: on

18. F. NO CHANGE
G. fishermen who rowed furiously, staked out beachheads, and casting
H. fishermen. Rowing furiously, staking out beachheads and casting
J. fishermen that rowed furiously, staking out beachheads and casting

19. The writer wishes to add a sentence here in order to make the description more vivid. Which of the following would most effectively accomplish this?
A. The struggle for valuable space is fierce.
B. Fishermen race to claim inviting pools and scowl at strangers.
C. Independently minded men guard their territory jealously.
D. The scene is like something out of a movie.

20. F. NO CHANGE
G. manage
H. have managed
J. had managed

21. A. NO CHANGE
B. many of
C. a complete outfit of
D. OMIT the underlined portion.

GO ON TO THE NEXT PAGE ➤

fly box are essential. And time, instead of melting into the river, <u>is being</u> reckoned with and <u>watched, guides</u>
22   23
are hired because the hours are limited, the fish must be caught, and the great outdoors must be enjoyed at least enough to warrant the expense.

<4>

(1) Even free time now demands efficient productivity. (2) This type of scene is repeated at national parks, ski resorts, tennis clubs and shopping malls. (3) The Friday morning after Thanksgiving, people <u>that</u>
24
<u>have</u> the day off line up in front of toy stores at six in the <u>morning, buying</u> this year's hottest gift. (4) No
25

wonder we don't know how to relax. [26]

<5>

Increasingly, we pay for consumer goods by racking up debt and bartering away our leisure time. Contrary to its promise, technology has made us work harder by blurring the boundaries between office and home, between work and play. [27] And technology itself is an expensive, ever-changing product most of us can't do without.

<6>

The desire to consume is rapidly replacing the desire for <u>leisure, in fact, is</u> being transformed into activities
28

22. F. NO CHANGE
    G. is
    H. must be
    J. has been

23. A. NO CHANGE
    B. watched, and guides
    C. watched; and guides
    D. watched: Guides

24. F. NO CHANGE
    G. with
    H. who have
    J. taking

25. A. NO CHANGE
    B. morning: buying
    C. morning, to buy
    D. morning to buy

26. Which of the following sequences of sentences will make paragraph 4 most logical?
    F. 2, 1, 3, 4
    G. 1, 3, 4, 2
    H. 4, 1, 3, 2
    J. 3, 2, 1, 4

27. At this point, the author wishes to insert a concise supporting sentence. Which of the following would be most effective?
    A. I remember setting out on a family vacation only to have my cell phone ring in the car.
    B. Computers, e-mail and cell phones have made it much more difficult to disconnect.
    C. Many of us take home work and call the office on our days off.
    D. The complex ramifications of technology are being slowly recognized.

28. F. NO CHANGE
    G. leisure, and in fact, it is
    H. leisure. In fact, it is
    J. leisure. In fact, leisure is

and products. What would you do if you had more free time? The very question is contrary to the definition of leisure. <u>It</u> used to mean spending a day doing almost

29

nothing. 30

Passage III

An Uncompromising Nature

\<1\>

<u>Since</u> his early photographs of soldiers in the Pacific

31

theater to his final book about the effects of pollution on a Japanese fishing village, the documentary photographs of W. Eugene Smith <u>are known to view-</u>

32

<u>ers</u> and critical acclaim. W. Eugene Smith, however, was never satisfied with his work and considered some to be an utter failure.

\<2\>

He was a difficult man who overcame great odds and little formal education to become one of America's

29. The writer wants to link the essay's opening and its conclusion. Which of the alternatives most successfully achieves this effect?

A. NO CHANGE

B. Relaxation

C. Going fishing

D. Before its decline, leisure

Item 30 poses a question about the essay as a whole.

30. Suppose the writer were to eliminate paragraph 1. This omission would cause the essay as a whole to lose primarily:

F. relevant details depicting the decline of leisure.

G. irrelevant details from a colorful anecdote.

H. background information that establishes the author's expertise.

J. the connection between fishing and the transformation of leisure.

31. A. NO CHANGE

B. Whereas

C. From

D. As of

32. F. NO CHANGE

G. have been known to viewers

H. have been praised by viewers

J. have won praise from viewers

GO ON TO THE NEXT PAGE ➤

best known photographers. His uncompromising nature and the desire for complete control over <u>his</u>
33
<u>negatives, prints and</u> all aspects of his published work led him to fight constantly with the magazine editors who hired him. He missed <u>deadlines,</u> he was
34
unwilling to take a few quick pictures in order to fulfill an assignment.

<3>

[35] He had to get to know his subject first. He

would spend a great deal of time in the company of

<u>country doctors, Spanish peasants, African-American</u>
36
<u>midwives</u> before he ever picked up his camera. The

idea was to <u>become friendly, friendly enough</u> that he
37
could turn almost invisible when he trained the camera on their lives. The results were intimate, heartfelt <u>portraits, a poetic homage to the human spirit.</u>
38

33. A. NO CHANGE
B. his negatives and prints
C. both his negatives and prints
D. OMIT the underlined portion.

34. F. NO CHANGE
G. deadlines because
H. deadlines and
J. OMIT the underlined portion.

35. Which of the following sentences, if added here, would provide the most logical transition between paragraphs 2 and 3?
A. Most photographers began photographing the day they arrived on location, but Smith couldn't work like that.
B. Smith was too independent a man to take orders from magazine editors who didn't know as much about photography as he did.
C. Smith considered himself to be an artist and only worked when he was inspired.
D. Unlike other photographers, Smith cared more about the quality of his work than the pay he received.

36. F. NO CHANGE
G. country doctors, Spanish peasants, and African-American midwives
H. country doctors; Spanish peasants; African-American midwives;
J. country doctors or Spanish peasants and African-American midwives

37. A. NO CHANGE
B. be friendly enough
C. become so familiar
D. become familiar, so

38. F. NO CHANGE
G. portraits, poetic works that pay homage to the human spirit.
H. portraits. Poetic works that pay homage to the human spirit.
J. portraits, which are a poetic homage to the human spirit.

<4>

(1) In 1955, <u>Smith, which was hired to take a series</u>
                                                          39
<u>of photographs</u> of Pittsburgh for the city's centennial

celebration. (2) The deadline came and went while

Smith wandered the <u>streets in which he read histories</u>
                                                          40

of the city. (3)The assignment was supposed to

last three weeks. (4) He became entranced by his

subject. [41]

<5>

His ambition grew to encompass <u>the many faces of</u>
                                                          42

<u>Pittsburgh: its steel industry and workers; its forgotten</u>

<u>neighborhoods; its backyards, bridges and parks.</u> He

set out to capture the very spirit of a time and a place.

His stay in Pittsburgh lasted nearly a year and he

took over 11,000 photographs. For years, he sorted

through the <u>prints, a huge task of trying</u> to put together
                                                          43

his masterpiece. When a small portion of the work was

finally published, he <u>considered that</u> a failure: the
                                                          44

39. A. NO CHANGE

B. Smith, who was hired to take a series of
   photographs

C. Smith, hired to take a series of photographs,

D. Smith was hired to take a series of photographs

40. F. NO CHANGE

G. streets and read histories

H. streets about which he read in histories

J. streets that were read about in histories

41. Which of the following sequences of sentences
    makes paragraph 4 most logical?

A. NO CHANGE

B. 1, 3, 2, 4

C. 1, 4, 3, 2

D. 3, 2, 1, 4

42. F. NO CHANGE

G. the many faces of Pittsburgh: it's steel industry and workers, it's forgotten neighborhoods;
   it's backyards, bridges and parks.

H. the many faces of Pittsburgh, its steel industry and workers, its forgotten neighborhoods,
   its backyards, bridges and parks.

J. the many faces of Pittsburgh—its steel industry and workers, its forgotten neighborhoods—its backyards, bridges and parks.

43. A. NO CHANGE

B. prints in a huge attempt

C. prints, trying

D. prints, trying in a huge attempt

44. F. NO CHANGE

G. considered it

H. considered what

J. considered that to be

GO ON TO THE NEXT PAGE

images did not do justice to the spirit he had spent so long pursuing. [45]

45. Which of the following, if added here, would most effectively conclude the essay and tie the conclusion to the beginning?

A. The world, however, is lucky to posses such an eloquent and uncompromising failure.

B. W. Eugene Smith was the harshest critic of his own work.

C. The Pittsburgh project was never completed, yet it still provides a powerful document of the 1950's.

D. W. Eugene Smith was an artist of the highest rank.

Passage IV

A Wondrous Moment

<1>

For the past two weeks, I've been a guest on board
46

46. F. NO CHANGE
   G. past, twice weeks
   H. past, two weeks
   J. past: two weeks

The Regina IV, a fully -equipped research vessel
47

hoping for a close-up view of sperm whales. From the scientists on board, I have gathered quite a bit of

47. A. NO CHANGE
   B. *The Regina IV*, a fully-equipped research vessel, hoping for a close-up view of sperm whales
   C. *The Regina IV*, a research vessel, hoping for a close-up view of sperm whales
   D. *The Regina IV*, hoping for a close-up view of sperm whales

information for my article, but until now we have not
48

been able to track a pod for observation.

48. F. NO CHANGE
   G. up until now
   H. so far
   J. as of late

<2>

We rush to the bridge and our binoculars are trained
49

49. A. NO CHANGE
   B. our binoculars train themselves on
   C. train our binoculars on
   D. through our binoculars we train on

on the sea. A group of sperm whales is floating close
50

50. F. NO CHANGE
   G. jammed together
   H. squeezed against each other
   J. packed together like sardines

together at the surface. Surprisingly, they don't dive
and barely seem to be in motion. Then we spot
the widening pool of blood, the oily slick created from
                            51
their blubber. The whales are gathered in a circle,
heads at the center, tails facing out like the spokes in

a wheel, it's a posture of defense.
           52

           <3>

[53] A group of killer whales, their dorsal fins

arched ominously above the waterline, race around
                           54
just outside the circle of sperm whales. One of the

killer whales cuts headlong between the thrashing tails
           55
and crunches into the flank of a sperm whale.

Almost before the killer whale can be seen in its
             56
retreat, fresh-blood oozes to the surface of the sea.
Then the posse of killer whales turns and moves
away from their prey. The sperm whales, however,
hold their defensive posture, as if they know it is a ruse.

51. A. NO CHANGE
    B. the widening pool of blood: the oily slick
       created from their blubber.
    C. the widening pool of blood and also the
       oily slick created from their blubber.
    D. the widening pool, blood, and the oily slick
       created from their blubber.

52. F. NO CHANGE
    G. wheel. It is a posture of defense.
    H. wheel, in a posture of defense.
    J. OMIT the underlined portion.

53. Which of the following sentences, if added here,
    would enhance the narrative flow and provide a
    satisfactory transition between paragraphs 2
    and 3?
    A. Never have I seen anything like it.
    B. Sperm whales have been known to do this
       when under attack.
    C. Soon the reason becomes apparent.
    D. None of us is prepared for what comes
       next.

54. F. NO CHANGE
    G. race
    H. raced around
    J. races around

55. A. NO CHANGE
    B. heading
    C. fast
    D. OMIT the underlined portion.

56. F. NO CHANGE
    G. retreats
    H. is seen retreating
    J. is seen to be retreating

GO ON TO THE NEXT PAGE

<4>

A few quiet minutes pass, <u>holding me with</u> a strange
                                                57

and awful suspense. On the one hand, I hope the killer

whales will disappear; on the other hand, I am

excited to witness an event that none of the researchers

on this boat has ever seen before.

<5>

Suddenly several killer whales charge out of the

distance. <u>Their is</u> a flurry of tails beating the water,
              58

followed by a heaving of the circle and a lone sperm

whale is dragged away from the circle.

<6>

Nature is supposed to be savage, but what happens

next is an act of heartwarming beauty. Despite open-

ing themselves up to attack, a pair of sperm whales

breaks from the circle and [59] escorts their maimed

57. A. NO CHANGE
    B. holding I with
    C. holding me to
    D. holding me in

58. F. NO CHANGE
    G. They are
    H. There are
    J. There is

59. Which of the following, if added here, would
    most effectively emphasize the emotion and
    meaning intended by the author in describing
    this event?

    A. with boundless courage in the face of
       disaster,

    B. with great speed and daring,

    C. like soldiers retrieving a fallen comrade
       from the line of fire,

    D. like the huge, unpredictable behemoths
       they are,

companion back to the floundering formation. ⑥⓪

Passage V

A Fall Harvest

<1>

Usually, it is wise to age a wine before you drink it. The *Beaujolais Nouveau* is an exception; it is best
  61
when young. In fact, time is of the essence with this

unique wine. Weeks after the grapes having been
          62
harvested, following a process of rapid fermentation and bottling, the new wine is ready to drink. At one minute past midnight, on the third Thursday of each
    63
November, bottles of *Beaujolais Nouveau* are sent out to shops and restaurants all over the world. This annual event is heralded by colorful banners that reads, in
         64
many languages, "The *Beaujolais Nouveau* has arrived!"

Item 60 poses a question about the essay as a whole.

60. Suppose the writer had been assigned to write an essay describing the method that killer whales employ to kill their prey. Would this essay successfully fulfill the assignment?

F. Yes, because the essay focuses on the way in which killer whales attack a pod of sperm whales.

G. Yes, because the essay describes the acts of the killer whales in great detail.

H. No, because the essay focuses primarily on the behavior of the sperm whales.

J. No, because the essay omits any mention of how the killer whales tracked their prey.

61. A. NO CHANGE
B. it, the
C. it. Because the
D. it, because the

62. F. NO CHANGE
G. are
H. being quickly
J. are being

63. A. NO CHANGE
B. passed
C. passing
D. past to

64. F. NO CHANGE
G. reads'
H. read
J. reading

GO ON TO THE NEXT PAGE ➤

<2>

Whenever I see most of these banners, I am re-
65

minded of the month I spent harvesting grapes in the

Beaujolais region of France. [66] Every day at the

crack of dawn, the grape pickers piled into a wagon

and rode out to the fields. In order to complete the

harvest in a hurry the owner of the vineyard had drawn
67

workers from many countries. In addition to Ameri-

cans like myself, they're were Algerians, Moroccans,
68

Poles and Bulgarians. Although everyone spoke some

French, the conversation that traveled through the

morning air was usually a jumble of languages.

<3>

(1) Harvesting grapes is difficult work. (2) To pass
69

the time, we would often tell each other about our

homes and families, sing our favorite songs, or even

dream out loud about the ideal menu for a special

dinner. (3) A long day in the fields would have allowed
70

plenty of time for learning about different cultures and

---

65. A. NO CHANGE
   B. few of these banners
   C. several of these banners
   D. one of these banners

66. Which of the alternatives best provides new, specific details about the *Beaujolais* region of France?
   F. NO CHANGE
   G. The *Beaujolais* region is located south of Macon and north of Lyon.
   H. The *Beaujolais* region is a specific region of France.
   J. While the *Beaujolais* is famous for wine, many regions in France are known for specific food items, such as a special sandwich in *Provence*.

67. A. NO CHANGE
   B. hurry, the owner of the vineyard had drawn
   C. hurry the owner of the vineyard, had drawn
   D. hurry, the owner of the vineyard had drawn,

68. F. NO CHANGE
   G. their were
   H. there were
   J. there are

69. A. NO CHANGE
   B. grapes, for this harvest, is
   C. grapes for this harvest is
   D. grapes in a jumble of languages, is

70. F. NO CHANGE
   G. will allow
   H. had allowed
   J. allowed

backgrounds. (4) Sometimes, <u>although</u>, we learned
                              71

that we were not so different after all. [72]

<4>

(1) One morning, while working alongside a young
man from Poland, I thought I recognized the song he
was singing. (2) The song was a popular American hit

<u>of the year's</u> before, Michael <u>Jacksons</u> *Billie Jean*.
       73   74
(3) We both knew all the words. (4) Hearing me, he
looked up and laughed. (5) Soon we were singing
together. (6) I quickly found myself humming

along. [75]

71. A. NO CHANGE
    B. however
    C. nevertheless
    D. even so

72. The writer wants to add the following descrip-
    tion of the work to paragraph 3:
    It involves much squatting and heavy lifting.
    This sentence would most logically be placed:
    F. before Sentence 1.
    G. after Sentence 1.
    H. before Sentence 3.
    J. before Sentence 4.

73. A. NO CHANGE
    B. of the years'
    C. from the years'
    D. from the year

74. F. NO CHANGE
    G. Jackson's
    H. Jacksons'
    J. Jackson

75. Which of the following sequences will make
    paragraph 4 most logical?
    A. 1, 4, 5, 2, 3, 6
    B. 1, 5, 3, 2, 4, 6
    C. 1, 6, 4, 5, 3, 2
    D. 1, 2, 5, 3, 6, 4

STOP

END OF SECTION 1. IF YOU HAVE ANY TIME LEFT, GO OVER YOUR
WORK IN THIS SECTION ONLY. DO NOT WORK IN ANY OTHER
SECTION OF THE TEST.

2. MATH TEST

60 Questions • Time—60 Minutes

Directions: Solve each problem below and mark the oval representing the correct answer on your answer sheet.

Be careful not to spend too much time on any one question. Instead, solve as many questions as possible, and then use any remaining time to return to those questions you were unable to answer at first.

You may use a calculator on any problem in this test; however, not every problem requires the use of a calculator.

Diagrams that accompany problems may or may not be drawn to scale. Unless otherwise indicated, you may assume that all figures shown lie in a plane and that lines that appear straight are straight.

1. If $\frac{x}{3}$, $\frac{x}{7}$, and $\frac{x}{9}$ are all positive integers, what is the least possible value of x?

   A. 21
   B. 27
   C. 36
   D. 63
   E. 189

2. In order to meet quality standards, a box of "Fruity Flakes" cereal must include at least 400 grams of cereal, but no more than 405 grams of cereal. If c represents the weight of the cereal, in grams, this standard can be indicated by which of the following inequalities?

   F. $400 < c < 405$
   G. $400 \leq c < 405$
   H. $400 \leq c \leq 405$
   J. $400 > c > 405$
   K. $400 \geq c \geq 405$

3. A certain town's police department gave out 4,860 tickets for violations over a one year period. If 70% of the issued tickets were for parking violations, how many of the tickets were issued for other violations?

   A. 1,458
   B. 2,430
   C. 2,592
   D. 3,402
   E. 4,560

4. If $2x + 4 = -4(x - 1)$, then $x = $?

   F. $-\frac{4}{3}$
   G. $-\frac{1}{6}$
   H. 0
   J. 1
   K. $\frac{4}{3}$

5. If $(vw^2)(xy)^2z^4 = 10$, which of the following CANNOT be negative?

   A. v
   B. w
   C. x
   D. y
   E. z

6. A line can be expressed in the slope-intercept form $y = mx + b$, where m and b are constants. What is the slope-intercept form of the equation $4x + 3y = 15$?

   F. $y = -\frac{4}{3}x + 5$
   G. $y = -\frac{4}{3}x + 1$
   H. $y = -\frac{3}{4}x - 5$
   J. $y = -\frac{3}{4}x + 5$
   K. $x = -\frac{3}{4}y + \frac{15}{4}$

7. The volume of a right cylinder can be expressed as $\pi r^2 h$, where r is the radius of the base of the cylinder and h is the height of the cylinder. What is the volume, in cubic inches, of a cylinder that has a base of radius 4 inches and a height of 8 inches?

    A. 16π

    B. 32π

    C. 64π

    D. 96π

    E. 128π

8. In the figure below, lines P and Q are parallel and line R is a transversal of lines P and Q. If $\angle x$ measures $80°$, what is the measure of $\angle y$?

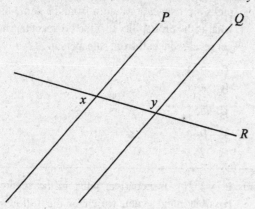

    F. $40°$

    G. $80°$

    H. $90°$

    J. $100°$

    K. $180°$

9. In the figure below, where points A, C, and D all lie on the same line, what is the measure of $\angle BCD$?

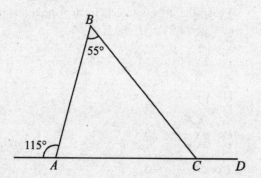

    A. $130°$

    B. $120°$

    C. $115°$

    D. $110°$

    E. $100°$

10. 10% of 10% = ?

    F. 10

    G. 1

    H. .1

    J. .01

    K. .001

11. $\sqrt{288} = ?$

    A. $8\sqrt{3}$

    B. $11\sqrt{3}$

    C. $7\sqrt{2}$

    D. $8\sqrt{2}$

    E. $12\sqrt{2}$

12. For all real numbers p and q, $(2p - 3q)^2 = ?$

    F. $36p^2q^2$

    G. $4p^2 + 9q^2$

    H. $4p^2 - 12pq + 9q^2$

    J. $4p^2 + 12pq + 9q^2$

    K. $4p^2 + 6pq - 9q^2$

13. The cost of 4 cookies, 6 doughnuts, and 3 boxes of doughnut holes is $8.15. The cost of 2 cookies, 3 doughnuts, and 4 boxes of doughnut holes is $7.20. What is the cost of a box of doughnut holes?

    A. $.85

    B. $.95

    C. $1.05

    D. $1.15

    E. $1.25

14. Which of the following lines is parallel to the line $2x + y = 6$?

    F. $2x + 2y = 6$

    G. $3x + y = 9$

    H. $4x + 2y = 10$

    J. $5x + 10y = 6$

    K. $6x + 4y = 12$

GO ON TO THE NEXT PAGE

15. A father and his young son have a combined weight of 240 pounds. If the father weighs 3 times as much as his son, what is the son's weight, in pounds?

    A. 40

    B. 60

    C. 80

    D. 160

    E. 180

16. What is the product of $\frac{3}{8}$ and .02 ?

    F. .75

    G. .075

    H. .0075

    J. .00075

    K. .000075

17. In the figure below, parallel lines m and n are crossed by transversals s and t. If the measures of $\angle B$ and $\angle C$ are 110° and 120°, respectively, what is the measure of $\angle A$?

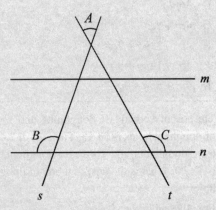

    A. 30°

    B. 50°

    C. 60°

    D. 70°

    E. 80°

18. In a student council executive board election, Aaron and Bonnie are running for president, Clarissa, Devon, and Edward are running for vice-president, and Francine and Gary are running for treasurer. If these are the only candidates, the only offices, and there are no ties, how many different executive boards are possible?

    F. 6

    G. 7

    H. 12

    J. 14

    K. 21

19. Salesperson A has already called 45 of the 120 names on her list of prospects. If salesperson B picks a prospect at random from the same list, what is the probability that the prospect has not yet received a call from salesperson A ?

    A. .375

    B. .45

    C. .55

    D. .625

    E. .75

20. If $y - \sqrt{11}$ is negative, what is the greatest possible integer value for y ?

    F. 1

    G. 2

    H. 3

    J. 4

    K. 5

21. The circumference of a circular garden is 20 meters. What is the radius, in meters, of the garden?

    A. 20π

    B. 40π

    C. $\dfrac{2\sqrt{5}}{\pi}$

    D. $\dfrac{10}{\pi}$

    E. $\dfrac{20}{\pi}$

22. For all positive $a, b,$ and c, $\left(\frac{3a^2b^4}{c^{-1}}\right)\left(\frac{3^{-1}a^{-3}c^{-2}}{b^3}\right) = ?$

   F. $\dfrac{b}{ac}$

   G. $\dfrac{9bc}{a}$

   H. $\dfrac{9b}{a^3c^3}$

   J. $\dfrac{bc}{9a}$

   K. $\dfrac{b}{9a^6c^2}$

23. A truck uses $\frac{3}{7}$ of a gallon of diesel fuel for each mile it travels. How many miles can the truck go with a full 300 gallon fuel tank?

   A. $128\frac{4}{7}$

   B. 210

   C. 300

   D. 540

   E. 700

24. Which of the following states the complete solution for the quadratic equation $x^2 - 4x = 5$?

   F. $x = -5$ or $x = 1$

   G. $x = -2$ or $x = 3$

   H. $x = -1$ or $x = 5$

   J. $x = 1$ or $x = 4$

   K. $x = 1$ or $x = 5$

25. What is the area, in square centimeters, of the figure shown below?

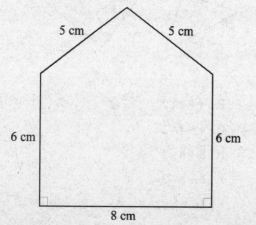

A. 48

B. 54

C. 60

D. 73

E. 88

26. Which of the following is an equation of the circle that has its center at (4,2) in the standard (x,y) coordinate plane and has a diameter of 8 units?

   F. $(x-4)^2 + (y-2)^2 = 16$

   G. $(x-4)^2 + (y-2)^2 = 64$

   H. $(x-2)^2 + (y-4)^2 = 64$

   J. $(x+4)^2 + (y+2)^2 = 8$

   K. $(x+4)^2 - (y+2)^2 = -64$

27. Which of the following is the slope-intercept form of the equation of the line that passes through the point (4,0) in the standard (x,y) coordinate plane and is perpendicular to the line $y = 2x + 3$?

   A. $y = -2x + 8$

   B. $y = -\dfrac{1}{2}x + 2$

   C. $y = -\dfrac{1}{2}x + 4$

   D. $y = \dfrac{1}{2}x - 2$

   E. $y = \dfrac{1}{2}x - \dfrac{1}{3}$

28. For all a and b where $(\sqrt{a^2 - b^2})(\sqrt{a - b})$ is defined, the expression is equivalent to:

   F. $(a-b)(\sqrt{a - b})$

   G. $(a-b)(\sqrt{a + b})$

   H. $(a-b)^2$

   J. $a^3 - b^3$

   K. $(\sqrt{a^3 - b^3})$

GO ON TO THE NEXT PAGE

29. A certain punch recipe calls for mixing cranberry juice and apple juice in a constant proportion. If 42 ounces of cranberry juice are needed to be mixed with 30 ounces of apple juice, how many ounces of cranberry juice would be needed to mix with 25 ounces of apple juice?

    A. 30

    B. 32.5

    C. 35

    D. 37.5

    E. 40

30. The diagonally opposite corners of a square have coordinates of (–1,2) and (5,2) in the standard (x,y) plane. Which of the following represents the coordinates of one of the other corners of the square?

    F. $(5 - 3\sqrt{2}, 2 - 3\sqrt{2})$

    G. $(5 - 3\sqrt{2}, 2 + 3\sqrt{2})$

    H. (–1,–2)

    J. (1,2)

    K. (2,–1)

31. Which of the following represents a simplification of the inequality $5 - x > 10 - 3(x - 2)$?

    A. $x < -\dfrac{1}{2}$

    B. $x > -\dfrac{1}{2}$

    C. $x < \dfrac{1}{4}$

    D. $x < \dfrac{11}{2}$

    E. $x > \dfrac{11}{2}$

32. If the lengths of the sides of the triangle below are shown in centimeters, how many centimeters long is $\overline{AC}$?

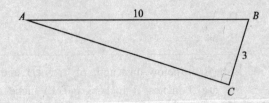

    F. 4

    G. 7

    H. 9

    J. $\sqrt{91}$

    K. $\sqrt{109}$

33. If $(2x + a)(2x + b) = 4x^2 - 4x + ab$, then $a + b$ = ?

    A. –4

    B. –2

    C. –1

    D. 2

    E. 4

34. Two 45°-45°-90° triangles are shown below. The smaller triangle has legs each 2 inches long and a hypotenuse x inches long. If the hypotenuse of the larger triangle is $2x\sqrt{2}$ inches long, what is the perimeter of the larger triangle, in inches?

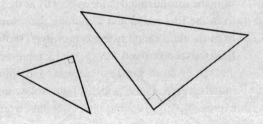

    F. $4 + 2\sqrt{2}$

    G. $4 + 4\sqrt{2}$

    H. $8 + 4\sqrt{2}$

    J. $8 + 8\sqrt{2}$

    K. $16 + 8\sqrt{2}$

35. If $\log_2 x = 5$, $x = ?$

    A. 10
    B. 16
    C. 25
    D. 32
    E. 64

36. In the figure below, the lengths of $\overline{AB}$, $\overline{AD}$, and $\overline{BC}$ are 5 inches, 4 inches, and 13 inches, respectively. What is the area, in square inches, of triangle BCD?

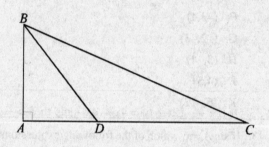

    F. 12
    G. 20
    H. 26
    J. 30
    K. 40

37. In a certain talent contest, contestants are rated on a scale of 1 to 10 in each of the 3 rounds of competition. In order to determine the contestants' final standing, a 1 to 10 point average score is determined by weighting the scores from the second round twice as heavily as those from the first round and weighting the scores from the third round twice as heavily as those from the second round. If S_1, S_2, and S_3 represent the scores from the first, second, and third rounds, respectively, which of the following expressions gives a contestant's weighted average?

    A. $\dfrac{S_1 + S_2 + S_3}{3}$

    B. $\dfrac{S_1 + 2S_2 + 2S_3}{3}$

    C. $\dfrac{S_1 + 2S_2 + 3S_3}{6}$

    D. $\dfrac{S_1 + 2S_2 + 4S_3}{3}$

    E. $\dfrac{S_1 + 2S_2 + 4S_3}{7}$

38. In the figure below, $\angle DCE$ measures 60° and $ABCE$ is a rectangle. What is the area, in square inches, of quadrilateral $ABCD$?

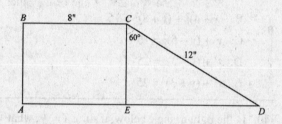

    F. $48 + 18\sqrt{3}$
    G. $40 + 15\sqrt{3}$
    H. $24 + 36\sqrt{3}$
    J. $66\sqrt{3}$
    K. 72

GO ON TO THE NEXT PAGE

39. Which of the following is an equation of the circle shown below in the standard (x,y) coordinate plane?

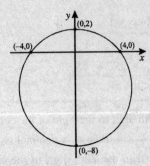

A. $(x-4)^2 + (y-2)^2 = 10$

B. $(x+4)^2 + (y+8)^2 = 16$

C. $x^2 + (y-5)^2 = 16$

D. $x^2 + (y-3)^2 = 25$

E. $x^2 + (y+3)^2 = 25$

40. In the right triangle below, if $\sin \angle X = \frac{1}{2}$, what is the value of $\cos \angle Y$?

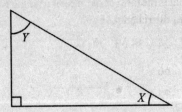

F. $\dfrac{x}{3}$

G. $\dfrac{1}{2}$

H. $\dfrac{\sqrt{3}}{2}$

J. $\dfrac{2\sqrt{2}}{3}$

K. $\sqrt{3}$

41. A line passes through the points $(3,2)$ and $(6,3)$ in the standard (x,y) coordinate plane. Which of the following points is also on this line?

A. $(4,6)$

B. $(9,5)$

C. $(10,5)$

D. $(12,6)$

E. $(15,6)$

42. In the standard (x,y) coordinate plane, which of the following is the center of the ellipse $2(x+3)^2 + 3(y-4)^2 = 15$?

F. $(-3,4)$

G. $(-2,-3)$

H. $(3,-4)$

J. $(4,3)$

K. $(6,-12)$

43. If $\sin A = x$, which of the following expressions is equal to x at all points for which it is defined?

A. $(1 - \cos^2 A)$

B. $(\cot A)(\cos A)$

C. $(\tan A)(\cos A)$

D. $\csc A - 1$

E. $\dfrac{\sec A}{\tan A}$

44. The graph below of a line in the standard (x,y) coordinate plane corresponds to which of the following equations?

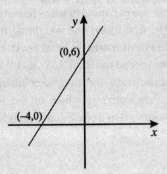

F. $y - 4x = 6$

G. $2y - 3x = 8$

H. $2y - 3x = 12$

J. $4y - 6x = 15$

K. $6y - 4x = 18$

45. In the figure below, $\overline{AB}$ and $\overline{AD}$ each are 4 meters long. If triangle BCD is equilateral, what is its area, in square meters?

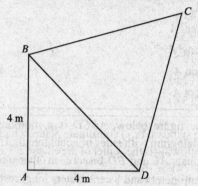

A. $4\sqrt{2}$

B. $4\sqrt{3}$

C. $8\sqrt{2}$

D. $8\sqrt{3}$

E. $16\sqrt{3}$

46. A large cube is made up of 27 equal smaller cubes. If the edge of each smaller cube has a length of 3 inches, what is the volume of the larger cube, in cubic inches?

F. 3^3

G. 3^6

H. 3^9

J. 3^{27}

K. 3^{51}

47. What positive value of a "completes the square" in the equation $9x^2 + ax + 16$?

A. 6

B. 12

C. 24

D. 36

E. 48

48. For what values of x is $2x^2 + 5x - 3$ negative?

F. $-5 < x < 1$

G. $-3 < x < \dfrac{1}{2}$

H. $-2 < x < 1$

J. $-1 < x < \dfrac{3}{2}$

K. $0 < x < 5$

49. The 20th digit to the right of the decimal point when $\frac{3}{11}$ is written as a decimal is how much greater than the 20th digit to the right of the decimal point when $\frac{7}{15}$ is written as a decimal?

A. 0

B. 1

C. 2

D. 3

E. 4

50. In the figure below, triangles ABC, DBF, and EGF are all equilateral. If $\overline{AD}$ is twice as long as $\overline{BD}$, and $\overline{EG}$ is one-half as long as $\overline{BD}$, then what is the ratio of the area of triangle EGF to the area of triangle ABC ?

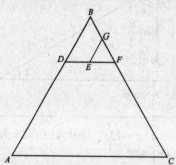

F. 1:36

G. 1:18

H. 1:16

J. 1:6

K. 1:4

51. The figure below is a regular octagon. What is the combined measure of all of the indicated angles?

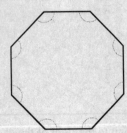

    A. 720°

    B. 960°

    C. 1,080°

    D. 1,220°

    E. 1,440°

52. If the graph of $\sin \theta$ is altered by having its amplitude multiplied by 6 and its period cut in half, then the new graph would be equivalent to the graph of which of the following expressions?

    F. $6\sin \dfrac{\theta}{2}$

    G. $6\sin 2\theta$

    H. $3\sin \dfrac{\theta}{2}$

    J. $3\sin 2\theta$

    K. $\dfrac{1}{3}\sin \theta$

53. If $x^2 = ax + 12a^2$, what are the 2 solutions for x in terms of a ?

    A. $-6a$ and $-2a$

    B. $-4a$ and $-3a$

    C. $-4a$ and $3a$

    D. $-3a$ and $4a$

    E. $-2a$ and $6a$

54. For values of A where $\sin A$, $\cos A$, and $\tan A$ are all defined, $\left(\dfrac{\cos^2 A}{\sin^2 A}\right)(\tan A) = ?$

    F. 1

    G. $\tan^3 A$

    H. $\cos^2 A$

    J. $\sin A$

    K. $\cot A$

55. In the figure below, $ABCD$ is a rhombus, a parallelogram with sides of equal length. If the diagonals $\overline{AC}$ and $\overline{BD}$ bisect each other and are 12 centimeters and 8 centimeters long, respectively, what is the perimeter of the rhombus, in centimeters?

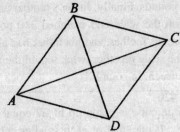

    A. 20

    B. $8\sqrt{13}$

    C. 40

    D. $16\sqrt{13}$

    E. Cannot be determined from the information given

56. For $y \neq 3$, what is the complete solution of the inequality $\dfrac{3}{y-3} < 3$?

    F. $y > 4$

    G. $y > 12$

    H. $y < -1$

    J. $y < 3$

    K. $y < 3$ or $y > 4$

57. A globe of radius 8" is to be placed into a square box for shipment. The globe's stand will be in a seperate container. What is the minimum inside volume that the box can be? (The formula for the volume of a sphere is $4\pi r^3$.)

   A. 32π cu. in.

   B. 512π cu. in.

   C. 2048π cu. in.

   D. 4096π cu. in.

   E. 4096 cu. in.

58. At a carnival weight-guessing booth, Jason and his mother got on the scale and weighed a combined 285 pounds. When Jason and his father got on the scale the combined weight was 345 pounds. Finally, Jason's mother and father got on the scale and weighed 310 pounds. If Jason, his mother, and his father had all gotten on the scale together, what would their weight have been, in pounds?

   F. 420

   G. 470

   H. 510

   J. 590

   K. 940

59. For which of the following values of c will there be only 1 distinct real solution to the equation $3x^2 + 8x + c = 0$?

   A. 0

   B. $\dfrac{4\sqrt{3}}{3}$

   C. $3\dfrac{1}{8}$

   D. $4\dfrac{1}{2}$

   E. $5\dfrac{1}{3}$

60. In the triangle below, $\overline{BC}$ has a length of a inches. If the slope of $\overline{AB}$ is b, which of the following expressions gives the length, in inches, of $\overline{AC}$?

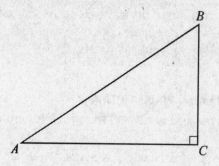

   F. $\dfrac{a}{b}$

   G. $\dfrac{b}{a}$

   H. ab

   J. $a^2 + b^2$

   K. $\dfrac{\sqrt{a^2 + b^2}}{b}$

STOP

END OF SECTION 2. IF YOU HAVE ANY TIME LEFT, GO OVER YOUR WORK IN THIS SECTION ONLY. DO NOT WORK IN ANY OTHER SECTION OF THE TEST.

3. READING TEST

40 Questions • Time—35 Minutes

Directions: This test consists of four passages, each followed by several questions. Read each passage, select the correct answer for each question, and mark the oval representing the correct answer on your answer sheet.

Passage I—PROSE FICTION

This passage is adapted from H.H. Munro's *Toys of Peace*.

James Cushat-Prinkly was a young man who had always had a settled conviction that one of these days he would marry; up to the age of thirty-four he had done nothing to justify that conviction. He liked and
(5) admired a great many women collectively and dispassionately without singling out one for special matrimonial consideration, just as one might admire the Alps without feeling that one wanted any particular peak as one's own private property. His lack of initia-
(10) tive in this matter aroused a certain amount of impatience among the sentimentally-minded women-folk of his home circle; his mother, his sisters, an aunt-in-residence, and two or three intimate matronly friends regarded his dilatory approach to the married state
(15) with a disapproval that was far from being inarticulate.

His most innocent flirtations were watched with the straining eagerness which a group of unexercised terriers concentrates on the slightest movements of a human being who may be reasonably considered likely
(20) to take them for a walk. No decent-souled mortal can long resist the pleading of several pairs of walk-beseeching dog-eyes; James Cushat-Prinkly was not sufficiently obstinate or indifferent to home influences to disregard the obviously expressed wish of his
(25) family that he should become enamoured of some nice marriageable girl, and when his Uncle Jules departed this life and bequeathed him a comfortable little legacy it really seemed the correct thing to do to set about discovering someone to share it with him.

(30)   The process of discovery was carried on more by the force of suggestion and the weight of public opinion than by any initiative of his own; a clear working majority of his female relatives and the aforesaid matronly friends had presented Joan Sebastable as the
(35) most suitable young woman in his range of acquaintance to whom he might propose marriage, and James

became gradually accustomed to the idea that he and Joan would go together through the prescribed stages of congratulations, present-receiving, Norwegian or
(40) Mediterranean hotels, and eventual domesticity. It was necessary, however, to ask the lady what she thought about the matter; the family had so far conducted and directed the flirtation with ability and discretion, but the actual proposal would have to be an
(45) individual effort.

Cushat-Prinkly walked across the Park towards the Sebastable residence in a frame of mind that was moderately complacent. As the thing was going to be done he was glad to feel that he was going to get it
(50) settled and off his mind that afternoon. Proposing marriage, even to a nice girl like Joan, was a rather irksome business, but one could not have a honeymoon in Minorca and a subsequent life of married happiness without such preliminary. He wondered
(55) what Minorca was really like as a place to stop in; in his mind's eye it was an island in perpetual half-mourning, with black or white Minorca hens running all over it. Probably it would not be a bit like that when one came to examine it. People who had been in Russia
(60) had told him that they did not remember having seen any Muscovy ducks there, so it was possible that there would be no Minorca fowls on the island.

His Mediterranean musings were interrupted by the sound of a clock striking the half-hour. Half-past four.
(65) A frown of dissatisfaction settled on his face. He would arrive at the Sebastable mansion just at the hour of afternoon tea. Joan would be seated at a low table, spread with an array of silver kettles and cream-jugs and delicate porcelain tea-cups, behind which her
(70) voice would tinkle pleasantly in a series of little friendly questions about weak or strong tea, how much, if any, sugar, milk, cream, and so forth. "Is it

one lump? I forgot. You do take milk, don't you? Would you like some more hot water, if it's too (75) strong?"

Cushat-Prinkly had read of such things in scores of novels, and hundreds of actual experiences had told him that they were true to life. Thousands of women, at this solemn afternoon hour, were sitting behind (80) dainty porcelain and silver fittings, with their voices tinkling pleasantly in a cascade of solicitous little questions. Cushat-Prinkly detested the whole system of afternoon tea. According to his theory of life a woman should lie on a divan or couch, talking with (85) incomparable charm or thinking unutterable thoughts, or merely silent as a thing to be looked on, and from behind a silken curtain a servant should silently bring in a tray with cups and dainties, to be accepted silently, as a matter of course, without drawn-out chatter about (90) cream and sugar and hot water. If one's soul was really enslaved at one's mistress's feet how could one talk coherently about weakened tea?

1. Which of the following places is mentioned as a potential location for a honeymoon?
   A. Minorca
   B. Russia
   C. Africa
   D. The Alps

2. The author compares James Cushat-Prinkly's mother, sisters, aunt and female friends to:
   F. a circle of energy.
   G. a comfortable park.
   H. an impressive mountain range.
   J. a group of anxious dogs.

3. It is most reasonable to infer that James does not like afternoon tea time primarily because:
   A. he is slightly allergic to many types of tea.
   B. it goes against his view of how women should act.
   C. the women he is courting cannot remember his tea preferences.
   D. he does not like the woman he is going to meet.

4. Given the way he is presented in the passage, James Cushat-Prinkly can best be described as:
   F. young and belligerent.
   G. ignorant of his relatives' wishes.
   H. passionate and enthused about marriage.
   J. not eager to propose marriage.

5. The third paragraph suggests that up until this time, James' courtship of Joan Sebastable has been:
   A. disregarded by members of James' family.
   B. found unsuitable by all of James' female friends.
   C. the only way James can make Uncle Jules proud.
   D. organized primarily by people other than James.

6. Which of the following conclusions about James' future plans with Joan is best supported by the details in the passage?
   F. After getting married, James plans on taking a honeymoon and then settling down.
   G. Joan and James plan on moving to the island of Minorca in the Mediterranean.
   H. James plans on marrying Joan as soon as he can be assured she is not after his money.
   J. James has no plans to propose to Joan.

7. What does the narrator suggest about James' previous associations with women?
   A. Though he has liked many women he never felt a strong enough attraction to be bound to one particular woman.
   B. Despite his attraction to various women, James did not wish to upset his delicate family with a marriage.
   C. James has asked numerous women for their hand in marriage, only to be denied because of his age.
   D. James' demanding job has kept him from closely associating with women.

GO ON TO THE NEXT PAGE

8. James imagines which of the following characterizations of Joan during afternoon tea?

   F. Her constant barrage of trivial questions is irritating.

   G. Her charming manner is incompatible with her common looks.

   H. Her lack of tact keeps her from being a good hostess.

   J. Her pleasant conversation is designed to avoid the topic of marriage.

9. One can reasonably infer from this passage that James is going to propose to Joan Sebastable because:

   A. she is the one thing in the world he has loved.

   B. she is the only women who can stand his mood swings.

   C. James is trying to get over his first failed marriage.

   D. James feels family obligations to get married.

10. From what sources does James draw his impressions of what afternoon tea is like?

    F. Movies he has seen.

    G. Books and personal experience.

    H. Conversations with his family.

    J. The opinions of his uncle.

Passage II—SOCIAL SCIENCE
This passage is adapted from a collection of essays concerning pertinent social issues.

Why has affirmative action, once advocated as a relatively painless method of correcting social injustice in America, been almost universally abandoned? What happened to our collective desire to eliminate (05) highly visible and agonizing hiring disparities among the races? Without a doubt it is because affirmative action programs have been vilified as bastions of "reverse discrimination." Because affirmative action programs in the 1970's and 1980's used timetables (10) and hiring quotas to help balance the races in professions that had obvious disparities, members of the Caucasian majority felt they were being treated as less

than human. This, some claimed, simply repeated the errors of discrimination, and even worse this new (15) "reverse discrimination" was written into law.

There is no denying that most Americans would like to see equality in hiring practices. Opinion polls and common sense lead us to this transparent conclusion. But what scares Americans even more than racism is (20) the loss of individuality. Being treated like a number and manipulated by an insensitive system: this drives Americans a little crazy, and likewise, drives them to the voting booths. As Bob Dole said during the 1994 campaign, "Why did 62 percent of white males vote (25) Republican in 1994? I think it's because of things like [affirmative action], where sometimes the best-qualified person does not get the job because he or she may be of one color, and I'm beginning to believe that may not be the way it should be in America." Granted, (30) Mr. Dole may be fishing for votes here, but his point is well taken. A vast majority of Americans, even minorities, do not think that affirmative action policies are effective ways of bettering society.

But the point that Dole and many conservative (35) thinkers miss is that although affirmative action has, on the whole, failed to ingrain itself in our social order, the impetus for affirmative action—a belief that hiring practices should be equal and fair, and that currently they are not—is still strongly subscribed to by almost (40) all Americans. Just because quota-based affirmative action policies have not been accepted does not mean that we should give up on the goal of improving equality in the workplace.

Democracy, we must remember, was an experiment (45) in government. Conjured up by social philosophers such as Rene Descartes and John Locke, the experiment of Democracy was set into motion in the late 1700's in North America with the stipulation that the experiment should remain that: an experiment. In (50) other words, the people conducting the experiment should be able to react to changes in their world and alter the rudimentary configuration of the experiment accordingly. To this end, the founders of this grand bit of research into human governance gave their sons and (55) grandsons the right, indeed the obligation, to create laws, make amendments to the rules of the experiment, and even change the basic drafted rules of the experiment (the Constitution) if necessary. We should embrace this responsibility and recognize that in order (60) to meet the end goal of the experiment—a society that equally promotes life, liberty, and the pursuit of happiness—we will have to constantly make adjustments to our laws. If a law or concept does not work out, or creates more problems than it solves, that does (65) not mean we can abandon our responsibility. Like a son or daughter who must take over the family business, we must take over this business of America and make it profitable. Of course, the profit we seek is not monetary, but nevertheless it is just as tangible. Our (70) profit is equality.

Our society is not a utopia; people of color still do not hold as many high-paying jobs as Caucasians do proportional to the size of their respective populations. Though we supposedly live in a meritocracy, the (75) lack of regulations to promote minorities keeps many highly skilled people of color from finding gainful employment.

At one time in our nation, segregation was seen as a way to keep our society from fragmenting. Jim Crow (80) laws kept blacks and whites supposedly "separate but equal" for decades. In 1896 the Supreme Court reaffirmed that Jim Crow laws were constitutionally valid in *Plessy v. Ferguson*. But in separate rulings in 1952 and 1954, the Court overturned its earlier decision and (85) proclaimed that "separate is inherently unequal." However, it wasn't until 1961, and President Kennedy's Executive Order 10952, that federal contractors were ordered to "take affirmative action to ensure that applicants are employed, and employees are treated (90) during their employment, without regard to race, creed, color or national origin." It is our responsibility to continue this tradition of expanded equality. To achieve this equality, some *action* must be taken. Ask Kennedy, ask Rosa Parks, and ask yourself; what *action* must we (95) take to *affirm* a better world.

11. The main point of the third paragraph is that although affirmative action has been rejected as a method of solving racial hiring disparities, it is still:

    A. possible that future generations will implement affirmative action policies.

    B. difficult to understand why affirmative action policies were used in the first place.

    C. important that we attempt to increase equality in the workplace.

    D. troublesome that many conservatives still reject affirmative action.

12. The author of the passage finds Bob Dole's statement (paragraph 2) pertinent, but feels that it is also an example of:

    F. affirmative action not working correctly.

    G. how politicians don't deal with the actual issues.

    H. the way conservatives are out of touch with minorities.

    J. Bob Dole trying to sway voters.

13. The author implies that one of the reasons Americans have rejected affirmative action is because:

    A. most Americans don't care about equality in the workplace.

    B. it made Americans feel as if they were losing their individuality.

    C. affirmative action was helping only certain minorities.

    D. Caucasians were not aware of how affirmative action was positively affecting the workplace.

14. The author states that in 1952 and 1954, the Supreme Court overturned:

    F. Kennedy's Executive Order.

    G. affirmative action.

    H. Plessy v. Ferguson.

    J. concepts of liberty.

15. The author implies that segregation was originally designed to keep society from:

    A. discriminating.

    B. regulating.

    C. fragmenting.

    D. being equal.

16. The author suggests that most Americans would like to see equality in the workplace and supports this statement by citing:

    F. Bob Dole's popularity.

    G. polls and common sense.

    H. examples of practical affirmative action programs.

    J. Jim Crow laws.

GO ON TO THE NEXT PAGE

17. As it is used in line 68, the word *profitable* is used to indicate the idea of:

    A. equality.

    B. money.

    C. happiness.

    D. politics.

18. According to the author, the experiment of Democracy was instituted in America with the assumption that:

    F. the Constitution would never be altered.

    G. without reasoned debate the experiment would fail.

    H. the rules of the experiment could be changed.

    J. skilled people would head the experiment.

19. Based on the passage it may be reasonably inferred that affirmative action was not supported by:

    I. Robert Kennedy.

    II. Bob Dole.

    III. most Americans.

    A. I only

    B. II only

    C. I and II only

    D. II and III only

20. The author's comment that "our society is not a utopia" refers to:

    F. young people trying to take over a difficult business.

    G. continued racial discrimination in the workplace.

    H. the use of the term *meritocracy*.

    J. conflicting Supreme Court rulings.

Passage III—HUMANITIES

This passage is adapted from *Guide to Life and Literature of the Southwest* by J. Frank Dobie.

In using the word intellectual, one lays himself liable to the accusation of having forsaken democracy. For all that, "fundamental brainwork" is behind every respect-worthy piece of writing, whether it be a
(5) lightsome lyric that seems as careless as a redbird's flit or a formal epic, an impressionistic essay or a great novel that measures the depth of human destiny. Nonintellectual literature is as nonexistent as education without mental discipline, or as "character build-
(10) ing" in a school that is slovenly in scholarship. Billboards along the highways of Texas advertise certain towns and cities as "cultural centers." Yet no chamber of commerce would consider advertising an intellectual center. The American populace has been
(15) taught to believe that the more intellectual a professor is, the less common sense he has; nevertheless, if American democracy is preserved it will be preserved by thought and not by physics. Editors of all but a few magazines of the country and publishers of most of the
(20) daily newspapers reinforce this attitude by crying out for brightness and vitality while at the same time shutting out critical ideas. They want intellect, but want it petrified. Happily, the publishers of books have not yet reached that form of delusion.

(25)   In 1834 Davy Crockett's *Autobiography* was published. It is one of the primary social documents of America. It is as much Davy Crockett, whether going ahead after bears in a Tennessee canebrake or going ahead after General Andrew Jackson in Congress, as
(30) the equally plain but also urbane *Autobiography of Franklin* is Benjamin Franklin. It is undiluted regionalism. It is provincial not only in subject but in point of view.

        No provincial mind of this day could possibly write
(35) an autobiography or any other kind of book equal in value to Crockett's "classic in homespun." In his time, Crockett could exercise intelligence and still retain his provincial point of view. Provincialism was in the air over his land. In these changed times, something in the
(40) ambient air prevents any active intelligence from being unconscious of lands, peoples, struggles far beyond any province.

        Biographies of regional characters, stories turning on local customs, novels based on an isolated society,
(45) books of history and fiction going back to provincial simplicity will go on being written and published. But I do not believe it possible that a good one will henceforth come from a mind that does not in outlook transcend the region on which it is focused. That is not
(50) to imply that the processes of evolution have brought

all parts of the world into such interrelationships that a writer cannot depict the manners and morals of a community up Owl Hoot Creek without enmeshing them with the complexities of the Atlantic Pact. Aware-
(55) ness of other times and other wheres, not insistence on that awareness, is the requisite.

James M. Barrie said that he could not write a play until he got his people off on a kind of island, but had he not known about the mainland he could never have
(60) delighted us with the islanders—islanders, after all, for the night only. Patriotism of the right kind is still a fine thing; but, despite all gulfs, canyons, and curtains that separate nations, those nations and their provinces are all increasingly interrelated.

(65) Nothing is too trivial for art, but good art treats nothing in a trivial way. Nothing is too provincial for the regional writer, but he cannot be provincial-minded toward it. Being provincial-minded will prevent him from being a representative or skillful interpreter.
(70) Horace Greeley said that when the rules of the English language got in his way, they did not stand a chance. We may be sure that if by violating the rules of syntax Horace Greeley sometimes added forcefulness to his editorials, he violated them deliberately and not in
(75) ignorance. Luminosity is not stumbled into. The richly savored and deliciously unlettered speech of Thomas Hardy's rustics was the creation of a master architect who had looked out over the ranges of fated mankind and looked also into hell. Thomas Hardy's ashes were
(80) placed in Westminster Abbey, but his heart, in accordance with a provision of his will, was buried in the churchyard of his own village. A provincial writer must, above all, remain true to his foundations.

21. As it is used in line 31, the word *undiluted* most nearly means:

   A. trapped.

   B. pure.

   C. forsaken.

   D. trivial.

22. The author's assertions about Davy Crockett's *Autobiography* are supported by all of the following statements EXCEPT that the *Autobiography*:

   F. was a work limited in its point of view.

   G. showed Crockett's intelligence.

   H. is not considered an important work.

   J. was published in 1834.

23. One of the author's main points is that it is currently impossible to write a good regional biography or story without:

   A. having a sense of how real people talk and act.

   B. several years of sustained effort and rewriting.

   C. violating the trust that people place in an author as chronicler.

   D. some awareness of the interconnected world we live in.

24. The main emphasis of the first paragraph regarding the use of the word "intellectual" is on:

   F. why schools no longer attempt to create intellectuals.

   G. changing the way people use the word "intellectual."

   H. how to make magazines and newspapers more intellectual.

   J. how all good writing is in some sense intellectual.

25. As it is used in line 20, the phrase *crying out* most nearly means:

   A. ignoring.

   B. advocating.

   C. paying.

   D. learning.

GO ON TO THE NEXT PAGE ➡

26. The example of Horace Greeley is presented in the sixth paragraph in order to reinforce the notion that:

    F. one must have general knowledge in order to effectively interpret specific things.

    G. no matter how hard young writers try, they will always depict characters from a provincial viewpoint.

    H. good art deals with issues that are not provincial in nature.

    J. writers must follow accepted rules of grammar in order to communicate sensibly.

27. The author claims that true education cannot occur without:

    A. mental discipline.

    B. strong morals.

    C. an open-minded approach.

    D. bowing to local customs.

28. The author contends that magazine and newspaper editors around the country do not wish to publish:

    F. autobiographies.

    G. provincial views.

    H. critical views.

    J. regional stories.

29. The description of Thomas Hardy's unique burial, in which his heart was buried in his village and his body was buried in Westminster Abbey, is intended to show:

    A. how Hardy never felt comfortable with his church.

    B. that Hardy felt a strong connection with his provincial roots.

    C. the lack of faith that Hardy had that his heirs would fulfil his requests.

    D. how intelligence is in direct opposition with provincialism.

30. The author believes that James M. Barrie could not have written so well about characters on a hypothetical "island" if Barrie had not been aware of:

    F. Thomas Hardy.

    G. the effects of patriotism.

    H. what living on an island was like.

    J. the "mainland."

Passage IV—NATURAL SCIENCE

This passage is adapted from a magazine article about the evolution of birds.

For more than a century, paleontologists have been in heated debate about how birds evolved. This debate still fills the journals and classrooms of those who study the present for clues to the distant past.

(5) While it has been popularly reported that birds descended from diminutive carnivorous dinosaurs like Archaeopteryx, there is a problem with this theory. About 65 million years ago, at the end of the Cretaceous Period, Archaeopteryx, along with thousands of (10) other dinosaur species, abruptly became extinct.

So, what happened to birds during this great extinction? Did many species survive the extinction, or are all modern birds descended from a few species that were able to scratch out livings on the coasts of ancient (15) continents? The answer to this question would seem to lie in the fossil record. However, the fossil record seems to be in conflict with the genetic evidence extracted from modern birds.

The general consensus among evolutionary biolo-(20) gists is that modern bird species developed before the Cretaceous Period extinction occurred. Evidence for this conjecture comes from the distribution of bird groups in the modern world. Ostriches, rheas and emus all belong to an order of birds called the ratites, (25) yet ostriches come from Africa, rheas come from South America, and emus are found in Australia. The ratites cannot fly, so the assumption has been that at some point in the distant past a common ancestor to modern ratites lived on the supercontinent (30) *Gondwanaland* before it fragmented.

It is believed that about 80 million years ago all of the continents were pressed together to form a "super-continent" called *Gondwanaland*. As this gigantic landmass fragmented over the next 80 million years, (35) animals of the same species and order were trapped on different continents and each group evolved along different paths.

Alan Fediccia, an ornithologist at the University of North Carolina, believes that he has found evidence (40) that disputes that view. He believes that only one small group of bird fossils from the Cretaceous looks like modern birds. These birds, which Fediccia believed lived in a narrow ecological niche along shorelines during the Cretaceous, look like modern stone (45) curlews.

Along with this discovery, Fediccia points out that there are numerous examples of *enantiornithine* fossils from the Cretaceous Period. The name *enantiornithine* means "opposite bird" and refers to (50) the fact that these "birds" had strange elongated foot bones, fleshy tails like lizards, and teeth. This hints that these "birds" were not the ancestors of modern birds. The *enantiornithine* are found in the fossil record right after Archaeopteryx originated, and like (55) the Archaeopteryx the *enantiornithine* completely died out in the vast Cretaceous extinction.

This, says Fediccia, suggests the only birds that survived the Cretaceous extinction were shoreline birds that lived on hardy marine life. Fediccia as-(60) sumes, as many scientists do, that the Cretaceous extinction was precipitated by a massive asteroid impact that darkened the sky and brought about a sudden global climatic change. Only these shore birds, Fediccia argues, were able to live through this massive (65) cooling of the planet by feeding on marine animals like crabs that were able to adjust to the rapidly chilling environment.

After the asteroid hit, animals that were able to survive had to evolve swiftly, and birds, according to (70) Fediccia and other researchers, did just that. Over the next 10 million years water and land-birds jump into the fossil record: penguins, flamingos, parrots, hawks, owls. Ancestors of these birds are not found in the Cretaceous fossil record, which means that in all (75) probability these birds did not evolve until after the extinction.

One disclaimer should be made: any theory about the distant past can be upset by one discovery. Every fossilized bird that is discovered either slightly sup-(80) ports a theory or completely capsizes it.

In fact, other scientists believe that the only reason no fossils of Cretaceous birds have been found is because paleontologists just haven't found them yet. These scientists believe that until thorough surveys of (85) Cretaceous fossil gold mines like Antarctica and New Zealand are conducted, it is premature to advance theories that depend on the non-existence of most birds in the Cretaceous Period.

But what really calls Fediccia's theory into doubt, (90) some biologists contend, is genetic evidence. As a species evolves, its genes accumulate various muta-tions. Scientists have been able to measure how these mutations differ between species, and from this mea-surement they have been able to create a family tree (95) that reveals how species differ genetically.

Based on this genetic evidence, many scientists have concluded that it is impossible for so many bird species to have evolved from a common ancestor in so short a time (10 million years). Of course, the genetic (100) evidence itself can be called into question, since it only looks at a relatively small portion of the actual DNA chain and extrapolates its findings over millions of years of evolution.

As more data is brought to light, no doubt other (105) theories will emerge as to when and how our avian brethren evolved. One day, it is hoped, an agreement will emerge between geneticists and paleontologists. Such an agreement is unlikely without more detailed information from the genetic and fossil records.

31. The reason that Alan Fediccia believes that most modern birds evolved from a common ancestor is because he has found evidence that certain shoreline birds from the Cretaceous Period:

    A. were made extinct by the Cretaceous asteroid impact.

    B. have not been examined by modern biologists.

    C. wiped out opposing bird populations.

    D. resemble modern birds.

GO ON TO THE NEXT PAGE

32. According to the passage, the Cretaceous Period ended with the:

    F. widespread extinction of dinosaurs.

    G. formation of a supercontinent.

    H. introduction of the ostrich to Africa.

    J. genetic diversification of the *enantiornithine*.

33. According to the passage, a good place to look for fossils from the Cretaceous Period is:

    I. New Zealand.

    II. South America.

    III. *Gondwanaland*.

    A. I only

    B. II only

    C. I and II only

    D. I and III only

34. According to Alan Fediccia, shoreline birds were able to survive in a radically altered environment (paragraph 8) because they could:

    F. fly faster and further than their land-based counterparts.

    G. consume marine creatures that adjusted quickly to the changing environment.

    H. easily attract mates using their simple vocal mechanisms.

    J. avoid extinction by finding hovels in geologically immature regions.

35. Which of the following best describes the conclusion of the passage as to what more is needed to resolve the debate about how birds evolved?

    A. More genetic and fossil data is needed before an agreeable theory can be advanced.

    B. What is needed is a theory that explains the appearance of birds before the end of the Cretaceous Period.

    C. Any more genetic or fossil data would further muddle the issue about the origin of modern birds.

    D. Biologists would greatly benefit from a close study of the most well-preserved fossil specimens.

36. It can be inferred from the passage that all of the following statements about *Gondwanaland* are true EXCEPT that it:

    F. began to fragment around 80 million years ago.

    G. was a gigantic landmass composed of other continents.

    H. is believed to have been the home to a common ancestor of modern ratites.

    J. began to fragment after the end of the Cretaceous Period.

37. The main reason many scientists doubt Fediccia's theory of bird evolution is because genetic evidence suggests that:

    A. it is unlikely that one species could evolve so quickly without massive inbreeding and, as a result, reduced intelligence.

    B. when a species evolves it must choose one direction, and birds have evolved into countless forms.

    C. Ostriches, emus and rheas are in fact not descended from a common ancestor.

    D. it takes much longer than 10 million years to accumulate the genetic mutations currently found in the DNA of various bird species.

38. The passage suggests that the debate about how birds evolved is:

    F. easily resolved.

    G. poorly understood.

    H. based on circumstantial evidence.

    J. at least 100 years old.

39. If a group of fossils were discovered that showed that before the Cretaceous Period Extinction there were already distinct species of penguins, parrots, and owls, this would support the theory:

   I. advanced by Alan Fediccia in the passage.

   II. that these birds evolved from *enantiornithine*.

   III. that these birds did not evolve from ancient shorebirds.

   A. II only

   B. III only

   C. I and II only

   D. I and III only

40. It can reasonably be inferred from the passage that Alan Fediccia believes that *enantiornithine* are NOT the ancestors of modern birds because *enantiornithine*:

   F. were extinct long before Archaeopteryx originated.

   G. are physically different from modern fowl.

   H. took more that 10 million years to evolve fully.

   J. are difficult to find in the fossil record of the Cretaceous.

STOP

END OF SECTION 3. IF YOU HAVE ANY TIME LEFT, GO OVER YOUR WORK IN THIS SECTION ONLY. DO NOT WORK IN ANY OTHER SECTION OF THE TEST.

4. SCIENCE REASONING TEST

40 Questions • Time—35 Minutes

Directions: This test consists of seven passages, each followed by several questions. Read each passage, select the correct answer for each question, and mark the oval representing the correct answer on your answer sheet. You may NOT use a calculator on this test.

Passage I

Biochemical tests are used to identify the presence of organic molecules in solution. To perform a biochemical test, an agent is added to a solution and, if a particular organic molecule is present, the agent will react with the organic molecule. The reaction can be seen because the agent changes color as a result of chemical bonds being broken and reformed. If no organic molecule is present, then no chemical bonds are broken upon the addition of the agent.

Three common biochemical tests are the Benedict's test, Iodine test, and Biuret test. A positive result for a Benedict's test is obtained only if the agent added changes from clear blue to a cloudy greenish, yellow, orange, red, or brown. A positive Iodine test is indicated only if the agent added changes from yellow to a deep blue-black color. A positive Biuret test is indicated only when the agent added changes from light blue to a purple or pink color. Each test is used to identify exactly one of the following types of organic molecules: monosaccharides, polysaccharides, or proteins.

Experiment 1

The three tests were performed on known organic molecules to determine which biochemical test identifies which organic molecule. Individual test tubes were filled with 3 ml of only one of the following four substances: monosaccharide, polysaccharide, protein, or water. The tests were done using water as a control. Each test was performed on a different set of four test tubes with the above-mentioned substances. Table 1 summarizes the results.

Table 1

Solution	Benedict's Test		Iodine Test		Biuret Test	
	Before	After	Before	After	Before	After
Mono-saccharide	clear	blue	clear	dark purple	clear	light blue
Poly-saccharide	clear	orange	clear	yellow	clear	light blue
Protein	cloudy	purple/ blue	cloudy	yellow	cloudy	purple
Water	clear	blue	clear	yellow	clear	light blue

Experiment 2

The three biochemical tests were then applied to unknown solutions to determine the composition of the unknown solutions. The data was recorded in Table 2.

Table 2

Solution	Benedict's Test		Iodine Test		Biuret Test	
	Before	After	Before	After	Before	After
A	cloudy	purple/ blue	cloudy	purple	cloudy	purple
B	cloudy	blue	cloudy	purple	cloudy	light blue
C	cloudy	orange	cloudy	yellow	cloudy	purple
D	clear	purple/ blue	clear	yellow	clear	light blue
E	clear	orange	clear	yellow	clear	light blue

1. On the basis of Experiment 1, which of the following substances reacted positively to the Benedict's test?

   A. Monosaccharide

   B. Polysaccharide

   C. Protein

   D. Water

2. Protein reacted positively with which of the following tests?

   I. Benedict's

   II. Iodine

   III. Biuret

   F. I only

   G. II only

   H. III only

   J. I and III only

3. Which of the following lists accurately states which tests are used to identify monosaccharide, polysaccharide, and protein, respectively?

   A. Iodine, Biuret, Benedict's

   B. Iodine, Benedict's, Biuret

   C. Biuret, Benedict's, Iodine

   D. Benedict's, Iodine, Biuret

4. Based on the results of Experiment 2, which of the following substances tested positively for monosaccharide?

   F. Solution B

   G. Solution C

   H. Solution D

   J. Solution E

5. Which of the following pairs of substances tested positively for more than one organic molecule?

   A. A and C

   B. B and D

   C. C and D

   D. B and E

6. Some of the solutions showed a change in color that was not consistent with the change expected for a positive test result. Which statement best accounts for the color changes in the non-reactive solutions?

   F. Chemical bonds are broken to change the color of the added solution.

   G. The added substances have their own distinct color that diffuses through the non-reactive solutions.

   H. Benedict solution, Iodine solution, and Biuret solution are all colorless before being added to any solution.

   J. Benedict solution, Iodine solution, and Biuret solution become colorless when added to a non-reactive solution.

Passage II

Industrial melanism, the spread of darkly colored moths and butterflies near polluted, industrial centers, was observed in the late 1840s in England. Before the 1840s, tree trunks throughout Britain were a whitish color due to the growth of lichens on the trees. These lichens are sensitive to airborne pollutants and are unable to survive near major industrial centers. In the polluted areas, the lack of lichen on the trees results in the trees being darker than in the unpolluted areas.

The peppered moth (*Biston betularia*) began to appear more and more in its melanic form in the polluted areas. In certain areas, the darker moths constituted 98% of the population. Scientists hypothesized that the cause of the decline in the light colored moths was due to predation by birds and not a result of the pollution itself.

Scientists performed an experiment to determine the selective force that caused the appearance of the darker moths. They distributed light and melanic moths in polluted and non-polluted areas and recorded the results shown in the table below.

GO ON TO THE NEXT PAGE ▶

	Light	Melanic
Dorset, England		
Woodland (light background)		
Released	496	473
Recaptured	62	30
Percent Recaptured	12.5	6.3
Birmingham, England		
Woodland (dark background)		
Released	137	447
Recaptured	18	123
Percent Recaptured	13.1	27.5

The scientists noted that they were also able to see birds capturing a higher proportion of moths that did not match their background. Scientists were also able to determine that the change in color is due to a genetic mutation. Once the mutation occurs, the new coloration is dominant and can therefore more successfully be passed to a greater percentage of offspring.

7. How many melanic moths were recaptured from the polluted region, according to the experimental data?

A. 18

B. 30

C. 62

D. 123

8. The fact that at least 100% more moths survived if they matched the background of the trees supports which of the following hypotheses?

F. The presence of pollution negatively affects the survival of melanic moths.

G. The existence of lichen on trees increases the survival of all moths.

H. Birds eat more moths that differ in color from their background trees than those moths that do not.

J. Birds are not selective as to the moths they eat.

9. If the scientist did not observe birds capturing a greater number of moths that did not match their backgrounds, all of the following could explain the data observed EXCEPT:

A. Appearance of lichen increases the likelihood for moth survival.

B. The pollution itself causes the light moth's difficulty with survival.

C. A selective force selects against the melanic moths in the unpolluted area and light moths in the polluted area.

D. Too few light moths were released in the polluted areas to make a valid comparison.

10. A critic of the experiment would point out that the scientists have not adequately accounted for which of the following?

F. With a light background, a greater percentage of light moths survived compared to the percentage of melanic moths.

G. Light moths were recovered in approximately the same percentage regardless of background color.

H. With a dark background, an increased percentage of melanic moths survived compared to the percentage of light moths.

J. Over both trials, the percentage of melanic moths recovered is close to the percentage of light moths recovered.

11. The increase in the percentage of melanic moths recaptured in polluted areas is consistent with which of the following?

A. Selection can be strong enough to nearly complete a color change in a species in a short time frame.

B. Moths depend on lichen for survival in polluted and non-polluted areas.

C. Pollution is the cause of the demise of the moth as a species.

D. The survival rate for the melanic moth is the same regardless of pollution.

12. If it were determined that, as a result of decreased pollution, the lichens were increasing in many areas, the scientists would probably suggest that:

   F. the number of melanic moths would increase and the number of light moths would decrease.

   G. the number of melanic moths would decrease and the number of light moths would increase.

   H. the number of both melanic moths and light moths would remain the same.

   J. the number of both melanic moths and light moths would decrease.

Passage III

Public health experts realize that educating the public about hazardous activities can be just as important as identifying those risks. One method of educating the public is by simplifying complex scientific analysis into easy to understand guidelines. Teaching people how to follow these guidelines allows them to avoid undue health risks.

For example, both cold and sun pose a health risk to the skin. Frostbite can result due to exposure to extreme cold and wind, and sunburn and, ultimately, skin cancer may result from prolonged exposure to ultraviolet radiation from the Sun. The wind chill factor and the UV Index are guidelines used by public health experts to inform people of these two risks.

Wind chill factor is the effect that wind velocity has on temperature. The actual temperature may be quite different than the effective temperature because wind velocity will lower the effective temperature. Wind chill increases the rate of heat loss and can change effective temperature significantly.

Table 1 below summarizes the effect of wind velocity on effective temperature. Temperatures in the range of –30°C to –55°C, are moderately dangerous and temperatures in the range of –60°C to –85°C are extremely dangerous. Exposed flesh can freeze in a minute at an effective temperature of –30°C. Effective temperatures below –60°C can cause freezing within seconds.

Table 1

Wind Speed (km/hr)	Actual Temperature (°Celsius)						
0	–10	–15	–20	–25	–30	–35	–40

Wind Speed (km/hr)	Effective Temperature (°Celsius)						
10	–15	–20	–25	–30	–35	–40	–45
20	–20	–25	–35	–40	–45	–50	–55
30	–25	–30	–40	–45	–50	–60	–65
40	–30	–35	–45	–50	–60	–65	–70
50	–35	–40	–50	–55	–65	–70	–75

The UV Index is an estimate of the amount of ultraviolet radiation that hits the Earth's surface at noon at a given location. Many factors go into the calculation of the index. Latitude, season, and elevation are all used to produce the single value. These factors are then combined with local weather forecasts, since it is the amount of sunshine that breaks through any clouds that plays the most significant role in the index. All other factors being equal, altitude can also have a large impact on the UV Index. A higher altitude means less atmosphere to absorb UV rays prior to their reaching the ground. Table 2 below summarizes the classification of different UV Index levels. Higher values indicate exposure to greater levels of ultraviolet radiation and a higher level of risk for sunburn.

Table 2

UV Index	Exposure Level
0 – 2	Minimal
3 – 4	Low
5 – 6	Moderate
7 – 9	High
10 and greater	Very High

GO ON TO THE NEXT PAGE

13. What would the effective temperature be if the actual temperature was –25°C and the wind speed was 30 km/hr?

    A. –40°C

    B. –45°C

    C. –50°C

    D. –60°C

14. On a windless day, if a skier skis down a mountain at 30 km/h, the effective temperature would be classified as moderately dangerous if the actual temperature was which of the following?

    I. –10°C

    II. –15°C

    III. –25°C

    F. I only

    G. II only

    H. I and II only

    J. II and III only

15. If the wind speed were 57 km/h, what would be the approximate effective temperature at actual temperature of –23°C?

    A. –40°C

    B. –45°C

    C. –50°C

    D. –55°C

16. A hiker plans to take an overnight camping trip in the mountains in the middle of winter. If the hiker is uncertain about the wind speed on the mountain but knows that it does not exceed 50 km/hr, what is the lowest that the temperature can be without the hiker risking exposure at the moderately or extremely dangerous effective temperatures?

    F. 0°C

    G. –10°C

    H. –20°C

    J. –30°C

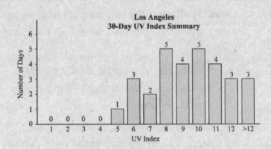

17. The graph above shows the number of days in a certain 30-day period for which the UV Index was at a given level. A local weather forecaster issues a warning if the UV Index falls in the high range or above. On how many days would the forecaster have issued warnings over this period?

    A. 7

    B. 11

    C. 18

    D. 26

18. Cities A and B are 75 miles apart. The UV Index for city A on a given day is 6, while the UV Index for city B is 9. Which of the following best explains this difference?

    F. City A is at an altitude 6,000 thousand feet above city B.

    G. The weather forecast for city A is for scattered showers, whereas forecasters are predicting sun for city B.

    H. City A's annual average UV Index is lower than city B's.

    J. City A is windier than city B.

Passage IV

Respiration is the process that takes place within a cell to convert glucose to energy. Oxygen is required for this process and carbon dioxide is a byproduct. An experiment was performed to determine the effect of temperature on the rate of respiration. Before the experiment was performed, a test tube was calibrated so that the amount of carbon dioxide produced during the experiment could be measured.

Calibration

A known volume of water was added to a small test tube and the length of the test tube filled with water was measured. This was done for several volumes and the results are presented in Table 1.

Table 1

Volume (ml)	Length (cm)
3	2.1
5	3.5
8	5.6
10	7.0

Experiment

The following experiment was performed to test the hypothesis that increasing the temperature will increase the rate of cellular respiration. Yeast was added to a sugar solution and a small test tube filled with the solution was inverted into a larger test tube, also filled with the solution. No air bubbles were present in the inverted test tube at the beginning of the experiment. As cellular respiration takes place, the inverted test tube will collect carbon dioxide, which will rise to the top of the inverted test tube. At different times, the length of the bubble was measured and, based on the calibration above, the volume of the bubble was determined. This procedure was repeated at two different temperatures.

Table 2

Elapsed Time (hrs.)	Test Tube 1 at 23° C		Test Tube 2 at 35° C	
	Length (cm)	Volume (ml)	Length (cm)	Volume (ml)
0	0	0	0	0
2	0.7	1.0	4.1	5.9
4	3.5	5.0	11.9	17.0
6	8.1	11.6	12.7	18.1
8	11.2	16.0	12.7	18.1
24	12.7	18.1	12.7	18.1

19. If the calibration had been performed with 6 ml of water, to approximately what length would this have corresponded?
   A. 2.4 cm
   B. 4.2 cm
   C. 6.0 cm
   D. 8.4 cm

20. What was the volume of carbon dioxide in the test tube after six hours at 23°C?
   F. 5.7 ml
   G. 8.9 ml
   H. 11.6 ml
   J. 18.1 ml

21. If readings were taken at 0 hours and 24 hours only, which of the following hypotheses could be supported?
   A. Temperature has no effect on the rate of respiration.
   B. Increased temperature increases the rate of respiration.
   C. Increased temperature decreases the rate of respiration.
   D. Cellular respiration does not emit carbon dioxide as a byproduct.

22. Which statement best describes the effect of temperature in the experiment?
   F. Increased temperature decreases the initial rate of carbon dioxide production.
   G. Increased temperature increases the initial rate of carbon dioxide production.
   H. Increased temperature decreases total carbon dioxide production.
   J. Increased temperature increases total carbon dioxide production.

GO ON TO THE NEXT PAGE

23. Comparing Test Tube 1 to Test Tube 2, approximately how many times greater is the measured length of carbon dioxide released after two hours?

    A. 2

    B. 3

    C. 4

    D. 6

24. Which of the following would explain why after six hours the volume of carbon dioxide in Test Tube 2 no longer increased?

    F. Cellular respiration does not release carbon dioxide.

    G. Yeast does not convert sugar through cellular respiration.

    H. The yeast had converted all available sugar.

    J. The yeast had not converted all available sugar.

Passage V

When two objects are placed near or next to one another and they are at different temperatures, energy is transferred to the cooler object. As a result of this energy transfer, the temperature of the cooler object rises. The ratio of the amount of energy transferred to the temperature change is called heat capacity. Table 1 summarizes the specific heat for various substances.

Table 1

Substance	Specific Heat Capacity (kJ/kgK)
Aluminum	0.898
Steel	0.447
Lead	0.130

An experiment was done to illustrate the temperature changes that are observed when substances with different heat capacities are subjected to the same procedures. In this experiment, 1 kg of water at 27°C was placed in an insulated container. A 0.2 kg piece of metal was placed in the water after the metal was heated to a particular temperature. The final temperature of the water and piece of metal were then recorded and summarized in Table 2.

Table 2

Initial Temperature (°Celsius)	Final Temperature (°Celsius)			
	Aluminum	Lead	Steel	Unknown
50	27.95	27.14	27.48	27.25
75	28.98	27.29	28.01	27.53
100	30.01	27.45	28.53	27.81
150	32.08	27.76	29.58	28.36
200	34.14	28.07	30.63	28.92

25. Which metal underwent the greatest temperature change when the starting temperature was 50°C?

    A. Aluminum

    B. Unknown

    C. Lead

    D. Steel

26. If the test was repeated with aluminum heated to an initial temperature of 250°C, which of the following is most likely to have been the final temperature?

    F. 28.47°C

    G. 29.52°C

    H. 31.74°C

    J. 36.21°C

27. For each of the trials, as initial temperature of the metal increased, the final temperature of the metal and water:

    A. increased

    B. decreased

    C. remained constant

    D. varied depending on the metal

28. Diamond has a specific heat capacity of 0.518 kJ/kgK. If the experiment had been performed using diamond, what would the expected temperature range be in °C if the starting temperatures ranged from 50°C to 200°C as in the other trials?

   F. 26.95 to 27.82

   G. 27.19 to 28.52

   H. 27.55 to 31.20

   J. 28.12 to 34.88

29. As the specific heat capacity for a substance increases, what observable effect is there on the range of final temperature readings?

   A. There is no observable difference in the range of temperatures.

   B. There is a greater range of final temperature readings.

   C. There is a smaller range of final temperature readings.

   D. The range of the final temperature readings is constant for all heat capacities.

30. Based on the temperature readings for the unknown metal, what would the estimated specific heat capacity of the unknown substance be?

   F. 0.120 kJ/kgK

   G. 0.234 kJ/kgK

   H. 0.682 kJ/kgK

   J. 0.953 kJ/kgK

Passage VI

Although astronomers have a general outline for the steps that lead up to the formation of the wide-ranging interplanetary bodies called *comets*, there remain as yet many questions of where and exactly *how* comets were formed. The major points of dispute involve the location of their formation and the processes by which the comets were drawn into the Oort Cloud becoming permanent members of our Solar System. Three astronomers describe their views on this process.

Astronomer 1

The flattened, rotating disk of the nebula* out of which our Sun and its companion planets were formed is the ideal place for comets to have been born. The

long, slow collapse of a nebula that evolved into a planetary system included the type of compression that would facilitate the accretion of the icy specks of matter into comet pellets. At a certain concentration level, these pellets began to clump into cometesimals and later aggregated into larger bodies. When our Solar System was formed, the bodies which formed in the outskirts became the population of comets known as the Oort cloud. Those comets that formed among the planets likely collided with the giant members of the Sun's family, coalescing into them. There is sufficient evidence of significant disturbance among the outer giant planets and their companion satellites in the early solar system to support this theory.

A nebula is a vast cloud of interstellar gas and dust.

Astronomer 2

We may reasonably suspect that the nebula out of which our Sun formed was at least twice the mass of the Sun at its current stage. We believe that the processes that formed the inner Solar System worked rapidly and were completed within 100,000 years. The remaining, less thoroughly coalesced matter was blown into the outer regions of the infant Solar System. The larger masses eventually became the four outer gas giants—Jupiter, Saturn, Uranus and Neptune. The smaller masses were thrown much farther, forming the Oort cloud. Here, so distant from the gravitational influence of their parent sun, they were much more subject to the random forces of other nearby stars. Some of them are pushed in towards us, making their periodic and sometimes spectacular visits; others are pushed out to wander unseen in the vast galaxy.

Astronomer 3

The interstellar clouds out of which stars are formed are more vast, cold, and formless than can easily be imagined. In the absence of evidence that all the members of the Solar System arose out of the same nebula, it is difficult to explain the birth of the wandering comets. The most likely scenario based on the actual evidence available is that icy grains of matter in these vast gas-molecular clouds slowly grew by aggregation as they wandered in cold, dark space. Eventually the masses would grow large enough to be deemed cometary. When the Sun compressed and ignited, it possessed enough gravity to capture a large number of these cometary masses, forming a captive population of comets now orbiting far beyond the realm of the other Solar companions.

GO ON TO THE NEXT PAGE ➤

31. Which of the following statements about the formation of comets would be most consistent with the views of Astronomer 1 and not Astronomer 2?

    A. Gravity from other stars is a crucial factor in the birth of comets.

    B. Comets were not originally members of our Solar System.

    C. The Sun, planets, and comets formed out of the same nebula.

    D. Comets previously existed in the same region as the planets.

32. Astronomer 2 would most likely criticize the theory of Astronomer 3 by saying that:

    F. evidence shows that the formation of comets was outside our Solar System.

    G. the influence of forces from other stars is ignored.

    H. the formation of the Sun was too slow and lengthy to account for the formation of comets.

    J. the role of the Sun's gravity is ignored.

33. What is Astronomer 3's chief objection to the views of Astronomers 1 and 2?

    A. They do not account for the vast amount of gas and dust in interstellar space.

    B. There is no evidence that the formation of the Sun and the planets was a very rapid process.

    C. They do not account for the formation of the Oort cloud.

    D. There is no evidence that comets formed out of the same nebula from which the Sun and planets formed.

34. The theory of Astronomer 2 depends heavily on which of the following assumptions?

    F. The time needed to complete the formation of the outer regions of the Solar System was greater than for the inner Solar System.

    G. The outer planets and there companions experienced violent collisions during their formative stages.

    H. The comets were not originally members of our Solar System.

    J. The formation of the inner Solar System was a slow, lengthy process.

35. The theory of Astronomer 1 does not conflict with the theories of either Astronomer 2 or Astronomer 3 regarding:

    A. the formation of comets outside our Solar System.

    B. the role of the Sun or other stars influencing the orbit of comets.

    C. the quickness with which the nebula would have collapsed to form comets.

    D. the evidence of comets in the inner part of our Solar System.

Passage VII

A scientist wanted to determine the relationship, if any, between a mass placed on the end of a spring and the force exerted by the mass on the spring.

Various weights were placed on the end of a spring and the force measured, in Newtons (N), that was exerted on the spring. The maximum displacement of the weight, called the amplitude, was measured by recording the extension of the spring. The time needed for one oscillation back and forth for the weight to return to its original position was also recorded. The results are shown in Table 1.

Table 1

Mass (kg)	Square (root of Mass)	Force (N)	Extension (cm)	Time (sec)
1	1.0	9.8	5	1.20
2	1.4	19.6	15	1.68
3	1.7	29.4	25	2.04
4	2.0	39.2	35	2.40

36. Based on the data presented in the table, if a weight with mass 2.7 kg were placed on the end of the spring, the force exerted on the spring would be approximately:

    F. 9 N

    G. 13 N

    H. 26 N

    J. 33 N

37. Which of the following best represents the relationship between the force exerted on the spring and the extension of the spring?

    A.

    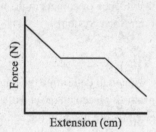

    B.

    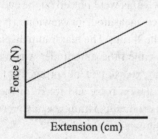

    C.

    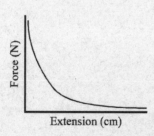

D.

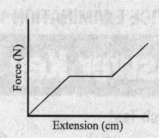

38. Approximately how long would a weight with mass 5 kg take for one oscillation?

    F. 0.8 sec

    G. 1.4 sec

    H. 1.9 sec

    J. 2.7 sec

39. Which of the following provides the best explanation as to why the scientist noted the square root of the mass?

    A. The mass is inversely proportional to the force exerted on the spring.

    B. The mass is directly proportional to the time of one oscillation.

    C. The square root of the mass is directly proportional to the time of one oscillation.

    D. The square root of the mass is directly proportional to the force exerted on the spring.

40. Which of the following suggests that the extension of the spring reaches a maximum value?

    F. When a force of 2 N is applied, there is no extension in the spring.

    G. When a force of 20 N is applied, the extension is 16 cm.

    H. When a force greater than 40 N is applied, the extension is greater than 35 cm.

    J. When a force greater than 40 N is applied, the extension is equal to 35 cm.

STOP

END OF SECTION 4. IF YOU HAVE ANY TIME LEFT, GO OVER YOUR WORK IN THIS SECTION ONLY. DO NOT WORK IN ANY OTHER SECTION OF THE TEST.

PRACTICE EXAMINATION 1

Answer Key

1. English Test

1. B	16. H	31. C	46. F	61. A
2. H	17. A	32. J	47. D	62. G
3. D	18. F	33. D	48. H	63. A
4. H	19. B	34. G	49. C	64. H
5. A	20. H	35. A	50. F	65. D
6. J	21. D	36. F	51. A	66. G
7. D	22. G	37. C	52. G	67. B
8. F	23. D	38. G	53. C	68. H
9. A	24. H	39. D	54. J	69. A
10. G	25. D	40. G	55. A	70. J
11. D	26. F	41. B	56. G	71. B
12. F	27. B	42. F	57. D	72. G
13. B	28. J	43. C	58. J	73. D
14. H	29. C	44. G	59. C	74. G
15. C	30. F	45. A	60. H	75. C

2. Math Test

1. D	13. E	25. C	37. E	49. B
2. H	14. H	26. F	38. F	50. F
3. A	15. B	27. B	39. E	51. C
4. H	16. H	28. G	40. G	52. G
5. A	17. B	29. C	41. E	53. D
6. F	18. H	30. K	42. F	54. K
7. E	19. D	31. E	43. C	55. B
8. J	20. H	32. J	44. H	56. K
9. B	21. D	33. B	45. D	57. E
10. J	22. F	34. J	46. G	58. G
11. E	23. E	35. D	47. C	59. E
12. H	24. H	36. G	48. G	60. F

3. Reading Test

1. A	9. D	17. A	25. B	33. A
2. J	10. G	18. H	26. F	34. G
3. B	11. C	19. D	27. A	35. A
4. J	12. J	20. G	28. H	36. J
5. D	13. B	21. B	29. B	37. D
6. F	14. H	22. H	30. J	38. J
7. A	15. C	23. D	31. D	39. B
8. F	16. G	24. J	32. F	40. G

4. Science Reasoning Test

1. B	9. A	17. D	25. C	33. D
2. H	10. G	18. G	26. J	34. F
3. B	11. A	19. B	27. A	35. B
4. F	12. G	20. H	28. H	36. H
5. A	13. B	21. A	29. B	37. B
6. G	14. J	22. G	30. G	38. J
7. D	15. D	23. D	31. D	39. C
8. H	16. F	24. H	32. G	40. J

PRACTICE EXAMINATION 1

Explanatory Answers

1. English Test

Passage I

1. **B** is correct. *Because* is the subordinating conjunction that indicates the reason language schools are booming.

2. **H** is correct. The period is needed to separate the sentences. *Unless* logically belongs to the second sentence.

3. **D** is correct. The present continuous tense is necessary in this context.

4. **H** is correct. This option cuts out unnecessary words that make for awkward phrasing.

5. **A** is correct. *There* is the right word in this context.

6. **J** is correct. Dashes set off the countries, which serve as examples, from the rest of the sentence.

7. **D** is correct. This option is clearest because it cuts out unnecessary and awkward phrasing.

8. **F** is correct. *What remains unsaid* is the subject of the sentence. The verb *is* follows the subject as it should.

9. **A** is correct. This sentence effectively links the idea of what remains unsaid to a concrete example and thus provides a smooth transition between paragraphs while developing the theme of differences between high and low-context cultures.

10. **G** is correct. This sentence explains the meaning of the example given in the previous sentence.

11. **D** is correct. *He* and *she* are the third person singular pronouns and must be used in place of *someone*.

12. **F** is correct. *Even* modifies handshakes to indicate that they cannot be taken for granted while leaving the sentence structure intact.

13. **B** is correct. *Who* is the relative subject pronoun used for *someone*. *Someone who does not know this* is the subject of the sentence.

14. **H** is correct. This is the only option that refers to *codes* as opposed to the more restrictive *gestures*. The essay covers gestures and language.

15. **C** is correct. The essay makes the distinction between "high-context" and "low-context" cultures in order to show that language training is not as important as cultural training. The essay does not explore the differences cited above as its purpose.

Passage II

16. **H** is correct. A relative pronoun is required and *that* is correct because *a scene that I witnessed* is a single identifying phrase—the object of *picture*.

17. **A** is correct. No punctuation is needed before the prepositional phrase that begins with *on*.

18. **F** is correct. The underlined portion is part of a single sentence, and the parallel structure of *rowing, staking,* and *casting* is required because this series of modifiers refers to the same noun—*fishermen*.

19. **B** is correct. This is the most specific option. *Race* and *scowl* are vivid verbs, while *pools* is a noun that can be pictured. All the other answers use vague or abstract language.

20. **H** is correct. The present perfect tense, have managed, indicates that the anglers did something in the past that is relevant to the present moment. They have carved time out in order to fish.

21. **D** is correct. This option gets rid of unnecessary words and keeps the sentence clear all the way to its end. It also maintains the parallel between *the right clothes* and *the gear*.

22. **G** is correct. *To reckon* is the verb and it is used in passive form.

23. **D** is correct. The colon is needed to indicate the series of examples that illustrates the reckoning of time.

24. **H** is correct. *Who* is the relative pronoun that indicates people.

25. **D** is correct. A verb form is required, not a modifier, and because there is already a conjugated verb—*people line up*—the second verb must be in the infinitive form (*to buy*), which cannot be separated by punctuation.

26. **F** is correct. Sentence 2 belongs first because "This type of scene . . ." refers to the description in the previous paragraph. It works as a transition from the scene to the idea that free time must be efficiently spent.

27. **B** is correct. This sentence gives specific examples of technology that blur the boundary between work and play and thus directly supports the previous sentence.

28. **J** is correct. The second sentence needs a subject and both are clearer when separated by a period. By repeating the word *leisure* D also avoids confusion over what *it* might refer to.

29. **C** is correct. *It* is ambiguous. A clear subject is needed. *Going fishing* is the best option because it maintains the link between the idea of leisure and the example of fishing that has been developed in the essay.

30. **F** is correct. The first paragraph is full of details that are relevant to the essay. It sets up the example that will be developed. It does not contain information establishing the author's expertise, nor does it explore a social or historical connection between fishing and the transformation of leisure.

Passage III

31. **C** is correct. The preposition *from* is needed to indicate the distance in time between the early photographs and the later photographs.

32. **J** is correct. To make this sentence clear, *viewers* and *critical acclaim* must both relate clearly to the verb. *Have won* makes *praise from viewers* parallel to *critical acclaim*. Both become objects of the verb.

33. **D** is correct. The underlined information is unnecessary and redundant because of the phrase *all aspects of his work*.

34. **G** is correct. *Because* gets rid of the comma splice and shows that the second clause provides the reason for his missing deadlines.

35. **A** is correct. This is the only option that clearly links the missing of deadlines with Smith's particular style of working.

36. **F** is correct. The commas between the adjective-noun combinations indicate that these are examples in series and that, in different instances, Smith took photographs of each of these groups. If *and* were added between the second and third groups in the series, the sentence would indicate that Smith spent time with these groups before every photo shoot.

37. **C** is correct. *Familiar* is better than friendly because it is associated with unobtrusive. Placing the modifier *so* before *familiar* increases the quality of familiarity and links it to *almost invisible*.

38. **G** is correct. This is the clearest construction. It maintains the integrity of the sentence and the plural from *portraits*.

39. **D** is correct. This answer links the subject *Smith* with the verb *was* to form a complete sentence.

40. **G** is correct. This is the clearest construction. It avoids awkward phrasing and keeps the subject *Smith* cleanly linked to the verbs *wandered* and *read*.

41. **B** is correct. Sentence 1 should come first because it introduces the year and the nature of the project. Sentence 3 states how long the assignment was to last, and this should be mentioned *before* the description of the deadline passing that occurs in Sentence 2.

42. **F** is correct. This is the only construction that properly separates *the many faces of Pittsburgh*. The colon indicates a list is coming. The semicolons separate the list into categories. Commas cannot be used for this separation because confusion would result in the final category where there is already a comma.

43. **C** is correct. This is the clearest, most succinct option. The others contain awkward phrasing such as *huge attempt* or redundancies such as *task of trying*.

44. **G** is correct. *It* refers to his work, which he thought a failure. *That* refers to the publication.

45. **A** is correct. This option concludes the story of the Pittsburgh project by addressing W. Eugene Smith's high standards and the value of his work

to the world, both of which are mentioned in the first paragraph.

Passage IV

46. **F** is correct. *Passed two weeks* is the only construction that correctly describes the amount of time spent on board the *Regina IV*.

47. **D** is correct. This construction is the clearest because it places the modifier *hoping* closer to the subject it modifies and avoids making it sound as if the ship is the subject being modified. It also eliminates redundant information.

48. **H** is correct. *So far* is the prepositional phrase used to mean *from the beginning to the present moment*.

49. **C** is correct. Parallel structure requires the verb to be active: We rush *and* train.

50. **F** is correct. It maintains the tone of the essay and is straightforward and correct.

51. **A** is correct. The comma separates the two different things that they see and keeps the sentence clear.

52. **G** is correct. This option gets rid of the comma splice and by creating a new sentence, maintains the clarity of the description.

53. **C** is correct. C is the only option that keeps the description of events flowing and also links the defensive posture of the whales with the sight of their attackers.

54. **J** is correct. Subject-verb agreement. A *group of killer whales* is a singular collective, so the correct form of the verb is *races*.

55. **A** is correct. *Headlong* is the only choice of an adverb to modify *cuts*. It adds a vivid quality to the description, and there is no reason to omit it.

56. **G** is correct. The active voice provides a clear, simple description of the action.

57. **D** is correct. The preposition *in* is used before the noun *suspense*.

58. **J** is correct. *There* is the right word and the verb *is* agrees with *a flurry*.

59. **C** is correct. The author wants to emphasize the *heartwarming* quality of the event, the apparent sense of compassion from the whales, which he finds almost human.

60. **H** is correct. The essay is primarily about the sperm whales. It opens with the hope of seeing sperm whales and concludes with a feeling of admiration for their behavior.

Passage V

61. **A** is correct. It provides punctuation (a period) that creates two complete sentences.

62. **G** is correct. Simple present tense is used to indicate the general reoccurring nature of the grape harvest.

63. **A** is correct. It uses the correct form of *past* in a descriptive phrase modifying *midnight*.

64. **H** is correct. Subject-verb agreement. *Banners* is a third person plural noun.

65. **D** is the correct answer. It is the most logical. The sight of only one banner is enough to remind the writer of her experience harvesting grapes.

66. **G** is correct. It provides new and specific information directly related to the region under discussion.

67. **B** is correct. It forms a complete sentence composed of a dependent clause and an independent clause separated by a comma.

68. **H** is correct. The verb form called for here is the past tense of the verb *to be* and the word *there* is neither a contraction nor a possessive pronoun.

69. **A** is correct. It makes the writer's point clearly and concisely without adding redundant and unnecessary words.

70. **J** is correct. The past tense of the verb is required because the writer is telling what *happened*, not what might have happened.

71. **B** is correct. *However* sets up the opposition to the previous sentence.

72. **G** is correct. The added sentence builds upon the idea that harvesting is difficult and should immediately follow the sentence in which that idea is introduced.

73. **D** is correct. It neither provides unnecessary punctuation, nor involves the use of a phrase that is unfamiliar in common usage.

74. **G** is correct. It supplies the correct singular possessive punctuation.

75. **C** is correct. Sentence 1 introduces the setting and characters described in the anecdote. Sentence 6 describes a tentative response to the events in Sentence 1 and should be placed before the narrator takes more vigorous action (singing out loud, for example). Sentence 4 describes the young Pole's response to her humming. Sentence 5, which describes the two workers singing together, cannot logically be placed before sentence 6, which describes the writer humming alone. Sentence 3, which introduces the fact that they both knew all the words to the song, logically follows the sentence in which they sing. Sentence 2 concludes the paragraph by revealing the name of the song.

2. Math Test

1. **D.** 63 is the least common multiple of 3, 7, and 9.

2. **H.** "At least" and "no more than" imply "greater than or equal to" and "less than or equal to," respectively.

3. **A.** The question asks how many tickets were issued for *other* violations, so the appropriate calculation is $(100\% - 70\%)(4,860) = (.3)(4,860) = 1,458$.

4. **H.** $2x + 4 = -4(x - 1)$
$$2x + 4 = -4x + 4$$
$$6x = 0$$
$$x = 0$$

5. **A.** A negative number raised to an even power gives a positive result. Only v is not raised to an even power. If v were negative, then the entire expression would be negative and could not equal 10.

6. **F.** $4x + 3y = 15$
$$3y = -4x + 15$$
$$y = -\frac{4}{3}x + 5$$

7. **E.** $\pi r^2 h = \pi(4^2)(8) = 128\pi$

8. **J.** When parallel lines are cut by a transversal, the sum of a created acute angle and a created obtuse angle is always 180°. If x measures 80°, then y must measure $180° - 80° = 100°$.

9. **B.** $\angle BAC = 180° - 115° = 65°$. An exterior angle of a triangle is equal to the sum of the opposite interior angles. $\angle BCD = \angle CBA + \angle BAC = 55° + 65° = 120°$.

10. **J.** 10% of 10% = (.1)(.1) = .01.

11. **E.** $\sqrt{288} = \sqrt{144 \times 2} = 12\sqrt{2}$

12. **H.** $(2p - 3q)(2p - 3q) = 4p^2 - 6pq - 6pq + 9q^2 = 4p^2 - 12pq + 9q^2$

13. **E.** Using the obvious notation, we have:

    $4c + 6d + 3h = 815$

    $2c + 3d + 4h = 720$

    Multiplying the second equation by –2 and adding the equations together yields $-5h = -625$; $h = 125$. Hence, the cost of a box of doughnut holes is $1.25.

14. **H.** Parallel lines have the same slope. The easiest way to determine the slope is to put each of the equations into the slope-intercept form of $y = mx + b$, where m is the slope. When converted to this form, you find that $2x + y = 6$ (or $y = -2x + 6$) and $4x + 2y = 10$ (or $y = -2x + 5$) both have a slope of –2.

15. **B.** The question gives two equations for the father (f) and son's (s) weight: $f + s = 240$ and $f = 3s$. Through substitution you solve for s:

    $3s + s = 240$

    $\qquad 4s = 240$

    $\qquad \ s = 60$

16. **H.** $\frac{3}{8}(.02) = (.375)(.02) = .0075$.

17. **B.** By using angle rules for supplementary angles, triangles, and vertical angles, you can solve for A as

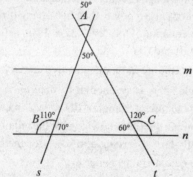

18. **H.** To obtain the total number of different executive boards, you multiply the number of possibilities for each office: president (2) × vice-president (3) × treasurer (2) = 12.

19. **D.** $\frac{120 - 45}{120} = \frac{75}{120} = .625$

20. **H.** $\sqrt{11} = 3.3$, so 3 is the greatest integer that still gives a negative result.

21. **D.** $2\pi r = 20$

    $y = \frac{20}{2\pi} = \frac{10}{\pi}$

22. **F.** $\left(\frac{3a^2 b^4}{c^{-1}}\right)\left(\frac{3^{-1}a^{-3}c^{-2}}{b^3}\right) = \left(\frac{3a^2 b^4 c}{3a^3 b^3 c^2}\right) = \frac{b}{ac}$

23. **E.** $\frac{300 \text{ gallons}}{\frac{3}{7} \text{ miles per gallon}} = 300 \times \frac{7}{3} = 700$ miles

24. **H.** $x^2 - 4x - 5 = 0$

    $(x + 1)(x - 5) = 0$

    $x + 1 = 0$ or $x - 5 = 0$

    $x = -1$ or $x = 5$

25. **C.** The area of the rectangular section of the diagram is (6)(8) = 48 square centimeters. Using the Pythagorean Theorem, you can determine that the height of the triangular section is 3 cm and its area is $\frac{1}{2}(3)(8) = 12$ square centimeters. The area of the entire figure is 12 + 48 = 60 square centimeters.

26. **F.** The formula of a circle can be generalized as $(x - a)^2 + (y - b)^2 = r^2$, where (a,b) is the center of the circle and r is the radius. Notice that the problem gives a diameter of 8, so the radius is 4. The circle with a center at (4,2) and a radius of 4 thus has an equation of $(x - 4)^2 + (y - 2)^2 = 16$.

27. **B.** This problem can be solved through process of elimination. Perpendicular lines have negative reciprocal slopes, so the correct answer must have a slope of $-\frac{1}{2}$. Only $y = -\frac{1}{2}x + 2$ meets this condition *and* passes through the point (4,0).

28. **G.** $\left(\sqrt{a^2 - b^2}\right)\left(\sqrt{a - b}\right) =$

    $\left(\sqrt{(a + b)(a - b)}\right)\left(\sqrt{a - b}\right)$

    $= \left(\sqrt{a + b}\right)\left(\sqrt{a - b}\right)\left(\sqrt{a - b}\right)$

    $= (a - b)\left(\sqrt{(a + b)}\right)$

29. **C.** You can solve this problem by setting up a proportion:

    $\frac{42}{30} = \frac{x}{25}$

    $30x = 1,050$

    $x = 35$

30. **K.** The diagonals of a square are perpendicular bisectors. The midpoint of one diagonal is thus the midpoint of the other diagonal. The midpoint of (–1,2) and (5,2) is (2,2) and this diagonal is parallel to the x-axis. The other diagonal must be parallel to the y-axis and pass through (2,2). Only (2,–1) satisfies this condition.

31. **E.** $5 - x > 10 - 3(x - 2)$
$5 - x > 10 - 3x + 6$
$-x + 3x > 16 - 5$
$2x > 11$
$x > \frac{11}{2}$

32. **J.** Use the Pythagorean Theorem to solve for $\overline{AC}$:
$3^2 + b^2 = 10^2$
$9 + b^2 = 100$
$b^2 = 91$
$b = \sqrt{91}$

33. **B.** $(2x + a)(2x + b) = 4x^2 - 4x + ab$
$4x^2 + 2(a + b)x + ab = 4x^2 - 4x + ab$
$2(a + b) = -4$
$a + b = -2$

34. **J.** This problem can be done fairly quickly if you remember that the relationship among the sides of a 45°-45°-90° triangle is $s, s, s\sqrt{2}$, where $s\sqrt{2}$ is the length of the hypotenuse. The smaller triangle has legs 2 inches long, so x, the length of the hypotenuse, must be $2\sqrt{2}$. The hypotenuse of the larger triangle is $2x\sqrt{2}$ or $(2\sqrt{2})(2\sqrt{2}) = 8$ inches long. The legs of the larger triangle are each $\frac{8}{\sqrt{2}} = 4\sqrt{2}$, so the perimeter is $4\sqrt{2} + 4\sqrt{2} + 8 = 8 + 8\sqrt{2}$ inches.

35. **D.** $\log_2 x = 5$
$2^5 = x$
$x = 32$

36. **G.** Using the Pythagorean Theorem you can obtain the length of $\overline{AC}$:
$5^2 + b^2 = 132$
$b^2 = 144$
$b = 12$
If $\overline{AC}$ is 12 inches long and $\overline{AD}$ is 4 inches, then $\overline{CD}$ is 8 inches. You now have both the height (5 inches) and base (8 inches) of triangle BCD. The area of the triangle is $\frac{1}{2}(5)(8) = 20$ square inches.

37. **E.** In order to weight the second round scores twice as heavily as the first, you need to count them twice. In order to weight the third round scores twice as heavily as the second round score, you need to count them 4 times. The weighted average is thus $\frac{S_1 + 2S_2 + 4S_3}{1 + 2 + 4} = \frac{S_1 + 2S_2 + 4S_3}{7}$.

38. **F.** Since triangle CDE is a 30°-60°-90° triangle, you can solve for $\overline{CE}$ as $\frac{12}{2} = 6$ inches and $\overline{DE}$ as $6\sqrt{3}$ inches. The rectangle $ABCE$ thus has an area

of $(6)(8) = 48$ square inches, and the triangle CED has an area of $\frac{1}{2}(6)(6\sqrt{3}) = 18\sqrt{3}$ square inches. The area of the entire quadrilateral is the sum of these two pieces.

39. **E.** The trick to solving this problem quickly is to realize that the center of the circle must have an x-coordinate midway between -4 and 4 and a y-coordinate midway between -8 and 2. The circle thus has a center at $(0,-3)$. Although it is possible to calculate the radius, you do not need to do so, since only the equation $x^2 + (y + 3)^2 = 25$ has the center in the correct spot.

40. **G.** The sine of a given angle is equal to the cosine of its complement (angles that add up to 90° are complements). Since X and Y are complementary angles, $\sin \angle X = \cos \angle Y$.

41. **E.** The equation for a line passing through $(3,2)$ and $(6,3)$ is $y = \frac{1}{3}x + 1$. Only $(15,6)$ also satisfies this equation.

42. **F.** An ellipse in the form $\frac{(x - h)^2}{a^2} + \frac{(y - k)^2}{b^2} = 1$ has a center at (h,k). The given ellipse would have a center at $(-3,4)$: $\frac{(x + 3)^2}{75} + \frac{(y - 4)^2}{5} = 1$.

43. **C.** An important trigonometric identity is that $\tan A = \frac{\sin A}{\cos A}$. Thus, $(\tan A)(\cos A) = \left(\frac{\sin A}{\cos A}\right)(\cos A) = \sin A$.

44. **H.** In many cases, it is easier to answer this type of problem by seeing which equation is satisfied by both given points than by solving directly for the equation. Only $2y - 3x = 12$ is satisfied by $(-4,0)$ and $(0,6)$.

45. **D.** Using the relationships in a 45°-45°-90° triangle, it is easy enough to determine that the hypotenuse of triangle ABD is $4\sqrt{2}$ meters long. You can then use knowledge of the relationship of a 30°-60°-90° triangle to solve for the height of the equilateral triangle:

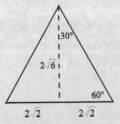

The area of the triangle is $\frac{1}{2}(4\sqrt{2})(2\sqrt{6}) = 4\sqrt{12} = 8\sqrt{3}$.

46. **G.** The small cubes each have a volume of 3^3 cubic inches. Since 27 (or 3^3) small cubes make up the large cube, the volume of the large cube is $(3^3)(3^3) = 3^6$ cubic inches.

47. **C.** $(3x + 4)^2 = 9x^2 + 24x + 16$, so a equals 24.

48. **G.** Factoring the expression gives $(x + 3)(2x - 1)$. The expression can only be negative if one of the factors is positive and one is negative. Thus:

$x + 3 > 0$ and $2x - 1 < 0$

$x > -3$ and $x < \frac{1}{2}$

$-3 < x < \frac{1}{2}$

Note that the alternative $(x + 3 < 0$ and $2x - 1 > 0)$ produces an empty set, so it does not effect the solution.

49. **B.** $\frac{3}{11}$ can be expressed as the repeating decimal $.27\overline{27}$, so the 20th digit, like all even-numbered digits, will be 7. $\frac{7}{15}$ can be expressed as $.46\overline{6}$, so the 20th digit is 6. The difference is 1.

50. **F.** If we call the length of a side of the smallest triangle x, then we can determine that $\overline{BD}$ is $2x$ long and that $\overline{AD}$ is twice that, or $4x$. Thus, the large triangle has sides of length $2x + 4x = 6x$. Since all of the triangles are similar, the ratio between the height of the largest triangle and height of the smallest triangle is 6, and the ratio between the base of the largest triangle and base of the smallest triangle is also 6. This means that the largest triangle has $(6)(6) = 36$ times the area of the smallest triangle. Expressed another way, the ratio of triangle EGF to triangle ABC is 1:36.

51. **C.** The sum of the interior angles of a polygon can be generalized by the formula $(N - 2)(180°)$, where N is the number of sides of the polygon. Thus, the sum of the interior angles of the octagon is $(8 - 2)(180°) = 1,080°$.

52. **G.** The graph of $6\sin 2\theta$ has 6 times the amplitude and half the period of the graph of $\sin \theta$.

53. **D.** $x^2 = ax + 12a^2$

$x^2 - ax - 12a^2 = 0$

$(x + 3a)(x - 4a) = 0$

$x = -3a$ or $x = 4a$

54. **K.** Use two basic trigonometric identities to reduce this equation:

$\tan A = \frac{\sin A}{\cos A}$ and $\cot A = \frac{\cos A}{\sin A}$.

$$\left(\frac{\cos^2 A}{\sin^2 A}\right)(\tan A) = \left(\frac{\cos^2 A}{\sin^2 A}\right)\left(\frac{\sin A}{\cos A}\right)$$

$$= \frac{\cos A}{\sin A}$$

$$= \cot A$$

55. **B.** The diagonals of a rhombus are perpendicular bisectors, so 4 equal right triangles are created. If the diagonals are 12 centimeters and 8 centimeters long, then the legs of each right triangle are 6 centimeters and 4 centimeters. The Pythagorean Theorem gives the length of a side of the rhombus:

$c^2 = 4^2 + 6^2$

$c^2 = 52$

$c = 2\sqrt{13}$

The perimeter of the rhombus is thus $4\left(2\sqrt{13}\right) = 8\sqrt{13}$.

56. **K.** The difficulty in this problem is that you must be sure to account for $y - 3$ being negative *or* positive, because it changes the direction of the inequality. First, assume that the quantity is positive:

$\frac{3}{y - 3} < 3$

$3 < 3y - 9$

$12 < 3y$

$y > 4$

On the other hand, if $y - 3$ is negative, then the inequality sign changes direction and you end up with $y < 4$. However, since values between 3 and 4, inclusive, do not make $y - 3$ negative, the solution for this part of the inequality is actually $y < 3$.

57. **E.** The box must be a cube of inside dimensions $16" \times 16" \times 16"$ (16" is the diameter of the sphere), or 4096 cubic inches.

58. **G.** The question gives 3 equations for the weights of Jason (J), his mother (M), and his father (F): $J + M = 285$, $J + F = 345$, and $M + F = 310$. The short-cut on this problem is to add up all three equations to obtain $2J + 2F + 2M = 940$. Thus, the combined weight of Jason, his mother, and his father is $\frac{940}{2} = 470$ pounds.

59. **E.** The discriminant ($b^2 - 4ac$) is the part of the quadratic formula underneath the radical that determines how many real roots a quadratic equation has. If the discriminant is equal to 0, then the two real roots are equal, so there is only 1 *distinct* real root.

$$b^2 - 4ac = 0$$
$$8^2 - 4(3)c = 0$$
$$64 - 12c = 0$$
$$12c = 64$$
$$c = \frac{64}{12} = \frac{16}{3} = 5\frac{1}{3}$$

60. **F.** Slope is equal to the "rise" over the "run".

$$\frac{rise}{run} = b$$
$$\frac{a}{AC} = b$$
$$\frac{a}{b} = \overline{AC}$$

3. Reading Test

1. **A.** A is the best answer because in paragraph 4 James mentions "a honeymoon in Minorca." B is incorrect because although Russia is mentioned in paragraph 4, it is not mentioned as a place to honeymoon. C is incorrect because Africa is not mentioned in the passage. D is incorrect because although the Alps are mentioned in paragraph 1, they are never suggested as a honeymoon spot.

2. **J.** F is incorrect because a circle of energy is never mentioned. G is incorrect because a park is never mentioned. H is incorrect because though the Alps are mentioned in paragraph 1, they are not mentioned in comparison to James' family members. J is the best answer because paragraph 1 and 2 state that the "women-folk of his home circle" including his "mother, sisters, and aunt-in-residence" watched with the "unrestrained eagerness" of "a group of unexercised terriers" (sentence 1, paragraph 2).

3. **B.** A is incorrect because James' allergies are not mentioned. B is the best answer because the final paragraph of the passage details how James' theory of how women should act contrasts strongly with the "solicitous little questions" and conversation of afternoon tea. C is incorrect because though Joan is shown to be forgetful of James' preferences in the fifth paragraph, it is the chatter itself that makes him dislike afternoon tea, not the forgetfulness. D is incorrect because we are never given any indication that James dislikes Joan.

4. **J.** F is incorrect because James is never presented as belligerent. G is incorrect because in the second Paragraph we learn that James "was not sufficiently obstinate or indifferent to home influences." H is incorrect because in paragraph 1 and 4 we learn that James is not enthralled with the idea of marriage and finds proposing "irksome." J is the best answer because in paragraph 4 James reveals that "proposing marriage . . . was a rather irksome business."

5. **D.** A is incorrect because the second paragraph mentions that James' family paid close attention to his "most innocent flirtations." B is incorrect because James' female friends support the choice of Joan (paragraph 3). C is incorrect because paragraph 2 tells us that Uncle Jules is already dead, and therefore cannot be made proud. D is the best answer because the last sentence of paragraph 3 tells us that "the family had so far conducted and directed the flirtation."

6. **F.** F is the best answer because in paragraph 3 we find that James has "became gradually accustomed to the idea that he and Joan would go together through the prescribed stages of congratulations, present-receiving, Norwegian or Mediterranean hotels, and eventual domesticity." Paragraph 4 also says that James will "propose marriage" and then have a life of "married happiness." G is incorrect because James only wishes to honeymoon in Minorca (paragraph 3), not move there. H is incorrect because nowhere in the passage do we find suggestion that Joan may be after James' money. J is incorrect because James does plan on proposing (paragraphs 3, 4, 5).

7. **A.** A is the best answer because paragraph 1 states that James "liked and admired a great many women" but did not wish to claim one for his own. B is incorrect because paragraphs 1, 2, and 3 suggest that James' family wished that he would get married. C is incorrect because the passage does not say that James has asked other women for their hand in marriage. D is incorrect because the passage does not contain information about James' job.

8. **F.** F is the best answer because paragraph 6 mentions that James "detests" afternoon tea, in part, because of the "drawn-out chatter" and the "solicitous little questions." G is incorrect because Joan's looks are not mentioned in the passage. H is incorrect because Joan is presented as someone with tact (paragraph 5). J is incorrect because the passage does not state that Joan is avoiding the topic of marriage.

9. **D.** A is incorrect because nowhere in the passage does it state that James loves Joan. B is incorrect because James is never presented as someone

with mood swings. C is incorrect because the passage never mentions a "first marriage" for James. D is the best answer because, as paragraph 3 states, James was influenced more by the "weight of public opinion than by any initiative of his own; a clear working majority of his female relatives and the aforesaid matronly friends had presented Joan Sebastable as the most suitable young woman in his range of acquaintance to whom he might propose marriage."

10. **G.** F is incorrect because "movies" are not mentioned in the passage. G is the best answer because the first sentence of the final paragraph of the passage states that James "had read of such things in scores of novels, and hundreds of actual experiences had told him they were true to life." H is incorrect because the passage does not mention conversations about afternoon tea James has had. J is incorrect because the passage does not mention the opinions of James' uncle.

11. **C.** A is incorrect because the passage does not say that affirmative action may be used in the future. B is incorrect because the author makes it clear throughout the passage that affirmative action was intended to increase equality in the workplace. C is the best answer because the final sentence in paragraph 3 states "Just because quota-based affirmative action policies have not been accepted does not mean that we should give up on the goal of improving equality in the workplace." D is incorrect because the author does not find it "troublesome" that conservatives rejected affirmative action.

12. **J.** F is incorrect because Dole's statement is in no way an example of affirmative action. G is incorrect because the author does not indicate that Dole is not dealing with the issue. H is incorrect because at the end of paragraph 2 we learn that in fact conservatives are in agreement with minorities in dismissing affirmative action as ineffective. J is the best answer because paragraph 2 states that "Mr. Dole may be fishing for votes here, but his point is well taken."

13. **B.** A is incorrect because paragraphs 2 and 3 make it clear that most Americans do support the idea of equality in the workplace. B is the best answer because paragraph 2 states that "what scares Americans even more than racism is the loss of individuality." C is incorrect because the fact that affirmative action helps only certain

minority groups is never mentioned. D is incorrect because a lack of knowledge is never cited as a reason affirmative action was rejected.

14. **H.** F is incorrect because Kennedy's Executive Order was not given until 1961. G is incorrect because the court's rulings in 1952 and 1954 set the stage for affirmative action. H is the best answer because the final paragraph states that "in separate rulings in 1952 and 1954, the Court overturned its earlier decision," referring to *Plessy v. Ferguson.* J is incorrect because the Court is not mentioned overturning concepts of liberty.

15. **C.** A is incorrect because limiting discrimination in society is not given as a reason for segregation. B is incorrect because limiting regulation in society is not given as a reason for segregation. C is the best answer because the final paragraph states that "segregation was seen as a way to keep our society from fragmenting." D is incorrect because keeping the society from being equal is not given as a reason for segregation.

16. **G.** F is incorrect because Bob Dole's popularity is not cited as support for the author's contention. G is the best answer because paragraph 2 states that "Opinion polls and common sense lead us to this transparent conclusion." H is incorrect because examples of affirmative action programs are not cited as support for the author's contention. J is incorrect because Jim Crow laws are not cited as support for the author's contention.

17. **A.** A is the best answer because paragraph 4 ends with "Of course, the profit we seek is not monetary, but nevertheless it is just as tangible. Our profit is equality." Thus, *profitable* in this context refers to equality. B is incorrect because paragraph 4 ends with "Of course, the profit we seek is not monetary, but nevertheless it is just as tangible. Our profit is equality." Thus, *profitable* in this context refers to equality, not money. C is incorrect because paragraph 4 ends with "Of course, the profit we seek is not monetary, but nevertheless it is just as tangible. Our profit is equality." Thus, *profitable* in this context refers to equality, not happiness. D is incorrect because paragraph 4 ends with "Of course, the profit we seek is not monetary, but nevertheless it is just as tangible. Our profit is equality." Thus, *profitable* in this context refers to equality, not politics.

18. **H.** F is incorrect because paragraph 4 implies that the Constitution can and should be altered. (See

explanation for H.) G is incorrect because the passage does not mention reasoned debate. H is the best answer because paragraph 4 states that "the founders of this grand bit of research into human governance gave their sons and grandsons the right, indeed the obligation, to create laws, make amendments to the rules of the experiment, and even change the basic drafted rules of the experiment (the Constitution) if necessary." J is incorrect because the skill of the people heading the experiment is never mentioned.

19. **D.** A is incorrect because I is incorrect: Paragraph 6 states that Kennedy implemented the first affirmative action programs. B is incorrect because although II is correct, III is also correct. (See explanation for D.) C is incorrect because although II is correct, I is not correct. (See explanation for A.) D is the best answer because I is incorrect. (See explanation for A.) II is supported by Dole's statement in paragraph 2 that "I'm beginning to believe that may not be the way it should be in America." The statement in paragraph 2 that "A vast majority of Americans, even minorities, do not think that affirmative action policies are effective ways of bettering society" supports III.

20. **G.** F is incorrect because the statement that "our society is not a utopia" does not refer to the metaphor presented in the previous paragraph. G is the best answer because the statement in question 20 is followed by "people of color still do not hold as many high-paying jobs as Caucasians do proportional to the size of their respective populations." H is incorrect because the statement that "our society is not a utopia" does not refer to the use of the word *meritocracy*. J is incorrect because the statement that "our society is not a utopia" does not refer to Supreme Court rulings, which are not mentioned until the next paragraph.

21. **B.** A is incorrect because undiluted means "not watered down" or *pure*. B is the best answer because undiluted means "not watered down" or *pure*. C is incorrect because undiluted means "not watered down" or *pure*. D is incorrect because undiluted means "not watered down" or *pure*.

22. **H.** F is incorrect because in paragraph 2 the author calls the work "provincial" which means limited in scope. G is incorrect because in paragraph 2 the author states that "Crockett could

exercise intelligence." H is the best answer because paragraph 2 states "It is one of the primary social documents of America." J is incorrect because in paragraph 2 the author says the work was published in 1834.

23. **D.** A is incorrect because the passage does not mention the speech patterns or actions of real people as being a prerequisite of a modern regional biography. B is incorrect because the passage does not mention sustained effort as being a prerequisite of a modern regional biography. C is incorrect because the passage does not mention violating trust as being a prerequisite of a modern regional biography. D is the best answer because paragraph 3 states "I do not believe it possible that a good one will henceforth come from a mind that does not in outlook transcend the region on which it is focused," and the end of the paragraph continues: "Awareness of other times and other wheres, not insistence on that awareness, is the requisite."

24. **J.** F is incorrect because the passage does not mention that schools no longer attempt to create intellectuals. G is incorrect because the passage does not discuss changing the way people use the word "intellectual." H is incorrect because the passage does not mention how magazines or newspapers could be made more intellectual. J is the best answer because the first paragraph states that "'fundamental brainwork' is behind every respect-worthy piece of writing."

25. **B.** A is incorrect because in this context *crying out* most nearly means advocating. B is the best answer because in this context *crying out* most nearly means advocating. C is incorrect because in this context *crying out* most nearly means advocating. D is incorrect because in this context *crying out* most nearly means advocating.

26. **F.** F is the best answer because the final paragraph states: "Nothing is too provincial for the regional writer, but he cannot be provincial-minded toward it . . . We may be sure that if by violating the rules of syntax Horace Greeley sometimes added forcefulness to his editorials, he violated them deliberately and not in ignorance." Thus, Greeley is presented as someone who could only provide a particular interpretation because he understood the greater context. G is incorrect because "young writers" are never mentioned. H is incorrect

because the final paragraph says; "nothing is too trivial for art." J is incorrect because Greeley is depicted breaking the rules of grammar and still communicating sensibly.

27. **A.** A is the best answer because paragraph 1 states that "Nonintellectual literature is as nonexistent as education without mental discipline." B is incorrect because strong morals are never mentioned in the passage. C is incorrect because the author never related open-mindedness to education. D is incorrect because the author never related local customs to education.

28. **H.** F is incorrect because the passage does not say that editors do not wish to publish autobiographies. G is incorrect because the passage does not say that editors do not wish to publish provincial views (on the contrary, paragraph 1 suggests that they do). H is the best answer because according to paragraph 1: "Editors of all but a few magazines of the country and publishers of most of the daily newspapers reinforce this attitude by crying out for brightness and vitality while at the same time shutting out critical ideas." J is incorrect because the passage does not say that editors do not wish to publish regional stories.

29. **B.** A is incorrect because how Hardy felt about his church is never discussed. B is the best answer because the final paragraph ends with the statement: "A provincial writer must, above all, remain true to his foundations." C is incorrect because the passage never suggests that Hardy had a lack of faith in his heirs. D is incorrect because the main point of the passage, as presented in paragraphs 1 and 2, is that intelligence and provincialism are not mutually exclusive.

30. **J.** F is incorrect because Hardy is not mentioned in relation to Barrie. G is incorrect because the author's reference to patriotism in paragraph 4 is not related to the island analogy presented by Barrie. H is incorrect because the point that the author makes is that Barrie had to have known what the mainland was like, not the island. (See explanation for J.) J is the best answer because paragraph 4 states "James M. Barrie said that he could not write a play until he got his people off on a kind of island, but had he not known about the mainland he could never have delighted us with the islanders."

31. **D.** A is incorrect because the passage does not say that the shoreline birds were made extinct; in fact,

paragraph 8 asserts that shoreline birds were the only birds to survive the impact. B is incorrect because the evidence Fediccia finds is not about modern biologists. C is incorrect because opposing bird populations are not mentioned in the passage. D is the best answer because, as paragraph 6 reveals, the evidence Fediccia finds is that only one certain shoreline bird fossil resembles modern birds.

32. **F.** F is the best answer because paragraph 2 tells us that "thousands of other dinosaur species, abruptly became extinct at the end of the Cretaceous Period." G is incorrect because we learn in paragraph 5 that the supercontinent began to fragment 80 million years ago, long before the end of the Cretaceous Period (65 million years ago). H is incorrect because the passage does not mention when the ostrich was introduced to Africa. J is incorrect because paragraph 7 states that the end of the Cretaceous Period brought the extinction of the *enantiornithine*, not the genetic diversification of it.

33. **A.** A is the best answer because only I is mentioned as a good place to look for fossils from the Cretaceous Period (paragraph 11: "Cretaceous fossil gold mines like Antarctica and New Zealand"). B is incorrect because II (South America) is not mentioned as a good place to find fossils from the Cretaceous Period. C is incorrect because II (South America) is not mentioned as a good place to find fossils from the Cretaceous Period. D is incorrect because III (*Gondwanaland*) is not mentioned as a good place to find fossils from the Cretaceous Period. In fact, *Gondwanaland* broke up before the Cretaceous Period even began (see paragraphs 4 and 5).

34. **G.** F is incorrect because their flight characteristics are never mentioned. G is the best answer because paragraph 8 states "Only these shore birds, Fediccia argues, were able to live through this massive cooling of the planet by feeding on marine animals like crabs that were able to adjust to the rapidly chilling environment." H is incorrect because the vocal mechanisms of birds are not mentioned in the passage. J is incorrect because bird hovels are not mentioned in the passage.

35. **A.** A is the best answer because the passage ends with the sentence "Such an agreement is unlikely without more detailed information from the

genetic and fossil records." B is incorrect because the passage does not suggest that a new theory is needed. (See explanation for A.) C is incorrect because the passage ends with a suggestion that more data is needed. (See explanation for A.) D is incorrect because the passage does not suggest that biologists need to closely study fossil specimens. (See explanation for A.)

36. **J.** F is incorrect because paragraph 5 confirms the fact that *Gondwanaland* fragmented 80 million years ago. G is incorrect because paragraph 4 confirms the statement that *Gondwanaland* was composed of other continents. H is incorrect because paragraph 4 states that *Gondwanaland* was probably the home to an ancestor of ratites. J is the best answer because according to paragraph 5, *Gondwanaland* began to fragment 80 million years ago and the Cretaceous Period ended 65 million years ago. Therefore, J is a false statement and the best answer for this EXCEPT question.

37. **D.** A is incorrect because inbreeding is never mentioned. B is incorrect because the "direction" of evolution is never mentioned. C is incorrect because according to paragraph 4, ostriches, rheas and emus are in fact related species. D is the best answer because paragraph 13 states genetic mutations build up in species, and paragraph 14 resolves that "Based on this genetic evidence, many scientists have concluded that it is impossible for so many bird species to have evolved from a common ancestor in so short a time (10 million years)."

38. **J.** F is incorrect because the passage ends with the conclusion that more data is needed, and any debate that lasts over a century must not be easy to resolve. G is incorrect because the passage does not suggest that the *debate* about bird evolution is poorly understood. H is incorrect because although *some* of the evidence for the bird debate *may* be considered circumstantial by some, the passage never mentions this. J is the best answer because the passage opens with the sentence "For more than a century, Paleontologists have been in heated debate about how birds evolved."

39. **B.** A is incorrect because II is incorrect. Paragraph 7 states that "the *enantiornithine* completely died out in the vast Cretaceous extinction," so it could not be the ancestor of birds whose fossils were found in a period before the Cretaceous. B is the best answer because if fossils of birds were found that proved their existence before the Cretaceous Extinction, then these birds would not have evolved from the shorebirds. In effect, the Fediccia theory would be negated by this discovery because it would show that ancient shorebirds are not the common ancestors of modern birds. C is incorrect because I is incorrect (see explanation for B) and because II is incorrect. Paragraph 7 states that "the *enantiornithine* completely died out in the vast Cretaceous extinction," so it could not be the ancestor of birds whose fossils were found in a period before the Cretaceous. D is incorrect because I is incorrect. (See explanation for B.)

40. **G.** F is incorrect because it contradicts the statement in paragraph 7 that "like the Archaeopteryx the *enantiornithine* completely died out in the vast Cretaceous extinction." G is the best answer because paragraph 7 states that "these 'birds' had strange elongated foot bones, fleshy tails like lizards, and teeth. This hints that these 'birds' were not the ancestors of modern birds." H is incorrect because the length of *enantiornithine's* evolution is never discussed. J is incorrect because the difficulty of finding fossils of *enantiornithine* is not provided as a reason for thinking they are not the ancestors of modern birds.

4. Science Reasoning Test

1. **B.** A positive Benedict's test is indicated with a change of the solution to green, yellow, orange, red, or brown. The only solution to turn any of those colors was the polysaccharide solution.

2. **H.** Protein showed a positive result to the Biuret test.

3. **B.** Monosaccharide reacts positively to the Iodine test, polysaccharide reacts positively to the Benedict's test and protein reacts positively to the Biuret test.

4. **F.** Monosaccharide is detected with the Iodine test and Solution B turned purple when it underwent the Iodine test.

5. **A.** Solution A reacted positively to the Iodine and Biuret tests and Solution C reacted positively to the Benedict's and Biuret tests.

6. **G.** Answer choices F, H, and J contradict information provided in the passage and the data. Through process of elimination, answer choice F is the only one that could possibly be right.

7. **D.** The Birmingham area is the polluted area and in that region 123 melanic moths were recovered.

8. **H.** Pollution does not negatively effect the survival of the melanic moths, therefore answer choice F is incorrect. Existence of lichen does not increase survival for all moths, therefore answer choice G is incorrect. Birds show selectivity based on the color of the moths according to the scientists' observations, therefore answer choice J is incorrect. The data supports that birds eat more moths that differ form their background. Therefore answer choice G is correct.

9. **A.** Appearance of lichen only increases the likelihood of survival for light moths but does not increase the likelihood of survival for melanic moths.

10. **G.** In both cases, light moths were recovered in almost equal percentages so it could be concluded that the light moths survive at the same levels regardless of pollution and presence of lichen.

11. **A.** Answer choices B, C, and D contradict the data presented.

12. **G.** The scientists concluded that the presence of lichen contributed to the success of the light moths. Therefore, if lichen reappeared, the light moths should be more successful than the melanic moths.

13. **B.** The table indicates that at an actual temperature of –25 degrees, the effective temperature would be –45 degrees if the wind is 30 km/hour.

14. **J.** To be moderately dangerous, the effective temperature would have to be between –30 and –55 degrees. When wind speed is 30 km/hour, actual temperatures of –15 and –25 degrees put the effective temperature within this range.

15. **D.** The effective temperature declines as the actual temperature declines and as the wind speed increases. Since –23 degrees and winds of 57 km/hour is colder than –20 degrees and windier than 50 km/hour, the answer must be less than –50 degrees.

16. **F.** Answer choices G, H, and J could all result in effective temperatures that are moderately dan-

gerous and extremely dangerous. Answer choice E is the only possible answer.

17. **D.** There are only 4 days over the 30-day period where the UV Index falls below the warning level.

18. **G.** A higher altitude would normally produce a higher UV Index, not a lower one, so answer choice F can be eliminated. The average index has no bearing on the index for a given day, so answer choice H is wrong. No correlation between wind and the UV Index is discussed in the passage, so answer choice J is not correct. Only answer choice F provides a plausible explanation for the difference.

19. **B.** Looking at Table 1, 6 ml would be between 4 ml and 8 ml, so the length would be between 3.5 cm and 5.6 cm.

20. **H.** Looking at Table 2, test tube 1 is the one at 23 degrees. The volume after six hours would be 11.6 ml.

21. **A.** At 0 hours, both test tubes had the same length and the same volume. At 24 hours, both test tubes again had the same length and same volume. It would appear based only on these two readings that temperature had no effect on the rate of respiration.

22. **G.** The total carbon dioxide is equal for both trials. When the temperature is greater, the maximum level of carbon dioxide is reached more quickly.

23. **D.** Comparing 0.7 cm, to 4.1 cm, the latter is about six times greater.

24. **H.** If the yeast had converted all of the available sugar, then there could be no further cellular respiration to occur and therefore the volume of carbon dioxide would not increase beyond that point.

25. **C.** Lead showed the greatest change in temperature when the starting temperature was 50 degrees.

26. **J.** When the initial temperature was 200 degrees, the final temperature was 34.14 degrees. If the initial temperature is 250 degrees, then the final temperature would be greater than 34.14 degrees.

27. **A.** The final temperature increases when the initial temperature increases for all of the metals.

28. **H.** Diamond's specific heat capacity is between that of aluminum and steel. The final temperatures for steel were lower than the final temperatures for aluminum for each different initial temperature. The range of temperatures for diamond should fall in between the range for aluminum and steel.

29. **B.** Aluminum has a range of final temperature readings greater than steel and steel has a range of temperature readings greater than lead.

30. **G.** Based on the temperature readings, the specific heat capacity of the unknown metal would fall between that of lead and steel.

31. **D.** Astronomer 1's theory includes the existence of comets in the region occupied by planets whereas Astronomer 2's theory allows for comets beyond the region of the planets.

32. **G.** Astronomer 2 believes that other stars influence the motion of the comets in the Oort Cloud, whereas Astronomer 3 believes that the Sun's gravity is responsible for the orbits.

33. **D.** Astronomer 3 points out that it cannot be known in certain terms whether all members of the Solar System arose from the same nebula.

34. **F.** Astronomer 2 describes how the inner Solar System formed rapidly and the ignition of the Sun blew lighter elements out to form the outer Solar System, so there was a difference in the time of formation for these two regions.

35. **B.** Astronomers 1 does not comment on the effect that the Sun or other stars have on the comets, so Astronomer 1 does not conflict with either Astronomer 2 or Astronomer 3.

36. **H.** A mass of 2.7 kg would exert a force in between the reading for mass of 2 kg and 3 kg.

37. **B.** As the force increases, the extension increases, and Answer B is the only graph that represents this increase.

38. **J.** A weight of 5 kg would take longer than a mass of 4 kg based on the trend shown in the table.

39. **C.** There is a direct linear relationship between the square root of the mass and the force exerted on the spring.

40. **J.** If the spring has a greater force applied and does not extend further than when a lesser force was applied, this is an indication that the spring extension has reached a maximum value.

PRACTICE EXAMINATION 2

Answer Sheet

1. English Test

1 Ⓐ Ⓑ Ⓒ Ⓓ	20 Ⓕ Ⓖ Ⓗ Ⓙ	39 Ⓐ Ⓑ Ⓒ Ⓓ	58 Ⓕ Ⓖ Ⓗ Ⓙ
2 Ⓕ Ⓖ Ⓗ Ⓙ	21 Ⓐ Ⓑ Ⓒ Ⓓ	40 Ⓕ Ⓖ Ⓗ Ⓙ	59 Ⓐ Ⓑ Ⓒ Ⓓ
3 Ⓐ Ⓑ Ⓒ Ⓓ	22 Ⓕ Ⓖ Ⓗ Ⓙ	41 Ⓐ Ⓑ Ⓒ Ⓓ	60 Ⓕ Ⓖ Ⓗ Ⓙ
4 Ⓕ Ⓖ Ⓗ Ⓙ	23 Ⓐ Ⓑ Ⓒ Ⓓ	42 Ⓕ Ⓖ Ⓗ Ⓙ	61 Ⓐ Ⓑ Ⓒ Ⓓ
5 Ⓐ Ⓑ Ⓒ Ⓓ	24 Ⓕ Ⓖ Ⓗ Ⓙ	43 Ⓐ Ⓑ Ⓒ Ⓓ	62 Ⓕ Ⓖ Ⓗ Ⓙ
6 Ⓕ Ⓖ Ⓗ Ⓙ	25 Ⓐ Ⓑ Ⓒ Ⓓ	44 Ⓕ Ⓖ Ⓗ Ⓙ	63 Ⓐ Ⓑ Ⓒ Ⓓ
7 Ⓐ Ⓑ Ⓒ Ⓓ	26 Ⓕ Ⓖ Ⓗ Ⓙ	45 Ⓐ Ⓑ Ⓒ Ⓓ	64 Ⓕ Ⓖ Ⓗ Ⓙ
8 Ⓕ Ⓖ Ⓗ Ⓙ	27 Ⓐ Ⓑ Ⓒ Ⓓ	46 Ⓕ Ⓖ Ⓗ Ⓙ	65 Ⓐ Ⓑ Ⓒ Ⓓ
9 Ⓐ Ⓑ Ⓒ Ⓓ	28 Ⓕ Ⓖ Ⓗ Ⓙ	47 Ⓐ Ⓑ Ⓒ Ⓓ	66 Ⓕ Ⓖ Ⓗ Ⓙ
10 Ⓕ Ⓖ Ⓗ Ⓙ	29 Ⓐ Ⓑ Ⓒ Ⓓ	48 Ⓕ Ⓖ Ⓗ Ⓙ	67 Ⓐ Ⓑ Ⓒ Ⓓ
11 Ⓐ Ⓑ Ⓒ Ⓓ	30 Ⓕ Ⓖ Ⓗ Ⓙ	49 Ⓐ Ⓑ Ⓒ Ⓓ	68 Ⓕ Ⓖ Ⓗ Ⓙ
12 Ⓕ Ⓖ Ⓗ Ⓙ	31 Ⓐ Ⓑ Ⓒ Ⓓ	50 Ⓕ Ⓖ Ⓗ Ⓙ	69 Ⓐ Ⓑ Ⓒ Ⓓ
13 Ⓐ Ⓑ Ⓒ Ⓓ	32 Ⓕ Ⓖ Ⓗ Ⓙ	51 Ⓐ Ⓑ Ⓒ Ⓓ	70 Ⓕ Ⓖ Ⓗ Ⓙ
14 Ⓕ Ⓖ Ⓗ Ⓙ	33 Ⓐ Ⓑ Ⓒ Ⓓ	52 Ⓕ Ⓖ Ⓗ Ⓙ	71 Ⓐ Ⓑ Ⓒ Ⓓ
15 Ⓐ Ⓑ Ⓒ Ⓓ	34 Ⓕ Ⓖ Ⓗ Ⓙ	53 Ⓐ Ⓑ Ⓒ Ⓓ	72 Ⓕ Ⓖ Ⓗ Ⓙ
16 Ⓕ Ⓖ Ⓗ Ⓙ	35 Ⓐ Ⓑ Ⓒ Ⓓ	54 Ⓕ Ⓖ Ⓗ Ⓙ	73 Ⓐ Ⓑ Ⓒ Ⓓ
17 Ⓐ Ⓑ Ⓒ Ⓓ	36 Ⓕ Ⓖ Ⓗ Ⓙ	55 Ⓐ Ⓑ Ⓒ Ⓓ	74 Ⓕ Ⓖ Ⓗ Ⓙ
18 Ⓕ Ⓖ Ⓗ Ⓙ	37 Ⓐ Ⓑ Ⓒ Ⓓ	56 Ⓕ Ⓖ Ⓗ Ⓙ	75 Ⓐ Ⓑ Ⓒ Ⓓ
19 Ⓐ Ⓑ Ⓒ Ⓓ	38 Ⓕ Ⓖ Ⓗ Ⓙ	57 Ⓐ Ⓑ Ⓒ Ⓓ	

2. Math Test

1 Ⓐ Ⓑ Ⓒ Ⓓ Ⓔ	16 Ⓕ Ⓖ Ⓗ Ⓙ Ⓚ	31 Ⓐ Ⓑ Ⓒ Ⓓ Ⓔ	46 Ⓕ Ⓖ Ⓗ Ⓙ Ⓚ
2 Ⓕ Ⓖ Ⓗ Ⓙ Ⓚ	17 Ⓐ Ⓑ Ⓒ Ⓓ Ⓔ	32 Ⓕ Ⓖ Ⓗ Ⓙ Ⓚ	47 Ⓐ Ⓑ Ⓒ Ⓓ Ⓔ
3 Ⓐ Ⓑ Ⓒ Ⓓ Ⓔ	18 Ⓕ Ⓖ Ⓗ Ⓙ Ⓚ	33 Ⓐ Ⓑ Ⓒ Ⓓ Ⓔ	48 Ⓕ Ⓖ Ⓗ Ⓙ Ⓚ
4 Ⓕ Ⓖ Ⓗ Ⓙ Ⓚ	19 Ⓐ Ⓑ Ⓒ Ⓓ Ⓔ	34 Ⓕ Ⓖ Ⓗ Ⓙ Ⓚ	49 Ⓐ Ⓑ Ⓒ Ⓓ Ⓔ
5 Ⓐ Ⓑ Ⓒ Ⓓ Ⓔ	20 Ⓕ Ⓖ Ⓗ Ⓙ Ⓚ	35 Ⓐ Ⓑ Ⓒ Ⓓ Ⓔ	50 Ⓕ Ⓖ Ⓗ Ⓙ Ⓚ
6 Ⓕ Ⓖ Ⓗ Ⓙ Ⓚ	21 Ⓐ Ⓑ Ⓒ Ⓓ Ⓔ	36 Ⓕ Ⓖ Ⓗ Ⓙ Ⓚ	51 Ⓐ Ⓑ Ⓒ Ⓓ Ⓔ
7 Ⓐ Ⓑ Ⓒ Ⓓ Ⓔ	22 Ⓕ Ⓖ Ⓗ Ⓙ Ⓚ	37 Ⓐ Ⓑ Ⓒ Ⓓ Ⓔ	52 Ⓕ Ⓖ Ⓗ Ⓙ Ⓚ
8 Ⓕ Ⓖ Ⓗ Ⓙ Ⓚ	23 Ⓐ Ⓑ Ⓒ Ⓓ Ⓔ	38 Ⓕ Ⓖ Ⓗ Ⓙ Ⓚ	53 Ⓐ Ⓑ Ⓒ Ⓓ Ⓔ
9 Ⓐ Ⓑ Ⓒ Ⓓ Ⓔ	24 Ⓕ Ⓖ Ⓗ Ⓙ Ⓚ	39 Ⓐ Ⓑ Ⓒ Ⓓ Ⓔ	54 Ⓕ Ⓖ Ⓗ Ⓙ Ⓚ
10 Ⓕ Ⓖ Ⓗ Ⓙ Ⓚ	25 Ⓐ Ⓑ Ⓒ Ⓓ Ⓔ	40 Ⓕ Ⓖ Ⓗ Ⓙ Ⓚ	55 Ⓐ Ⓑ Ⓒ Ⓓ Ⓔ
11 Ⓐ Ⓑ Ⓒ Ⓓ Ⓔ	26 Ⓕ Ⓖ Ⓗ Ⓙ Ⓚ	41 Ⓐ Ⓑ Ⓒ Ⓓ Ⓔ	56 Ⓕ Ⓖ Ⓗ Ⓙ Ⓚ
12 Ⓕ Ⓖ Ⓗ Ⓙ Ⓚ	27 Ⓐ Ⓑ Ⓒ Ⓓ Ⓔ	42 Ⓕ Ⓖ Ⓗ Ⓙ Ⓚ	57 Ⓐ Ⓑ Ⓒ Ⓓ Ⓔ
13 Ⓐ Ⓑ Ⓒ Ⓓ Ⓔ	28 Ⓕ Ⓖ Ⓗ Ⓙ Ⓚ	43 Ⓐ Ⓑ Ⓒ Ⓓ Ⓔ	58 Ⓕ Ⓖ Ⓗ Ⓙ Ⓚ
14 Ⓕ Ⓖ Ⓗ Ⓙ Ⓚ	29 Ⓐ Ⓑ Ⓒ Ⓓ Ⓔ	44 Ⓕ Ⓖ Ⓗ Ⓙ Ⓚ	59 Ⓕ Ⓖ Ⓗ Ⓙ Ⓚ
15 Ⓐ Ⓑ Ⓒ Ⓓ Ⓔ	30 Ⓕ Ⓖ Ⓗ Ⓙ Ⓚ	45 Ⓐ Ⓑ Ⓒ Ⓓ Ⓔ	60 Ⓐ Ⓑ Ⓒ Ⓓ Ⓔ

3. Reading Test

1 (A) (B) (C) (D)	11 (A) (B) (C) (D)	21 (A) (B) (C) (D)	31 (A) (B) (C) (D)
2 (F) (G) (H) (J)	12 (F) (G) (H) (J)	22 (F) (G) (H) (J)	32 (F) (G) (H) (J)
3 (A) (B) (C) (D)	13 (A) (B) (C) (D)	23 (A) (B) (C) (D)	33 (A) (B) (C) (D)
4 (F) (G) (H) (J)	14 (F) (G) (H) (J)	24 (F) (G) (H) (J)	34 (F) (G) (H) (J)
5 (A) (B) (C) (D)	15 (A) (B) (C) (D)	25 (A) (B) (C) (D)	35 (A) (B) (C) (D)
6 (F) (G) (H) (J)	16 (F) (G) (H) (J)	26 (F) (G) (H) (J)	36 (F) (G) (H) (J)
7 (A) (B) (C) (D)	17 (A) (B) (C) (D)	27 (A) (B) (C) (D)	37 (A) (B) (C) (D)
8 (F) (G) (H) (J)	18 (F) (G) (H) (J)	28 (F) (G) (H) (J)	38 (F) (G) (H) (J)
9 (A) (B) (C) (D)	19 (A) (B) (C) (D)	29 (A) (B) (C) (D)	39 (A) (B) (C) (D)
10 (F) (G) (H) (J)	20 (F) (G) (H) (J)	30 (F) (G) (H) (J)	40 (F) (G) (H) (J)

4. Science Reasoning Test

1 (A) (B) (C) (D)	11 (A) (B) (C) (D)	21 (A) (B) (C) (D)	31 (A) (B) (C) (D)
2 (F) (G) (H) (J)	12 (F) (G) (H) (J)	22 (F) (G) (H) (J)	32 (F) (G) (H) (J)
3 (A) (B) (C) (D)	13 (A) (B) (C) (D)	23 (A) (B) (C) (D)	33 (A) (B) (C) (D)
4 (F) (G) (H) (J)	14 (F) (G) (H) (J)	24 (F) (G) (H) (J)	34 (F) (G) (H) (J)
5 (A) (B) (C) (D)	15 (A) (B) (C) (D)	25 (A) (B) (C) (D)	35 (A) (B) (C) (D)
6 (F) (G) (H) (J)	16 (F) (G) (H) (J)	26 (F) (G) (H) (J)	36 (F) (G) (H) (J)
7 (A) (B) (C) (D)	17 (A) (B) (C) (D)	27 (A) (B) (C) (D)	37 (A) (B) (C) (D)
8 (F) (G) (H) (J)	18 (F) (G) (H) (J)	28 (F) (G) (H) (J)	38 (F) (G) (H) (J)
9 (A) (B) (C) (D)	19 (A) (B) (C) (D)	29 (A) (B) (C) (D)	39 (A) (B) (C) (D)
10 (F) (G) (H) (J)	20 (F) (G) (H) (J)	30 (F) (G) (H) (J)	40 (F) (G) (H) (J)

TEAR HERE

Practice Examination 2

1. ENGLISH TEST

75 Questions • Time—45 Minutes

Directions: This test consists of five passages in which particular words or phrases are underlined and numbered. Alongside the passage, you will see alternative words and phrases that could be substituted for the underlined part. You must select the alternative that expresses the idea most clearly and correctly or that best fits the style and tone of the entire passage. If the original version is best, select "No Change."

The test also includes questions about entire paragraphs and the passage as a whole. These questions are identified by a number in a box.

After you select the correct answer for each question, mark the oval representing the correct answer on your answer sheet.

Passage I

Traveling Blues

<1>

I had been in Europe for three weeks, <u>seeing</u> twenty-
                                        1
five cities in six countries and sat on an infinite number

of trains. The <u>thought and idea</u> of going to yet
                2

another crowded tourist site was not <u>appealing, how</u>
                                       3
<u>ever,</u> my traveling companions assured me that

Florence, <u>the most charming city</u> in Europe, would cure
           4
my growing distaste for travel.

1. A. NO CHANGE
    B. was seeing
    C. seen
    D. saw

2. F. NO CHANGE
    G. thought
    H. possibility
    J. idea and thought

3. A. NO CHANGE
    B. appealing, and however,
    C. appealing, however:
    D. appealing. However,

4. F. NO CHANGE
    G. the charmingest
    H. the most charmed
    J. the by far most charming

GO ON TO THE NEXT PAGE

<2>

(1) We arrived in the dead of night long after the last restaurant had closed, and trudged

5

to the nearest pensione for a room. (2) My friends insisted that in the morning one look at the Piazzale Michelangelo would revitalize me.

(3) All that night I slept on a lumpy bed, trying

6

to ignore the rhythmic growling of my stomach. [7]

5.　A. NO CHANGE
　　B. long after the last restaurant had closed in the dead of night
　　C. in the dead of night, long after the last restaurant had closed,
　　D. dead in the night and long after the last restaurant had closed

6.　F. NO CHANGE
　　G. Through all
　　H. During all
　　J. OMIT the underlined portion.

7.　The writer wishes to add the following detail to Paragraph 2:

We had eaten no dinner.

The sentence would most logically be inserted:
　　A. before sentence 1.
　　B. before sentence 2.
　　C. before sentence 3.
　　D. after sentence 3.

<3>

The morning came all too soon; my ever-

8

eager travel companions shaking me awake hours earlier than I thought reasonable. I stepped into twice-worn clothes while they babbled on about the piazzale's stunning charm.

It was a bright sunny morning, and my friends wanted to walk. I would have been perfectly happy to snooze on a bench. Rather we hiked up a steep road for

9

8.　F. NO CHANGE
　　G. all too soon,
　　H. all too soon.
　　J. OMIT the underlined portion.

9.　A. NO CHANGE
　　B. Instead
　　C. But no,
　　D. OMIT the underlined portion.

what seemed like hours, sweating in the lovely

sunshine. [10]

<4>

Finally, we reached the piazzale. I gasped, but not

with delight. Tourists teemed across the square like

lemmings, jostling one another to take photos and

videos of the spectacular domed Cathedral and <u>its</u> bell

11

tower. "Isn't this place amazing?" my friends cooed.

They were already snapping pictures and seemed

impervious to my glares.

<5>

I leaned against a wall to sulk and <u>stare, at the throngs</u>

12

in front of the Cathedral. Suddenly, a sweet, mysterious

smell wafted up from behind the wall. My spirits lifted

as I inhaled. I looked over to see thousands of roses

basking in the glow of mid-morning. The garden was

empty save for one lone, happy soul.

<6>

[13] I climbed over the wall and slipped into the

garden. I stretched out on empty bench and gently

touched the plump petals of a yellow rose. <u>Solitude</u>

14

<u>embraced me</u>. For the first time in days, I gazed out

10. The purpose of Paragraph 3, as it relates to the remainder of the essay, is primarily to:

   F. continue developing the travel conflict between the narrator and her companions.

   G. suggest how difficult the narrator was acting.

   H. demonstrate the difficulties of traveling on a budget.

   J. belittle the narrator's companions for being excited about Florence.

11. A. NO CHANGE

     B. it's

     C. its'

     D. his

12. F. NO CHANGE

     G. stare: at the throngs

     H. staring at the throngs

     J. stare at the throngs

13. Should the writer begin a new paragraph at this point?

     A. Yes, because the following sentence introduces a new argument.

     B. Yes, because the narrator is about to do something new and pivotal.

     C. No, because Paragraph 5 is too short.

     D. No, because the events of Paragraph 5 lead to her climbing over the wall.

14. F. NO CHANGE

     G. Solitude overcame me.

     H. I was overwhelmed by solitude.

     J. Over me came solitude.

GO ON TO THE NEXT PAGE ➤

at the beautiful skyline and smiled. [15]

Item 15 poses a question about the essay as a whole.

15. The writer wishes to insert the following material into the essay:

I wondered why traveling was considered fun.

The sentence would most logically be inserted into Paragraph:

A. 1, after the last sentence.

B. 3, after the last sentence.

C. 4, before the first sentence.

D. 6, before the first sentence.

Passage II

The Slow Birth of Agriculture

<1>

New digs and the development of techniques to glean more information from the scant evidence of ancient settlements, are changing our view of the distant

16

past. Anatolia, for instance, was thought to be the

earliest known agricultural-based city. With a

17

corresponding division of labor. Recent evidence, however, indicates that hunting and gathering continued to be key to survival way after the dense settlement

18

was built.

<2>

This may have seemed like a debate limited

19

16. F. NO CHANGE
    G. settlements are
    H. settlements, will be
    J. settlements had been

17. A. NO CHANGE
    B. city: with
    C. city, and with
    D. city with

18. F. NO CHANGE
    G. forever after
    H. long after
    J. much after

19. A. NO CHANGE
    B. be seeming
    C. seemingly be
    D. seem

to the archaeological community, but in fact, what is at stake is the theory of the rise of civilization <u>that</u> we were

20

taught in school. For several decades archaeologists have postulated that the birth of agriculture paved the way for the Neolithic Revolution. [21] The scenario states that agriculture was born in the Fertile Crescent at the end of the last ice age when humans learned to domesticate plants. A stable food supply led to dense cities. Food surpluses not only allowed more children to reach adulthood, but also resulted in a division of labor that evolved political and priestly classes, as well as

soldiers and urban laborers. The <u>benevolence</u> of

22

agriculture were obvious, and the techniques spread quickly, giving rise to civilization as we know it.

<3>

[23] This story has begun to crumble from an onslaught of new data. Gene analysis of plants has enabled

scientists to track changes in ancient <u>grains, technologi-</u>

24

<u>cal</u> advances allow for more accurate <u>ways of dating</u> the

25

remains at different levels of ancient settlements. Rye fields were apparently cultivated in regions of the Near East four thousand years before the arrival of the classic agricultural economy. Squash in tropical

20. F. NO CHANGE
G. which is what
H. that is what
J. how

21. Would it contribute to the understanding of the essay to define here the term "Neolithic Revolution"?
A. Yes, because it is unclear and essential to the theory being discussed.
B. No, because the focus of the essay is on agriculture, not revolution.
C. No, because the meaning of the term can be inferred from the rest of the paragraph.
D. No, because the term is jargon and extraneous to the focus of the essay.

22. F. NO CHANGE
G. benefits
H. benefit
J. beneficence

23. Which of the following sentences would be the most effective opening for Paragraph 3?
A. NO CHANGE
B. This theory was believed for several decades.
C. It was a very attractive hypothesis.
D. This idea was recently disproved.

24. F. NO CHANGE
G. grains: technological
H. grains. Technological
J. grains, but technological

25. A. NO CHANGE
B. methods of dating
C. measurements of dating
D. dating

GO ON TO THE NEXT PAGE

forests of the Americas and rice in China <u>seems</u> to
26

have been domesticated much earlier than the

rise of settlements in these regions. <u>On the other</u>
27

<u>hand</u>, several dense settlements like Anatolia

have been excavated to levels that show no

evidence of domesticated food sources. Instead,

remains point to a hunting and gathering economy.

<4>

Scientists now believe that agriculture was born

slowly, in fits and starts, and that the first successes in

plant domestication <u>co-existed in</u> hunter-gather
28

economies. Instead of revolution, there was probably

an evolution of food gathering techniques, and the first

cities were probably built from an impulse other than

agricultural surpluses. 29　30

26. F. NO CHANGE
G. seem
H. seemed
J. seeming

27. A. NO CHANGE
B. In addition,
C. However,
D. As a consequence,

28. F. NO CHANGE
G. co-existed with
H. co-existed, in
J. co-existed before

Items 29 and 30 pose questions about the essay as a whole.

29. Suppose the writer wished to more closely examine evidence that supports the idea that agriculture was slowly incorporated into human economies. In order to expand on material already present there, this information would most logically be added to Paragraph:

A. 1.
B. 2.
C. 3.
D. 4.

30. The essay consists of four paragraphs. Which of the following is the best description of their relationship?

   F. Introduction to subject; previous thinking on the subject; evidence contrary to the previous thinking; present thinking on the subject.

   G. Introduction to subject; discussion of one aspect of subject; discussion of second aspect; conclusion.

   H. Statement of purpose; elaboration of one reason for viewpoint; elaboration of a second reason; conclusion.

   J. Explanation of one viewpoint; explanation of opposing viewpoint; reconciliation of views; conclusion.

Passage III

Mount Vinson

At 16,076 feet, Mount Vinson is the highest peak in Antarctica. The views from its summit are <u>spectacular.</u>

             31

<u>An unobstructed panorama</u> of the numerous nearby mountains. Vinson is twelve hundred miles from the northern tip of the Antarctic Peninsula and six hundred miles <u>away from</u> the South Pole. The polar <u>ice cap's</u>

     32   33

high-pressure system controls Vinson's cold, relatively

stable climate. <u>However,</u> because Vinson is in an arctic

       34

climate, snow and terrific winds are always feasible.

31.   A. NO CHANGE

    B. spectacular; an unobstructed panorama

    C. spectacular: an unobstructed panorama

    D. spectacular. Undoubtedly an obstructed panorama

32.   F. NO CHANGE

    G. away to

    H. from

    J. near

33.   A. NO CHANGE

    B. ice caps'

    C. ice caps

    D. ice-capped

34.   F. NO CHANGE

    G. Since

    H. Moreover,

    J. In addition,

GO ON TO THE NEXT PAGE

Summer runs from November through <u>January, dur-</u>
35

<u>ing</u> this time, the sun shines twenty-four hours a day.

The average midsummer temperature is minus twenty

degrees Celsius. Despite this below-freezing tempera-

ture, the intensity of the sun often melts <u>into</u> a thin
36

layer of snow, and you can walk around in a tee shirt if

there is no wind. During the winter months, tempera-

tures can dip to minus one hundred degrees Celsius.

Despite these adverse conditions, <u>or maybe</u>
37

<u>that is the reason why,</u> there are still people

eager to climb to the top of Mount Vinson

<u>because</u> it is the highest of the Antarctic peaks
38

and has had less than four hundred people at its summit.

Vinson's stunning landscape <u>of the wind-carved</u> ice
39

and snowdrifts also attracts thrill seekers.

<u>To survive</u> a trek up Vinson, you must have
40

prior skiing and climbing experience and be prepared

to withstand extreme weather conditions. During the

height of winter, it can get cold enough for fillings to

fall out of your teeth, for metal to stick to exposed

flesh and for kerosene to turn to jelly. However, the

inevitable bouts with brutal winds can be more danger-

ous than the cold. When winds are fierce, <u>one must</u> pile
41

on layer upon layer of clothing because any exposed

35. A. NO CHANGE
    B. January,
    C. January, but during
    D. January, and during

36. F. NO CHANGE
    G. up
    H. around
    J. OMIT the underlined portion.

37. A. NO CHANGE
    B. or maybe because of them,
    C. or perhaps with them in mind,
    D. OMIT the underlined portion.

38. F. NO CHANGE
    G. though
    H. despite the fact
    J. because of the fact

39. A. NO CHANGE
    B. full of wind-carved
    C. of wind-carved
    D. made of wind-carved

40. F. NO CHANGE
    G. Surviving
    H. Survival of
    J. Having to survive

41. Which of the choices is most consistent with the style established in this essay?
    A. NO CHANGE
    B. it is necessary to
    C. you must
    D. one is supposed to

skin, particularly on your <u>extremities; ears, nose, cheeks,</u>
42

<u>fingers or toes—</u>is susceptible to

instantaneous frostbite.

   Suffice it to say that if you want to climb

Mount Vinson, you need <u>more than a warm coat</u>
43

<u>and a pair of mittens.</u> [44] 45

42.   **F.** NO CHANGE

       G. extremities—ears, nose, cheeks, fingers or toes—

       H. extremities: ears, nose, cheeks, fingers or toes—

       J. extremities, ears nose, cheeks, fingers or toes

43.   Suppose the writer were to substitute "to be prepared" for the underlined portion of this sentence. If made, this change would cause the sentence to be:

       A. more dramatic

       B. more informative

       C. less effective

       D. less straightforward

44.   Which of the following sentences, if added here, would provide the best conclusion to this essay?

       F. The effort, however, will reward you with one of the most stunning views on earth.

       G. You must begin preparations and physical training months in advance of your departure.

       H. You should think carefully before undertaking such a formidable expedition.

       J. The magnificence of Mount Vinson and its panorama are hard to match anywhere in the world.

Item 45 poses a question about the essay as a whole.

45.   The writer has been asked by a mountaineering magazine to write an essay that would prepare climbers who wish to ascend Mount Vinson. Would this essay fulfill that assignment?

       A. Yes; the writer focuses on the specific obstacles and conditions that a climber is likely to face on Mount Vinson.

       B. Yes; the writer focuses on the best viewpoints and ascent routes up the mountain.

       C. No; the writer focuses on arctic conditions in general without particular regard to Mount Vinson.

       D. No; the writer focuses on the appeal of Mount Vinson, offering a general description of its climate and setting.

GO ON TO THE NEXT PAGE ▶

Passage IV

I'd Rather Read the Book

Today, Hollywood <u>is adapting</u> more classic novels,
46

like Victor Hugo's *Les Miserables,* into films than <u>ever</u>

<u>before in the past.</u>
47

<u>This is because</u> more and more people think they can
48

watch film adaptations <u>which are the director's</u>
49

<u>interpretations,</u> and still have the same experience.

These people don't <u>get it</u> that there is no replacing
50

the classics. You must read them to appreciate them.

   Because film is a visual medium, characters bore

you with soliloquies and can only show you what they

think and feel through dramatic <u>action.</u> Your experi-
51

ences with the characters are limited because you

can't get inside <u>they're</u> heads. In a novel,
52

46. F. NO CHANGE
     G. has adapted
     H. adapted
     J. will adapt

47. A. NO CHANGE
     B. previously in the past.
     C. ever before.
     D. they have in the past.

48. F. NO CHANGE
     G. Despite this,
     H. Fortunately,
     J. However,

49. A. NO CHANGE
     B. of these time-proven classics
     C. on the big screen
     D. without reading the novels

50. F. NO CHANGE
     G. grasp the self-evident concept
     H. sense
     J. realize

51. A. NO CHANGE
     B. slow down the film by showing you what
        they think and feel through dramatic
        action.
     C. can only show you what they think and
        feel through dramatic action or risk boring
        you with soliloquies that slow down the
        film.
     D. in order not to risk boring you, slow down
        the film with soliloquies and show you
        what they think and feel through dramatic
        action.

52. F. NO CHANGE
     G. their
     H. there
     J. the many

either an <u>omnipresent</u> narrator, a third character,

       53

or the characters themselves can go into great detail about inner emotions and thoughts, enabling us to not only get inside those characters but to become them.

    Additionally, when a novel is made into a film, many of the characters and much of the story are cut to fit the novel into a two-hour format. <u>Producing an oral presen-</u>

       54

<u>tation of</u> an entire novel takes a lot longer than two hours. If you read the novel before you watch the film adaptation, you'll probably find yourself wondering what happened to your favorite minor characters and most of the story. Chances <u>are; they</u> just didn't fit.

       55

[56] When watching a film, you are visually spoon fed story and character development, a process that requires little complex thought on your part. Reading

a novel requires you to <u>recreate and interpret</u> that

       57

novel in your mind's eye. You, not the film, are the active element here.

    Finally, while the visuals of a good film are stimulating and exciting, there is no substitute for literature, which uses the <u>poetry, power</u> of

       58

53.   A. NO CHANGE
       B. omniscient
       C. omnipotent
       D. OMIT the underlined portion.

54.   F. NO CHANGE
       G. Talking about
       H. Reading
       J. Memorizing

55.   A. NO CHANGE
       B. are, they
       C. are they
       D. are: they

56.   For the sake of the unity and coherence of this essay, Paragraph 4 should be placed:
       F. where it is now.
       G. before Paragraph 1.
       H. after Paragraph 1.
       J. before Paragraph 3.

57.   A. NO CHANGE
       B. think about and consider
       C. challenge and compare
       D. debunk and manifest

58.   F. NO CHANGE
       G. poetry or power
       H. poetry, which has the power to impact strongly,
       J. poetry and power

GO ON TO THE NEXT PAGE

words to evoke our imaginations and lead us into new worlds. [59] 60

59. The writer wishes to add a concluding sentence that will provide a link to the opening paragraph. Which of the alternatives most successfully achieves this effect?

    A. In conclusion, an educated person is one who has read the classics.

    B. Finally, the best films are those that are produced from original screenplays.

    C. The obvious conclusion to my argument is that reading is a better use of time than watching films.

    D. So the next time somebody tells you watching a film adaptation is the same as reading the novel, tell them, "I'd rather read the book."

Item 60 poses a question about the essay as a whole.

60. Which of the following alternatives best summarizes the argument presented in this essay?

    F. Because they have been translated into films so often, classic books have lost their power to move us.

    G. Good books make for slow and boring films.

    H. Classic novels often lose a great deal of their power when adapted into films.

    J. Most directors haven't read the books they adapt into films.

Passage V
Prince Rainier III of Monaco

<1>

When asked to imagine an existence of ease and luxury, many people immediately think of the life of a prince or princess. The benefits of such a life include servants waiting to attend to your every desire; a

61

61.   A. NO CHANGE

    B. desire:

    C. desire,

    D. desire

magnificent <u>dwelling of many rooms and corridors,</u>

62

jewels and expensive clothes. It is hard to imagine that

a prince or princess could ever have a day of sadness or

stress.

<2>

[63] Perched on the Riviera and blessed

with 300 sunny days a year, it truly seems that

Monaco is a wonderful place in which to be

royal. This wealthy <u>indeed</u> tiny country

64

(Monaco is less than 500 acres) is currently ruled

by Prince Rainier III. The prince's family name

is Grimaldi and one or another of his relatives

<u>has ruled</u> Monaco for hundreds of years. In fact,

65

the Grimaldi family is the oldest ruling family in

Europe.

<3>

The <u>Grimaldi's</u> are more than an ancient

66

royal family, however. They are the reason

62. F. NO CHANGE
    G. palace
    H. house
    J. domicile

63. The writer wants to begin Paragraph 2 with a sentence that will focus the topic of the essay and provide a smooth transition from paragraph 1. Given that all are true, which of the following would most effectively accomplish this?

    A. Of all the countries in the world that are ruled by a monarchy, the small land of Monaco is perhaps the one that brings that fantasy most to mind.

    B. Because of its lenient tax policy, the land of Monaco has long been a playground of the rich and famous.

    C. When asked for the name of a member of royalty, many people think of Diana, the former Princess of Wales.

    D. France is an example of a country that was once, but is no longer, ruled by monarchy.

64. F. NO CHANGE
    G. moreover
    H. in addition
    J. but

65. A. NO CHANGE
    B. will have ruled
    C. is ruling
    D. ruled

66. F. NO CHANGE
    G. Grimaldis
    H. Grimaldis'
    J. Grimaldis, Monaco's rulers,

GO ON TO THE NEXT PAGE ▶

Monaco exists at all. Many people know
67

Monaco for its casinos; one was even featured in

a James Bond movie. A treaty signed in 1918

states that, should the Grimaldis all die at the
68

same time, Monaco will become a French state.

But when I think about the fact that the Prince
69

has three children and several grandchildren, the

end of the Grimaldi family is not something that

is likely to happen soon.

<4>

The prince's wife and the mother of his three children

was an american movie actress named Grace Kelly.
70

Beautiful and poised, two fantasies were merged into
71

one when she married Prince Rainier, becoming both a

star and a princess. Sadly, Princess Grace died in an auto

accident in 1982, when she was in the prime of
72

her life. The tragic story of Princess Grace, and that of

the husband whom mourns her still, reminds us all that
73

even a prince's life can be destroyed by sorrow. 75
74

67. A. NO CHANGE
     B. The capital of which is Monte Carlo.
     C. Hundreds of years ago, Monaco was still a vacation destination for the very rich.
     D. OMIT the underlined portion.

68. F. NO CHANGE
     G. kick the bucket
     H. no longer exist as a family on this earth
     J. die out

69. A. NO CHANGE
     B. considering
     C. the reason is
     D. OMIT the underlined portion.

70. F. NO CHANGE
     G. an American
     H. An American
     J. a American

71. A. NO CHANGE
     B. she became the ideal woman
     C. she merged two fantasies into one
     D. as the mother of his children

72. F. NO CHANGE
     G. would have been
     H. might have been
     J. still a young woman

73. A. NO CHANGE
     B. of the husband who mourns her still,
     C. of the husband who mourns her still
     D. of the husband who'll mourn her still,

74. F. NO CHANGE
     G. complicated
     H. enhanced
     J. marred

Item 75 poses a question about the essay as a whole.

75. Suppose the writer had been assigned to write an essay comparing the lives of royalty to those of ordinary people. Would this essay successfully fulfill the assignment?

A. Yes, because this essay discusses how tragedy can strike in the lives of both royalty and ordinary people alike.

B. Yes, because this essay discusses the images that ordinary people think of when asked to imagine a royal life.

C. No, because this essay restricts its focus to Prince Rainier III and his family.

D. No, because this essay does not mention ordinary people at all, even indirectly.

STOP

END OF SECTION 1. IF YOU HAVE ANY TIME LEFT, GO OVER YOUR WORK IN THIS SECTION ONLY. DO NOT WORK IN ANY OTHER SECTION OF THE TEST.

2. MATHEMATICS TEST

60 Questions • Time—60 Minutes

Directions: Solve each problem below and mark the oval representing the correct answer on your answer sheet.

Be careful not to spend too much time on any one question. Instead, solve as many questions as possible, and then use any remaining time to return to those questions you were unable to answer at first.

You may use a calculator on any problem in this test; however, not every problem requires the use of a calculator.

Diagrams that accompany problems may or may not be drawn to scale. Unless otherwise indicated, you may assume that all figures shown lie in a plane and that lines that appear straight are straight.

1. The regular price for a certain suit is $250. If a sale reduces the price by 25%, what is the sale price of the suit?

   A. $187.50
   B. $200.00
   C. $222.50
   D. $225.00
   E. $312.50

2. A contractor is building a house with a rectangular foundation 60 feet long and 20 feet wide. What is the foundation's perimeter, in feet?

   F. 1,200
   G. 160
   H. 140
   J. 120
   K. 80

3. If $a = -3$ and $b = -2a$, what is the value of the expression $ab - 3a$?

   A. -27
   B. -12
   C. -9
   D. 9
   E. 27

4. In a rose garden, 18 of the 48 rose bushes are red roses. What percentage of the rose bushes are red roses?

   F. 2%
   G. 18%
   H. 25%
   J. 37.5%
   K. 40%

5. If $n = 5$, then $3n^2 - 2n + 7 = ?$

   A. 12
   B. 22
   C. 27
   D. 72
   E. 81

6. Five templates cut out of paper are shown below. Each template is made up of 6 equal squares, and they are only to be folded along the dotted lines. Which template could be folded, without tearing, to form a complete cube?

F.

G.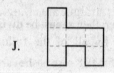

H.

J.

K.

7. If $(x + 2)(x - 5) = 8$, then which of the following must be true?

A. $x + 2 = 0$

B. $x - 2 = 0$

C. $x - 5 = 0$

D. $x - 5 = 8$

E. $x - 6 = 0$

8. On a certain state's drivers' exam, an applicant must get at least 70% of the 400 possible points in order to pass. If an applicant raises his score on his second attempt by 25 points and passes with the minimum required score, what score did he receive on his first attempt?

F. 255

G. 260

H. 265

J. 280

K. 305

9. A copy shop offers copies on 5 colors of paper, each of which comes in 4 finishes. If a company gets 2 newsletters copied on different papers, there are how many distinct possible combinations of newsletter, color, and finish?

A. 40

B. 20

C. 11

D. 10

E. 5

10. The graphs below represent the solutions of two inequalities. Which of the following specifies the intersection of the two graphs in algebraic form?

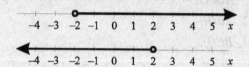

F. $x \ \ 2$ or $x > -2$

G. $x < 2$ or $x \ \ -2$

H. $-2 < x < 2$

J. $-2 < x \ \ 2$

K. $-2 \ \ x < 2$

11. How many inches long is the radius of a circle whose area is 24π square inches?

A. 12

B. $4\sqrt{6}$

C. 6

D. $2\sqrt{6}$

E. 4

GO ON TO THE NEXT PAGE

12. Six points are drawn to scale below. Which four points could be connected in order to form a parallelogram?

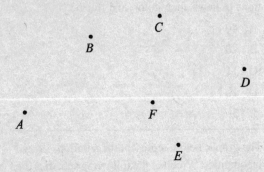

   F. *ABCD*

   G. *ABDE*

   H. *BCDE*

   J. *BCDF*

   K. *CDEF*

13. For all real numbers m and n, $3(m+n) - 2(m-3n)$ = ?

   A. $m + 9n$

   B. $m - 3n$

   C. $5m$

   D. $5m + 9n$

   E. $5m - 3n$

14. The hypotenuse of a right triangle is 5 inches long. What is the perimeter of the triangle in inches?

   F. 6

   G. 10

   H. 11

   J. 15

   K. Cannot be determined from the given information

15. In the (x, y) coordinate plane, at which y-value does the line $x + 3y = 6$ intersect the y-axis?

   A. 0

   B. 1

   C. 2

   D. 3

   E. 6

16. In a certain parking lot, 540 cars have in-state license plates, while the remaining 180 have out-of-state license plates. What percent of the cars in the parking lot have out-of-state license plates?

   F. 20%

   G. 25%

   H. 30%

   J. $33\frac{1}{3}\%$

   K. $66\frac{2}{3}\%$

17. $s = (2)(4)(6)(9)t$

   If t is a positive integer, then s must be divisible, with no remainder, by all of the following EXCEPT?

   A. 12

   B. 24

   C. 30

   D. 54

   E. 72

18. A rectangle has a length of $(3x + 2)$ centimeters and a width of $(5x - 3)$ centimeters. Which of the following expressions must represent the area, in square centimeters, of the rectangle?

   F. $8x - 1$

   G. $15x^2 - 6$

   H. $15x^2 - 9x - 6$

   J. $15x^2 + x - 6$

   K. $15x^2 + 19x - 6$

19. The equation $4x^2 = 6x + 4$ is equivalent to which of the following equations ?

   A. $(2x + 1)(x - 2) = 0$

   B. $(2x - 4)(2x - 1) = 0$

   C. $(4x - 1)(x + 4) = 0$

   D. $(4x - 2)(x - 2) = 0$

   E. $(4x + 2)(x + 2) = 0$

20. The lengths of the sides of one triangle are 5 inches, 10 inches, and x inches, respectively. The length of the sides of a similar triangle are $2.5x$ inches, $5x$ inches, and $4x$ inches, respectively. What is the value of x ?

   F. 2

   G. 8

   H. 12

   J. 16

   K. 32

21. If $\frac{x}{10} - 4.2 = .2x + 3.3$, then $x = ?$

   A. −75

   B. −45

   C. 9

   D. 45

   E. 75

22. A plane left New York for San Francisco, a distance of about 3,000 miles, at 3pm traveling at 350 mph. An hour later, a plane left San Francisco flying in the opposite direction at 450 mph. At what time will they pass each other?

   F. 7:03 pm

   G. 7:18 pm

   H. 7:33 pm

   J. 7:48 pm

   K. 8:03 pm

23. If $(x-a)(x+b) = x^2 + 2x - 4b$, then $b = ?$

   A. −2

   B. 0

   C. 2

   D. 4

   E. 6

24. $\dfrac{3.2 - 1.557}{2(1 - .5 - .375)} = ?$

   F. 8.413

   G. 6.572

   H. 3.119

   J. .9488

   K. .41075

25. If $12x^2 - ax - a = (3x+1)(4x-2)$, what is the value of a ?

   A. −2

   B. 2

   C. 3

   D. 4

   E. 6

26. The expression "rationalizing the denominator" refers to eliminating radicals from a denominator. Which of the following expressions represents $\frac{x\sqrt{3}}{x - \sqrt{3}}$ with a rationalized denominator?

   F. $x + \sqrt{3}$

   G. $x^2\sqrt{3} + 3x$

   H. $\dfrac{3x}{x - 3}$

   J. $\dfrac{3x^2}{x^2 + 3}$

   K. $\dfrac{x^2\sqrt{3} + 3x}{x^2 - 3}$

27. If $ABCD$, not shown, is a rectangle, then which of the following must be true?

   I. $ABCD$ is a quadrilateral

   II. $ABCD$ is a rhombus

   III. $ABCD$ is a parallelogram

   A. I only

   B. II only

   C. I and II only

   D. I and III only

   E. I, II, and III

GO ON TO THE NEXT PAGE

28. Work is defined in physics as force times distance and can be measured in joules. If it requires 150 joules to move an object 20 feet, how far would the object be moved with 180 joules?

    F. 24

    G. 25

    H. 26

    J. 28

    K. 30

29. In the right triangle ABC, illustrated below, the sine of $\angle B$ is $\frac{4}{9}$. What is the sine of $\angle A$?

    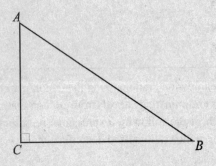

    A. $\dfrac{9}{4}$

    B. $\dfrac{\sqrt{65}}{4}$

    C. $\dfrac{\sqrt{65}}{9}$

    D. $\dfrac{4\sqrt{65}}{9}$

    E. $\sqrt{65}$

30. If $n + 8 = 14 - 4(3 - n)$, then $n =$

    F. -3

    G. -1

    H. 0

    J. 1

    K. 2

31. What is the slope of a line that is parallel to the line with the equation $2x + 7y = 5$?

    A. $-\dfrac{7}{2}$

    B. $-\dfrac{2}{7}$

    C. $-\dfrac{2}{5}$

    D. $-\dfrac{5}{2}$

    E. $-\dfrac{7}{2}$

32. The diagram below shows the plan for a carpeted living room floor. What is the amount of carpet, in square feet, actually used to cover the floor?

    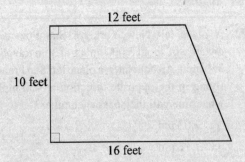

    F. 120

    G. 140

    H. 160

    J. 192

    K. 208

33. If $x + 10 = yz + 5$, where $xyz \neq 0$, which of the following expressions solves for y in terms of x and z ?

    A. $y = \dfrac{x + 5}{z}$

    B. $y = \dfrac{x + 15}{z}$

    C. $y = \dfrac{5 - x}{z}$

    D. $y = \dfrac{5}{2} - x$

    E. $y = \dfrac{x}{z} + 5$

34. What is the slope of the line $6x - 5y = 10$?

F. -2

G. $-\dfrac{6}{5}$

H. $-\dfrac{5}{6}$

J. $\dfrac{5}{6}$

K. $\dfrac{6}{5}$

35. If, in the diagram below, $\overline{AB}$ is 20 centimeters long, how many centimeters long is $\overline{BC}$?

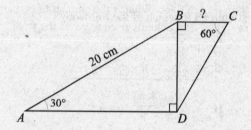

A. 5

B. 10

C. $\dfrac{5\sqrt{3}}{3}$

D. $\dfrac{10\sqrt{3}}{3}$

E. $\dfrac{20\sqrt{3}}{3}$

36. A circle with center at $C(0,5)$ and passing through the point $P(6,1)$ is in the standard (x,y) plane below. What is the area of the circle, in square units?

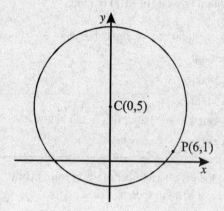

F. 12π

G. 25π

H. 37π

J. 52π

K. 104π

37. The line $y = \dfrac{5}{2}x + 1$ passes through all of the following points in the standard (x,y) plane EXCEPT:

A. $(-2,-4)$

B. $(0,1)$

C. $(3,8)$

D. $(5,13.5)$

E. $(8,21)$

GO ON TO THE NEXT PAGE

Use the following information to answer questions 38 and 39.

An advertisement for a men's clothing store reads, "Men's shirts $22 each; 3 for $55. Receive a 10% discount on any sale of $100 or more."

38. What is the total cost of eight shirts?

    F. $136.80

    G. $138.60

    H. $154.00

    J. $158.40

    K. $176.00

39. What is the greatest number of shirts you can buy if you have $100 to spend?

    A. 4

    B. 5

    C. 6

    D. 7

    E. 8

40. The lengths of the sides in the right triangle below are 10 inches, 24 inches, and 26 inches. What is the sine of $\angle B$?

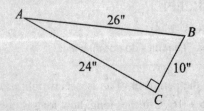

    F. $\dfrac{5}{13}$

    G. $\dfrac{5}{12}$

    H. $\dfrac{12}{13}$

    J. $\dfrac{13}{12}$

    K. $\dfrac{13}{5}$

41. Polynomial $P(x)$ is a 3rd degree polynomial with 3 distinct real roots. Polynomial $Q(x)$ is a 4th degree polynomial with 2 distinct real roots. If $y = P(x) \times Q(x)$ is graphed on the standard (x,y) coordinate plane, what is the maximum number of times the graph can intersect (touch or cross) the x-axis?

    A. 3

    B. 5

    C. 6

    D. 7

    E. 9

42. If $y^2 - x^2 \neq 0$, then $\dfrac{2x^2 - 4xy + 2y^2}{y^2 - x^2}$ can be simplified to which of the following?

    F. 2

    G. $2(x - y)$

    H. $\dfrac{2(x + y)}{x - y}$

    J. $\dfrac{2(x - y)}{x + y}$

    K. $\dfrac{2(y - x)}{x + y}$

43. What is the height of the equilateral triangle below?

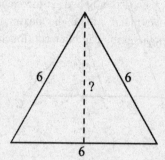

A. 3

B. $3\sqrt{2}$

C. $3\sqrt{3}$

D. 6

E. $6\sqrt{3}$

44. How many different real numbers are solutions for the equation $(x + 2)(x - 6) = 2x - 21$?

F. 0

G. 1

H. 2

J. 3

K. 4

45. Six students in a history class of x students received A's on their term papers. If the professor never gives A's to fewer than 20% of the class nor never more than 40%, how many different values of x are possible?

A. 16

B. 18

C. 20

D. 24

E. 30

46. A polynomial that has zeros of 0, 1, and 2 could be which of the following?

F. $3x + 3 = 0$

G. $x^2 + 2x - 3 = 0$

H. $x^3 + 2x - 2 = 0$

J. $x^3 - 3x^2 + 2x = 0$

K. $x^3 + 3x^2 + 2x = 0$

47. If $ABCE$ is a square with sides 6 inches long, then what is the area, in square inches, of triangle CDE ?

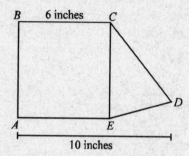

A. 6

B. 12

C. 18

D. 24

E. Cannot be determined from the given information.

48. At what point in the standard (x,y) coordinate plane do the lines $y = 4x - 4$ and $3x + y = 10$ intersect?

F. $(0,-4)$

G. $(2,4)$

H. $(8,-14)$

J. $(14,52)$

K. The lines do not intersect.

49. If the perimeter of an isosceles right triangle is $16 + 16\sqrt{2}$ inches long, how long is one of the perpendicular sides?

A. $4\sqrt{2}$

B. 4

C. $8\sqrt{2}$

D. 8

E. $16\sqrt{2}$

GO ON TO THE NEXT PAGE

50. If $x = \dfrac{2 - \sqrt{3}}{2 + \sqrt{3}}$ and $y = \dfrac{2 + \sqrt{3}}{2 - \sqrt{3}}$, what is the value of $x + y$?

    F. 1

    G. 14

    H. $8\sqrt{3}$

    J. $\dfrac{4}{2 + \sqrt{3}}$

    K. $\dfrac{4 - 2\sqrt{3}}{4 + 2\sqrt{3}}$

51. If there are no real numbers that satisfy the inequality $3x - k(x + 2) \geq 10 - 3(1 + x)$, where k is a constant, what is the value of k ?

    A. 0

    B. 1

    C. 2

    D. 4

    E. 6

52. During a week at a certain software company, the orders per day climbed at a constant rate from 40 on Monday to 60 on Friday. If the average order size decreased at a constant daily rate from a high of $250 on Monday to a low of $210 on Friday, on what day did the company first record at least $12,000 in orders?

    F. Monday

    G. Tuesday

    H. Wednesday

    J. Thursday

    K. Friday

53. In the figure below, K and J lie on triangle ABC, $\overline{JK}$ is parallel to $\overline{AB}$, and the lengths of the sides of quadrilateral $ABJK$ are in inches as indicated. What is the perimeter, in inches, of triangle ABC ?

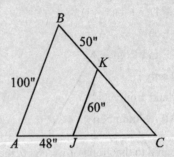

    A. 296

    B. 320

    C. 345

    D. 365

    E. 410

54. What is the maximum number of points of intersection between the graphs of a triangle and a circle?

    F. 1

    G. 2

    H. 3

    J. 4

    K. 6

55. For all real numbers a and b, which of the following must be true?

    I. $|a + b| = |a| + |b|$

    II. $\left|\dfrac{a}{b}\right| = \dfrac{|a|}{|b|}$

    III. $|ab| = |a| \times |b|$

    A. II only

    B. III only

    C. I and II only

    D. II and III only

    E. I, II, and III

56. What are the real numbers x such that $2x^5 - 2x = 2x(x^2 + 1)(x + 1)(x - 1)$?

    F. -1 only

    G. -1 and 1 only

    H. 0 only

    J. 0 and 1 only

    K. All real numbers

57. Compared to the graph of $y = \cos \theta$, the graph of $2y = \cos 2\theta$ has:

    A. half the period and half the amplitude

    B. half the period and twice the amplitude

    C. twice the period and half the amplitude

    D. twice the period and twice the amplitude

    E. the same period and the same amplitude

58. An ellipse with equation $9(x + 2)^2 + 4(y - 2)^2 = 36$ is inscribed in a circle. Which of the following is the equation of the circle?

    F. $x^2 + y^2 = 4$

    G. $x^2 + y^2 = 36$

    H. $(x + 2)^2 + (y - 2)^2 = 6$

    J. $(x + 2)^2 + (y - 2)^2 = 9$

    K. $(x - 4)^2 + (y - 9)^2 = 6$

59. The volume of a sphere with a radius of x inches is how many times the volume of a sphere with a radius of $\frac{x}{2}$ inches ?

    (*Note:* The volume of a sphere is $\frac{4}{3}\pi r^3$, where r is the radius)

    A. $\dfrac{1}{4}$

    B. 2

    C. 3

    D. 4

    E. 8

60. The angles of a triangle have measures of $x°$, $(2x)°$, and $(3x)°$. If the side opposite the smallest angle has a length of 4 units, how many units long is the perimeter of the triangle?

    F. $8\sqrt{3}$

    G. $8 + 4\sqrt{3}$

    H. $12 + 4\sqrt{3}$

    J. $16 + 8\sqrt{3}$

    K. 24

STOP

END OF SECTION 2. IF YOU HAVE ANY TIME LEFT, GO OVER YOUR WORK IN THIS SECTION ONLY. DO NOT WORK IN ANY OTHER SECTION OF THE TEST.

3. READING TEST
40 Questions • Time—35 Minutes

Directions: This test consists of four passages, each followed by several questions. Read each passage, select the correct answer for each question, and mark the oval representing the correct answer on your answer sheet.

Passage I

PROSE FICTION: This passage is adapted from Jack London's *Burning Daylight*.

In all lands where life is a hazard lightly played with and lightly flung aside, men turn, almost automatically, to gambling for diversion and relaxation. In the Yukon men gambled their lives for gold, and those that won (5) gold from the ground gambled for it with one another. Nor was Elam Harnish an exception. He was a man's man primarily, and the instinct in him to play the game of life was strong. Environment had determined what form that game should take. He was born on an Iowa (10) farm, and his father had emigrated to eastern Oregon, in which mining country Elam's boyhood was lived. He had known nothing but hard knocks for big stakes. Pluck and endurance counted in the game, but the great god Chance dealt the cards. Honest work for sure but (15) meager returns did not count. A man played big. He risked everything for everything, and anything less than everything meant that he was a loser. So for twelve Yukon years, Elam Harnish had been a loser. True, on Moosehide Creek the past summer he had taken out (20) twenty thousand dollars, and what was left in the ground was twenty thousand more. But, as he himself proclaimed, that was no more than getting his ante back. He had anted his life for a dozen years, and forty thousand was a small pot for such a stake—the price of a drink and (25) a dance at the Tivoli, of a winter's flutter at Circle City, and a grubstake for the year to come.

The men of the Yukon reversed the old maxim till it read: hard come, easy go. At the end of the reel, Elam Harnish called the house up to drink again. Drinks were (30) a dollar apiece, gold rated at sixteen dollars an ounce; there were thirty in the house that accepted his invitation, and between every dance the house was Elam's guest. This was his night, the day of his birth, and nobody was to be allowed to pay for anything.

(35) Not that Elam Harnish was a drinking man. Whiskey meant little to him. He was too vital and robust, too untroubled in mind and body, to incline to the slavery of alcohol. He spent months at a time on trail and river

when he drank nothing stronger than coffee, while he (40) had gone a year at a time without even coffee. But he was gregarious, and since the sole social expression of the Yukon was the saloon, he expressed himself that way. When he was a lad in the mining camps of the West, men had always done that. To him it was the (45) proper way for a man to express himself socially. He knew no other way.

He was a striking figure of a man, despite his garb being similar to that of all the men in the Tivoli. Soft-tanned moccasins of moose-hide, beaded in Indian (50) designs, covered his feet. His trousers were ordinary overalls, his coat was made from a blanket. Long-gauntleted leather mittens, lined with wool, hung by his side. They were connected in the Yukon fashion, by a leather thong passed around the neck and across the (55) shoulders. On his head was a fur cap, the ear-flaps raised and the tying-cords dangling. His face, lean and slightly long, with the suggestion of hollows under the cheek-bones, seemed almost Indian. The burnt skin and keen dark eyes contributed to this effect, though the bronze of (60) the skin and the eyes themselves were essentially those of a white man. He looked older than thirty, and yet, smooth-shaven and without wrinkles, he was almost boyish. This impression of age was based on no tangible evidence. It came from the abstracter facts of the man, (65) from what he had endured and survived, which was far beyond that of ordinary men. He had lived life naked and tensely, and something of all this smoldered in his eyes, vibrated in his voice, and seemed forever a-whisper on his lips.

(70) The lips themselves were thin, and prone to close tightly over the even, white teeth. But their harshness was retrieved by the upward curl at the corners of his mouth. This curl gave to him sweetness, as the minute puckers at the corners of the eyes gave him laughter. (75) These necessary graces saved him from a nature that was essentially savage and that otherwise would have

been cruel and bitter. The nose was lean, full-nostrilled, and delicate, and of a size to fit the face; while the high forehead, as if to atone for its narrowness, was splen-
(80) didly domed and symmetrical. In line with the Indian effect was his hair, very straight and very black, with a gloss to it that only health could give.

1. It can be reasonably inferred from the passage that Elam Harnish did not drink because:

   A. he did not like fraternizing with other men.

   B. he was too strong in mind and body.

   C. he had already spend too much of his life intoxicated.

   D. gambling was a better way to spend money.

2. According to the narrator, Elam's attraction to risky ventures was influenced most strongly by:

   F. a wavering belief in God.

   G. a lack of a mother to raise him.

   H. his difficult childhood.

   J. a misunderstanding of the rules of chance.

3. Elam looked like an Indian for which of the following reasons?

   I. His cheek bones were hollow.

   II. He often moved about barefoot.

   III. His hair was straight and black.

   A. I only

   B. III only

   C. I and III only

   D. I, II and III

4. The second paragraph suggests that Elam was buying alcohol for the people in the bar because:

   F. he owed them a large amount of money.

   G. his mine had just struck a lode of gold.

   H. it was his best chance of winning at cards.

   J. he was throwing a birthday party for himself.

5. Elam seemed older than thirty years old because Elam's:

   I. face showed signs of aging.

   II. age showed in his eyes.

   III. voice carried a sense of experience.

   A. I only

   B. II only

   C. II and III only

   D. I, II and III

6. As it is described in the first paragraph, Elam's Moosehide Creek mine was a venture that:

   F. did not yield as much as other nearby mines.

   G. more than made up for the twelve years Elam had worked on it.

   H. would potentially yield twenty thousand more dollars for Elam.

   J. was not profitable until Elam joined up with other miners.

7. In the fourth paragraph Elam is described as being dressed:

   A. much like everyone else in the region.

   B. in the same way as a boy would dress.

   C. similar to how visitors from the city would dress.

   D. in a ridiculous manner.

8. Elam liked to relax in saloons because, despite his non-drinking nature, the saloon was:

   F. a great place to find gamblers to swindle.

   G. the only place to hear local news.

   H. something held in reverence from Elam's childhood.

   J. the only place for men to socialize.

9. According to the narrator, the men of the Yukon, after mining gold from the ground, would:

   A. hoard it in hope of raising its value.

   B. then risk it in games of chance.

   C. not reveal to each other where their mines were.

   D. invest the gold in substantial business ventures.

GO ON TO THE NEXT PAGE

10. What does the author suggest is a central characteristic of Elam Harnish?

   F. Idiocy

   G. Barbarity

   H. Meekness

   J. Loving kindness

Passage II

SOCIAL SCIENCE: This passage is adapted from Owen Wister's *A Straight Deal*.

When you finished school, what idea did you have about the War of 1812? I will tell you what mine was. I thought we had gone to war because England was stopping American ships and taking American sailors
(5) out of them for her own service. I could refer to Perry's victory on Lake Erie and Jackson's smashing of the British at New Orleans; the name of the frigate Constitution sent thrills through me. And we had pounded old John Bull and sent him home a second time! Such was
(10) my glorious idea, and there it stopped.

Did you know much more than that about it when your schooling was done? Did you know that our reasons for declaring war against Great Britain in 1812 were not so strong as they had been three and four years
(15) earlier? That during those years England had moderated her arrogance, was ready to moderate further and wanted peace; while we, who had been nearly unanimous for war, and with a fuller purse in 1808, were now, by our own congressional fuddling and messing, without any
(20) adequate army, and so divided in counsel that only one northern state was wholly in favor of war? Did you know that our General Hull began by invading Canada from Detroit and surrendered his whole army without firing a shot? That the British overran Michigan and
(25) parts of Ohio, and western New York, while we retreated disgracefully? That though we shone in victories of single combat on the sea and showed the English that we too knew how to sail and fight on the waves as hardily as Britannia (we won eleven out of thirteen of
(30) the frigate and sloop actions), nevertheless she caught us or blocked us up, and rioted unchecked along our coasts? You probably did know that the British burned Washington, and you accordingly hated them for this barbarous vandalism—but did you know that we had
(35) burned Toronto a year earlier?

I left school knowing none of this—it wasn't in my school book, and I learned it in my more mature years with amazement. I then learned also that England, while she was fighting with us, had her hands full fighting
(40) Bonaparte, that her war with us was a sideshow, and that this was uncommonly lucky for us—as lucky as those ships from France under Admiral de Grasse, without whose help Washington could never have caught Cornwallis and compelled his surrender at Yorktown on
(45) October 19, 1781. Did you know that there were more French soldiers and sailors than Americans at Yorktown? Is it well to keep these things from the young?

My next question is what did you know about the Mexican War of 1846–1847 when you came out of
(50) school? The names of our victories, I presume, and perhaps of the heroes Zachary Taylor and Winfield Scott; and possibly the treaty of Guadalupe Hidalgo, whereby Mexico ceded to us the whole of Texas, New Mexico, and Upper California, and we paid her fifteen
(55) million. No doubt you know that Santa Anna, the Mexican General, had a wooden leg. Well, there is more to know than that, and I found it out much later.

I found out that General Grant, who had fought with credit as a lieutenant in the Mexican War, briefly
(60) summarized it as "iniquitous." I gradually, through my reading as a grown man, learned the truth about the Mexican War which had not been taught me as a boy; that in that war we bullied a weaker power, that we made her our victim, that the whole discreditable business had
(65) the extension of slavery at the bottom of it. More Americans were against it than had been against the War of 1812. But how many Americans ever learn these things? Do not most of them, upon leaving school, leave history also behind them, and become farmers, or mer-
(70) chants, or plumbers, or firemen, or carpenters, or whatever, and read little but the morning paper for the rest of their lives?

The blackest pages in our history would take a long while to read. Not a word of them did I ever see in my
(75) school textbooks. Those books were written on the premise that America could do no wrong. Only recently have our educators and textbook writers begun to real-ize that teaching the truth instills a greater sense of love for our great nation. Just as we love our friends in spite
(80) of their faults, and all the more intelligently because we know these faults, so our love of our country would be just as strong, and far more intelligent, were we honestly and wisely taught in our early years those acts and policies of hers wherein she fell below her lofty and
(85) humane ideals. Her character and her record on the

whole from the beginning are fine enough to allow the shadows to throw the sunlight into relief. To have produced at three different stages of our growth three such men as Washington, Lincoln, and Roosevelt, is (90) quite sufficient justification for our existence.

11. According to the passage, two fairly well-known heroes of the Mexican War of 1846–1847 are:

    A. Abraham Lincoln and Thomas Jefferson.

    B. George Washington and Admiral de Grasse.

    C. Zachary Taylor and Winfield Scott.

    D. Sam Bowie and Davy Crockett.

12. The author of the passage would most likely agree with which of the following statements?

    F. Students should learn about both the positive and negative aspects of American history.

    G. The best way to deal with horrific aspects of history in an educational setting is to avoid mentioning them, or mention them only in passing.

    H. The Mexican War was prompted by aggressive Mexican military action along the Texan border.

    J. Students who learn about War of 1812 seldom learn about the torching of Washington, D.C. by British troops.

13. It can be inferred from the first paragraph of the passage that when the author of the passage attended school, he was taught that the War of 1812 was instigated by:

    A. the Americans, who openly attacked British frigates.

    B. the Americans, who were in collusion with Napoleon Bonaparte.

    C. the English, who were taking sailors from American ships.

    D. the English, who had invaded Michigan and Ohio.

14. According to the second paragraph, the War of 1812 was fought by America in 1812 instead of 1808 despite:

    I. more support for the war in 1808.

    II. England's desire for peace in 1812.

    III. inadequate military resources in 1812.

    F. I only

    G. III only

    H. I and II only

    J. I, II, and III

15. The passage asserts that there were more French soldiers than American soldiers in which of the following battles?

    A. New Orleans

    B. Guadalupe Hidalgo

    C. Toronto

    D. Yorktown

16. The passage argues that, at the time of the Mexican War, a great many Americans felt that the war:

    F. was necessary.

    G. should not be fought.

    H. started by Santa Anna.

    J. kept the economy going.

17. One of the main ideas of the passage is that:

    A. learning about America's faults makes people love America in a more intelligent manner.

    B. what the author learned in school about America is essentially the correct view.

    C. education is only practical if it clearly has a nationalistic bias.

    D. the United States government benefits from the disingenuous education of its citizens.

GO ON TO THE NEXT PAGE

18. According to the passage, the Mexican War was fought by the United States primarily in order to:

    I. strengthen alliances.

    II. expand slavery.

    III. gain land.

    F. II only

    G. I and II only

    H. I and III only

    J. II and III only

19. It may reasonably be inferred from the passage that General Grant fought in:

    A. the War of 1812.

    B. the Revolutionary War.

    C. the Mexican War.

    D. World War II.

20. It may be inferred that the author believes that British troops burned Washington in response to which of the following events?

    F. The looting of London

    G. The Battle of New Orleans

    H. The victory in New York

    J. The burning of Toronto

Passage III

HUMANITIES: This passage is adapted from the article "The Education of the Child" by Edward Key.

The art of natural education consists of ignoring the faults of children nine times out of ten, avoiding immediate interference, which is usually a mistake, and devoting one's whole vigilance to the control of the (5) environment in which the child is growing up. The art also includes watching the education of the child, which is allowed to go on by itself. But educators who, day in and day out, are consciously transforming the environment and themselves are still a rare product. Most (10) people live on the capital and interest of an education, which perhaps once made them model children, but has deprived them of the desire for educating themselves.

Only by keeping oneself in constant process of growth, under the constant influence of the best things in one's (15) own age, does one become a companion half-way good enough for one's children. To bring up a child means carrying one's soul in one's hand, setting one's feet on a narrow path. It means the humble realization of the truth that the ways of injuring the child are infinite, (20) while the ways of being useful to him are few.

How seldom does the educator remember that the child is making experiments with adults, with marvelous shrewdness making his own valuations and reacting sensitively to each impression. The slightest mistrust, (25) the smallest unkindness, the least act of injustice or contemptuous ridicule, leave wounds that last for life in the finely strung soul of the child. While on the other side unexpected friendliness, kind advances, just indignation, make quite as deep an impression on those (30) senses which people term as soft as wax but treat as if they were made of cowhide.

Relatively excellent was the old education which consisted solely in keeping oneself whole, pure, and honorable. For it did not in the least depreciate person- (35) ality, although it did not form it either. By leading, not interfering, acting as an invisible providence through which the child obtains experience, that child may draw his own conclusions. The present practice is to impress one's own discoveries, opinions, and principles on the (40) child by constantly directing his actions. The last thing to be realized by the educator is that he really has before him an entirely new soul, a real self whose first and chief right is to think over the things with which he comes in contact. By a new soul he understands only a new (45) generation of an old humanity to be treated with a fresh dose of the old remedy. We teach the new souls not to steal, not to lie, to economize their money, to obey commands, say their prayers. But who teaches the new souls to choose for themselves the path they must tread? (50) Who thinks that the desire for this path of their own can be so profound that a hard or even mild pressure towards uniformity can make the whole of childhood a torment.

The new educator will, by regularly ordered experience, teach the child by degrees his place in the great (55) orderly system of existence. But in other respects, none of the individual characteristics of the child will be suppressed, so long as they do not injure the child himself, or others. Therefore, the educator should do anything but advise the child to do what everybody (60) does. He should rather rejoice when he sees in the child tendencies to deviation. Using other people's opinion as a standard results in subordinating one's self to their will. So we become a part of the great mass, led by the Superman through the strength of his will, a will which (65) could not have mastered strong personalities. For the progress of the whole of the species, as well as of society, it is essential that education shall awake the feeling of independence; it should invigorate and favor the disposition to deviate from the type in those cases (70) where the rights of others are not affected, or where deviation is not simply the result of the desire to draw attention to oneself.

Finally, the new educator must remember that the sensitive feelings of children are constantly injured by (75) lack of consideration on the part of grown people. Their easily stimulated aversions are constantly being brought out. Just as there are few better methods of teaching than to ask children, when they have behaved unjustly to others, to consider whether it would be pleasant for (80) them to be treated in that way, so there is no better corrective for the trainer of children than the habit of asking oneself: Would I consent to be treated as I have just treated my child? If it were only remembered that the child generally suffers twice as much as the adult, (85) parents would perhaps learn physical and psychological tenderness without which a child's life is a constant torment.

21. In line 23, the word shrewdness most nearly means:

   A. perceptiveness.

   B. cunning.

   C. stupidity.

   D. depravity.

22. According to the first paragraph of the passage, a good educator is:

   I. open to change and growth.

   II. intent on educating him/herself.

   III. aware that it is easier to harm children than help them.

   F. I only

   G. III only

   H. II and III only

   J. I, II, and III

23. In the third paragraph, it is possible to infer from the sentence "For it did not in the least depreciate personality, although it did not form it either" that:

   A. current education is better in every way than old education.

   B. the main flaw in old education is the fact that it suppressed personality.

   C. although the old education is superior in some ways to current education, it is still flawed.

   D. new education is not intent on forming personality.

24. Which of the following does the author assume is a fact of human nature rather than a precept of a sound educational philosophy?

   F. It is important to allow a child to express his or her individual characteristics.

   G. Children are exposed to both positive and negative adult influences.

   H. In order to be an effective educator, one must not interfere with children's natural faults.

   J. It is more important to teach children to go their own way than it is to teach them to conform to society.

25. In the fourth paragraph, the lines "So we become part of the great mass, led by the Superman through the strength of his will, a will which could not have mastered strong personalities" imply that:

   A. strong personalities are easy to develop in children, since educators encourage them.

   B. without individualism, instead of progressing and developing, society will become easy prey to strong personalities that don't have society's best interests at heart.

   C. education should help nurture the Superman personalities that are meant to run society.

   D. people need to conform their behavior to other people's opinions.

GO ON TO THE NEXT PAGE ➡

26. Which of the following statements best reflects the meaning of the phrase "those senses which people term as soft as wax but treat as if they were made of cowhide" from Paragraph 2?

    F. Children are able to ignore insensitive treatment.

    G. Adults are incapable of inflicting pain on children.

    H. Although many adults give lip service to children's sensitive natures, those same adults tend to treat children insensitively.

    J. Children are able to internalize good treatment more quickly than bad.

27. According to the author, a natural education:

    A. is determined by a parent's ability to reprimand a child fairly.

    B. means a child is allowed to do exactly as he or she pleases all the time, with no interference.

    C. enables a child to conform to societal expectations.

    D. is dependent on the educator's ability to recognize that encouragement of a child's individuality is more important than correcting a child's flaws.

28. In Paragraph 1, the phrase, "carry one's soul in one's hand, setting one's feet on a narrow path" refers to the author's belief that:

    F. in order to raise children successfully, you must be willing to recognize your flaws.

    G. child-rearing is a divine function few can master.

    H. child-rearing severely restricts one's life.

    J. raising children is unfulfilling.

29. According to the last paragraph of the passage, adults will treat children with greater care if they:

    I.   remember that children are highly sensitive to inconsiderate behavior.

    II. treat children as insubordinate creatures in need of guidance.

    III. asked themselves if they would want to be treated the way they treat children.

    A. II only

    B. III only

    C. I and III only

    D. I, II, and III

30. In line 36, *providence* most nearly means:

    F. manipulator.

    G. worrier.

    H. observer.

    J. influence.

Passage IV

NATURAL SCIENCE: This passage is adapted from an article about quantum mechanics.

Pick a random point in the universe and chances are you will find nothing. That is because the universe is mostly made up of empty space. Between the vastly spread out solar systems and galaxies are regions of
(5) interstellar space where there may be less than one atom per square mile. But even if you were to randomly pick a point near a sun or in an interstellar dust cloud, chances are that you would still come up with nothing. Think for a moment of how small our planets are in comparison to
(10) the total area of the solar system. Then recall that most of the nine planets are rotating on a thin disk around the sun. Running into matter in all this empty space is as unlikely as winning the lottery several dozen times in a row!

(15) It is no surprise that many physicists have spent a great deal of time trying to deduce the nature of the vacuum, since it makes up the vast bulk of the universe. For more than 2,500 years philosophers and scientists have attempted to comprehend what the vacuum is and
(20) if it even exists. In the early twentieth century Quantum mechanics experimentally determined that the vacuum isn't exactly empty. In fact, the vacuum is highly dynamic.

In 1925 quantum mechanics replaced classical
(25) Newtonian physics as the best way to describe the actions of subatomic particles. One of the crucial concepts of quantum mechanics is what is known as the uncertainty principle. Named after its discoverer Werner Heisenberg, the uncertainty principle basically states
(30) that you cannot know with certainty the speed and position of a subatomic particle at the same time. The more accurately you measure the speed of an electron,

for example, the less accurately you are able to determine its position at any given time. This is due to the (35) peculiar nature of subatomic particles.

The uncertainty principle makes more sense when you think of particles as constantly vibrating waves. No matter how much you try to slow them down, they always shake to some degree.

(40) This constant oscillation, which seems to be an inherent feature of the universe, also affects the vacuum. Even though a section of the universe may be empty of matter, it is nevertheless permeated with electromagnetic fields that constantly fluctuate on all wavelengths. (45) Since there is a potentially infinite amount of vacuum, the sum total of all of the energy fluctuations in the universe must be infinite.

"But if there is infinite energy in empty space, then we must be able to tap it and have unlimited energy re- (50) sources!" you may shout. The problem, most physicists will tell you, is that to tap the energy in the fluctuations of empty space you would have to break several basic laws of physics.

Even more incredible is the quantum mechanical (55) finding that occasionally the electromagnetic fluctuations of the vacuum lead to the materialization of new particles. You heard it right: sometimes, you can get something from nothing. Every once in a random while, for a split second, a negative electron and a paired (60) particle made of antimatter pop into existence and then annihilate each other a millisecond later.

One metaphor that has been proposed is that the dynamic vacuum is like the surface of a lake. Its surface is rippled with energy vacillations, with negative elec- (65) trons with their antimatter twins popping out of the surface of the lake like paired fish every few moments, only to disappear moments later.

These revelations severely alter the classical conception of the vacuum. Scientists from Aristotle to Newton (70) viewed the vacuum as being a stable medium filled with the "ether." Even after the existence of the ether was called into question in the 1887 by the work of Albert Michelson and Edward Morley, physicists felt that the ether was necessary for the movement of waves of light. (75) They used as their justification the premise that waves must have a medium to travel in. But in 1905 Einstein dispensed with the ether in his paper on the Special

Theory of Relativity. Dismissing the concept as super- fluous, Einstein showed that light waves (and all elec- (80) tromagnetic waves) were unlike waves in water or air because of their unique subatomic nature. With one fell swoop Einstein slay the great ether beast that had been loosed upon science by Aristotle.

31. The main idea of the passage is that:
    A. when electromagnetic particles collide there is sometimes a subatomic explosion.
    B. the vacuum of space is dynamic and fluctuating.
    C. the Special Theory of Relativity changed the way scientists thought about the universe.
    D. it may be possible to extract great amounts of energy from empty space.

32. The passage compares the vacuum to:
    F. a surface of a lake.
    G. a thin disk of matter.
    H. a dozen lotteries.
    J. a room full of oxygen.

33. The passage states that the uncertainty principle was formulated by:
    A. Einstein.
    B. Albert Michelson and Edward Morley.
    C. Heisenberg.
    D. Aristotle.

34. As it is used in line 40, the word oscillation most nearly means:
    F. rotation.
    G. speed.
    H. change.
    J. vibration.

GO ON TO THE NEXT PAGE ➤

35. According to the passage, which of the following is NOT a concept supported by quantum mechanics?

    A. It is impossible to be certain about both the speed and position of a subatomic particle.

    B. The vacuum is suffused with fluctuations in electromagnetic fields.

    C. The universe is pervaded by an electromagnetic medium called the ether.

    D. Sometimes new particles materialize in the vacuum of space.

36. With which of the following statements would the author of the passage most likely agree?

    F. Subatomic particles behave in much the same way as motes of dust behave.

    G. The vacuum is basically a static, unchanging electromagnetic medium.

    H. Waves of light behave like waves of sound under certain circumstances.

    J. The amount of vacuum in the universe far exceeds the amount of matter.

37. What, according to the passage, is the reason that it would be impossible to extract energy from the fluctuations of the vacuum?

    A. Einstein determined in 1905 that any attempt to extract energy from the vacuum would call the existence of the ether into question.

    B. Extracting energy from the vacuum is impossible because it is too difficult to find the place in the universe where random fluctuations are occurring.

    C. The laws of physics dictate that such an extraction of energy from empty space is impossible.

    D. Without the ability to channel the tapped energy, any attempt to harness this unlimited source of energy would result in a massive explosion.

38. The passage suggests that although interstellar space does indeed contain atoms of matter, these atoms are:

    F. grouped together.

    G. composed mainly of hydrogen.

    H. widely spaced.

    J. unlike atoms found on planets.

39. It may be reasonably inferred from the passage that the idea of the ether was popularized in a scientific context by:

    A. Aristotle.

    B. Einstein.

    C. Albert Michelson and Edward Morley.

    D. Werner Heisenberg.

40. What is the main idea of the fourth paragraph?

    F. Quantum mechanics has changed the way we think about reality.

    G. Subatomic particles are in constant motion.

    H. The speed of a subatomic particle is directly related to its position.

    J. In a vacuum, particles move much slower.

STOP

END OF SECTION 3. IF YOU HAVE ANY TIME LEFT, GO OVER YOUR WORK IN THIS SECTION ONLY. DO NOT WORK IN ANY OTHER SECTION OF THE TEST.

4. SCIENCE REASONING TEST

40 Questions • Time—35 Minutes

Directions: This test consists of seven passages, each followed by several questions. Read each passage, select the correct answer for each question, and mark the oval representing the correct answer on your answer sheet. You may NOT use a calculator on this test.

Passage I

Osmosis is the diffusion of water across a semi-permeable membrane. Water will move across a semi-permeable membrane if the concentration of solutes is different on the two sides of the membrane. Solutes are those particles present in solution. Water will always move from a region of lower concentration to a region of higher concentration. *Equilibrium* is the point at which the concentration of solutes is the same for the two regions divided by the semi-permeable membrane. Osmosis will continue until equilibrium is reached. When this equilibrium state is reached, the environment is said to be *isotonic*.

A scientist hypothesized that potato contained NaCl (table salt). When potato is submersed in an NaCl solution it would either release water to the solution or absorb water from the solution depending on the NaCl concentration in the solution. A series of experiments was performed to observe the effect that different NaCl concentrations would have on raw potato. Water with a particular NaCl concentration was prepared and a potato core was submersed in the water and NaCl solution. The potato cores were weighed before and after submersion. Also, the volume of the potato cores was determined before and after submersion. Table 1 shows the results of the experiment as well as the percent change observed for weight and volume.

Table 1

% NaCL conc. of sol.	Initial wt. (g)	Final wt. (g)	% chg. in wt.	Initial vol. (ml)	Final vol. (ml)	% chg. in vol.
0.0	2.80	3.25	16	2.62	3.28	25
0.5	2.75	2.80	2	2.57	2.67	4
1.0	2.74	2.47	−10	2.56	2.15	−16
1.5	2.81	2.30	−18	2.61	2.09	−20
2.0	2.82	2.20	−22	2.60	1.98	−24
3.0	2.77	2.08	−25	2.58	1.88	−27
5.0	2.78	2.00	−28	2.59	1.81	−30

1. According to data presented, what was the final weight and volume, respectively, of the potato core when it was submersed in an NaCl concentration of 1.5%?

   A. 2.30 g and 2.09 ml
   B. 2.47 g and 2.15 ml
   C. 2.81 g and 2.61 ml
   D. 2.82 g and 2.60 ml

2. Dividing the final weight of the sample by the final volume gives a measure of the density of the sample in g/ml. At which of the following salt concentrations did the final sample have a density less than 1 g/ml?

   F. 0.0%
   G. 0.5%
   H. 2.0%
   J. 5.0%

GO ON TO THE NEXT PAGE

3. Which of the following graphs best represents the percentage change in weight with increasing NaCl concentration.

A.

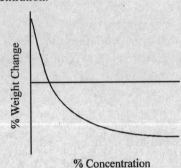

B.

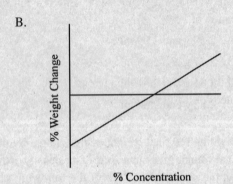

C.

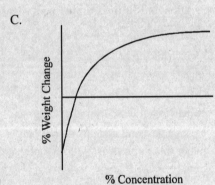

D.

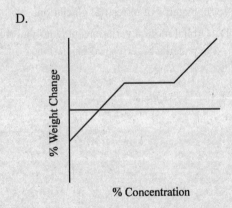

4. From the data in Table 1, at approximately what NaCl concentration do the cores reach an isotonic state?

F. 0.0%

G. 0.3%

H. 0.6%

J. 1.9%

5. What could you expect to happen if the cores were submerged in water with an NaCl concentration of 10%?

A. The weight would increase and volume would increase.

B. The weight would increase and volume would decrease.

C. The weight would decrease and volume would increase.

D. The weight would decrease and volume would decrease.

6. Which of the following observations supports the hypothesis that the cores contained some NaCl prior to the experimental procedure?

F. The cores absorbed water when placed in a solution with 0% NaCl concentration.

G. The cores released more water into solution as NaCl concentration increased.

H. The cores released less water into solution as NaCl concentration increased.

J. The cores released water into solution when solution was 5% NaCl concentration.

7. Another variety of potato was tested and its weight decreased from 2.72 g to 2.34 g in an NaCl concentration of 3.0%. In another trial, the initial weight increased from 2.73 g to 3.19 g in an NaCl concentration of 1.5%. How would the original NaCl concentration compare to the variety of potato used in the original experiment?

A. The original NaCl concentration would be lower in the second variety tested.

B. The original NaCl concentration would be higher in the second variety tested.

C. The original NaCl concentration would be comparable in the two potatoes.

D. The original NaCl concentration could be either greater or less than the original variety tested.

Passage II

Geologists have continued to engage in debate over the cause of major periods of glaciation, or Ice Ages, during the history of Earth. Although the mechanics of glacier formation are well understood in a general sense, the causes of the alternating periods of global-scale glaciation and intervening periods of glacial retreat have been the subject of some controversy. Two geologists present two different geological theories.

Geologist 1

The dramatic long-term cooling trends leading to widespread terrestrial glaciation depend upon the physics of the Earth's motion around the sun and around its own axis of rotation. The generally elliptical orbit of the Earth varies in shape, tending sometimes to a form that appears more circular, other times to a shape that has a more pronounced elliptical quality. This cycle of varying between a circular and elliptical trend is repeated on an average of about once every 100,000 years. When Earth's orbit is more elliptical, the Earth receives significantly less heat energy from the Sun. Also, the axis of the Earth's rotation fluctuates from a tilt of 21.5° to 24.5°, which influences the amount of heat the planet receives from the Sun.

Furthermore, there is a *precession*, or a kind of "wobbling" of the axis itself, which further contributes to fluctuations that must affect the global temperature on a scale that would lead to growth and retreat of the terrestrial ice caps. The precession of the Earth's axis operates on a 41,000 year cycle. Research to this date has provided ample evidence of glaciation and warming matching the cycles with cooling trends evident on both the 100,000-year and 41,000-year scales.

Geologist 2

It is now generally accepted that one of the larger mass extinctions to occur on Earth, the K-T boundary event of 65 million years ago, was the result of a massive asteroid or comet impact that caused a kind of "nuclear winter." It makes much sense then, if we keep in mind how common space junk is in our solar system, to infer that Earth's contact with dust and debris of a smaller and more plentiful nature would contribute to other cycles of cooling and warming. It is likely that these dustloadings may be random in nature, but not as random and rare as killer impacts on the scale of the K-T boundary event. These dustloadings are simply fluctuations in gross amounts of interplanetary dust in our region that may be affected by gravitational forces and other cosmic interactions that ebb and flow around us.

Furthermore, the planets orbit the sun in a plane—imagine a plate with the nine orbits drawn concentrically upon its surface. This angle changes ever so slightly, subtly altering the regions of space through which our Earth travels. So it is the change in position relative to clouds of cosmic dust, gas and meteoroids which limit the amount of solar energy reaching our planet. The scale on which this occurs is a better match to our evidence of 100,000 year cycles of glaciatian and warming.

8. If the 41,000 year cooling trends were substantiated with available evidence, whose theory would be supported?

   F. Geologist A's theory

   G. Geologist B's theory

   H. Both geologists' theories

   J. Neither geologist's theory

9. With which of the following statements would Geologist 1 and Geologist 2 agree?

   A. Cosmic dust and meteors play a major role in patterns of terrestrial glaciation.

   B. Cosmic dust and meteors do not play a major role in patterns of terrestrial glaciation.

   C. Orbital motion variations play a major role in patterns of terrestrial glaciation.

   D. Orbital motion variations play no real role in patterns of terrestrial glaciation.

GO ON TO THE NEXT PAGE

10. Geologist 2 might argue that Geologist 1 does not account for which of the following?

   F. The effect that the precession of the Earth has on the amount of heat received by Earth.

   G. The change of energy Earth receives from the Sun based on Earth's distance from the Sun.

   H. All cycles of terrestrial glaciation.

   J. The impact that extraterrestrial debris has on the temperature of the Earth.

11. If it was found that 70,000 years ago there was a major global cooling trend, Geologist 1 would most likely suggest that:

   A. the Earth's orbital tilt was a major influence on this episode of terrestrial cooling.

   B. the Earth passed through a cloud of cosmic dust and gas during that period.

   C. the Earth's orbit was less elliptical at that time.

   D. a large meteor could have struck the earth at that time.

12. Which of the following assumptions about the Earth's motions was made by Geologist 2?

   F. Changes in orbital angle and position have a negligible effect on terrestrial glaciation patterns.

   G. Changes to the size and shape of the Earth's orbit do not influence patterns of cooling and warming.

   H. Fluctuations of extraterrestrial debris are not a contributing factor to cooling trends.

   J. The tilt of the Earth's axis impacts the amount of energy received from the Sun.

Passage III

Acids are substances that increase the hydrogen ion concentration in aqueous solution. A convenient way to quantify the concentration of hydrogen ion in aqueous solution is with the pH scale. The pH range for most substances is between 0 and 14. The closer to 0 a substance is on the pH scale, the more acidic the solution is considered. The closer the solution is to 14 on the pH scale, the more basic it is considered. Table 1 shows the hydrogen ion concentration and pH for some common substances.

Table 1

Substance	Hydrogen ion conc. (mol/l)	pH
Sodium hydroxide	1.0×10^{-13}	13.0
Household ammonia	1.0×10^{-12}	12.0
Borax	4.0×10^{-10}	9.4
Seawater	3.0×10^{-9}	8.4
Blood	3.1×10^{-8}	7.5
Milk	1.0×10^{-7}	7.0
Coffee	1.0×10^{-5}	5.0
Wine	3.2×10^{-4}	3.5
Gastric juice	1.0×10^{-2}	2.0
Hydrochloric acid	1.0×10^{-1}	1.0

Indicators are substances that change color at different pH levels. The pH range of an indicator shows at what pH level the indicator will change color. When the pH level is lower than the range indicated, the indicator will be in its acidic form. When pH level is higher than the range indicated, the indicator will be in its basic form. The interval represents when the indicator is in the process of changing color. Table 2 summarizes the sensitivity of different indicators to different pH levels.

Table 2

Indicator	pH interval for color change	Acid color	Base color
methyl violet	0.0 – 2.0	yellow	violet
methyl yellow	1.2 – 2.3	red	yellow
methyl orange	2.9 – 4.0	red	yellow
methyl red	4.2 – 6.3	red	yellow
bromthymol blue	6.0 – 7.6	yellow	blue
thymol blue	8.0 – 9.6	yellow	blue
Phenolphthalein	8.3 – 10	colorless	pink
alizarin yellow G	10.1 – 12.0	yellow	red

13. For what substance is the concentration of hydrogen ion 1 x 10^{-5} moles/liter?

    A. Sodium hydroxide

    B. Coffee

    C. Gastric juice

    D. Hydrochloric acid

14. Thymol blue will turn completely blue when added to which of the following solutions?

    F. Blood

    G. Seawater

    H. Borax

    J. Household ammonia

15. According to Table 1 which of the following is the most basic?

    A. Gastric juice

    B. Coffee

    C. Milk

    D. Borax

16. Which of the following indicators requires the greatest change in pH to complete its conversion from acid to base form?

    F. Methyl violet

    G. Alizarin yellow G

    H. Methyl red

    J. Phenolphthalein

17. If bromthymol blue were blue, which of the following solutions could be added to convert it to its acidic form?

    A. Sodium hydroxide

    B. Milk

    C. Coffee

    D. Seawater

Passage IV

Substances can generally exist in 3 phases: solid, liquid, and gas. A phase change is the transition of a substance from one phase to another. If pressure remains constant and temperature is increased, the substance will increase in temperature until it reaches the point where the phase change occurs. The temperature will not increase further until the substance completely changes from one phase to another.

The energy absorbed or liberated in a phase changed is called the *latent heat*. The *latent heat of fusion* (L_f) refers to the heat needed to convert a substance from solid to liquid phase. The melting point is the temperature at which this phase change takes place at atmospheric pressure. The *latent heat of vaporization* (L_v) refers to the heat needed to convert a substance from liquid to gaseous phase. The boiling point is the point at which this phase change takes place at atmospheric pressure.

The table below lists the latent heats of fusion and vaporization, melting points, and boiling points for several substances at atmospheric pressure. The latent heats of fusion and vaporization indicate the heat needed to change 1 kg from one phase to another.

Substance	Melting Point (°C)	Heat of Fus. (kJ/kg)	Boiling Point (°C)	Heat of Vap. (kJ/kg)
Helium			–269	21
Nitrogen	–210	25.5	–196	201
Ethyl alcohol	–114	104	78	854
Water	0	333	100	2,255
Lead	327	24.5	1,620	912
Silver	960	88.3	2,193	2,335
Gold	1,063	64.4	2,660	1,580

18. Once 1 kg lead is at a temperature of 327°C, how much energy is required to convert it from solid to liquid phase?

    F. 24.5 kJ

    G. 912 kJ

    H. 1,620 kJ

    J. 2,335 kJ

GO ON TO THE NEXT PAGE

19. Which of the following substances can exist in a liquid phase over the widest range of temperatures?

    A. Nitrogen

    B. Ethyl Alcohol

    C. Water

    D. Gold

20. Which of the following 2 substances have the smallest difference between their latent heats of vaporization?

    F. Nitrogen and Helium

    G. Lead and Ethyl Alcohol

    H. Silver and Lead

    J. Water and Gold

21. The values for the latent heat of vaporization of water and silver contradict which of the following hypotheses?

    A. The substance with the highest boiling point has the greatest latent heat of vaporization.

    B. The substance with the lowest melting point has the smallest latent heat of fusion.

    C. Of the seven substances, helium has the lowest heat of vaporization.

    D. Latent heat of vaporization is independent of melting point.

22. If placed in an oven at 1,000°C, which of the following would remain in liquid form?

    F. Nitrogen and water

    G. Helium and lead

    H. Ethyl Alcohol and water

    J. Lead and silver

23. Which of the following hypotheses is supported by the data?

    A. As melting point increases, latent heat of fusion increases.

    B. As boiling point increases, latent heat of fusion increases.

    C. As melting point decreases, boiling point decreases.

    D. As boiling point decreases, latent heat of vaporization decreases

Passage V

An antigen is a substance that can elicit a specific immune response when introduced into an animal with a functioning immune system. Proteins, polysaccharides and nucleic acids can serve as antigens if they are injected into an animal that normally does not have those substances as normal constituents. Antibodies are specific molecules that the body produces as an immune response to the introduction of an antigen.

An antigen can also be mixed with pure antibody that is directed against that antigen to form a precipitate containing antigen-antibody complexes. Because it is possible to directly measure precipitate formed, it is also possible to determine the amount of antibody present when a known amount of antigen is added.

An experiment was performed to determine the amount of antibody produced as part of an immune response. The scientist followed a procedure that allowed the harvest of antibody in serum from two rabbits. A different antibody was harvested from each rabbit. A series of test tubes were prepared with samples of the antibody in serum and different levels of antigen were added. Polysaccharide antigen was used to precipitate one antibody and protein antigen was used to precipitate the other.

The graphs below show the results of the relationship between the amount of antigen added and the amount of antibody precipitated. Figure 1 shows when polysaccharide was used and the Figure 2 when protein was used.

Figure 1

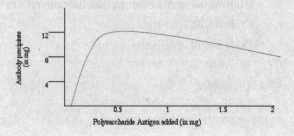

Figure 2

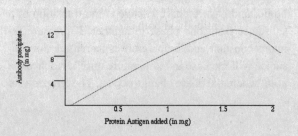

24. When 0.4 mg of polysaccharide were added, how much antibody precipitate formed?

    F. 1 mg
    G. 5 mg
    H. 8 mg
    J. 12 mg

25. Approximately what 2 amounts of protein antigen could be added to yield 8 mg of antibody precipitate?

    A. 0.1 mg and 2 mg
    B. 0.4 mg and 1.6 mg
    C. 0.8 mg and 2 mg
    D. 1.2 mg and 1.5 mg

26. The zone of equivalence is the point at which there is maximal precipitation and there is no excess antigen and no excess antibody. This zone in Figure 2 was reached when antigen added equaled which of the following?

    F. 0.4
    G. 1.0
    H. 1.5
    J. 2.0

27. If the trial using polysaccharide antigen was repeated and the antigen was added only in increments of 1 mg, how would the equivalence zone appear compared to the actual equivalence zone.

    A. It would shift to the left and up.
    B. It would shift to the right and down.
    C. It would shift right and up.
    D. It would remain the same.

28. When only 0.2 mg of either polysaccharide and protein antigen are added, which of the following statements could be supported by the data?

    F. There was an excess of antibody compared to antigen in both cases.
    G. There was an excess of antigen compared to antibody in both cases.

    H. There was an excess of antigen in Figure 1 and an excess of antibody in Figure 2.
    J. There was an excess of antibody in Figure 1 and an excess of antigen in Figure 2.

29. Which of the following best explains the drop in antibody precipitate when the level of polysaccharide was greater than 0.5 mg?

    A. There was more antibody present in the test tubes in which 0.5 mg of polysaccharide was used.
    B. The amount of antibody was constant in all the test tubes that were tested with polysaccharide antigen.
    C. The presence of less than 0.5 mg of antigen caused the excess to interfere with the formation of the antigen-antibody complexes and therefore inhibited the formation of a precipitate.
    D. The presence of more than 0.5 mg of antigen caused the excess to interfere with the formation of the antigen-antibody complexes and therefore inhibited the formation of a precipitate.

Passage VI

Atoms are composed of protons, neutrons, and electrons. Protons and neutrons reside in the nucleus or inner core of the atom and the electrons reside outside the nucleus. Electrons are negatively charged particles that occupy orbital shells around the nucleus. In a neutral atom, the number of electrons is equal to the number of protons, the positively charged particles. The atomic number for an element indicates how many protons are in the nucleus of a given element.

If an electron is removed from an atom, the atom will become positively charged. The energy required to remove an electron is referred to as the ionization energy. The table below summarizes the ionization energies for several elements with respect to the removal of the first three electrons. Successive ionization energies are designated with a subscript consistent with which electron is being removed.

GO ON TO THE NEXT PAGE

Ele-ment	Atomic Rad.	Atomic Num.	Electrons in Outer Shell	Ionization Energy (kJ/mol)		
				I_1	I_2	I_3
Sodium	1.60	11	1	490	4,560	N/A
Mag.	1.40	12	2	735	1,445	7,730
Alum.	1.30	13	1	580	1,815	2,740
Silicon	1.20	14	2	780	1,575	3,220
Phos.	1.10	15	3	1,060	1,890	2,905
Sulfur	1.05	16	4	1,005	2,260	3,375
Chlor-ine	1.00	17	5	1,255	2,295	3,850

30. What is the ionization energy, in kJ/mol, to re-move the first electron in silicon?

    F. 580

    G. 780

    H. 1,575

    J. 3,220

31. Which element has the greatest difference in ionization energies for the removal of the first two electrons?

    A. Sodium

    B. Aluminum

    C. Phosphorus

    D. Chlorine

32. It was hypothesized that energy required to re-move the first electron from a neutral atom in-creases as atomic radius decreases. Which pair of elements from the table would contradict this hypothesis?

    F. Sodium and Chlorine

    G. Magnesium and Silicon

    H. Aluminum and Sulfur

    J. Phosphorus and Chlorine

33. Which of the following statements is supported by the data?

    A. Ionization energy remains constant as electrons are removed from an atom.

    B. Ionization energy decreases as electrons are removed from a neutral atom.

    C. Atomic radii increase as atomic numbers decrease.

    D. Atomic radii decrease as atomic numbers decrease.

34. After removal of electrons from the outer shell, ionization energies more than triple relative to when the elements contained electrons in the outer shell. The data from which of the elements supports this statement?

    I. Sodium

    II. Magnesium

    III. Aluminum

    F. I only

    G. II only

    H. I and II only

    J. I, II, and III

Passage VII

A chemist, a biologist and a doctor spent several years studying and measuring their respective populations in an Alaskan fishing community. Some of their observa-tions are recorded below.

Chemist: Seawater Salinity*/Temperature (°C) (Seasonal Average)

	Winter	Spring	Summer	Fall
Surface	0/–1°	25/1°	32/12°	15/2°
5 meters deep	0/–1°	29/5°	32/7°	26/7°
20 meters deep (ocean floor)	39/4°	32/5°	32/6°	34/5°

* Seawater salinity is measured in parts/thousand.

Biologist: Population Counts (Seasonal Average)

Bay (free-swimming)	Winter	Spring	Summer	Fall
Fur seals (number successfully hunted)	6.3	3.0	5.4	2.2
Salmon (tonnage caught)	0	122.5	1,152.6	4,259.5
Gray whales (number observed)	0	29.8	32.4	1.4

Bay (bottom-dwelling amphipods)

	Winter	Spring	Summer	Fall
Gammarus duebeni (sample count in one gallon of seawater)	50	25	15	60
Gammarus locusta (sample count in one gallon of seawater)	340	5	5	260

Land species

	Winter	Spring	Summer	Fall
Kodiak Bears (number observed)	0	4	11	21
Humans (number counted)	63	66	85	117

Doctor: Number of Medical Complaints (Seasonal Average)

	Winter	Spring	Summer	Fall
Dehydration-related illnesses	0.0	0.0	3.4	0.9
Bear attacks	0.0	0.2	1.1	2.2
Protein deficiency-related illnesses	10.4	4.1	1.0	0.0

35. Between which seasons was the greatest change in salinity at a depth of 5 meters observed?
    - A. Winter to Spring
    - B. Spring to Summer
    - C. Summer to Fall
    - D. Fall to Winter

36. The temperature and salinity readings at the ocean floor support which of the following conclusions?
    - F. *Gammarus duebeni* is sensitive to temperature changes.
    - G. *Gammarus locusta* is sensitive to temperature changes.
    - H. *Gammarus locusta* is sensitive to salinity changes
    - J. Both species of *gammarus* are equally sensitive to salinity changes.

37. Which graph best expresses the relationship between the seasonal salmon catch and the incidence of protein-deficiency–related illnesses in the doctor's data?

    A.

    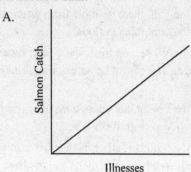

    B.

    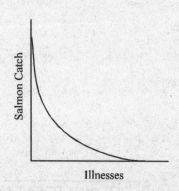

GO ON TO THE NEXT PAGE

C.
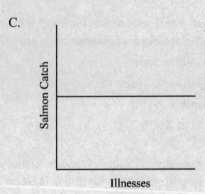

D.
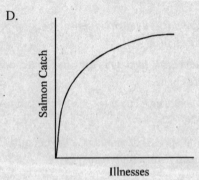

38. Which of the following supports the trend observed with respect to dehydration-related illnesses?

  F. In the Fall, there is ample fresh water due to frequent rainy periods.

  G. In the Winter, all fresh water reserves are frozen and cannot be accessed as drinking water.

  H. In the Spring, not enough ice has melted to provide enough fresh water.

  J. In the Summer, all of the ice that stores fresh water reserves melts and the fresh water is lost to the ocean.

39. Which of the following statements is NOT supported by the evidence?

  A. Whales are most commonly seen in the area in the Spring and Summer.

  B. Summer and Fall are the primary salmon fishing seasons.

  C. Spring and Summer are the primary fur seal hunting seasons.

  D. Bear attacks are uncommon in the winter.

40. A biologist wants to isolate the effect on bear population due to salmon levels from the effect due to human influence, in particular, the availability of an alternative food source in the village. What could the biologist do to help obtain the most accurate measure of the bear population when they have access only to their natural salmon food supply?

  F. Feed the bears salmon to replace their intake of village garbage and food.

  G. Ensure that the village's garbage containers and food storage containers are kept locked.

  H. Remove the salmon from the area and measure the effect on the bears.

  J. Increase the frequency of the bear population survey from weekly to daily.

STOP

END OF SECTION 4. IF YOU HAVE ANY TIME LEFT, GO OVER YOUR WORK IN THIS SECTION ONLY. DO NOT WORK IN ANY OTHER SECTION OF THE TEST.

PRACTICE EXAMINATION 2

Answer Key

1. English Test

1. C	16. G	31. C	46. F	61. C
2. G	17. D	32. H	47. C	62. G
3. D	18. H	33. A	48. F	63. A
4. F	19. D	34. F	49. D	64. J
5. C	20. F	35. D	50. J	65. A
6. J	21. C	36. J	51. C	66. G
7. B	22. G	37. B	52. G	67. D
8. G	23. A	38. F	53. B	68. J
9. B	24. H	39. C	54. H	69. B
10. F	25. D	40. F	55. B	70. G
11. A	26. G	41. C	56. H	71. C
12. J	27. A	42. G	57. A	72. F
13. B	28. G	43. C	58. J	73. B
14. F	29. C	44. F	59. D	74. J
15. B	30. F	45. D	60. H	75. C

2. Math Test

1. A	13. A	25. B	37. C	49. C
2. G	14. K	26. K	38. G	50. G
3. C	15. C	27. D	39. C	51. E
4. J	16. G	28. F	40. H	52. J
5. D	17. C	29. C	41. B	53. C
6. K	18. J	30. K	42. K	54. K
7. E	19. A	31. B	43. C	55. D
8. F	20. G	32. G	44. G	56. K
9. A	21. A	33. A	45. A	57. A
10. H	22. G	34. K	46. J	58. J
11. D	23. E	35. D	47. B	59. E
12. G	24. G	36. J	48. G	60. H

3. Reading Test

1. B	9. B	17. A	25. B	33. C
2. H	10. G	18. F	26. H	34. J
3. C	11. C	19. C	27. D	35. C
4. J	12. F	20. J	28. F	36. J
5. C	13. C	21. A	29. C	37. C
6. H	14. J	22. J	30. J	38. H
7. A	15. D	23. C	31. B	39. A
8. J	16. G	24. G	32. F	40. G

4. Science Reasoning Test

1. A	9. C	17. C	25. C	33. C
2. F	10. J	18. F	26. H	34. J
3. A	11. A	19. D	27. B	35. A
4. H	12. G	20. G	28. F	36. H
5. D	13. B	21. A	29. D	37. B
6. F	14. J	22. J	30. G	38. J
7. B	15. D	23. C	31. A	39. C
8. F	16. H	24. J	32. H	40. G

PRACTICE EXAMINATION 2

Explanatory Answers

1. English Test

Passage I

1. **C** is correct. *I had* is understood to be the first part of the verb and this structure requires the second part of the verb to be in the past participle. The series should read: *I had been, . . . seen . . . and sat.*

2. **G** is correct. This option gets rid of redundancy without changing the meaning.

3. **D** is correct. A period is needed to separate the two sentences.

4. **F** is correct. This is the superlative form of *charming.*

5. **C** is correct. The phrase *long after the last restaurant had closed* modifies *the dead of night* and therefore is placed directly after *night* with commas separating the modifier from the rest of the sentence.

6. **J** is correct. *All* is unnecessary and no new words need to be added to make the sentence clear.

7. **B** is correct. First, they arrive in Florence. Then, after learning that the restaurants are closed, we can be told that they haven't eaten dinner. This detail describes one of the reasons the narrator is unhappy and should come before sentence 2 where the narrator's friends try to console her.

8. **G** is correct. The portion beginning *my ever-eager travel companions . . .* is not a sentence and so should only be separated by a comma. *All too soon* should not be omitted because it shows the narrator's irritation.

9. **B** is correct. *Instead* is the right word to indicate the opposition between the narrator's desires and that of her companions while providing a smooth transition between the sentences.

10. **F** is correct. This paragraph illustrates the narrator's basic unhappiness with the choices her companions continue to make on their trip.

11. **A** is correct. The possessive pronoun for an object is *its.*

12. **J** is correct. The verbs are in the infinitive—*to sulk and stare*—and the object of the verb (*throngs*) should not be separated from the verb by a comma.

13. **B** is the correct answer. This should be a new paragraph because it describes a new and pivotal action in the story. In the previous paragraph the narrator stands outside the wall to the garden. In this paragraph the narrator finally follows his or her impulse and climbs into the garden.

14. **F** is correct. *Embraced* is the best verb because the connotation is one of warmth and happiness. The active sentence is clean and direct.

15. **B** is correct. The material emphasizes the narrator's discomfort and should therefore be placed after the description of something that helps to create this discomfort. By placing the material at the end of Paragraph 3, it becomes a summary statement of how the narrator feels as she walks uphill in the hot sun after too little sleep.

Passage II

16. **G** is correct. There should not be a comma separating the subjects from the verb, which is in the present continuous tense.

17. **D** is correct. The prepositional phrase (*with . . .*) belongs to the previous sentence and should not be separated.

18. **H** is correct. *Long after* is the accepted idiom. *Way after* is too colloquial. The other options are wrong.

19. **D** is correct. The sentence is in the present tense and requires that form of the verb *to seem.*

20. **F** is correct. *That* is the right choice of relative pronoun. It identifies the theory and adds no unnecessary words.

21. **C** is correct. While the term is not defined, the context makes it clear that the revolution involved a sudden transformation to an agricultural economy and the rise of cities.

22. **G** is correct. While *benefit* is the right noun for this context, the verb *were* demands the plural form.

23. **A** is correct. This is the only sentence that links the old thinking with the evidence against it—gene analysis, etc.—without going too far and claiming that the old theory was definitively disproved at a certain moment in the past.

24. **H** is correct. The two sentences should be separated. The second does not define the first, which would justify a colon, nor is there an opposition to justify the conjunction *but*.

25. **D** is correct. The preposition *of* after the underlined portion excludes all other possibilities. *Dating of the remains* is the only phrase that makes sense.

26. **G** is correct. Subject-verb agreement. There are two subjects, *Squash* and *rice*, and therefore the verb is conjugated in third person plural.

27. **A** is correct. There are two sides to the evidence: that which shows plant domestication before the rise of settlements; and that which shows settlements before the rise of plant domestication. *On the other hand* indicates this distinction between the evidence in the previous sentence and the evidence that follows.

28. **G** is correct. Two things co-exist *with* each other, one alongside the other.

29. **C** is correct. Paragraph 3 already includes several pieces of evidence against the swift rise of agriculture. Therefore, it is the best place to more fully examine why this evidence points to the slow development of large-scale agriculture.

30. **F** is correct. This is the only option that describes the basic tension of the essay between the previous and present day thinking on the subject. The specific pattern of the essay is exactly described. The other options are either too vague (G). or simply wrong (H and J).

Passage III

31. **C** is correct. The fragment beginning, *an unobstructed panorama*, explains the spectacular views from the previous sentence and should, therefore, be linked by a colon.

32. **H** is correct. This option gets rid of an unnecessary word and maintains the sense of distant isolation.

33. **A** is correct. The construction calls for the possessive. *The polar ice cap* is singular and therefore the apostrophe comes before the *s*.

34. **F** is correct. *However* is the only option that indicates a contrast to the *relatively stable climate* mentioned in the preceding sentence.

35. **D** is correct. There are two separate sentences that need to be linked. This can be done with a comma and a conjunction. *But* does not work because it indicates a contrast where there is none.

36. **J** is correct. There is no need for a preposition between the verb and its object.

37. **B** is correct. This option clarifies the sentence by maintaining a straightforward conceptual and grammatical link with the opening phrase. *Despite* indicates that people are not put off by the *adverse conditions*; *or because of them* offers the possibility that people may even be attracted by these conditions. The other options are either awkward or alter the meaning of the sentence.

38. **F** is correct. The subordinating conjunction *because* creates a causal link between the two clauses. The subject (*it*) of the subordinate clause follows the conjunction to maximize clarity and avoid awkwardness.

39. **C** is correct. This option is the clearest because it avoids redundancy and leaves out the definite article *(the)* which incorrectly indicates that the *snowdrifts* have been mentioned before.

40. **F** is correct. This option makes it clear that the discussion is about what must be done in order *to survive* a trek up Vinson.

41. **C** is correct. Throughout the paragraph, the writer employs the informal *you* to address the reader about what must be done to climb Vinson.

42. **G** is correct. Dashes are used to set off an explanation in the middle of a sentence, in this case, examples of *extremities*.

43. **C** is correct. The underlined portion makes the point in a humorous way by citing specific examples that are clearly insufficient for arctic mountain climbing.

44. **F** is correct. This is the only sentence that relates the effort involved in making a climb to the reward. The essay has spent a great deal of time describing both.

45. **D** is correct. This essay provides an interesting and informative description that is directed toward a general audience.

Passage IV

46. **F** is correct. The sentence describes something that is currently taking place.

47. **C** is correct. This option gets rid of redundant phrasing.

48. **F** is correct. According to the passage, the adaptation of books into movies *is caused* by the belief that stories can be told just as well on film.

49. **D** is correct. This answer avoids redundancy and makes the writer's point that the audience has not read the book in advance of seeing the film.

50. **J** is correct. This option avoids unnecessary words and overly colloquial language.

51. **C** is correct. This is the only option that clearly conveys the author's point that there is no effective way to explore the mind of a character on film.

52. **G** is correct. The reference is to the heads of the characters and therefore the possessive pronoun is required.

53. **B** is correct. The word *omniscient* means all-knowing.

54. **H** is correct. *Reading* is the only option that translates the actual length of a novel into time.

55. **B** is correct. A comma separates the clauses for the sake of clarity.

56. **H** is correct. Paragraph 4 introduces the idea that films spoon feed character development to the audience. That idea is elaborated on in Paragraph 2.

57. **A** is correct. This option is the most logical given the writer's emphasis on the reader's imagination.

58. **J** is correct. This option conveys the idea that words are both poetic and powerful without making the sentence awkward.

59. **D** is correct. This option restates the main idea of the essay, which is the writer's desire to persuade the reader to read classic novels rather than watch film adaptations of them.

60. **H** is correct. The writer's argument centers on the problems inherent in adapting classic novels for the screen and not on the comparative value of books and films.

Passage V

61. **C** is correct. The word *desire* is part of a series, and the series should be separated by commas.

62. **G** is correct. This choice avoids unnecessary words and is neither overly technical nor overly vague.

63. **A** is correct. This sentence links the idea of fantasy, from Paragraph 1, with Monaco.

64. **J** is correct. The conjunction *but* indicates that the combination *wealthy* and *tiny* might go against expectation.

65. **A** is correct. The present perfect implies correctly that the family ruled in the past and continues to do so.

66. **G** is correct. No possessive punctuation is required here. *Grimaldis* is a plural noun.

67. **D** is correct. Any addition here of extraneous information would interrupt the logic of the paragraph, which focuses on the Grimaldis.

68. **J** is correct. This option avoids unnecessary words and inappropriate changes in tone.

69. **B** is correct. This choice maintains the third person style of the essay and the logic of the sentence.

70. **G** is correct. Nationalities are capitalized. *An* is necessary to avoid consecutive vowels.

71. **C** is correct. *Beautiful* and *poised* refer to Princess Grace; she is the subject of the verbs.

72. **F** is correct. The past tense is appropriate here. The sentence describes something that did in fact happen.

73. **B** is correct. The pronoun *who* correctly implies that Prince Rainier is the subject of the verb *to mourn*. A comma is required following the word *still* in order to separate this clause from the next.

74. **J** is correct. It implies a negative impact of the tragedy without exaggerating it.

75. **C** is correct. This essay does not fulfill the assignment as it only refers to ordinary people indirectly.

2. Mathematics Test

1. **A.** The sale price of the suit is $250 - (.25)($250) = $187.50.

2. **G.** The perimeter of the foundation is equal to twice the length plus twice the width or $2(60) + 2(20) = 160$ feet.

3. **C.** If $a = -3$, then $b = (-2)(-3) = 6$. The expression $ab - 3a$ equals $(-3)(6) - 3(-3) = -18 + 9 = -9$.

4. **J.** $\frac{18}{48} = .375 = 37.5\%$ of the bushes are red roses.

5. **D.** $3(5^2) - 2(5) + 7 = 75 - 10 + 7 = 72$.

6. **K.** None of the other templates can be folded into a cube without violating the rules of the question.

7. **E.** $(x + 2)(x - 5) = 8$
$$x^2 - 3x - 10 = 8$$
$$x^2 - 3x - 18 = 0$$
$$(x - 6)(x + 3) = 0$$
$$x - 6 = 0 \text{ or } x + 3 = 0$$

8. **F.** The minimum passing score is $(400)(.7) = 280$ points. If the applicant raised his score by 25 points and received 280, then his first score was $280 - 25 = 255$.

9. **A.** The number of different combinations can be obtained by multiplying the number of variations on each variable—color, finish, and newsletter. The number of distinct combinations is $(5)(4)(2) = 40$.

10. **H.** The first graph illustrates $x > -2$ and the second graph illustrates $x < 2$. The intersection of these inequalities is $-2 < x < 2$.

11. **D.** $\pi r^2 = 24\pi$
$$r^2 = 24$$
$$r = \sqrt{24} = 2\sqrt{6}$$

12. **G.** A parallelogram is a quadrilateral with two sets of parallel sides. *ABDE* satisfies these conditions.

13. **A.** $3(m + n) - 2(m - 3n) = 3m + 3n - 2m + 6n = m + 9n$

14. **K.** Knowing only the hypotenuse of a right triangle is not enough information to determine the lengths of the legs.

15. **C.** A line intersects the y-axis where $x = 0$, so substitute $x = 0$ into the equation and solve for y:
$$0 + 3y = 6$$
$$3y = 6$$
$$y = 2$$

16. **G.** There are $180 + 540 = 720$ cars in the parking lot, so $\frac{180}{720} = .25 = 25\%$ have out-of-state plates.

17. **C.** If $t = 1$ the product $(2)(4)(6)(9)t$ is divisible by all of the answers except 30.

18. **J.** The area of a rectangle is length times width:
area $= (3x + 2)(5x - 3)$
$$= 15x^2 - 9x + 10x - 6$$
$$= 15x^2 + x - 6$$

19. **A.** $\qquad 4x^2 = 6x + 4$
$$4x^2 - 6x - 4 = 0$$
$$2x^2 - 3x - 2 = 0 \text{ (divide both sides by 2)}$$
$$(2x + 1)(x - 2) = 0$$

20. **G.** You can determine that the sides of the second triangle are all 4 times as long as the sides of the first triangle, because you are given that two of the similar sides are x and $4x$. You can then use this fact to solve for x. The side that is $5x$ is 4 times the side of length 10, so $5x = 40$ or $x = 8$.

21. **A.** Multiplying both sides of the equation by 10 gets rid of the fractions and decimal points:
$$x - 42 = 2x + 33$$
$$-x = 75$$
$$x = -75$$

22. **G.** First plane left at $t + 1$. Second plane (t) left at 4 pm.
$$350(t + 1) + 450t = 3000$$
$$350t + 350 + 450t = 3000$$
$$800t = 3000 - 350 = 2650$$
$$t = 3.3$$
That's 3.3 hours after 4 pm or 7:18 pm.

23. **E.** $(x - a)(x + b) = x^2 + 2x - 4b$
$x^2 + (b - a)x - ab = x^2 + 2x - 4b$
From the above equation, you know that $ab = 4b$, or $a = 4$. Given that $a = 4$, you can solve for b:
$$b - a = 2$$
$$b - 4 = 2$$
$$b = 6$$

24. **G.** $\frac{3.2 - 1.557}{2(1 - 5 - 375)} = \frac{1.643}{.25} = 6.572$

25. **B.** $12x^2 - ax - a = (3x + 1)(4x - 2)$
$12x^2 - ax - a = 12x^2 - 2x - 2$
$a = 2$

26. **K.** $\frac{x\sqrt{3}}{x - \sqrt{3}} \times \frac{x + \sqrt{3}}{x + \sqrt{3}} = \frac{x^2\sqrt{3} + 3x}{x^2 - 3}$

27. **D.** A rectangle is a four-sided polygon, so it is a quadrilateral. It has two sets of parallel sides, so it is a parallelogram. However, a rhombus has 4 equal sides, and a rectangle does not (unless it is a square).

28. **F.** Solve for the distance by setting up a proportion:
$$\frac{20}{150} = \frac{x}{180}$$
$$150x = 3,600$$
$$x = 24$$

29. **C.** Since sine is defined as $\frac{\text{opposite}}{\text{hypotenuse}}$, you can assume that $\overline{AC}$ is 4 and $\overline{AB}$ is 9. Solving for $\overline{BC}$ using the Pythagorean Theorem gives $\sqrt{65}$. The sine of $\angle A$ is thus $\frac{\sqrt{65}}{9}$.

30. **K.** $n + 8 = 14 - 4(3 - n)$
$$n + 8 = 14 - 12 + 4n$$
$$-3n = -6$$
$$n = 2$$

31. **B.** Parallel lines have equal slope. Put the original equation into the form $y = mx + b$, where m is the slope:
$$2x + 7y = 5$$
$$7y = -2x + 5$$
$$y = -\tfrac{2}{7}x + \tfrac{5}{7}$$

32. **G.** You can divide the room into a rectangular section with an area of $(10)(12) = 120$ square feet and a triangular section with an area of $\frac{1}{2}(4)(10) = 20$ square feet. The amount of carpet used is $120 + 20 = 140$ square feet.

33. **A.** $x + 10 = yz + 5$
$$x + 5 = yz$$
$$\frac{x + 5}{z} = y$$

34. **K.** Determine the slope by putting the equation into the form $y = mx + b$, where m is the slope:
$$6x - 5y = 10$$
$$-5y = -6x + 10$$
$$y = \tfrac{6}{5}x - 2$$

35. **D.** The relationship among the sides of a 30°-60°-90° triangle is x, $x\sqrt{3}$, and $2x$, respectively. You can use these relationships to determine the lengths of the sides of the triangles.

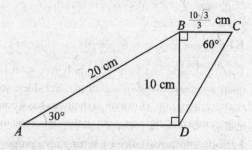

36. **J.** Use the distance formula to determine the radius of the circle:
$$r = \sqrt{(0 - 6)^2 + (5 - 1)^2}$$
$$= \sqrt{36 + 16}$$

$$= \sqrt{52}$$
The area of the circle is $\pi r^2 = \pi(\sqrt{52})^2 = 52\pi$.

37. **C.** Substitute the x and y values into the equation and you find that only $(3,8)$ does not satisfy the equation of the line.

38. **G.** Eight shirts are two sets of three, plus two singles, which will cost $110 plus $44, or $154. Then you get a $15.40 discount (10%), bringing the final cost to $138.60.

39. **C.** If you buy five shirts, you get three for $55 plus two more for $22 each, for a total of $99. But if you buy six shirts (two sets of three), you pay $110 less a 10% discount of $11, bringing your cost down to $99. The extra shirt is free!

40. **H.** Sine is equal to $\frac{\text{opposite}}{\text{hypotenuse}}$, so $\sin \angle B = \frac{24}{26} = \frac{12}{13}$.

41. **B.** A graph of a polynomial intersects the x-axis at each real root. If the 3 real roots of $P(x)$ are different from the 2 real roots of $Q(x)$, then the graph would intersect the x-axis at 5 points.

42. **K.** $\dfrac{2x^2 - 4xy + 2y^2}{y^2 - x^2} = \dfrac{2(x - y)(x - y)}{(y + x)(y - x)}$
$$= \frac{-2(x - y)(y - x)}{(y + x)(y - x)}$$
$$= \frac{-2(x - y)}{(y + x)}$$
$$= \frac{2(y - x)}{(x + y)}$$

43. **C.** You can use the relationships of a 30°-60°-90° triangle to solve for the height, or you can apply the Pythagorean Theorem:
$$3^2 + b^2 = 6^2$$
$$9 + b^2 = 36$$
$$b^2 = 27$$
$$b = \sqrt{27} = 3\sqrt{3}$$

44. **G.** $(x + 2)(x - 6) = 2x - 21$
$$x^2 - 4x - 12 = 2x - 21$$
$$x^2 - 6x + 9 = 0$$
$$(x - 3)^2 = 0$$
$$x = 3$$
There is only one real number that solves the equation.

45. **A.** If the 6 students represent exactly 20% of the class, then there are $\frac{6}{.2} = 30$ students in the class. If the 6 students represent exactly 40% of the class, then there are $\frac{6}{.4} = 15$ students in the class. Since any number of students between 15 and 30 is also possible, there are a total of 16 different values of x.

46. **J.** A zero is a real root—a point at which the function has a y-value of 0. If a polynomial has zeros of 0, 1, and 2, then the polynomial could be as follows:

$$(x - 0)(x - 1)(x - 2) = 0$$
$$x(x^2 - 3x + 2) = 0$$
$$x^3 - 3x^2 + 2x = 0$$

47. **B.** To determine the area of a triangle, you need to know its base and its height. You can call the side shared with the square the base, and you know that it is 6 inches long. Although the height is not given directly, you are given that the entire horizontal distance from A to D is 10 inches. Thus, the height of the triangle is $10 - 6 = 4$ inches. The area is $\frac{1}{2}(6)(4) = 12$.

48. **G.** You can substitute each of the points into the equations, or you can solve the simultaneous equations:

$$y - 4x = -4$$
$$-y + 3x = 10$$
$$-7x = -14$$
$$x = 2$$

49. **C.** In an isosceles right triangle, if a leg has a length of x, then the hypotenuse has a length of $x\sqrt{2}$. Given the perimeter, you can solve for the length of x:

$$x + x + x\sqrt{2} = 16 + 16\sqrt{2}$$
$$(2 + \sqrt{2})x = 16 + 16\sqrt{2}$$
$$x = (2 + \sqrt{2})8\sqrt{2}$$
$$x = 8\sqrt{2}$$

50. **G.** $x + y$ can be found by getting a common denominator for the two fractions:

$$\frac{2 - \sqrt{3}}{2 + \sqrt{3}} + \frac{2 + \sqrt{3}}{2 - \sqrt{3}} = \frac{(2 - \sqrt{3})(2 - \sqrt{3})}{(2 + \sqrt{3})(2 - \sqrt{3})} + \frac{(2 + \sqrt{3})(2 + \sqrt{3})}{(2 - \sqrt{3})(2 + \sqrt{3})}$$
$$= \frac{4 - 4\sqrt{3} + 3}{4 - 3} + \frac{4 + 4\sqrt{3} + 3}{4 - 3}$$
$$= \frac{14}{1} = 14$$

51. **E.** $3x - k(x + 2) \geq 10 - 3(1 + x)$
$$3x - kx - 2k \geq 10 - 3 - 3x$$
$$6x - kx \geq 7 + 2k$$
$$(6 - k)x \geq 7 + 2k$$

If k equals 6, then the inequality is $0 \geq 19$, which cannot be true.

52. **J.** The orders per day on Monday through Friday are 40, 45, 50, 55, and 60. The average order sizes are $250, $240, $230, $220, and $210. The first day that the company has sales of at least $12,000 is Thursday: $(55)(\$220) = \$12,100$.

53. **C.** Triangles ABC and CJK are similar. If $\overline{CJ}$ is x, then you can solve as follows:

$$\frac{x}{x + 48} = \frac{60}{100}$$
$$100x = 60x + 2,880$$
$$40x = 2,880$$
$$x = 72$$

You can then solve for $\overline{CK}$ as y:

$$\frac{y}{50} = \frac{72}{48}$$
$$48y = 3,600$$
$$y = 75$$

The perimeter of the triangle is $100 + 72 + 48 + 75 + 50 = 345$ inches.

54. **K.** If the triangle extends just beyond the circle at the three vertices, then there are 6 points of intersection.

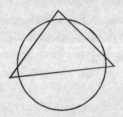

55. **D.** I is not always true. For example, if a is negative and b is positive, II is always true. The expressions will always be positive and will always be equal. III is always true, as well.

56. **K.** $2x^5 - 2x = 2x(x^2 + 1)(x + 1)(x - 1)$
$$2x(x^4 - 1) = 2x(x^2 + 1)(x + 1)(x - 1)$$
$$x^4 - 1 = (x^2 + 1)(x^2 - 1)$$
$$x^4 - 1 = x^4 - 1$$

The equation is true for all values of x.

57. **A.** $2y = \cos 2\theta$ can be rewritten as $y = \frac{\cos 2\theta}{2}$. The amplitude of this expression is half that of $y = \cos \theta$ and so is its period.

58. **J.** First, you may want to rewrite the ellipse in the standard form:

$$\frac{(x + 2)^2}{4} + \frac{(y - 2)^2}{9} = 1$$

One way of thinking about this problem is to realize that a circle is simply an ellipse with equal denominators. Thus, the equation of the circle that inscribes the ellipse is

$$\frac{(x + 2)^2}{9} + \frac{(y - 2)^2}{9} = 1 \text{ or } (x + 2)^2 + (y - 2)^2 = 9.$$

59. **E.** $\frac{\frac{4}{3}\pi x^3}{\frac{4}{3}\pi(\frac{x}{2})^3} = \frac{x^3}{\frac{x^3}{8}} = 8$

60. **H.** First, solve for x:

$$x + 2x + 3x = 180$$
$$6x = 180$$
$$x = 30$$

What you have, then, is a 30°-60°-90° triangle. If the side opposite the 30° angle has a length of 4, then the side opposite the 60° angle has a length of $4\sqrt{3}$. The side opposite the 90° angle has a length of 8. The perimeter of the triangle is $12 + 4\sqrt{3}$.

3. Reading Test

1. **B.** A is incorrect because we learn in the third paragraph that Elam was "gregarious." B is the best answer because the second sentence in the third paragraph tells us "he was too vital and robust" to be inclined toward drinking. C is incorrect because the passage does not mention Elam drinking. D is incorrect because although Elam did gamble, nowhere in the passage does it say he preferred it to drinking.

2. **H.** F is incorrect because Elam's religious conviction is never mentioned. G is incorrect because Elam's mother is never mentioned. H is the best answer because the first paragraph states "he had known nothing but hard knocks for big stakes" and "Environment had determined what form that game should take" in reference to Elam's gambling nature. J is incorrect because nowhere does it state that Elam misunderstood games of chance.

3. **C.** A is incorrect because although I is mentioned in paragraph 4, III is mentioned in paragraph 5. B is incorrect because although III is mentioned in paragraph 5, I is mentioned in paragraph 4. C is the best answer because I is mentioned in the middle of paragraph 4 and III is mentioned at the end of in paragraph 5. D is incorrect because II is never mentioned.

4. **J.** F is incorrect because owing money is never mentioned. G is incorrect because though Elam's mine is mentioned in paragraph 1, he had struck gold "the past summer." H is incorrect because playing cards is not mentioned. J is the best answer because at the end of the second paragraph it mentions it was "the day of his birth."

5. **C.** A is incorrect because paragraph 4 states that Elam was "without wrinkles." B is incorrect because III is also mentioned in paragraph 4. C is the best answer because II and III are both mentioned in paragraph 4. D is incorrect because paragraph 4 states that Elam was "without wrinkles", so I is incorrect.

6. **H.** F is incorrect because the yield from Elam's mine is not compared to other mines. G is incorrect because paragraph 1 states that the Moosehide Creek mine allowed Elam to "no more than get his ante back." H is the best answer: paragraph 1 states that "what was left in the ground was twenty thousand more." J is incorrect because other miners are not mentioned.

7. **A.** A is the best answer because the first sentence of paragraph 4 tells us that "despite his garb being similar," Elam was striking. B is incorrect because though the paragraph says Elam looks boyish, it does not say he dresses that way. C is incorrect because visitors from the city are not mentioned in the passage. D is incorrect because Elam dressing in a "ridiculous manner" is not mentioned.

8. **J.** F is incorrect because swindling gamblers is never mentioned. G is incorrect because local news is not mentioned in the passage. H is incorrect because though the "mining camps" of Elam's youth are mentioned, there is no suggestion that Elam held them in "reverence." J is the best answer because paragraph 3 tells us "it was the proper way for a man to express himself socially" and that Elam "knew no other way."

9. **B.** A is incorrect because raising the value of gold is not mentioned. B is the best answer because paragraph 1 states "those that won gold from the ground gambled for it with one another." C is incorrect because "revealing mines" is never mentioned. D is incorrect because "investment" is never mentioned.

10. **G.** F is incorrect because nothing said about Elam suggests he was an idiot. G is the best answer because the final paragraph of the passage says Elam's nature was "essentially savage." H is incorrect because nowhere does it say Elam was meek. J is incorrect because the final paragraph of the passage says Elam's nature was "essentially savage," which is incongruous with the suggestion that he is full of "loving kindness."

11. **C.** A is incorrect because Jefferson is not mentioned in the passage, and Lincoln is not mentioned as being a war hero. B is incorrect because although Washington and de Grasse are mentioned in the passage, neither is mentioned in connection with the Mexican War. C is the best answer because paragraph 4 mentions the heroes "Zachary Taylor and Winfield Scott." D is incorrect because Sam Bowie and Davy Crockett are not mentioned in the passage.

12. **F.** F is the best answer because the last paragraph of the passage states that students should be taught "those acts and policies of [America] wherein she fell below her lofty and humane ideals." G is incorrect because it contradicts the statement mentioned above. H is incorrect because paragraph 5 makes clear that the Mexican war was started by the United States with the purpose of "the extension of slavery." J is incorrect because in the last sentence of paragraph 2 the author states "you probably know that the British burned Washington," referring to students who know something about the War of 1812.

13. **C.** A is incorrect because paragraph 1 clearly states that the author was taught the British started the War of 1812. B is incorrect because paragraph 1 clearly states that the author was taught the British started the War of 1812. C is the best answer because the author says in paragraph 1 that "I thought we had gone to war because England was stopping American ships and taking American sailors out of them for her own service." D is incorrect because the author does not mention Michigan or Ohio as reasons the War of 1812 began.

14. **J.** F is incorrect because II and III are also correct (see explanation for J). G is incorrect because I and II are also correct (see explanation for J). H is incorrect because II is also correct (see explanation for J). J is the best answer because I, II, and III are all supported by the sentence "That during those years [between 1808 and 1812] England had moderated her arrogance, was ready to moderate further and wanted peace; while we, who had been nearly unanimous for war, and with a fuller purse in 1808, were now, by our own congressional fuddling and messing, without any adequate army, and so divided in counsel that only one northern state was wholly in favor of war?"

15. **D.** A is incorrect because the passage does not say there were more French soldiers than American soldiers at the Battle of New Orleans. B is incorrect because the passage does not say there were more French soldiers than American soldiers at the Battle of Guadalupe Hidalgo. C is incorrect because the passage does not say there were more French soldiers than American soldiers at the Battle of Toronto. D is the best answer because the second to the last sentence in paragraph 3 mentions that there were more French soldiers than American soldiers at the Battle of Yorktown.

16. **G.** F is incorrect because the paragraph 5 states "More Americans were against it than had been against the War of 1812." G is the best answer because paragraph 5 states "More Americans were against it than had been against the War of 1812." H is incorrect because the passage does not say that Santa Anna started the war. J is incorrect because the passage does not mention the economy.

17. **A.** A is the best answer because it is a paraphrase of the statement from the final paragraph that "our love of our country would be just as strong, and far more intelligent, were we honestly and wisely taught in our early years those acts and policies of hers wherein she fell below her lofty and humane ideals." B is incorrect because throughout the passage the author asserts that he did not learn the whole story of American history in school. C is incorrect because the author never makes statements that support the concept of "nationalistic bias." D is incorrect because in the last paragraph the author argues that the country would be better off if people were taught the whole truth about American history.

18. **F.** F is the best answer because only II is correct, supported by the contention presented in paragraph 5 that "the whole discreditable business had the extension of slavery at the bottom of it." G is incorrect because I is wrong; the passage does not mention "strengthening alliances." H is incorrect because I is wrong; the passage does not mention "strengthening alliances." J is incorrect because although, in reality, statement III may have been true, this fact is not mentioned or supported anywhere in the passage.

19. **C.** A is incorrect because paragraph 5 begins with the phrase "General Grant, who had fought with credit as a lieutenant in the Mexican War." B is

incorrect because paragraph 5 begins with the phrase "General Grant, who had fought with credit as a lieutenant in the Mexican War." C is the best answer because paragraph 5 begins with the phrase "General Grant, who had fought with credit as a lieutenant in the Mexican War." D is incorrect because paragraph 5 begins with the phrase "General Grant, who had fought with credit as a lieutenant in the Mexican War."

20. **J.** F is incorrect because London is not mentioned in the passage. G is incorrect because the Battle of New Orleans is not mentioned in connection with the burning of Washington. H is incorrect because the victory in New York is not mentioned in connection with the burning of Washington. J is the best answer because paragraph 2 ends with the sentence "You probably did know that the British burned Washington, and you accordingly hated them for this barbarous vandalism—but did you know that we had burned Toronto a year earlier," that infers a connection between the attack on Toronto and the burning of Washington.

21. **A.** A is the best answer because the context of "shrewdness" supports a child's ability to evaluate adult behavior. B is incorrect because "cunning" implies a sneakiness the author never attributes to children. C is incorrect because a child's intelligence and/or stupidity is not mentioned in this passage. D is incorrect because "depravity" implies unnatural behavior on a child's part that is not discussed in the passage.

22. **J.** F is incorrect because although I is correct (see explanation for J), so are II and III (see explanation for J). G is incorrect because although III is correct (see explanation for J), so are I and II (see explanation for J). H is incorrect because although II and III are correct (see explanation for J), so is I (see explanation for J). J is the best answer because I, II and III are all correct. I is supported by the phrase in paragraph 1, "educators who, day in and day out, are consciously transforming the environment and themselves." II is supported by the sentence in paragraph 1, "Most people live on the capital and interest of an education, which perhaps once made them model children but has deprived them of the desire for educating themselves." The implication here is that, unless one maintains this desire for education, one can't be a good educator. III is supported by the sentence in paragraph 1, "It means

the humble realization of the truth that the ways of injuring the child are infinite, while the ways of being useful to him are few."

23. **C.** A is incorrect because this sentence is used as an example of an attribute of old education that current education does not have. B is incorrect because while the context of the sentence implies the old education did not necessarily develop personalities, is does not imply anywhere that old education meant to suppress such development. C is the best answer because, although the sentence prior to this one implies that the old education did have excellent qualities, the fact that it "did not form" personality is depicted as a negative quality in the rest of the passage, which stresses the importance of developing children's individual personalities. D is incorrect because it is contradicted by the sentence in paragraph 4, "it is essential that education shall awake the feeling of independence; it should invigorate and favor the disposition to deviate from the type." This sentence stresses that new education does try to form personality.

24. **G.** F is incorrect because it is explicitly mentioned in the passage as a precept of the author's philosophy of education. G is the best answer because it is an assumed fact of human nature and the only answer which is not a directive explicitly mentioned within the author's philosophy of education. H is incorrect because it is explicitly mentioned in the passage as a precept of the author's philosophy of education. J is incorrect because it is explicitly mentioned in the passage as a precept of the author's philosophy of education.

25. **B.** A is incorrect because the context of paragraph 4 does not discuss how easy or difficult it is to develop any type of personality in children, much less strong ones. B is the best answer because the statement in paragraph 4, "for the progress of the whole of the species, as well as of society, it is essential that education shall awake the feeling of independence" supports the idea that without individualism, society will weaken. The sentence in paragraph 4, "Using other people's opinion as a standard results in subordinating one's self to their will" implies that if one tries to conform, the danger is that one will be under the power of other, stronger personalities. C is incorrect because although the context of the phrase encourages the development of personality in children, the Superman

personalities are presented as a negative influence that people end up subordinating themselves to, as the phrase, "Using other people's opinion as a standard results in subordinating one's self to their will" in paragraph 4 implies. D is incorrect because the whole point of paragraph 4 is that people do not conform their behavior to others but rather they develop their individuality.

26. **H.** F is incorrect because in paragraph 2, insensitive behavior is stated to "leave wounds that last for life in the finely strung soul of the child," indicating that insensitive treatment affects children regardless of their outward reaction to it. G is incorrect because the phrase from paragraph 5, "the sensitive feelings of children are constantly injured by lack of consideration on the part of grown people" directly contradicts it. H is the best answer because it is supported by the phrase from paragraph 5, "the sensitive feelings of children are constantly injured by lack of consideration on the part of grown people." J is incorrect because in the second paragraph, kind treatment of children is said to "make quite as deep an impression" as negative treatment does, indicating that children internalize good and bad treatment equally.

27. **D.** A is incorrect because how fairly a parent reprimands a child is not mentioned in this passage. B is incorrect because the first paragraph states natural education should ignore "the faults of children nine times out of ten," implying that children should not be allowed to do what they want *all* the time. C is incorrect because the fourth paragraph specifically states that a new educator "rejoice when he sees in the child tendencies to deviation" from society, indicating that natural education enables a child to deviate from, not conform to society. D is the best answer because the first phrase in paragraph 1, "the art of natural education consists in ignoring the faults of children nine times out of ten" supports the idea that fault control is not important to natural education, while the entire fourth paragraph is devoted to the importance of developing a child's individuality.

28. **F.** F is the best answer because the phrase that directly follows it, "the humble realization of the truth that the ways of injuring the child are infinite, while the ways of being useful to him are few" implies adult flaws injure children. G is incorrect because, while the first paragraph states,

"educators who . . . are consciously transforming the environment and themselves are a rare product," indicating that there are few people truly good at child-rearing, no where in the passage is child-rearing referred to as divine. H is incorrect because although "setting one's feet on a narrow path" in paragraph 1 may seem to indicate a limitation, the line that follows it, "the humble realization of the truth that the ways of injuring the child are infinite, while the ways of being useful to him are few," indicates that the narrow path is actually the educator's navigation of the treatment of children. J is incorrect because in paragraph 4, the phrase referring to child rearing and education as being "for the progress of the whole of the species, as well as of society" implies that such an outcome is indeed fulfilling.

29. **C.** A is incorrect because II is incorrect. B is incorrect because, although III is, I is also correct. C is the best answer because I and III are correct and II is incorrect. I is supported by the statement in the fifth paragraph that "the new educator must remember that the sensitive nature of children are constantly injured by lack of consideration on the part of grown people." III is supported by the statement in paragraph 5, "Would I consent to be treated as I have just treated my child." II is incorrect because although the passage does imply that children are in need of guidance, it does not portray children as disobedient creatures but rather as sensitive, fallible beings. D is incorrect because, although I and III are correct, II is not correct.

30. **J.** F is incorrect because "manipulator" implies an underhanded, conscious desire on the part of a good educator to control the child, which directly contradicts one of the main points of the passage—that an educator must sensitively guide a child towards individuality. G is incorrect because no where does the passage stress the educator as a "worrier." H is incorrect because the context of "providence" implies that the educator will be invisibly guiding the child through his example, not merely observing the child's behavior. J is the best answer because the context of "providence" supports the image of the educator as an influential figure from whose example the child learns.

31. **B.** A is incorrect because although the passage mentions matter and antimatter annihilating each other in paragraph 7, it is only a small portion of the

passage. B is the best answer because paragraph 2 ends with the statement that the vacuum is dynamic and paragraphs 3–8 deal with the different ways the vacuum fluctuates. C is incorrect because although the Special Theory of Relativity is mentioned in paragraph 9, it is not the main idea of the passage. D is incorrect because though extracting energy from space is mentioned in paragraph 6, it is mentioned nowhere else in the passage.

32. **F.** F is the best answer because paragraph 8 states "One metaphor that has been proposed is that the dynamic vacuum is like the surface of a lake." G is incorrect because although a thin disk of matter is mentioned in paragraph 1 it is used to describe the planets. H is incorrect because "a dozen lotteries" is used in paragraph 1 of the passage to describe the chances of finding matter, not to describe the actual vacuum. J is incorrect because a room full of oxygen is never mentioned in the passage.

33. **C.** A is incorrect because Einstein did not formulate the uncertainty principle. (see explanation for C) B is incorrect because Michealson and Morley did not formulate the uncertainty principle. (see explanation for C) C is the best answer because paragraph 3 states "Named after its discoverer Werner Heisenberg, the uncertainly principle basically states." D is incorrect because Aristotle did not formulate the uncertainty principle. (see explanation for C)

34. **J.** F is incorrect because rotation means spin, and the particles are vibrating. G is incorrect because speed means to quick movement, and the particles are vibrating. H is incorrect because the particles are vibrating, not changing. J is the best answer because paragraph 3 states that we should "think of particles as constantly vibrating waves."

35. **C.** A is incorrect because the statement is supported by paragraph 3 (the uncertainty principle). B is incorrect because the statement is supported by the information in paragraph 5. C is the best answer because the ether was disproved by Einstein in 1905 so it could not be part of the theory of quantum mechanics, which was developed in the 1920's. D is incorrect because the statement is supported by the information in paragraph 7.

36. **J.** F is incorrect because according to the third paragraph subatomic particles have a "peculiar nature" that makes them unlike visible objects like motes of dust. G is incorrect because the entire passage makes reference to the vacuum as a dynamic, fluctuating entity. H is incorrect because according to the final paragraph of the passage, waves of light behave unlike other waves. J is the best answer because paragraph 1 states that "the universe is mostly made up of empty space." This idea is repeated in paragraph 2.

37. **C.** A is incorrect because no connection is made in the passage between Einstein and tapping the fluctuation of energy in the vacuum. B is incorrect because finding where the fluctuations take place is not mentioned in paragraph 6 as a reason tapping the energy cannot be accomplished. C is the best answer because according to paragraph 6, in order to "tap the energy" you would need to "break several basic laws of physics." D is incorrect because a "massive explosion" resulting from the tapped energy is not discussed.

38. **H.** F is incorrect because the passage does not say that atoms are grouped together. (see explanation for H) G is incorrect because the passage does not say that most atoms in interstellar space are hydrogen. Although this may be truthful, it is not suggested by the passage and it therefore an incorrect answer choice. (see explanation for H) H is the best answer because according to paragraph 1: "Between the vastly spread out solar systems and galaxies are regions of interstellar space where there may be less than one atom per square mile." J is incorrect because the passage does not say that atoms in interstellar space are different than other atoms.

39. **A.** A is the best answer because the passage ends with a reference to "the great ether beast that had been loosed upon science by Aristotle." B is incorrect because Einstein refuted the idea of the ether (final paragraph). C is incorrect because Michelson and Morley attacked the idea of the ether (final paragraph). D is incorrect because Heisenberg is not mentioned in reference to the ether.

40. **G.** F is incorrect because the fourth paragraph does not mention the way people perceive reality. G is the best answer because the fourth paragraph mentions "constantly vibrating waves" and that particles "always shake to some degree." H is incorrect because though the statement in H is supported by the information in paragraph 3, it is not the main idea of paragraph 4. J is incorrect because nowhere

in the passage does it state that a vacuum slows down the movement of particles.

4. Science Reasoning Test

1. **A.** Looking at the table, at 1.5% salt concentration, the final weight was 2.30 g and the final volume was 2.09 ml.

2. **F.** In the 0.0% NaCl solution, the final weight is 3.25 g and the final volume is 3.25 ml. This is the only sample that gives a density less than 1 g/ml.

3. **A.** The percentage weight change at lower concentrations is positive and the percentage weight change at higher concentrations is negative.

4. **H.** The isotonic state is the point at which there is no net movement of water between the semi-permeable membrane. This would have occurred in between 0.5% and 1.0% salt concentration according to the data in the table.

5. **D.** According the table, if the NaCl concentration were increased above 5%, the volume and weight of the potato core should decrease.

6. **F.** When the core was submerged in water with no NaCl concentration, the weight and volume of the core increased. Water will move toward the area of greater solute concentration. The core had to have some NaCl concentration, otherwise the water would not have been absorbed.

7. **B.** The isotonic state for the second variety would be reached at a higher NaCl than the other variety, therefore the initial NaCl concentration in the second variety would be higher than in the first.

8. **F.** Only Geologist 1 accounts for the 40,000 year cycles.

9. **C.** Both geologists believe that orbital motion has an effect on cooling trends. The two geologists only differ as to the mechanism for cooling.

10. **J.** Geologist 1 does not address the impact of extraterrestrial debris on Earth's temperature.

11. **A.** Geologist 1 proposes that orbital tilt can affect the amount of heat the Earth receives form the Sun.

12. **G.** Geologist 2 assumes that the orbit of the earth does not contribute to cooling trends.

13. **B.** Looking at Table 1, coffee has the indicated hydrogen ion concentration.

14. **J.** Thymol blue will turn in the presence of pH greater than 9.6. Household ammonia is the only substance listed with a pH this high.

15. **D.** The most basic substance will have the highest pH. Of the four substances, Borax has the highest pH.

16. **H.** Methyl violet needs a pH change of 2, alizarin yellow g needs a pH change of 1.9, methyl red needs a pH change of 2.1, and phenolphthalein needs a pH change of 1.7.

17. **C.** To be converted to its acidic form, the pH level would need to be 6.0 or lower. Coffee is the only substance among the answers with a pH low enough.

18. **F.** Looking at the table, lead requires 24.5 kJ/kg to change from the solid to liquid phase. Since 1 kg is being changed, 24.5 kJ is required.

19. **D.** Liquid phase exists between melting point and boiling point. Gold is liquid over the widest range of temperatures.

20. **G.** Look at the table and compare the substances. Nitrogen and helium have a difference of 180 kJ/kg, lead and ethyl alcohol have a difference of 58 kJ/kg, silver and lead have a difference of 1,423 kJ/kg, and water and gold have a difference of 675 J/kg.

21. **A.** If silver and water were not considered, the greater the boiling point, the greater the heat of vaporization would be.

22. **J.** Lead and silver are both liquid at 1,000 degrees.

23. **C.** The only hypothesis that is supported by the data is that as melting point decreases, boiling point decreases.

24. **J.** Look at Figure 1 at the point at which 0.4 mg of antigen was added. The graph shows that the amount of precipitate would be close to 12 mg.

25. **C.** Look at Figure 2 and see at what levels the antigen must be to yield 8 mg of precipitate.

26. **H.** The zone of equivalence was reached when 1.5 mg of antigen was added. The graph is at its maximum at this point.

27. **B.** The equivalence zone would shift to the right and down because the point at 1 mg antigen would yield the most precipitate. It would appear that all of the available antibody and antigen were used at an antigen level of 1 mg.

28. **F.** When 0.2 mg of either antigen was added, there was antibody present that did not precipitate because there was not enough antigen added relative to the amount of antibody present.

29. **D.** As antigen levels were increased above 0.5 mg, the antigen took up too much space relative to the antibody; the antibody could not sufficiently bind to the antigen to form the precipitate.

30. **G.** From the chart, the first ionization energy for silicon is 780 kJ/mol.

31. **A.** Look at the table at each element and look at the difference between I_1 and I_2. The difference for sodium is 4,070 and is greater than any of the other elements.

32. **H.** If aluminum and sulfur were not considered, the ionization energies would increase as atomic radius decreases.

33. **C.** The table shows that as atomic radius decreases, atomic number increases and visa versa.

34. **J.** All three elements have ionization energies that increase by at least a factor of three after the electrons in the outer shell are removed.

35. **A.** From Winter to Spring, the salinity changed from 0 to 29.

36. **H.** As salinity changes at the ocean floor, the number of *gammarus locusta* changes the most drastically.

37. **B.** When the salmon catch is high, the number of protein deficiency-related illnesses is low and when the salmon catch is low, the number of protein deficiency-related illnesses is high.

38. **J.** This is the only answer that is consistent with the number of illnesses recorded.

39. **C.** There is no primary season for fur seal hunting, since they seem to be caught at fluctuating levels throughout the year.

40. **G.** This would force the bears to depend upon their natural food supply and not rely on the food taken from the village.

PRACTICE EXAMINATION 3

Answer Sheet

1. English Test

1 (A) (B) (C) (D)   20 (F) (G) (H) (J)   39 (A) (B) (C) (D)   58 (F) (G) (H) (J)
2 (F) (G) (H) (J)   21 (A) (B) (C) (D)   40 (F) (G) (H) (J)   59 (A) (B) (C) (D)
3 (A) (B) (C) (D)   22 (F) (G) (H) (J)   41 (A) (B) (C) (D)   60 (F) (G) (H) (J)
4 (F) (G) (H) (J)   23 (A) (B) (C) (D)   42 (F) (G) (H) (J)   61 (A) (B) (C) (D)
5 (A) (B) (C) (D)   24 (F) (G) (H) (J)   43 (A) (B) (C) (D)   62 (F) (G) (H) (J)
6 (F) (G) (H) (J)   25 (A) (B) (C) (D)   44 (F) (G) (H) (J)   63 (A) (B) (C) (D)
7 (A) (B) (C) (D)   26 (F) (G) (H) (J)   45 (A) (B) (C) (D)   64 (F) (G) (H) (J)
8 (F) (G) (H) (J)   27 (A) (B) (C) (D)   46 (F) (G) (H) (J)   65 (A) (B) (C) (D)
9 (A) (B) (C) (D)   28 (F) (G) (H) (J)   47 (A) (B) (C) (D)   66 (F) (G) (H) (J)
10 (F) (G) (H) (J)   29 (A) (B) (C) (D)   48 (F) (G) (H) (J)   67 (A) (B) (C) (D)
11 (A) (B) (C) (D)   30 (F) (G) (H) (J)   49 (A) (B) (C) (D)   68 (F) (G) (H) (J)
12 (F) (G) (H) (J)   31 (A) (B) (C) (D)   50 (F) (G) (H) (J)   69 (A) (B) (C) (D)
13 (A) (B) (C) (D)   32 (F) (G) (H) (J)   51 (A) (B) (C) (D)   70 (F) (G) (H) (J)
14 (F) (G) (H) (J)   33 (A) (B) (C) (D)   52 (F) (G) (H) (J)   71 (A) (B) (C) (D)
15 (A) (B) (C) (D)   34 (F) (G) (H) (J)   53 (A) (B) (C) (D)   72 (F) (G) (H) (J)
16 (F) (G) (H) (J)   35 (A) (B) (C) (D)   54 (F) (G) (H) (J)   73 (A) (B) (C) (D)
17 (A) (B) (C) (D)   36 (F) (G) (H) (J)   55 (A) (B) (C) (D)   74 (F) (G) (H) (J)
18 (F) (G) (H) (J)   37 (A) (B) (C) (D)   56 (F) (G) (H) (J)   75 (A) (B) (C) (D)
19 (A) (B) (C) (D)   38 (F) (G) (H) (J)   57 (A) (B) (C) (D)

2. Mathematics Test

1 (A) (B) (C) (D) (E)   16 (F) (G) (H) (J) (K)   31 (A) (B) (C) (D) (E)   46 (F) (G) (H) (J) (K)
2 (F) (G) (H) (J) (K)   17 (A) (B) (C) (D) (E)   32 (F) (G) (H) (J) (K)   47 (A) (B) (C) (D) (E)
3 (A) (B) (C) (D) (E)   18 (F) (G) (H) (J) (K)   33 (A) (B) (C) (D) (E)   48 (F) (G) (H) (J) (K)
4 (F) (G) (H) (J) (K)   19 (A) (B) (C) (D) (E)   34 (F) (G) (H) (J) (K)   49 (A) (B) (C) (D) (E)
5 (A) (B) (C) (D) (E)   20 (F) (G) (H) (J) (K)   35 (A) (B) (C) (D) (E)   50 (F) (G) (H) (J) (K)
6 (F) (G) (H) (J) (K)   21 (A) (B) (C) (D) (E)   36 (F) (G) (H) (J) (K)   51 (A) (B) (C) (D) (E)
7 (A) (B) (C) (D) (E)   22 (F) (G) (H) (J) (K)   37 (A) (B) (C) (D) (E)   52 (F) (G) (H) (J) (K)
8 (F) (G) (H) (J) (K)   23 (A) (B) (C) (D) (E)   38 (F) (G) (H) (J) (K)   53 (A) (B) (C) (D) (E)
9 (A) (B) (C) (D) (E)   24 (F) (G) (H) (J) (K)   39 (A) (B) (C) (D) (E)   54 (F) (G) (H) (J) (K)
10 (F) (G) (H) (J) (K)   25 (A) (B) (C) (D) (E)   40 (F) (G) (H) (J) (K)   55 (A) (B) (C) (D) (E)
11 (A) (B) (C) (D) (E)   26 (F) (G) (H) (J) (K)   41 (A) (B) (C) (D) (E)   56 (F) (G) (H) (J) (K)
12 (F) (G) (H) (J) (K)   27 (A) (B) (C) (D) (E)   42 (F) (G) (H) (J) (K)   57 (A) (B) (C) (D) (E)
13 (A) (B) (C) (D) (E)   28 (F) (G) (H) (J) (K)   43 (A) (B) (C) (D) (E)   58 (F) (G) (H) (J) (K)
14 (F) (G) (H) (J) (K)   29 (A) (B) (C) (D) (E)   44 (F) (G) (H) (J) (K)   59 (F) (G) (H) (J) (K)
15 (A) (B) (C) (D) (E)   30 (F) (G) (H) (J) (K)   45 (A) (B) (C) (D) (E)   60 (A) (B) (C) (D) (E)

3. Reading Test

1 Ⓐ Ⓑ Ⓒ Ⓓ	11 Ⓐ Ⓑ Ⓒ Ⓓ	21 Ⓐ Ⓑ Ⓒ Ⓓ	31 Ⓐ Ⓑ Ⓒ Ⓓ
2 Ⓕ Ⓖ Ⓗ Ⓙ	12 Ⓕ Ⓖ Ⓗ Ⓙ	22 Ⓕ Ⓖ Ⓗ Ⓙ	32 Ⓕ Ⓖ Ⓗ Ⓙ
3 Ⓐ Ⓑ Ⓒ Ⓓ	13 Ⓐ Ⓑ Ⓒ Ⓓ	23 Ⓐ Ⓑ Ⓒ Ⓓ	33 Ⓐ Ⓑ Ⓒ Ⓓ
4 Ⓕ Ⓖ Ⓗ Ⓙ	14 Ⓕ Ⓖ Ⓗ Ⓙ	24 Ⓕ Ⓖ Ⓗ Ⓙ	34 Ⓕ Ⓖ Ⓗ Ⓙ
5 Ⓐ Ⓑ Ⓒ Ⓓ	15 Ⓐ Ⓑ Ⓒ Ⓓ	25 Ⓐ Ⓑ Ⓒ Ⓓ	35 Ⓐ Ⓑ Ⓒ Ⓓ
6 Ⓕ Ⓖ Ⓗ Ⓙ	16 Ⓕ Ⓖ Ⓗ Ⓙ	26 Ⓕ Ⓖ Ⓗ Ⓙ	36 Ⓕ Ⓖ Ⓗ Ⓙ
7 Ⓐ Ⓑ Ⓒ Ⓓ	17 Ⓐ Ⓑ Ⓒ Ⓓ	27 Ⓐ Ⓑ Ⓒ Ⓓ	37 Ⓐ Ⓑ Ⓒ Ⓓ
8 Ⓕ Ⓖ Ⓗ Ⓙ	18 Ⓕ Ⓖ Ⓗ Ⓙ	28 Ⓕ Ⓖ Ⓗ Ⓙ	38 Ⓕ Ⓖ Ⓗ Ⓙ
9 Ⓐ Ⓑ Ⓒ Ⓓ	19 Ⓐ Ⓑ Ⓒ Ⓓ	29 Ⓐ Ⓑ Ⓒ Ⓓ	39 Ⓐ Ⓑ Ⓒ Ⓓ
10 Ⓕ Ⓖ Ⓗ Ⓙ	20 Ⓕ Ⓖ Ⓗ Ⓙ	30 Ⓕ Ⓖ Ⓗ Ⓙ	40 Ⓕ Ⓖ Ⓗ Ⓙ

4. Science Reasoning Test

1 Ⓐ Ⓑ Ⓒ Ⓓ	11 Ⓐ Ⓑ Ⓒ Ⓓ	21 Ⓐ Ⓑ Ⓒ Ⓓ	31 Ⓐ Ⓑ Ⓒ Ⓓ
2 Ⓕ Ⓖ Ⓗ Ⓙ	12 Ⓕ Ⓖ Ⓗ Ⓙ	22 Ⓕ Ⓖ Ⓗ Ⓙ	32 Ⓕ Ⓖ Ⓗ Ⓙ
3 Ⓐ Ⓑ Ⓒ Ⓓ	13 Ⓐ Ⓑ Ⓒ Ⓓ	23 Ⓐ Ⓑ Ⓒ Ⓓ	33 Ⓐ Ⓑ Ⓒ Ⓓ
4 Ⓕ Ⓖ Ⓗ Ⓙ	14 Ⓕ Ⓖ Ⓗ Ⓙ	24 Ⓕ Ⓖ Ⓗ Ⓙ	34 Ⓕ Ⓖ Ⓗ Ⓙ
5 Ⓐ Ⓑ Ⓒ Ⓓ	15 Ⓐ Ⓑ Ⓒ Ⓓ	25 Ⓐ Ⓑ Ⓒ Ⓓ	35 Ⓐ Ⓑ Ⓒ Ⓓ
6 Ⓕ Ⓖ Ⓗ Ⓙ	16 Ⓕ Ⓖ Ⓗ Ⓙ	26 Ⓕ Ⓖ Ⓗ Ⓙ	36 Ⓕ Ⓖ Ⓗ Ⓙ
7 Ⓐ Ⓑ Ⓒ Ⓓ	17 Ⓐ Ⓑ Ⓒ Ⓓ	27 Ⓐ Ⓑ Ⓒ Ⓓ	37 Ⓐ Ⓑ Ⓒ Ⓓ
8 Ⓕ Ⓖ Ⓗ Ⓙ	18 Ⓕ Ⓖ Ⓗ Ⓙ	28 Ⓕ Ⓖ Ⓗ Ⓙ	38 Ⓕ Ⓖ Ⓗ Ⓙ
9 Ⓐ Ⓑ Ⓒ Ⓓ	19 Ⓐ Ⓑ Ⓒ Ⓓ	29 Ⓐ Ⓑ Ⓒ Ⓓ	39 Ⓐ Ⓑ Ⓒ Ⓓ
10 Ⓕ Ⓖ Ⓗ Ⓙ	20 Ⓕ Ⓖ Ⓗ Ⓙ	30 Ⓕ Ⓖ Ⓗ Ⓙ	40 Ⓕ Ⓖ Ⓗ Ⓙ

Practice Examination 3

1. ENGLISH TEST

75 Questions • Time—45 Minutes

Directions: This test consists of five passages in which particular words or phrases are underlined and numbered. Alongside the passage, you will see alternative words and phrases that could be substituted for the underlined part. You must select the alternative that expresses the idea most clearly and correctly or that best fits the style and tone of the entire passage. If the original version is best, select "No Change."

The test also includes questions about entire paragraphs and the passage as a whole. These questions are identified by a number in a box.

After you select the correct answer for each question, mark the oval representing the correct answer on your answer sheet.

Passage I

The Names of Flowers

<1>

I <u>look and stare</u> at the first green shoots
1

sprouting up through the dead leaves.

The sight sets me trembling <u>with anticipation,</u>
2

and I kneel <u>down</u> toward the earth to make
3

sure I've seen right. Yes, the daffodils

<u>are already pushing</u> toward the sun. As if in a
4

<u>fever I forget my work and wander</u> about the
5

garden inspecting the mulched beds. Winter

is almost over, and I can taste the coming

delirium of flowers.

1. A. NO CHANGE
    B. look, staring
    C. looking and staring
    D. stare

2. F. NO CHANGE
    G. to anticipate
    H. and anticipating
    J. OMIT the underlined portion.

3. A. NO CHANGE
    B. forward
    C. downward
    D. OMIT the underlined portion.

4. F. NO CHANGE
    G. have already pushed
    H. could already be pushing
    J. push

5. A. NO CHANGE
    B. fever, I forget my work and wander
    C. fever, I forget my work, and wander
    D. fever I forget my work, and wander

GO ON TO THE NEXT PAGE ➡

<2>

Gardening is something new to me, a

delight this city boy never imagined. Raised

in an apartment in New York, it <u>seems</u> enough to
                                    6

know that there were flowers and trees. <u>Culture</u>
                                                    7

<u>marked even more than the seasons were by</u>
                      7

<u>nature.</u> In autumn, we played football in the
    7

street, or when I was older, tried to pick the peak

foliage weekend to go camping. We were

familiar with the highlights that marked each

season, <u>whereas</u> the subtle particulars, the
          8

gradual way one transformed into another.

That intimacy was reserved for buildings,

crowds, and subway trains. [9]

<3>

Now the twilight of summer is marked for

me by budding chrysanthemums that spill over

the retaining wall <u>on</u> the side of the house. In
                    10

two seasons, they've grown huge and

sprawling. At the height of autumn they are

as <u>bright yellow and red and purple</u> as
        11

any foliage and the season ends when they turn

brown, when the last rose buds on the climbers

leaning up the porch fail to open.

6. F. NO CHANGE
   G. does seem
   H. did seem
   J. seemed

7. A. NO CHANGE
   B. Even culture was marked more than the seasons were by nature.
   C. Even the seasons were marked more by culture than by nature.
   D. Seasons were marked more even by culture than by nature.

8. F. NO CHANGE
   G. though not
   H. even though not
   J. while not

9. The purpose of Paragraph 2 as it relates to the remainder of the essay is primarily:
   A. to provide background that helps to explain the significance of the garden to the writer.
   B. to provide background that explains why the writer feels lucky to have escaped the city.
   C. to portray the writer's childhood as vividly as the writer's garden.
   D. to establish the writer's sensitive personality and ability to appreciate flowers.

10. F. NO CHANGE
    G. over
    H. for
    J. at

11. A. NO CHANGE
    B. bright, yellow, and red and purple
    C. bright, yellow, and red, and purple
    D. bright yellow, and red, and purple

<4>

Daffodils along the front walk <u>mark</u> the
                                12

beginning of a long Missouri spring that unfolds with

crocuses and tulips, irises and peonies under my study

window, forsythia and spirea around the edges of the

lawn. Summer means daisies swaying on the hill, and

later, black-eyed susans jostling along the fence.

<5>

At thirty-five, I'm beginning to learn the

names of flowers, and more than just the names.

Names are our entry into the world, and I feel a

fresh side of myself come alive as I become

familiar with the words <u>standing</u> for all those
                              13

vivid scents and colors springing from the

ground. It's nice to know that one can keep

on growing, finding enough space inside for

gardens and for subway trains. [14] [15]

12. F. NO CHANGE
     G. have marked
     H. marks
     J. marked

13. A. NO CHANGE
     B. that stand
     C. who stand
     D. whose stand

Items 14 and 15 pose questions about the essay as a whole.

14. Is the writer's use of contractions appropriate
     in the essay?
     F. No; it creates confusion when the writer
         switches from the present to the past.
     G. No; it creates an informal tone that is
         inappropriate for the subject.
     H. Yes; it creates an informal tone that is
         appropriate for the intimate nature of the
         subject.
     J. Yes; it helps to focus the essay on the
         specific flowers in the garden.

15. The writer wishes to insert the following detail
     into the essay:
     I could tell you there were pines, but not distin-
     guish them from cedar.
     The sentence would most logically be inserted
     into Paragraph:
     A. 1
     B. 2
     C. 3
     D. 4

GO ON TO THE NEXT PAGE ➤

Passage II

Pasta and Tomatoes

<1>

As trade goes, <u>so also</u> goes the world. In
                16
these days of global markets where people and
goods crisscross the world, the idea that a
development in Asia can have a major effect
on America is <u>taken for granted</u>. Less
                                17

commonly understood <u>was</u> the fact that
                          18

exchange has always been a motor force in
world affairs.

<2>

[19] Agricultural techniques developed in
the Near East spread deeper into Asia, as well as
Europe and Africa, evolving form as they went.

<u>Goods, religion, knowledge, all of these things</u>
                        20

<u>have moved</u> about through the ages, adopted
      20

here by one people, forced on another people
there, and every wealth of interchange, saw too a
wealth of transformation.

16. F. NO CHANGE
     G. So therefore,
     H. also
     J. so

17. A. NO CHANGE
     B. not taken for granted
     C. not well understood
     D. hard to fathom

18. F. NO CHANGE
     G. is
     H. had been
     J. could be

19. Which of the following sentences, if inserted at
     this point, would provide the most effective
     transition to the second paragraph?
     A. Throughout history, agriculture has
         always played a major role in the
         development of civilizations.
     B. Throughout history, the movement of
         people and goods has been a major factor
         in changing human societies.
     C. Many examples can be found in the
         history of trade during the past fifty
         years.
     D. However, this phenomenon was never as
         important as it is in the modern world.

20. F. NO CHANGE
     G. Goods, religion, knowledge: all of these
         things have moved
     H. Movement has occurred in goods,
         religion, and knowledge
     J. Goods, religion and knowledge have all
         moved

<3>

That is why Herodotus could marvel at the different practices he found upon his <u>tour, of</u> the [21]

ancient Mediterranean, and why too his impressions <u>had been</u> passed on to generations [22]

born two millennium later. In fact, the ancient Greeks, <u>whom</u> were well aware of the influences [23] of Egypt on their civilization, did not pass their wealth of knowledge directly on to Modern Europe who claims Greece as its root. Greek thought was kept alive by Arab scholars at the height of Islam's <u>power, Greek</u> texts had to be [24] translated from Arabic into Latin before the likes of Thomas Aquinas could open the intellectual door to the European Renaissance.

<4>

But perhaps the clearest examples of this exchange and transformation lay in a realm less heady and much closer to the stomach.

<u>How would modern Italy be</u> without [25]

pasta and tomatoes? <u>Imagine</u> Switzerland [26]

without chocolate or Ireland and Eastern Europe without potatoes. [27]

21. A. NO CHANGE
    B. tour—of
    C. tour; of
    D. tour of

22. F. NO CHANGE
    G. have been
    H. are
    J. will be

23. A. NO CHANGE
    B. that
    C. who
    D. which

24. F. NO CHANGE
    G. power, and Greek
    H. power, but Greek
    J. power, therefore Greek

25. A. NO CHANGE
    B. What would modern Italy be like
    C. Where would modern Italy be
    D. Would modern Italy be

26. F. NO CHANGE
    G. Can you imagine
    H. Try to imagine
    J. Isn't it strange to imagine

27. Which of the alternatives provides the most logical conclusion for Paragraph 4?
    A. Yet none of these familiar staples were known in the Europe of the Middle Ages.
    B. These staples have become part of the very identity of these nations.
    C. They would not be the same countries that they are today.
    D. Cuisine is an important element of every culture.

GO ON TO THE NEXT PAGE

<5>

Marco Polo brought pasta back to Europe

from China. Tomatoes, potatoes and <u>cacao,</u>
                                        28

<u>they</u> were all brought back from the Americas
28

and transformed into something else.

<u>Therefore</u> while neither pasta nor tomatoes is
29

originally Italian, <u>one cannot think of pasta</u>
                          30

<u>and tomato sauce in all its glorious forms</u>
               30

<u>without thinking of Italy</u>.
        30

Passage III
The Uncharted Waters of Alternative Medicine

<1>

Enter any large Natural foods store, head to

the homeopathic section, and you are liable to

find yourself bewildered by a sea of herbal

<u>remedies, each</u> claiming a variety of medicinal
        31

properties. It is very difficult to know which

works and <u>what</u> doesn't. Often, the choice
              32

comes down to trial and error mixed with a

good dose of faith.

<2>

The same can be said of techniques like

<u>the one called acupuncture</u>. No one has
        33

28. F. NO CHANGE
     G. cacao,
     H. cacao
     J. cacao, which

29. A. NO CHANGE
     B. Because
     C. Since
     D. For

30. Which of the alternatives would conclude this
     sentence so that it supports the writer's point
     about culture ?
     F. NO CHANGE
     G. they have been adapted by Italians.
     H. they are now important in Italian cooking.
     J. one cannot forget that they were once
         unknown in Italy.

31. A. NO CHANGE
     B. remedies; each
     C. remedies, and each
     D. remedies each

32. F. NO CHANGE
     G. who
     H. which
     J. why it

33. A. NO CHANGE
     B. that which is called acupuncture
     C. acupuncture
     D. anything such as acupuncture

ever been able to prove the existence of energy
paths in the body, the theory upon which
acupuncture is based. Yet a video clip of a
Chinese woman giving birth while eating a
                    34
bowl of rice is very convincing as to
acupuncture's effectiveness against pain.

<3>

(1) Yet perhaps one of the reasons that
alternative medicine is booming today
has been precisely because in an era in which
 35
invasive medical procedures and antibiotics
are prescribed at the drop of hat, people have
become less trusting of medical science. (2) The
medical profession has traditionally scoffed at
the claims of alternative medicine. (3) When
anecdotal evidence of it's successes is trotted
                    36
out, doctors have routinely put it down to the
placebo effect. (4) Clearly drugs and
technology, as valuable as they are, all the
                    37
answers to health do not hold. [38]
 37

<4>

The antagonism between medical science
and alternative medicine is older, than
                    39
most people know. In fact, the American
Medical Association was founded in 1846
mostly in response to the nation's first medical

34. F. NO CHANGE
     G. that gives birth
     H. who gave birth
     J. to give birth

35. A. NO CHANGE
     B. is
     C. are
     D. will be

36. F. NO CHANGE
     G. its'
     H. its
     J. OMIT the underlined portion.

37. A. NO CHANGE
     B. hold not all the answers to health
     C. don't pertain to all the answers for health
     D. do not hold all the answers for health

38. Which of the following sequences will make
     Paragraph 3 most logical?
     F. NO CHANGE
     G. 2, 3, 1, 4
     H. 2, 4, 1, 3
     J. 4, 1, 2, 3

39. A. NO CHANGE
     B. older; than
     C. older than
     D. older: than

GO ON TO THE NEXT PAGE

association, the American Institute of
Homeopathy. The A.M.A. set the standard for
medical <u>licenses; and</u> was quick to exclude
            40
any doctor who had even associated with
someone practicing homeopathy.

<5>

[41] Younger doctors are beginning to
acknowledge the limits of bio-medical
understanding and admit that there

<u>might or might not indeed</u> be healing properties
            42
in plants or treatments that may be effective even
if we don't know how they work. Recently, a
major drug company signed a contract with
China to develop pharmaceuticals from
traditional Chinese medicine. Finally, we are
beginning to see serious attempts to evaluate
alternative medicine, instead of simply
dismissing it. Perhaps within the next decade,
when <u>you approach</u> that sea of herbal remedies,
            43
we will have a better sense of which ones
really work and why. 44 45

40. F. NO CHANGE
     G. licenses. And
     H. licenses and
     J. licenses; and

41. Which of the following sentences, if inserted at
     this point, would provide the most effective
     transition to Paragraph 5?
     A. Homeopathy is still not fully accepted by
         the medical establishment.
     B. The rules of the A.M.A. are not as strict
         as they once were.
     C. However, alternative medicine is making
         a comeback.
     D. Only now are there signs that this deep
         schism in the field of health is beginning
         to heal.

42. F. NO CHANGE
     G. is some possibility to
     H. might or might not
     J. might

43. Which of the choices is most consistent with the
     style established in the essay?
     A. NO CHANGE
     B. one approaches
     C. you are approached by
     D. approach is intended to

Items 44 and 45 pose questions about the essay as a whole.

44. If this essay were revised to include a paragraph on the philosophy of homeopathic remedies, the new paragraph would most logically follow Paragraph:

F. 2.

G. 3.

H. 4.

J. 5.

45. Suppose the writer had been assigned to write an essay exploring the reasons for the present popularity of alternative medicine. Would this essay successfully fulfill the assignment?

A. Yes, because the essay focuses on people's dissatisfaction with the medical establishment.

B. Yes, because the essay touches on the reasons for alternative medicine's popularity in Paragraph 3.

C. No, because the essay focuses on the question of the value of alternative medicine.

D. No, because the essay restricts its focus to the antagonism of doctors toward alternative medicine.

Passage IV

A Professional Lesson

<1>

When I first began working as a journalist in the 1970's, there are few women in the
46

field who are taken seriously. I had
46

no illusions, I would have to prove myself again
47

and again.

46. F. NO CHANGE

G. there are few women in the field who is taken seriously.

H. there were few women in the field who are taken seriously.

J. there were few women in the field who were taken seriously.

47. A. NO CHANGE

B. no illusions: I

C. no illusion in which I

D. no illusion that I

GO ON TO THE NEXT PAGE ➡

<2>

Editors were surprised when my work
turned to out to be first rate. It took me a long
time to understand that the reason had to do with
the way I carried myself, <u>not to mention the fact</u>
                                                    48

<u>that I was making no attempt with which to</u>
                    48

<u>conceal my anxieties.</u> I had not yet learned to
              48

put on a professional face.

<3>

<u>Editors who would try to hand me the</u>
                            49

<u>softer stories,</u> or the stories with a "woman
      49

angle."

"Maybe you <u>could do a piece on the charity</u>
                                  50

<u>work of</u> the First Lady." I was undaunted by
    50

these incidents, and by the inevitable tasteless
jokes and innuendoes. After all, I had chosen a
career that meant <u>not breaking ground</u> in a
                              51

traditional male bastion. Determination and a
thick skin were required.

<4>

There <u>was, however;</u> an aspect of
              52

professional life for which many of us were not
prepared. I remember that when I was working
on a difficult assignment and I checked in with
the editor, I would tell him about my worries,
describe the obstacles I had yet to surmount, or

48. F. NO CHANGE
   G. not to mention the fact that I made no
      attempt to conceal my anxieties
   H. with the fact that I made no attempt to
      conceal my anxieties
   J. I made no attempt to conceal my anxieties

49. A. NO CHANGE
   B. Editors would try to hand me the softer
      stories,
   C. The softer stories, the ones editors would
      try to hand me,
   D. Editors who tried to hand me the softer
      stories,

50. F. NO CHANGE
   G. could do the charity work of
   H. could be doing it on the charity work of
   J. could do a piece on charity work for

51. A. NO CHANGE
   B. breaking ground in
   C. it broke ground in
   D. broken ground in

52. F. NO CHANGE
   G. was however
   H. was, however,
   J. was; however,

sometimes even <u>complaining </u>about the minor
53

frustrations that had made for a bad day. I

thought of it as communication, being honest in

my work. I never doubted that I would get past

these problems. They merely represented the

moment to moment process of doing my job.

After all, life was like that too—full of

difficulties that I discussed with friends as a way

of getting through them. [54]

<5>

I noticed, <u>therefore</u>, that when my male
55

colleagues spoke to editors, no matter what

doubts they had, they always said that everything

was under control. It seemed like lying. What

were these men afraid of? I didn't realize that

<u>by behaving the way in which I'd been acting,</u>
56

my honesty was making a negative impression

on my editors. Editors assumed that if I were

speaking about my difficulties, then I must really

be in trouble. Like all managers, they wanted to

know that everything was under control. By

sharing the struggles that are part of the process

of all work, I made my editors worry, and at the

53. A. NO CHANGE
     B. was complaining
     C. complained
     D. complain

54. Would it add to the effectiveness of the essay if the writer inserted a paragraph at this point describing the way in which she discussed problems with a close friend?

     F. No, it would be superfluous because the writer's description of how she interacted with her editor is already clear.

     G. No, because such a description belongs just before this paragraph.

     H. Yes, because the writer needs to more fully illustrate how she interacts with other people.

     J. Yes, because the writer needs to show why she wanted the "softer stories" she was assigned.

55. A. NO CHANGE
     B. somewhat
     C. in support of my ideas
     D. though

56. F. NO CHANGE
     G. my behavior and
     H. my behaving in that way and
     J. OMIT the underlined portion.

GO ON TO THE NEXT PAGE

same time reinforced all those stereotypes about

women <u>that</u> can't stand the pressure. 58 59 60
  57

57. A. NO CHANGE
     B. who
     C. whom
     D. what

Items 58 through 60 ask questions about the essay as a whole.

58. For the sake of unity and coherence, Paragraph 2 should be placed

     F. where it is now.
     G. before Paragraph 1.
     H. after Paragraph 4.
     J. after Paragraph 5.

59. Suppose the writer were to eliminate Paragraph 4. This omission would cause the essay as a whole to lose primarily:

     A. relevant details about the mistakes the writer made that led to her ultimate realization.
     B. historical information regarding women in the workplace.
     C. relevant details regarding the writer's male colleagues' behavior.
     D. an irrelevant anecdote about the writer's experience with her friends.

60. Which of the following assignments would this essay most clearly fulfill?

     F. Write a persuasive essay about the benefits of holding a job.
     G. Write an essay comparing current versus past business environments for women.
     H. Write an essay about a lesson you learned from a professional experience.
     J. Write an essay about an experience in which your personal integrity was challenged.

Passage V

Edwidge Danticat, A Born Writer

Those who live in countries where a large proportion of the population <u>is illegible,</u>
61

share their stories orally. In Haiti, <u>it being a</u>
62

<u>small country,</u> when someone has a tale to tell
62

he or she will call out *Krik?* <u>Neighbors:</u> friends
63

and relatives will then gather around with

an answering call of *Krak!,* signaling <u>there</u>
64

willingness to listen.

The Haitian-born writer, Edwidge Danticat,

<u>would have been</u> only twenty-six when she
65

took these two words and made them the title for

her collection of stories. The nine stories in

Krik?Krak! focus on the hardships of living

<u>alongside a</u> dictatorship and the struggles
66

encountered by families who flee Haiti and seek

new <u>lives, in</u> the United States. The book
67

received <u>much</u> critical acclaim and even became
68

a finalist for the National Book Award.

61. A. NO CHANGE
     B. are ineligible
     C. is illiterate
     D. are illiterate

62. F. NO CHANGE
     G. as one of the world's smaller countries
     H. it being a small country
     J. OMIT the underlined portion.

63. A. NO CHANGE
     B. Neighbors;
     C. Neighbors
     D. Neighbors,

64. F. NO CHANGE
     G. they're
     H. their
     J. they are

65. A. NO CHANGE
     B. having been
     C. was being
     D. was

66. F. NO CHANGE
     G. under a
     H. without a
     D. in spite of a

67. A. NO CHANGE
     B. lives' in
     C. lives in
     D. life in

68. F. NO CHANGE
     G. many
     H. too much
     J. negative

GO ON TO THE NEXT PAGE

Born in Port-au-Prince in 1969, Danticat moved to New York City when she was twelve. She spoke little as a new immigrant, because when she did speak, <u>you may find this hard to</u>
<u>believe,</u> other children made fun of her heavily-
69

accented English. [70] Her thesis in graduate school later became the novel *Breath, Eyes, Memory.* That novel, which was subsequently chosen by Oprah Winfrey for her book club, featured a heroine who, like the author, moved from Haiti to New York City at the age of twelve. Danticat's third book, *The Farming of*

Bones, is also set <u>in a small Caribbean country</u>
71
<u>called Haiti.</u>
71

This young <u>authors</u> chosen subject
72
matter, as well as the Creole-accented language she uses to tell her stories, show that while she has left Haiti for her adopted country of

69. A. NO CHANGE
   B. you may find this hard to believe
   C. as hard to believe as you may find this
   D. OMIT the underlined portion.

70. Which of the following sentences, if added here, would best provide a transition from the description of Danticat as a young girl to that of Danticat as an author?
   F. Danticat refrained from criticizing them in return, however, and was successful in the end.
   G. Most Haitians speak Creole and the language is quite different from American English.
   H. Many writers have had difficult childhoods.
   J. Although she was silent much of the time, Danticat watched and remembered, as if already thinking like a writer.

71. A. NO CHANGE
   B. in the country of the author's birth, which is called Haiti.
   C. in Haiti, which shares a border with the Dominican Republic.
   D. in Haiti.

72. F. NO CHANGE
   G. authors'
   H. author's
   J. author

America, she has forgotten <u>both the land of her</u>
                                    73

<u>birth and its</u> brave people. 74 75
   73

73. A. NO CHANGE
     B. the land of her birth, its people
     C. neither the land of her birth nor its
     D. neither the land of her birth and its

Items 74 and 75 ask questions about the essay as a whole.

74. The writer wishes to open the essay with a
     sentence that will set the theme and tone of the
     essay. Which of the following would most
     effectively accomplish this?

     F. Whether or not they can read, people all
         over the world love stories.

     G. One of my favorite books is a collection
         of stories set in Haiti.

     H. The problem of illiteracy results in a
         variety of consequences for people all
         over the world.

     J. Have you ever wondered what it feels
         like to not be able to read?

75. The writer wishes to give this essay a different
     title. Which of the following alternatives would
     be most appropriate?

     A. How Edwidge Danticat Overcame
         Struggles as an Immigrant

     B. Life in Haiti

     C. A New Voice in Literature

     D. The Haiti I Will Never Forget

STOP

END OF SECTION 1. IF YOU HAVE ANY TIME LEFT, GO OVER YOUR
WORK IN THIS SECTION ONLY. DO NOT WORK IN ANY OTHER
SECTION OF THE TEST.

2. MATHEMATICS TEST

60 Questions • Time—60 Minutes

Directions: Solve each problem below and mark the oval representing the correct answer on your answer sheet.

Be careful not to spend too much time on any one question. Instead, solve as many questions as possible, and then use any remaining time to return to those questions you were unable to answer at first.

You may use a calculator on any problem in this test; however, not every problem requires the use of a calculator.

Diagrams that accompany problems may or may not be drawn to scale. Unless otherwise indicated, you may assume that all figures shown lie in a plane and that lines that appear straight are straight.

1. Thirty-two of the 80 children at a daycare center missed at least one day because of illness in January. What percent of the children at the center missed at least one day due to illness in January?

   A. 4%

   B. 16%

   C. 24%

   D. 32%

   E. 40%

2. Three lines intersect to form the triangle below. What is the measure of ∠X ?

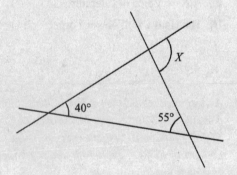

   F. 65°

   G. 75°

   H. 85°

   J. 95°

   K. 105°

3. A businessperson calculates that it costs her P dollars per hour in parts costs and L dollars per hour in labor costs to operate a certain piece of machinery. Which of the following expressions would provide her with the total cost of operating this machine for x hours?

   A. PLx

   B. $(Px)(Lx)$

   C. $(P + L)x$

   D. PL

   E. $P + L$

4. In the standard (x,y) coordinate plane, a straight line segment is drawn to connect (0,0) and (4,4). Which of the following sets of points, when connected by a straight line segment, will intersect the original segment?

   F. (−3,3) and (3,4)

   G. (0,−1) and (4,3)

   H. (0,1) and (4,5)

   J. (1,0) and (8,4)

   K. (2,1) and (2,5)

5. A phone company charges $1 per calling card call plus 25 cents per minute for the length of the call. If Jacob makes 10 calling card calls, half of which last exactly 1 minute and half of which last exactly 3 minutes, what is his cost for the 10 calls?

    A. $5

    B. $10

    C. $15

    D. $20

    E. $25

6. Which of the following is one of the factors of $x^2 + x - 30$?

    F. $x + 10$

    G. $x + 6$

    H. $x + 5$

    J. $x + 3$

    K. $x + 2$

7. Which of the following is equal to the sum of $\frac{2}{5}$, $\frac{1}{8}$, and .177 ?

    A. .656

    B. .677

    C. .689

    D. .692

    E. .702

8. In the figure below, $\overline{BC}$ is 2 inches long, $\overline{CD}$ is 8 inches long, and B, C, and D are collinear. If the area of triangle ABC is 5 square inches, what is the area of triangle ACD, in square inches?

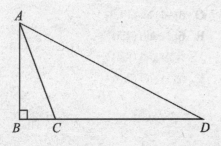

    F. 10

    G. 15

    H. 20

    J. 25

    K. 30

9. What is the value of $m^2 - 4mn + n$ when $m = -1$ and $n = -3$?

    A. −15

    B. −14

    C. −11

    D. 8

    E. 10

10. $(3 + \sqrt{2})(4 - \sqrt{2}) = ?$

    F. 10

    G. 14

    H. $8 - \sqrt{2}$

    J. $10 + \sqrt{2}$

    K. $14 + 7\sqrt{2}$

11. What is the measure of one of the interior angles of a regular hexagon?

    A. 60°

    B. 90°

    C. 100°

    D. 110°

    E. 120°

12. What is the least possible integer that is separately divisible by each of 2, 4, 6, and 10 (with no remainder)?

    F. 12

    G. 30

    H. 60

    J. 120

    K. 480

13. A store charges $20 for a box of 40 computer diskettes, $13 for a box of 25 diskettes, and $8 for a box of 10 diskettes. What is the least amount of money, excluding tax, for which a customer can buy at least 100 diskettes from this store?

    A. $60

    B. $58

    C. $56

    D. $54

    E. $53

GO ON TO THE NEXT PAGE

14. $(.01)^4 = ?$

    F. 10^{-8}

    G. 10^{-4}

    H. 10^{-2}

    J. 10^4

    K. 10^8

15. In the figure below, $\overline{AD}$ and $\overline{BC}$ intersect at E and $\overline{AB}$ is parallel to CD. The measure of $\angle ABE$ is 60° and the measure of $\angle CDE$ is 40°. What is the measure of $\angle CED$?

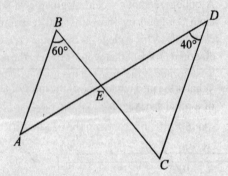

    A. 30°

    B. 40°

    C. 60°

    D. 80°

    E. Cannot be determined from the given information

16. For all a, $(2a - 3)^2 = ?$

    F. $4a - 6$

    G. $4a^2 - 9$

    H. $4a^2 - 6a + 9$

    J. $4a^2 - 12a + 9$

    K. $4a^2 + 9a - 6$

17. What is the slope-intercept form of the line $3x + y - 2 = 0$?

    A. $y = 3x - 2$

    B. $y = 3x + 2$

    C. $y = \dfrac{1}{3}x + \dfrac{1}{2}$

    D. $y = -3x + 2$

    E. $y = -3x - 2$

18. A painter calculates that one side of a house requires exactly 4 large cans of paint OR exactly 6 small cans of paint. If all 4 sides of the house require identical amounts of paint, which collection of paint cans will cover all 4 sides with no waste?

    F. 2 large and 24 small

    G. 4 large and 18 small

    H. 6 large and 16 small

    J. 8 large and 8 small

    K. 12 large and 12 small

19. At what value of x does the expression $|x - 5| + 2$ reach its minimum?

    A. –5

    B. –2

    C. 0

    D. 2

    E. 5

20. What is the smallest positive integer for which $x - \sqrt{5} > 5$ is true?

    F. 9

    G. 8

    H. 7

    J. 6

    K. 5

21. If $x + 6$ is a factor of $x^2 + bx - 6$, then $b = ?$

    A. 1

    B. 2

    C. 3

    D. 5

    E. 6

22. In the figure below, triangle *ABC* and triangle *DEF* are similar. If the lengths of the sides are indicated in units, how many units long is $\overline{DE}$?

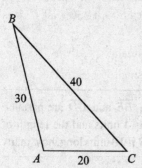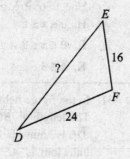

F. 25

G. 28

H. 30

J. 32

K. 40

23. What is the area of the right triangle below, in square centimeters?

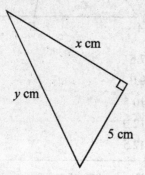

A. $\frac{5}{2}x$

B. $\frac{5}{2}y$

C. $5x$

D. $5y$

E. $5xy$

24. It took Rene exactly 9 minutes and 20 seconds to download a 1,400 kilobyte file from the internet onto her computer. At that same rate, how long would it take Rene to download a 2,000 kilobyte file?

F. 11 minutes

G. 12 minutes and 10 seconds

H. 12 minutes and 40 seconds

J. 13 minutes

K. 13 minutes and 20 seconds

25. A college campus's central green is a square lawn bordered by footpaths 100 feet long on each side. The college is debating creating a diagonal footpath that would connect the south-west corner of the green to the northeast corner of the green. Approximately how many feet shorter would the new path be than taking the shortest possible route on the existing paths?

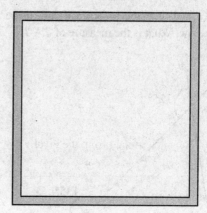

A. 20

B. 40

C. 60

D. 80

E. 140

GO ON TO THE NEXT PAGE

26. If $x < 0$ and $3x^2 - 7x = 6$, then $x = $?

    F. -6

    G. -3

    H. -2

    J. $-\dfrac{3}{2}$

    K. $-\dfrac{2}{3}$

27. For all a and b, $\sqrt{3^4 a^3 b^2}$ = ?

    A. $9a^{\frac{2}{3}}b^1$

    B. $9a^{\frac{3}{2}}b^1$

    C. $9a^{-\frac{3}{2}}b^0$

    D. $27a^3b^2$

    E. $27a^6b^4$

28. Lines p, q, and r intersect to form a triangle in the figure below. What is the measure of $\angle A$?

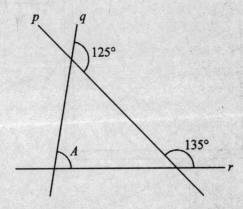

    F. 70°

    G. 75°

    H. 80°

    J. 85°

    K. Cannot be determined from the given information

29. $\dfrac{.018}{.12}$ is equal to how many thousandths?

    A. 1.5

    B. 15

    C. 60

    D. 150

    E. 667

30. Which of the following inequalities gives the complete solution set for $|x - 1| \le 2$?

    F. $-3 \le x \le 3$

    G. $-1 \le x \le 3$

    H. $0 \le x \le 2$

    J. $0 \le x \le 3$

    K. $x \le 3$

31. In the figure below, $\overline{BE}$ and $\overline{CD}$ are parallel. The length of $\overline{BC}$ is 4 units and the length of $\overline{DE}$ is 3 units. If $\overline{AB}$ is 10 units long, how many units long is $\overline{AE}$?

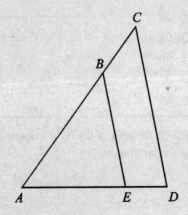

    A. 7.5

    B. 9.0

    C. 10.5

    D. 12.0

    E. 12.5

32. For $0° < \theta < 90°$, if $\cos \theta = \frac{5}{7}$, then $\tan \theta = $?

    F. $\dfrac{2}{7}$

    G. $\dfrac{7}{5}$

    H. $\dfrac{2\sqrt{6}}{7}$

    J. $\dfrac{2\sqrt{6}}{5}$

    K. $\dfrac{24}{7}$

33. The average of x numbers is 15. If two of the numbers are each increased by y, the new average will be increased by how much?

    A. $2y$

    B. y

    C. $\dfrac{x}{2y}$

    D. $\dfrac{y}{x}$

    E. $\dfrac{2y}{x}$

34. What is the slope of the line passing through the points $(-1,4)$ and $(2,-5)$ in the standard (x,y) plane?

    F. -3

    G. $-\dfrac{1}{3}$

    H. 0

    J. $\dfrac{1}{9}$

    K. 9

35. A 12 foot ladder is propped against a 10 foot house as outlined below. What is the best approximation for how many feet the base of the ladder is from the wall of the house?

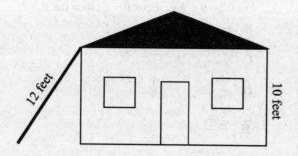

    A. 2.0

    B. 4.0

    C. 5.5

    D. 6.6

    E. 7.1

36. A circle with a radius of 3 feet has a circumference how many feet long?

    F. $\dfrac{3}{2}\pi$

    G. 3π

    H. 6π

    J. 9π

    K. 12π

37. If $\dfrac{3}{5}n + \dfrac{2}{7} = \dfrac{3}{7}n - \dfrac{2}{5}$, then $n = ?$

    A. -4

    B. -3

    C. 0

    D. 2

    E. 3

38. A line in the standard (x,y) coordinate plane is parallel to the y-axis and passes through the point $(2,3)$. Which of the following is an equation of this line?

    F. $x = 2$

    G. $y = 3$

    H. $y = 2x$

    J. $y = 2x - 3$

    K. $y = x + 1$

39. If the lengths of the sides are shown in units in the triangle below, $\sin x° = ?$

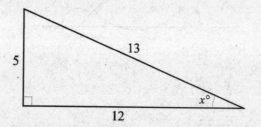

    A. $\dfrac{5}{13}$

    B. $\dfrac{5}{12}$

    C. $\dfrac{12}{13}$

    D. $\dfrac{13}{12}$

    E. $\dfrac{13}{5}$

GO ON TO THE NEXT PAGE

40. If the quadrants in the standard (x,y) plane are numbered as below, the graph of the circle defined by $(x-4)^2+(y+6)^2=25$ lies entirely in which quadrants?

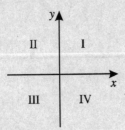

F. I and II

G. I and IV

H. II and III

J. II and IV

K. III and IV

41. If the circle below has center at C and a radius of 9 feet, what is the length, in feet, of arc XYZ?

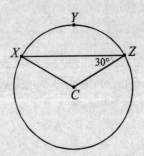

A. $\dfrac{3\pi}{2}$

B. 3π

C. 6π

D. 18π

E. 27π

42. What is the least possible value for the product xy if $x + y = 24$ and x and y are both prime numbers?

F. 23

G. 44

H. 95

J. 119

K. 143

43. The area of a circle is 64 square inches. What is the diameter, in inches, of the circle?

A. 8

B. 16

C. $\dfrac{8}{\pi}$

D. $\dfrac{8}{\sqrt{\pi}}$

E. $\dfrac{16}{\sqrt{\pi}}$

44. If $2x = 4x + 1$, then $6x - 2 = ?$

F. −5

G. −3

H. −1

J. 2

K. 4

45. In the isosceles right triangle below, what is the value of $\tan x°$?

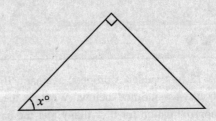

A. $\dfrac{\sqrt{2}}{2}$

B. 1

C. $\sqrt{2}$

D. $\dfrac{\sqrt{3}}{2}$

E. $\sqrt{3}$

46. What is the area of the rectangle shown below in the standard (x,y) coordinate plane?

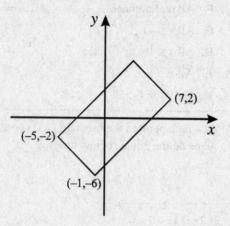

F. $32\sqrt{2}$

G. 64

H. 88

J. 128

K. 144

47. If $\frac{x^3y^2}{z}$ is positive, then which of the following may be true?

 I. x and z are both negative

 II. x is negative and z is positive

 III. x is zero

A. I only

B. II only

C. I and II only

D. II and III only

E. I, II, and III

48. The average of 6 test scores is 80. When 2 more tests are included, the average for all 8 tests is 85. What is the average score on the 2 added tests?

F. 70

G. 85

H. 90

J. 95

K. 100

49. If x is inversely related to y and y is directly related to z, which of the following expressions gives one possibility for y in terms of x and z ?

A. $y = \dfrac{x}{z}$

B. $y = \dfrac{z}{x}$

C. $y = zx$

D. $y = x^z$

E. $y = z^x$

50. A circle exists such that its center is at $C(1,-1)$ and it passes through $P(5,2)$ in the standard (x,y) coordinate plane below. Which equation determines the circle described?

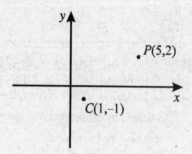

F. $(x-5)^2 + (y-2)^2 = 25$

G. $(x+5)^2 + (y+2)^2 = 25$

H. $(x-1)^2 + (y+1)^2 = 25$

J. $(x+1)^2 + (y-1)^2 = 25$

K. $(x+1)^2 + (y+1)^2 = 25$

51. If $-[(x-4)-(3-2x)] = 3 - (5x+6)$, what is the value of x ?

A. -6

B. -5

C. -4

D. -3

E. -2

GO ON TO THE NEXT PAGE

52. What is the period of the graph of $y = 3\sin \frac{x}{2}$?

    F. $\dfrac{\pi}{2}$

    G.

    H. $\dfrac{3\pi}{2}$

    J. 2π

    K. 4π

53. If exactly one real value of x satisfies the equation $x^2 + ax + 16 = 0$, which of the following is a possible value of a ?

    A. -8

    B. -4

    C. 4

    D. 6

    E. 10

54. A positive number x is increased by 20 percent and then the result is decreased by 30 percent. The final result is equal to which of the following?

    F. x decreased by 50 percent

    G. x decreased by 16 percent

    H. x decreased by 10 percent

    J. x increased by 10 percent

    K. x increased by 25 percent

55. A 50 foot wire is attached to the top of an electric pole and is anchored on the ground. If the wire rises in a straight line at a 70° angle from the ground, how many feet tall is the pole?

    A. $50 \sin 70°$

    B. $50 \cos 70°$

    C. $50 \tan 70°$

    D. $\dfrac{\cos 70°}{50}$

    E. $\dfrac{50}{\cos 70°}$

56. What is the complete solution set for the equation $|1 - x| = x - 1$?

    F. All real numbers

    G. All $x \le -1$

    H. All $x \le 1$

    J. All $x \ge 1$

    K. Only $x = 1$

57. At which point in the standard (x,y) coordinate plane do the 2 lines below intersect?

    $$\frac{x}{2} + y = 2$$
    $$2x + y = 2$$

    A. $(2,1)$

    B. $(1,-2)$

    C. $(0,2)$

    D. $(-1,-1)$

    E. $(-2,0)$

58. Lines m and n are perpendicular in the standard (x,y) coordinate plane below. Which of the following is the equation for line n ?

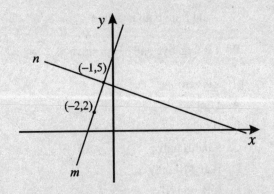

    F. $y = -x + 5$

    G. $y = -2x + 3$

    H. $2y = -x - 4$

    J. $3y = -x + 14$

    K. $3y = x + 16$

59. Five cards lettered A through E are placed in a hat. If two cards are drawn at random from the hat, what is the probability that the B and C cards will both be drawn?

 A. .05

 B. .1

 C. .125

 D. .2

 E. .4

60. While shopping at a clothing store, Ben finds that a shirt and two ties cost $105, while two shirts and one tie cost $135. If the store charges the same price for all of its shirts and the same price for all of its ties, what is Ben's cost if he wants to buy just one tie?

 F. $20

 G. $25

 H. $30

 J. $35

 K. $40

STOP

END OF SECTION 2. IF YOU HAVE ANY TIME LEFT, GO OVER YOUR WORK IN THIS SECTION ONLY. DO NOT WORK IN ANY OTHER SECTION OF THE TEST.

3. READING TEST

40 Questions • Time—35 Minutes

Directions: This test consists of four passages, each followed by several questions. Read each passage, select the correct answer for each question, and mark the oval representing the correct answer on your answer sheet.

Passage I

PROSE FICTION: This passage is adapted from Theodore Dreiser's *Sister Carrie*.

Once across the river and into the wholesale district, Carrie glanced about her for some likely door at which to apply. As she contemplated the wide windows and imposing signs, she became conscious of being gazed
(05) upon and understood for what she was—a wage-seeker. She had never done this thing before, and lacked courage. To avoid a certain indefinable shame she felt at being caught spying about for a position, she quickened her steps and assumed an air of indifference
(10) just as if she were upon an errand. In this way she passed many manufacturing and wholesale houses without once glancing in. At last, after several blocks of walking, she felt that this would not do, and began to look about again, though without relaxing her pace.
(15) A little way on she saw a great door which, for some reason, attracted her attention. It was ornamented by a small brass sign, and seemed to be the entrance to a vast hive of six or seven floors.

"Perhaps," she thought, "they may want someone,"
(20) and crossed over to enter. When she came within a score of feet of the desired goal, she saw through the window a young man in a gray checked suit. That he had anything to do with the concern, she could not tell, but because he happened to be looking in her direction
(25) her weakening heart departed her and she hurried by, too overcome with shame to enter. Over the way stood a great six-story structure, labeled Storm and King, which she viewed with rising hope. It was a wholesale dry goods concern and employed women. She could
(30) see them moving about now and then upon the upper floors. This place she decided to enter, no matter what. She crossed over and walked directly toward the entrance. As she did so, two men came out and paused in the door, looking in her direction. A messenger in
(35) blue dashed past her and up the few steps that led to the entrance and disappeared. Several pedestrians out of

the hurrying throng which filled the sidewalks passed about her as she paused, hesitating. She looked helplessly around, and then, seeing herself observed, re-
(40) treated. It was too difficult a task. She could not go past them.

So severe a defeat told sadly upon her nerves. Her feet carried her mechanically forward, every foot of her progress being a satisfactory portion of a flight
(45) which she gladly made. Block after block passed by. Upon streetlamps at the various corners she read names such as Madison, Monroe, La Salle, Clark, Dearborn, State, and still she went, her feet beginning to tire upon the broad stone flagging. She was pleased
(50) in part that the streets were bright and clean. The morning sun, shining down with steadily increasing warmth, made the shady side of the streets pleasantly cool. She looked at the blue sky overhead with more realization of its charm than had ever come to her
(55) before.

Her cowardice began to trouble her in a way. She turned back, resolving to hunt up Storm and King and enter. On the way, she encountered a great wholesale shoe company, through the broad plate windows of
(60) which she saw an enclosed executive department, hidden by frosted glass. Without this enclosure, but just within the street entrance, sat a gray-haired gentleman at a small table, with a large open ledger before him. She walked by this institution several times
(65) hesitating, but, finding herself unobserved, faltered past the screen door and stood humbly waiting. "Well, young lady," observed the old gentleman, looking at her somewhat kindly, "what is it you wish?"

"I am, that is, do you—I mean, do you need any
(70) help?" she stammered.

"Not just at present," he answered smiling. "Not just at present. Come in some time next week. Occasionally we need someone."

(75) She received the answer in silence and backed awkwardly out. The pleasant nature of her reception rather astonished her. She had expected that it would be more difficult, that something cold and harsh would be said—she knew not what. That she had not been put to shame and made to feel her unfortunate position,
(80) seemed remarkable.

With the wane of the afternoon went her hopes, her courage, and her strength. She had been astonishingly persistent. So earnest an effort was well deserving of a better reward. On every hand, to her fatigued senses,
(85) the great business portion grew larger, harder, more stolid in its indifference. It seemed as if it was all closed to her, that the struggle was too fierce for her to hope to do anything at all. Men and women hurried by in long, shifting lines. She felt the flow of the tide of
(90) effort and interest—felt her own helplessness without quite realizing the wisp on the tide that she was. She cast about vainly for some possible place to apply, but found no door which she had the courage to enter. It would be the same thing all over. The old humiliation
(95) of her plea, rewarded by curt denial. Sick at heart and in body, she turned to the west, the direction of Minnie's flat, which she had now fixed in mind, and began that wearisome, baffled retreat which the seeker for employment at nightfall too often makes.

1. The firm of Storm and King is described in the passage as a:
   A. department store.
   B. wholesale shoe company.
   C. sweat shop.
   D. wholesale dry goods store.

2. When Carrie attempts to get a job at the shoe company, she is met with what could best be described as:
   F. apathetic dismissal.
   G. angry rebuttal.
   H. congenial rejection.
   J. exasperated disdain.

3. As she walks along the street in the late afternoon, Carrie feels as if she:
   A. has made a mistake in moving to the city.
   B. deserves a better reward for her hard work.
   C. is ready to look all night for a job if necessary.
   D. knows that employment is a waste of time.

4. In order to overcome her embarrassment while looking for work, Carrie pretends that:
   F. she is a spy carrying out a secret mission.
   G. she is performing an appointed task.
   H. she is the boss of a large company.
   J. she is rich and doesn't really need a job.

5. In the third paragraph all of the following Street names are mentioned EXCEPT:
   A. Monroe.
   B. Block.
   C. Madison.
   D. State.

6. As it is used in line 16, the word *ornamented* most nearly means:
   F. complicated.
   G. lacking.
   H. withdrawn.
   J. adorned.

7. Given the way she is presented in the passage, Carrie's mental state can best be described as:
   A. irate.
   B. compassionate.
   C. despondent.
   D. mechanical.

8. In the final paragraph of the passage the narrator suggests that Carrie's failure to find work has:
   F. affected her physical well-being.
   G. filled her with vanity.
   H. made her feel wholesome.
   J. given her a renewed sense of purpose.

GO ON TO THE NEXT PAGE ➤

9. After Carrie asks him for work, the old gentleman at the shoe company tells Carrie that she:

   A. will not be able to find work in the city.

   B. should seek out an employment agency.

   C. has no marketable skills.

   D. should come back next week.

10. What keeps Carrie from entering the wholesale dry goods store mentioned in the second paragraph?

   F. The messengers are entering and leaving the building.

   G. The pedestrians are rushing down the street.

   H. The men are standing in the doorway watching her.

   J. She cannot find the entrance to the store.

Passage II

SOCIAL SCIENCE: This passage is adapted from a sociological study of traditional Fiji culture conducted by Dr. Alfred Goldsborough Mayer.

Land tenure in traditional Fijian culture is a subject so complex that heavy volumes could be written about it. In general it may be said that the chief could sell no land without the consent of his tribe. In traditional Fiji (05) society, cultivated land belonged to the man who originally farmed it, and was passed undivided to all his heirs. Waste land was held in common. Native settlers who were taken into the tribes from time to time were permitted to farm some of the waste land, (10) and for this privilege they and their heirs paid a yearly tribute to the chief either in produce or in service. In essence, this amounted to paying rent to the chief.

Fijians appear never to have been wholly without a medium of exchange, for sperm-whale's teeth always (15) had a recognized purchasing power. They were also were especially regarded as a means of expressing good will and honesty of purpose. A whale's tooth was as effective to secure compliance with the terms of a bargain in ancient Fiji as a signed contract is with (20) modern Americans. Given Americans' penchant for wiggling their way out of contracts, a whale's tooth from a Fijian probably generated much more trust that the agreement would be fulfilled.

As in all communities, including our own world of (25) finance, a man's wealth consisted not only of what he possessed but even more so of the number of people from whom he could beg or borrow. Wilkes records an interesting example of this, for he found that the rifle and other costly presents he had presented to King (30) Tanoa were being seized by Tanoa's nephew who, as his *vasu*, had a right to take whatever he might select from the king's possessions. Indeed, in order to keep his property in sight, Tanoa was forced to give it to his own sons, thus escaping the rapacity of his nephew.

(35) In a traditional Fiji, tribe an individual as such can hardly be said to own property, for nearly all things belong to his family or clan, and are shared among cousins. This condition is partially responsible for the absence of personal ambition which once struck (40) Westerners as so illogical, but which was nevertheless the dominant feature of the social fabric of traditional Polynesians, and which prevented the introduction of "ideals of modern progress" until well into the twentieth century. The Fijians, for much of the last few (45) centuries, were relatively happy; why should they work when every reasonable want was already supplied? None were rich in material things, but none were beggars except in the sense that all were such. No one could be a miser, a capitalist, a banker, or a (50) promoter in such a community, and thieves were almost unknown. Indeed, the honesty of the traditional Fijians was one of those virtues that promoted the comment of travelers in previous centuries.

During Professor Alexander Agassiz's cruises in (55) the late 1800's, in which he visited nearly every island of the Fijis, the natives came on board by the hundreds and not a single object was stolen, although things almost priceless in native estimation lay loosely upon the deck. Once, indeed, when the deck was deserted by (60) both officers and crew and fully a hundred natives were on board, the Professor found a man who had been gazing wistfully for half an hour at a bottle which lay upon the laboratory table. Somehow he had managed to acquire a shilling, a large coin in Fiji at the (65) time, and this he offered in exchange for the coveted bottle. As Agassiz tells us: "One can never forget his shout of joy and the radiance of his honest face as he leaped into his canoe after having received it as a gift."

As these Fijians said to Professor Agassiz, "The (70) white man possesses more than we, but his life is full of toil and sorrow, while our days are happy as they pass."

But this was the Fiji of the past, when life was an evanescent thing, and only as real as the murmur of the
(75) surf when the sea breeze comes in the morning. This was Fiji before capitalism took hold, before the forests were slashed and burned to make more land available for farming, and before the young people began to leave their ancient islands to look for "a better life."
(80) This life usually entails hoarding wealth and becoming enmeshed in the rat race of modern civilization. Sadly, this race rarely has a happy ending.

Hoarded wealth inspired no respect in the Fiji of previous centuries, and indeed, were it discovered, its
(85) possession would have justified immediate confiscation. Yet man must raise idols to satisfy his instinct to worship things above his acquisition, and thus rank was more revered because respect for property was low. Among traditional Fijian tribes chiefs were greatly
(90) revered, and names themselves had more power than worldly goods.

One aspect to note is that names in traditional Fijian culture could change throughout one's life, depending on any important events that occurred. For instance,
(95) Chief Thakombau began life as "Seru," then after the civil war in which he overcame his father's enemies and reestablished Tanoa's rule in Mbau he was called "Thakombau" (evil to Mbau). At the time he also received another name, "Thikinovu" (centipede) in
(100) allusion to his stealth in approaching to bite his enemy, but this designation, together with his given Christian name "Ebenezer," (he was converted by British missionaries) did not survive the test of usage.

11. The passage specifies that in traditional Fijian society individual property was, for the most part:

   A. taken by Western explorers.

   B. collectively owned by the family or clan.

   C. owned solely by the chief of the tribe.

   D. thought to be possessed of evil phantoms.

12. Based on information in the passage, a contract from a traditional Fijian would most likely take the form of which of the following?

   F. a burnt offering to the gods.

   G. a semiprecious stone.

   H. the granting of a Fijian name.

   J. a whale's tooth.

13. The anecdote about King Tanao's nephew described in the third paragraph is presented in order to illustrate the principle that:

   A. Western civilization has decimated traditional Fijian values.

   B. the right to take or borrow from another was a notable indication of wealth in Fijian culture.

   C. all communities that value personal property levy heavy sanctions against theft.

   D. trust was not easily gained among Fijian tribes.

14. The author of the passage appears to feel that the answer to the question "what does modern civilization mean for the people of Fiji?" is best answered by the assertion that:

   F. Fiji, like most island civilizations, must give up its insular culture in order to compete in world markets.

   G. capitalism will help the people of Fiji profit from their traditional values of honesty and egalitarianism.

   H. modern civilization will not make the people of Fiji any happier than they previously were.

   J. there is little chance that modern civilization will ever have an impact on the way of life enjoyed by most Fijians.

GO ON TO THE NEXT PAGE

15. The author states in paragraph 4 that "the intro-
    duction of 'ideals of modern progress'" was
    prevented "well into the twentieth century" in
    Fiji because of a lack of:

    A. a sense of personal ownership.

    B. established religious customs.

    C. codified land laws.

    D. Western cultural indoctrination.

16. As it is used in line 18, the word *compliance*
    most nearly means:

    F. agreement.

    G. introduction.

    H. withdrawal.

    J. inconsistency.

17. According to the passage, Chief Thakombau
    was granted his name after he:

    A. was born to distinguished parents.

    B. hoarded a large amount of wealth.

    C. was converted by British missionaries.

    D. restored Tanoa's rule in Mbau.

18. The author's analysis of traditional Fiji culture
    includes details concerning:

    I. ownership of land.

    II. how capitalism has changed Fijian culture.

    III. the shortage of natural resources in Fiji.

    F. I only

    G. I and II only

    H. II and III only

    J. I, II, and III

19. It can reasonably be inferred from the informa-
    tion in the first paragraph that a Fijian chief did
    not have the right to:

    A. declare war.

    B. start a new community on the same
       island.

    C. cultivate land.

    D. sell tribal land without the tribe's
       permission.

20. One of the main points made in the fourth para-
    graph (lines 35–53) is that although traditional
    Fijians did not have strong ambitions to acquire
    personal wealth, one benefit of this was the:

    F. lack of good jobs.

    G. promotion of industrialization.

    H. scarcity of theft in Fijian society.

    J. growth of friendship between Fijian
       chiefs.

Passage III

HUMANITIES: This passage is adapted from
The Physical Michelangelo by James Frederick
Rogers.

Had Michelangelo been less poetic and more explicit in his language, he might have said there is
nothing so conducive to mental and physical wholeness as saturation of body and mind with work. The
(05) great artist was so prone to over-anxiety and met
(whether needlessly or not) with so many rebuffs and
disappointments, that only constant absorption in
manual labor prevented spirit from fretting itself free
from flesh. He toiled "furiously" in all his mighty
(10) undertakings that body and mind remained one and in
abundant health for nearly four score and ten years.

Michelangelo's life was devoted with passion to art.
Art became his religion and required of him the
sacrifice of all that might keep him below his highest
(15) level of power for work. His father early warned him
to have a care for his health. Said he, "In your profession, if once you were to fall ill you would be a ruined
man." To one so intent on perfection and so keenly
alive to imperfection such advice must have been
(20) superfluous, for the artist could not but observe the
effect upon his work of any depression of his bodily
well-being. He was, besides, too thrifty in all respects
to think of lapsing into bodily neglect or abuse. He was
severely temperate, save in those times when devotion
(25) to work caused him to sleep with his clothes on, so that
he might not lose time in seizing the chisel when he
awoke. He ate to live and to labor. When intent on
some work he usually confined his diet to a piece of
bread which he ate in the middle of his labors. Few
(30) hours were devoted to sleep. He ate comparatively
little and slept less than many men because he worked
better. He dressed for comfort and not to mortify the

flesh, sometimes leaving his high dog-skin boots on for so long that when he removed them the scarf skin (35)came away like the skin of a molting serpent.

His intensity of purpose and fiery energy expressed themselves in his features and form. His face was round, his brow square, ample, and deeply furrowed; the temples projected much beyond the ears; his eyes (40)were small rather than large, of a dark color and peered, piercingly, from under heavy brows. The flattened nose was the result of a blow from a rival apprentice. He evidently looked the part, though for such mental powers one of his colossal statues would (45)seem a more fitting mold.

It was not until the age of seventy that an illness which seemed to mark any weakening of his bodily powers came upon Michelangelo. At seventy-five, symptoms of calculus (a disease common in that day (50)at fifty) appeared, but, though naturally pessimistic, he writes, "In all other respects I am pretty much as I was at thirty years." He wielded the brush and the chisel with consummate skill in his seventy-fifth year. With the later loss of his energy, he found vent more (55)in the planning and supervising of architectural works, culminating in the building of St. Peter's. But even in these later years he took up the chisel as an outlet for superfluous energy and to induce sleep. Though the product of his hand was not good, his health was the (60)better for this mutual exercise of mind and body.

In his eighty-sixth year he is said to have sat drawing for three consecutive hours until pains and cramps in his limbs warned him that he had not the endurance of youth. For exercise, when manual labor proved a (65)disappointment, he often took horseback rides. There was no invalidism about this great spirit, and it was not until the day before his death that he would consent to go to bed.

His temperance, manual industry, and his extraordi-(70)nary blamelessness in life and in every action had been his source of preservation. He was miserly, suspicious, quarrelsome and pessimistic, but the effects of these faults were balanced by his better habits of thought and action. That he, like most great men, felt (75)keenly the value of health, is evidenced not only by his own practice, but by his oft repeated warnings to his nephew when choosing a wife to see that whatever other qualities she might have she be healthy. One of

those who looks beneath unusual human phenomena (80)for signs of the pathologic finds Michelangelo "affected by a degree of neuropathy bordering closely upon hysterical disease." What a pity that more of us do not suffer from such degrees of neuropathy and how much better for most of us if we had such (85)enthusiasm for perfection, and such mania for work, at least of that health-bringing sort in which there is absorbing unity of brain and hand. True it is that "there is no better way of keeping sane and free from anxiety than by being mad."

21. According to the passage, Michelangelo had to maintain his physical health because:
    A. poor health ran in his family.
    B. his father demanded that he did.
    C. if he got sick, he wouldn't be able to work.
    D. he could get seriously injured.

22. The author of the passage would most likely agree with which of the following statements?
    F. Michelangelo used the physicality of his work to help relieve his many anxieties and frustrations.
    G. Michelangelo was an easygoing, carefree man who possessed a unique genius for art.
    H. In order to be successful, all artists have to have the same passion Michelangelo had.
    J. Michelangelo's artistic skills remained completely intact until he died.

23. The passage says that Michelangelo began planning and supervising more architectural works when he was:
    A. under thirty
    B. eighty-six
    C. under seventy
    D. over seventy-five

GO ON TO THE NEXT PAGE

24. According to the third paragraph, Michelangelo's physical appearance reflected:

    I. a coarse sense of humor.

    II. fierce devotion to his work.

    III. enormous mental capacity.

    F. I only
    G. III only
    H. II and III only
    J. I, II and III

25. It can be inferred from the second paragraph that by limiting his food and sleep, Michelangelo was:
    A. able to fully realize his potential as an artist.
    B. driven to madness.
    C. unable to be as prolific as he might otherwise have been.
    D. able to control his health.

26. In line 32, *mortify* most nearly means:
    F. bruise
    G. darken
    H. beautify
    J. warm

27. The main idea of the passage is that:
    A. to live a long, healthy life, one must make the same sacrifices Michelangelo did.
    B. Michelangelo's supreme devotion to his work enabled him to live to a ripe old age with a unique merging of mind and spirit.
    C. through sheer force of will, Michelangelo was able to stay healthy.
    D. Michelangelo was insane.

28. According to paragraph 6, Michelangelo's "source of preservation" was due in part to his:

    I. ascetic living style.

    II. miserly nature.

    III. pessimistic outlook.

    F. I only
    G. I and II only
    H. I and III only
    J. II and III only

29. Based on the information in the passage, which of the following is a fact rather than an opinion?
    A. Michelangelo's last sculptures were not of the same artistic caliber as his earlier works.
    B. Michelangelo's bad qualities were balanced by his good ones.
    C. We would all be better off if we had the same keen desire for perfection that Michelangelo did.
    D. Michelangelo did not rest until the day before his death.

30. The phrase "one of his colossal statues would seem a more fitting mold" in paragraph 3 implies:
    F. many of Michelangelo's sculptures were self-portraits.
    G. Michelangelo's actual appearance was not as impressive as his work.
    H. his intellectual skills were not as great as his sculptural ability.
    J. Michelangelo didn't create small-scale sculptures.

Passage IV

NATURAL SCIENCE: This passage is adapted from an excerpt of a biology text.

Imagine for a moment that you are a plant living in a bog. You strain to extract the nitrogen you need from the soil, but it's simply too acidic for the bacteria that break down dead plant matter to grow in.

(05) So where do you get the nitrogen you need? If you're a pitcher plant, you get it from insects that you catch.

Like the Venus flytrap, the sundew and the bladderwort, the pitcher plant is able to trap and consume (10)insects. But unlike these other carnivorous plants, the pitcher plant does not produce enzymes to digest the captured insects itself. Instead, the pitcher plant absorbs nutrients that are the result of a complex interaction between insect larvae that grow in the pitcher (15)plant's deadly interior.

A pitcher plant has a sweet-smelling flower and purple-veined leaves that form "pitchers" by curving in on themselves. These leaves have tiny downward-pointing hairs on them to prevent any insects that (20)happen to wander into the pitcher's clutches from wandering out again. Below the downward-pointing hairs is a highly slippery part of the leaf. When insects reach this slippery section, they fall into the heart of the pitcher plant: a highly acidic mixture of water and (25)the plant's own secretions.

First, an insect is attracted to the pitcher plant by the sugary smell of its flower. Once the victim has drowned in the deadly water, the pitcher plant has its own unique system of extracting needed nutrients from the (30)deceased insect. Inside the pitcher plant, living in the deadly acid reservoir, are the larva of three distinct insect species. The larvae of a fly, a mosquito, and a midge species all live in the noisome fluid of the pitcher plant. These larvae, which are astoundingly (35)found nowhere else in nature, work together to break down the victim insects into base components that can be absorbed by the plant, and along the way the larvae also receive needed sustenance. Within the pitcher plant is a tiny ecosystem of plants and animals (40)working together.

Each larva has a life span of about a year, which is also the life span of each pitcher plant leaf. In July adult insects deposit their young in the pitcher plant where for four months the larva consume insects (45)unlucky enough to fall into the watery pit. Then the larvae spend the cold winter months frozen inside of the pitcher plant. With the spring thaw, the larvae resume their feast until early July. At that point they are fully mature insects, ready to fly off from their (50)botanic home, find a mate and lay their eggs in a new pitcher plant receptacle.

The three different insect species do not actually compete for the insects that fall into the clutches of the pitcher plant. The fly larvae are much larger than (55)the midge and mosquito larvae. Floating at the top of the pitcher pool, the fly maggot chews on insects when they first enter the pool and drown. Underneath the fly maggot the mosquito and midge larvae lurk, waiting for carcasses or parts of carcasses that escape the (60)greedy jaws of the maggot.

Then the midge gets to work, gnawing on insects that sink below the fly. The mosquito has to wait for the midge to finish eating, since the mosquito can only consume very small particles of insect that the midge (65)chews up first. The mosquito larvae also consume the bacteria that grow on the surface of these insect particles.

Field biologists were able to examine the interaction of these species by taking clear plastic tubes, filling (70)them with water from actual pitcher plants, and then sticking these tubes into bogs. These tubes were then used in a variety of experiments to determine just how the insect larvae in pitcher plants process their food.

In one experiment, a fixed numbers of midges and (75)mosquitoes were placed in various plastic pitchers. After a week, the plastic tubes were taken to a lab and analyzed. Measurements were made of the amount of food particles in each tube, how much bacteria was in each pool, and the number of midges and mosquitoes (80)that survived. Each midge and mosquito larva was also weighed to determine how healthy it was.

Biologists found that the more midges there were in a pitcher plant, the better off the mosquitoes were. This is because instead of competing for resources (85)with the mosquitoes, the midges were actually preparing food for mosquitoes to consume. This is a unique interaction in the animal kingdom. Usually when animals are in a symbiotic relationship they both benefit in some way, but in this case the mosquito (90)population did not positively effect the midges in the experiments conducted. But since the mosquitoes brought no harm to the midges, this could not be considered a parasitic relationship. This relationship, where one species produces food for another species, (95)has been termed a "processing chain" by some biologists.

GO ON TO THE NEXT PAGE ➤

31. The passage mentions that biologists have conducted experiments demonstrating that mosquito larvae in the pitcher plant benefit from:

    A. an absence of midge larvae in the plant's basin.

    B. a dearth of fly larvae in the plant's basin.

    C. an increase in the number of midge larvae in the plant's basin.

    D. any change in the amount of bacteria in the plant's basin.

32. According to the passage, the pitcher plant has:

    I. long, penetrating roots.

    II. a sweet-smelling flower.

    III. leaves with tiny hairs on them.

    F. I only

    G. II only

    H. I and II only

    J. II and III only

33. The passage suggests that a pitcher plant leaf lives for approximately:

    A. one month.

    B. four months.

    C. one year.

    D. ten years.

34. It can reasonably be inferred from the passage that the water found in the basin of a pitcher plant is all of the following EXCEPT:

    F. full of enzymes produced by the pitcher plant.

    G. the home for several species of insect larvae.

    H. highly acidic in nature.

    J. the fluid from which the pitcher plant absorbs needed nutrients.

35. According to the passage, fly larvae differ from mosquito and midge larvae because fly larvae:

    A. do not present a danger to field biologists.

    B. always live on the bottom of the pitcher plant's basin.

    C. directly affect the number of midge larvae in the pitcher plant.

    D. are larger than mosquito and midge larvae.

36. The reason that the pitcher plant cannot extract nitrogen from the soil of a bog is due to:

    F. the pitcher plant's immature root system.

    G. the surplus of water found in boggy locations.

    H. the lack of a certain type of bacteria in the soil.

    J. the insect larvae living in the plant's interior.

37. According to the passage, mosquito larvae cannot eat insect parts until the insects have first been:

    A. broken down by the midge larva in the pitcher plant.

    B. completely absorbed by the pitcher plant.

    C. frozen for several months in the interior of the pitcher plant.

    D. completely consumed by the fly larva in the pitcher plant.

38. The passage states that biologists used plastic tubes in order to:

    F. trap mosquito larvae for testing.

    G. test the acidity of the soil found in the bog.

    H. simulate the form of the pitcher plant.

    J. give fly larvae a chance to compete with the midges and mosquitoes.

39. Based on information from the passage, the leaves of the pitcher plant have all of the following characteristics EXCEPT that pitcher plant leaves do not have:

    A. downward-pointing hairs.

    B. a way to produce digestive enzymes.

    C. purple veins on them.

    D. a section that is highly slippery.

40. Which of the following would be the best example of a "processing chain" that mirrors the midge and mosquito relationship found in the interior of the pitcher plant?

    F. A human farmer grows grains to be consumed by both humans and farm animals.

    G. A vulture can only eat a moose after it has been killed and partially consumed by a wolf.

    H. A certain fish survives by eating the bacteria found on a shark's skin and the shark benefits from this relationship with healthier skin.

    J. A bird feeds her young by taking food from other smaller birds.

STOP

END OF SECTION 3. IF YOU HAVE ANY TIME LEFT, GO OVER YOUR WORK IN THIS SECTION ONLY. DO NOT WORK IN ANY OTHER SECTION OF THE TEST.

4. SCIENCE REASONING TEST

40 Questions • Time—35 Minutes

Directions: This test consists of seven passages, each followed by several questions. Read each passage, select the correct answer for each question, and mark the oval representing the correct answer on your answer sheet. You may NOT use a calculator on this test.

Passage I

As power is supplied to a circuit, current flows through the circuit. An ammeter is the device used to measure the current and many ammeters measure current in milliamps (mA). The voltage responsible for the current can be measured by a voltmeter and is measured in volts. When a resistor is placed in a circuit, it dampens the current flowing through a circuit at a given voltage.

If there is a linear relationship between current and voltage when a resistor is placed in the circuit, the resistor is considered an *ohmic device*. If the temperature of the resistor changes, then it is not considered an ohmic device. Some resistors are sensitive to small external temperature changes and will show a change in resistance as a result of these temperature changes. These resistors are called *thermistors*. The change in resistance exhibited by a thermistor can be detected by a change in the observed current at a given voltage.

The following procedure was performed to investigate whether different resistors acted as ohmic devices in a circuit. The circuit was constructed as shown in Figure 1.

Figure 1

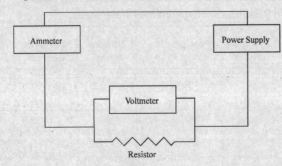

After each resistor was connected to the circuit, the resistor was submerged in water to detect any changes in temperature as well its sensitivity to different beginning temperatures. The power source was turned on and the voltage of the power source and the resulting current were recorded. The voltage was changed several times and the corresponding current was noted.

Table 1 summarizes the results when 3 different resistors were tested at 2 different temperatures. In all cases, no change in water temperature was observed.

Table 1

Voltage (V)	Resistor A 23°C Current (mA)	Resistor A 25°C Current (mA)	Resistor B 23°C Current (mA)	Resistor B 25°C Current (mA)	Resistor C 23°C Current (mA)	Resistor C 25°C Current (mA)
0.25	25	25	150	150	5	4.5
0.50	50	50	195	195	10	9.0
1.00	100	100	230	230	20	18.0
2.00	200	200	295	295	40	36.0
3.00	300	300	345	345	60	54.0
4.00	400	400	405	405	80	72.0
4.50	450	450	420	420	90	81.0
5.00	500	500	445	445	100	90.0

1. When the voltage is 3.0 volts and the temperature 23°C, what is the current of the circuit when Resistor B is used?

   A. 54 milliamps
   B. 60 milliamps
   C. 300 milliamps
   D. 345 milliamps

2. If 6.0 volts were used in the circuit with Resistor C at 25°C, approximately what would the current have read?

   F. 108 milliamps

   G. 140 milliamps

   H. 485 milliamps

   J. 600 milliamps

3. According to the data, which of the following resistors is not sensitive to temperature?

   I. Resistor A

   II. Resistor B

   III. Resistor C

   A. I only

   B. III only

   C. I and II only

   D. II and III only

4. Which of the following observations supports that one of the resistors is a thermistor?

   F. Resistor A showed a change in resistance when introduced to two different temperatures.

   G. Resistor B had a greater measured current than Resistor A.

   H. Resistor C had a change in resistance when introduced to two different temperatures.

   J. Resistor C had a lower observed current than Resistor A.

5. Based on the data in Table 1, Resistor B does not appear to be an ohmic device because:

   A. at a constant voltage the current varies with temperature.

   B. the current is unaffected by temperature.

   C. the voltage and current have a linear relationship.

   D. the voltage and current do not have a linear relationship.

6. Which of the following hypotheses would be disproved if there had been a noted temperature change in the water for all six trials?

   F. Resistor A is an ohmic device because of its linear relationship between voltage and current.

   G. Resistor B is affected by different starting temperatures.

   H. Resistor C is not an ohmic device because it does not have a linear relationship between voltage and current.

   J. Resistor C is not affected by different starting temperatures.

Passage II

A state forestry commission engaged a group of ecologists to study the nutrient flow in a forest on federal lands that was being considered for lease to a logging company. They were also asked to study the effects of clear-cutting in selected areas to predict what the long-term effects on the nutrient budget might be. The scientists selected several small sections of the forest for observation and experiment.

The first task was to estimate the average nutrient flow within the entire forest area. Table 1 shows their estimate based on 6 experimental areas chosen within the forest. Nutrients enter the forest ecosystem via precipitation, so rain gauges were set up in various locations in the study areas. Nutrients exit the ecosystem through runoff from streams and rivers, so the ecologists measured stream flows in the designated areas.

Table 1   Average Concentrations of Dissolved Substances in Bulk Precipitation and Stream Water in 6 Undisturbed Experimental Watersheds.

Substance	Precipitation	Stream Water	Percent Change
Calcium	0.21	1.51	–619%
Magnesium	0.05	0.37	–640%
Potassium	0.10	0.23	–130%
Sodium	0.12	0.94	–683%
Aluminum	0.01	0.24	–2,300%
Ammonium	0.22	0.05	340%
Sulfate	3.10	6.20	–100%
Nitrate	1.30	1.14	12%

continued

Table 1   (cont.)

Substance	Precipitation	Stream Water	Percent Change
Chloride	0.42	0.64	–52%
Dissolved Silica	0.03	4.59	–15,300%

Notes: Data is given in kilograms per dry weight of materials per hectare of the watershed. Basin-caught materials are coarse, net-caught materials are fine and filter-caught materials are super-fine.

After estimating the overall nutrient flow in this forest, the ecologists had one 15-hectare* area cleared of trees in order to determine the amount of increase that would occur in runoff. The trees were removed from the area, but nothing else was disturbed. For the first two years after the logging, an herbicide was applied so that no vegetation would grow back. The ecologists then compared this cleared watershed with one of the intact watersheds under study. They measured the stream flow for the first three years after the logging took place. Table 2 summarizes the amounts of organic and inorganic matter found at the watershed basin. A net and filter system was utilized to catch finer matter as the runoff exited the watershed area.

*A hectare is a metric unit of measure equal to 2.471 acres.

Table 2   Annual Losses of Particulate Matter

Source of Output	Year	Watershed 1 Undisturbed Area		Watershed 2 Deforested Area	
		Organic	Inorganic	Organic	Inorganic
Ponding Basin	1	4.62	8.30	35.41	158.32
Net	1	0.43	0.02	0.26	0.01
Filter	1	2.64	2.80	4.23	4.80
Ponding Basin	2	11.39	31.00	45.13	321.88
Net	2	0.43	0.02	0.25	0.03
Filter	2	3.32	3.70	6.24	7.10
Ponding Basin	3	3.83	5.78	53.72	540.32
Net	3	0.42	0.01	0.27	0.04
Filter	3	2.61	2.97	8.73	12.98

Notes: Data is given in kilograms per dry weight of materials per hectare of the watershed. Basin-caught materials are coarse, net-caught materials are fine and filter-caught materials are super-fine.

7. Based on the figures reported in Table 1, which is apparently true of the nutrient budget as estimated using the 6 experimental areas?

A. There is a net loss for all measured nutrients entering the ecosystem.

B. There is a net gain for all measured nutrients entering the ecosystem,

C. There is a net loss for all measured nutrients except for ammonium and nitrate.

D. There is a net gain for all measured nutrients except for ammonium and nitrate.

8. According to the data obtained, which substances are most dramatically depleted in this ecosystem?

F. Sodium and Calcium

G. Silica and Aluminum

H. Magnesium and Potassium

J. Chloride and Nitrate

9. Which of the following best explains why the scientists chose to use three different collection methods?

A. It enabled them to collect particulate matter at different water sheds.

B. It enabled them to collect particulate matter of different sizes.

C. All of the collected particulate matter was quite coarse.

D. The collected particulate matter was dissolved in water.

10. Which of the following hypotheses concerning the effects of logging on the forest ecosystem is supported by the data?

F. Logging decreases the loss of organic and inorganic matter from the forest ecosystem.

G. Logging increases the loss of organic matter, but has no effect on inorganic matter in the forest ecosystem.

H. Logging increases the loss of inorganic matter, but has no effect on organic matter in the forest ecosystem.

J. Logging increases the loss of organic and inorganic matter from the forest ecosystem.

11. Based on the trend in the numbers over the first 3 years of observing the undisturbed and logged watershed areas reported in Table 2, it would be reasonable to predict that the runoff:

    A. would vary from year to year within narrow limits in the undisturbed area, but steadily increase in the logged area.

    B. in both experimental areas would steadily increase over the years.

    C. in both experimental areas would vary from year to year.

    D. in the undisturbed area would remain constant, but the runoff in the logged area would vary from year to year.

12. The ecologists inform the state officials that the bark in trees contains a significant proportion of nutrients. If the state officials are committed to leasing a set amount of this federal land to a logging company, they might reduce the nutrient loss in that region by:

    F. removing all remains from the trees after they are cut down so that the area is clear for new growth.

    G. applying herbicide immediately after any logging operation.

    H. allowing the logging companies to use the cleared areas for roads.

    J. stripping the bark from all logged trees and leaving it behind in the cleared area.

Passage III

Elements are categorized to help understand the similarities and differences between them. One way is to consider their similarities based on the number of negatively charged particles in a particular orbit. Alkali metals are reactive elements that contain one electron in what is considered an *s* orbital. Scientists have been able to observe different characteristics in alkali metals. Atomic number is the number of positively charged particles (protons) in an element. These positively charged particles are balanced with the same number of electrons in a neutrally charged atom.

Table 1 contains data for the alkali metals, including the atomic number, atomic weight, melting point, and density.

Table 1

Element	Atomic Number	Atomic Weight (amu)	Melting Point (°C)	Density (g/cm³)
Lithium	3	6.9	181	0.53
Sodium	11	23.0	98	0.97
Potassium	19	39.1	63	0.86
Rubidium	37	85.5	39	1.53
Cesium	55	132.9	29	1.87

13. The element with atomic weight of 85.5 amu has a melting point of:

    A. 29°C
    B. 37°C
    C. 39°C
    D. 63°C

14. According to the table, which of the following elements has a density of approximately twice that of sodium?

    F. Lithium
    G. Potassium
    H. Rubidium
    J. Cesium

15. The data seems to indicate that as atomic number increases, melting point:

    A. increases
    B. decreases
    C. remains constant
    D. decreases, then increases

16. It was hypothesized that the density will increase as atomic weight increases. Based on the data in the table, which of the following pairs of substances supports this hypothesis?

    I. Sodium and Potassium

    II. Rubidium and Cesium

    III. Lithium and Potassium

    F. I only
    G. III only
    H. I and II only
    J. II and III only

GO ON TO THE NEXT PAGE ➤

17. If an alkali metal existed with an atomic number greater than that of cesium, which of the following would be the best predicted measurements for its melting point and density?

   A. Melting point would be greater than 29°C and density would be greater than 1.87 g/cm³.

   B. Melting point would be less than 29°C and density would be less than 1.87 g/cm³.

   C. Melting point would be greater than 29ϒC and density would be less than 1.87 g/cm³.

   D. Melting point would be less than 29ϒC and density would be uncertain.

Passage IV

By studying rock samples, geologists can reconstruct much of an area's geologic history. Table 1 lists rock samplings taken along a line proceeding east and inland from a shoreline, in 20-mile intervals. The sampled rock found at each altitude and distance is shown, and the crystallization temperature and ages typical of each type of rock are listed. Figure 1 shows the cross-sectional area of measurement.

Table 1

Distance East (miles)	Altitude (ft)	Type of Rock in Sample	Crystallization Temp* (°C)	Estimated Age (millions of years)
0 (shoreline)	0	Rhyolite	750°	10.0
20	6,000	Diorite	850°	250.0
40	5,000	Peridotite	1,200°	200.0
60	90	Shale	750°	0.1
80	−10	Limestone	800°	6.0
100	25	Breccia	750°	0.5
120	75	Andesite	950°	3.6
140	2,000	Andesite	900°	4.0
160	3,300	Gabbro	1,100°	300.0
180	13,900	Granite	700°	400.0

*(Crystallization temperature is based on the mineral composition of the rock)

Figure 1

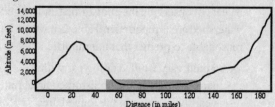

18. What is the relationship between the ages of rocks and altitude?

   F. The oldest rocks are generally found at lower altitudes.

   G. The oldest rocks are generally found at higher altitudes.

   H. There is no relationship between altitude and rock ages.

   J. Rocks less than 100 million years old are only found in areas less than 1,000 feet in altitude.

19. If higher crystallization temperatures generally produce darker-colored rocks, which of the following rocks is most likely to be dark-colored?

   A. Limestone

   B. Shale

   C. Gabbro

   D. Granite

20. Which of the following measurements is shown on the vertical axis in Figure 1?

   F. Altitude

   G. Distance inland from shoreline

   H. Temperature

   J. Age of rocks

21. Iron ore is usually found in rocks that crystallize at higher temperatures. From the data shown, how far east of the shoreline would a miner try to find large concentrations of iron?

   A. 40 miles

   B. 100 miles

   C. 120 miles

   D. 180 miles

22. Based on the data provided, what is the relationship between distance from shoreline and the ages of the rock samples?

    F. Rocks closer to the shoreline are always younger.

    G. Rocks closer to the shoreline are always older.

    H. The age of rocks gradually increases farther inland.

    J. There is no consistent relationship between the distance from shore and the ages of the rock samples.

23. Limestone is *sedimentary* rock that develops from the accumulated deposits of sea organisms with shells. Andesite is *igneous* rock deposited by lava flows from volcanoes. Which of the following is the best hypothesis about the geologic record of the shaded area?

    A. Part of this area was once a sea while volcanoes erupted to the east.

    B. Part of this area was once a sea; later, volcanoes erupted to the east.

    C. A volcano arose west of an inland sea in this area.

    D. A sea existed in part of this area after nearby volcanoes became extinct.

Passage V

The apparent bird-dinosaur evolutionary connection has been a source of considerable debate among paleontologists during the second half of the twentieth-century. This association was proposed on the basis of numerous anatomical similarities, and has been supported by the discovery of fossils of a small number of seeming transitional forms uncovered in Europe and Asia. Yet scientists differ in their interpretation of the significance of these similarities and the nature of the fossil evidence as well.

Paleontologist A

The discovery of fossil reptiles equipped with feathers, wings and beak-like snouts may be significant, but more likely provides only limited support for the dinosaurs-into-birds hypothesis. Convergent evolution often provides animals of very distant lineages with similar appendages—witness, for example, the similarities in the body shape and presence of fins in fish and cetaceans such as whales and dolphins. We would never put forth the idea that orcas evolved from sharks based on the morphological similarities of these creatures; it would be immediately deemed absurd.

It is more likely the case that birds and dinosaurs share a very distant common ancestor, perhaps from among the thecodonts. These prototypical reptiles of the late Permian survived the largest mass extinction recorded in the planet's history to bring forth many more recent lines; crocodiles, dinosaurs, pterosaurs and birds are the most notable among these.

Paleontologist B

In our studies of numerous dinosaur fossils, it has become obvious that the lifestyles of dinosaurs were amazingly varied. No longer is it acceptable to view dinosaurs only as lumbering, cold-blooded monsters; indeed, the most frightening dinosaurs did not lumber at all. They were agile, swift and deadly predators, who could run, leap, kick and shred to pieces an animal they were intent upon consuming. Lightweight muscular body structure would be crucial to the success of this type of predator.

Based upon this observation, along with a number of obvious physical similarities and evidence from the fossil record, we are convinced that birds evolved from small, carnivorous dinosaurs called theropods. A mere examination of the forelimb, hindlimb and feet of a theropod fossil, and a comparison to one of the five available specimens of *Archaeopteryx** will bear this out. In addition, more recent discoveries of fossil dinosaurs with bird-like traits and habits, particularly the finds uncovered in the Liaoning province of China, lend further credible support for our position that birds are for all intents and purposes actual members of the lineage Dinosauria living and thriving in our midst.

*Archaeopteryx was a feathered reptile of the late Jurassic Era thought to represent an intermediate form between dinosaurs and birds.

GO ON TO THE NEXT PAGE

24. According to Paleontologist A, similarities in the body forms of dinosaurs and birds:

    F. represent a failed experiment of evolution.

    G. are the products of convergent evolution.

    H. are completely without significance.

    J. helped both types of organism survive a large mass extinction.

25. Which of the following types of evidence, if found, would lend strong support to the position of Paleontologist A?

    A. Discovery of thecodont fossils with characteristics of modern birds and existing dinosaur fossils.

    B. Discovery of another possible intermediate form between dinosaurs and birds from the Jurassic Era.

    C. Discovery of an avian prototype dating back to before the beginning of the era of dinosaur dominance.

    D. A careful examination of several sets of theropod fossil remains.

26. Which of the following is a criticism that Paleontologist A would make of the avian evolutionary hypothesis of Paleontologist B?

    F. It ignores the possibility of the existence of transitional forms.

    G. It ignores the impact of a very large mass extinction.

    H. It assumes that morphological similarities are a result of a direct lineage.

    J. It proposes that dinosaurs and birds arose from distant lineages.

27. Which of the following perspectives would be consistent with the views of Paleontologist B?

    A. Convergent evolution produces similar forms in diverse lineages.

    B. Dinosaurs and birds may be related via a common ancestor.

    C. Birds and dinosaurs arose out of completely separate lineages.

    D. Birds arose out of a lineage of dinosaurs.

28. If genetic evidence was established to date the avian lineage 85 million years prior to the rise of *Archaeopteryx*, this finding would tend to:

    F. support the theory of Paleontologist A.

    G. support the theory of Paleontologist B.

    H. support the theories of both paleontologists.

    J. refute the theories of both paleontologists.

29. If Paleontologist B could confirm that birds appeared much later in evolutionary history than any dinosaurs, which of the following statements would reconcile this fact with the theory of Paleontologist A?

    A. The ancestors of birds and the ancestors of dinosaurs were exposed to specific environmental conditions at the same time and this caused the development of similar characteristics.

    B. The ancestors of birds and the ancestors of dinosaurs were exposed to specific environmental conditions that caused the development of similar characteristics, but the dinosaur ancestors were exposed to these environmental conditions later than the bird ancestors were.

    C. The rate of evolutionary change from the thecodont ancestor was much slower for the lineage that resulted in birds than for the lineage that resulted in dinosaurs.

    D. The rate of evolutionary change from the thecodont ancestor was much faster for the lineage that resulted in birds than for the lineage that resulted in dinosaurs.

Passage VI

Ecology graduate students wished to experiment with levels of diversity in a simple community to observe the relationship between increasing complexity and stability of populations. In particular, they were interested in the impact of changing certain conditions in a community on populations of two species of *Paramecium*, a common ciliated protozoan.

A *trophic level* is the number of steps a species is away from the producer species in a community. Producers are organisms that synthesize energy out of chemical products into nutrients. Table 1 shows the trophic level occupied by each type of organism involved in the experiments, and the number of species that would be used on each level.

Table 1

Trophic Level	Organism	Number of Species Studied
First	Bacteria	3
Second	Paramecia	2
Third	Amoebae (predator of protozoa)	2

Experiment 1

The graduate students wished to study the relationship between one species of *Paramecium* and the number of species of bacteria available for consumption in the community. They created 300 "microcosms"—100 cultures each populated with communities of one, two or three species of bacteria and one of the *Paramecium* species. After 20 days, they examined the cultures individually. The results are displayed in Table 2.

Table 2

Number of Bacterium Species	Number of Cultures in Which Paramecia Survived
1	32/100
2	61/100
3	70/100

Experiment 2

The students then decided to study how two species of Paramecium would be affected when different combinations of Paramecium and bacteria were mixed in the cultures. They created 100 dishes each of six separate types of communities—600 cultures with different combinations of the Paramecium and the three bacteria species. After 20 days, they examined the cultures and recorded their results. These results are reproduced in Table 3.

Table 3

Number of Bacterium/ Paramecium Species	Number of Cultures in which Paramecia Survived
1/1	35/100
2/1	58/100
3/1	65/100
1/2	20/100
2/2	26/100
3/2	31/100

Experiment 3

The last condition that the graduate students studied was the addition of a third trophic level to their microcosms. They introduced two different species of *Amoebae* that feed on *Paramecium*. They decided to use five different versions in 100 culture dishes each, creating 500 communities for this last experiment. They allowed them to grow undisturbed for 20 days, and then examined the cultures and recorded their results in Table 4 displayed below.

Table 4

Number of Bacterium/ Paramecium/ Amoeba Species	Number of Cultures in Which Paramecia Survived
1/1/1	22/100
2/1/1	15/100
2/2/1	8/100
2/2/2	6/100
3/2/2	2/100

30. Which of the following factors was varied in Experiment 1?

F. The species of *Paramecium* in the community.

G. The number of species of bacteria present in the community.

H. The medium used to culture the microbes.

J. The number of trophic levels in the community.

GO ON TO THE NEXT PAGE

31. According to the results of Experiments 1 and 2, increasing the number of bacteria species present in the community:

    A. decreased the survival rates of the *Paramecium* in the community.

    B. increased the survival rates of the *Paramecium* in the community.

    C. had no effect on any species in the community.

    D. decreased the survival rates of one type of bacteria in the community.

32. According to the results of Experiment 2, increasing the number of *Paramecium* species in the community was related to:

    F. decreased survival rates for the *Paramecium* depending on the number of bacteria species present in the community.

    G. decreased survival rates for all species present in the community.

    H. decreased survival rates for the *Paramecium* independent of the number of bacteria species present in the community.

    J. increased survival rates for the *Paramecium* depending on the number of bacteria species present in the community.

33. What new factor was introduced in Experiment 3?

    A. An additional species of bacteria.

    B. A longer time for incubation of the experimental cultures.

    C. A new method for culturing the experimental microbes.

    D. An additional trophic level.

34. After examining the results of Experiment 3, it would be reasonable to conclude that increased diversity in the experimental communities:

    F. was beneficial to all species present in the communities.

    G. had no effect on any species in the communities.

    H. had a detrimental effect on the survival rate of one species of *Amoebae* only.

    J. had a detrimental effect on the survival rates of both species of *Paramecium* under study.

Passage VII

The nine planets of our solar systems were categorized as planets as each was discovered. Scientists have observed some differences among the planets that have caused them to reconsider whether all of the planets should retain their current categorization.

There has been the discovery and classification of objects call Trans-Neptunian Objects that do not fit into the existing categories of planets, satellites (moons), comets, or asteroids. Some of the characteristics that make these objects distinct include size, orbital inclination, and orbital eccentricity. Orbital inclination is the amount the orbit is tilted with respect to the plane of the solar system. Orbital eccentricity refers to the amount that the orbit deviates from a circular orbit. The difficulty that scientists face is that the wide variation among the planets and among the Trans-Neptunian Objects on these characteristics makes it difficult to create numerical classifications upon which everyone can agree.

The table below summarizes many of the qualities of the nine planets, as well as those of the Earth's Moon for comparison.

	Mass (kg)	Mean Density (kg/m³)	Black-body Temp. (°K)	Orbital Inclination (°)	Orbital Eccentricity	Rotation Period (hrs)
Planet						
Mercury	3.3×10^{23}	5,427	442.5	7.000	0.2056	1,407.60
Venus	4.9×10^{24}	5,204	238.9	3.390	0.0068	5,832.50
Earth	6.0×10^{24}	5,520	247.3	0.000	0.0167	23.93
Mars	6.4×10^{23}	3,933	216.6	1.850	0.0934	24.62
Jupiter	1.9×10^{27}	1,326	90.6	1.305	0.0484	9.93
Saturn	5.7×10^{26}	687	63.9	2.484	0.0542	10.50
Uranus	8.7×10^{25}	1,318	35.9	0.770	0.0472	17.24
Neptune	1.0×10^{26}	1,638	33.2	1.769	0.0086	16.11
Pluto	1.3×10^{22}	2,050	42.7	17.140	0.2488	153.29

	Mass (kg)	Mean Density (kg/m³)	Black-body Temp. (°K)	Orbital Inclination (°)	Orbital Eccentricity	Rotation Period (hrs)
Satellite						
Earth's Moon	7.3 × 10²²	3,340	274.5	5.145	0.0549	655.73

35. Neptune has a density greater than which of the following planets?

    A. Mars, Venus, and Mercury

    B. Saturn, Uranus, and Jupiter

    C. Earth, Jupiter, and Pluto

    D. Venus, Saturn, and Earth

36. Black-body temperature is the temperature that would result from the planet absorbing all received electromagnetic radiation without reflection. If black-body temperatures are higher for objects closer to the Sun, which of the following would be considered furthest from the Sun based on the data presented?

    F. Mercury

    G. Uranus

    H. Pluto

    J. Neptune

37. If an astronomer proposed that Trans-Neptunian Objects would be defined based solely on having an orbital inclination greater than 5 degrees and orbital eccentricity of 0.2, how many of the current planets would be recategorized as Trans-Neptunian Objects?

    A. 4

    B. 3

    C. 2

    D. 1

38. If scientists were to define planets based only on a minimum mass requirement and the mass designated would be greater than that of the Earth's Moon, which of the current planets would lose its designation as a planet?

    F. Mercury

    G. Mars

    H. Pluto

    J. Jupiter

39. It was hypothesized that Jupiter, Saturn, Neptune, and Uranus were gaseous planets, whereas the others were composed of solid material. Which of the following statements best supports this hypothesis?

    A. Jupiter, Saturn, Neptune, and Uranus have lower temperatures than most of the other planets.

    B. Jupiter, Saturn, Neptune, and Uranus have densities much smaller than the densities of the other planets.

    C. Jupiter, Saturn, Neptune, and Uranus have greater masses than the other planets.

    D. Jupiter, Saturn, Neptune, and Uranus have rotation periods that are much shorter than the other planets.

40. Which of the following statements is NOT supported by the data?

    F. Mercury and Venus exhibit the longest rotation periods of all the planets.

    G. Rotation period decreases as black-body temperature decreases.

    H. The two planets with the greatest mass have the shortest rotation periods.

    J. Mars and Earth have rotation periods within one hour of length of each other.

STOP

END OF SECTION 4. IF YOU HAVE ANY TIME LEFT, GO OVER YOUR WORK IN THIS SECTION ONLY. DO NOT WORK IN ANY OTHER SECTION OF THE TEST.

PRACTICE EXAMINATION 3

Answer Key

1. English Test

1. D	16. J	31. A	46. J	61. C
2. F	17. A	32. H	47. B	62. J
3. D	18. G	33. C	48. H	63. D
4. F	19. B	34. F	49. B	64. H
5. B	20. J	35. B	50. F	65. D
6. J	21. D	36. H	51. B	66. G
7. C	22. G	37. D	52. H	67. C
8. G	23. C	38. G	53. D	68. F
9. A	24. G	39. C	54. F	69. D
10. J	25. B	40. H	55. D	70. J
11. A	26. F	41. D	56. J	71. D
12. F	27. A	42. J	57. B	72. H
13. B	28. H	43. A	58. J	73. C
14. H	29. D	44. F	59. A	74. F
15. B	30. F	45. C	60. H	75. C

2. Mathematics Test

1. E	13. E	25. C	37. A	49. B
2. J	14. F	26. K	38. F	50. H
3. C	15. D	27. B	39. A	51. B
4. K	16. J	28. H	40. K	52. K
5. C	17. D	29. D	41. C	53. A
6. G	18. G	30. G	42. H	54. G
7. E	19. E	31. A	43. E	55. A
8. H	20. G	32. J	44. F	56. J
9. B	21. D	33. E	45. B	57. C
10. J	22. J	34. F	46. G	58. J
11. E	23. A	35. D	47. A	59. B
12. H	24. K	36. H	48. K	60. G

3. Reading Test

1. D	9. D	17. D	25. A	33. C
2. H	10. H	18. G	26. H	34. F
3. B	11. B	19. D	27. B	35. D
4. G	12. J	20. H	28. F	36. H
5. B	13. B	21. C	29. D	37. A
6. J	14. H	22. F	30. G	38. H
7. C	15. A	23. D	31. C	39. B
8. F	16. F	24. H	32. J	40. G

4. Science Reasoning Test

1. D	9. B	17. D	25. A	33. D
2. F	10. J	18. G	26. H	34. J
3. C	11. A	19. C	27. D	35. B
4. H	12. J	20. F	28. F	36. J
5. D	13. C	21. A	29. C	37. C
6. F	14. J	22. J	30. G	38. H
7. C	15. B	23. B	31. B	39. B
8. G	16. J	24. G	32. F	40. G

PRACTICE EXAMINATION 3

Explanatory Answers

1. English Test

Passage I

1. **D** is correct. This option gets rid of the redundant phrasing caused by two similar verbs.

2. **F** is correct. *With* is the appropriate preposition in this common phrase. The phrase should not be omitted because it explains the writer's trembling.

3. **D** is correct. *Kneel* indicates a downward motion, and therefore no other word is necessary.

4. **F** is correct. The action is in the process of happening, therefore the present continuous tense is appropriate.

5. **B** is correct. A comma is needed after *fever* to separate the introductory phrase from the main clause of the sentence. No comma is needed before *and* because both verbs belong to the same subject.

6. **J** is correct. The past tense is appropriate because the writer is describing his childhood.

7. **C** is correct. This option clearly states the writer's point that in New York, culture was the dominating element even when it came to marking the passage of the seasons.

8. **G** is correct. *Though* is the appropriate conjunction to indicate the contrast between knowing the highlights and knowing the particulars of the seasons.

9. **A** is correct. Paragraph 2 tells us that the writer grew up knowing little about nature. This fact is essential to understanding the garden's effect on the writer.

10. **J** is correct. The retaining wall is located *at* the side of the house. It is not attached to the house, nor is it dangling in air, as *over* would suggest.

11. **A** is correct. No commas should be used because *bright* modifies yellow and all the other colors. No commas are needed to separate the colors because the writer has chosen to link them with the conjunction *and.*

12. **F** is correct. The present tense is appropriate for a general situation that is repeated year after year. The plural, *Daffodils,* demands the third person plural form of the verb.

13. **B** is correct. A relative pronoun is needed to link the words with what they stand for. *That* is appropriate for objects.

14. **H** is correct. The tone of the essay is personal and informal.

15. **B** is correct. This detail is an example of how little the writer knew about nature and therefore belongs in the paragraph that discusses growing up in New York.

Passage II

16. **J** is correct. The idiomatic expression is: *as x goes, so goes y.* The other options either add unnecessary words or are simply awkward.

17. **A** is correct. From the following sentence, it is clear that the writer means that this phenomenon is *well understood* when applied to the present, but not when applied to the past.

18. **G** is correct. The writer is speaking about our present understanding of trade in the past. It is an assertion without any sense of the conditional.

19. **B** is correct. This is the only sentence that stresses the historical importance of exchange and thereby links the previous paragraph to the examples of this phenomenon presented in paragraph 2.

20. **J** is correct. The clearest construction lists the subjects and proceeds directly to the verb without punctuation or unnecessary words.

21. **D** is correct. No punctuation should separate the noun from the prepositional phrase that identifies it.

22. **G** is correct. The present perfect tense indicates the connection between the past and the present, between antiquity and today.

23. **C** is correct. *Greeks* is the subject of the relative clause, and therefore the relative pronoun *who* is appropriate.

24. **G** is correct. A coordinating conjunction is needed to link the two independent clauses. *And* is the best choice because it indicates the consequential relationship between the clauses. *Therefore* also expresses this relationship but cannot be used to link two independent clauses.

25. **B** is correct. This phrasing properly indicates that the question is about the character of modern Italy. The other options ask different questions.

26. **F** is correct. The imperative form avoids unnecessary words and maintains the authoritative tone of the essay.

27. **A** is correct. This sentence makes the point that these foods are not indigenous to the nations that rely on them, and this point is crucial to the main idea of the essay.

28. **H** is correct. As in question 20, the sentence begins with a series of subjects and should then proceed to the verb without punctuation or unnecessary words.

29. **D** is correct. *For* creates a smooth transition from the previous sentence without changing the meaning. *Therefore* would wrongly indicate that the way we think of Italy is a direct consequence of the transformation of exchanged goods.

30. **F** is correct. This option emphasizes the creative transformation of tomatoes and pasta by Italian cooking.

Passage III

31. **A** is correct. A comma is necessary to separate the modifying phrase from *remedies*, the noun it modifies. The other options that separate would only work if the final phrase were an independent clause.

32. **H** is correct. *Which* is used to ask a question involving a choice of many. In this case it is also required by parallel structure.

33. **C** is correct. This option avoids unnecessary words and is the clearest.

34. **F** is correct. There is no need for a conjugated verb (which would have to be in the continuous tense). The gerund phrase describes what the woman is doing and keeps the sentence flowing.

35. **B** is correct. The present tense is needed because the sentence speaks about today. *One of the reasons* is singular, so the third person singular is required.

36. **H** is correct. This option supplies the possessive pronoun for alternative medicine.

37. **D** is correct. This option is the most straightforward and avoids awkward phrasing.

38. **G** is correct. *Yet* indicates the contrasting nature of sentence 1. By placing it after sentence 3, it counters the position of the medical establishment and serves as a bridge to the conclusion that medical science does not hold all the answers.

39. **C** is correct. *Than* is part of a comparison and should come directly after the comparative form of the adjective.

40. **H** is correct. The sentence has only one subject, and the verb should not be separated from it by punctuation.

41. **D** is correct. This sentence declares that the antagonism of the previous paragraph is lessening and paves the way for the examples that follow.

42. **J** is correct. This option expresses the intended possibility while avoiding unnecessary words.

43. **A** is correct. The reader was addressed directly as *you* in the opening sentence, which is referred to here.

44. **F** is correct. Paragraph 2 mentions the theory behind acupuncture and provides an example of its use. In addition, Paragraph 2 is the only option that discusses homeopathy without also mentioning medical science. Therefore, an exploration of homeopathy's philosophy should follow here.

45. **C** is correct. The essay discusses alternative medicine in terms of its possible but unproven value in the field of health.

Passage IV

46. **J** is correct. The phrase refers to the past and so the verbs must be in the past tense. The plural subject demands the third person plural form of the verb.

47. **B** is correct. The first sentence of the paragraph tells us that the writer must prove herself in reality. This answer is the only one that maintains such a meaning, and is correctly punctuated with a colon to separate the two related independent clauses.

48. **H** is correct. This option maintains the parallel structure set up by the preposition *with* and thus indicates that the two factors mentioned are sides of the same problem.

49. **B** is correct. This option turns the fragment into a complete sentence.

50. **F** is correct. This option makes it clear that the writer is being asked to write a piece about the First Lady's charity work.

51. **B** is correct. The gerund phrase acts as a noun, in this case the object of the verb *meant,* creating a correct sentence. The form should be positive because the essay makes it clear that the author did break ground.

52. **H** is correct. Commas are required to set "however" apart from the rest of the sentence.

53. **D** is correct. The verb *would tell* in the previous part of the sentence sets up a parallel structure that requires *describe* and *complain.*

54. **F** is correct. The suggested paragraph would add details that are unnecessary in making the writer's point and would therefore constitute a digression.

55. **D** is correct. This is the only answer choice that indicates that the writer is contrasting her behavior in the previous paragraph to the behavior of her male colleagues.

56. **J** is correct. This option avoids unnecessary wording and correctly conveys the writer's feeling that her complete honesty was inappropriate for her workplace.

57. **B** is correct. The relative subject pronoun is needed because *women* is the subject of the relative clause.

58. **J** is correct. The opening sentence of the paragraph indicates that the writer has set some kind of expectation up that her work will not be first rate. Therefore, in order for this paragraph to be most effective, it should come at the end of the passage, after the writer has shown us what she has done to set up such an expectation. In addition, the last line of the paragraph serves to point out the lesson that has been learned, concluding the essay.

59. **A** is correct. The writer sets up important, relevant information regarding her behavior that ultimately helped her to understand why she needed to put on a professional face.

60. **H** is correct. The writer is conveying an experience she had in her professional life that led to a personal revelation.

Passage V

61. **C** is correct. *Illiterate* means unable to read, and *population* is a singular noun.

62. **J** is correct. The size of the country is irrelevant here.

63. **D** is correct. The word *neighbors* is part of a list and should be separated from the next item by a comma.

64. **H** is correct. The *willingness* refers to that of the neighbors, friends and relatives and so the possessive pronoun is called for here.

65. **D** is correct. The sentence describes the age of the author at the time referred to, requiring the simple past tense of the verb *to be.*

66. **G** is correct. *To live under* a dictatorship is the idiomatic phrase.

67. **C** is correct. No punctuation is needed before the prepositional phrase that begins with *in.*

68. **F** is correct. The modifier indicates a quantity of critical acclaim, and *acclaim* is a singular noun. *Too much* would give the sentence an unwanted negative connotation.

69. **D** is correct. The underlined portion is irrelevant and deviates from the tone of the essay.

70. **J** is correct. This option links Danticat's childhood behavior with her development as a writer.

71. **D** is correct. This option avoids unnecessary words and irrelevant facts.

72. **H** is correct. Only one author is being referred to and the possessive form is used to indicate that the subject matter belongs to the author.

73. **C** is correct. This option is the most logical because of the author's subject matter. The negative construction requires the conjunctions *neither, nor*.

74. **F** is correct. This option introduces the informative, impersonal tone of the essay and provides an introduction to the theme of storytelling.

75. **C** is correct. The essay is primarily about an emerging writer.

2. Mathematics Test

1. **E.** $\frac{32}{80} = .4 = 40\%$ of the children missed at least one day in January.

2. **J.** An exterior angle of a triangle is equal to the sum of the two opposite interior angles. The measure of $\angle X$ is $40° + 55° = 95°$.

3. **C.** The machine costs $P + L$ to operate each hour, so if it operates for x hours. The expression would be $(P + L)x$.

4. **K.** If you sketch each of the segments on a coordinate plane, you'll find that only the segment connecting $(2,1)$ and $(2,5)$ intersects with the original segment.

5. **C.** Jacob's cost is $5(1 + .25(1)) + 5(1 + .25(3)) = 6.25 + 8.75 = 15.00$ dollars.

6. **G.** $x^2 + x - 30 = (x + 6)(x - 5)$

7. **E.** $\frac{2}{5} + \frac{1}{8} + .177 = .4 + .125 + .177 = .702$.

8. **H.** If the area of triangle ABC is 5 square inches, then you can solve for its height:

$$\frac{1}{2}(2)h = 5$$
$$h = 5$$

Triangle ACD has the same height, so its area is $\frac{1}{2}(8)(5) = 20$ square inches.

9. **B.** $(-1)^2 - 4(-1)(-3) + (-3) = 1 - 12 - 3 = -14$.

10. **J.** $(3 + \sqrt{2})(4 - \sqrt{2}) = 12 - 3\sqrt{2} + 4\sqrt{2} = 10 + \sqrt{2}$

11. **E.** The sum of the interior angles of a polygon can be generalized by the formula $(N - 2)(180°)$, where N is the number of sides of the polygon. The sum of the interior angles of a hexagon is $(6 - 2)(180°) = 720°$. In a regular hexagon the six interior angles are all equal, so each angle is $\frac{720°}{6} = 120°$.

12. **H.** The least common multiple of 2, 4, 6, and 10 is 60.

13. **E.** It is cheapest not to buy exactly 100 diskettes, but to buy 105 diskettes by purchasing two boxes of 40 and one box of 25. The total cost is $2(\$20) + \$14 = \$54$.

14. **F.** $(.01)^4 = (10^{-2})^4 = 10^{-8}$

15. **D.** When parallel lines are cut by a transversal, the alternate interior angles are equal. Thus, $\angle DCE$ measures 60°. Since the angles in a triangle add up to 180°, $\angle CED$ measures $180° - 40° - 60° = 80°$.

16. **J.** $(2a - 3)(2a - 3) = 4a^2 - 6a - 6a + 9 = 4a^2 - 12a + 9$.

17. **D.** The slope-intercept form of a line is $y = mx + b$.
$$3x + y - 2 = 0$$
$$y = -3x + 2$$

18. **G.** If painting one side of the house requires 6 small cans, then all 4 sides requires 24 small cans. Given the relationship of 4 large cans = 6 small cans, you can convert large cans to small by multiplying by $\frac{6}{4} = 1.5$. Thus, 4 large cans and 18 small cans is equivalent to the 24 small cans required.

19. **E.** Since an absolute value can never be negative, its minimum is at 0. $x - 5$ equals 0 if x is 5.

20. **G.** $8 - \sqrt{8}$ 5.17

21. **D.** $(x + 6)(x - 1) = x^2 + 5x - 6$, so $b = 5$.

22. **J.** Set up a proportion between similar sides:

$$\frac{24}{30} = \frac{x}{40}$$
$$30x = 960$$
$$x = 32$$

23. **A.** The area of a triangle is $\frac{1}{2}bh$. The legs of a right triangle can always be considered the base and height, so the area of the triangle is $\frac{1}{2}5x = \frac{5}{2}x$.

24. **K.** Convert the time to seconds and set up a proportion:

$$\frac{560}{1,400} = \frac{x}{2,000}$$

$1,400x = 1,120,000$

$x = 800$ seconds $= 13$ minutes and 20 seconds

25. **C.** The current paths require a trip of 200 feet. A diagonal path would form an isosceles right triangle with the existing paths. By the rules of 45°-45°-90° triangles, the length of the path would be $100\sqrt{2}$ feet or approximately 140 feet. The new path would shorten the route by about $200 - 140 = 60$ feet.

26. **K.** $3x^2 - 7x - 6 = 0$

$(3x + 2)(x - 3) = 0$

$3x + 2 = 0$ or $x - 3 = 0$

$x = -\frac{2}{3}$ or $x = 3$

Since the question states that $x < 0$, $x = -\frac{2}{3}$.

27. **B.** $\sqrt{3^4 a^3 b^2} = (3^4 a^3 b^2)^{\frac{1}{2}} = 3^2 a^{\frac{3}{2}} b^1 = 9a^{\frac{3}{2}} b^1$

28. **H.** Given that there are 180° in a line and in a triangle, you can solve for the angles in the triangle:

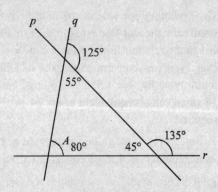

29. **D.** $\frac{.018}{.12} = .150$ or 150 thousandths.

30. **G.** When solving for an absolute value, you need to account for the possibility that the expression is positive (in which case it will be unchanged by the absolute value) or negative (in which case its sign will be changed by the absolute value). First, assume that $x - 1$ is positive:

$x - 1 \leq 2$

$x \leq 3$

If $x - 1$ is negative, then the absolute value changes the signs:

$-(x - 1) \leq 2$

$-x + 1 \leq 2$

$-x \leq 1$

$x \geq -1$

The complete solution is thus $-1 \quad x \quad 3$.

31. **A.** You are dealing with similar triangles, so you can set up a proportion between the segments:

$$\frac{10}{4} = \frac{x}{3}$$

$4x = 30$

$x = 7.5$

32. **J.** If $\cos\theta = \frac{5}{7}$, then you can create a right triangle with an adjacent side of 5 and a hypotenuse of 7. Solving for the opposite leg gives

$5^2 + b^2 = 7^2$

$b^2 = 49 - 25$

$b = \sqrt{24} = 2\sqrt{6}$

Tangent is equal to opposite over adjacent or $\frac{2\sqrt{6}}{5}$.

33. **E.** Average is equal to $\frac{\text{total}}{\text{number}}$. The new average is

$\frac{15x + 2y}{x} = 15 + \frac{2y}{x}$, or $\frac{2y}{x}$ more than the old average.

34. **F.** Slope is equal to the change in y over the change in x:

$$\left(\frac{4 - (-5)}{-1 - 2}\right) = \left(\frac{9}{-3}\right) = -3$$

35. **D.** The ladder forms a right triangle with the house and the ground, so you can use the Pythagorean Theorem to solve for the distance:

$10^2 + b^2 = 12^2$

$b^2 = 144 - 100$

$b = \sqrt{44} \approx 6.6$

36. **H.** Circumference $= 2\pi r$. The radius is 3 feet, so the circumference is $2\pi(3) = 6\pi$ feet.

37. **A.** Multiplying both sides of the equation by 35 eliminates the fractions:

$\left(\frac{3}{5}n + \frac{2}{7}\right)35 = \left(\frac{3}{5}n - \frac{2}{7}\right)35$

$21n + 10 = 15n - 14$

$6n = -24$

$n = -4$

38. **F.** In order for a line to be parallel to the y-axis, it must have the same x-coordinate at all points. Since the line passes through (2,3), its equation must be $x = 2$.

39. **A.** Sine is equal to opposite over hypotenuse. so $\sin x° = \frac{5}{13}$ in the given triangle.

40. **K.** The given circle has a center at (4,–6) and a radius of 5. The circle is centered in quadrant IV and of the circle would also go into quadrant III, but it would not reach quadrants I or II.

41. **C.** If $\angle Z$ measures 30°, then $\angle X$ also measures 30°, and $\angle C$ must measure $180° - 30° - 30° = 120°$. Arc XYZ is thus $\frac{120°}{360°} = \frac{1}{3}$ of the entire circumference of the circle. The circumference is $2\pi(9) = 18\pi$ feet, so arc XYZ has a length of 6π feet.

42. **H.** Three pairs of prime numbers add to 24: (5,19), (7,17), (11,13). $(5)(19) = 95$ is the least possible value of xy. Note that 1 is NOT a prime number.

43. **E.** Area $= \pi r^2$
    $$\pi r^2 = 64$$
    $$r^2 = \frac{64}{\pi}$$
    $$r = \frac{8}{\sqrt{\pi}}$$
    The diameter is twice the radius or $\frac{16}{\sqrt{\pi}}$ inches.

44. **F.** First, solve for x:
    $$2x = 4x + 1$$
    $$-2x = 1$$
    $$x = -\frac{1}{2}$$
    Substituting this value into the second equation gives $6(-\frac{1}{2}) - 2 = -5$.

45. **B.** Tangent equals opposite over adjacent. In an isosceles right triangle the opposite and adjacent sides are equal, so $\tan x° = 1$.

46. **G.** You can solve for the width and length of the rectangle using the distance formula:
    $$w = \sqrt{(-5-(-1))^2 + (-2-(-6))^2}$$
    $$= \sqrt{16+16}$$
    $$= \sqrt{32} = 4\sqrt{2}$$

$$l = \sqrt{(-1-7)^2 + (-6-2)^2}$$
$$= \sqrt{64+64}$$
$$= \sqrt{128} = 8\sqrt{2}$$
The area of the rectangle is $\left(4\sqrt{2}\right)\left(8\sqrt{2}\right) = 64$.

47. **A.** In order for the expression to be positive, x and z must either both be negative or both be positive.

48. **K.** Average $= \frac{\text{Total}}{\text{Number}}$ or, alternatively, Total = (Average)(Number). The total of the 6 original scores is $(6)(80) = 480$ points. The total of all 8 tests is $(8)(85) = 680$ points. The average of the 2 added tests is $\frac{680-480}{2} = 100$.

49. **B.** $y = \frac{z}{x}$ describes a direct relationship between y and z, but an inverse relationship between x and y.

50. **H.** The generalized formula for a circle is $(x-h)^2 + (y-k)^2 = r^2$, where (h,k) is the center of the circle and r is the radius. Of the equations given, only $(x-1)^2 + (y+1)^2 = 25$ has a center at $(1,-1)$.

51. **B.** $-[(x-4) - (3-2x)] = 3 - (5x+6)$
    $$-(x-4-3+2x) = 3 - 5x - 6$$
    $$-(3x-7) = -5x - 3$$
    $$-3x + 7 = -5x - 3$$
    $$2x = -10$$
    $$x = -5$$

52. **K.** The graph of sine has a period of 2π. However, if you graph $\sin \frac{x}{2}$ the period doubles in length to 4π.

53. **A.** In order for the equation to have only one real root, it must be a double root. Given the values in the equation, the only possibilities are $(x+4)^2$ and $(x-4)^2$. Only $(x-4)^2$ gives a value for a that is one of the answer choices:
    $$(x-4)^2 = x^2 - 8x + 16$$
    $$a = -8$$

54. **G.** $x + .2x = 1.2x$
    $$1.2x - (.3)(1.2x) = .84x$$
    This is equivalent to decreasing x by 16%:
    $$x - .16x = .84x$$

55. **A.** As shown in the diagram below, the height of the pole, x, is opposite 70° and the hypotenuse is 50. Since sine equals opposite over hypotenuse:

$$\frac{x}{50} = \sin 70°$$

$$x = 50\sin 70°$$

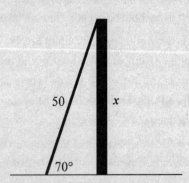

56. **J.** When solving for an absolute value, you must account for the expression within the absolute value being positive or negative. If it is positive, then the absolute value does not change the expression:

$$1 - x = x - 1$$
$$-2x = -2$$
$$x = 1$$

If the expression is negative, then the absolute value changes the sign of the expression:
$$-(1 - x) = x - 1$$
$$x - 1 = x - 1$$

The last equation seems to indicate that it is true for all values. However, it is only true if the expression within the absolute value is negative. $1 - x$ is only negative when $x > 1$. Thus, the complete solution of the equation is $x = 1$ or $x > 1$, which can be simplified as $x \geq 1$.

57. **C.** The easiest way of solving this problem is to test each point and see which one satisfies both equations. Otherwise, you can solve the question using simultaneous equations:

$$2x + y = 2$$
$$-\frac{x}{2} + y = 2$$
$$\overline{}$$
$$\frac{3}{2}x = 0$$
$$x = 0$$
$$y = 2$$

58. **J.** The equation for line m is $y = 3x + 8$. Since line n is perpendicular to m, it must have a slope of $-\frac{1}{3}$. You can see that $3y = -x + 14$ has a slope of $-\frac{1}{3}$ when you put it into the slope-intercept form: $y = -\frac{1}{3}x + \frac{14}{3}$.

59. **B.** The probability that you will draw either B or C out of the hat on the first draw is $\frac{2}{5}$. Your odds of drawing the remaining card on the second draw is $\frac{1}{4}$. The probability of both of these events happening is $\frac{2}{5} \times \frac{1}{4} = \frac{2}{20} = \frac{1}{10}$.

60. **G.** The problem provides you with 2 equations for the prices of a shirt (s) and a tie (t): $s + 2t = 105$ and $2s + t = 135$. You can solve for t using simultaneous equations. If you multiply both sides of the first equation by 2, then you get the following:

$$2s + 4t = 210$$
$$-2s + t = 135$$
$$\overline{}$$
$$3t = 75$$
$$t = 25$$

3. Reading Test

1. **D.** A is incorrect because in the middle of the second paragraph we learn that Storm and King is a "wholesale dry goods concern." B is incorrect because in the middle of the second paragraph we learn that Storm and King is a "wholesale dry goods concern." C is incorrect because in the middle of the second paragraph we learn that Storm and King is a "wholesale dry goods concern." D is the best answer because in the middle of the second paragraph we learn that Storm and King is a "wholesale dry goods concern."

2. **H.** F is incorrect because in paragraphs 4–7 the old gentleman treats her "kindly" and Carrie is surprised at her "pleasant reception," even though she is told there is no work. G is incorrect because the old gentleman in paragraph 4 is not angry. H is the best answer because in paragraphs 4–7 the old gentleman treats her "kindly" and Carrie is surprised at her "pleasant reception," even though she is told there is no work. J is incorrect because the old gentleman in paragraph 4 shows Carrie no disdain.

3. **B.** A is incorrect because the passage makes no reference to Carrie believing her move into the city was a "mistake." B is the best answer because the second sentence of the final paragraph states "so earnest an effort was well deserving of a better reward." C is incorrect because the passage ends with Carrie going homeward, making a "baffled retreat." D is incorrect because nowhere in the passage does Carrie express an opinion that looking for work is a "waste of time."

4. **G.** F is incorrect because the passage does not mention Carrie pretending she is a spy. G is the best answer because in the first paragraph we learn that Carrie "assumed an air of indifference just as if she were upon an errand." H is incorrect because the passage does not mention Carrie pretending she is a boss. J is incorrect because the passage does not mention Carrie pretending she is rich.

5. **B.** A is incorrect because "Monroe" is mentioned in paragraph 3. B is the best answer because "Block" is not mentioned as a street name in paragraph 3. C is incorrect because "Madison" is mentioned in paragraph 3. D is incorrect because "State" is mentioned in paragraph 3.

6. **J.** F is incorrect because *ornamented*, in this context, means "adorned." G is incorrect because *ornamented*, in this context, means "adorned." H is incorrect because *ornamented*, in this context, means "adorned." J is the best answer because *ornamented*, in this context, means "adorned."

7. **C.** A is incorrect because Carrie is never described as being irate. B is incorrect because the passage never mentions Carrie's feelings for other workers. C is the best answer because in the final paragraph we learn that Carrie has lost "her hopes, her courage, and her strength," and that she "felt her own helplessness." D is incorrect because Carrie's despondent feelings, as mentioned in the final paragraph, show that she is not being mechanical about her job search.

8. **F.** F is the best answer because the last sentence of the passage tells the reader that Carrie was "sick at heart and in body." G is incorrect because though Carrie looked "vainly" for work (final paragraph), that does not equate to "vanity" or self-love. H is incorrect because the last sentence of the passage tells the reader that Carrie was "sick at heart and in body," consequently not "wholesome." J is incorrect because the last sentence of the passage tells the reader that Carrie was "sick at heart and in body," so she would not have a "renewed sense of purpose."

9. **D.** A is incorrect because the old gentleman never mentions Carrie not finding work. B is incorrect because the old gentleman never mentions an employment agency. C is incorrect because the old gentleman never mentions Carrie's skills. D is the best answer because the old gentleman says, "Come in some time next week" in paragraph 6.

10. **H.** F is incorrect because paragraph 2 tells us "two men came out and paused in the door . . . She looked helplessly around, and then, seeing herself observed, retreated. It was too difficult a task. She could not go past them." "Them" in the final sentence refers to the men in the doorway, not the messenger. G is incorrect because paragraph 2 tells us "two men came out and paused in the door . . . She looked helplessly around, and then, seeing herself observed, retreated. It was too difficult a task. She could not go past them." "Them" in the final sentence refers to the men in the doorway, not the pedestrians on the street. H is the best answer because paragraph 2 tells us "two men came out and paused in the door . . . She looked helplessly around, and then, seeing herself observed, retreated. It was too difficult a task. She could not go past them." "Them" in the final sentence refers to the men in the doorway. J is incorrect because paragraph 2 does not mention Carrie not being able to find the entrance to the store.

11. **B.** A is incorrect because the passage does not say that Westerners had taken Fijian property. B is the best answer because paragraph 4 begins by stating that "In a traditional Fiji tribe an individual as such can hardly be said to own property, for nearly all things belong to his family or clan." C is incorrect because, according to the first paragraph, the chief cannot sell land without "the consent of his tribe." Furthermore, paragraph 4 states that property belongs to the "family or tribe." D is incorrect because the passage does not mention evil phantoms or spirits.

12. **J.** F is incorrect because burnt offerings to the gods are not mentioned in the passage. G is incorrect because semiprecious stones are never mentioned in the passage. H is incorrect because the granting of a Fijian name is not mentioned as a way to represent a contract. J is the best answer because paragraph 2 states that a whale's tooth expressed "good will" and was comparable with "a signed contract."

13. **B.** A is incorrect because Western destruction of Fijian values is not mentioned in the passage. B is the best answer because paragraph 3 begins with the statement: "As in all communities, including our own world of finance, a man's wealth consisted not only in what he possessed but even more so in the number of people from whom he could beg or borrow," then presents the Tanao story as an example of this principle. C is incorrect because theft is not mentioned until paragraph 4. D is incorrect because the anecdote is not presented to show the difficulty of obtaining Fijian trust (see explanation for B).

14. **H.** F is incorrect because competition in world markets is not mentioned in the passage. G is incorrect because paragraph 7 tells us that instead of profiting from capitalism, Fijians instead are "becoming enmeshed in the rat race of modern civilization. Sadly, this race rarely has a happy ending." H is the best answer because paragraph 7 shows that the author believes that modern civilization (capitalism) "entails the hoarding of wealth and becoming enmeshed in the rat race of modern civilization. Sadly, this race rarely has a happy ending." J is incorrect because paragraph 7 clearly shows that modern civilization has had an impact on the lives of Fijians.

15. **A.** A is the best answer because paragraph 4 clearly links the lack of personal property to the difficulty in introducing "ideals of modern progress" in Fiji. B is incorrect because religious customs are never discussed. C is incorrect because land laws are never mentioned in relation to the introduction of "ideals of modern progress." D is incorrect because Western cultural indoctrination is never mentioned in relation to the introduction of "ideals of modern progress."

16. **F.** F is the best answer because the paragraph discusses contracts and uses the word *compliance* to signify *agreement*. G is incorrect because *compliance* would never mean "introduction." H is incorrect because *compliance* would never mean "withdrawal." J is incorrect because *compliance* would never mean "inconsistency."

17. **D.** A is incorrect because the final paragraph in the passage does not mention Chief Thakombau's parents. B is incorrect because the final paragraph in the passage does not mention Chief Thakombau's hoarded wealth, and the eighth paragraph tells us the hoarded wealth was not respected in Fiji. C is incorrect because the final paragraph in the passage says that Chief Thakombau's Christian name was "Ebenezer." D is the best answer because the final paragraph says "Chief Thakombau began life as "Seru," then after the civil war in which he overcame his father's enemies and reestablished Tanoa's rule in Mbau he was called "Thakombau" (evil to Mbau).

18. **G.** F is incorrect because although I is discussed in paragraph 1, II is also discussed (see explanation for G). G is the best answer because I is mentioned in paragraph 1 ("land tenure"), II is mentioned in paragraph 7 ("Fiji before capitalism took hold"), and III is not mentioned. H is incorrect because although II is discussed in paragraph 7, III is never discussed (see explanation for G). J is incorrect because although I is mentioned in paragraph 1 ("land tenure"), and II is mentioned in paragraph 7 ("Fiji before capitalism took hold"), III is never mentioned in the passage.

19. **D.** A is incorrect because the passage does not say that chiefs may not declare war. B is incorrect because the passage does not mention starting communities on the same island. C is incorrect because the passage makes no reference to chiefs cultivating land. D is the best answer because the second sentence of the passage states "In general it may be said that the chief could sell no land without the consent of his tribe."

20. **H.** F is incorrect because the lack of jobs in Fiji is never presented as a benefit of the lack of ambition to acquire personal property. G is incorrect because the lack of ambition would not promote industrialization, but would rather have the opposite effect. H is the best answer because paragraph 4 ends with the statement that "No one could be a miser, a capitalist, a banker, or a promoter in such a community, and thieves were almost unknown."

J is incorrect because the passage does not mention friendship between Fijian chiefs.

21. **C.** A is incorrect because there is no indication in the passage that anyone in Michelangelo's family was in poor health. B is incorrect because although Michelangelo's father advised his son to take care of his health, there is nothing in the passage that implies Michelangelo's father meant this advice as a demand. C is the best answer because in paragraph 2, Michelangelo's father states, "In your profession, if once you were to fall ill you would be a ruined man." D is incorrect because although Michelangelo's work was extremely physical and the possibility of injury existed, this possibility is never mentioned, nor does it have any bearing on whether or not he maintained his long-term health.

22. **F.** F is the best answer because it paraphrases the statement in paragraph 1, "The great artist was so prone to over-anxiety and met (whether needlessly or not) with so many rebuffs and disappointments, that only constant absorption in manual labor prevented spirit from fretting itself free from flesh." G is incorrect because it contradicts the above statement and because, in paragraph 6, the author describes him as "miserly, suspicious, quarrelsome and pessimistic." H is incorrect because nowhere does the passage make reference to other artists or how they might aspire to Michelangelo's greatness. J is incorrect because in paragraph 4, the lines "though the production of his hand was not good," imply that Michelangelo was not able to produce work as skillfully and artistically impressive as he once had.

23. **D.** A is incorrect because answer D is correct (see explanation for D). B is incorrect because answer D is correct (see explanation for D). C is incorrect because answer D is correct (see explanation for D). D is the best answer because, paragraph 4 states that, while the artist still painted and sculpted with the skill of a genius at age seventy-five, he later lost the required energy for such work and so turned to such works as St. Peter's and other architectural projects.

24. **H.** F is incorrect because I is incorrect. Although reference is made to the coarse nature of Michelangelo's dress habits (he left his boots on for so long that when he took them off, the author

says they came away "like the skin of a molting serpent"—paragraph 2), no mention is made of his sense of humor. In fact, from the description the author gives of Michelangelo in the last paragraph, one might think the artist had no sense of humor at all. G is incorrect because although III is correct (see explanation for H) I is incorrect (see explanation for F). H is the best answer because both II and III are supported by paragraph 3 with the phrases, "his intensity of purpose and fierce energy" and "for [Michelangelo's] mental powers one of his colossal statues would seem a more fitting mold." J is incorrect because, although II and III are correct (see explanation for H), I is incorrect (see explanation for F).

25. **A.** A is the best answer because the beginning of paragraph 2, specifically the lines "art became his religion and required of him the sacrifice of all that might keep him below his highest level of power for work," indicate that the rest of the paragraph will describe the elements that Michelangelo sacrificed for his work. Sleep and food are two of these elements. B is incorrect because although in paragraph 6, the lines "Michelangelo [was] affected by a degree of neuropathy bordering closely upon hysterical disease" imply that Michelangelo was not of sound mind, the next lines "What a pity that more of us do not suffer from such degrees of neuropathy and how much better for most of us if we had such enthusiasm for perfection" implies that, to the author, such madness is desirable. C is incorrect because there is no indication in the passage that Michelangelo was anything *but* prolific. In fact, in the first paragraph, the lines "He toiled 'furiously' in all his mighty undertakings that body and mind remained one and in abundant health for nearly four score and ten years," indicate that, since Michelangelo worked throughout his almost ninety years, he was indeed prolific. D is incorrect because, although Michelangelo was intent on controlling his health, the implication of the second paragraph is that he limited his food and health in order to devote every minute possible to his art.

26. **H.** F is incorrect because dress cannot bruise the flesh. G is incorrect because dress cannot darken the flesh. H is correct because the context of "mortify" makes it clear that Michelangelo's dress

habits had little to do with beautification. J is incorrect because, if mortify meant warmth, Michelangelo would be more likely to take the boots off than leave them on for long periods of time.

27. **B.** A is incorrect because although the passage may imply that living the way Michelangelo did may help other people live as long as Michelangelo did, it is not the main idea of the passage. B is the best answer because it is a paraphrase of the first paragraph, in particular, the lines "there is nothing so conducive to mental and physical wholeness as saturation of body and mind with work." C is incorrect because in paragraph 2, the author states that Michelangelo remained healthy not simply because he wished to but because he took scrupulous care of himself. He knew if he did not remain healthy, he could not work. Also, in paragraph 5, the author implies that Michelangelo stayed healthy because he remained active even when he couldn't pursue manual labor as he once had. D is incorrect because, although in paragraph 6 the author refers to Michelangelo's devotion to his art as a type of madness, the author clearly does not consider the artist truly mad because he states that such devotion is an admirable, beneficial state of mind. In addition, the question of the artist's sanity is not the main idea of the passage.

28. **F.** F is the best answer because only I is correct, supported by the statement in paragraph 2 that "he ate comparatively little and slept less than many men because he worked better." G is incorrect because, although I is correct (see explanation for F), II is wrong; paragraph 6 indicates that Michelangelo's miserliness was an undesirable quality that his good qualities, the ones that helped preserve him, balanced out. H is incorrect for the same reason that G was incorrect. Michelangelo's pessimism was an undesirable quality that his good qualities, the ones that helped preserve him, balanced out. J is incorrect because II is wrong (see explanation for G) and III is wrong (see explanation for H).

29. **D.** A is incorrect because whether or not Michelangelo's last sculptures were not as great as his earlier work is a matter of opinion. There are some that disagree completely with that statement. B is incorrect because whether or not

Michelangelo's good qualities balanced out his bad is a matter of opinion. There are some who believe that certain bad qualities can never be outweighed by any good. C is incorrect because, again, the statement is a matter of opinion and impossible to determine for certain. D is the best answer because the statement is a fact, supported by paragraph 5.

30. **G.** F is incorrect because no reference is made in the passage to the subject matter of Michelangelo's work. G is the best answer because the description the author gives of Michelangelo in paragraph 3 is of a man whose appearance is flawed and not as befitting a man of his genius as one of his statues would be. H is incorrect because several references are made to Michelangelo's great intellectual capacity. In paragraph 1, it is stated that his "body and mind remained one and in abundant health for nearly four score and ten years." In paragraph 3, reference is made to his mental powers being the equivalent in size to "one of his colossal statues." J is incorrect because, although reference is made to Michelangelo's statues as "colossal" (paragraph 3), this does not mean he never created smaller scale statues.

31. **C.** A is incorrect because paragraph 11 says that mosquitoes benefit from more midge larvae. B is incorrect because the passage does not mention the effect that fly larvae have on mosquitoes. C is the best answer because paragraph 11 begins with the statement that "Biologists found that the more midges there were in a pitcher plant, the better off the mosquitoes were." D is incorrect because the passage does not suggest that mosquitoes benefit from "any change" in the amount of bacteria. Since mosquitoes eat the bacteria, it may be assumed that a decrease in the amount of bacteria would harm them.

32. **J.** F is incorrect because I is wrong: the roots of the pitcher plant are never mentioned. G is incorrect because although II is correct, III is also correct (see explanation for J). H is incorrect because I is wrong: the roots of the pitcher plant are never mentioned. J is the best answer because II is correct (supported by information in paragraph 4) and III is correct (supported by information in paragraph 4).

33. **C.** A is incorrect because paragraph 6 states that "Each larva has a life span of about a year, which is also the life span of each pitcher plant leaf." B is incorrect because paragraph 6 states that "Each larva has a life span of about a year, which is also the life span of each pitcher plant leaf." C is the best answer because paragraph 6 states that "Each larva has a life span of about a year, which is also the life span of each pitcher plant leaf." D is incorrect because paragraph 6 states that "Each larva has a life span of about a year, which is also the life span of each pitcher plant leaf."

34. **F.** F is the best answer because paragraph 3 says the "pitcher plant does not produce enzymes." G is incorrect because paragraphs 5–8 discuss the insect species living in the pitcher plant. H is incorrect because paragraph 4 states that the plant has "a highly acidic mixture." J is incorrect because paragraph 3 states that the pitcher plant "absorbs nutrients" from its internal ecosystem.

35. **D.** A is incorrect because the passage does not mention fly larvae being a danger to anyone. B is incorrect because the according to paragraph 7, fly larvae float on the top of the pitcher pool. C is incorrect because paragraph 11 says "since the mosquitoes brought no harm to the midges" which suggests that the mosquitoes did not affect the midges. D is the best answer because paragraph 7 states "The fly larvae are much larger than the midge and mosquito larvae."

36. **H.** F is incorrect because the plant's root system is never mentioned. G is incorrect because the surplus of water is not mentioned as a reason that the pitcher plant cannot extract nitrogen from the soil. H is the best answer because the first paragraph says "it's simply too acidic for the bacteria that break down dead plant matter to grow in." J is incorrect because the insect larvae are not mentioned as a reason that the pitcher plant cannot extract nitrogen from the soil.

37. **A.** A is the best answer because paragraph 8 states "The mosquito has to wait for the midge to finish eating, since the mosquito can only consume very small particles of insect that the midge chews up first." B is incorrect because the pitcher plant only absorbs the nutrients after they have been completely broken down by the larvae. C is incorrect because the passage does not say that the insect parts must be frozen to be eaten by the mosquito larvae. D is incorrect because if the insect parts were completely consumed by the fly larvae, there would be no parts left for the midge or mosquito larvae to eat.

38. **H.** F is incorrect because the passage does not say the tubes were used to trap mosquitoes. G is incorrect because the passage does not say the tubes were used to test the acidity of the bog soil. H is the best answer because according to paragraph 9, "These tubes were then used in a variety of experiments to determine just how the insect larvae in pitcher plants process their food." It can be assumed that since the tubes were filled with pitcher plant water and used to examine the interactions within the plant, the tubes were designed to simulate the form of the plant. J is incorrect because the passage does not say that fly larvae compete with other larvae in the pitcher plant.

39. **B.** A is incorrect because downward-pointing hairs are mentioned in paragraph 4. B is the best answer because paragraph 3 states that the "pitcher plant does not produce enzymes." C is incorrect because purple veins are mentioned in paragraph 4. D is incorrect because a highly slippery section of the leaf is mentioned in paragraph 4

40. **G.** F is incorrect because unlike a person producing food for others, the midge and fly larvae consume what comes to them, leaving the scraps for the mosquito larvae. G is the best answer because the vulture example is the only example where the consumer of the processed food (the vulture) eats what is left over by the original consumer (the wolf), which mirrors the relationship between midge and mosquito larvae as described in the passage. H is incorrect because the shark benefits from the fish's cleaning, and the midge does not benefit from its food processing for the mosquito (see paragraph 11). J is incorrect because it describes a competitive system (the "taking of food from other smaller birds"), which paragraph 7 and 11 clearly state that midges and mosquitoes do not compete for resources in the pitcher plant.

4. Science Reasoning Test

1. **D.** Looking at the table, Resistor B has a current of 345 milliamps when the temperature is 23 degrees and the voltage is 3 volts.

2. **F.** Current for Resistor C at 5 volts and 25 degrees was 90 milliamps, and for every 1 volt increase, the current increases by 18 milliamps. The current at 6.0 volts would be 108 milliamps.

3. **C.** When exposed to different temperatures, Resistor A and Resistor B are not affected.

4. **H.** A thermistor is a device that shows different resistances based on sensitivity to temperature, therefore Resistor C could be the one thermistor.

5. **D.** Resistor B does not have a linear relationship between voltage and current.

6. **F.** Resistor A seems to be an ohmic device because there is a linear relationship between voltage and current. If Resistor A released heat into the water, it would not be considered an ohmic device.

7. **C.** Answer choice C is correct because although most nutrients are decreasing, the table shows a net gain for these two.

8. **G.** Review Table 1 to see that the largest percentage decreases are shown for G, Silica and Aluminum.

9. **B.** The purpose of using the different techniques was to insure that the scientists could capture the different sizes of material exiting the ecosystem.

10. **J.** This experiment was designed to track the effects of logging on watersheds that were already losing nutrients. The design of the experiment and the design/display of the results in Table 2 show the ecologists' concern about loss of nutrients to be of crucial importance. Answer H is the only option that reflects this concern.

11. **A.** Close examination of the results displayed in Table 2 show that there is no pattern to the loss of substances in the undisturbed watershed and that the loss is relatively small. The logged area is losing nutrients and this is increasing year to year. The only answer which reflects this comparison is A.

12. **J.** Nutrients are more dramatically depleted in the logged area, so a way to retain some of the nutrients would be useful. If tree bark contains many nutrients, keeping it in the system would help towards this end.

13. **C.** The element with the atomic weight of 85.5 is rubidium and its melting point is 39 degrees.

14. **J.** Sodium's density is 0.97 g/cm^3 and cesium's density is 1.87 g/cm^3, which is nearly twice that of sodium.

15. **B.** According to the table, as atomic number increases, melting point decreases.

16. **J.** Cesium has a higher atomic number than rubidium and a higher density. Potassium has a higher atomic weight than lithium and has a higher density.

17. **D.** Melting point seems to decrease with increase of atomic number. If another metal existed with a greater atomic number, the melting point would be higher than that of cesium. Density does not clearly increase as atomic number increases, so it would be difficult to predict the density of the element.

18. **G.** The oldest rocks are at the higher altitudes according to the table.

19. **C.** Gabbro has the highest crystallization temperature of the rocks listed.

20. **F.** The vertical axis is the altitude.

21. **A.** The highest crystallization temperatures are found with peridotite. Peridotite is found 40 miles inland.

22. **J.** The age of rocks is not related to the distance from the shore that the rocks are found. The oldest rocks are found closest to the coast and furthest from the coast.

23. **B.** Limestone is found 80 miles inland and andesite is found 120 to 140 miles inland. The andesite is further east than the limestone. The limestone is 6.0 million years old. The andesite is 3.6 to 4.0 million years old. Andesite from volcanoes would have had to erupt after the deposit of the limestone.

24. **G.** Paleontologist A believes that morphological (body) similarities can just as reasonably be assumed to represent the effects of convergent evolution on distant lineages inhabiting similar environments.

25. **A.** Paleontologist A believes that dinosaurs and birds share a common ancestor. A fossil find from before the age of the dinosaurs with common features would support this view.

26. **H.** Paleontologist B assumes that the body similarities between dinosaurs and early birds must be evidence that birds came forth from the dinosaur lineage. This view does subscribe to the idea of transitional forms. Mass extinction is not relevant to this view.

27. **D.** Paleontologist B believes that birds arose out of a lineage of dinosaurs.

28. **F.** This contradicts the theory of Paleontologist B because Paleontologist B suggests that birds arose from dinosaurs. Paleontologist A suggested that the two arose from an extremely distant ancestor and the theory of convergent evolution is not inconsistent with birds appearing before dinosaurs.

29. **C.** Paleontologist A postulates the existence of a very distant common ancestor for birds and dinosaurs. The development of birds much later than that of dinosaurs might seem to refute this argument. However, the rate of evolutionary change is not constant across different lineages. Dinosaurs may have developed relatively rapidly from thecodonts, for example, whereas birds did not evolve until much later.

30. **G.** Close examination of Table 2 shows that the only factor being changed is the number of species of bacteria present.

31. **B.** Examining the results in Tables 1 and 2 shows that although in experiment #2 fewer paramecium survived overall when their number of species was increased from 1 to 2, increasing the number of species of their food sources, the bacteria, did produce a relative increase in their survival rate.

32. **F.** Looking at Tables 1 and 2, it appears that increasing the number of species of paramecium from one to two was most detrimental to their overall survival.

33. **D.** Experiment 3 added a predator of paramecia. The number of bacteria species remained at 3; we have no information that the time or the culture method was changed.

34. **J.** The results of this experiment suggest that increasing diversity in terms of trophic levels was ultimately harmful to the survival of the paramecium species under study. It was not beneficial to all species because of the decreasing survival rates for the paramecia.

35. **B.** Neptune's density is 1,638 kg/m³. Saturn has a density of 687 kg/m³, Uranus has a density of 1,318 kg/m³, and Jupiter has a density of 1,326 kg/m³.

36. **J.** Neptune has the lowest temperature so, based on that measure, it would seem to be the furthest from the Sun.

37. **C.** Mercury has an orbital inclination of 7.000 degrees and an orbital eccentricity of 0.2056. Pluto has an orbital inclination of 17.14 degrees and an orbital eccentricity of 0.2488. Therefore, there are two planets that would be re-categorized.

38. **H.** Pluto would lose its designation as a planet because its mass is smaller than that of Earth's Moon.

39. **B.** The gaseous planets would be expected to be less dense than the ones made of solid material.

40. **G.** Venus and Mercury do have the longest rotation periods. Mars and Earth do have similar rotation periods. The planets with the greatest mass do have the shortest rotation period. As black-body temperature decreases, the rotation periods do no necessarily decrease.

PART
5

Life After the ACT Assessment

PREVIEW

Applying to the College of Your Choice

WHEN TO APPLY

After you've narrowed your list of possible colleges down to a handful of schools, it's time to start the application process. So, when should you start?

All schools fall into one of three types of admission categories:

- **Selective admission,** with firm applications deadlines, generally these fall in January.
- **Rolling admission,** where there is no firm application deadline, and applicants are accepted (and rejected) until the freshman classes are full.
- **Open admission,** used by many two-year colleges, where there is no admission deadline and the schools accept anyone with a high school diploma until classes begin.

All that said, you should probably start preparing your applications in November and December, and submit all your applications no later than January. There is little benefit to submitting much earlier than that, and there is a downside if you submit later. When in doubt, contact the college of your choice to find out its recommended application date.

ABOUT THE EARLY ACTION AND EARLY DECISION OPTIONS

Some colleges offer Early Action and/or Early Decision plans that enable you to apply to your first-choice schools early and receive early notification of your acceptance or rejection—often as early as December. These plans have benefits for both you and the schools. Early applicants get the first chance at financial aid packages, fellowships, and student housing, and they can put the whole college application process behind them and enjoy the rest of their senior year. The colleges get to start constructing their freshman class profile—with a group of students who are really committed to attending *their* school. The plans have drawbacks, as well, so let's look at them in a bit more detail.

ROAD MAP

- *Learn When to Apply*
- *Learn How to Apply*
- *Understand What Materials You Must Submit with Your Application*
- *Learn the Best Sidebars for Applying Online*
- *Review Your College Admissions Timeline*

NOTE

There is one general exception to the application rule. Many schools offer honors programs and honors scholarships, and these programs and scholarships often have earlier application deadlines, sometimes as early as the fall.

Under most Early Action plans, you can apply to schools as early as November and receive notification of acceptance as early as January or February. Most Early Action plans require that you accept or reject admission by May 1. You can apply to a number of schools (if they offer this plan, that is) and compare the financial aid packages and offers before you accept. If you are relatively certain of which schools you're really interested in attending, and if you fit the "profile" of their average applicant, Early Action gives you a chance to compete in a smaller applicant pool and let your first-choice schools know right up front that you're interested in them. If you need time to shop around, though, or if you need as much as time as possible to boost your academic performance, Early Action might not be for you. Check each college's published guidelines for its Early Action plan before you commit to this route.

Early Decision plans offer many of the same benefits as Early Action, but they involve some restrictions, too. As a rule, you make your Early Decision applications in November, and receive notification as early as December. Under most Early Decision plans you can only have one Early Decision application underway at any one time. You can apply to other schools, but only under their regular admissions plan. And, most Early Decision plans require you to accept admission if it is offered to you and if it's accompanied by an adequate financial aid package. If you're accepted by your first-choice school, you have to withdraw all other outstanding applications. Obviously, this plan can prevent you from comparing financial aid offers from other schools. Because it might be a binding agreement, Early Decision is right for a more select group of students. It's well worth considering if:

- You know with certainty your first-choice school, and you fit its applicant profile.
- You don't need time to boost your academic performance prior to applying.
- You don't need to negotiate the highest possible financial aid package.

And, as with Early Action plans, before you decide to participate in Early Decision, carefully read the college's published guidelines for the program.

HOW TO APPLY

When you're ready to apply, what is involved? Although each school has its own specific admissions guidelines (and you should contact each school to get a copy of these), there are some general guidelines used by most major institutions. In fact, many colleges are now using something called the Common Application, an eight-page form created by the National Association of Secondary School Principals.

For any school using the Common App, you only have to fill out one form, which can then go to multiple colleges. You can get copies of the Common

App from your high school guidance office; you'll have to get institution-specific application forms from the individual schools.

In addition, many schools now accept applications either via software or online forms. (See "Applying Online," for more information on applying online.) If your school is one of those that let you apply online, take advantage of the opportunity—at the very least, it will save you a few stamps!

FILLING OUT THE APPLICATION

The Common App and most private application forms include the following sections:

TIP
You really should visit your first-choice school before you opt for its Early Decision plan (the summer before your senior year is a good time to visit the colleges that you think you might want to attend). If you commit to an Early Decision plan without first having visited the campus, you're committing yourself to a largely unknown academic destination. Take the time to look before you leap!

- **Personal Data,** including information such as your name, address, possible areas of concentration, language spoken, and whether or not you'll be applying for financial aid.

- **Educational Data,** such as the school you currently attend, your graduation date, the name of your high school counselor, etc.

- **Test Information,** specifically your SAT or ACT Assessment scores.

- **Family,** information about your family—father's name, mother's name, where they went to school, their occupations, that sort of thing.

- **Academic Honors,** where you should describe any scholastic distinctions or honors you have won (since the ninth grade).

- **Extracurricular, Personal, and Volunteer Activities,** where you get to impress the judges with all the things you do *outside* of school. This is more important than it might sound, most often the second item read by admission officers, who want to make sure you have a well-rounded background. Make sure you include sports, volunteer work (*not* paid work!), and other non-academic activities—and list them in order of importance.

- **Work Experience,** where you list all the jobs you've held during the past three years. Don't forget to fill in the section where you elaborate on the most important of these activities (work and other) and why they were important to you.

- **Personal Statement,** otherwise known as *the essay*. Some schools require this, many don't. For those that do, you're often asked to evaluate an important experience in your life; discuss a national, local, or personal issue; or describe how one person has influenced your life. Take your time with these, and make sure what you write has *meaning*, and is written well.

OTHER MATERIALS TO SUBMIT

In addition to the application form, you'll also need to submit some or all of the following, depending on school guidelines:

- **Recommendation letters** from one or more of your teachers (although some colleges have predefined forms they use instead of free-form letters).

TIP

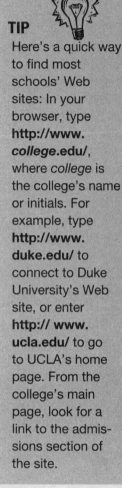

Here's a quick way to find most schools' Web sites: In your browser, type **http://www. college.edu/**, where *college* is the college's name or initials. For example, type **http://www. duke.edu/** to connect to Duke University's Web site, or enter **http:// www. ucla.edu/** to go to UCLA's home page. From the college's main page, look for a link to the admissions section of the site.

- **Counselor form** (also known as the School Report), often a separate form that must be completed by your school counselor.
- **SAT/ACT Assessment results,** which some colleges require to be submitted directly by your high school.
- **Major-specific requirements.** Some individual schools and majors have their own specific requirements. For example, most schools require music majors to arrange and pass an audition.
- **Application fee.**

You should submit these materials directly to the admissions offices of the colleges you have selected—unless you're applying online.

APPLYING ONLINE

Applying online is often easier than applying on paper. There are several Web sites that let you fill out a single application form that can then be submitted to multiple colleges. Here's a short list of these application-oriented sites:

- **Apply!** (http://www.weapply.com)
- **CollegeEdge Web Apps** (http://apply.collegeedge.com/WebApps/)
- **CollegeNET ApplyWeb** (http://www.applyweb.com/aw/)
- **CollegeView AppZap** (http://www.collegeview.com/appzap/)
- **E-Apps Undergraduate Admissions** (http://www.eapp.com/univ/uglist.htm)
- **XAP College Admissions Applications Online** (http://www.xap.com/xapWWW/eduX.html)

In addition, many individual schools let you apply directly from their own Web sites. For a listing of individual schools' application pages, try the **Yahoo! Online Applications: Individual Schools** page at http://dir.yahoo.com/Education/Higher_Education/College_Entrance/Online_Applications/Individual_Schools/.

COLLEGE ADMISSIONS TIMELINE

Taking into account everything discussed in this appendix (and a lot more!), the following table provides you with a detailed timeline to plan your college admissions activities.

College Admissions Timeline

When	What to do
Junior Year of High School	
September	Make sure that PSAT/NMSQT registration is handled by your guidance counselor staff (except in regions where ACT Assessment test is prevalent). Find out and save the date.

When	What to do
	Ask your guidance department about college fairs in your area and college admission-representative visits to the school. Attend fairs and sessions with reps at school.
	Familiarize yourself with guidance-office resources.
October	Make sure PSAT/NMSQT date is on your calendar. Read the student bulletin and try the practice questions.
	Schedule a day trip to visit nearby colleges. Don't worry if these are places where you won't apply; the goal is to explore different types of schools, so aim for variety. Discuss which characteristics are attractive and which aren't.
December	Questions about PSAT scores? Contact your guidance counselor. If necessary, discuss strategies for improving weak areas. Evaluate different SAT prep options, as needed.
	Take advantage of college students home for vacation. Ask them questions.
	Take an introductory look at financial aid forms, just to see what you'll need by this time next year.
January	Evaluate your academic progress so far. Are your grades up to par? Are course levels on target? Do your study habits need improvement?
	Begin thinking about worthwhile summer plans (job, study, camp, volunteer work, travel, etc.).
	Mark projected SAT I & II or ACT Assessment test dates on your calendar. Also mark registration deadlines.
February	Look ahead to SAT or ACT Assessment registration deadlines for the tests you plan to take. Are you about to miss one? Mark appropriate dates on your calendar. (A few juniors have reason to take the SAT I in March. If you will do so, heed February registration deadline.) Buy a general guidebook to U.S. colleges and universities. Start checking out prospective schools via their Web sites.
March	Consider and plan spring-vacation college visits.

continues

College Admissions Timeline (cont.)

When	What to do
March (cont.)	Begin listing target colleges in a notebook or computer spreadsheet or database.
	Begin calling, writing, or e-mailing target colleges to request publications.
	Set aside an area for college propoganda. Invest in folders for materials from front-runner schools.
	Look ahead to SAT or ACT Assessment registration deadlines for the tests you plan to take. Are you about to miss one? Mark appropriate test and registration dates on your calendar.
	Make sure you discuss plans to take Advanced Placement exams with teachers and/or guidance counselor as needed.
April	Look ahead to SAT or ACT Assessment registration deadlines for the tests you plan to take. Are you about to miss one? Mark appropriate test and registration dates on your calendar.
	Decide on senior-year classes. Include at least one math course or lab science, as well as the most challenging courses possible. Recognize that colleges weigh senior classes and grades as heavily as the junior record.
	Update your activities record.
May	Look ahead to SAT or ACT Assessment registration deadlines for the tests you plan to take. Are you about to miss one? Mark the appropriate test and registration dates on your calendar.
	Assess the need for and affordability of special services such as standardized test-prep courses, independent college counselors, and private group-tour programs.
	Do you need to take the TOEFL (Test of English as a Foreign Language)? Select date and oversee registration.
June	Look ahead to SAT or ACT Assessment registration dead-lines for the tests you plan to take. Are you about to miss one? Mark the appropriate test and registration dates on your calendar.
Summer	Make sure you have a job or constructive activities throughout most of the summer. Study, jobs, and volunteer work always rate high with admission officials.
	Consider and plan summer and fall college visits.

When	What to do
	Request publications from additional target colleges.
	Plan and execute supplemental submissions such as audition tapes and art slides/portfolio, if required and/or appropriate.
	Review and update target college list. Include pros and cons. Make tentative plans for fall visits.
	Begin to explore Early Action and Early Decision options at first-choice schools. Get the materials you need and read them carefully.
Senior Year of High School	
September	Discuss plans and goals for the months ahead; pros and cons of target schools.
	Look ahead to SAT or ACT Assessment registration for the tests you plan to take. Are you about to miss one? Mark the appropriate test and registration dates on your calendar.
	Ask your guidance counselor about college fairs in your area and college admission representative visits to the school. Make certain that you attend fairs and sessions with representatives at schools.
	Finalize fall college-visit plans. Include campus overnights, where possible. Visit!
	Request additional publications and applications from target colleges.
	If applicable, take appropriate Early Action and Early Decision application steps, as outlined in the published guidelines of your first-choice schools.
October	Look ahead to SAT or ACT Assessment registration for the tests you plan to take. Are you about to miss one? Mark the appropriate test and registration dates on your calendar.
	Draw up a master schedule of application and financial aid due dates, and then put them on your calendar.
	Begin considering essay topics and requesting teacher recommendations.
	Visit colleges. Include interviews on campus (or with local alumni representatives).
	Attend college fairs.

continues

College Admissions Timeline *(cont.)*

When	What to do
October *(cont.)*	For another look at college life, rent a movie like *Animal House* or *School Daze*.
	Again, review at Early Decision and Early Action options and requirements, and take appropriate actions.
November	Look ahead to SAT or ACT Assessment registration for the tests you plan to take. Are you about to miss one? Mark the appropriate test and registration dates on your calendar.
	Reduce target college long list to a short list, where applications will be made.
	Plan a Thanksgiving break that includes college visits (to almost-empty campuses).
	What is the status of your applications? Get someone to proofread your applications and essay(s).
December	Look ahead to SAT or ACT Assessment registration for the tests you plan to take. Are you about to miss one? Mark the appropriate test and registration dates on your calendar.
	Pick up financial aid material from guidance office and attend planning workshops, if available. Check out financial aid resources on the Internet.
	Make sure that teachers and guidance counselors are up-to-date with reference forms and that transcripts are being sent to all short-list colleges.
	Some Early Decision notifications may be sent this month—be on the lookout if you've applied under this plan.
January	**Begin filling out financial-aid forms.** Finish and mail these forms as soon as possible and *never late*.
	Complete all applications, including those with later deadlines. Don't forget to photocopy everything and save it in accordian files.
	If SATs are being taken this month, are "Rush" scores required? Ask target colleges, if you're not certain.
February	Unless confirmations have been received, call colleges to check on completion of applications. Record the name of the person with

When	What to do
	whom you spoke. Track down missing records.
	If you've made Early Action applications, colleges should send notifications by the end of this month. Be on the lookout for yours, and follow up if necessary.
March	WAIT!
April	Keep in mind that "thin" letters aren't always rejections. Some schools send out enrollment forms later.
	Rejoice in acceptances; keep rejections in perspective.
	Plan "crunch-time" visits to campuses, as needed, to help prompt final decisions.
	Compare financial aid decisions, where applicable. Contact financial aid offices with questions.
	Make sure you return Wait-List cards, as needed. Contact admission offices to check on Wait-List status. Send updated records and other information, if available. Write an upbeat "Please take me, and this is why you should" letter.
	Make your final decision. Have your parents send the required deposit. Don't dawdle and miss the May 1 deadline or colleges can give away your place. Also notify those schools you won't be attending, especially if an aid offer was made.
May	Take AP exams, if appropriate.
	Stay abreast of housing choices, etc. When will forms be mailed? Should you be investigating living-situations options? When is a freshman orientation? (Some schools have spring and summer programs.) When is course registration?
June	Write a thank-you note to anyone who might have been especially helpful. Guidance counselors are often unsung heroes. Don't forget teachers who wrote recommendations, admission counselors or secretaries, tour guides, or other students.

continues

College Admissions Timeline *(cont.)*

When	What to do
June *(cont.)*	Consider summer school if you want to accelerate or place out of requirements. ALWAYS check with colleges first to make sure credits will count. Get permission in writing when it's questionable.
	Make sure that a final high school transcript is sent to the college you will attend. (Most schools do this automatically.)

Finding Financial Aid

FIGURING OUT FINANCIAL AID

After you know what different schools might cost, it's time to work out what you and your family can afford to pay. Then you'll know how much financial aid you can apply for. The principle behind financial aid is that students who can't afford the full cost of college should still have the opportunity to go.

WHAT YOU WILL PAY

Taking the difference between what the college costs (including room and board, books, and other supplies) and what you can afford to pay gives the amount of your need. This deceptively simple term, "need," doesn't necessarily mean what you think it ought to mean, or what you would like for it to mean. It's a specific, technical term for the amount you cannot pay on your own—the amount left after your **Expected Family Contribution (EFC)** is subtracted from your cost of education.

Your EFC is the total amount that you, as a family, are expected to contribute toward college costs. This number is determined by analyzing your overall financial circumstances and comparing them to the circumstances of other families. Family income is the major factor in determining your EFC, *not* the balances of your savings accounts or the worth of trust funds and other assets.

Your EFC figure might vary from school to school, depending on which formula the college uses to determine financial need. Although your EFC might seem to be an unattainable amount, it can be financed if you carefully plot out a strategy that combines different economic sources, including loans, savings, a part-time job for the student, and current income.

WHAT'S COVERED BY FINANCIAL AID

Financial aid, which makes up the difference between the EFC and the cost of attending the school of your choice, comes in three basic flavors:

- **Grants and scholarships** don't need to be repaid or maintained by a job. Grants are usually based on need alone, while scholarships are given to students who have met some criteria, such as academic or athletic merit.

- **Loans** are the most widely available source of financial aid. They must be repaid some day, but the interest rates for student loans are often lower than for commercial loans, and payments are deferred until the student has completed college.
- **Work-study** lets students work 10 to 15 hours per week in order to gain the money to pay for school.

You and the financial aid officer at the college of your choice will negotiate a financial assistance package that will probably contain a combination of all three of these varieties of aid.

SOURCES OF FINANCIAL AID

Your aid will most likely come from a number of sources, from the most massive federal programs down to institutional funds unique to your school. Aid might come from the state, private foundations, the college, or even an employer. If the aid comes from a federal government program or a state agency, it is known as public aid; sources like employers, donors, and foundations are known as private aid.

FEDERAL AID

The federal government is by far the largest source of financial aid, providing nearly 70 percent of the aid that is awarded each year. In 1997–98, the federal government, through the Department of Education, made available more than $42 billion dollars in student aid. So, it pays to know something about the major federal programs, since they will be your first source of aid.

Pell Grants

The Pell Grants program was once known as the Basic Educational Opportunity Grant program, and you might still see it referred to as such in older materials. Pell Grants are distributed based on family need and education costs at your school. The maximum grant available in the 1998–99 school year was $3,000 per year, but this figure changes from year to year depending on how Congress funds the program.

Eligibility for Pell Grants is determined by the standard Federal Methodology formula that was passed into law by Congress and is used to calculate your EFC. If that figure falls below a certain threshold, you'll be eligible for a Pell Grant. After you've applied for aid, you'll receive a Student Aid Report that gives your EFC number and tells you if you qualify. The amount of the grant you may receive is not standardized. Different schools, with their varying tuitions, disburse different amounts.

Federal Loan Programs

There are two main kinds of low-interest loans for students and parents: the Federal Direct Student Loans (Direct Loan) program; and the Federal

Family Education Loan (FFEL) program. Collectively, they're called Stafford Loans.

Direct Loans come directly from the federal government. FFEL loans involve private lenders like banks, credit unions, and savings and loans. Aside from that difference, the two loan programs are pretty much the same; the program from which you get your money depends on the program in which your school participates. The interest rate on these loans varies from year to year, but the maximum is 8.25 percent, and often the interest rate is lower while you're in school. You'll also have to pay a fee of up to 4 percent, deducted from each loan disbursement; this money goes to the federal government to help reduce the cost of the loans.

If financial need remains after subtracting your EFC, your Pell Grant eligibility, and aid from other sources, you can borrow a Stafford Loan to cover all or part of the remaining need. This is a subsidized loan; the government pays the interest while you're in school and for six months after you graduate.

Even if you have no remaining need, you can still borrow a Stafford Loan for your EFC or the annual Stafford Loan borrowing limit, whichever is less. (The borrowing limit ranges from $2,625 to $10,500 a year, depending on a number of factors, including your year in school and whether you're classified as an independent or dependent student.) However, this is an unsubsidized loan; you're responsible for paying all of the interest.

Parents who are applying for the financial aid go for what are called PLUS Loans. Like the Stafford Loans, PLUS Loans are available from both the Direct Loan and the FFEL program. The yearly borrowing limit on PLUS Loans is equal to the cost of attending the college *minus* any financial aid you get; so if it costs $6,000 per year to attend college and the student has received $4,000 in other financial aid, that student's parents can borrow up to $2,000. The interest rate varies from year to year, but the maximum is 9 percent. For the 1997–98 fiscal year, the interest rate was 8.98 percent.

Campus-Based Programs

"Campus-based" simply means that financial aid officers at each school administer the programs. Three of the federal programs are campus-based (not all schools participate in all three programs):

- **Federal Supplemental Educational Opportunity Grants (FSEOG):** These grants are awarded to undergraduates based on financial need: "exceptional financial need" is the way the government brochures put it. Pell Grant recipients with the lowest EFCs will be the first in line for one of these grants. Depending on your need, when you apply, and the funding level at your school, you might receive between $100 and $4,000 a year.
- **Federal Work-Study (FWS):** This is basically a part-time job. Most undergraduates are paid by the hour and often at minimum wage

(graduate students might receive a salary). Jobs are awarded based on need, the size of FWS funds at your school, and the size of your aid package. The program encourages community service work and work related to your field of study, so it can also help you get your foot in the door by giving you work experience in your chosen field.

- **Federal Perkins Loans:** These are low-interest loans for students with "exceptional" financial need. They're also an exceptionally good deal at just 5 percent interest, and you don't have to start repaying until nine months after you graduate. Undergraduates can borrow $3,000 a year, up to a total of $15,000.

How much aid you receive from a campus-based program is based on your financial need, how much other aid you're receiving, and the availability of funds at your school. Unlike Pell Grants or Stafford Loans, the campus-based programs aren't entitlement programs. The government gives each school a set amount of cash; when it's gone, it is really gone—no more campus-based aid can be had until the next year's allotment comes through. Not every eligible student will receive aid from these programs. The schools set their own deadlines, so ask at your school's financial aid office and apply as early as possible to catch some of the money before it runs out.

Other Federal Aid

The Department of Education is not alone in providing financial aid; the federal government has several other ways of helping students get through school. Scholarships, loans, job training, and money to pay back existing loans are all available from a variety of federal programs, including the following:

- The branches of the Armed Forces maintain ROTC units on many campuses, which are a rich lode of scholarships geared toward helping minority students and boosting the number of students entering important-but-strained career fields, such as the health professions. For more information, call (800) USA-ROTC.
- The Department of Veterans Affairs (VA) offers aid for veterans, reservists, those who serve in the National Guard, and widows and orphans of veterans. For more information on these programs, call (800) 827-1000 and speak with a Veterans Benefits Counselor.
- The Corporation for National and Community Service administers a program called AmeriCorps, which enables students to pay for education in exchange for one year of public service.
- The U.S. Public Health Service provides a variety of loan, scholarship, and loan repayment programs to students studying to enter the health professions.
- The Department of Labor administers the Job Training Partnership Act, a tuition aid program for the economically disadvantaged and others facing employment barriers. To request more information, write to:

Office of Employment and Training Programs
Rm. N4469
U.S. Department of Labor
200 Constitution Ave. NW
Washington, DC 20210

STATE AID

It's part of a continuing trend among the states to increase their support for higher education, and all fifty states offer grant aid. However, each state is different, and some states spend far more than others. Five states—California, Illinois, New Jersey, New York, and Pennsylvania—award about 60 percent of the national total, $1.5 billion altogether in undergraduate need-based aid.

COLLEGE FUNDS

This money includes everything from athletic to academic (or merit) scholarships, which don't take need into account; merit aid is used by colleges to attract the students that they want. Next to the federal government, colleges are the largest sources of aid, awarding approximately $8 billion each year.

The last few years have also been building years for college and university endowments, with hundreds of millions of dollars flowing into schools as diverse as Harvard University and the University of Washington. Some, but certainly not all, of this endowment money has gone into scholarship funds. Other college funds might find their way to students in the form of tuition discounts for prepayment, aid in receiving loans, and other innovative programs. Most schools also keep funds on hand for short-term emergency loans for students.

EMPLOYERS

Many employers help put students through college through the burgeoning field of cooperative education, in which students alternate semesters of school with semesters of work. Not only does this provide professional skills and a leg up in the employment game, but it also puts money into the student's pocket. It is best developed at technical and engineering schools like Georgia Tech, which places hundreds of students into positions in a five-year degree program, but all kinds of institutions offer cooperative education programs—almost 1,000 schools boast such programs.

PRIVATE SCHOLARSHIPS

This is a relatively small part of the financial aid picture, and many carry daunting eligibility requirements—the old "red-haired Methodist from Georgia" problem. There's a lot more money to be drawn from federal and

CAUTION

A warning about Web site addresses: They change. The Internet is a very active place, and Web page addresses can be ephemeral things. That's why it's important to familiarize yourself with Internet search tools so that you can always find the information you want without the hassles of following a rabbit trail in cyberspace.

state programs, but hundreds of millions of dollars are nonetheless available in private scholarships—not an amount to turn up your nose at. Just remember to go after the big money first and early, and then look around for whatever private scholarships you can pick up.

FINDING FINANCIAL AID ONLINE

The Internet contains a treasure trove of financial aid resources, including applications that you can file electronically, in-depth information about grants and loans, college connections, scholarship searches, and more.

Almost every financial aid agency that you'll deal with—from the Department of Education to your college's financial aid office—maintains a Web site that provides applications, deadline dates, the latest news, and more important information that you need to know. There are also numerous Web sites from "unofficial" third-party sources that can also help you with researching financial aid; these sites often include insider advice, tips, and tricks that the official sources won't give you.

THE DEPARTMENT OF EDUCATION

A great place to start looking into the nuts and bolts of student financial aid is the source of so much of it—the federal government. The Department of Education maintains three separate Web sites that provide a great deal of reliable information:

- **The Office of Postsecondary Education** will tell you about the different kinds of federal aid and how to go about applying for that aid. You'll also find a free electronic version of the federal financial application that you can submit directly from the site. Go to http://www.ed.gov/offices/OPE/Students/index.html.

- **Project EASI** (Easy Access for Students and Institutions) is a Department of Education program aimed at streamlining the financial aid process. The Web site takes you step-by-step through the entire process and offers down-to-earth, straightforward advice. Go to http://easi.ed.gov/.

- **Think College** is the Department of Education's college preparation information resource. This site provides information about recently enacted government programs that help pay for college, such as the higher education tax credits of the Taxpayer Relief Act. The site also offers good advice geared toward parents and high school students on how to prepare for paying for college. Go to http://www.ed.gov/thinkcollege/.

THE COLLEGE BOARD

There is probably no better online resource for pre-college students and their parents than the College Board's Web site at http://www.collegeboard.org/. The financial aid section of this immense site archives tons of useful information on paying for college. The following are some of the most beneficial services of the site:

- **CSS/Financial Aid PROFILE:** This program helps students create a "profile" of themselves that schools and scholarship programs use to award aid funds. Many schools require this form as part of the financial aid application. You can fill out the form online or order a printed copy. Go to http://profileonline.cbreston.org/.
- **CollegeCredit Loans:** The College Board has partnered with Sallie Mae to provide low-interest Stafford and PLUS loans, as well as private loans, for students and parents. Go to http://www.collegeboard.org/finaid/fastud/html/collcred/collcred.html.
- **Expected Family Contribution Calculator:** Use a free, online calculator to figure out your family's EFC. Go to http://www.collegeboard.org/finaid/fastud/html/efc.html
- **Financial Aid Calculators:** Other calculators help you determine how your college savings will grow over time, parents' capacities to take on extra debt in the form of education loans, monthly loan payments, and realistic borrowing amounts for students. Go to http://www.collegeboard.org/finaid/fastud/html/fincalc/fcintro.html.
- **Financial Aid Services:** Besides all of the services that I've already told you about, you'll also find a plethora of facts, news, and advice pertaining to financial aid. Go to http://www.collegeboard.org/finaid/fastud/html/intro.html.

TIP
To talk with others who are going through the financial aid process, join the Usenet newsgroup soc.college.financial-aid. You might net some valuable advice from parents who have already been through it or just find support and sympathy.

STATE PROGRAMS

Many states have begun innovative financial aid programs, such as prepaid tuition funds and college savings plans. And of course, you can find up-to-date information about the majority of these programs on the Web.

For a comprehensive list of college savings programs by state, go to the listing at the **College Savings Plan Network** Web site (http://www.collegesavings.org/yourstate.htm). In addition, you might find more information about such plans by contacting your state's financial aid office.

SALLIE MAE AND OTHER LENDERS

And then there's Sallie Mae, the company that provides much of the money that goes into higher education loans. Sallie Mae's Web site has an introductory guide to financial aid. The site is very well adapted to the multimedia environment with plenty of links, illustrations, and other bells and whistles that make it as entertaining as it is informative. You'll also find many planning tools, including calculators that help you determine how much you can safely borrow or work out a budget for college, and free access to a comprehensive database of scholarships and other financial aid resources. In addition, you can access a borrower's account after you obtain a loan. Go to http://www.salliemae.com/.

TIP

Here's a quick way to find most schools' Web sites: In your browser, type **http://www. college**.edu/, where *college* is the college's name or initials. For example, type **http://www. duke.edu/** to connect to Duke University's Web site, or enter **http:/ /www.ucla.edu/** to go to UCLA's home page. Look for the financial aid page somewhere in the admissions section of the site.

The **National Financial Services Network** has published an online directory of lenders who provide education loans, organized by state. Searching the directory is probably the fastest way to locate a lender. Go to http://www.nfsn.com/Educatio.htm.

COLLEGE WEB SITES

It's getting hard to find a college these days that doesn't have a home page on the Web to advertise itself to prospective students. Of course, surfing the Web sites of schools that you're interested in is a fun—and effective—way to narrow down your list. But many colleges' sites also have pointers to the information provided by the school's financial aid office. This online financial aid "office" can be an extremely valuable resource, giving you access to up-to-date application deadlines, required forms, available scholarships, and more for your school of choice. So, surf over to your new school and check out its Web site!

To get started, search for the Web sites of specific college aid offices at the **FinAid** site (http://www.finaid.org/finaid/fao-web.html).

THIRD-PARTY RESOURCES

There's a great deal of excellent unofficial information on the Web as well. The best place to start is **FinAid,** produced by Mark Kantrowitz, author of the *Prentice Hall Guide to Scholarships and Fellowships for Math and Science Students*. The Web page is a gold mine. It includes access to scholarship and fellowship databases, information on grants and loans, an extensive bibliography, and links to school financial aid offices. Like all good Web pages, this one contains links to most of the other important sources of financial aid information contained on other computer systems. So we won't go into a long list of Web page addresses here, because one leads to the other. Go to http://www.finaid.org/.

Another nice resource is the full text of the current edition of the popular book, *Don't Miss Out: The Ambitious Student's Guide to Financial Aid* by Robert and Anna Leider.

Finally, the **College Guides and Aid Home Page** at http:// www.collegeguides.com/ is a unique financial aid resource. It aims to save you time and money by pointing you to only the best of the rest of the resources, including Web sites, books, CD-ROMs, and more. Each resource is thoroughly reviewed, so you'll know what you're getting before you spend any time or money on it.

SCHOLARSHIP SEARCHES

A number of Web sites now offer to quickly hook students up with scholarship money, and many of them are making good on that offer. The best scholarship search services turn out to be free! Take the increasingly popular **FastWEB** (http://www.fastweb.com/), which scans 180,000 sources of financial aid to find the ones that match the profile that you submitted and sends updates to your electronic mailbox as new sources become available. It's truly awesome—by far the largest free database of scholarships, grants, and other financial aid resources available on the Web. A few other sites offer similar services (remember, you can't apply for too many scholarships!); they're listed in the following table.

Free Scholarship Searches on the Web

Scholarship Search	Web Address
CASHE	http://scholarships.salliemae.com/
College Board	http://www.collegeboard.org/fundfinder/html/ssrchtop.html
CollegeNET	http://www.collegenet.com/mach25/
FastWEB	http://www.fastweb.com/
FreeSch!	http://www.freschinfo.com/
Peterson's	http://www.petersons.com
Scholarship Resource Network	http://www.srnexpress.com/execsrch.htm

A STEP-BY-STEP GUIDE TO APPLYING FOR FINANCIAL AID

Althought the financial aid application process might seem dauntingly complex, when you break it down into its separate steps, there's really not that much to it. Much of your time will be spent filling out the requisite financial aid forms and then waiting to see what you get.

BEFORE YOU APPLY: ASSEMBLING THE PAPERWORK

Before you start accumulating forms and wearing down the point of your number-two pencil, you should prepare for your applications by assembling the following records, necessary for many of the common aid forms:

- Earned income for the year
- Federal taxes paid for the year
- Untaxed income received (such as Social Security benefits)
- Money held in checking and savings accounts
- Value of any current investments
- Value of any business or farm owned by your family

CAUTION
Some scholarship search services are excellent resources, but others are scams, according to the FTC. The biggest tip-off is money: If somebody wants a lot of it in order to conduct a search for you, you're probably dealing with the wrong folks. The bills can quickly outstrip the value of scholarships discovered—and often, they aren't finding anything that you wouldn't come across with some smart online searching of your own.

TIP

One of the best sites for finding things online is Yahoo! (http://www.yahoo.com/), which organizes a gigantic directory of Web sites in outline form so that you can track down information by category. You can get directly to Yahoo!'s financial aid resources by going to http://dir.yahoo.com/Education/Financial_Aid/. You can also search the entire Web for certain words or phrases by using such sites as Altavista (http://www.altavista.com/), Excite (http://www.excite.com/), and HotBot (http://www.hotbot.com/).

For each item on this list, you'll need both the student's and the parents' records, unless you're an independent student—in which case you'll need these records for you and for your spouse.

GETTING AND FILLING OUT FINANCIAL AID FORMS

The forms that you'll need to fill out to apply for financial aid vary from state to state and from institution to institution, depending on the "need analysis service" used by that state or institution. Your school will let you know which forms you must complete and will provide them to you. Although they're not easy, none of these forms are impossible to fill out on your own.

The most common forms are the following:

- The U.S. Department of Education's Free Application for Federal Student Aid (FAFSA)
- The College Scholarship Service's CSS Financial Aid PROFILE (available in high school guidance counselor offices, college financial aid offices, and online at http://www.collegboard.com/)
- The Pennsylvania Higher Education Assistance Agency's Application for Pennsylvania State Grant and Federal Student Aid (PHEAA)
- The Student Aid Application for California (SAAC)
- The Illinois State Scholarship Commission's Application for Federal and State Student Aid (AFSSA)

Your school's application instructions will give you the information you need about applying for other forms of aid—several states, for instance, require that you fill out still more forms to apply for their own aid programs. It's also a good idea for students applying for private or institutional funds to check with the schools in which they are interested to see if additional forms are required or if other procedures must be followed. The school's own application and the state applications might have separate deadlines that you have to meet.

After you've applied, the processing agency will take between four and six weeks to turn your application around. You might be asked to confirm information or to correct the forms and then return them to be processed again. The reprocessing will add another two or three weeks to your wait.

Getting the FAFSA

There are a number of ways to apply for federal financial aid—but it all starts with the FAFSA. You have several options for getting a copy of the FAFSA and submitting it to a federal aid processing center:

- You can apply electronically through your school.
- You can apply electronically through the Department of Education's Web site, http://www.fafsa.ed.gov/.

- You can use the FAFSA Express software; it runs on computers that use the Windows operating system and have a modem. Computers with the FAFSA Express program can be found at many high schools, public libraries, and Educational Opportunity Centers. Or you can order the software on diskette by calling (800) 801-0576, or download a copy yourself from the Department of Education's Web site by going to http://www.ed.gov/office/OPE/express.html.

- You can forego technology altogether and get the version of the form that comes on old-fashioned paper. Ask at your high school guidance office, college financial aid office, or write directly to

Federal Student Aid Information Center
P.O. Box 84
Washington, DC 20044
(800) 4-FEDAID

TIP
Some schools offer financial aid applications in electronic form, so you don't have to worry about your eraser rubbing through the paper. You can also submit forms faster electronically and have the computer check for errors before you submit the forms.

Filling Out the FAFSA

Be as accurate and as neat as you can when completing the FAFSA. Use a pen with black ink or a number-two pencil that can easily be read by a computer. Don't jot notes in the margin that might interfere with processing the form. And don't attach any explanatory documents like tax returns—they'll just wind up in the shredder.

KEEPING TRACK OF PAPERWORK: WHAT TO DO WITH THE STUDENT AID REPORT

After processing your data, you'll begin to receive a lot of paper. Your application for federal aid through the FAFSA or the other forms will be used to generate a **Student Aid Report (SAR),** which arrives within four weeks after submitting the FAFSA. The SAR compares all your data and generates a **Student Aid Index** number (which lets you know whether you qualify for a Pell Grant) and an **Estimated Family Contribution (EFC)** number (which will be used to see whether you qualify for campus-based programs like FSEOG, Federal Work-Study, Federal Perkins Loans, and the Stafford Loan programs).

If you qualify for a Pell Grant, your SAR will arrive in three parts:

- Part 1, the Information Summary, tells you how to check the SAR for errors.
- Part 2, the Information Review Form, is used to correct any errors in the SAR.
- Part 3, the Pell Grant Payment Document, is used by your school to decide how much money you will receive.

TIP
Always save a copy of your application and worksheets as a backup, whether filing electronically or submitting a paper form. The school might need to see these copies later, or you might need to refer to them if you find errors in your aid package.

Immediately make copies of Part 1 and send one to the financial aid office of each school to which you applied. You'll submit all three parts of the SAR to the school that you ultimately decide to attend.

Didn't get the Pell Grant? Don't worry—very few applicants do. But now you have something very important—your EFC number. Send that information to your financial aid administrator, who will use it to figure out whether you qualify for other federal student aid.

RECEIVING YOUR AWARD LETTER

After the school has all the information it needs, it can put together an aid package that will probably include a combination of grants (precious few), loans (too many), and work-study employment. You're notified of what your aid package contains in an award letter. This document gives you an idea of your probable cost of attendance, how your need was determined, what your need turned out to be, and the composition of that aid package. If you're satisfied with the aid package, you sign the documents that come with the form and send them back to the school.

Even if you haven't decided which school to attend, you should move quickly to accept the aid package from each school that offers one. Accepting the aid package does not obligate you to attend the school, but it's the only way to keep your options open. Schools set response deadlines: If you don't respond to your aid letter within that time, you could miss out on the funds that have been offered to you. This isn't to say that you should keep a number of colleges on a string—choose your college as quickly as possible so that the schools you don't choose can distribute the money to other students.

But before you leap to accept that award letter, evaluate your offers with a cold eye. Don't be fooled by big numbers; pay special attention to how much of the offer is made up of grants and how much is made up of loans. Are all the costs of attending the school listed in the aid package, or will the costs of books, personal expenses, and travel add on to that amount? Which schools are tossing in special awards for academic or athletic merit? If scholarships are offered, are they renewable or are they one-shot wonders that will leave you high and dry next year? Break out your calculator and compare the loan interest rates offered by different institutions, and check out whether the payback requirements for those loans are especially onerous. And as for work-study offers, keep in mind the study load before you, and ask yourself whether you'll be able to juggle work and school right off the bat. And remember, financial aid offers might be negotiable. Compare all of the offers that you receive, then contact the admissions office of any school with which you want to negotiate. Your offer might be non-negotiable, but you won't know until you ask.

PUTTING IT ALL TOGETHER: THE FINANCIAL AID CALENDAR

The following table presents a calendar of important dates to remember when applying for college and for financial aid. Use this calendar as a checklist to ensure that you get everything done on time; to get the most aid, get applications in early.

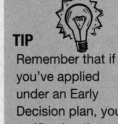

TIP
Remember that if you've applied under an Early Decision plan, your notification time—and subsequent obligations—differ. See Appendix A, "About Early Action and Early Decision Options," for more details.

Calendar of Important Financial Aid Dates

When	What to Do
Junior Year of High School	
October	Take the PSAT/NMSQT.
Fall/Winter	Send for college brochures and financial aid information.
Spring	Begin campus tours; talk to financial aid advisers at colleges.
	Sign up for AP courses for senior year, if available.
Senior Year of High School	
September–December	Narrow down your college choices.
	Ask schools for admission applications and financial aid forms.
	Get a copy of the FAFSA.
	Send in applications for admission to college.
	Take the SAT or ACT Assessment.
January 1	Send in the FAFSA and other required financial aid applications.
February–March	Make sure that the colleges received your applications and that you've completed all the required financial aid applications for each college.
April 1	Most college acceptances and rejections have been sent out by now; send in your nonrefundable deposit to the college of your choice.
May	Take any AP tests.
	Follow up with housing, financial aid, and other college offices.

continues

TIP

Remember that the money from campus-based programs, state programs, and the college's own awards are often given out much earlier than the June 30 deadline for filing your FAFSA. Get your financial aid applications in as soon after January 1 as possible to have more of your need met.

Calendar of Important Financial Aid Dates *(cont.)*

When	What to Do
June 30	Your financial aid application must be received by the processing agency listed on the form.
	Your school's financial aid office must have received your application and student aid report.

Choosing the Right College

WHICH COLLEGE IS RIGHT FOR YOU?

Choosing a college is a long and arduous process—but it can also be a lot of fun.

You know that this will be one of the most important decisions you'll ever make. You're choosing where you're going to spend the next four (or more!) years of your immediate life, where you're going to learn the skills you'll need for your adult life, and where you'll meet friends you will cherish for *all* of your life. You don't want to make the wrong choice, but still have to make *a* choice—and probably sooner than you'd like!

So, how do you determine which is the right college for you?

First, make sure you choose the college that offers the best mix of academics, environment, and extracurricular activities for your particular needs and wants. Don't choose a school just on its academic merits; remember, you'll be spending the next four years of your life there, so you better make sure you enjoy the non-academic life on campus, too!

You also have to take into account *where* the college is (how far away from your parents do you *really* want to be?) and *how much* it costs to attend. Your dream school might be too far away or simply cost too much to make it practical. (Although even if a college appears out of reach monetarily, you should always evaluate the potential for financial aid at that institution.)

If you have an idea of what career you wish to pursue after graduation, you should look for universities that are known for their excellence in the field that interests you. When comparing the merits of different schools, be sure to examine the caliber of the faculty, average class size in upper division courses, its academic reputation, and finally, the facilities. Visiting the prospective campus can be the most decisive factor in your choice of a school.

Even if a school meets *your* requirements, though, you might not meet *theirs*. You should examine the admissions requirements of each school that you are interested in very carefully to determine which offer the most realistic opportunities for gaining admission. Consider the school's SAT and ACT

ROAD MAP

- *Find the College That's Right for You*
- *Tips for Campus Visits—What to Do and How to Get the Most from Your Trip*
- *Learn How to Get Student-Views of the Campus, Online*
- *Use our College Search Sites List to Find College Home and Information Web Sites*

Assessment standards, whether or not they require an interview, that sort of thing. Don't waste your time, money, or hope applying to schools that you have little, if any, chance of getting into.

In a nutshell, then, here are some of the key points to consider when choosing a college:

- **Size.** Are you more comfortable at a college (1,000–2,500 population), a small university (2,500-6,000), or a big university (7,000 and up)? Colleges and small universities might offer a more comfortable environment with more extracurricular camaraderie, while big universities offer more extracurricular activities, period—and more class and subject selection.

- **Location.** Do you prefer a school situated in a rural setting, a town, a small city, or a megalopolis. Does the location of the school in any way enhance the curriculum? How far away from home do you want to be— one hour, one gas tank, or one airplane ticket? How much will it cost you to travel home—and how often will you be making the trip? What are the local transportation options? Can you park a car on campus—or do you have to take the bus?

- **Curriculum.** Which is most important to you, a liberal arts, professional, or technical degree? What is the school known for? What are its academic strengths and weaknesses? Do they offer the courses and the degree track that you really want?

- **Faculty.** What percentage of the faculty has attained the terminal degree (Ph.D., master's, etc.) in their field? Are professors available to meet with students outside of their classrooms? How many classes will actually be taught by a professor, vs. a teaching assistant? Is there an academic advising program? What about tutoring?

- **Job placement.** What percentage of students have job offers when they graduate? What percentage of alums continue on to graduate school? How strong is the alumni network?

- **Admissions requirements.** Are they academically rigorous? Too much so? Can you pass muster—or can *too many others* pass muster?

- **Costs and financial aid.** Can you afford this particular institution? What financial aid can you obtain to help you afford it? Are there any "hidden" costs of living on this campus?

- **Housing/food.** Are there different types of on-campus housing options? Do you *have* to live in a dorm? With how many roommates? What off-campus housing is available? What about fraternities and sororities? What are your dining options? Just how bad is the dorm food? Where is the closest pizza place—and do they deliver?

- **Extracurricular activities.** What do you like to do *outside* of class? What sports activities are available for non-athletic majors? What about music, theater, and clubs? Where are the closest nightspots?

- **Social atmosphere/student body.** Is this a fun place to live? Too much fun? Is the school known as a "party" campus? Is it elitist or populist? Are the students there people you'd choose to hang out with, given the choice?

How do you find the answers to all these questions? There are numerous sources of information available to you, from official university brochures to comprehensive college selection Web sites. However, the best sources of information are often the college's students—and you can meet them either on campus or online.

TIPS ON VISITING CAMPUSES

You should try to visit as many schools as possible before deciding where to apply. This is helpful in many ways, especially if you get accepted into more than one school and have to choose between them. A campus visit is even more important if you're applying under an Early Decision Plan and must commit to that school if you're accepted. Remember, the school you choose is going to be your home for the next four to five years; make sure it's a place you really want to live.

Walking and talking, observing and interacting are things you can *only* do in person. Here are some things to look for when you visit a school:

- **Walk around.** By all means, check out the campus. Walk around, take in the sights. Does it seem cold and impersonal, or warm and friendly? Is this a campus you'll remember twenty years from now? Visit the student center, and find out what activities the university has to offer— free movies, games, lectures, etc. See whether or not the classrooms and lecture halls are relatively close together. Will you have to do a great deal of walking? What is the campus transportation like? How do you get to your favorite *off-campus* places, for shopping, eating, drinking, and socializing?

- **Check out the weather.** What's the weather like? Learn the weather patterns of the area. What are the winters like? How cold does it get— and how much snow will you have to hike through between classes? How much rain can you expect? When does it start warming up—and how hot does it get? What about the humidity? Make sure that, weather-wise, this can be a comfortable place for you to live.

- **Visit the dorms.** Take a look at everything—the bathrooms, bedrooms, lounges, you name it. Are the rooms big enough? Are they clean? Quiet enough for studying? If possible, stay the night and take a trip to the dining hall and try the food. Can you keep it down? If there is more than one dorm or dining area, then check out several, and determine your preferences.

- **Visit the classrooms.** Stop by the departments that you might be majoring in, and pick up their course lists. Take the time to ask questions of the people working in each department. Find out a little about the first-year professors you might have.

- **Talk to people!** Most importantly, stop and strike up conversations with some of the students. Ask them what they think about the school, their coursework, the social scene, the Greek system, the dorms, the dorm food, or anything else that you were wondering about. Find out from the students what are the best dorms, which places have the best pizza,

TIP

Don't forget that you can get a lot of information about a college by checking out its campus newspaper. Almost every college journalism department produces a campus 'rag.' The school's web site may have contact information for the campus newspaper, or you can ask the Admissions Office for information on how you can get a copy. While you're at it, find out the name of the local city newspaper and get a copy of it, too. You'll learn a lot from these papers about the cultural climate, the cost of living, and other critical aspects of the school's locale.

where are the best parties, who are the best professors. Maybe you'll even make a few new friends and exchange phone number or email addresses. Students are your best resource—use them!

When you do visit, visit during the school year, not during spring, summer, or Christmas break. You should also try to avoid making visits during midterms and finals, or during the first few weeks of a new school year, before students are truly settled in. Also, it's probably better to visit during the week, if you can; a lot of students go home on weekends, and the atmosphere isn't quite the same.

HANGING OUT WITH OTHER STUDENTS ONLINE

If you can't hang out with college students in person, you can do so online, in *Usenet newsgroups* and in *e-mail mailing lists*. Newsgroups and mailing lists are like topic-specific discussion groups, where you post messages (called *articles*) and read articles posted by similarly-interested users; they're a great way to interact with others, electronically.

USENET NEWSGROUPS

Usenet newsgroups are the easiest discussion forums to find and to use. Since Usenet is part of the Internet, you need a computer and Internet access to visit them. You'll also need a *newsreader* software program. Two of the most popular newsreader programs are **Microsoft Outlook Express** (included free with both Windows 98 and Microsoft Internet Explorer) and **Netscape Messenger** (included free with the Netscape Communicator suite, which also includes the Netscape Navigator Web browser). If you access the Internet via America Online, just go to the keyword **newsgroups** to use AOL's built-in newsreader.

Newsgroups are arranged in *hierarchies*, so that all "alternative" newsgroups start with **alt.**, and alternative newsgroups related to colleges start with **alt.college.**, and on down the hierarchy. Here are some of the better newsgroups to peruse:

- alt.college
- alt.college.food
- alt.college.fraternities
- alt.college.greek.organizations
- alt.college.sororities
- alt.college.us
- alt.education.higher.stu-affairs
- alt.penpals.college
- alt.student.affairs.net
- soc.college

- soc.college.admissions
- soc.college.financial-aid

E-MAIL MAILING LISTS

You can also communicate with college students through email mailing lists. Mailing lists are like newsgroups, except you do all your message posting and reading via normal e-mail, and the lists are typically moderated (resulting in less unwanted "noise" and spam).

You can find a master list of all available mailing lists at the **Liszt** Web site (http://www.liszt.com); some of the more appropriate mailing lists for your needs include:

- **college_tips**, for students who want to share ideas that have improved their college life. For more information to http://www.geocities.com/CollegePark/Lab/1616/.
- **fresch**, the weekly newsletter of scholarship and financial aid information. Go to http://freschinfo.com/index.phtml for more information.
- **noirsurblanc**, a list about higher education, universities, and students. For more information, send an email to noirsurblanc@sorengo.com with the word **info** in the subject line of the message.
- **oncourse**, presenting innovative strategies for helping college students achieve their potential. For more information, send an e-mail to majordomo@ari.net with the phrase **info oncourse** in the subject line of the message.
- **studentactivism**, for students who want to become more active in issues affecting the world. For more information, go to http://www.studentactivism.listbot.com.
- **student-parents**, for parents who are also students. Go to their Web site at http://www.eGroups.com/list/student-parents/ for more information.
- **Students-Online**, for students and others interested in a variety of educational topics. To get more information, send an email to listcaster@listserv.rogersu.edu with the phrase **info Students-Online** in the subject line of the message.

CHECK OUT COLLEGE AND STUDENT WEB PAGES

Almost every college has its own Web site. These sites often include a lot of good information about the school, the faculty, the classes, and the campus. In many cases you'll also be able to access individual student Web pages directly from the main college Web site.

To search for college Web sites, go to **Yahoo! College Search**, at http://dir.yahoo.com/Education/Higher_Education. Enter the name of the college you're looking for and click the **Find Colleges** button. You can also search for search for schools by major, location, enrollment, and "wiredness" (level of PC use on campus).

In addition to the official college Web sites, it's also fun and informative to check out the Web pages created by students of a particular college. While you can access some student pages from some college Web sites, you can also find listings of student pages at the following independent sites:

- **Personal Page Direct** (http://www.student.com/feature/ppd/), from Student.com, listing more than 200,000 student Web pages.

- **Personal Pages Worldwide** (http://www.utexas.edu/world/personal/index.html), which links to collections of personal pages at colleges and universities worldwide.

- **Student Homepages** (http://www.westegg.com/students/), listing student pages from more than 300 different colleges.

COLLEGE SEARCH SITES ON THE INTERNET

You'll also find dozens, if not hundreds, of sites on the Web devoted to helping you learn more about and choose a college. Here's just a small list of the best and/or most popular of these college selection sites.

- **Admissions Offices** (http://www.yahoo.com/Education/Higher_Education/College_Entrance/Admissions_Offices/), Yahoo's comprehensive list of links to college admissions offices across the U.S.

- **All About College** (http://www.allaboutcollege.com), compiling thousands of links to college and university Web sites around the world. Includes admissions office e-mail addresses for most schools.

- **Best College Picks** (http://www.bestcollegepicks.com). After completeing a survey, BCP will match you with colleges that fit your interests and future goals.

- **Campus Tours** (http://www.campustours.com), online virtual tours of thousands of college campuses, complete with interactive maps, college webcams, QuickTime VR tours, campus movies, and pictures. A great way to "tour" a school without actually being there!

- **college base** (http://library.advanced.org/17038), a site (created by two high school students!) that offers help for the SAT/ACT Assessment, a collection of college stories written by college students, and an appraisal section which evaluates colleges from the student's perspective.

- **College Board Online** (http://www.collegeboard.org), the official web site of the non-profit college organization that sponsors the SAT. Includes a College Search database of more than 3200 two- and four-year colleges, a Scholarship Search service, a Career Search service, and online prep for the SAT.

- **College Bound.net** (http://www.cbnet.com), a resource that bills itself as "a student's interactive guide to college life," with sections like Money, College Profiles, Sports, and Food.

- **College E-Mail Addresses** (http://www.qucis.queensu.ca/FAQs/college-email/college.html), an extremely useful site that explains how to find email addresses for undergraduate and graduate students, faculty, and staff at various colleges and universities.

- **College Is Possible** (http://www.collegeispossible.org), a resource guide for parents, students, and education professionals, prepared by the Coalition of America's Colleges and Universities. A good reference for preparing for, choosing, and paying for college.

- **College Spot** (http://www.collegespot.com), dedicated to helping high school students through the college selection and application process. Includes a college search engine, admissions info, scholarship info, and financial aid info.

- **College411** (http://www.college411.org), a collection of links to other college-oriented Web sites.

- **CollegeDegree.com** (http://www.collegedegree.com), which lists all available distance learning courses available at major colleges and universities.

- **CollegeEdge** (http://www.collegeedge.com), with college planning advice, a campus tour, a scholarship search, a financial calculator, and an extensive careers and majors section. This site offers one of the most comprehensive college search databases with 5850 two- and four-year colleges (plus vocational/technical schools) generating extensive (30+ pages) profiles of admissions, tuition, financial aid, curriculum, minority enrollment, and campus life. Make sure you check out the Pack and Go section, with adivce on how to pack for school, what to do your first semester, and how to get along with your roommate.

- **CollegeNET** (http://www.collegenet.com), offering school searches by major, location, and tuition. You can also search by state for four-year colleges and community, technical, and junior colleges. Includes virtual tours of selected colleges, complete with live "campus cams."

- **Colleges & Careers Center** (http://www.usnews.com/usnews/edu/), from U.S. News Online. Includes a full-color Class Scheduler, a sophisticated College Planner to help you find the right college for you, a Find a Scholarship service, and the ability to compare up to four schools on features such as admissions, demographics, and financial aid. Most important, this is the source of the famous (or infamous) yearly College Rankings.

- **Colleges.com** (http://www.colleges.com), a "virtual campus" that provides an online community for college students across the country. Sections include Entertainment, Academics, Sports, Music, Books, Games, Research, and Search Engines.

- **CollegeView** (http://www.collegeview.com), with sections on financial aid, careers, resume writing, and interviewing, as well as a searchable database of all accredited colleges and universities in the U.S. and Canada. Inlcudes an online self-assessment test to help you determine your best career options, as well as virtual tours of hundreds of schools.

- **CollegeXpress** (http://www.collegexpress.com), profiling private and independent institutions (no state universities or community colleges). You can search for schools by location or programs offered, get an overview of financial aid and scholarships, and read about the admissions process. Includes a section for parents.

CAUTION
A warning about Web site addresses: They change. The Internet is a very active place, and Web page addresses can be ephemeral things. That's why it's important to familiarize yourself with general Internet search engines (such as Yahoo!, at http://www.yahoo.com) so that you can always find the information you want without the hassles of following a rabbit trail in cyberspace.

- **Critical Comparisons of American Colleges and Universities** (http://www.memex-press.com/cc/), incorporating data from the U.S. Department of Education's IPEDS database, studies conducted by the National Research Council, and assorted crime statistics. Offers interactive graphs and statistical analyses to help you compare and contrast various schools.

- **Educational Resources Information Center** (http://www.accesseric.org), the site of the National Library of Education. Includes the ERIC Database, the world's largest source of education information, wtih more than 950,000 abstracts of documents and journal articles. This site also lets you access a large inventory of brochures for parents.

- **ETS Net** (http://www.ets.org), the official site of the Educational Testing Service. Includes information on colleges and universities, careeers and jobs, and disabilities and testing, as well as a variety of articles about colleges, college preparation, and college life.

- **Getting Ready for College Early** (http://www.ed.gov/pubs/GettingReadyCollegeEarly/), an online handbook for parents of students in the middle and junior high school years, from the U.S. Government.

- **GoCollege** (http://www.gocollege.com), offering a college search based on your desired major, test scores, class rank, location, and tution. Includes free online SAT/ACT Assessment practice tests, and the capability to apply to 850 colleges directly online.

- **Kaplan** (http://www.kaplan.com), from the giant test prep company, with a site packed wtih free information, including several free newsletters, financial aid information, and à college search engine.

- **Mapping Your Future** (http://mapping-your-future.org), which guides you from paying for school, selecting a school, and planning a career. Includes guided tours for middle and high school students, non-traditional students, and parents.

- **National Association for College Admission Counseling** (http://www.nacac.com), a site created by the education association of secondary school counselors, college and university admission officers, other student counselers. This assocation sponsors the National College Fair program, and the site includes a comprehensive listing of college fairs.

- **Petersons.com** (http://www.petersons.com), an online database of academic programs, colleges and universities, and scholarship programs as well as test-prep information.

- **Power Students Network** (http://www.powerstudents.com), a resource for students and parents on hot to get into, pay for, and succeed in college.

- **Preparing Your Child for College** (http://www.ed.gov/pubs/Prepare/), an online resource for parents, from the U.S. Government.

- **The Student Survival Guide** (http://www.luminet.net/~jackp/survive.html), last but far from least, a wonderful little self-published resource guide for success in college. Includes 10 Tips for Survival in the Classroom, 10 Campus Organizations to Look Into, 10 Tips for

Surviving the Registration Process, 10 Tips for Deciding On or Changing Your Major, 10 Ways to Improve Your Social Life, and numerous other lists of "10s" to help you make your way through your first year at school.

As you can see, there are a lot of resources available for you to use on the Internet. It's best to take your time, settle back with a soft drink or glass of juice, and cruise through a number of these Web sites to see what they have to offer. At the end of your Web surfing, you'll be a lot more informed about where you want to go than you were when you first started out!

Using Other Study Aids

The book you're reading right now offers you one of the most proven methods for preparing for the ACT Assessment. But as competition for college admission in-creases, so does the number of preparation tools used by the average student. Many students today are using multiple methods to prepare for the ACT Assessment, and those include guides (such as *Master The ACT Assessment,* 2002 edition), local or national courses, software packages, and individual tutoring programs. This appendix lists some of the more popular offerings within each of these groups. But remember, only *you* can judge your ACT Assessment preparation needs. Don't feel pressed into a panicky buying spree of study aids, just because they're available. Use the tools in this book to build your skills and to determine your progress and readiness. If you think you'd benefit from additional study aids, you might find some of interest in this appendix.

ONLINE STUDY AIDS

The Internet is becoming an ever more important source of test preparation. There are numerous sites related to the ACT Assessment and SAT online, although you'll probably want to augment your online studying with more traditional sources.

Here is a short list of some of the more prominent Web sites related to the ACT Assessment and SAT:

- **ACT Assessment Home** (http://www.act.org), the official Web site of the ACT, Inc., offers a selection of sample test questions and information about recommended test-taking strategies.
- **College Board Online** (http://www.collegeboard.org), the official Web site of the non-profit college organization that sponsors the SAT, offers a "test question of the day" and EssayPrep, an online evaluation of essay answers.
- **College PowerPrep** (http://www.powerprep.com) provides a number of online tools for preparing for the SAT and ACT Assessment.
- **Kaplan** (http://www.Kaplan.com), from the preparation course company, offers some online practice tests for the SAT and ACT Assessment, a list of "1000 Most Common SAT/ACT Words," and free downloadable "diagnostic" software.

ROAD MAP

- *Learn About the Best Online Study Aids*
- *Understand the Pros and Cons of Software Study Aids*
- *Learn About Test-Prep Coaching Courses and Individual Tutoring Programs*

- **Number 2** (http://www.number2.com), as in "number-two pencils," offers the SAT Companion tutorial, online practice tests for the SAT.
- **Petersons.com** (http://www.petersons.com) allows you to download practice ACT Assessment software.
- **SAT Math** (http://www.satmath.com) offers an "intelligent diagnostic" testing for the SAT math exam.
- **Test.com** (http://www.test.com) lets you practice for the SAT online.
- **TestPrep.com** (http://www.testprep.com), from Stanford Testing Systems, offers a free online testing and preparation service called **WebWare.** You begin by taking a sample SAT (using the College Board's *Taking the SAT* booklet), entering your answers into the WebWare for the SAT Answer Sheet, and then the WebWare service shows which math and verbal skills you need to work on. The site then guides you to a series of SAT math and verbal skill review lessons—as well as some SAT-based games and cartoons.

One thing to note about these online test prep sites—they're not all completely free. Some offer free samples or viewings, but then charge for more in-depth practice. Make sure you "try before you buy" from one of these sites.

SOFTWARE STUDY AIDS

In addition to the online study resouces, you might want to consider using one of the many software packages available to supplement your study and practice program. You'll probably need a CD-ROM drive, because most test-prep software is currently packaged in that form; most programs are available in either Windows or Macintosh versions.

By comparison with a book, software has certain advantages and disadvantages. Many students who use computers daily are very comfortable with the mouse, keyboard, and monitor, and they enjoy the rapid interactivity that software offers: you do something, and the computer responds quickly. The relatively vast memory capacity of a CD-ROM means that a large amount of information—thousands of sample test questions, for example—can be stored in a tiny disk, which is easier to carry around than a fat paperback book. And, of course, when you take a sample test on your computer, it can be instantly and accurately scored by the machine, and diagnosis of your strengths and weaknesses can be equally rapid.

A possible drawback in using software to prepare for the SAT or ACT Assessment is that the tests themselves are not computerized exams. Therefore, when you practice on a computer, you are distancing yourself to some degree from the actual test-taking experience. It's a bit like training for your driver's test using a joystick and a video monitor—useful practice, maybe, but not quite the same as the real thing.

And, if you don't have access to a portable computer, the software can actually be *less* portable than a book. If you aren't certain that you will always be able to access a computer when you have the time (and desire) to study for the exam, you might want to use both a book and a software prep package.

That said, software preparation is gaining in popularity, and here are some of the best-selling software packages:

- **Acing the New SAT** and **Acing the ACT,** is from Princeton Teaching Associates Software. Includes three practice tests and 500 questions. Go to http://www.ptas.com for more information.
- **Higher Score for the SAT/ACT**, from Kaplan, offers five practice tests and 2700 questions. Go to http://www.kaptest.com/catalog/product.jhtml?ProdID=115416&CATID=0 for more information.
- **Score Builder for the SAT and ACT,** from The Learning Company, offers three practice tests and 500 questions. Go to http://www.learningco.com for more information.

In addition to these commercial software programs, there are also *freeware* and *shareware* programs available for download from the Internet. These programs, while often not as polished or sophisticated as their more expensive cousins, can be yours either for free or for a token registration fee.

For a good selection of freeware and shareware test-prep programs, check out the following Web sites:

- **CNET's Download.com** (http://www.download.com; search for either "SAT" or "ACT")
- **ZDNet Software Library: Study Aids** (http://www.zdnet.com/downloads; search for "ACT")

COACHING COURSES

Generally speaking, there are four kinds of coaching courses available: one-on-one **tutoring, school-based** programs, **local** commercial courses, and **national** commercial courses. Each type of course is discussed in the following sections.

INDIVIDUAL TUTORING

In this kind of course, you work one-on-one with an individual teacher, at times and at places you mutually choose. How do you find a teacher to provide individual tutoring for the SAT or ACT Assessment? Usually through informal networking—ask your friends, or have your parents inquire through their grapevine. Check your local advertising media, too; look for flyers in the supermarket or ads in the neighborhood newspaper or pennysaver. You might also ask your favorite teacher at school if he or she knows a good tutor; perhaps there's a colleague or friend he or she can recommend.

TIP

Videotape and audiotape learning are a small part of the test-preparation business, although there are products available from several companies. As with online and software test prep, the instructional medium is quite different from the medium of the test itself; but if you find it more interesting to learn through the voice of a "live" instructor, you might want to look for video or audio programs.

Individual tutoring can be a good way to prepare for an exam. Scheduling is likely to be flexible, and when "crunch time" comes and you need or want intensive work for a week or two, you might be able to arrange extra hours. The cost will depend on your tutor's credentials, of course, but generally speaking, tutoring can be a cost-effective option: you pay only for the hours you need and want.

An individual tutor might be your best choice if there is a particular area of the exam on which you want to focus and you can find a tutor with special expertise in that topic. For example, if you have a weakness in the area of algebra, a tutor who is a skilled, experienced, and empathetic high school math teacher might be exactly what you need. On the other hand, if you need general instruction in several areas of the test, it might be impossible to find one individual who is equally knowledgeable in all areas. A classroom course might be a better choice in that case.

SCHOOL-BASED PROGRAMS

Many high schools now offer SAT/ACT Assessment-preparation courses for their students, either during the school day or at some special time—before or after classes begin, at lunch hour, or on Saturday morning, for example. These courses are often free of charge, so if your school offers such a course, you might want to consider attending it.

A school-based program might be a good choice for you if you feel you'll benefit from the convenience of classes held right in your own school, and if the idea of working with teachers (and classmates) you know appeals to you. On the other hand, if you're fed up with the same old faces and places by the end of the regular school day, this "advantage" might be really turn out to be a disadvantage.

LOCAL COMMERCIAL COURSES

These are courses that are run as for-profit businesses by local companies, staffed by area residents. Local commercial courses are often offered by individuals who have worked as tutors and subsequently expanded their businesses to include classroom courses.

A local commercial course differs from individual tutoring in that it involves group study, a fixed class schedule, and a prearranged curriculum, usually covering all areas of the exam. Classes can be held at any available local site—a storefront, an office, rented space in a school or community center, or even the teacher's home.

Local commercial courses offer some definite advantages. The classes are usually taught by the same small staff of teachers who own and operate the business, generally people with high school teaching experience. This means you will usually know in advance who your teacher will be, and you can get a sense of his or her personality by asking friends, family, or teachers for a recommendation. The classes are usually small (five to fifteen students), which allows a fair amount of give-and-take, and individual tutoring is usually available to supplement the classroom work (for an additional fee).

Consider a local commercial course if your community has one with a good reputation. If you don't need the individual attention that a tutor can offer, and if you want a program that covers all of the topics and skill areas on the exam, then a local course might be a good choice for you.

NATIONAL COMMERCIAL COURSES

These programs bear much the same relationship to the local commercial courses as McDonald's bears to your neighborhood hamburger place. The national courses are big businesses operating in standardized fashion throughout the country, offering a product that's generally consistent and reliable in quality. You might not get the individual attention that a local tutor or teacher offers, but there are advantages that, for many students, outweigh any negatives.

There are two major national test-prep schools offering SAT and ACT Assessment courses. The larger and older is **Kaplan Educational Centers;** the newer and somewhat smaller center, though also widely available, is **Princeton Review.**

The books, lesson plans, and study guides used by Kaplan's teachers are developed by a large staff of writers and editors who constantly monitor changes in the exams and update the materials frequently. In addition to classroom lesson plans, Kaplan creates many other materials: diagnostic tests (generally using actual SAT and ACT Assessment test questions) to measure student strengths and weaknesses, homework materials including sample tests and math and verbal study guides, and instructional materials on CD-ROM and videotape.

A typical Kaplan course includes twelve class sessions, each three to four hours long. Three of the sessions are devoted to full-length practice tests. Students also have many opportunities for additional study and practice; office hours when students can visit are scheduled, workshops on particular topics are offered, and libraries of videotaped classes and workshops as well as computerized exams for self-testing purposes and available in Kaplan centers.

In mid-1998, Kaplan's basic SAT course was offered in New York City at a fee of $749. Princeton Review is quite competitive with Kaplan in terms of the number, kind, and quality of their course materials.

NOTES